Florida
and The Bahamas

"And in order to better describe it
I wish to tell of the expanse,
of the beauty and loveliness
of this fertile paradise,
of its people and nature.
It is a new world
full of charms and comely
with many diverse colors,
a flowered and delightful meadow
with birds of a thousand kinds."

Bartolomé de Flores, 1571,
Obra nuevamente compuesta
(Newly Composed Work)
Translated by William Richard Jackson

Travel Publications

Michelin North America
One Parkway South, Greenville SC 29615, U.S.A.
℡ 1-800-423-0485
www.ViaMichelin.com
TheGreenGuide-us@us.michelin.com

Manufacture française des pneumatiques Michelin
Société en commandite par actions au capital de 304 000 000 EUR
Place des Carmes-Déchaux – 63 Clermont-Ferrand (France)
R.C.S. Clermont-Fd B 855 200 507

Typesetting: Nord Compo, Villeneuve-d'Ascq
Printing : I.M.E., Baume-les-Dames
Binding : I.M.E., Baume-les-Dames

Cover design: Carré Noir, Paris 17ᵉ arr.

THE GREEN GUIDE:
The Spirit of Discovery

Leisure time spent with The Green Guide is also a time for refreshing your spirit, enjoying yourself, and taking advantage of our selection of restaurants, hotels and other places for relaxing. Immerse yourself in the local culture, discover new horizons, experience the local lifestyle— The Green Guide opens the door for you.

Each year our writers go touring: visiting the sights, devising the driving tours, identifying the highlights, selecting the hotels and restaurants, checking the routes for our maps and plans.

Each title is compiled with great care, giving you the benefit of regular revisions and Michelin's first-hand knowledge. The Green Guide responds to changing circumstances and takes account of its readers' suggestions; all comments are welcome.

Come share our enthusiasm for travel, which has led us to discover over 60 destinations around the world. Let yourself be guided by the best motive for travel-the spirit of discovery.

Contents

Dear Reader

Introduction

Flagler College, St. Augustine

Art Deco Detail

4

Tropical Drink

Caribbean Flamingo

5

Maps and Plans

COMPANION PUBLICATIONS

Map 492 Eastern USA and Eastern Canada

Large-format map providing detailed road systems; includes driving distances, interstate rest stops, border crossings and interchanges.
– Comprehensive city and town index
– Scale: 1:2,400,000 (1 inch = approx. 38 miles)

Map 930 USA Road Map

Covers principal US road network while also presenting shaded relief detail of overall physiography of the land.
– State flags with statistical data and state tourism office telephone numbers
– Scale: 1:3,450,000 (1 inch = approx. 55 miles)

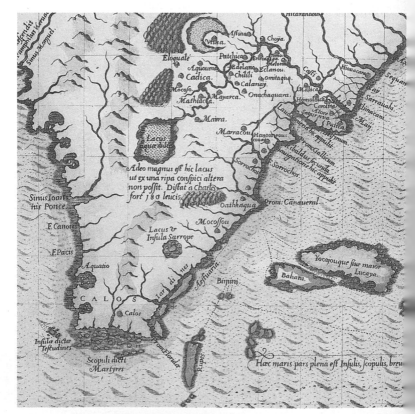

Map of Florida (16C) by Jacques Le Moyne

LIST OF MAPS AND PLANS

Using this guide

● The guide is organized into 12 regions of Florida (listed alphabetically) and one section on The Bahamas. Within these sections, each **Entry Heading** is followed by a population figure, map reference, tourist information phone number and Web site when available.

● In the text, useful information such as sight location or street address, opening hours, admission charge, telephone number and Web site appears in *italics*. In addition, symbols indicate wheelchair access &; on-site eating facilities ✕; camping facilities ⚠; on-site parking ▣; sights of interest to children [Kids]; and long lines ||||. The presence of a swimming pool is indicated by the symbol ⊼ in Address Books.

● Many entries feature **digressions**—entertaining breaks from sightseeing that are marked by a purple bar and indicated on maps by a black dot ❶ with the corresponding map reference number.

● Sections with a blue background offer practical information, such as available transportation, contact information for visitors bureaus and recreation opportunities, for a city or region. Blue sections edged in a marbleized band contain an **Address Book** describing suggested hotels and restaurants.

● At the back of the guide, the section of blue pages offers **Practical Information** on planning your trip, getting there and getting around, basic facts and tips for international visitors.

Addresses, phone numbers, opening hours and prices published in this guide are accurate at press time. We welcome corrections and suggestions that may assist us in preparing the next edition. Please send your comments to:

Michelin Travel Publications
Editorial Department
P. O. Box 19001
Greenville, SC 29602-9001
Email: TheGreenGuide-us@us.michelin.com
Web site: www.ViaMichelin.com

© Jerry Mesmer/FOLIO, Inc.

Key

	Sight	Seaside Resort	Winter Sports Resort	Spa
Worth a journey	★★★	�ののの	✴ ✴ ✴	⚕ ⚕ ⚕
Worth a detour	★★	のの	✴ ✴	⚕ ⚕
Interesting	★	の	✴	⚕

Sight symbols

▭ ◉ ▬▬▬▬ ▬▬▬▬ Recommended itineraries with departure point

🏛 ✡ ⊡	Church, chapel – Synagogue	▬▬	Building described
○	Town described	▬▬	Other building
AZ B	Map co-ordinates locating sights	▪	Small building, statue
▪ ▲	Other points of interest	◎ ⁘	Fountain – Ruins
⚒ ⌒	Mine – Cave	🛈	Visitor information
🕎 ⚲	Windmill – Lighthouse	⚓ ⚓	Ship – Shipwreck
☆ ⛪	Fort – Mission	⁂ ⩔	Panorama – View

Other symbols

🛡80	Interstate highway (USA)	🛡225	US highway	⬭180	Other route
🍁	Trans-Canada highway	▣401	Canadian highway	◈	Mexican federal highway
▬	Highway, bridge			═══	Major city thoroughfare
═══	Toll highway, interchange			═══	City street with median
═══	Divided highway			◄──	One-way street
═══	Major, minor route			▬▬	Pedestrian Street
╲ **15 (21)**	Distance in miles (kilometers)			∋∷∈	Tunnel
2149/655 ╲╱	Pass, elevation *(feet/meters)*			▬▬▪▬▬	Steps – Gate
△6288(1917)	Mtn. peak, elevation *(feet/meters)*			⚠ ⛴	Drawbridge - Water tower
✈ ✛	Airport – Airfield			🅿 ✉	Parking – Main post office
⛴	Ferry: Cars and passengers			▤ ✚	University – Hospital
⛴	Ferry: Passengers only			🚆 🚌	Train station – Bus station
←< ▢	Waterfall – Lock – Dam			● ⌂	Subway station
—··—··	International boundary			❶ ⌂	Digressions – Observatory
─ ─ ─ ─	State boundary, provincial boundary			▦ ▭	Cemetery – Swamp
🍇	Winery			⊪⊪⊪	Long lines

Recreation

▪–o–o–o–▪	Gondola, chairlift	(⌐⌐⌐)	▶	Stadium – Golf course
🚂	Tourist or steam railway	❀		Park, garden
⛵ ⚓	Harbor, lake cruise – Marina	🌐		Wildlife reserve
🏄 ⛵	Surfing – Windsurfing	◐⩔		Wildlife/Safari park, zoo
🤿 🛶	Diving – Kayaking	─ ─ ─ ─		Walking path, trail
⛷ ⛷	Ski area – Cross-country skiing	🚶		Hiking trail
	🔵	Sight of special interest for children		

Abbreviations and special symbols

NP	National Park	NMem	National Memorial	NMS	National Marine Sanctuary
NF	National Forest	NHS	National Historic Site	NWR	National Wildlife Refuge
SP	State Park	NHP	National Historical Park	SWP	State Wildlife Preserve
SF	State Forest	NPres	National Preserve	SAS	State Archaeological Site
SR	State Reserve	NM	National Monument	SAP	State Archeological Park
SPres	State Preserve	NVM	National Volcanic Monument	SRA	State Recreational Area
SHS	State Historic Site			NRA	National Recreation Area

🛡 National Park 🛡 State Park 🌲 National Forest 🌲 State Forest

All maps are oriented north, unless otherwise indicated by a directional arrow.

Principal Sights

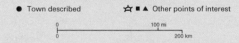

HIGHLY RECOMMENDED	★★★
Recommended	★★
Interesting	★

Place names in black type indicate the cities and sights
described in this guide *(see Index)*.

● Town described   ☆ ■ ▲ Other points of interest

```
0                    100 mi
0                         200 km
```

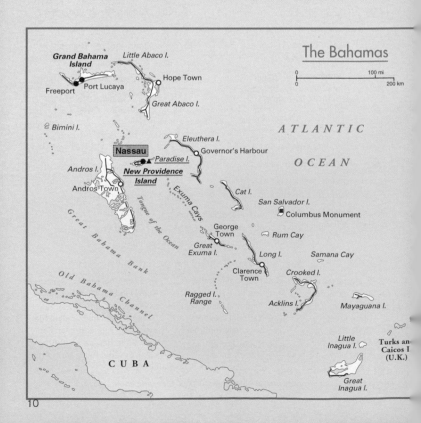

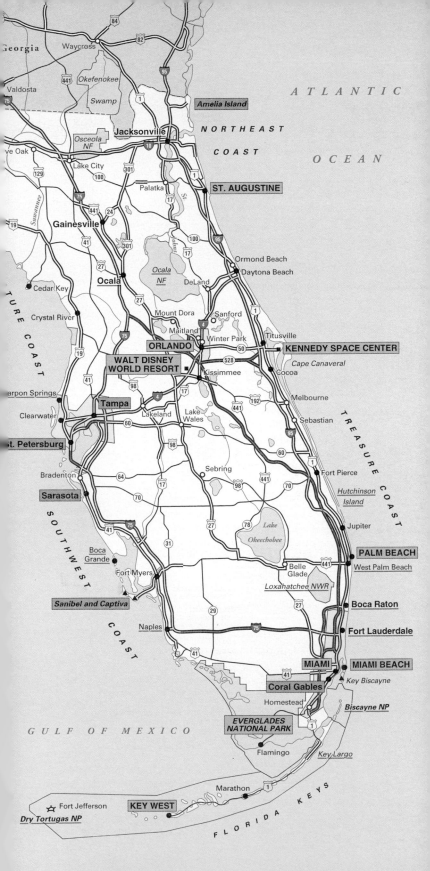

Regional Driving Tours

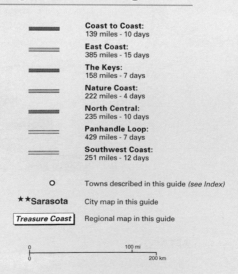

Coast to Coast:
139 miles - 10 days

East Coast:
385 miles - 15 days

The Keys:
158 miles - 7 days

Nature Coast:
222 miles - 4 days

North Central:
235 miles - 10 days

Panhandle Loop:
429 miles - 7 days

Southwest Coast:
251 miles - 12 days

○   Towns described in this guide *(see Index)*

★★**Sarasota**   City map in this guide

Treasure Coast   Regional map in this guide

0   100 mi
0   200 km

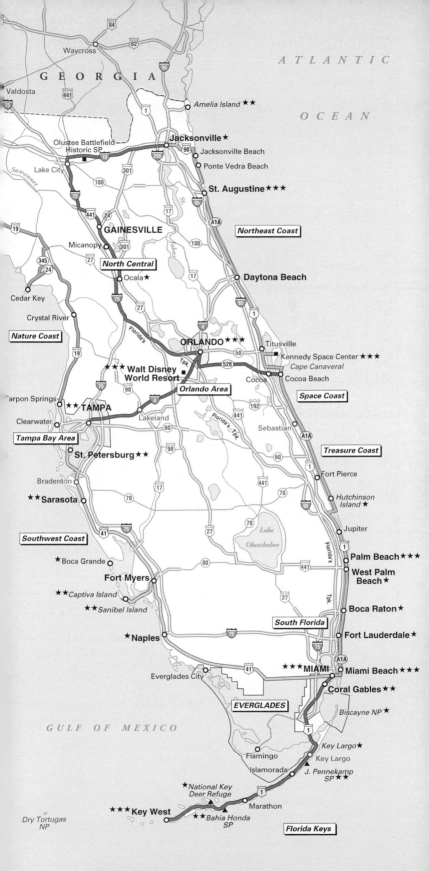

ATLANTIC

OCEAN

Amelia Island ★★

GEORGIA

Waycross

Valdosta

Olustee Battlefield
Historic SP
Lake City

Jacksonville ★
Jacksonville Beach
Ponte Vedra Beach

St. Augustine ★★★

Northeast Coast

GAINESVILLE

Micanopy

North Central

Ocala ★

Daytona Beach

Cedar Key

Crystal River

Nature Coast

ORLANDO ★★★

Titusville
Kennedy Space Center ★★★
Cape Canaveral
Cocoa
Cocoa Beach

★★★ Walt Disney
World Resort

Orlando Area

Space Coast

arpon Springs

★★ TAMPA

Lakeland

Clearwater

Tampa Bay Area

Sebastian

Treasure Coast

St. Petersburg ★★

Fort Pierce

Bradenton

*Hutchinson
Island* ★

★★ Sarasota

Jupiter

Southwest Coast

*Lake
Okeechobee*

★ Boca Grande

Palm Beach ★★★

Fort Myers

West Palm
Beach ★

★★ *Captiva Island*

★★ *Sanibel Island*

Boca Raton ★

South Florida

★ Naples

Fort Lauderdale ★

★★★ MIAMI
Miami Beach ★★★

Everglades City

Coral Gables ★★

EVERGLADES

Biscayne NP ★

GULF OF MEXICO

Key Largo ★
Key Largo

Flamingo

J. Pennekamp
SP ★★

Islamorada

★ *National Key
Deer Refuge*

★★★ Key West

Marathon

Dry Tortugas
NP

★★ *Bahia Honda
SP*

Florida Keys

Regional Maps and Distance Chart

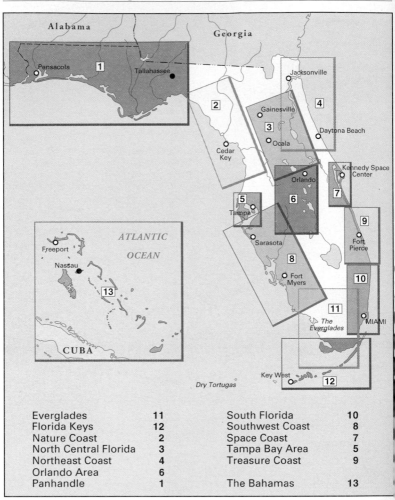

Everglades	11	South Florida	10
Florida Keys	12	Southwest Coast	8
Nature Coast	2	Space Coast	7
North Central Florida	3	Tampa Bay Area	5
Northeast Coast	4	Treasure Coast	9
Orlando Area	6		
Panhandle	1	The Bahamas	13

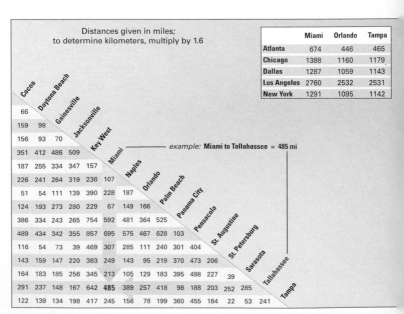

Distances given in miles;
to determine kilometers, multiply by 1.6

	Miami	Orlando	Tampa
Atlanta	674	446	465
Chicago	1388	1160	1179
Dallas	1287	1059	1143
Los Angeles	2760	2532	2531
New York	1291	1095	1142

example: **Miami to Tallahassee = 485 mi**

Cocoa	Daytona Beach	Gainesville	Jacksonville	Key West	Miami	Naples	Orlando	Palm Beach	Panama City	Pensacola	St. Augustine	St. Petersburg	Sarasota	Tallahassee
66														
159	98													
156	93	70												
351	412	486	509											
187	255	334	347	157										
226	241	264	319	236	107									
51	54	111	139	390	228	187								
124	193	273	280	229	67	149	166							
386	334	243	265	754	592	481	364	525						
489	434	342	355	857	695	575	467	628	103					
116	54	73	39	469	307	285	111	240	301	404				
143	159	147	220	383	249	143	95	219	370	473	206			
164	183	185	256	345	213	105	129	183	395	498	227	39		
291	237	148	167	642	**485**	389	257	418	98	188	203	252	285	
122	139	134	198	417	245	156	78	199	360	455	184	22	53	241

Useful Addresses and Web Sites

Visit Florida
P.O. Box 1100
Tallahassee FL 32302
☎ 850-488-5607 or 888-735-2872
www.flausa.com.

Florida Department of Environmental Protection
Division of Recreation & Parks
3900 Commonwealth Blvd.
Tallahassee FL 32399-3000
☎ 850-488-9872
www.dep.statc.fl.us./parks

Office of Fisheries Management
3900 Commonwealth Blvd.
Tallahassee FL 32399-3000
☎ 850-922-4340
www.myflorida.com

Office of Greenways and Trails
2600 Blair Stone Rd.
Tallahassee FL 32399-2400
☎ 850-487-4784
www.myflorida.com

Florida Association of RV Parks & Campgrounds
340 Vickers Rd.
Tallahassee FL 32303-3041
☎ 850-562-7151
www.floridacamping.com

Florida Department of Transportation
605 Suwannee St.
Tallahassee FL 32399
☎ 850-487-1200
www.dot.state.fl.us

Florida Sports Foundation
2964 Wellington Circle North
Tallahassee FL 32308
☎ 850-488-8347
www.flasports.com.

US Forest Service
325 John Knox Rd.
Tallahassee FL 32303-4160
☎ 850-942-9300
www.fs.fed.us

Other helpful Web sites:
www.myflorida.com
State of Florida information including state parks
www.flheritage.com State Division of Historical Resources information includes museum network, preservation news, etc.
www.floridasecrets.com Accommodations, restaurants, fun facts and more
www.see-florida.com Attractions, lodgings, dining and recreation
www.beachdirectory.com Information on accommodations, restaurants and attractions available in five languages

Admission prices shown throughout this guide are for a single adult only; children's admission prices are typically less. Discounts may be available for students, seniors, military personnel and others.

Courtesy Lee Island Coast V&CB

Saw Grass and Mangroves at Sunrise, Everglades National Park

Introduction
to Florida

Florida Landscapes

Distinguished by its 1,197-mile coastline—second after Alaska among the 50 states—Florida is surrounded by the sea: the Atlantic Ocean to the east, the Straits of Florida to the south and the Gulf of Mexico to the west. On land, to the north and northwest, lie Georgia and Alabama, whose narrow corridor to the Gulf Coast reaches around Florida's extreme northwestern border along the Perdido River. Thanks to the state's peninsular shape, no point is more than 80mi from salt water. Land elevations vary only slightly—from sea level to a peak of 345ft in the Panhandle. Ranking 22nd in area, the state comprises 59,988sq mi—including 5,991sq mi of water. With an estimated 30,000 lakes, including Lake Okeechobee, the nation's third-largest freshwater lake, Florida claims more lakes than any US state south of Wisconsin. Most of the lakes are natural, many the result of sinkholes. In addition, nearly a quarter of the nation's first-magnitude springs (those that discharge 64.6 million gallons or more of water per day) surface in Florida.

Geologic Past

Lacking the telltale exposed strata of eroded mountain outcrops, Florida reveals its geology much less readily than other states. Early efforts at peering into the geological past were mainly a side benefit from deep well borings and other commercial explorations below the land's surface. The evidence amassed by earth scientists over the years has helped sketch a composite portrait of what is probably the youngest region in the continental US—that is, the last to emerge from a primordial, subtropical sea only 10 to 15 million years ago.

Origins – During the late Paleozoic era, Florida was part of the supercontinent Pangea, a C-shaped, crustal conglomerate formed by the earth's colliding major landmasses some 280 million years ago. Straddling the equator, Pangea split along a north-south axis 130 million years later and began to break up into the modern continents of Eurasia, Africa, North and South America, Antarctica and Australia. The Atlantic Ocean was born as the larger continental plates drifted away from the sea's mid-ocean ridge. Precambrian Florida was one of the many terranes, or smaller crustal pieces, set afloat among the larger continents. Tracking northwards, it was grafted onto the much larger North American plate at a time when a chain of volcanic islands erupted off the mainland and arced into what are now the Bahamas.

Over time balmy shallow seas covered this bedrock. While dinosaurs roamed the great landmass to the north, silts and clays washed down from the Appalachian Mountains and fanned out into extensive submarine deltas along Florida's northern shore. To the

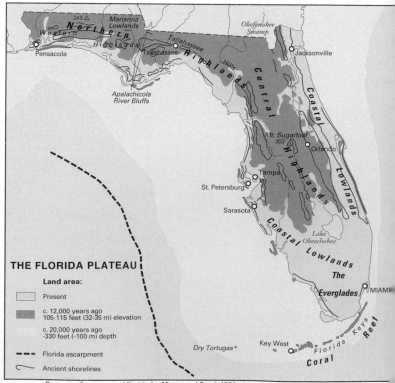

THE FLORIDA PLATEAU

Land area:

☐ Present

■ c. 12,000 years ago
105-115 feet (32-35 m) elevation

■ c. 20,000 years ago
-330 feet (-100 m) depth

-- -- Florida escarpment

〜 Ancient shorelines

south, marine shells mixed with microscopic carbonate fragments accumulated in a massive layer of limestone and dolomite. In places 13,000ft to 18,000ft thick, these sedimentary rocks cover much of the Florida Plateau from the Gulf escarpment to the Atlantic Ocean.

During the late Oligocene, the plateau broke the surface of the sea. As Ice Age glaciers locked up more and more of the earth's water, Florida's land area grew—possibly to twice its present-day size. During the early Pleistocene, this part of the continent became a haven for mammoths, mastodons, saber-toothed tigers, sloths and other large mammals retreating overland from the frozen north.

The Florida Plateau Today – As the continental ice sheets melted and refroze, the sea level rose and fell several times, etching successive terraces into ancient shorelines that are still visible today. Though much the same size, the plateau now lies half submerged again, its edges defining the continental shelf which surrounds Florida at some 300ft below the sea. Deepwater harbors on the Gulf side result from a pronounced westward dip of the plateau that continues to this day: the plateau's surface rises about 6ft at Miami, and it tilts downward about 30ft at Pensacola.

Regional Landscapes

For the most part a flat terrain with sandy and clay soils, Florida holds within its boundaries an astonishing diversity of landscapes, each exhibiting its own distinct characteristics. From hardwood forests to freshwater marshes, from coastal dunes and barrier islands to tropical coral reefs, the Sunshine State promises great variety to travelers of both highway and footpath.

Northern Highlands – Encompassing much of the Panhandle between the Alabama state line and the Withlacoochee River, this hilly area of forests and rivers unrolls as a 250mi-long and 30mi-wide band from west to east. Florida's natural apex—at 345ft, not even as high as some of the state's urban skyscrapers—stands 25mi north of De Funiak Springs in Walton County near the Alabama border. Encased by scrub and high pine as well as temperate hardwood forests, Florida's principal rivers course through this sparsely populated, largely rural region. The state's largest springs also originate here.

Ranging from the Perdido River to the Apalachicola River, the **Western Highlands** form a south-sloping complex dissected by narrow stream valleys with steep bluffs. An open overstory of longleaf pines and deciduous oaks above a ground cover of perennial grasses characterizes the vegetation of this region. The life cycle of longleaf pine is indelibly linked to fire. Lightning-sparked blazes foster seed germination and enhance pine forest regeneration.

Encompassing most of the upstream drainage basins of the Chipola and Choctawhatchee rivers, the **Marianna Lowlands** may have been the first area of Florida to emerge from the sea. Composed of Eocene sedimentary rocks, the rolling landscape wedged into this corner of the Inland Panhandle features numerous springs, scattered limestone outcrops, and countless sinkholes, lakes and ponds.

One of the state's unusual geographical features, **sinkholes** occur when the limestone foundation erodes under topsoil, leaving a bowl-shaped depression in the earth. Whereas a solution sinkhole forms gradually, a collapse sinkhole happens suddenly when an underground cavern caves in. Sinks often result from either drought or heavy rain—both of which can weaken the underlying limestone structure. Many become basins for swamps, ponds or lakes.

Just to the east of the Marianna Lowlands, the **Tallahassee Hills** stretch 100mi from the Apalachicola River to the Withlacoochee River. This region of gentle rises and forested valleys slopes upward to form a 300ft-high plateau west of Tallahassee near the Georgia border. Its fertile clay soils nourish hardwood forests (cypress, live oak, magnolia and hickory) more extensive than those found anywhere else in the state.

One of Florida's most remarkable geological formations can be found on this area's western border. The **Apalachicola River Bluffs**, a series of steep bluffs and ravines, line the eastern shore of the Apalachicola River in Gadsden and Liberty counties. Parts of this river system, which rose in the Appalachian Mountains during the early Cenozoic era, have been above sea level for as long as 24 million years. Forests along these bluffs shelter the native Torreya trees. Now near extinction, *Torreya taxiflora* is preserved in Torreya State Park.

Central Highlands – The green spine of Florida runs down the middle of the peninsula from the southernmost reaches of the Okefenokee Swamp (which dips across the Georgia border into northeast Florida) for 250mi to Lake Okeechobee. Though the northern section bulges to 60mi in width, the re-

---

■ Sinkholes

In 1981 a 300ft-wide sink opened up in Winter Park, engulfing six vehicles, a house and parts of two streets. The largest sink on record in Florida, it measures 100ft deep. (It's no wonder that sinkhole insurance has become a popular financial instrument in the state.) Between 400 and 4,000 new sinkholes develop in Florida every year, most less than 20ft wide.

gion tapers to a point in the south, where it converges with the Everglades and the Coastal Lowlands. Characterized by longitudinal ridges and upland plains and valleys, this region boasts thousands of lakes.

The world's heaviest concentration of **citrus trees** flourishes along a 100mi-long ridge (1mi to 25mi wide and 240ft high) from Leesburg to Sebring. "The Ridge," acclaimed science writer John McPhee notes, "is the Florida Divide, the peninsular watershed, and, to hear Floridians describe it, the world's most stupendous mountain range after the Himalayas and the Andes...." This infamous ridge reaches its pinnacle at 302ft Mount Sugarloaf.

Northern reaches of the Central Highlands also claim a high concentration of natural **springs**. The combination of warm climate, heavy humidity, abundant decayed vegetation and a thick limestone bedrock makes north Florida ideal terrain for spring formation. South of Lake Okeechobee, where the limestone peters out, no springs exist. Bubbling up from the Floridan Aquifer, these clear pools provide soothing, therapeutic waters for thousands of visitors each year.

Coastal Lowlands – Harboring nearly all the state's major commercial, industrial and resort areas, the flat, low-lying areas rimming the peninsula spread inland as much as 60mi in some places and include the Florida Keys and the Everglades. Dominated by pastureland and extensive farming, the region's interior contrasts sharply with its glittering margins, where the state's environment-based tourism and recreational activities are focused. Florida's fine quartz and calcium carbonate (shell fragments) sand makes dazzling white beaches. The oldest, finest—and purest quartz—sand, washed over the eons to a powdery texture, can be found on Florida's west coast near Sarasota and along the Panhandle coast.

Beach in Northwest Florida

Blessed with a gentle climate and warm Gulf and Atlantic waters, the state's coastal areas encompass a variety of natural environments. **Estuaries**, the most productive marine habitat in Florida, line nearly the entire coast where fresh water mingles with salt water. These shallow-water communities are vital for the development of a tremendous number of marine organisms. Another nursery for fish and shellfish, **mangrove swamps** edge the southeast and southwest coasts. More than 200 different types of fish and 180 bird species find habitat here, as do the endangered American crocodile and Florida manatee. Wind-blown **dunes** and their backdrop of **maritime forest** harbor sea oats and 22 other native plant species, as well as hosts of shorebirds.

Along both the Atlantic and Gulf coasts, strings of narrow, elongated sandy spits form protective **barrier islands** sheltering the mainland's many inlets, bays and estuaries. In addition to the periodic damage caused by hurricanes and violent winter storms, their ecological survival is severely tested by coastal development.

The Everglades – Considered a separate ecosystem, the broad expanse of the Everglades is covered by a shallow, slow-moving river that flows southward from Lake Okeechobee to the Florida Bay. Freshwater marshes, saw grass prairies, swamps and hardwood hammocks cover this depression. The youngest part of Florida, the area south of Lake Okeechobee emerged from the sea upon built-up layers of live coral clinging to submerged oolitic limestone. With the eventual formation of sand dunes that sealed out the ocean, a new freshwater basin filled with marine plant life and eventually became the peat- and boglands that served as the forerunner to the Everglades—a territory unlike any other in the world.

Scattered along the southern end of the Everglades, small rocky hammocks—designated as **South Florida Rockland**—give rare shelter to pines and broad-leaved tropical plants among barren limestone outcrops.

Tropical Coral Reefs – Vital to Florida's economy, **coral reefs** extend in a 150mi-long curve from near Miami to the Dry Tortugas, 69mi west of Key West. Commercial and recreational fishing industries depend on the reef ecosystems, as do diving and snorkeling enthusiasts. Found nowhere else in the continental US, these spectacular underwater worlds are composed of calcified limestone secreted by invertebrate coral polyps. The formations began forming some 7,000 years ago. Colorful fans, coral branches and plumes on the reef create intricate forests inhabited by diverse communities of tropical fish, sponges, spiny lobsters and other exotic sea creatures, making the Keys one of the world's most popular diving destinations.

Balancing Act – With one of the fastest growing populations in the country, Florida faces the likelihood of ever-greater loss of its wildlife, native vegetation and natural resources. Coral reefs and other marine environments contend with oil drilling and contamination; wetlands are lost to drainage, filling and development; and upland forests and flatwoods are reduced by logging and conversion to citrus groves. In response, state and private organizations have begun to buy more and more land to be set aside for conservation and recreation. Public awareness of the importance of these environments has also helped strike a balance between nature and mankind. Programs like the state-funded Preservation 2000, which commands a $300 million annual budget for purchasing environmentally sensitive land, offer Florida a fighting chance of preserving for future residents and visitors a few wild landscapes washed by balmy breezes and timeless subtropical seas.

Climate

Considered by many its most important natural resource, Florida's climate generally remains pleasant from January to December, drawing tourists year-round. Conditions vary from tropical in the Keys and subtropical in the central region to temperate in the Panhandle. Positioned at a more southerly latitude than any US state except Hawaii, Florida claims the country's highest average year-round temperatures, with Key West ranking as the hottest city in the nation at an average of 77.4°F. The warm Gulf Stream, which flows around the Florida Straits and north up the Atlantic coast from the tropics, tempers the prevailing easterly wind that blows over the peninsula. More than half the average annual rainfall of 52in a year falls between the beginning of June and the end of September (the month when most hurricanes occur). These hot, humid summers bring hordes of mosquitoes to the forests and marshes. Winter, the main tourist season, enjoys mild and relatively dry weather—especially in central and south Florida. The Panhandle suffers a more continental winter, with a higher frequency of freezing temperatures. Snowfall is almost nonexistent, though several inches—a dusting of which reached as far south as Miami Beach—were recorded in the north part of the state in 1977.

The combination of moist air and sun-heated land and water surfaces in Florida provides ideal conditions for the formation of **thunderstorms**. In fact, the state experiences more thunderstorms than anywhere in the world except East Africa. On summer days, hot air rises over the peninsula. When it meets with damp air from the Gulf and the Atlantic, converging airstreams force air upward, where it condenses into towering thunderheads. Parts of south Florida have more than 90 storms a year; Fort Myers leads the state with an annual average of 100 days with lightning.

Hurricanes – Florida also lies in the path of intense tropical cyclones spawned in the Atlantic, the Caribbean or the Gulf of Mexico. Most common in August and September when weak low-pressure systems develop over warm water, hurricanes can measure upwards of 500mi in diameter and contain winds of up to 200mph (a tropical depression officially becomes a hurricane once its winds reach a speed of 74mph). These doughnut-shaped storms commonly churn across the Atlantic coast between Cape Canaveral and the Keys (a corridor popularly known as "hurricane alley"), though in recent decades the Panhandle has received a significant share of these storms as well. An average of one hurricane a year, usually of low or moderate intensity, strikes Florida. Several devastating storms have hit in this century: a hurricane in 1926 scored a direct hit on Miami, causing the worst city damage in history; two years later, another storm took some 2,000 lives when floodwaters breached levees around Lake Okeechobee; the Labor Day hurricane of 1935—holding the record for the highest sustained winds and storm tide—struck the Keys and ripped into the Gulf, killing more than 400 people. More recently, Hurricane Andrew mowed an 8mi swath across south Miami-Dade County in 1992, leaving in its wake 85 dead, 10,000 injured, and $30 million in damage. In early October 1995, Hurricane Opal—the 15th named storm of that season—pummeled the Panhandle coast, racking up over $2 billion worth of damage and washing away some of the area's famous dunes.

An average hurricane drops more than 2.4 trillion gallons of rain during each day of its existence and releases enough energy in one day to supply electricity for the entire US for six months.

On the positive side, Florida's epic storms invigorate its natural environment. High winds often distribute plant seeds over a wide expanse. The combination of winds and heavy rains stirs up sediments and nutrients on the bottoms of bays and backwaters. When hurricanes level forests and other protective ground cover, sun-loving plants and small animals quickly exploit the newly available niches, thus generating a whole new cycle of life.

Water Resources

Floridians have one of the highest per capita rates of water use in the country, thanks to the seemingly inexhaustible reserves of the **Floridan Aquifer**, the state's largest and only artesian aquifer (characterized by water that is forced up through cracks in non-porous rock by hydrostatic pressure). Called "Florida's rain barrel," the Floridan underlies the entire state and varies in depth up to 2,000ft in the areas surrounding Jacksonville and Orlando. Along with the shallower **Biscayne Aquifer**, which serves southeast Florida, the Floridan provides nearly 90 percent of the state's water for drinking, recreation, irrigation and waste disposal. These layers of porous limestone serve as underground reservoirs that give Florida more groundwater than any other state. Water levels are replenished by an abundant annual rainfall—the greatest amount falling in the extreme northwest and southeast corners of the state.

One of the largest sources of surface water in the state, **Lake Okeechobee** (Seminole for "big water") supplies south Florida's cities and farms, as well as the Everglades. At 700sq mi it ranks as the state's largest lake. After Okeechobee inundated nearby farming communities as a result of hurricanes in 1926 and 1928, the US Army Corps of Engineers began taming the lake with a new system of canals, dikes, pumping stations and spillways. Now its waters can be manipulated to control flooding of surrounding fields and towns. With an ever-increasing population in south Florida, Lake Okeechobee today lies at the heart of many complex land-use controversies which pit environmentalists against the area's farmers.

Flora

Dubbed by Ponce de León "Isle of Flowers" (for the Spanish *Pascua florida* Eastertime feast), Florida boasts an abundance of lush vegetation. Early botanists catalogued over 3,000 types of indigenous flowering plants, from tiny orchids to showy magnolias. To this total thousands of tropical and subtropical plants have been added over the years. Positioned between 24°30'N and 30°N latitude—the same latitude as Egypt—Florida juts southward from the temperate zone into warm tropical seas. This location produces a unique inversion: temperate-zone plants bloom in winter and the tropical varieties flower in summer. Furthermore, Florida's regional climatic variations contribute to the great diversity of native botanical species found in the state, from the high pine forests of the northwest to the saw grass marshes of the Everglades. The state's vegetation is generally distributed among seven habitats—hammocks, pinelands, flatwoods, scrublands, swamps, savannas and salt marshes. Together they contain about half the tree species north of Mexico.

Hammocks and Flatwoods – Occurring in the north and central regions, **hardwood hammocks** are raised islands of hardwoods and broad-leaved shrubs surrounded by prairie

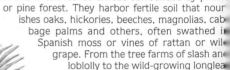

or pine forest. They harbor fertile soil that nourishes oaks, hickories, beeches, magnolias, cabbage palms and others, often swathed in Spanish moss or vines of rattan or wild grape. From the tree farms of slash and loblolly to the wild-growing longleaf of the uplands and the scrub pine of flat sandy areas, the state's many species of pine constitute Florida's most common tree.

Flatwoods containing boggy soil are found all over Florida and contain a number of blooms including 64 kinds of terrestrial **orchids**. Found in the central peninsula and along the coastal dunes, **scrublands** are characterized by thick stands of evergreen live oaks, saw palmetto and blackjack. Much of this land has been converted to vast groves of oranges and grapefruit. The savannas, or grasslands, in central Florida support a variety of marine grasses, including turtle, eel and manatee grasses.

Sabal Palm

R. Corbel/MICHELIN

A Profusion of Palms – Symbol of a luxuriant lifestyle, the **palm** also proliferates in Florida, which claims several hundred species—more than any other state. The cabbage or **Sabal palm**, one of only 15 native palms, is Florida's official state tree and flourishes throughout the state; early settlers harvested its crunchy edible bud, which was said to taste like cabbage. Among other notable natives, the tall royal palm graces many prominent boulevards and the low-lying palmetto forms dense thickets in the flatlands, varying in color from light green to grayish blue. The coconut palm massed lavishly in south Florida until an outbreak of lethal yellowing disease in the 1970s, when more than five million palms around Miami were destroyed. Many of the coconut palms were replaced by the hybrid Maypan and the coconut-bearing Malayan Dwarf.

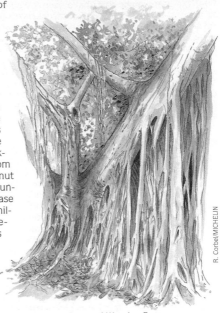

R. Corbel/MICHELIN

Aerial Roots of Weeping Banyan

The Marvelous Mangrove – The only known trees that can survive in salt water, mangroves have received much attention in recent decades, rising in status from developers' nuisance to coastal guardian. **Red mangroves** *(Rhizophora mangle)* thrive in the tidal zones; **black mangroves** *(Avicennia germinans)*, distinguished by short fingerlike aerating branches called pneumatophores that project above the soil, are found slightly more inland. **White mangroves** *(Laguncularia racemosa)* generally grow at the highest elevations. All have the ability to withstand the salt water of wind spray and high tide. Their cagelike root systems can stabilize a shoreline better than a seawall, as well as providing sanctuary for hundreds of species of fish. The most well known of the three Florida varieties, the red mangrove grows near the water on reddish aerial roots that absorb oxygen and fresh water and filter out salt. (Indians dubbed the red mangroves "walking trees," because the above-ground roots look like legs wading out into the water.) Black and white mangroves excrete salt by means of glands on the surface of their leaves.

Natives and Exotics – Among the 350 different types of trees found in Florida are the thick, coppery **gumbo-limbo** and the **manchineel**, one of the continent's most poisonous plants (often mistaken for poisonwood or poison sumac). Manchineel trees grow in swamps and produce a sap so toxic that even water dripping from their leaves can irritate the skin. A type of ficus native to the Sunshine State, the **strangler fig** wraps around its host (often a Sabal palm) and eventually kills it. The deciduous **bald cypress**, commonly found in Florida swamps, is named for its leafless winter appearance. A fig tree native to East India, the distinctive **banyan** tree is recognizable by its numerous trunks that appear like vertical bars of a prison cell. The tree's branches send out shoots that grow down to the soil and root to create additional trunks *(can be seen on grounds of Ringling Museum and Edison Ford Winter Estates)*.

© Al Messerschmidt

Cypress Trees

Over the years, **exotic plants** have been introduced to Florida, threatening the survival of many native species. Parks and conservation areas have implemented programs to rid their locales of such imported exotics, which now constitute 27 percent of all the plant species in the state. Trees such as the Brazilian pepper, imported for shade and ornamentation, have spread from backyards to wilderness, crowding out indigenous vegetation. Likewise, the Australian pine provides wonderful shade but also prevents anything from growing underneath its dense branches. The fire-resistant **Melaleuca** (also called the tea tree or cajeput), native to Australia and New Guinea, was planted in the Everglades in the 1930s to help dry up the wetlands; since then this uncontrollable pest has conquered tremendous acreage. Dade County now prohibits the planting or sale of any of these three species.

Fauna

Florida's gentle winters and warm sunshine support a bursting variety of animal life, including some 100 species of mammals and more than 400 species and subspecies of birds. While the increasing human population continues to reduce available territory for wildlife, an ardent segment has arisen to ensure that in the 21C Florida will carry on its ark with as many wild creatures as possible.

If you visit the Florida coast, you're likely to see bottle-nosed **dolphins**—a perennial favorite with visitors and residents—frolicking offshore. These sleek mammals frequent the shallow waters of the Gulf of Mexico as well as the Atlantic. Once hunted almost to extinction, **alligators** have enjoyed a renaissance in Florida and now number more than a million. Though often viewed as menacing, the giant reptiles help control populations of snakes and small mammals.

Perhaps the most easily observed animals, dozens of species of water birds make permanent or part-time homes in Florida. Of the species more likely to be found in Florida than anywhere else, the long-necked **anhinga** is known for its skill in spearing fish with its beak. Bird-watchers may also add **roseate spoonbills** to their must-see lists; sometimes mistaken for flamingos, spoonbills are shorter and are characterized by the flat, spoon-shaped beaks for which they are named. They flock in pink clouds over the wildlife refuges on Sanibel and Merritt islands. Another rare find, the **purple gallinule** frequents marshy waterways in the Everglades. This small bird is recognizable by its bright purple and blue feathers. The **brown pelican** makes a graceful sight skimming along the Atlantic and Gulf coasts. The pelicans' prevalence in Florida is misleading: outside the state they are rare, their numbers diminished by pesticides.

© Lynn M. Stone

Florida Panther

Florida provides haven to more than 67 species of threatened or endangered animals. Prominent on the endangered list are the reclusive **Florida panther**; the West Indian **manatee**; the diminutive **Key deer**; the **wood stork**, a wading bird once prevalent in mangrove and cypress swamps; and the Florida **sandhill crane**, another long-legged wader. The five kinds of **sea turtles** that nest in Florida are all either endangered or threatened; and the aggressive **American crocodile**, nearly extinct in the US, lives only in southern Florida.

While the high number of endangered species may seem to indicate a losing battle, Florida has actually made progress in slowing, and sometimes reversing, the decline of some animals. For instance, leatherback turtles, for the first time in a decade, have recently begun nesting as far north as St. Augustine and Jacksonville. Conservation organizations, wildlife hospitals, state parks and concerned citizens all appear determined to provide for Florida's wild kingdom for many years to come.

History

Prehistoric and Native Floridians

Prehistoric peoples probably inhabited the area of North America that now includes Florida as early as 10,000 BC. While it has long been thought that Ice Age nomads filtered southeast after crossing the Bering land bridge from Siberia into Alaska between 20,000 and 15,000 BC, there is now speculation that those who reached the Florida peninsula may have come instead from Central and South America through the Antilles. The earliest Indians here were hunter-gatherers whose diet included the meat of saber-toothed tigers, mastodons, bison and other Pleistocene animals. (Divers in northern Florida rivers often discover fluted stone spearheads, known as Clovis or Suwannee points, used by prehistoric hunters.)

The first semipermanent settlements began to spring up along Florida's waterways around 5000 BC. Evidence can be found in ancient **midden mounds**—or trash heaps— containing the discarded shells of shellfish, which had become increasingly important to the Indians' diet. Agriculture, including the cultivation of squash, beans and corn introduced from South America or Mexico, began when the population became more sedentary around 1000 BC. Archaeologists have also found some 14,000 **burial** mounds throughout the state (many lost to modern development). In these mysterious mounds, thought to reflect the influence of the Hopewell cultures of Illinois and Ohio, the bodies of chiefs or religious leaders were found resting face-up toward the sun. Other important tribal figures were buried face-down above them. By the Christian era, some of the ceremonial sites had developed into large complexes comprising several individual mounds connected by an intricate system of canals and roadways.

By the time European explorers visited the Florida peninsula in the 16C, the native population numbered an estimated 100,000. There were six main groups: the **Timucua** (occupying northeast Florida as far south as present-day Cape Canaveral); the **Apalachee** (Panhandle), the **Ais** (central and southeast coast), the **Tequesta** (southeast coast), the **Tocobaga** (Tampa Bay area) and the **Calusa** (southwest region). Developing independently, each group maintained a separate culture with specific social orders and sophisticated religious and political institutions. The northern Indians subsisted by farming, while those south of the Everglades generally hunted game and fished for seafood.

Within 250 years of European colonization, intertribal wars, Spanish slave raids and European-imported diseases such as smallpox, influenza and measles had decimated most of the Indian population. The few hundred remaining Timucua and Apalachee left Florida for Cuba with the Spanish in 1763. Today the only remaining traces of Florida's earliest native cultures are archaeological.

St. Augustine Historical Society

Timucuan Indians Taking Crops to Granary (16C). Drawing by Jacques Le Moyne

First Spanish Period 1513-1763

European explorers and fortune hunters began making forays into the Caribbean and Florida Straits in the 15C. Soon after Christopher Columbus discovered Hispaniola in 1492, Italian-born cartographer **Giovanni Caboto** (also known as John Cabot), commissioned by England's King Henry VIII, ventured into the New World to chart his findings. Although there is no specific record of it, Cabot and his son Sebastian probably sighted the Florida peninsula in 1497 or 1498. At least three European maps made between 1502 and 1511 indicate that others soon followed. Accounts that early explorers encountered Spanish-speaking Indians on the Florida peninsula support the theory that Spanish slave hunters from the West Indies had been there as well.

In 1513 explorer **Juan Ponce de León**, awarded with a Spanish patent to colonize any lands he found, made the first recorded—and officially sanctioned—landfall. De León, who was looking for the island of Bimini, went ashore somewhere between present-day St. Augustine and the St. Johns River in early April. He gave the name *La Florida* to an area that covers most of the present-day Southeast, west to the Mississippi River and north into the Carolinas. When de León returned to the southwest coast in 1521, he was gravely wounded in an Indian attack; he then sailed to Cuba where he died within a few weeks.

Subsequent Spanish colonization attempts also failed miserably. **Pánfilo de Narváez** set sail from Spain in 1527 with a patent to settle Florida—a reward from Emperor Charles V for de Narváez' service in the Spanish conquest of Cuba. In 1528 de Narváez landed in Tampa Bay, and with over half his cadre of 400 men, marched north by foot to Apalachee in search of gold, sending his ships up the coast to wait for him. When the men reached the coast, they found no ships so they set out for Mexico in several crude boats. De Narváez and all but 80 of his men subsequently met their end in a storm off the coast of Texas. Accomplished conquistador **Hernando de Soto's** legendary three-year search (1539-41) for riches in the New World also proved disastrous. After trekking several thousand miles with his 600 men—throughout central and northern Florida and as far west as present-day Oklahoma—de Soto died from fever. The remaining dispirited fortune-hunters—some 300 survivors—eventually found their way back to Spain. Next to try his luck, wealthy Spanish viceroy **Tristán de Luna** followed de Soto in 1559. Plagued by storms, hunger and dissension among his soldiers, de Luna was forced to abandon his effort to establish a settlement at Pensacola Bay.

Finding plenty of trouble but none of the anticipated riches, Spain (already importing gold and silver from Mexico and Peru) temporarily lost interest in colonizing *La Florida*. The peninsula's strategic location on the Florida Straits, however, was vital to protecting the country's Caribbean trade routes from pirates. In 1562, a French expedition led by the ardent Calvinist **Jean Ribault** entered the St. Johns River in search of a site for a Huguenot colony. When Ribault's fledgling settlement completed building Fort Caroline near the river's mouth in 1565, an alarmed Spain moved to reclaim her hold. Accordingly, later that year **Pedro Menéndez de Avilés** sailed into the Florida Straits and founded St. Augustine (to be the first permanent European settlement in Florida). He then massacred the French at Fort Caroline. At least one

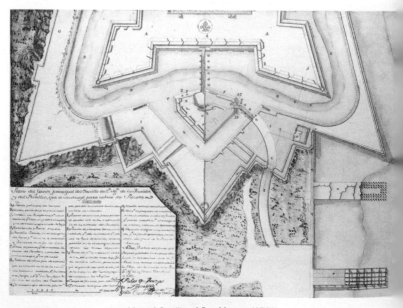

Map of Castillo of San Marcos (1763)

important legacy survives the French defeat: the published drawings and descriptions of the native population by French illustrator **Jacques Le Moyne** remain one of the most detailed accounts of early Florida history.

The Mission Chains – Although Spain retained her power in Florida for the next two centuries, the region attracted few independent settlers outside the military and the Catholic Church. Besides two garrisons at Pensacola and St. Augustine, the Spanish presence consisted of about 100 missions. Begun in 1565, the first of two chains led north from St. Augustine along the coast of present-day Georgia and South Carolina. A second string, built from the early 1600s to 1704, stretched west across the Panhandle to the Apalachee Bay region. At its center stood powerful San Luis de Talimali, built in 1656 near present-day Tallahassee, which included a church, a convent for the friars, cemetery and block houses, as well as an Apalachee Indian village and ball field. The missions functioned primarily as a strategic defensive system, designed to convert, centralize—and thus control—the Indians, who were coerced into labor and defense of the Spanish frontier. Ultimately the system failed, succumbing to both internal power struggles among the Franciscan friars and to external attack. By the early years of the 18C, most missions had been burned in raids—supported by defecting Indians—led by British soldiers from the English colony of South Carolina. Remaining structures, fashioned from perishable wooden frames roofed with palm thatch, quickly deteriorated, and soon all traces of the missions had disappeared.

British Period 1763-1783

The 1763 **Treaty of Paris** ending the Seven Years War between England and France marked a decisive turning point in Florida history. Under the treaty's provisions, the Spanish colony was ceded to Britain in exchange for Havana, Cuba, which England had captured the previous year. Florida was then split into two parts. East Florida, with a capital at St. Augustine, included the peninsula and the Panhandle as far as the Apalachicola River. West Florida, with Pensacola as its capital, was bounded on the north by the present state line, and on the west by the Mississippi River. By British charter in 1764, Florida gained a section between the Mississippi and Chattahoochee rivers extending north to present-day cities of Jackson, Mississippi, and Montgomery, Alabama.

In contrast to Spain, Britain attempted a self-supporting colony. Sugar, rice, indigo and cotton plantations were established along the St. Johns River. Export subsidies and generous land grants drew Protestant settlers from Great Britain as well as Tory sympathizers who left Georgia and South Carolina after the Revolution. The new population also included a 1768 colony of some 2,000 Greeks, Italians and Minorcans at New Smyrna, about 75mi south of St. Augustine. By the 1720s, a number of different loosely organized Indian groups (later known as the Creek Confederacy), pushed by settlers out of Georgia, Alabama and South Carolina, had also begun to filter into northern Florida. From the Creeks, two main nations, the Hitchiti-speaking **Miccosukee** and the Muskogee-speaking **Seminoles**, emerged.

Second Spanish Period 1784-1821

British occupation of Florida was to last only 20 years. With Britain's forces engaged in Revolutionary War battles farther north, Spain (participating in the war indirectly as a French ally) took advantage of Florida's weakened defenses and recaptured Pensacola in 1781. Under the **Second Treaty of Paris** (1783) ending the Revolution, the remainder of Florida reverted to Spanish control—excluding the northern section added above the Panhandle in 1764. By about 1800, Seminole villages were scattered from Apalachicola east to the St. Johns River and from south Georgia down to the Caloosahatchee River. During the War of 1812, violence erupted repeatedly between white settlers and Indians, who were resented for harboring runaway slaves and controlling valuable land. In 1814, a battle with the Upper Creeks at Horseshoe Bend ended in Indian defeat and a treaty opening 20 million acres of Creek land to US settlement. From 1817 to 1818, Gen. Andrew Jackson led a special US command against the Seminoles, initiating a series of raids later known as the **First Seminole War** and attacking several Spanish settlements.

By this time it was clear that Spain could neither govern nor police its increasingly turbulent territory effectively. Its power thus diminished, Spain negotiated the **Adams-Onís Treaty** in 1819. This agreement transferred the land east of the Mississippi to the US and formalized the boundaries of present-day Florida with the Panhandle terminating at the Perdido River. The treaty was ratified in 1821 and the two Floridas were handed over to General Jackson in Pensacola on July 17.

Early Settlement and the Seminole Wars

In 1822 President Monroe unified the two Floridas into a single territory with two counties: Escambia and St. Johns. Two years later, the first Territorial governor, William P. DuVal, named Tallahassee as the capital. In the new US Territory, the government recognized all land grants made before 1818, pending fulfillment of the original terms. Congress also granted the right of pre-emption to settlers, allowing squatters to remain if they purchased 80 acres of land at $1.25 an acre. With the area now open to settlers, tensions mounted over the Indian presence.

In the 1820s the US government attempted to contain the native population on a single tract of land in central Florida. When this effort failed, Jackson, now president, signed the **Indian Removal Act** in 1830, in hopes of resolving Indian conflicts once and for all by relocating eastern tribes to a designated area west of the Mississippi River. This law specified that the Indians must consent to moving, that they would be paid for their land and they would hold perpetual title to their new territories in the west. The Seminole demonstrated the greatest resistance to this infamous forced exodus, known as the **Trail of Tears**. In 1832 a small group (unauthorized by their leaders) signed the **Treaty of Payne's Landing**, requiring the Indians to relinquish their land and relocate to a reservation in Arkansas (now Oklahoma). At the end of a three-year grace period, however, not a single Seminole had left.

Osceola (c. 1837). Portrait by John Rogers Vinton

US troops arrived in 1835 to enforce the treaty. In December Seminoles ambushed the command of Maj. Francis Dade near Bushnell, precipitating the **Second Seminole War**. The leader of the Seminole resistance was **Osceola**. Still remembered for his cunning and courage, this great man met a bitter end. In late 1837, he was tricked into entering a US army camp near St. Augustine. There under a flag of truce, he was imprisoned and transferred to Fort Moultrie in Charleston, South Carolina, where he died in 1838. The Seminole Wars ended in 1842, when at least 3,000 Indians and blacks were sent to Oklahoma. For every two Indians removed, one white soldier was killed; the cost to the federal government was $20 million. Eluding capture, several hundred Seminoles melted into the Everglades. In 1845 Florida was admitted to the Union as the 27th state. Indian rights remained unresolved, as Floridians kept pressing the US government for total removal of the Seminoles from the state. Increasing incursions of the white man into Indian reservation land eventually led to the **Third Seminole War** of 1855-58, an inconclusive series of swamp skirmishes that ended with the surrender of Seminole chief Billy Bowlegs and never resulted in a formal treaty with the US government.

The Plantation Belt – During early statehood, settlement remained primarily between the Suwannee and Apalachicola rivers in an area called Middle Florida, where pioneers and cattle drivers established small farms. The dark, sandy loam there also proved excellent for **cotton** cultivation and hundreds of plantations flourished by 1850, building a cotton economy comparable to that of antebellum Georgia. (In 1834 the first railroad incorporated in Florida connected the cotton market of Tallahassee to the port of St. Marks. It was built for the express purpose of shipping cotton to textile mills in New England and overseas.) Eventually, this plantation belt spread southeastward, encompassing Alachua and Marion counties by 1860. Aside from cotton, timber, turpentine and sugarcane were common plantation products. Sugarcane plantations were concentrated along the St. Johns and Manatee rivers.

While plantation size varied from 1,000 to 5,000 acres, wealth was measured not by acreage but by the number of slaves one owned. "Planters" were defined as those who owned 20 or more slaves. The number of planters who owned 30 or more slaves doubled between 1850 and 1860. This elite group set the local political, economic and social tone.

The Steamboat Age – The riverboat industry was critical to Florida's economic development and settlement. The first steamboat service was offered in 1827 on the Apalachicola River. This waterbody, along with the Chattahoochee and Flint rivers, formed an important cotton outlet. Lumber, then a major export, was also ferried via steamer. During the Second Seminole War, the government chartered 40 steamboats to transport troops and supplies. By 1848 service from Jacksonville connected Palatka and Enterprise on the St. Johns River. With the steamers came Florida's first winter tourists, a major portion of whom were northerners whose doctors had recommended a sunny clime to cure their ailments. Sick and healthy passengers alike slept in elegantly furnished staterooms and dined on fine food, while the exotic foliage, Spanish moss and alligators sighted on the banks of the dark, winding waterways held the promised trappings of a wilderness adventure.

Civil War and Reconstruction

A steady flow of settlers and the sound plantation economy increased Florida's population of 34,700 in 1830 to 140,400 in 1860. Almost half of them were "non-white." To protect its one-sided economy, which relied heavily on slave labor, the state seceded from the Union in 1861 and became an important supplier of beef, cotton and salt to the Confederacy. The major Civil War clash on Florida soil was the 1864 battle at Olustee near Lake City; there on February 20, Confederate troops drove back the Union soldiers and preserved supply lines to Georgia. A second important victory occurred the next year, when Tallahassee—the only southern capital to escape capture—was successfully defended in the Battle of Natural Bridge.

The war put the state into near bankruptcy, but reconstruction brought new investors from the north, ready to finance business, land speculation, transportation and tourism. Sharecroppers and tenant farmers, including freed blacks, took over the plantations. Cotton, timber and cattle sales helped boost the economy. In the late 1860s, some 6,000 Cubans immigrated to Florida at the start of Cuba's Ten Years' War of Independence (1868-78), establishing Key West as a major cigar-making center. Soon thereafter, the commercial sponge market, established in Key West in 1849, moved its hub north after new beds were discovered off Tarpon Springs in the 1870s. And the commercial citrus industry increased and thrived—until two terrible freezes in the winter of 1894-95 obliterated about 90 percent of the crop.

The Railroad Boom – Florida's late 19C growth was closely linked to its rapid railroad development, spurred by the state's 1881 sale of four million acres of swamp and overflow land in central Florida to Philadelphia entrepreneur **Hamilton Disston**. Most importantly, this sale provided funds to clear the titles of state-owned land from earlier railroad promotions and opened the way for subsidies and land grants to new railroad builders. The undisputed leaders in the field—and in Florida development —remain two of the most colorful figures in the state's history: railroad tycoons **Henry Bradley Plant** and **Henry Morrison Flagler**. Plant consolidated and expanded numerous existing short lines and extended track to Tampa in 1884 to create an important link to northern markets. The Plant system merged with the Atlantic Coast Line in 1902 to complete a network of about 2,250mi of track originating in Richmond, Virginia. Flagler concentrated on the **Florida East Coast Railway** (FEC), extending it from Jacksonville to St. Augustine in 1886 and subsequently to Palm Beach (1894), Miami (1896) and Key West (1912). As the railway system expanded to link Florida to the rail lines crossing the US, it also spurred the state's winter production of fruit and vegetables.

Extravagant hotels strategically placed at each new railhead, such as the sprawling Ponce de Leon in St. Augustine, the Royal Poinciana in Palm Beach (the dining room seated 1,600), and Miami's Royal Palm (with its circular six-hole golf course) became fashionable resort destinations for the northern social set in the late 19C.

20C DEVELOPMENT

The early 20C was Florida's gilded age, a brief period of glamour, extravagance and no income or inheritance tax. Millionaire industrialists luxuriated in fabulous villas, while movie stars arrived from Hollywood to make films in Jacksonville, then a leading motion-picture production center. The economy had benefited from the 1898 **Spanish-American War**, when embarkation camps for American troops were located in Tampa, Miami and Jacksonville. After the US won its bid to gain Cuban independence from

© CAMERA GRAPHICS

Bathing Beach at the Breakers Hotel, Palm Beach (c.1928)

Spain, many soldiers returned to Florida with their families. For the first time, good roads—the Florida Road Department was established in 1915—and the affordable Model T automobile made vacations accessible to people who could not afford luxury hotels. Modest, family-operated motels and tourist courts sprouted on the Florida roadside. By the 1920s "tin-can tourist camps," filled with Tin Lizzies outfitted as campers, had appeared in every major Florida city.

Dozens of land speculators, including Carl Fisher in Miami Beach and George Merrick in Coral Gables, not only peddled Spanish bungalows, but also a new lifestyle and a rosy future in the "Empire of the Sun." From 1920-25, the state grew four times faster than any other state. As real-estate agent and self-proclaimed con-man Wilson Mizner (younger brother of architect Addison Mizner) assessed the situation: "Right up to January 1926, it was only necessary to point carelessly to a mudhole and tell a client that there was his future. He could not deny it, and even the salesman was in deadly fear that he spoke the truth."

Unfortunately, the bust was just as rapid as the boom. The real-estate crash came in 1926 on the heels of overspeculation and a destructive hurricane that beheaded palm trees, leveled cheaper construction and stopped new building in its tracks. A ruinous Mediterranean fruit fly invasion in 1929 devastated the citrus industry. And the onset of the national Depression that same year only confirmed what Floridians already knew.

Effects of World War II – Despite the lean years, Florida's population had grown to around two million by 1940. This number was supplemented by another three million tourists annually. World War II stimulated the economy with defense-related industry, road-building, and new and revitalized naval bases. After the war, servicemen who trained on the beaches of Daytona, Miami and St. Petersburg returned to find jobs or enroll in Florida colleges under the GI bill. The economy diversified. Frozen citrus juice concentrates became a major industry by 1950. The same year, the US inaugurated a long-range, missile-testing program at Cape Canaveral, followed by a new space satellite program eight years later.

After World War II, a strong Florida government made a concerted effort to bring corporate industry to the state. In addition, millions of people began to vacation here as the two-week paid vacation became standard. To accommodate them, more new hotels appeared in Greater Miami between 1945 and 1954 than in all the other US states combined. In 1958 the first US domestic jet service, from New York to Miami, opened the way for more tourists. Highway travel increased, too, and with it small attractions—featuring everything from alligators to mermaids—mushroomed along the Florida roadside. These private businesses were the forerunners of modern corporate-run theme parks, including the ever-expanding Disney empire. Today, some 70 million visitors come to Florida each year.

During the same period, Florida hosted another growing population: foreign refugees. Most notably, the 1959 Cuban Revolution sent waves of exiles into Dade County in that year and again in 1961. Between 1965 and 1973, a series of Cuban government-controlled airlifts—that came to be known as "Freedom Flights"—carried thousands more refugees to Florida. In 1980 the Cuban government again allowed emigration. This time, more than 125,000 residents of the port of Mariel, among them criminals released from Cuban prisons, landed on Miami's shores. The number of Cubans in Florida climbed to about 670,000 in 1990, infusing the state's culture with a strong Latin flavor.

Contemporary Florida

Only a few decades ago, Florida was seen as a region of infinite potential. "So many of Florida's resources are as yet undeveloped, so much wealth lies hidden in her soil, so great an area of wilderness beauty is yet to be discovered and appreciated," boasted a 1930 promotional booklet. Many would argue that during the next half-century, those same resources were not only overdeveloped, but exhausted. The boom cycles, transportation advancements and population influxes that define Florida history also brought the inevitable housing complexes, strip malls, high-rise beach development and traffic jams—making it difficult to believe that the peninsula was a beckoning frontier as recently as the early 20C. The state's proximity to South America means that much of the illegal drug trade entering the US filters through Florida. And immigration remains a sensitive subject, as the influx of Cuban exiles, Haitians, Nicaraguans, Jamaicans, Vietnamese, Cambodians and many other groups continues. Another type of immigrant—northern retirees—has also made an indelible mark on the Florida landscape, boosting the economy yet crowding roads and towns.

Florida's resources still abound, however, and in recent decades a trend toward preserving them has been emerging. Begun in 1981, the award-winning planned town of Seaside on the Panhandle has become an international model of environmentally sensitive contextual design. A proposal to remove some of the man-made locks and spillways in the Everglades in an effort to restore the natural water flow is being implemented. Politically active Seminole Indians are working to revive and preserve the cultural traditions. To be sure, any economy so dependent on tourism will always struggle to maintain the delicate balance between modern development and conservation of the land and people that constitute its natural resources.

Time Line

10,000-8,000 BC	First migration of prehistoric Indians to the Florida peninsula.
5000 BC	First semipermanent Native American settlements in Florida.
1492	Christopher Columbus lands in the region of the present-day Bahamas.
1513	Spanish explorer **Juan Ponce de León** lands in the area of present-day St. Augustine and names the land "*La Florida.*"
1521	Ponce de León returns to the southwestern coast of the Florida peninsula and attempts to establish a colony.
1528	Explorer **Pánfilo de Narváez** goes ashore at Tampa Bay and marches to Apalachee in search of gold.
1539-1541	Conquistador **Hernando de Soto** explores the Florida interior, trekking north and west into the continent.
1559	Spanish nobleman **Tristán de Luna** attempts to establish a settlement at Pensacola Bay.
1562	French Protestant **Jean Ribault** explores the banks of the St. Johns River as a possible site for a Huguenot colony; led by René de Laudonnière, the colony is established in 1564.
1565	**Pedro Menéndez de Avilés** founds San Augustine, the first permanent European settlement in America.

Courtesy of St. Augustine Historical Society

Juan Ponce de León   Hernando de Soto   Pedro Menéndez de Avilés

1565-1704	Spain founds about 100 **missions** in two chains stretching north and west from St. Augustine.
1672	Work begins on the **Castillo de San Marcos** at St. Augustine, the first stone fort built by the Spanish in Florida.
1702	British colonel James Moore destroys St. Augustine but fails to capture the Castillo de San Marcos. Britain begins attacks on Spanish missions two years later.
1719	French soldiers capture Pensacola but soon return the colony to Spain. France occupies the Gulf Coast west of Pensacola.
1720s	First migration of Creek groups—later called the Seminoles and **Miccosukee**—from Georgia into Florida.
1740	The British military invades Florida from Georgia.
1763	**Treaty of Paris** ends the Seven Years War (1756-63) between Britain and France. Britain gains Florida from Spain and splits the region into two provinces divided by the Apalachicola River.
1768	Minorcan, Italian and Greek colonists establish a colony at New Smyrna.
1781	Spanish recapture Pensacola from the British.
1783	The **Second Treaty of Paris** ends the American Revolution. Florida returns to Spanish control.
1814	Driven from their land in Alabama, homeless Creeks migrate to Florida, doubling that territory's Indian population.
1817-1818	Gen. Andrew Jackson initiates a series of raids against the Seminoles, later known as the **First Seminole War**.
1818	US gains Pensacola and pushes for Spanish withdrawal from the region.
1821	Spain gains the Texas territory and relinquishes Florida to the US under the terms of the **Adams-Onís Treaty**. Jackson is elected the first governor of the two Florida colonies.
1822	President Monroe unifies East and West Florida into one territory and settlement begins. Jacksonville is founded.
1824	Tallahassee is chosen as the state capital. Key West becomes a US naval station.

1827	The first steamboat service is established on the Apalachicola River.
1830	President Andrew Jackson signs the **Indian Removal Act** authorizing the relocation of eastern tribes to an area west of the Mississippi River.
1831	First cigar factory is built in Key West.
1832	US claims Seminole lands in Florida under the **Treaty of Payne's Landing**.
1834	Florida's first railroad, the mule-drawn Tallahassee-St. Mark's line, is incorporated.
1835-1842	US military forces and Florida Indians clash in the **Second Seminole War**. At least 3,000 Indians and blacks are relocated to Arkansas and Kissimmee area is opened to white settlement.
1837	Seminole leader **Osceola** is imprisoned under a flag of truce at a St. Augustine army base.
1838	Osceola dies at age 34 in a South Carolina dungeon. First Constitutional Convention held in St. Joseph (Port St. Joe).
1841	Yellow fever epidemic hits the Panhandle.
1845	Florida becomes the 27th US state under President John Tyler. William D. Moseley is elected the first governor.
1849	The first commercial sponge market opens in Key West.
1851	Dr. John Gorrie patents the process of making ice artificially.
1855	Under Florida's **Internal Improvement Act**, undeveloped Florida land is made available to investors.
1855-1858	Billy Bowlegs—the last chief under whom all Seminoles were united—leads the Indian resistance in the **Third Seminole War**.
1860	The first east-west Florida railroad, linking Cedar Key with Fernandina Beach, is completed.
1861	Florida secedes from the Union.
1864	Confederate troops win the **Battle of Olustee** near Lake City, Florida, preserving interior supply lines to Georgia.
1865	Florida militia repulse Union forces at **Natural Bridge**, saving Tallahassee from capture.
1868	New Florida constitution is adopted.
1875	The city of Orlando is incorporated.
1881	Philadelphia industrialist **Hamilton Disston** buys four million acres of land in central Florida and begins the first private land development in the state.
1883	The first all-black high school is founded in Jacksonville.
1884	**Henry Plant** completes a rail line into Tampa.
1885	**Henry Flagler** begins building a rail line between Jacksonville and St Augustine and establishes the Florida East Coast Railway.
1886	Fire destroys the entire commercial district of Key West. Labor disputes cause the cigar industry to relocate from Key West to Tampa.
1894-1895	Winter freezes destroy citrus crops in central and north Florida and force the citrus industry to move south.
1896	In April, Flagler extends railroad to Miami; three months later, the City of Miami is incorporated.
1898	Embarkation camps for American troops are established in Tampa, Miami and Jacksonville during the **Spanish-American War**.
1901	Fire destroys most of Jacksonville, gutting more than 2,000 buildings.
1906	Drainage of the Everglades begins, spearheaded by Florida governor Napoleon Bonaparte Broward.
1912	Flagler's **Overseas Railroad** from Homestead (near Miami) to Key West is completed.
1914	First regularly scheduled commercial airline flight is made by pilot Tony Jannus between St. Petersburg and Tampa.
1917-1918	World War I soldiers and aviators train in Florida.
1926	Miami takes a direct hit from a deadly September hurricane.
1927	Pan American Airways inaugurates commercial service with a flight from Key West to Havana, Cuba.
1928	The Tamiami Trail (US-41) across the Everglades is opened.
1929	A Mediterranean fruit-fly infestation destroys citrus crops in 20 central Florida counties.
1935	A devastating Labor Day hurricane batters Key West, destroying the Overseas Railroad.
1941-1945	Defense-related industry boosts the Florida economy during **World War II**.
1947	University of Florida opens to female students. President Harry S Truman dedicates **Everglades National Park**.

Overseas Railroad (c.1920)

1950	Frozen citrus concentrates become a major Florida business. US inaugurates long-range missile-testing program at Cape Canaveral.
1954	The Sunshine Skyway bridge connects St. Petersburg with Manatee County to the south.
1955	Florida legislature authorizes the construction of a turnpike to run the length of the state.
1958	Newly formed National Aeronautics and Space Administration (NASA) begins operations at Cape Canaveral and launches first US satellite.
1959	The first regularly scheduled domestic air flights begin between New York and Miami.
1959-1962	Thousands of refugees flee Cuba for Florida to escape Fidel Castro's communist regime.
1961	NASA launches the first American astronaut, Alan Shepard, into space from Cape Canaveral.
1962	The first black students are admitted to undergraduate schools at Florida State University and the University of Florida.
1964	Race riots break out in Jacksonville and St. Augustine.
1969	On July 16, the first manned moon launch lifts off from Cape Kennedy.
1971	Walt Disney World opens near Orlando.
1972	Miami Beach hosts the Democratic and Republican national conventions.
1973	Freedom flights from Cuba to Miami end after bringing over 250,000 refugees to the US.
1979	The Miami Beach Art Deco district is designated a National Register Historic District.
1980	Some 125,000 Cuban refugees land in Miami. Riots erupt in Miami after four white policeman are acquitted in the beating death of a black man.
1981	On April 12, the Kennedy Space Center launches the first space shuttle, *Columbia*.
1983	A Christmas freeze strikes central Florida citrus groves; losses exceed $1 billion.
1986	Space shuttle *Challenger* explodes shortly after take-off from Cape Canaveral, killing all seven crew members aboard.
1989	Serial killer Theodore Bundy—who confessed to 31 murders in nine states—is executed in Florida's electric chair.
1990	Senator Gwen Margolis, a Democrat from Miami Beach, is elected first woman president of the Florida Senate.
1992	**Hurricane Andrew** smashes into Dade County on August 24, sending 80,000 citizens into shelters.
1993	President Clinton names Janet Reno, State Attorney of Dade County, as US Attorney General. Nine foreign tourists are murdered in Florida within 12 months.
1994	Florida Legislature passes the **Everglades Forever Act**, authorizing removal of agricultural pollutants from the area's waters.
1995	Hurricane Opal wreaks havoc along the Panhandle coast in October.

1996	Vice President Al Gore announces a comprehensive seven-year plan to restore the Everglades ecosystem in south Florida.
1998	Environmental advocate **Marjory Stoneman Douglas**, champion of the Everglades, dies at the age of 108. Major grass fires ravage northeast Florida, forcing 70,000 residents to evacuate their homes.
2000	The state holds the outcome of US presidential elections in the balance for six weeks as its ballots are painstakingly recounted. Florida's secretary of state reads the final tally, with George W. Bush receiving the majority of votes. The Supreme Court declares Bush the next president.
2001	By summer's end, 24 of the 42 shark attacks worldwide occur off Florida's coast, several at New Smyrna Beach.

Economy

By the time Florida became part of the US in 1821, it already had a thriving plantation economy in the northern part of the state, where most of the people lived. After the Civil War, new and diverse industries sprang up: timber, citrus, shipping, cattle and cigar-making helped establish Florida's importance in the national marketplace. Once the railroads linked the state with the rest of the country in the late 19C, Florida's economy began to blossom. Speculative land sales rocketed in the 1920s, but ended just as suddenly several years later. The subsequent downturn in real estate activity, followed by the Depression, slowed the state's growth until after World War II. Since then Florida's population has expanded rapidly, with retirees and young families fueling a healthy economy that varies from high-tech electronics and finance to agriculture and fishing.

Industry – Florida's **service** industries as a whole are projected to account for about 90 percent of new jobs created in the next decade. Leading this list are community and personal services, such as health care and tourist-related enterprises. About 30 percent of the state's employees work in this sector, earning one-quarter of the gross revenues.

Economists forecast that with Florida's aging population, **health care** will be one of the fastest growing industries in the next decade. The second biggest service industry, **retail** generates over 12 percent of the state's revenue in some of the country's largest department stores, malls, car dealerships, service stations and grocery stores. Enlisting about 13 percent of all workers, **government** extends its hand into schools, hospitals and the military.

Another big wedge of the service pie belongs to **finance and real estate**. Real estate in particular has mushroomed with the state's population growth, and now employs more than double the national average. Although Miami has recently topped Jacksonville as the state's leading financial center, Jacksonville still reigns as the insurance king, with several major insurance company headquarters located there. Transportation and foreign trade round out the service sector, with the latter expected to be one of Florida's hottest industries in upcoming years.

Highlighting the transportation field, **air travel** helps make large-scale tourism possible, while **trucks** transport most of the state's industrial and agricultural products. And some 15 deepwater **ports** serve Florida's international clients, with Tampa doing the largest volume of business.

Entertainment, now a subset of the service industry, has in the last 15 years made exciting moves: Universal and Disney-MGM have opened studios in Orlando. Motion picture, television, commercial and music video productions have injected some $3.9 billion into the local economy.

Because of Florida's distance from major US cities, **manufacturing** has traditionally taken a back seat to tourism and other service industries. With only 10 percent of the gross state product, manufacturing plays a small role here. Yet, since the beginning of the space program in the late 1950s, **high-technology** products have become a staple of the state's economy. National firms have opened branches here for the manufacture of communications devices, x-ray equipment, semiconductors and other computer components. Florida also engages in a sizable **food production** business that includes canned fruit juice, canned fruits and packaged vegetables. The **construction industry** has fluctuated with speculation based on the availability of loans as well as the predicted need of new housing.

Natural Resources – With Florida's waters claiming more than 700 species of fish, the **commercial fishing** industry nets the state more than $200 million a year, led by catches of shrimp, lobster, crab and snapper. Other important local species include grouper, swordfish, tuna and mullet. Ten percent of the total US shrimp harvest comes from Florida, and the state's Gulf estuaries—particularly off Apalachicola and the Big Bend coast—produce about 6 percent of the US oyster catch. Unfortunately, over fishing, foreign competition and contamination have caused a recent decline in the shellfish haul, and Florida has made some attempts at aquaculture to provide a more reliable harvest.

Forests cover about half of Florida's total land area, or almost 16 million acres. The north part of the state is the most densely timbered—commercial forests occupy 75 percent of the northwest region. Since the early 19C, **forestry** has held a significant place in the state's economy. In the years before the Civil War, hardwoods were cut for lumber and pines were tapped for turpentine and rosin used in shipbuilding. By the 1920s the **turpentine industry** had already peaked, but pulp mills were on the rise. Between 1889 and 1933, more than one billion board feet were sawed every year in Florida's great virgin forests before a division of forestry was established to manage this precious resource. Slash pine today ranks as the top commercial tree; common hardwoods include magnolia, black tupelo and oak. Among valued trees harvested almost to extinction are pecky cypress (a porous wood, resistant to termites and rotting) and Dade County pine, both popular local building materials during the early 20C.

Heading the list of mineral deposits, **phosphate** was discovered in the southwest part of the state in 1881. Florida now produces 80 percent of the country's phosphate—an essential ingredient in fertilizer. Florida also leads the nation in production of rutile and zircon, heavy minerals found in ancient beach deposits and used in ceramics, metals and chemicals. Found in greater quantities here than in any other state, **peat** is prized as a soil conditioner. Florida also boasts extensive amounts of **limestone** (its most prevalent mineral). All of Florida's mining operations combined account for less than one-half of one percent of the gross state product.

Agriculture – Leading the southeastern US in farm sales, Florida produces a variety of fruits, vegetables and nursery plants that it transports fresh to northern markets in the winter and spring. **Citrus fruits**, first introduced to Florida around 1570, outpace all Florida's other agricultural products, with oranges claiming over three-quarters of the total citrus sales. Florida invariably leads the nation in orange and grapefruit production, and supplies the vast majority of its orange juice. (Hard freezes in the 1980s destroyed thousands of acres of citrus groves in central Florida, forcing the state to import juice concentrate from Brazil.) Among Florida's many popular varieties of citrus are Valencia oranges (the world's most ubiquitous juice orange), Temple oranges, and Duncan grapefruit (its white flesh is considered the most flavorful).

While it is the single biggest crop, citrus makes up only a third of the state's total crop sales. Florida stands as the nation's top producer

Robert Torrez/Tony Stone Images

Citrus Fruit Sorted for Shipping

of **sugarcane**. Sugar plantations of the late 18C and early 19C were largely destroyed during the Seminole Wars, but the industry held on until finally receiving a big boost when US trade relations with Cuba soured in 1961. Now Florida produces nearly half the country's sugar, primarily in the area just south of Lake Okeechobee.

Only California beats out Florida in total production and value of fresh **vegetables**. Major local crops include tomatoes, sweet corn, green peppers, snap beans and cucumbers. The state's dairy and beef industries generate a quarter of its total farm income, making Florida the largest cattle state east of the Mississippi.

Tourism – From the time railroads linked Florida's grand east coast resorts in the late 19C, visitors have been flocking to the Sunshine State to escape the cold winters of more northern climes. With the widespread use of automobiles and the increase in small-scale tourist facilities, more people could afford an excursion to Florida. After World War II, the advent of indoor air-conditioning made south Florida a year-round destination. Now more than 70 million people visit the state annually, lured by clear subtropical seas, white-sand beaches and world-class tourist attractions. The opening of Walt Disney World in 1971 outside Orlando meant a greater distribution of tourists among the non-coastal areas; the Orlando area now attracts some 43 million tourists annually.

Visitors spend a total of $50 billion a year and generate work for 843,000 Floridians—about 12 percent of the state's jobs. Employing people in travel, restaurants, hotels, retail stores and recreational facilities, tourism continues to be the state's top economic resource. Winter remains the busiest tourist season, while spring lures hordes of vacationing college students to Daytona Beach and Panama City. Summertime brings auto-touring families to beaches and theme parks, but autumn sees the fewest visitors. Among foreign travelers to Florida, Canadians account for nearly two million.

Economic Outlook – Like the rest of the country, Florida has been weakened by recessionary trends surfacing in 2001 and by the accelerated economic downturn resulting from terrorist attacks on US soil on September 11 of that year. Significant job cuts by major companies across the US have had an impact on the state's economy. Lower interest rates have meant less income for dividend-receiving retirees, which translates to less cash flow and fewer new jobs. With a projected slowdown in population growth, job and income growth rates in Florida may be sluggish over the next 15 years. One sector of the economy that forecasters claim could outperform tourism in the next decade is **international trade**. Florida's proximity to Latin American and Caribbean markets coupled with its international ports and modern airports give the state an edge in this burgeoning field.

As for regional growth, look for Orlando to lead in population increase and housing starts. Southeast Florida, the most populous region, will likely maintain a healthy economic climate. Smaller areas on the move include Naples, Fort Walton Beach, Panama City, Ocala, Fort Myers, Fort Pierce and Port St. Lucie.

People

Four out of five Floridians are not native to the state. As a group, residents of Florida have in common the identity of "newcomer" more than anything else, and beyond that identity lies a hodgepodge of races, ages, origins and attitudes that sometimes sits uneasily side-by-side in this growing state. Yet along with their status as newcomers, Floridians as a whole share a sense of hope. Some come here seeking new job opportunities and others political freedom; but all come looking for a piece of the American good life, a place in the sun.

Florida's phenomenal growth has outstripped most of the country: in 1900 the state ranked 33rd in population; by 1960 it had risen to 10th. With nearly 16 million people, it now ranks as the fourth-largest state in the nation. And the population has redistributed itself as the south Florida wilderness has yielded to the dreams of pioneers and developers. In 1900 north Florida held 66 percent of the population, compared to 5 percent in south Florida. Today the north has shrunk to 20 percent, while the south carries 37 percent—with one-third of the entire state living on the 65mi strip from Miami to West Palm Beach known as the Gold Coast.

Early Minorities – One of the smallest ethnic groups, the **Seminoles** are themselves relatively new to Florida. They coalesced from various southeastern tribes and moved into Florida in the 18C to escape harassment by white settlers. Though most were relocated to Oklahoma in the mid-19C, about 2,000 Seminoles still live and maintain elements of their culture on reservations in and around the Everglades. The percentage of **African-Americans** decreased from 44 percent of the population in 1900 to about 13 percent in 1990. In the intervening decade, their numbers have grown to some 2.3 million, or about 14 percent of Florida's population.

North and South – If some Floridians consider the label "Cracker" a slur, most proudly acknowledge it as an ethnic identity that extols the frontier virtues of independence and self-reliance. The term—probably deriving from the snapping noise of whips used by early Florida cowboys—refers loosely to descendants of native white Floridians who

Miami Beauties

owned small farms or ranches in the north part of the state. Whereas the peninsula has funneled in Yankees from the northeast over the past 50 years, north Florida has retained the flavor and drawl of neighbors Georgia and Alabama. The north, with its large concentration of military retirees, takes conservative political stances, while the south, claiming a high number of Jews and northeasterners, tends toward a more liberal outlook.

Old and New – Add to this complex mélange senior citizens, Hispanics and numerous smaller groups, and the portrait of Florida becomes even richer and more difficult to delineate. Since the end of World War II, the elderly have pushed in from less hospitable climes, until Florida now claims a higher percentage of **seniors** than any other state. This group has made southwest Florida one of the fastest-growing areas in the country. Another large number of retirees, known as "snowbirds," migrate to Florida for the winter, then return home in the spring.

The most influential group of arrivals to Florida in recent times, **Hispanics** have swirled up from Cuba and other places south with the frequency of tropical storms ever since the Cuban revolution in 1959. From that time to this, more than 750,000 people from the Caribbean have moved to Florida, giving the state one of the largest populations of Hispanics in the country: almost 2.7 million, or nearly 17% of the state's population. About 72 percent live on the Gold Coast, imparting their lively language and customs to the Miami region.

Over the Hill – Florida's population explosion may finally see some relief in the next decade. As the over-65 age group dwindles, fewer retirees will move to the Sunshine State. Of course, along with slower growth and less crowding comes a less robust economy. The Gold Coast area, already near capacity, suffered in the early 1990s from a high crime rate brought on, in part, by a heated mixture of diverse people jostling for the promised good life. Other areas of Florida stand ready to usher in the next wave of arrivals, from wherever they may come, and residents and visitors alike will have the opportunity to witness a state in the exciting process of defining itself.

Architecture

For a relatively young state, Florida claims a remarkably rich and diverse heritage of building traditions incorporating the practical, the outrageous, the witty— and the bizarre—in equal measure. Ever since 17C Spanish colonization, a strong Mediterranean current has run through the architectural landscape here. The tropical terrain and climate also influenced early design and continue to do so today as a new generation of architects begins to discover and reinvent the past.

Native Structures – The traditional dwelling of the Miccosukee and Seminole tribes is the **chickee**, an open-air shelter framed with rot-resistant cypress poles and thatched with palmetto fronds. Well-adapted to the swampy glades where the tribes hid their camps, the practical structures featured a platform floor of split logs or sawn boards elevated about 3ft off the ground to provide protection from snakes, alligators and flood tides. A compound comprised several individual chickees for sleeping, cooking, communal eating and religious rites.

R. Corbel/MICHELIN

Seminole Chickee

Early Spanish Building – Although Dominican and Franciscan friars were the true founders of Spanish colonial architecture in Florida, scant archaeological traces remain of some 100 wooden mission compounds established here beginning in 1565. The oldest extant Spanish-built edifice in Florida is the 1695 Castillo de San Marcos in St. Augustine. The massive structure of quarried **coquina** (native shellstone) is considered the best surviving example of a type of European fortress introduced after gunpowder was invented in the late Middle Ages.

Most early Spanish colonial houses were simple one-story, two-room palmetto-thatched shelters built of wood planks or coquina blocks and rough **tabby** plaster—made of oyster shells and lime. Only the more substantial two-story 18C coquina structures have survived. Following Spanish tradition, the houses in Florida's two Spanish garrisons, St. Augustine and Pensacola, fronted directly onto the street and were part of private, walled compounds entered by a gate. Loggias, or galleries, captured cooling summer breezes and the low winter sun. The glass-paned double-hung windows (replacing earlier wood *rejas*, or open window grills), hipped roofs, dormers and clapboard upper stories seen on many 18C St. Augustine houses were probably introduced by the British during the 1763-83 occupation.

Dogtrot Cracker Dwelling

19th Century – The term "Cracker" is believed to have originated with the whip-cracking cattle drivers who began crossing into Florida in the early 19C. The first so-called **Cracker houses** of the Panhandle and central Florida regions were log cabins of several standard types: **single-pen** (one room), **saddlebag** (two rooms and a central chimney) or **dogtrot** (two rooms and a central breezeway). Such structures were raised off the damp ground on blocks made of limestone, heart pine or rot-resistant cedar. Florida's pioneer houses took on a number of interesting variations after the **balloon frame** (a system of framing a wooden building by nailing together lightweight wood studs) was invented in the 1830s and began to replace the more expensive and labor-intensive pegged-timber frame throughout the US. A typical balloon-frame Cracker house is the 1.5-story farmhouse, with vertical board-and-batten siding and a pitched roof (often of inexpensive sheet metal) sloping over a broad porch. The **four-square** Cracker house, named for the shape of its floor plan, incorporates a porch and hipped roof (four slopes), often vented with a rooftop cupola designed to draw warm air up and out of the interior. **Shotgun** houses served as cheap housing for laborers along the Gulf Coast in south Florida's early Bahamian settlements. This narrow one-room-wide structure with a long row of back-to-back rooms is thought to be an African form that evolved on Haitian sugar plantations. It was said that if a shotgun were fired through the front door, the load would pass straight through the line of rooms and out the back door.

Built from the 1830s to 1920s, the **Conch house** of Key West is named for the Bahamian islanders—colloquially known as "Conchs"—who settled in the Keys in the 19C. The earliest Conch houses were framed by ships' carpenters using a pegged-and-braced timber system borrowed from shipbuilding, but most of those remaining are balloon-frame structures. The one- or two-story clapboard Conch house is usually raised on stone or brick piers and topped by a peaked roof (shingled or tin) with the gable end facing front; louvered blinds at the doors and windows block the heat of the fierce tropical sun.

The first **plantation houses** built after Florida became a US Territory in 1821 were unpretentious two-story, wood-frame structures. In the antebellum years these were replaced by imposing **Greek Revival** mansions fronted by columned two-story porches.

Gingerbread House, Key West

Dating from the late 19C, when many citrus and railroad fortunes were made, elaborate **Queen Anne** houses—featuring asymmetrical facades, turrets, ample verandas, recessed balconies, gingerbread trim, spindles, turned railings and decorated gables—may be found throughout the state. Look also for the charming white board-and-batten Carpenter Gothic churches from the same period, distinguished by their pointed-arch windows.

Early 20th Century – The building boom of the early 20C coincided with the rise of the **Mediterranean Revival** style, which borrowed loosely from medieval Moorish and Spanish architecture. The style became popular after California featured a Spanish-style pavilion at the widely publicized California-Pacific Exposition in 1915. Although other period revivals were also fashionable at the time, the Mediterranean mode caught on especially well in California and Florida where Spanish roots were strong. Pastel-colored stucco walls, red-clay roof tiles, arcaded loggias, towers, arched windows and ornate wrought-iron detailing not only suited Florida's tropical landscape, but also "...express[ed] the spirit of a land dedicated to long, carefree vacations," as a 1925 issue of *House Beautiful* described it. The style became the unifying design theme for dozens of Florida's boom-era developments, including Carl Fisher's Miami Beach, George Merrick's model suburb Coral Gables, and Addison Mizner's 1,600-acre architectural playground, Boca Raton. Indeed, many society architects, among them Mizner, Carrère and Hastings, and Walter DeGarmo (Florida's first registered architect) made their names with commissions for the luxurious Mediterranean Revival villas that still dominate Florida's early seaside resorts.

Resort Hotels – Perhaps the most distinctive symbols of Florida's heyday are the great resort hotels of the pre-Depression era. The tradition of extravagant hospitality catering to affluent northerners started in the late 19C. The friendly rivalry of railroad magnates Henry Bradley Plant and Henry Morrison Flagler extended to gigantic (and often unprofitable) hotels located at each major railhead. The first was Flagler's 1888 Ponce de Leon Hotel in St. Augustine (now Flagler College), designed by Thomas Hastings (later a partner in the prestigious New York firm of Carrère and Hastings). Plant countered with the 500-room brick, minaret-crowned Tampa Bay Hotel in 1890. Subsequent hotels were built of less costly wood, and consequently most of these were later claimed by fire. Plant's multi-gabled, 600-room Belleview Hotel, opened near Clearwater in 1897, may be the sole survivor.

The Biltmore Hotel, Coral Gables

A second wave of posh resorts reached its peak in the 1920s. By this time, the Mediterranean Revival style was considered the apex of architectural design, and most of these enormous structures were built of masonry, adorned with decorative tiles, stone carvings, frescoes and woodwork. While many of the hotels fell into disrepair after the economic crash of 1926, a recent restoration movement has returned a few choice examples to their original luster. St. Petersburg boasts both the **Vinoy Park** (now the Renaissance Vinoy Resort), restored in 1992, and Henry Du Pont's **Don CeSar**, a five-story pink stucco confection with bell towers and red-clay roof tiles. Others include the majestic Coral Gables **Biltmore Hotel**, the Palm Beach **Breakers Hotel**, and Mizner's **Cloister Inn** in Boca Raton. Originally built as a 100-room hotel, the Cloister now forms the east wing of the Boca Raton Resort & Club.

Modern Movements – The first widely popular style in the US to purposely break with traditional historical revivals, **Art Deco** transformed hundreds of gas stations, diners, theaters, houses, hotels, motel courts and storefronts across the US into eye-catching streamlined designs between the late 1920s and into the 1940s. An offshoot of the **International Style** with its simple forms and austere surfaces, Deco adopted the sleek lines, cubic massing and new materials of the technology-oriented modernist

Art Deco Hotels, Miami Beach

aesthetic that was emerging in Europe after World War I. At a time when they were trying to bury memories of the recent war and Depression, Americans welcomed the fresh contemporary look of Art Deco buildings. Rather than reject ornament, as pure modernists did, Florida's Deco designers embraced fanciful decoration wholeheartedly—in particular exotic motifs (palmettos, chevrons and ziggurats) inspired by ancient Egyptian, Aztec and Mayan design.

A later phase of Art Deco, called **Streamline Moderne**, took on an even more futuristic look. Beginning in the 1930s, buildings were stripped of surface decoration and angular elevations were also smoothed with rounded corners, horizontal bands ("speed lines") and porthole windows inspired by contemporary streamlined trains, planes and ocean liners. New mass-produced materials—steel, chrome, glass block and concrete block—made it possible to build quickly and cheaply. These benefits proved a plus for developers of post-war boom towns like Miami Beach, which now possesses the largest and best-preserved concentration of Art Deco and Streamline Moderne buildings in the world.

By the 1950s Florida was better known for its glitzy resort architecture, most notably **Morris Lapidus'** stupendous movie-set Miami Beach hotels, such as the Fontainebleau and the Eden Roc. More recently, however, renowned modern architects have helped make metropolitan skylines here as sophisticated as any in the US. Downtown Miami boasts landmarks by I.M. Pei (International Place, 1985), Skidmore, Owings & Merrill (First Union Financial Center, 1984) and John Burgee and Philip Johnson (Miami-Dade Cultural Center, 1982). Florida's best-known architectural firm, Miami's **Arquitectonica**, features witty, brash designs incorporating both high-tech and historical references rendered in bold geometry and bright colors. Their work—described by critics as "beach blanket Bauhaus"—includes the exuberant Miracle Center Mall in Coral Gables as well as three extravagant luxury apartment towers erected during Miami's "Mondo-Condo" building boom of the early 1980s: the Palace, the 21-story Atlantis, and the Imperial.

The most notable example of the **New Urbanist** movement (which emphasizes human scale, historical references and the relationship of a building to its neighbors) is found in the Panhandle coast town of **Seaside**. Following the lead of developer Robert S. Davis, Miami architects Elizabeth Plater-Zyberk and Andres Duany created the master plan for this model beach community in 1981. Seaside observes traditional town-planning concepts by placing houses, shops and offices in close proximity to encourage a pedestrian community. The nostalgic pastel wood-frame buildings intentionally recall Florida's 19C Cracker houses and reflect a growing appreciation for the state's early vernacular architecture. Seaside has inspired other traditional developments, including Disney's Celebration, as well as sprawling suburban communities that borrow the style of New Urbanism (gabled roofs, front porches, clapboard siding), while ignoring its compact planning.

More recently, the development of Walt Disney World has added "entertainment architecture" to Florida's mélange of styles. Resembling larger-than-life cartoons, the **Dolphin and Swan hotels** (1990, Michael Graves) near Epcot illustrate the Disney sense of whimsy: each is crowned with a pair of its namesake animals. The literal symbolism combines the irony of post-Modernism with the elan of contemporary advertising. Also near Orlando, the **Team Disney** building (1991, Arata Isozaki) presents a riveting cluster of bright geometric shapes that create intriguing optical illusions. With the traditionally laid-out town of **Celebration** (1994), located south of Walt Disney World, the famed mega-entertainment giant joined the New Urbanist movement, offering traditional homestyles, technological sophistication and human-scale planning. Disney's Celebration has attracted notable architects Michael Graves, Philip Johnson, Cesar Pelli, Jaquelin Robertson and Robert A.M. Stern, and despite criticism of its restrictions, lack of diversity and high cost, has become the focus for the New Urbanist experiment nationwide.

Gwen Cannon/MICHELIN

Seaside

The Arts

Though most visitors venture to Florida for its resorts and outdoor recreation, they may be surprised to find that the state claims a growing number of artists and cultural exhibitions, as well as more than 30 museums of fine art. Indeed, vibrant arts scenes now exist within Miami, Sarasota, Tampa and other smaller cities. And with the recent population explosion of Caribbean immigrants, the Miami area has become a cradle for innovations in Latin and West Indian music.

Visual Arts – A number of 19C painters visited Florida and captured its sun-drenched landscapes on canvas. Among them were Boston artist **William Morris Hunt** (1824-1879), who sought Florida's subtropical climate in 1873 as a balm for his jangled nerves; British painter **Thomas Moran** (1837-1926), who chose Fort George Island to illustrate an issue of *Scribner's Monthly*; **Martin Johnson Heade** (1819-1904), a Pennsylvanian from the Luminist school who favored Florida's salt marshes; and George Inness Jr. (1854-1926), who wintered and painted in Tarpon Springs.

Honoring those who have made significant contributions in the state, the Florida **Artists Hall of Fame** recognizes several nationally and internationally famous artists, including **Robert Rauschenberg**, a modern experimental painter who has lived off and on in Florida for many years. The abstract expressionist creations of **Hiram Williams**, a University of Florida faculty member, have earned him a national reputation. Also at the University of Florida, surrealist photographer **Jerry Uelsmann** has exerted a widespread influence on his field.

West Palm Beach's **Norton Museum of Art** and Winter Park's **Charles Hosmer Morse Museum of American Art** are among museums with fine collections of art by Floridians.

Sunset, Tropical Marshes (c. 1880) by Martin Johnson Heade

Performing Arts – Florida's performing arts have also blossomed in the last few decades. Since the founding of the **Greater Miami Opera** in 1941, six more companies have sprung up around the state. Florida now offers some 78 theater companies as well as 33 professional dance groups, including the **Miami City Ballet**, which has been performing classical and modern dance in south Florida since the mid-1970s.

Most of Florida's major cities have professional symphony orchestras, and numerous regional and university music ensembles present frequent concerts. The **Florida West Coast Symphony** performs for audiences in Bradenton and Sarasota. Florida's official teaching festival, the **Sarasota Music Festival** takes place every June, attracting talented young professionals from around the world. Young musicians (age 21 to 30) also fill the ranks of the Miami Beach-based **New World Symphony**. Moving up the coast, the **Florida Philharmonic Orchestra** plays in Fort Lauderdale and southeast Florida, while the **Jacksonville Symphony Orchestra** entertains music-lovers farther north.

Fueled by the success of singer **Gloria Estefan** and her producer-husband Emilio, Miami Beach has become the national capital for the Latin music boom. The Estefans' Sony Building in the Art Deco Historic District has full music- and video-production facilities. Another longtime Florida resident is singer-songwriter **Jimmy Buffett**, whose vagabond-sailor persona has beguiled an international following.

Film and Television – Famous for its theme parks that celebrate film and TV, Florida has carved out a solid niche for itself in the **movie industry**. After years of providing the jungle backdrop for such early films (1940s and 50s) as the Tarzan series and the

Creature from the Black Lagoon. Florida welcomed Universal and Disney-MGM studios in the late 1980s. Operating as both theme parks and actual production facilities, these two Orlando operations add to the smaller studios in Miami to create an attractive milieu for filmmaking. Recent big-budget pictures filmed in Florida include *Heartbreakers*, *Ocean's 11* and *Sunshine State*. Over the years, the state has also hosted a number of television series, including *Flipper*, *Miami Vice*, *SeaQuest*, *Sins of the City* and several Latin soap operas.

Folk Arts – Ethnic and regional **folk arts** are kept alive through numerous festivals, apprenticeships and grants. The annual Florida Folk Festival, held each May at the **Stephen Foster State Folk Culture Center** in White Springs, illustrates regional folklife through music, dancing and farm crafts. Namesake of the Folk Culture Center, Pennsylvania-born composer **Stephen Collins Foster** (1826-1864) immortalized Florida's Suwannee River in his 1851 song *Old Folks At Home*. In 1935 this folk tune was officially designated as the state song.

Ranking third (after New York and California) in state appropriations for the arts, Florida hands out $32 million every year in grant awards to artists, many of whom preserve the traditions of folklife maintained in the state's numerous ethnic groups. **Cubans** in Key West, Miami and Tampa's Ybor City make woodcarvings and *guayaberas*—shirts decorated with pleating and embroidery. Caribbean transplants continue a rich maritime craft tradition with handmade boats, sails and fishing gear. **Greeks**, who have maintained a vibrant presence in Tarpon Springs since the early 1900s, bring their own nautical arts to modern Florida, along with sponge diving, Greek folk dance, colorful embroidery and music.

Charles Hosmer Morse Museum of American Art

South Florida is also home to tribes of **Seminole** and **Miccosukee** Indians, who still craft bracelets, bead necklaces, palmetto-fiber dolls, painted wood tomahawks, pine-needle and sweet-grass baskets, and dazzling calico clothing. The latter boasts colorful patchwork designs suggesting lightning, arrows, diamonds and other symbols. These Native American wares are plied in reservation gift shops and at arts fairs in the Everglades' Miccosukee Indian Village and Ah-Tha-Thi-Ki Museum.

Literature

Long after gaining statehood Florida remained largely an untamed frontier. The sense of mystery and raw natural beauty of the unfamiliar landscape lured both adventurers and romantics—writers among them—and have proved enduring themes in the region's literature.

Early Voices – Naturalists were among the first visitors to chronicle Florida and its native inhabitants. Appointed "Royal Botanist of the Floridas" by King George III, **John Bartram** (1699-1777) traveled from Philadelphia into the tropical wilderness in 1765-66, documenting unknown species of flora and fauna in *A Description of East Florida* (1769). His son William Bartram followed with *Travels Through North and South Carolina, Georgia, East and West Florida* in 1791.

During the 19C, magazine fiction and travel stories constituted a major body of Florida writing. In the 1830s and 40s, the monthlies *Knickerbocker* and *Graham's* published Florida adventure tales by such popular figures as **Washington Irving** and **James Fenimore Cooper**. In 1897 **Stephen Crane** (1871-1900), author of *The Red Badge of Courage* (1896) and a brief resident of Jacksonville, wrote *The Open Boat*. This dramatic story was based on a shipwreck he survived off New Smyrna Beach on his way to Cuba to fight in the Spanish-American War.

Contemporary travel guides were pivotal in bringing settlers and tourists to Florida. Among the classics now coveted by collectors are *Florida for Tourists, Invalids, and Settlers* (1881) by George Barbour (a phenomenal best-seller in its day) and *Florida: Its Scenery, Climate, and History* (1875) by the acclaimed southern poet **Sydney Lanier** (1842-1881).

One of the many travelers who returned to Florida to live was author **Harriet Beecher Stowe** (1811-1896), who spent winters in Mandarin, just outside Jacksonville, from 1868 to 1884. Her widely read *Palmetto Leaves* (1873) celebrated the beauty of the St. Johns River and attracted hundreds of curious travelers to the area.

Black Voices – Black writers have also helped shape the state's literary tradition. Jacksonville native **James Weldon Johnson** (1871-1938) was the author of several books, poems and songs. His works include *Autobiography of an Ex-Colored Man* (1912) and *Lift Every Voice and Sing*, which has been called the black national anthem. Eatonville's master story-teller **Zora Neale Hurston** (1891-1960) is acclaimed for fiction and essays that celebrate black culture and bespeak the honest values of rural southern life. They include the autobiographical *Dust Tracks On A Road* (1942) and *Their Eyes Were Watching God* (1937), considered one of the first black feminist novels of this century.

Zora Neal Hurston

Yale Collection of American Literature, Beinecke Library

20C – Remaining unspoiled well into the 20C, the rugged beauty of backwoods Florida captivated many northern transplants, including **Marjorie Kinnan Rawlings** (1896-1953). Rawlings settled in the hamlet of Cross Creek in 1928, and shaped many of her novels and stories around characters and settings inspired by her rural surroundings. The 1938 classic *The Yearling*—the story of a young boy and his pet deer in the Big Scrub (now Ocala National Forest)—won a Pulitzer Prize in 1939. Other Florida-inspired Rawlings titles include *South Moon Under* (1933) and *Cross Creek* (1942). A longtime resident of Coconut Grove, **Marjory Stoneman Douglas** (1890-1998) arrived in Miami in 1915 and became one of the state's first environmentalists. Her 1947 volume, *The Everglades: River of Grass*, remains an eloquent warning against the exploitation of this imperiled natural resource. During the 1930s and 40s, novelist **Hervey Allen** (1889-1949) and America's then-Poet Laureate **Robert Frost** (1874-1963) taught at the University of Miami's Winter Institute of Literature.

Call of the Keys – Key West also proved a magnet for writers. **Wallace Stevens** (1879-1955), who frequented the island on his yearly travels south from Connecticut, touted the tropical lushness of South Florida in his poetry anthology, *Harmonium* (1923). **Ernest Hemingway**, Florida's favorite literary son, spent most of the 1930s in Key West. Among the many works he wrote there, *To Have and Have Not* (1937) evokes the dignity and despair of the Depression-era life in the then-hard-bitten fishing village. Cultivated during his Key West years, Hemingway's fascination with the physical and intellectual challenge of deep-sea fishing was later reflected in *The Old Man and the Sea* (1952). Poet **Elizabeth Bishop** (1911-1979) made Key West her home in the late 1930s and early 1940s. Among the plays **Tennessee Williams** (1911-1983) wrote in his Duncan Street studio were *The Rose Tattoo* (1950) and *Night of the Iguana* (1961). Other well-known literary figures attracted to Key West include Thornton Wilder—who penned *The Matchmaker* there in 1954—poet and playwright Archibald MacLeish, humorist S.J. Perelman, and poet Richard Wilbur. Contemporary Key West writers include Philip Caputo, Ralph Ellison and Thomas McGuane (whose 1978 novel *Panama* is set in Key West).

Elsewhere in Florida, mystery writer and former Sarasota resident **John D. MacDonald** (1916-1986), author of *Condominium* (1977) and *The Lonely Silver Rain* (1985), used Florida's Gold Coast as the backdrop for the exploits of his fictional private eye, Travis McGee. Kurt Vonnegut, Gore Vidal and Alison Lurie number among the other novelists, short-story writers and essayists attracted to the Sunshine State, which continues to inspire literary themes ranging from ecological and social concerns to pure adventure.

Recreation

World-famous for over a century, Florida's glorious **beaches** continue to top the heap of the state's recreational venues. With their fine white sand, rolling dunes and gentle clear blue surf, these beaches attract hordes of sun-worshippers and swimmers. Sanibel Island and other Gulf Coast beaches offer **shelling** unparalleled anywhere in the country, and over the past several years, 15 Florida beaches have ranked among the top 20 in the nation in an annual independent survey. Variously rated for their beauty, water and air temperatures, sand softness, water clarity and solitude, beaches that have been awarded the highest marks include those at Florida's state parks such as St. George Island, Grayton Beach, Caladesi Island and St. Joseph Peninsula.

In and On the Water – Water sports of all types abound along both coasts, with **surfing** concentrated on the Atlantic side and **sailing** and **windsurfing** on the calmer Gulf. Florida manufactures more pleasure boats than any other state in the country; many of them are used for **waterskiing** or for taking fishing parties out to cast for such deep-sea denizens as mackerel, marlin, bonefish, sailfish and tarpon. Inland, the state's numerous rivers, lakes and springs provide ample opportunity for freshwater **fishing**, as well as **canoeing** through primeval swamplands. The Florida Canoe Trail system boasts 950mi of routes along 36 waterways. **Snorkelers** don fins and masks along both coasts to explore ancient wrecks and exotic fish. For sheer underwater beauty, **scuba divers** head to the coral reef that stretches off the shores of the Florida Keys. Divers also plunge into the mysterious underwater caves located in many of Florida's crystal-clear springs, where they encounter such creatures as American eels and blind crayfish.

© Al Messerschmidt

Windsurfing in Biscayne Bay

Back On Land – Florida claims over 1,000 **golf courses**, more than any state in the union, and most of which are open to the public. Another year-round sport, **tennis** is played throughout the state; many hotels and resorts offer vacation packages that include tennis lessons with resident pros. A significant number of tourists also escape to Florida to take advantage of its many **spas**, which promise rest for the weary and rejuvenation for the aged.
Backcountry in the Everglades and the Panhandle attracts **campers** to vast acreages of national and state parks. And **hiking** is becoming a more and more popular activity, with over 2,300mi of developed trails in the state. In the years ahead, state officials hope to link the **Florida National Scenic Trail** with the Appalachian Trail, thus extending the latter from Alabama and Georgia to the Everglades. The Florida trail currently traverses some 1,000mi through swampland, scrub and hardwood forest. And agencies plan to add more footpaths to the Lake Okeechobee area and to convert the state's old railroad beds into bike trails.

Spectator Sports – Among the spectator sports in the state, **jai alai** is perhaps the most uniquely Floridian. Originating in the Basque region of Spain and imported from Cuba, the world's fastest game is played on six *frontons* (176ft courts) throughout Florida, including America's oldest, the 1926 Miami Jai-Alai Fronton. Players hurl *pelotas* (balls) against curved walls at speeds of 170mph or more and catch them in *cestas* (baskets) attached to their arms. Spectators may wager on games. **Auto racing**, which started on the beach near Daytona in 1902, continues on the Daytona International Speedway with the famous Daytona 500 and other events. Racing fans can also watch greyhounds or horses run on tracks throughout the state. Miami's Hialeah Park (1925) remains one of the most popular venues for horse racing in Florida. **Professional sports** teams bring some of the country's top athletes to Florida. Since 1901 the state has been a favorite location for major league **baseball spring training camps**. Twenty teams train here and hold exhibition games, while several minor league clubs provide summertime ballpark excitement.

Culinary Traditions

Taking advantage of the bounty of its offshore waters, its year-round growing season and the influence of its Latin and Caribbean immigrants, the Sunshine State offers a crazy-quilt of cuisines that vary regionally from north to south. Whether your tastes run to "down-home" cooking or haute cuisine, you can find it in Florida.

Cracker Cooking – Saltpork, cornmeal, molasses and turnip greens were staples in the diets of Florida's early settlers. Known as "Crackers"—supposedly for the sound of the cattle ranchers' whips—these pioneers hunted squirrel, deer and raccoon to add to their tables. Freshwater fish, caught in local rivers and springs, was pan-fried. The ubiquitous Sabal palm was harvested for its edible bud, said to taste like raw cabbage. Called "swamp cabbage" by the settlers, this same delicacy is known today by the more elegant appellation "hearts of palm."

In the Panhandle and northeastern regions, dishes still echo this early style of cooking, replete with the southern accents of neighbors Georgia and Alabama. Steamed Apalachicola Bay oysters, broiled amberjack (a mild, flaky white fish), fried catfish or Gulf shrimp, hush puppies (small balls of deep-fried cornmeal dough) and grits (a bland gruel made from ground white corn) constitute typical northern fish-house fare. A menu in these restaurants might also include fried alligator and frog legs, as well as spicy Cajun creations such as the thick seafood stew called gumbo, and jambalaya, a hearty variety of meats and shellfish cooked together with rice.

Tropical Melting Pot – South Florida cooking takes its cues from the fresh vegetables, exotic fruits, and the bountiful numbers of commercial fish harvested in the state. Here you can sample smoked mullet and freshly caught grouper (tried it grilled or as a fish sandwich), pompano, snapper and mahi mahi—all often paired with tropical fruit salsas. Succulent stone crab claws, chewy conch fritters (made from the mollusk found inside Florida's once abundant state shell) and clawless spiny lobster constitute some of the state's unique shellfish dishes. Although renowned for its citrus fruit— over 20 varieties are grown here—Florida has added exotics such as passion fruit, papaya, mango and carambola to its expanding list of produce. In addition Florida claims the small, yellowish, bracingly tart key limes used in making **key lime pie**. A simple mixture of egg yolks, sweetened condensed milk and key lime juice in a graham-cracker crust, the state's famed dessert is served topped with either whipped cream or fluffy meringue.

Ever-evolving Florida cuisine is generously peppered with foreign flavors. Cubans have introduced plantains (a cousin to the banana), yuca (a mild-tasting root vegetable) and boniato (a nutty Cuban sweet potato) to grocery stores. And such dishes as black beans and rice; *arroz con pollo* (chicken with yellow rice); and *ropa vieja* (Spanish for "old clothes"), shredded beef dressed with tomatoes, peppers, onions, garlic and white wine, appear as entrées on many restaurant menus. Miamians have even come to favor the strong, dark *café Cubano* now available throughout the city. Nicaraguans, Peruvians, Haitians and other ethnic groups have also influenced Florida's culinary scene. One of the best-known Nicaraguan contributions is *tres leches* (three-milks cake), a dessert made with a mixture of fresh milk, evaporated milk and sweetened condensed milk.

Speciality of the House at Joe's Stone Crab

■ On the Wild Side: Florida's Exotic Fruits

South Florida's subtropical climate nurtures a plethora of little-known fruits from around the world. What follows is a sampling of Florida's exotic bounty.

Carambola – Each slice of the yellow-green, ridged carambola forms a star, thus its more popular moniker, star fruit. Hailing from East India, the crunchy carambola has a fresh, slightly acidic flavor that enhances desserts and salads.

Kumquat – Eaten raw, this Chinese quail-egg-size citrus fruit tastes tart and its rind bitter. Chefs recommend poaching kumquats in sugar syrup to render them more palatable.

Lychee – Another China native, resembling a small red ball with knobby skin, the lychee grew in Florida as early as 1886. Its honeyed, fragrant white flesh is often served for dessert in Chinese restaurants.

Mango – The dark, oval fruit has been cultivated in tropical East Asia for over 6,000 years. Florida growers stagger ripening times so mango-lovers can enjoy this peachy treat for as long as five months a year.

Passion Fruit – Encased in a hard, bitter-tasting, yellow or purple shell, the juicy edible pulp of the passion fruit is studded with tiny black seeds. The South American native caught on as a commercial fruit in the 1980s.

Plantain – This jumbo cousin of the banana originated in Africa. Rarely eaten raw, plantains—an essential ingredient in Cuban cuisine—are usually served fried, boiled or baked.

Sapodilla – Fans of the egg-shaped, brown-skinned sapodilla claim it tastes like a pear infused with maple syrup. This fruit grows wild in parts of Mexico and Central America.

Ugli Fruit – A cross between a tangerine and a grapefruit, the ugli is named for its unappealing thick yellow-green skin. Despite its appearance, this pear-shaped native of Jamaica boasts a sought-after, tart-sweet flavor.

Surprise Celebration Parade, Walt Disney World Resort

Sights

Everglades

River of Grass — Uniphoto Picture Agency

Renowned throughout the world, the vast "river of grass" known as the Everglades covers the southern end of the Florida peninsula in a subtropical wetland. It is home to hosts of rare birds, mammals and reptiles. The 50mi-wide sheet of moving water stretching from Lake Okeechobee to the Florida Bay began to form during the last Ice Age, when a shallow tropical sea intermittently covered the area, creating the limestone bedrock that now underlies it. Waters draining from the Kissimmee Basin to the north gradually inundated the land. This slow-moving river—averaging 6in in depth and losing only 2in of elevation for every mile it slopes down toward the Gulf of Mexico—gives rise to diverse ecosystems: coastal and saw grass prairies, mangrove swamps, tree islands, pinelands, hardwood hammocks and coastal estuaries. All of these communities depend upon the seasonal rhythm of the flow of water feeding them. Heavy rains nourish the area during the wet season, from May to October, while the landscape becomes increasingly parched during the dry winter months.

Calusa Indians were the first known people to inhabit what they called Pa-hay-okee, or "Grassy Waters." Archaeological evidence indicates that the Calusa lived in these coastal areas for as long as 2,000 years, disappearing from southern Florida only after the arrival of the Spanish in the 16C.

Small bands of Miccosukee and Seminoles took refuge in the Glades in the mid-19C, to escape the Seminole Wars and to avoid being sent west to reservations by the federal government. The remaining Indians developed a subsistence culture here and were virtually the area's sole inhabitants until the late 19C. At that time a few intrepid white settlers braved the heat and mosquitoes to settle along the coastal periphery of the Everglades.

Animals and plants in the Everglades today belong to a complex, interdependent cycle of water, fire, grasses and soils that has been interrupted in recent decades by the human manipulation of water flow. During floods too much water is channeled into the Everglades from urban and agricultural areas to the north; during droughts not enough water is allowed to flow south to the Gulf. Recent legislation seeks to address the increasingly complicated demands of this unique ecosystem in the dawn of a new century.

PRACTICAL INFORMATION ....Area Code: 305

When to Go

The best time to visit is in **winter** *(the dry season, Nov-mid-Apr)*, when daytime temperatures range from 60°-80°F, mosquitoes are tolerable, and wildlife is easier to spot. The busiest week is Dec 25-Jan 1. Make lodging and tour reservations several months in advance. Although the park is less crowded in **summer** *(the wet season, May-Oct)*, temperatures often soar to 95°F and the hot, humid weather brings clouds of mosquitoes and other biting insects. Insect repellent is recommended year-round. During the wet season, flooding may cause some park facilities and trails to close.

Getting There

By Air – **Miami International Airport (MIA):** ☎ 876-7000, www.miami-airport.com: closest commercial airport, 34mi north of Homestead. Shuttle service to Homestead: **Super Shuttle** *(24hr service; one-way $41 first passenger, $12 second passenger)*, for reservations: ☎ 871-2000, www.supershuttle.com; **The Airporter** *(3 times daily; one-way $25)*, for reservations ☎ 852-3413 or 800-830-3413. Major rental car agencies *(p 343)* are located at the airport.

By Car – There are two entrances to **Everglades National Park:** to reach the southern terminus at Flamingo, take Route 9336 east then south from Florida City *(directions from Miami p 54)*. US-41 (Tamiami Trail) borders the northern part of the park. Shark Valley entrance is accessible from US-41.

By Bus – Four trips daily between Miami and Homestead. **Greyhound bus station:** 5 N.E. 3rd St., Homestead *(☎ 800-231-2222; www.greyhound.com)*.

General Information

Visitor Information – **Park Headquarters**, 40001 State Rd. 9336, Homestead FL 33034 *(☎ 242-7700; www.nps.gov/ever)*. The park is open daily year-round. Entrance fee is $10/vehicle; ⚠ ♿. **Ernest F. Coe Visitor Center:** 11mi southwest of Homestead on Rte. 9336 *(open year-round daily 8am-5pm)* ☎ 242-7700. Additional visitor centers: **Royal Palm** on US-41 *(open year-round daily 8am-4:15pm;* ☎ *242-7700)*; **Flamingo** at terminus of Rte. 9336 *(open Dec-Apr 7:30am-5pm; rest of the year daily 9am-5pm;* ☎ *941-695-2945)*; **Shark Valley** on US-41 *(open year-round daily 8:30am-5:15pm; $8/vehicle;* ☎ *221-8776)* and **Gulf Coast** in Everglades City *(open year-round daily 7:30am-5pm;* ☎ *941-695-3311)*. Rangers lead wildlife walks, canoe trips and evening programs Dec-Apr; for schedules check the park newspaper or visitor centers. **Everglades Area Chamber of Commerce** *(PO Box 130, Everglades City FL 34139;* ☎ *941-695-3941 or 800-941-6355)* and **Tropical Everglades Visitor Assn.** *(160 Hwy. 1, Florida City, FL 33934;* ☎ *800-388-9669; www.tropicaleverglades.com)* provide information on local lodging, gas stations and recreation.

Accommodations – **Flamingo Lodge, Marina & Outpost Resort** facilities include motel rooms *($65-$95)*, cottages *($89-$135)*, full-service marina, houseboat rental *(Nov-Apr; 2-7 days $575-$1,375, fully equipped)* and restaurant. For reservations: #1 Flamingo Lodge Hwy., Flamingo FL 33034-6798, ☎ 941-695-3101 or 800-600-3813, www.flamingolodge.com. Everglades City, Homestead and Florida City offer hotels, motels, campgrounds and RV parks. *Rates quoted are average prices for a double room in high season (lower in summer)*.

Tours – Narrated tours (reservations suggested) leaving from Flamingo: **Bald Eagle Florida Bay cruise** departs from marina *(Nov-Apr daily 10am-dusk; rest of the year daily 1:30pm; round-trip 1hr 30min; commentary; $10)*. **Pelican Backcountry cruise** departs from the marina *(Nov-Apr daily 8am-4pm; rest of the year daily 10:30am & 4:30pm; round-trip 2hrs; commentary; $16)*; the *Dolphin* (seats 6) departs from the marina for a backcountry tour *(year-round daily 8am & 1:30pm; round-trip 4hrs; commentary; $39)*. Also available at Flamingo Lodge are canoe *($22/half day, $32/day)*, skiff *($65-$100 half day, $90-$155/day)*, kayak *($27-$38/half day, $43-$54/day)* and bicycle rentals *($8/half day, $14/day)*, as well as charter fishing with experienced guides. Schooner *Windfall* departs from marina and sails the Florida Bay *(☎ 941-695-3101)*. **Shark Valley tram tours** *(☎ 221-8455)*.

Sports and Recreation – **Camping** at Long Pine Key and Flamingo *($14/camp site; group rate for 15-20 people $28/camp site; no camping fees Jun-Aug; reservations:* ☎ *800-365-2267)*. **Backcountry** is accessible by boat, canoe and on foot only. A permit *($10-$30)*, obtainable at the visitor centers, is required for all overnight trips. A Florida **fishing** license, available at local bait and tackle shops, is required for fresh- and saltwater fishing. Flamingo Lodge offers fishing charters *($250/half day, $325/day)*.

Seven **canoe** trails thread the southern park region. Rental canoes are available at Nine-Mile Pond through TW Recreational Services, Inc. *(☎ 941-695-3101)*. **Boat tours** of Ten Thousand Islands *(☎ 941-695-2591;www.enpbt.com)*. Canoe the Wilderness Waterway with **North American Canoe Tours** *(Nov-Apr; day trip $40-$60/person; 4 or 7 days $450-$800/person; reservations required; ☎ 941-695-4666; www.evergladesadventures.com)*. **Sea kayak tours** *(Dec-Jan, 4-day minimum, $500-$875/person; reservations required)* by Wilderness Southeast *(☎ 912-897-5108)*. Eight **hiking** trails fan out from Flamingo; for maps and trail information, contact park headquarters.

American Alligator

■ Rap on Reptiles

● Sluggish-looking alligators can sprint at speeds nearing 15mph for distances of 50 yards.

● There are six types of poisonous snakes in Florida: Pygmy Rattlesnake *(Sistrurus miliarius barbouri)*; Eastern Diamondback Rattlesnake *(Crotalus adamanteus)*; Canebrake Rattler *(Crotalus horridus articaudatus)*; Coral Snake *(Micrurus fulvius)*; Florida Cottonmouth, a.k.a. Water Moccasin *(Agkistrodon piscivorus conanti)*; and Southern Copperhead *(Agkistrodon contortrix contortrix)*.

● Alligators have been clocked swimming at speeds of 14 knots, or 16mph.

● The small dark lizards you see everywhere in Florida are Cuban Brown Anoles *(Anolis sagrei sagrei)*, a species introduced into the state from the West Indies. Its lesser-seen relative, the Green Anole *(Anolis carolinensis)*, is a Florida native.

● Alligators' jaws can crush their prey with 3,000 pounds of pressure per square inch!

● Rattlesnakes and other pit vipers grow new fangs on the average of one set every three months.

EVERGLADES NATIONAL PARK★★★

Map p 59
Tourist Information: www.nps.gov/ever ☎ 305-242-7700

One of only a few American parks that enjoys UNESCO status as a World Heritage Site and falls within an International Biosphere Reserve, the 1.5-million-acre Everglades National Park attracts birding enthusiasts, canoeists, fishermen and those who simply want to drink in the spectacle of an aquatic wilderness that remains unique in the world.

Historical Notes

Ecosystem in Jeopardy – The timeless rhythm of the Everglades was seriously compromised in the early 20C, when **Napoleon Broward**, a Florida gubernatorial candidate, proposed draining the soggy area to provide water for agriculture and land for urban development. Broward won the election and, in the following decades, water was diverted from the Glades through some 1,400mi of man-made canals that drain the Everglades' water for farmland and suburban drinking water.

Though early grassroots conservationists protested the desecration, their efforts generally proved ineffective. In 1916, however, the first Everglades preserve—the roughly 2,000-acre **Royal Palm State Park**—was established, thanks in large part to the efforts of the Florida Federation of Women's Clubs. Even so, development also rolled on. In 1928 the **Tamiami Trail** (US-41), so called because it connects Tampa to Miami, was completed, cutting through the heart of the Everglades and blocking the water's southerly flow. Today these "grassy waters" lie mostly in private hands.

Preserving Pa-hay-okee – The establishment of the park in 1947 stemmed the tide of development that threatened to destroy this fragile ecosystem. About the same time, *The Everglades: River of Grass* appeared. This popular work by late Florida journalist **Marjory Stoneman Douglas** explained the need to protect the Glades, while extolling the beauty of "their vast glittering openness ... the racing free saltness and sweetness of their massive winds, under the dazzling blue heights of space." Douglas remained in the forefront of the ongoing fight to preserve the Everglades and return their natural flow of water until her death in 1998 at the age of 108. Since the park's establishment, its boundaries have been increased several times, most recently with the 1989 **East Everglades Expansion Act**, which added an additional 107,600 acres to the park.

A Balancing Act – Now the third-largest national park in the continental US after Death Valley and Yellowstone, the area still suffers from its proximity to major farming and urban centers that introduce toxins—such as the 200 annual tons of phosphates from agricultural fertilizers and pesticides—into this wilderness. The Everglades ecosystem also has natural enemies. Exotic plants—like the fire-resistant Australian Melaleuca tree, one acre of which sucks up the area's precious water at a rate of 2,100gal per hour—that have been introduced into the Glades threaten to overtake native vegetation, thus upsetting the delicate ecological balance.

Florida's Legislature began removing agricultural and other pollutants from the area's waters following the passage of the **Everglades Forever Act** in 1994; two years later, the federal government announced a comprehensive seven-year plan to restore the Everglades ecosystem. Construction projects to reestablish water flow are ongoing.

Whitewater Bay, Southern Everglades

The decline in fresh water flowing through the Everglades has similarly damaged the fragile environment in Florida Bay, along the park's southern rim, fouling once-pristine sea grass flats and crippling the area's delicate ecosystem. Federal restoration plans for the Everglades are designed to help the bay as well. Balancing human needs against natural ones continues to be problematic, but fortunately policymakers now acknowledge Douglas' contention that "there are no other Everglades in the World."

SOUTHERN EVERGLADES (DRIVING TOUR)
76mi round-trip within park

While you can see the highlights in a day, to best experience and understand the Everglades you must spend some time hiking its trails and boating on its waters. Sights in the southern part of the national park are organized as a driving tour, going from north to south.

Everglades Regulations

▲ Water-skiing is prohibited.

▲ Firearms and hunting are prohibited.

▲ Smoking on trails is not permitted.

▲ Pets are not allowed on trails.

▲ All vehicles must stay on designated roads; off-road vehicles are not permitted.

▲ Reduce speed in marked wildlife areas.

Safety Tips

■ Exercise extreme care when burning campfires, permitted in fire rings in campground areas only.

■ Do not disturb or feed wildlife.

■ When hiking, advise someone of your itinerary.

■ Owing to abundant wildlife in freshwater ponds and poor underwater visibility, swimming is not encouraged.

■ Watch for sudden weather changes, especially when boating, that can produce heavy thunderstorms with dangerous lightning and high winds.

■ Always wear a sunscreen and protective clothing.

From Miami, take Florida's Turnpike (I-75) south until it dead-ends at Florida City. Turn right on Rte. 1 south to Palm Dr. (Rte. 9336). Follow Rte. 9336 about 1.5mi and turn left on 192nd Ave. Continue 2mi to 376th St. S.W. Turn right and follow the road 5.6mi to park entrance. Route 9336 then continues 38mi to its terminus in Flamingo.

Ernest F. Coe Visitor Center *– Just inside park entrance on right. Park open year-round daily 8am-5pm. $10/vehicle* ♿ 🅿 ☎ *305-242-7700. www.nps.gov/ever. Visitor center open year-round daily 8am-5pm.* ♿. The new Coe Visitor Center, named for one of the park's early champions, was dedicated in 1996 to replace a previous visitor center destroyed by Hurricane Andrew. Its hipped, metal roof and wood siding enable it to blend inconspicuously into the natural environment. Exhibits and films educate visitors not only on the Everglades, but also on the environmental crises confronting the greater South Florida ecosystem. An information desk provides details on recreational activities within the national park; administrative offices are located in an adjacent building.

Continue 2mi on Rte. 9336 and turn left at the sign for Royal Palm Visitor Center and the Gumbo Limbo and Anhinga trails.

★★**Anhinga Trail** *– .5mi. Begins at rear of visitor center. Ranger-led walks and lectures are held here several times daily (first-come, first-served).* One of the park's most popular areas, this trail begins as a wide paved path, which follows a portion of the Old Ingraham Highway. A boardwalk then leads across Taylor Slough (pronounced "slew"), a shallow, slow-moving river that channels through a marsh dense with willow thickets and punctuated by a palm hammock. Alligators, turtles and myriad birds congregate here, particularly in the dry winter months.

★**Gumbo Limbo Trail** *– .4mi.* This trail weaves through the luxuriant vegetation of historic Paradise Key Hammock, the area that formed the original **Royal Palm State Park**. A typical tropical island of hardwood trees, Paradise Key supports a rich variety of ferns, lianas, orchids, royal palms and, of course, gumbo-limbo trees. The latter is known in Florida as the "tourist tree" because its red, peeling bark resembles sunburned skin.

Return to Rte. 9336 and continue 4.4mi.

Pinelands Trail *– .3mi.* A paved trail here circles through a rocky, drier landscape that supports one of the few existing forests of **Florida slash pine**, also known as Dade County pine. Highly prized for its durability, slash pine was extensively logged earlier in the 20C. That logging, and the suppression of forest fires, which allow the fire-resistant pine to compete with hardwoods, has led to the demise of the pine forests that once covered much of southern Florida. Only a total of 20,000 acres of slash pine remain, making this species the continent's most endangered member of the pine family.

Continue 6.3mi to the turn-off for Pa-hay-okee Overlook.

★★ **Pa-hay-okee Overlook** – This elevated platform provides a sweeping **view**★★ of the Everglades' seemingly endless saw grass prairie, interrupted only by sporadic islands of trees. Saw grass *(Cladium jamaicense)*, part of the sedge family, is by far the most dominant flora in the Everglades. Though its long blades are razor-sharp, its soft roots are edible.

Return to Rte. 9336 and drive 7mi; turn right at sign for Mahogany Hammock.

Mahogany Hammock – *.3mi. May be temporarily closed.* Tunneling through a lush display of ferns and mahogany trees, the boardwalk trail passes the largest known mahogany tree in the country. Unfortunately, this landmark was damaged by Hurricane Donna in 1960 and again by Hurricane Andrew in 1992.

Return to Rte. 9336 and continue 11.3mi; turn right to parking area for West Lake.

★ **West Lake Trail** – *.3mi.* Follow the boardwalk here along the edge of West Lake across a watery mangrove swamp. The dense concentration of mangroves, with their complex tangle of roots and branches, typifies Florida's coastal areas, where fresh water and salt water mix. Three types of mangroves grow in the Everglades: red, distinguished by their reddish arcing roots; black, whose bases are surrounded by spiky breathing tubes called pneumatophores; and white, generally found on drier ground.

Continue 3.6mi.

Mrazek Pond – Right beside the road, this watering hole is popular with birders. At dawn and dusk, waterbirds such as grebes, herons, egrets, ibis and roseate spoonbills congregate here to feast on fish and shellfish.

Continue 3.5 mi to Flamingo.

Flamingo – *Located at the southern terminus of Rte. 9336 (38mi from park entrance).* A small outpost overlooking Florida Bay serves as the hub of visitor services in the southern Everglades, providing the only food and accommodations in this part of the park. The **visitor center** *(open Dec-Apr daily 7:30am-5pm, rest of the year daily 9am-5pm;* ⚠ ✂ ♿ 🅿 ☎ *941-695-2945)* houses a small display area with natural history exhibits. The adjacent marina serves as the boarding point for a variety of **cruises**★★ *(p 51)* that tour the backcountry canals and the open waters of Florida Bay. Cruise guides point out wildlife and natural features of the landscape.

Man-made **Eco Pond**★ *(.9mi west of visitor center)* is a bird-watcher's paradise, particularly at dawn and dusk when flocks of waterfowl and wading birds gather to feed. The **observation platform** provides an excellent vantage point. *Bring binoculars.*

NORTHERN EVERGLADES

Completed in 1928, the Tamiami Trail (US-41) cuts across the Everglades, linking Miami with Naples on the west coast. Land along this strip of swampland and saw grass prairie is maintained under the jurisdictions of Everglades National Park, neighboring Big Cypress National Preserve and the South Florida Water Management District. The main entrance into the national park along this route is at Shark Valley.

★★ **Shark Valley (Park Entrance)** – *30mi west of Miami, entrance on south side of US-41. Park open year-round daily 8:30am-5:15pm. $8/vehicle.* ♿ 🅿 ☎ *305-221-8776. www.nps.gov/ever. Maps and detailed park information available at kiosk adjacent to the parking lot.* Named for the shallow, slow-flowing slough that empties into the brackish—and shark-infested—Shark River to the southwest, Shark Valley is actually a basin that lies a few feet lower than the rest of the Everglades. The waters that drain this valley flow into the Gulf of Mexico.

★ **Tram Tour** – *Ticket booth adjacent to parking lot. Tours depart from parking lot Dec-May daily 9am-4pm. Rest of the year daily 9:30am-3pm. 2hrs round-trip. Commentary. Reservations suggested. $10.50.* ♿ 🅿 *($8) Shark Valley Tram Tours* ☎ *305-221-8455. Bring drinking water on tram. Bicycle rentals available.* The 15mi loop road here—part of which was constructed by early oil prospectors—cuts through open fields of grassy wetland. The easiest way to traverse this route is via the park's open-air trams. Along the way, park naturalists point out some of the local denizens: snail kites, egrets, herons, alligators and gar fish, to name a few. At the halfway point, the tram stops at a concrete **observation tower**, so visitors can view the expansive landscape.

A Haven for Wildlife

One of the major wetlands left on this continent, the Everglades supports some 600 species of animals—including 350 types of birds, 60 species of mosquitoes and 26 kinds of snakes—some of which are found nowhere else in the world. The southern Everglades, in fact, is the only place in the world where you'll find both alligators and crocodiles. Birds provide the greatest spectacle in the park, with herons, egrets, ibis, cranes and other waterbirds almost always within sight. Bald eagles and ospreys nest here, and white pelicans—largest birds on the continent, with a wingspan of 9ft—winter here. The following creatures number among those that make their home in the Glades.

American Alligator *(Alligator mississippiensis)* – Once a species with a poor prognosis for survival, the alligator has made a strong comeback and is routinely seen gliding silently through freshwater channels and marshes. Reaching lengths of up to 16ft, male alligators rank as the largest reptiles on the continent. Mating occurs in the spring, after which the female will build a nest and deposit up to 80 eggs. Incubation requires between 9 and 10 weeks. For these cold-blooded reptiles, the sex of the hatchlings is determined by the temperature at which the egg incubates: temperatures below 87°F will produce females; temperatures above 89°F will yield males. The young are black with yellow bands; adults are black. Efficient predators, gators also contribute to the survival of other animals. As the dry season approaches, the reptiles dig out "gator holes," depressions that fill with underground water and help sustain many kinds of animals during the dry months.

American Crocodile *(Crocodylus acutus)* – Cousin to the alligator, the endangered American crocodile has been reduced to a few hundred animals, concentrated in the salty mangrove inlets in the southern part of Everglades National Park and in Crocodile Lake National Wildlife Refuge on the northern end of Key Largo. Crocodiles can be distinguished from alligators by their lighter gray-green coloring, long pointed snout, and the lower incisors that protrude from either side of their jaw when their mouth is closed. On land, these reptiles move with an agile swaying motion, enabling them to reach speeds of 15mph. Generally considered more aggressive than the alligator, American crocs tend to avoid humans, unless molested or protecting their young.

56

Anhinga *(Anhinga anhinga)* – This long-necked denizen of the Everglades has become its symbol, often spotted in trees with its black wings outstretched. Lacking the oil covering that other birds have on their wings, the anhinga must air dry its wings in order to fly again after it has emerged from a feeding foray. To obtain food, the anhinga dives underwater and spears fish with its pointed bill. When swimming, only the bird's sinuous neck is exposed above the water; thus it is sometimes called the "snakebird."

Florida Panther *(Felis concolor coryl)* – Experts believe that only 30 of these big tawny-brown cats—designated Florida's state animal—still roam the state's wetlands, the only habitat left for them in the eastern US. The panther's birthrate of two to four kittens every other spring has been diminished by infertility caused by mercury-contaminated prey. Once widespread, these members of the cougar family have been squeezed down to the tip of the peninsula, mostly into the protected lands of Big Cypress Swamp and Everglades National Park. Secretive and difficult to spot, adults stand about 2ft high and weigh between 60 and 130 pounds.

Snail Kite *(Rostrhamus sociabilis plumbeus)* – This small, shy, gray-brown hawk survives exclusively on Pomacea, or apple, snails. With its curved beak, it extracts the snail from its shell. While snail kites are common in some parts of Central and South America, in North America these endangered birds are found only in central and southern Florida. Draining the Everglades has killed the kite's main source of food; it is estimated that fewer than 900 snail kites remain in Florida.

Miccosukee Indian Village – *.5mi west of Shark Valley entrance, on south side of US-41. Open year-round daily 9am-5pm. $5 (includes optional guided tour). Airboat rides (30min) $10.* ✕ ♿ 🅿 ☎ *305-223-8380. www.miccosukeetribe.com.* Since the mid-19C Miccosukee Indians have inhabited the Everglades. Originally a part of the Creek Confederation, this tribe shares some similarities with the Seminoles but remains a distinct group with its own language and traditions. Now numbering some 500 people, the Miccosukee are concentrated in the northern Everglades, where they maintain a residential enclave and attempt to preserve their native culture.

Miccosukee Indian Village, a commercial venture, re-creates a traditional settlement of chickees—palm-thatched, open-sided structures once used as shelters. Natives demonstrate crafts such as beadwork and the bright patchwork for which the Miccosukee are renowned. A **museum** displays reproductions of traditional clothing, tools and baskets, as well as historic photographs. In the village's **alligator arena**, wrestlers demonstrate the bare-handed way in which Miccosukee hunters once captured alligators *(11am & 12:30pm, 1:30pm, 3pm, 4:30pm).* Since meat spoils so quickly in the tepid subtropical climate, the animals had to be kept alive until the Indians were ready to eat them. Thus it was necessary to subdue the alligator and tie its feet before bringing it back to the village to await the tribe's next meal.

Everglades City – *4mi south of US-41 on Rte. 29. Gulf Coast Visitor Center (Everglades National Park information) open year-round daily 7:30am-5pm;* 🅿 ☎ *941-695-3311.* Established in the 1920s as a headquarters site for the building of the Tamiami Trail, Everglades City now serves as an access point to the watery domain of the northwestern Everglades. The town's most famous institution remains the **Rod and Gun Club** *(200 Waterside Dr.).* Serving as a fishing and hunting club since the late 19C, this structure was originally the residence of one of the area's first settlers, W.S. Allen. The rambling white-frame Victorian, with its rich interior paneling, gained world renown in the 1930s as one of the most exclusive sports clubs in the nation. Then owned by **Barron Collier**, the land speculator largely responsible for the building of the Tamiami Trail, the club played host to a number of dignitaries. It now operates as an inn.

★★**Cruises of the Ten Thousand Islands** – *Cruises depart from the ranger station on Rte. 29 (from US-41, take Rte. 29 south 4mi to traffic circle; stay on Rte. 29—3/4 turn around circle—and continue .5mi to Everglades National Park Gulf Coast Visitor Center on right) year-round daily 8:30am-5pm. Round-trip 1hr 30min. Commentary. $16. Everglades National Park Boat Tours* ✕ ♿ 🅿 ☎ *941-695-2591 www.enpbt.com.* Park-sponsored tours offer a look at the marine world of Chokoloskee Bay. Countless small islets here are covered collectively with one of the largest mangrove forests in the world. During the cruise you may see dolphins, manatees and numerous waterbirds, including ospreys, herons and perhaps even nesting bald eagles.

Historic Smallwood Store – *360 Mamie St. From Everglades City, continue south on Rte. 29 about 3mi onto Chokoloskee Island; turn right on Smallwood Dr. and left on Mamie St.; follow Mamie to end. Open Dec-Apr daily 11am-5pm, rest of the year daily 10am-4pm. Closed major holidays. $2.50.* ☎ *941-695-2989. www. florida-everglades.com/chokol/smallw.htm.* Perched at the edge of Chokoloskee

Miccosukee Indian Child in Traditional Dress

Bay, this weathered wooden structure functioned as a trading post and general store from 1906 to 1982. Named for C.S. "Ted" Smallwood, the Collier County pioneer who founded it, the store now functions as a museum. It displays turn-of-the-century wares—90 percent of which are original to the store—and recalls the atmosphere of an earlier era in southern Florida.

Wilderness Waterway – A paradise for boaters and canoeists, this watery inland course twists 99mi through protected rivers and bays, from Flamingo to Everglades City. Markers designate the waterway, and campsites (some furnished with chickee shelters) punctuate the route. *National Park Service permits are required for overnight camping; course takes 6-8hrs by motorboat and 8-10 days by canoe. Pick up permit (no more than 24hrs before start of trip) and maps at the ranger station in Flamingo ☎ 941-695-2945 or Gulf Coast Visitor Center (in Everglades City) ☎ 941-695-3311.*

Big Cypress National Preserve – *Accessible from US-41 and I-75. Open daily year-round. △ ☎ 941-695-4111. www.nps.gov/bicy.* Contiguous to the northern Everglades, the 729,000-acre preserve protects a portion of the 2,400sq mi **Big Cypress Swamp**, a rich variegated wetland covered with forests of bald cypress trees. Few giant cypress still stand, having been heavily logged early last century, and much of the terrain is now covered with dwarf cypress and saw grass prairie. In the 1960s, developers hatched plans to drain the vast swamp and build on its lands. In 1974, however, the government—recognizing that this area was a critical link in south Florida's wetlands wilderness—established a 500,000-acre preserve. A major habitat for much of the same wildlife found in the Everglades, Big Cypress is particularly favored by dwindling numbers of the endangered Florida panther.

The **Oasis Visitor Center** *(19 mi west of Shark Valley on US-41; open year-round daily 8:30am-4:30pm; closed Dec 25; ☐ ☎ 941-695-4111)* shows a 15 min movie on the geology, flora and fauna of Big Cypress. Behind the center, the **Florida National Scenic Trail** leads 21mi into the heart of the preserve. A 26mi loop road *(Rte. 94 from Forty Mile Bend to Monroe Station)* circles through haunting cypress swamps in the southern part of the preserve.

An unpaved **northern loop** *(16.5 mi)* begins at Route 839 and travels through wide-open saw grass prairie *(follow Turner River Rd./Rte. 839 north 7.3mi; turn left on Rte. 837 to Birdon Rd./Rte. 841, which leads back to US-41).*

★**Fakahatchee Strand Preserve State Park** – *Open year-round daily dawn-dusk ☎ 941-695-4593. Big Cypress Bend trail parking located 7mi west of Rte. 29; look for a brown park sign on right.* Adjacent to Big Cypress National Preserve, Fakahatchee features a 20mi-long and 3- to 5mi-wide swamp forest containing a dense and exotic mix of vegetation. Its flora includes the largest stand of native **royal palm** in the US, as well as the greatest concentration and diversity of **orchid** *(different species can be seen blooming year-round)*; 15 species of bromeliads; and a variety of epiphytes, or air plants. A boardwalk *(1 mi round-trip)* at **Big Cypress Bend**★★ leads through an eerily beautiful virgin cypress forest, ending at a primeval swamp frequented by alligators. *Bring mosquito repellent.*

The Keys

Curving southwest 220mi from Biscayne Bay to the Dry Tortugas, the thousand-some islands and islets that compose the Florida Keys scribe a narrow archipelago separating the waters of the Atlantic from Florida Bay and, farther south, the Gulf of Mexico. Not far from the bustle of Miami some 50mi north, the Keys maintain a laid-back atmosphere throughout, though the character of the individual islands varies. The upper and middle Keys serve as a jumping-off point for sportfishermen, divers, snorkelers and wildlife enthusiasts interested in the wealth of marine life on the offshore **coral reef**. The lower Keys are dominated by the town of Key West, an internationally renowned destination with its own distinctive flavor.

With the exception of the northernmost sand islands, the Keys consist of the remains of coral reefs that began forming as early as 10 to 15 million years ago, when the area was covered by a shallow sea. Until the 20C, most of these "chaotic fragments of coral reef, limestone, and mangrove swamps," as one early writer called the Keys, supported only a small, scattered population of Indians and, later, indomitable fishermen and farmers. In the 1800s the islands were a less than hospitable place because of the plague of mosquitoes that blackened the sides of homes and forced residents to burn perpetual smudge pots. In these early days, boats were the only means of transportation among the Keys. Then in 1904, railroad magnate **Henry Flagler** launched plans to extend his Florida East Coast Railway south from Miami to Key West. Although the construction of "Flagler's Folly," as the **Overseas Railroad** was popularly known, was thwarted from the beginning by hurricanes, Flagler persisted; in 1912 the first train pulled into Key West. At the end of the train's maiden voyage in January, Flagler—who had just turned 82—proclaimed, "Now I can die in peace." The following year he passed away. For 23 years Flagler's railroad provided transportation to the Keys. Disaster struck in September 1935, when a killer hurricane destroyed the line. Flagler's successors at the Florida East Coast Railway decided not to rebuild the line that had never been a money-maker. In 1938 the current **Overseas Highway** was completed along the former railroad bed. Crossing 43 bridge/causeways (only one of them over land), this southernmost stretch of US-1 offers fine views of the Atlantic to the east and the shallow, aquamarine waters of Florida Bay to the west.

The other event critical to the Keys' modern development was the installation in 1982 of a 36in water pipeline, which follows the highway from the mainland to Key West. The new pipeline made possible the development of hundreds of acres of land in the Keys, where fresh water is increasingly difficult to find.

PRACTICAL INFORMATION ....Area Code: 305

When to Go

The months from December through April are considered high season; afternoon temperatures range from 73°F to 79°F. The rest of the year they run 75°F to 85°F; annual average temperature is 77.4°F. Rainfall is considerably less than on the mainland and falls in brief thunderstorms during summer afternoons. March is the pinnacle of Spring Break, when hordes of young people descend on the Keys, and travelers are likely to encounter substantial mayhem.

Getting There

By Air – **Marathon Airport** *(information: ☎ 743-2155)* in the Middle Keys and **Key West Airport** *(information: ☎ 296-5439)* are serviced by most domestic airlines as well as charters. Rental car agencies *(p 343)* are located at both airports. International flights connect through Miami International Airport.

By Car – Small green mile-marker **(MM)** posts, sometimes difficult to spot, are used to delineate locations of sites along US-1 (Overseas Highway) giving distances from Key West. The **Mile-Marker system** begins in Florida City (MM 127) on the mainland, and crosses a causeway to Key Largo (MM 110). From here it drops down through the Keys to its terminus in Key West (MM 0). Much of the route is two-lane, and traffic can be heavy, particularly in the high season (Dec-Apr) and on weekends. Allow 3 hrs for the drive. The best places along US-1 to find lodging, restaurants and other amenities (marinas, recreational facilities) are: Key Largo (MM 110-87), Islamorada (MM 86-66), Marathon (MM 65-40), Big Pine Key (MM 39-9) and Key West (MM 0).

By Bus – Greyhound **bus** makes scheduled stops in Key Largo, Islamorada, Marathon, Big Pine Key, Ramrod Key and Key West. *(information: ☎ 800-FLA KEYS or 800-231-2222; www.greyhound.com)*. A number of **shuttle** services offer on-demand transport to the Keys from Miami International, including Keys Shuttle *(☎ 800-830-3414)* and Go Tours *(☎ 800-689-3304)*.

By Boat – **Intracoastal Waterway** allows travel by boat from Miami into Florida Bay.

Visitor Information	MM	Hours	☎
Florida Keys Visitor Information www.fla-keys.com		24hrs/7 days	800-FLA-KEYS
Key Largo Chamber of Commerce 105950 Overseas Hwy. Key Largo 33037	106	9am-6pm daily	451-1414 or 800-822-108.
Islamorada Chamber of Commerce PO Box 915 Islamorada FL 33036 www.islamoradachamber.com	82.5	Mon-Fri 9am-5pm Sat-Sun 9am-2pm	664-4503 or 800-322-5397
Marathon Chamber of Commerce 12222 Overseas Hwy. Marathon 33050 www.floridakeysmarathon.com	53.5	9am-5pm daily	743-5417 or 800-842-9580
Lower Keys Chamber of Commerce PO Box 430511 Big Pine Key 33043	31	Mon-Fri 9am-5pm Sat 9am-3pm	872-2411 or 800-872-3722
Greater Key West Chamber of Commerce 402 Wall Street, Mallory Square Key West 33040 www.keywestchamber.org		8:30am-5pm daily	294-2587 or 800-527-8539

Accommodations – **Area visitors' guides** including lodging directories are availabl (free) from area Chambers of Commerce. Accommodations include hotels, mote and **resorts** *($95-$500)*. **Reservation services**: Welcome Center of Florida Key *(☎ 296-4444 or 800-352-8538)*; AA Accommodation Center *(☎ 800-732 2006)*. **Apartment and condo rentals** are available through local propert management groups. **Camping** and **RV parks** are located throughout the Keys an offer full hookups, and in some cases, beaches, freshwater pools, marinas an rental boats. KOA Kampground at Fiesta Key *(☎ 664-4922)* and Sugarloaf Ke *(☎ 745-3549)*; America Outdoors Camper Resort, Key Largo *(☎ 852-8054* The three state parks in the Keys—John Pennekamp *(☎ 451-1202)*, Long Ke *(☎ 664-4815)* and Bahia Honda *(☎ 872-2353)*—also offer dozens of camp sites, but reservations are essential well in advance, sometimes as much a

11 months for peak travel periods. A different way of exploring the Keys is to rent a **houseboat** *($950-$1,375/weekend; $1,495-$2,300/week fully equipped; advance reservations required):* Houseboat Vacations, Islamorada ☎ 664-4009. *Rates quoted are average prices per night for a double room and are subject to seasonal variations.*

Sports and Recreation – Visitors can enjoy many activities including sailing, snorkeling, fishing, scuba diving and boating. **Diving** in the Florida Keys is best from March-July. Dive shops rent equipment and offer day trips and package deals as well as instruction. Outfitters' boats that include a captain and mate leave daily year-round *(round-trip 4hrs; advance reservations strongly recommended; divers can bring their own equipment):*

Marina Del Mar	MM 100	Key Largo	☎ 451-4107 or 800-451-DIVE
Sea Dwellers Dive Shop	MM 100	Key Largo	☎ 451-3640 or 800-451-3640
Halls Diving Center	MM 48	Marathon	☎ 743-5929 or 800-331-4255
Strike Zone Charters	MM 29.5	Big Pine Key	☎ 872-9863 or 800-654-9560
Looe Key Reef Resort	MM 275	Ramrod Key	☎ 872-2215

Scuba and snorkel cruises:Theater of the Sea MM 84.5, Islamorada *(year-round daily 8:30am and 1pm; round-trip 4hrs; commentary; purchase tickets in advance at Theater of the Sea; $49.95 including equipment rental; ☎ 664-2431).* **Underseas Inc.** MM 30.5, Big Pine Key *(depart from Dive Shop year-round daily 9am & 1pm; round-trip 4hrs; commentary; reservations required; $25-$40; $55 including equipment rental; ☎ 872-2700 or 800-446-5663).*
To explore the **backcountry**—Key West National Wildlife Refuge and the Great White Heron National Wildlife Refuge—visitors should engage a reputable guide.
Area **golf** courses: **Key West Golf Club** (MM 5) *(☎ 294-5232);* **Key Colony Beach** (MM 53.5), **Marathon** *(☎ 289-1533).*

Dolphin encounter sites – Visitors participate in a marine orientation seminar *(30min-3hrs 30min, depending on facility)* followed by a swim *(30min)* with Atlantic bottlenose dolphins. Participants must be at least 8 years old (5 years old if with parent in the water), be good swimmers in deep water and be experienced in the use of mask and fins. Reservations should be made 4-8 weeks in advance. Prices range from $85-$125/person.

Site	MM/ City	www	☎
Dolphin Research Center	MM 59/Marathon	dolphins.org	289-1121
Dolphin Adventure **Theater of the Sea**	MM 84.5/ Windley Key	theaterofthe sea.com	664-2431
Dolphins Plus	MM 100.5/ Key Largo	pennekamp.com/ dolphins-plus	451-1993
Dolphin Cove	MM 102/ Key Largo	dolphinscove.com	451-4060

Meeting a Dolphin at Pennekamp State Park

Sportfishing Tournaments

Season	Tournament	☎
	General sportfishing information	888-FISH-KEYS
late March	Islamorada All-Tackle Spring Bonefish Tournament	852-1694
late Apr-early May	Texaco Key West Classic	294-4042
Apr-Nov	Key West and Lower Keys Fishing Tournament	800-970-9056
June	Women's World Invitational Tarpon Fly Championship Tournament	664-2080
late June	TNT/Golden Fly Invitational Tarpon Championship	664-2080
late Sept	Little Palm Island Grand Slam	664-2002
mid-Oct	Sloppy Joe's/Galleon Marina Fish Roundup	296-7182
	George Bush/Cheeca Lodge Bonefish Tournament	664-4651
late Nov	WCA Light Tackle Billfish Classic, Marathon	743-6139
late Nov	Marathon Small Boat Billfish Tournament	743-6139
Dec-May	Metropolitan South Florida Fishing Tournament Mini-Met	569-0066

ADDRESS BOOK

Address Book for Key West p 76. For a legend of price listings for hotels and restaurants, see p 76. Information about Florida hotel chains is in the Practical Information section at the back of this guide.

Staying in the Keys

Cheeca Lodge – *Mile Marker 82, Overseas Hwy., Islamorada.* ✗ ⟋ ▣ ✈ ☎ *305-664-4651 or 800-327-2888. www.cheeca.com. 203 rooms.* $$$$$ Colonial Bahamian elegance permeates the grounds of this deluxe resort, favored by former president George H. Bush as a base for his bonefishing excursions. Broad lawns and a 9-hole golf course surround the stucco-and-tile buildings, creating the ambience of an estate. Tennis courts, two pools and a saltwater lagoon entice adult guests, as do sailboarding and other water activities; extensive children's programs keep the younger set occupied.

Hawk's Cay Resort – *61 Hawk's Cay Blvd., Duck Key.* ✗ ⟋ ▣ ✈ ☎ *305 743-7000 or 800-432-2242. www.hawkscay.com. 180 rooms.* $$$$ A full-scale family resort, Hawk's Cay's 60-acre complex offers every imaginable tropical activity, including swimming with dolphins. One of the two pools is reserved for adults; the saltwater lagoon boasts its own small beach. Two- and three-story buildings house the guest units, done in cool blue and white to echo the view of the Atlantic Ocean from their balconies.

Jules' Undersea Lodge – *51 Shoreland Dr., Key Largo.* ▣ ☎ *305-451-2353 www.jul.com. 1 unit (maximum 6 people).* $$$$ You have to don scuba gear (but you don't have to be an expert diver) to reach your room at this unique establishment near John Pennekamp Reef Park. Situated 21ft below the surface of a little lagoon, 100ft from shore, Jules' advertises itself as the world's only undersea lodge. Guest accommodations are fully equipped with TV, microwave, telephone and air conditioning. Dinner and breakfast must be ordered in advance, if you choose not to bring your own food.

Kona Kai Resort – *97802 Overseas Hwy., Key Largo.* ⟋ ▣ ✈ ☎ *305-852-7200 or 800-365-7829. www.konakairesort.com. 11 cottages.* $$$$ Set in a small, lushly landscaped compound, this collection of low-slung stucco cottages and cabanas is well off the highway, facing westward, and overlooking Florida Bay and its spectacular sunsets. All suites feature ceiling fans, tile baths and compact kitchens. Relax in the secluded pool or hot tub, sheltered by dense tropical foliage.

Conch Key Cottages – *62250 Overseas Hwy., Marathon.* ⟋ ▣ ✈ ☎ *305 289-1377 or 800-330-1577. www.conchkeycottages.com. 12 cottages.* $$ Bright bougainvillea and hibiscus surround these cozy stucco cottages, which occupy their own private key in the Atlantic Ocean. Clad in island prints and furnished in rattan and wicker, the cottages come complete with kitchenettes. There's a tranquil pool, a small beach, and lots of palm-shaded hammocks in which to enjoy the profusion of peace and quiet.

Largo Lodge – *101740 Overseas Hwy., Key Largo.* ⟋ ▣ ☎ *305-451-0424 or 800-468-4378. www.largolodge.com. 8 cottages.* $$ Equipped with kitchens, screened porches and living rooms, Largo Lodge's rustic cottages are spacious, comfortable and economical. A private beach and boat dock offer access to the Gulf of Mexico; the no-children policy enhances the serenity. Make reservations months in advance for winter weekends.

KEY LARGO★

Map p 67

Tourist Information: www.fla-keys.com/keylargo ☎ 305-451-1414 or 800-822-1088

Called *Cayo Largo*, or "Long Island," by 16C Spanish explorers, Key Largo is the first and largest in this chain of coral rock isles. The real beauty of this island, which spans 26mi in length but only one mile at its widest point, can be found along its shoreline and underneath its crystal blue waters. Immediately to the east lies the vast windswept Atlantic Ocean; to the west, the calm shallow Florida Bay serves as a nursery for birds and marine life. Mangrove swamps and tropical hammocks—slightly elevated areas—envelop the island's shores, where turtles, crocodiles and great white herons reside. The commercial strip of US-1 runs down the spine of Key Largo, taking in the small community of Tavernier.

Key Largo saw its first settlers in the early 19C, primarily pirates and pioneers. When Henry Flagler's railroad pulled into Key Largo in 1906, Rock Harbor—as Key Largo was originally called—was already established. Hoping for greater access to markets for their produce, farmers longed for the tracks to reach Key West. However, Key West soon outstripped Rock Harbor and Planter (now Tavernier) as a produce shipping center. During the 1920s, ferries brought visitors to the local taverns that operated freely despite Prohibition. Although US-1 was completed between the mainland and Key Largo in 1938, the island did not see its first boom until after World War II. Real-estate promoters petitioned to rename the town for *Key Largo*, the popular 1948 movie that focused attention on the small island.

Fortunately, the Nature Conservancy and the Fish and Wildlife Service rescued some of the land from development when they bought it in 1979 to form the **Crocodile Lake National Wildlife Refuge** *(not open to the public)*. Here along Card Sound Road, some 500 crocodiles—the largest concentration of these reptiles in North America—dwell in 6,686 acres of mangrove swamp and upland jungle.

SIGHTS

★★**John Pennekamp Coral Reef State Park** – *MM 102.5. Park hrs & fees p 350. Open year-round daily 8am-dusk. $4/vehicle; 50¢ per person. △ (reservations suggested) ✗ ✗ ▯ ☎ 305-451-1202.* Stretching along Key Largo's coastline and reaching 3mi into the ocean, America's first underwater park encompasses a dazzling kaleidoscope of vivid coral and sea creatures. Established in 1960, the park is named for the *Miami Herald* associate editor who lobbied to preserve the reef and was instrumental in creating Everglades National Park. Informative displays relating to the reef and its marine life in the **visitor center** *(open year-round daily 9am-5pm)* provide an excellent introduction to the undersea world offshore. Of the 150 species of tropical fish that feed here, the most colorful

Snorkeling off Key Largo

© Stephen Frink/Tony Stone Images

and conspicuous are angelfish, parrot fish, triggerfish and snapper. Sea fans, whips, plumes and sponges cling to the coral. Since 96 percent of the park lies underwater, snorkeling and scuba diving are the best ways to experience this site. A variety of water craft can be rented. Or take a glass-bottom boat tour of the reef *(tours depart from the marina year-round daily 9:15am, 12:15pm & 3pm; round-trip 2hrs 30min; commentary; reservations suggested; $18; for tours and equipment rental: Coral Reef Park Co. ☎ 305-451-1621; www.dep.state.fl.us/parks).*
Near the visitor center, a small rocky beach edges a shallow lagoon ideal for swimming and snorkeling, and several nature trails wind through tropical hammocks.

Florida Keys Wild Bird Rehabilitation Center – *MM 93.6 in Tavernier. Open year-round daily dawn-dusk. Contribution suggested. ✗ ▯ ☎ 305-852-4486.* At this bird recovery center alongside Florida Bay, wooden boardwalks wind above a

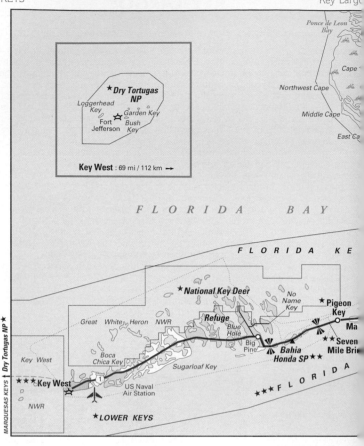

mangrove swamp past spacious enclosures where dozens of winged waterbird shorebirds and Florida raptors (such as hawks and ospreys) recuperate fro injuries, most inflicted by fishing lines and hooks.

■ Preserving the Reef

The coral reef that lies off Key Largo forms part of the **Florida Reef★★★** tract. the largest living coral reef system in North American waters and third-largest barrier reef in the world (after Australia's Great Barrier Reef and the Belize Barrier Reef off Central America). The reef protects almost 200mi of coastline from Fowey Rock (south of Miami) to the Dry Tortugas. Descending to depths of nearly 80ft, it consists of calcium carbonate (limestone) secreted over thousands of years by colonies of small, soft-bodied coral polyps (members of the coelenterate phylum) and associated organisms.

This fragile system, including coral reefs, sea-grass meadows and mangrove forests, is protected by the expansive **Florida Keys National Marine Sanctuary**, which protects the waters surrounding the Keys from Biscayne National Park to the Dry Tortugas, encompassing the former Key Largo National Marine Sanctuary as well. The sanctuary provides mooring buoys at various dive sites to prevent boaters from anchoring on the reef.

In order to remain healthy, coral requires water of a certain salinity, temperature and clarity. Over the years, pollution, overharvesting and careless use have adversely affected the Florida Reef. A comprehensive management plan and water-quality protection program developed for the Keys sanctuary is attempting to reverse the destructive trend and restore this national treasure to full health. The effort extends all the way "upstream" to the Everglades, which a massive federal and state program is attempting to revive. Water from the Everglades flows south into Florida Bay—also an endangered environment—through the narrow channels to the reefs that depend on the purity of this flow.

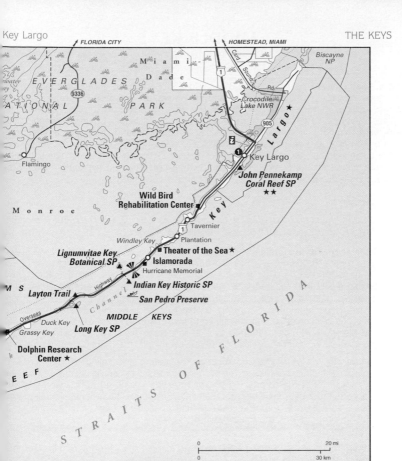

FLORIDA CITY

HOMESTEAD, MIAMI

Biscayne NP

Miami-Dade

EVERGLADES

Card Sound

9336

Crocodile Lake NWR

ATIONAL   PARK

905

Key Largo

Flamingo

Key Largo

John Pennekamp
Coral Reef SP
★★

Monroe

Wild Bird
Rehabilitation Center

Tavernier

Windley Key

Plantation

Lignumvitae Key
Botanical SP

Theater of the Sea ★

Islamorada

Hurricane Memorial

M S

Layton Trail

Indian Key Historic SP

San Pedro Preserve

Overseas

Duck Key

MIDDLE   KEYS

Grassy Key

Long Key SP

Dolphin Research
Center ★

E E F

STRAITS   OF   FLORIDA

0   20 mi

0   30 km

The Key Lime Tree

Map above. Overseas Hwy. (east side of highway) in town of Key Largo.
☎ *305-853-0378 or 800-870-1780.* This roadside Key Largo shop carries
just about everything imaginable made from key limes, including admirably
tart iced smoothies that are perfect refreshers before continuing the long drive
north out of the Keys. Key limes are good for much more than their famous
namesake pies or these blended drinks. Introduced to the Caribbean by
Christopher Columbus on his second voyage in 1493, lime trees became
endemic in the West Indies, evolving into a distinctive variety called Key Lime
in the Keys. Most backyards in the Keys have a lime tree or two, and a small
cottage industry has sprung up to make use of the fruit. The lime's astringent
juice is a principal ingredient in soothing lotions, bracing soaps and shampoos,
and sauces and marinades that range from savory to stinging.

MIDDLE KEYS

The Middle Keys reach from MM 85 to MM 45. Sportfishing enthusiasts favor these islands—especially Islamorada—casting their waters for such deep-sea trophies as sailfish, tarpon, marlin and shark. Below MM 80, US-1 crosses a series of viaducts, causeways and bridges connecting myriad individual islands. Driving through them, however, you'll have less a sense of separate bodies of land than an overall impression of water, as sweeping **views**★★★ of the cerulean Atlantic Ocean and Florida Bay fan out on either side of the road. Development returns with the roadside shopping plazas, motels and eateries in Marathon. Just past Marathon at the south end of Vaca Key, Seven-Mile Bridge spans the distance to the Lower Keys.

SIGHTS

South of Key Largo, you'll pass through the hamlets of Tavernier and Plantation. Just past Plantation (MM 85), you'll come to Windley Key.

★**Theater of the Sea** – 🔲 *Windley Key, MM 84.5. Open year-round daily 9:30am–4pm (open 10:30am Dec 25). Reservations required for special programs. $17.25.* ♿ 🅿 ☎ *305-664-2431. www.theaterofthesea.com.* This 17-acre marine park, second oldest in the US after St. Augustine's Marineland, was established in 1945 in an old railroad quarry. Its small, open-air pools house sharks, turtles and fish. At two larger lagoons, visitors are invited to participate in shows featuring dolphins and sea lions. Continuous guided tours through the park explain the behavior and biology of different animals as well as the threats posed to their survival by the modern world. The park also offers a swim-with-the-dolphins program.

Islamorada – *MM 84-80.* Early Spanish explorers named this place islas moradas ("purple islands"), because of the profusion of violet sea snails *(Janthina janthina)* they found here. Islamorada ("EYE-la-ma-RAH-da") is noted for **charter fishing** and hosts a number of sportfishing tournaments. Seafood restaurants and small motels line US-1 here. At MM 81.7 a roadside **Hurricane Memorial** *(east side of highway)* of local limestone marks the mass grave of the 400-some people killed in the 1935 hurricane.

Layton Trail – *Long Key, MM 68, trailhead marked by Long Key Fishing Club historic marker on right side of US-1.* Administered by the Long Key State Recreation Area, this dirt path *(.25mi)* tunnels through a low-hanging, dense tangle of tropical vegetation at the edge of Florida Bay. Botanical labels identify species that include gumbo-limbo, wild lime, coffee, poisonwood and Jamaica dogwood.

■ Bonefishing

The shallow, flat waters surrounding the Keys are home to several types of highly prized, and legendarily elusive, gamefish—including the famed bonefish. Bonefishing is an arcane and demanding art. Success therein depends on skill, expertise, concentration and more than a little luck. The bonefish flats in Florida Bay, northwest of the Keys, range from 3ft to 8ft deep; thus, shallow-hull boats are necessary, and visitors must rely on knowledgeable guides to find their way through the maze of channels, flats and islands that, to an outsider, seem indistinguishable. The sun invariably blazes down, and afternoon winds prowl the waters; polarized sunglasses are needed to pick out the fish cruising the flats for prey. Anglers cast streamer flies (designed to look like small prey) ahead of the fish, and when hooked, memorable fights ensue on the light tackle typically used. Aside from bonefish, snook, tarpon and redfish are often caught; sea trout and sharks are secondary targets. The bonefish guiding community has begun to promote a catch-and-release conservation ethic, as the environmental problems besetting Florida Bay have curtailed the fishery somewhat. Even if you don't catch a bonefish, the area is a waterfowl haven, where osprey, eagles, pelicans and herons are common sights; flamingoes are less often seen in this semi-wilderness habitat unique to this part of the Keys.

A day of guided bonefishing costs $350 or more *(rods and gear supplied by the guide).* It's essential to patronize guides whose principles include safeguarding the delicate environment of the Keys backcountry. *Conservation-minded guides include Adam Redford, who specializes in upper Florida Bay and the Everglades (☎ 800-632-0394); and Mike Collins in Islamorada (☎ 305-852-5837). In Key West, the Salt Water Angler (243 Front St.; ☎ 305-294-3248) can arrange trips with reputable and ethical guides.*

■ Where are the Beaches?

Outsiders picture the Keys as a tropical paradise of white strands of sand, breeze-tossed palms and languid waters. That they are, but the archipelago's beaches often puzzle first-time visitors. The beaches that do exist are fairly scant, and even those are often not ideal for swimming, given their very shallow depths and wind-roiled water. The explanation is topographical: the waters surrounding the Keys, both Gulf and Atlantic, are almost invariably shallow, and bounded by reefs on the Atlantic side. The reefs block the currents that bring large quantities of sand to the high shore and scour the near-shore bottom, creating the typical ocean beach found worldwide. Most of the major resort complexes have "made" their own beaches, often by manufacturing saltwater lagoons on their property, or sometimes by dredging near-shore waters.

There are a few public beaches where visitors can enjoy water deep enough to swim. **Anne's Beach**, right along US-1 at MM 73 on Lower Matecumbe Key, offers clean sand and a series of swimming holes at the south end of the beach. **Sombrero Beach** in Marathon has clean water and sand and a pleasant park that is largely uncrowded. **Bahia Honda State Park**, MM 36.8, is well-known for the best beach in the Keys—famed enough to draw long lines of cars on weekends and holidays.

Long Key State Park – *Long Key, MM 67.5. Park hrs & fees p 350.* △ ▯ ▨ *305-664-4815.* The shorelines of the 965-acre park touch both ocean and bay waters and offer swimming, snorkeling, fishing and camping. The **Golden Orb Spider Trail** *(1mi)* begins as a boardwalk across a mangrove creek, where a low observation platform allows views of the lush treetops. It then crosses a narrow beach habitat and enters a shady tropical hammock.

★**Dolphin Research Center** – Kids *Grassy Key, MM 59. Open year-round daily 9am-4pm. Closed major holidays. $12.50.* ᴋ ▯ ▨ *305-289-1121. www.dolphins.org.* Combining research with public education and entertainment, the Dolphin Research Center maintains a population of roughly 15 dolphins in holding pens in Florida Bay. Visitors watch trainers work with several groups of dolphins as guides explain dolphin behavior, socialization and physiology. The facility has been used in the filming of several dolphin movies, including the 1960s classic *Flipper*. They also offer a swim-with-the-dolphins program *(reservations required)*.

Marathon – *MM 50 on Vaca Key.* Commercial and administrative hub for the Middle Keys, Marathon began as a base camp for laborers on Flagler's Florida East Coast Railway. The town's name derives from those early days, when crews stationed here engaged in a "marathon" effort to complete the rail to Key West before Flagler's death. After the camp was abandoned, the settlement languished until the 1950s, when a Detroit developer planned Marathon's first subdivisions. Marathon's **Sombrero Beach** is a fairly good swimming spot *(follow Sombrero Rd. 2mi east of the main highway)*.

★**Tropical Crane Point Hammock** – *MM 50 in Marathon. Open year-round Mon-Sat 9am-5pm, Sun noon-5pm. Closed major holidays. $7.50.* ▯ ▨ *305-743-9100. www. thefloridakeys.com/marathon/museum.htm.* Trails that wind through 63 acres of tropical forest connect a **Museum of Natural History**, the adjoining **Florida Keys Children's Museum** Kids and the **Adderly Village Historic Site**. Displays in the yellow stucco natural-history museum limn local flora and fauna (much of it now rare or endangered), including marine life on the coral reef and collections of native tree snails and butterflies, as well as Middle Keys history. At the Children's Museum, youngsters visit habitats for iguanas, hawks and scorpions. Restoration work at Adderly Village, a site pioneered in 1903, includes George Adderly's Bahamian Conch house, a reconstructed outdoor kitchen and culinary gardens. A pleasant trail *(1mi)* winds out and back through the hammock's dense scrub forest.

★**Pigeon Key** – *MM 45 on Knight Key. Visitor center on the east side of US-1; turn left just before Seven-Mile Bridge. Watch for signs marking the turn; if you miss it, you have to cross the bridge and return.* From the visitor center, housed in a railroad car, a shuttle takes visitors across a 2.2mi span of the **Old Seven-Mile Bridge** to the former railroad work camp on Pigeon Key *(trams depart year-round daily on the hour 10am-3pm, except Thanksgiving Day & Dec 25; round-trip 2hrs; commentary; $7.50;* ᴋ ▯ ▨ *305-743-5999; passengers may remain on Pigeon Key and return later; visitors may walk across bridge-no private vehicles allowed)*. Completed in 1912, the bridge formed a vital link in the rail line. It was laid on 546 concrete foundation piers anchored in bedrock as deep as 28ft underwater. In Pigeon Key's heyday, the village was home to some 410 people. A cluster of modest, turn-of-the-last-century houses on the four-acre islet is all that remains of construction crew residences. Tour guides take visitors through one of the unfurnished houses.

★★**Seven-Mile Bridge** – *MM 47-40, from Knight Key to Little Duck Key.* Considered an engineering masterpiece, this sweeping bridge ranks as the longest segmental bridge in the world. Its 135ft-long sections—some 288 of them—link the Middle and Lower Keys. Completed in 1982 to replace Flagler's concrete and steel marvel, the new span is both wider and higher than the Old Seven-Mile Bridge, providing a 65ft clearance for vessels to pass underneath. Its heights afford expansive **views**★★ of the open ocean.

OFFSHORE EXCURSIONS

Lignumvitae Key Botanical State Park – *Accessible by boat only; departs from Robbie's Marina MM 77.5 year-round Thu-Mon 9:30am & 1:30pm. Round-trip 1hr 30min. Commentary. Reservations suggested. $15.* ☐ *Robbie's Rent-a-Boat:* ☏ *305-664-9814, www.robbies.com. Mosquitoes can be numerous; wear clothing that covers your arms and legs and bring insect repellent.* A rare **virgin forest**★ covers much of this 280-acre Florida Bay island with lignumvitae, gumbo-limbo, strangler fig and other flora characteristic of a tropical hammock. The modest **Matheson House** (1919), made of coral rock, served as a caretaker's home when the island was owned by William Matheson, a wealthy resident of Key Biscayne who brought yachting entourages to the island.

Indian Key Historic State Park – *Accessible by boat only; departs from Robbie's Marina MM 77.5 year-round Thu-Mon 8:30am & 12:30pm. Round-trip 1hr 30min. Commentary. Reservations suggested. $15.* ☐ *Robbie's Rent-a-Boat:* ☏ *305-664-9814. www.robbies.com.* Now uninhabited, the 11-acre island off the east coast of Lower Matecumbe Key played a critical role in the history of the Keys, thanks to a New Yorker named **Jacob Housman**. Arriving in Florida in the 1830s, Housman became involved in Key West's wrecking business. Seeking autonomy from local laws there, he came north and established a small salvaging town on Indian Key. In 1836 Housman convinced local authorities to create Dade County, appointing his town as the county seat. (Indian Key is now part of Monroe County.) Unfortunately, Housman's ambitious little community was short-lived—Seminole Indians attacked and burned it in 1840.

Dirt lanes of the former 19C village still grid the island, but little else remains save a few crumbling foundations and a re-creation of the tombstone that marked Housman's grave. An observation platform affords a panorama of the island and surrounding waters. Offshore breezes sweep the island, keeping it blessedly free of mosquitoes.

San Pedro Underwater Archaeological Preserve State Park – *1.25 nautical miles south of Indian Key. Accessible via private boat only. For rental, contact Robbie's Rent-a-Boat* ☏ *305-664-9814.* Located in 18ft of water on a sand bottom, the remains of the *San Pedro*, a Dutch-built merchant vessel that sank in July 1733, are now protected as an underwater archaeological preserve. The ship was part of a 21-vessel convoy sailing from Havana to Spain. Caught in a hurricane off the Keys on Friday the 13th, all but one vessel in the flotilla was lost in the storm. Salvaging at the wreck sites went on for years; in recent decades, the *San Pedro* has been rediscovered and more of its treasure recovered. Popular with divers and snorkelers, the *San Pedro* site contains a mound of ballast stones and attracts a colorful array of marine life.

LOWER KEYS★

Map p 66

Tourist Information: www.fla-keys.com/lower keys ☏ 305-872-2411

Scrub and slash pine characterize this handful of wooded islands extending from MM 45 to the outskirts of Key West at MM 5. Their low, wet land and surrounding waters provide refuge for a variety of wildlife, including the great white heron and the diminutive Key deer. For sun worshippers, Bahia Honda boasts one of the few sand beaches in the Keys; for those who prefer to be underwater, the unusually clear waters of the reef at **Looe Key**, a parcel of the Florida Keys National Marine Sanctuary *(7 mi offshore in the Atlantic)*, constitute a diver's paradise.

■ Kayaking the Keys

The shallow waters, mangrove thickets and innumerable islands of the lower Keys are prime territory for sea kayakers. The **Great White Heron National Wildlife Refuge** northeast of Key West, for example, is a kayaker's delight. Here visitors can paddle for hours in quiet backwaters where fish splash, turtles lurk and herons, pelicans, osprey and dozens of other birds roost in the mangroves. Although afternoon breezes shuffle the open waters, they keep insects at bay. Narrow channels (called "creeks," though they are not) in the mangroves offer protection and solitude—and occasional deep holes where adventurous paddlers can slip from their kayaks for a plunge into warm waters sometimes sluiced by cool fresh water from deep springs. Although experienced kayakers can find their way with the aid of detailed maps, local guides know the best routes. They can also provide commentary on the profusion of wildlife, including the shallow underwater community of sponges, fishes and sea grass, and on the environmental challenges that beset this fragile habitat. Visitors to the refuge must maintain a respectful distance from nesting birds, and not disturb any of the other rare animals found within, such as sea turtles. The rewards for a backwater trek are profound peace and solitude and an enhanced understanding of a unique tropical domain. *For guided kayak trips, contact Crystal Seas* ☏ *877-SEAS-877 or Florida Keys visitor information* ☏ *800-FLA-KEYS.*

SIGHTS

Once across the Seven-Mile Bridge, you enter Bahia Honda Key.

★★**Bahia Honda State Park** – *Bahia Honda Key, MM 36.8. Park hrs & fees p 350.* ⚠ 🅿 ☏ *305-872-2353. The park can be especially crowded on weekends and holidays; it closes when it reaches full occupancy.* Named by the Spanish for its "Deep Bay," Bahia Honda Key encompasses one of the largest stretches of rare sand **beach**⚐ in the chain. (The Keys owe their lack of high surf and sandy beaches to the existence of the reef. It serves as an offshore barrier, breaking the impact of Atlantic waves before they reach shore.) This popular park covers 524 acres and includes a lagoon, mangrove forest and a tropical hardwood hammock.

Bahia Honda State Park

Stroll through these diverse communities on the **Silver Palm Trail** *(.25mi)*, where you'll glimpse such unique West Indian specimens as yellow satinwood and Jamaica morning glory. At the southern tip of the park, you can walk out on a segment of the original **Bahia Honda Bridge**, erected for Flagler's railroad and later remodeled for the Overseas Highway. Because of the water's depth here, this bridge was the most difficult to build. From its vantage point high over the ocean stretch **views★** of stately palms swaying above tranquil turquoise water.

★**National Key Deer Refuge** – *MM 30.5, on Big Pine Key. Turn right onto Key Deer Blvd. (Rte. 940) and follow it .3mi to the refuge office in shopping center on right. The refuge is 3mi west on Key Deer Blvd. The 30mph speed limit is strictly enforced; stay alert for deer crossing the road. Open year-round daily dawn-dusk.* 🚻 🅿 ☎ *305-872-2239. http://nationalkeydeer.fws.gov.* This National Wildlife Refuge was established in 1954 to protect Key deer. Since then, the Key deer population has grown and stabilized. Two trails within the refuge provide good opportunities for deer sightings, particularly at dawn and dusk, when the shy animals come out to feed. At **Blue Hole** *(west side of Key Deer Blvd., 1.25mi north of intersection with Watson Blvd.)*, visitors may see deer drinking in this old rock quarry now filled with water. The pond is also home to alligators, turtles and sunfish. The **Jack C. Watson Wildlife Trail** *(continue .3mi north on Key Blvd.)* weaves .6mi through a thicket of slash pines and palms, a favorite Key deer habitat.

A short drive across less populous **No Name Key** *(turn east on Watson Blvd., which dead-ends at Ave. B; turn left and cross bridge; road dead-ends at east end of No Name Key)* often rewards visitors with views of tiny deer feeding on the sides of the road.

■ Key Deer

The unique **Key deer** *(Odocoileus virginianus clavium)* is found only in the lower Florida Keys. Smallest of all North American deer, the members of this subspecies of Virginia white-tailed deer measure about 2ft high at the shoulder and weigh from 50 to 100 pounds. How the deer came to occupy the Keys is unknown, but it is believed that they migrated here from the mainland thousands of years ago. Uncontrolled hunting and land development reduced the number of deer to less than 50 in the 1940s. Since the establishment of the national refuge, the population has grown. Today some 600 Key deer inhabit Big Pine Key. Conflict has inevitably arisen among conservationists, area developers, and local residents who view the animals as foliage-consuming pests. The most pressing threat to Key deer, however, is highway traffic.

R. Corbel/MICHELIN

Key Deer

KEY WEST★★★

Population 25,478
Map p 81
Tourist Information: www.fla-keys.com/keywest ☎ 305-294-2587 or 800-527-8539

Pirates, wreckers, writers, US presidents and Cuban freedom fighters have at one time found a haven on this small island at the southernmost tip of the continent. Closer to Havana than Miami, Key West cultivates an atmosphere of sublime laissez-faire that encourages an eclectic mix of residents, from old-time "conch" families (descended from the island's original settlers) to a more recently arrived gay community. Well established is the lush landscape here, where banyan trees and palms shade older neighborhoods, while the scent of tropical flowers fills the evening air. Key West is undeniably commercial, yet it possesses a charm and long-standing independent spirit that still appeal to writers and artists, as well as to the droves of tourists who come here each year.

Historical Notes

Early Prosperity – When Ponce de León arrived in 1513, he claimed the island for Spain and named it *Cayo Hueso*, ("Island of Bones"), apparently for the abundance of Indian bones he found there. (The English later transformed *Cayo Hueso* into Key West.) Through the 18C the island remained largely the domain of the Calusa and Ais Indians. In 1822 Key West became permanently American and a customs house was established.

■ The Conch Republic

The tradition of autonomy that pervades the Florida Keys dates back to the 18C, when pirates prowled the islands and salvagers first began to profit from the many reef wrecks along the Atlantic side of the Keys. In 1980 the Mariel boatlift brought thousands of Cuban refugees to Key West. Though most refugees dispersed, the town still maintains a palpable Cuban presence. When the US Board Patrol set up a roadblock on Highway 1 (US-1) north of town, Key West residents did not take kindly to this interference with their freedom. All outbound vehicles were being checked for guns, illegal aliens and drugs. On April 23, 1982, at high noon in Mallory

© Eric P. Lucas

Flying the Conch Republic Flag

Square, community activists declared their own country, the Conch Republic. The outraged Conchs, as native Key Westers call themselves (after the mollusk that once thrived in local waters and whose meat provided the mainstay of the settlers' diet) announced they were seceding from the US. A blue Key West flag was raised, speeches peppered the afternoon air, and a loaf of bread was pitched aloft as a declaration of war. It was mostly tongue-in-cheek. Republic leaders quickly "surrendered" to seek foreign aid from the state of Florida. As local writer Joy Williams put it in her definitive book *The Florida Keys*, "There were T-shirts, of course, and flags and border passes.... And there was a party which lasted a week."

The spirit of the Conch Republic lives today in two conspicuous facets of Key West life. **Conch Independence Days** each April is one of the city's three main festivals (October's **Fantasy Fest** and **Hemingway Days** in July are the other two). And hundreds of homes throughout the city still fly the azure Conch Republic flag, asserting at least their cultural, if not political, perspective.

In the late 1820s Key West served as headquarters for a lucrative enterprise called **wrecking**—salvaging goods from ships that ran aground on the Florida reef. By mid-century a new industry, **cigar making**, had begun. These industries thrived to the extent that, by 1889, the combined revenues from the fishing, sponging, wrecking and cigar-making industries had made Key West the wealthiest town per capita in the country. During the Civil War the military used Key West to control ship traffic through the Florida Straits, but the island saw no serious action. After the war Cuban cigar barons, disaffected with Spanish control of Cuba, moved here and opened factories, attracting Cuban workers and revolutionaries. By 1890 the largest cigar-manufacturing city in the world was also a hotbed of Cuban revolutionary activity. Cuban liberator **José Martí** (1853-1895) soon headquartered himself here. In 1898 the *USS Maine* departed Key West for Havana and exploded there, precipitating the short-lived **Spanish-American War**. In 1912 Henry Flagler's Overseas Railroad finally reached its terminus in Key West, connecting the island with the rest of the continent. Designed by the eminent New York firm Carrère and Hastings, the deluxe **Casa Marina** hotel *(see Address Book)* opened here nine years later, equipped with a hurricane-proof reinforced concrete exterior.

Chic Resort – Poor and rundown during the Depression, the town maintained its charm nonetheless, for in 1931 author **Ernest Hemingway**—destined to become Key West's most celebrated son—bought a house here, beginning a literary tradition that continues today. The town has been home to writers John Dos Passos, Tennessee Williams, Elizabeth Bishop, Robert Frost, Philip Caputo, John Ciardi, James Merrill, Thomas McGuane, Wallace Stevens, Ralph Ellison and John Hersey, among others. *(The Key West Literary Seminar sponsors a weekly Writer's Walk through Old Town; see Sightseeing opposite.)*

Using federal funds, local volunteers transformed the shabby town into an attractive tourist destination. However, a violent hurricane in 1935 destroyed the railroad to Key West. The town languished for three years before the **Overseas Highway** was completed on the old rail bed, making Key West more accessible to travelers than ever before. In mid-century President **Harry Truman** became enamored of Key West, escaping to his Little White House on the Navy base there.

In the past several decades, the island has undergone a slow transformation from renegade outpost to fashionable resort. The town's overtly commercial main stem, 14-block-long **Duval Street**, is named for William Pope DuVal, the first governor of the Florida Territory. Amid the eateries, bars and boutiques that line the north end of Duval, Key West still cultivates its eccentricity. By night, live music fills the streets, spilling out of bars frequented over the years by such notables as authors Ernest Hemingway and Truman Capote, and singer-songwriter Jimmy Buffett.

■ Key West Architecture

Diverse 19C and early 20C architectural styles found in Key West's Old Town range from gracious Neoclassical houses to gingerbread-trimmed Victorians, to Caribbean-influenced "Conch cottages."

Given the New England background of many of the 19C seafarers who settled here, much of Key West's architecture follows the Classical Revival style. Among the indigenous features added to this style to adapt it to a subtropical climate, the "eyebrow" is unique. This West Indian element consists of eaves that partly overhang second-story windows, thus resembling a brow over squinting eyes. Like an awning, the "eyebrow" blocks out direct sunlight, thus keeping the house cool. Among the 50-some **eyebrow houses** extant in Key West are the residences at 401 and 525 Frances Street, 643 William Street and 1211 Southard Street.

Bahamian features, such as wide, breeze-catching verandas, also figure in the architectural mix. Due to a lack of trees on the island, some early settlers from the Bahamas actually dismantled their houses and floated them to Key West. A couple of classic examples of imported **Bahama Houses** still stand.

The many vernacular buildings found throughout the city are locally known as **Conch houses**. Built from the 1830s to 1920s, this type of dwelling is named for the Bahamian islanders—colloquially known as "Conchs"—who settled in the Keys in the 19C. While these houses take varied forms, in general they are wood frame, devoid of ornamentation, and only a story or two high with a porch across the front. Distinguishing features are the front porch (running full-height on two-story houses) and widow's walk, which may be borrowed from the New England houses seen by Key West seafarers. The narrow, single-story **shotgun house**, a variation on this style, is only one room wide, with a roofline that runs perpendicular to the street. Many of these plain dwellings were built by cigar makers for their workers. A good sampling of Conch cottages can be found in the 600 and 700 blocks of Elizabeth Street. You'll also find a number of elegant Queen Anne structures on the island, among them the George Patterson House and the Southernmost House.

PRACTICAL INFORMATION ....Area Code: 305

Getting There

By Air – **Key West Airport (EYW)**: serviced by most domestic airlines as well as charters *(information:* ☎ *296-5439)*. Transportation to Old Town by **taxi** *($5-$15)* and hotel courtesy shuttles. Major **Rental car** agencies *(p 343)* are located at airport.

Getting Around

Local **bus service** travels two routes *(Mon-Fri 6am-10:30pm, weekends 9:15am-6:30pm; 75¢; schedule and route information:* ☎ *292-8160)*. The best way to get around Old Town Key West is on foot as most attractions are within easy walking distance of each other. The Bone Island **Shuttle** route takes in Mallory Sq., Duval St. and the Seaport *($5)*. Legal for city street use, two- and four-seat Key West Cruisers can be rented *($169/day;* ☎ *294-4724)*. Another good means of transport is **bicycle** or **scooter**: Adventure Scooter & Bike Rental *(*☎ *293-9933)*; Bicycle Center *(*☎ *294-4556)*; Caribbean Scooter Rental *(*☎ *293-9971)*. Daily rentals average $4-$10 for a bike and $23-$35 for a scooter.

Taxi service: Friendly Cab *(*☎ *292-0000)*; **Maxi Taxi** *(*☎ *296-2222)*. Gas prices are higher in Key West than on the mainland. **Parking** is limited in Old Town area; public parking lots average 75¢/hr; Mallory Square parking garage: $2/hr.

General Information

Visitor Information – **Greater Key West Chamber of Commerce**, 402 Wall St., Key West FL 33040, provides information on lodging, shopping, entertainment, festivals and recreation *(open year-round Mon-Fri 8:30am-6pm, weekends 8:30am-5pm;* ☎ *294-2587 or 800-527-8539; www.keywestchamber.org)*.

Accommodations – A variety of lodgings from large **hotels** and **resorts** *($100-$350)* to small **motels** *($75-$150)* are offered. Most accommodations in Old Town Key West are **guest houses** and **bed-and-breakfast inns** *($65-$275)*. **Reservations** can be made through the Welcome Center of Florida Keys *(*☎ *296-4444 or 800-352-8538)*. **Youth Hostel** *($17-$20;* ☎ *296-5719)*. **Camping and RV park**: Boyd's Key West Campground *(*☎ *294-1465)*.
Rates quoted are average prices per night for a double room and are subject to seasonal variations.

Sightseeing – **Conch Train Tour** *(departs from Mallory Square or Roosevelt Blvd. year-round daily 9am-4:30pm; round-trip 1hr 30min; commentary; $18;* ♿ ☎ *294-5161)*. **Old Town Trolley Tour** *(departs from various locations year-round daily 9am-4:30pm; round-trip 1hr 30min; commentary; $18; free reboarding;* ☎ *296-6688)*. **Key West Writer's Walk** *(departs from Heritage House Museum Dec-May Sat 10:30am, from Hemingway House Dec-May Sun 10:30am; 1hr; $10; purchase tickets from Heritage House Museum;* ☎ *293-9291)*.

Entertainment – Consult the arts and entertainment section in the *Key West Citizen* (Fridays), *Travelhost* and *See Florida Keys* (available free at hotels and restaurants) for schedule of cultural events and addresses of principal theaters. **Tennessee Williams Fine Arts Center**: Broadway shows, concerts, jazz *(*☎ *296-1520)*; **Red Barn Theater**: plays *(*☎ *296-9911)*; **Waterfront Playhouse**: plays, musicals *(*☎ *294-5015)*.

© Eric P. Lucas

Conch Train Tour

Useful Numbers

Police/Ambulance/Fire	**911**
Police (non-emergency) Key West	294-2511
Florida Highway Patrol	289-2300
US Coast Guard Boating and Safety Hotline	292-8700
Visitor Assistance Program (multilingual)	*(Florida only)* 800-771-KEYS

ADDRESS BOOK

The accommodations listed below were selected for their ambience, location and/or value for money. Prices reflect the average cost for a standard double room (two people) in high season (not including any applicable city or state taxes). Room rates may be considerably lower in off-season and hotels sometimes offer discounted weekend rates. The presence of a swimming pool is indicated by the ⌇ symbol. For information about hotel chains in Florida, see the Practical Information section at the back of this guide.

$$$$$	over $300	$$	$75-$125
$$$$	$200-$300	$	less than $75
$$$	$125-$200		

Staying in Key West

Paradise Inn – *819 Simonton St.* ⌖ ▣ ⌇ ☏ *305-293-8007 or 800-888-9648. www.theparadiseinn.com. 18 units.* **$$$$$** Distinguished by decorator touches such as pine Shaker beds and custom-made armoires, this collection of shimmering white cottages and suites is set back from the street. More modern in flavor than most Key West guest houses, sleeping quarters are appointed with French doors, ceiling fans, marble baths, and bars. The extensive grounds showcase night-blooming jasmine and myriad other tropical plants.

Gardens Hotel – *526 Angela St.* ⌖ ▣ ⌇ ☏ *305-294-2661 or 800-526-2664. www.gardenshotel.com. 17 units.* **$$$$** The luxuriant gardens that fill much of this walled Old Town compound were once a private botanical preserve harboring tropical species collected around the world. Composed of three restored historic structures and two new additions, the complex harbors tastefully decorated rooms featuring wood floors and marble baths—many with Jacuzzi tubs and steam showers. Rates include a buffet continental breakfast served in the sunlit Garden Room.

Hotel Marquesa – *600 Fleming St.* ✗ ⌖ ▣ ⌇ ☏ *305-292-1919 or 800-869-4631. www.marquesa.com. 27 rooms.* **$$$$** Comprising four 1884 Conch houses encircling two pools and a palm-filled garden, this favored lodging in the historic district is listed on the National Historic Register. Breezy guest rooms mix soft tropical colors with Chippendale pieces and West Indies wicker; several of the poolside rooms have sitting areas and patios. The hotel's **Cafe Marquesa** specializes in Caribbean-inspired dishes with Asian and Central American influences; try the pan-seared jumbo scallops served with foie gras and squash coulis, or the pistachio-encrusted rack of lamb with rosemary-pinot noir reduction.

Pier House Resort – *One Duval St.* ✗ ⌖ ▣ ⌇ ☏ *305-296-4600 or 800-327-8340. www.pierhouse.com. 142 rooms.* **$$$$** One of Key West's original landmark resorts, the Pier House has recently remodeled and upgraded to maintain top-drawer status. Its location at Mile Zero is ideal for visiting Old Town sights, especially Mallory Square. Housed in attractive white buildings, the rooms are airy, comfortable and spacious, and many look out over Key West Harbor. A full-service spa and health club, located in a separate building, supplement the pool and private beach.

Simonton Court – *320 Simonton St.* ⌖ ⌇ ☏ *305-294-6386 or 800-944-2687. www.simontoncourt.com. 27 units.* **$$$$** Although it's just two blocks from Duval Street, this secluded enclave of former cigar-makers' cottages is elegant and lush. Oleander, bougainvillea and hibiscus shade the two small pools—one placed within the foundation of a ruined brick house. Individually decorated rooms feature Florida pine furnishings and marble baths. Ask the knowledgeable staff anything you want to know about Key West.

Wyndham Casa Marina Resort – *1500 Reynolds St.* ✗ ⌖ ▣ ⌇ ☏ *305-296-3535 or 800-626-0777. www.casamarinakeywest.com. 464 rooms.* **$$$$** Tile roofs, massive, hurricane-proof stucco walls and Spanish Renaissance styling mark the hotel that Henry Flagler envisioned as the endpoint resort for his Overseas Railroad. Darkly elegant black cypress encases the lobby; rooms are decorated in sunny pastels, light woods and rattan. On the expansive grounds you'll find almost every imaginable amenity, including two pools, an 1,100ft private beach, and numerous cabanas and bars. Shuttles run guests to downtown Key West.

Island City House Hotel – *411 William St.* & ⌇ ☎ *305-294-5702 or 800-634-8230. www.islandcityhouse.com. 24 units.* **$$$** This small hotel encompasses three multistory late-19C clapboard buildings, with exterior stairs and balconies. Guest-room decor ranges from bright island fabrics and white wicker to Victorian antiques and lace curtains. Some of the cozy suites include kitchenettes. The family-friendly complex encloses a palm-shaded pool with a hot tub. Continental breakfast is served outside in the courtyard.

Merlinn Inn – *811 Simonton St.* & ⌇ ☎ *305-296-3336 or 800-642-4753. www.merlinnkeywest.com. 20 units.* **$$$** A landscaped courtyard is the central focus of the moderately priced Merlinn, located one block off Duval Street. Rooms are compact and sparely decorated, but comfortable. Start the day with a top-notch continental breakfast poolside and take refuge in the song-filled aviary after a busy day of sightseeing.

Key West Hostel & Seashell Motel – *718 South St.* & ☐ ☎ *305-296-5719. www.keywesthostel.com. 92 beds. 15 rooms.* **$$** This pleasant lodging, a member of Hostelling International, is one of the most economical anywhere near Old Town Key West. Located in a residential neighborhood, it offers a peaceful stay, even during the chaos of Spring Break. Rooms are dorm style, but private motel rooms are also available. Amenities include kitchen facilities and a game room, and lockers and bikes are available for rent.

Spanish Gardens Motel – *1325 Simonton St.* & ☐ ⌇ ☎ *305-294-1051. 26 rooms.* **$$** Conveniently located near Duval Street and Old Town, this classic small motel offers standard but clean rooms equipped with refrigerators and television sets. Tile bathrooms and ceiling fans help to keep the rooms cool.

Dining in Key West

The establishments listed below were selected for their ambience, location and/or value for money. Prices indicate the average cost of an appetizer, an entrée and dessert for one person (not including tax, gratuity or beverages). Call for information regarding reservations and opening hours.

$$$$	over $50	**$$**	$15-$30
$$$	$30-$50	**$**	less than $15

Louie's Backyard – *Vernon & Waddell Sts.* & ☎ *305-294-1061.* **$$$$** Continental. Louie's deluxe, Florida-flavored cuisine (like roasted salmon with mustard seeds, bacon and spaetzle or the annatto-rubbed grouper with black-bean salsa) is matched by the sensational setting, overlooking the Atlantic. The late-19C house containing the restaurant has been crisply refurbished, but the best spots are in the namesake backyard. Outside tables are at a premium, though, so go early.

Key Lime Pie

A&B Lobster House – *700 Front St.* & ☎ *305-294-5880.* **$$$** Seafood. One of Key West's longest-established seafood restaurants, the upscale A&B specializes in Maine and Caribbean lobster, as well as in traditional Keys favorites like grouper stuffed with crabmeat and topped with mango bearnaise sauce. The restaurant's downstairs sibling, **Alonzo's Oyster Bar,** offers a more economical seafood menu and a boisterous setting along the harbor walkway. It's a good place to people-watch. *Dinner only.*

© Michael Ventura/FOLIO, Inc.

Caladesi Catch – *530 Simonton St.* ♿ *305-295-9300.* **$$$ Seafood.** Caladesi's inventive, Key West-raised chef greets passersby on the outside step of this Neoclassical building to promote his unique menu, which melds Conch cuisine with Asian and Caribbean influences. Tuna sashimi, for instance, is accompanied by ginger cream, chile paste and wasabi; mahi mahi is blackened with French spices and served with couscous. *Dinner only.*

Pepe's Café – *806 Caroline St.* ♿ *305-294-7192.* **$$$ Pub Fare.** The decor in this publike cafe focuses on autographed celebrity photos, including a picture of Harry S Truman playing the piano. At midday the vine-covered patio becomes a cool retreat. The burgers, fried oysters and other tavern-type offerings here are reliable, and the key lime pie gets local raves.

Seven Fish – *632 Olivia St..* ♿ *305-296-2777.* **$$$ Seafood.** Big crowds gather almost every night at this popular restaurant, where rich seafood preparations—such as red snapper with a curry cream sauce—contrast markedly with the sparse decor. Culinary influences are global, from Japanese to Northern Italian. The key lime curd over shortbread is Seven Fish's estimable version of key lime pie. *Dinner only.*

Blue Heaven – *729 Thomas St.* ♿ *305-296-8666.* **$$ Bahamian.** A former Hemingway hangout, Blue Heaven's popularity now revolves around its food. Breakfast, lunch and dinner are served in the dirt courtyard, where chickens peck under the tables and a huge mango tree provides shade. Waiting diners often engage in a friendly game of ping-pong. The menu is a West Indies hybrid—with dishes like jerk chicken with brown rice and black beans, and fish sandwiches with brown rice, black beans and cornbread. Save room for the key lime pie.

Camille's – *703 Duval St.* ♿ *305-296-4811.* **$$ American.** Camille's reliable, no-fuss comfort food draws crowds for breakfast. Enjoying a great vantage point on Duval, the compact, friendly cafe serves standard morning fare, such as buckwheat pancakes, corned-beef hash and buttermilk waffles, on generous platters. At lunchtime, try the chicken salad sandwich.

El Siboney – *900 Catherine St.* ♿ *305-296-4184.* **$$ Cuban.** Housed in a brick building on a back street, this traditional Cuban restaurant offers a down-home atmosphere (red gingham tablecloths), efficient service, and filling platters of shredded beef or pork, rice and beans and *plátanos.* Try the rich, flavorful conch chowder and be sure to order a cup of Cuban coffee, thick, strong and heavily sweetened.

OLD TOWN WALKING TOUR *1.5mi. See map.*

The 200-square-block area of **Old Town★★** designated a National Historic District ranks as one of the largest, boasting more than 3,000 significant historic structures. In addition there are a number of museums and attractions—some of which are housed in historic buildings—that draw Key West visitors.

Begin at the intersection of Duval and Front Sts. (northwest end of Duval St.).

Ornate brickwork and balcony of the striking **First Union Bank** building on the far corner *(422 Front St.)* reflect the origins of the Cuban cigar manufacturers who financed its construction in 1891.

Continue west 2 blocks on Front St.; turn right on David Wolkowsky St.

Mallory Square – *Behind Mallory Market on Front St.* Overlooking Key West Harbor, this former warehouse area is named for Stephen Mallory, Florida's fourth US senator and son of one of the island's oldest families. It now harbors souvenir vendors, craft shops and eateries, and its adjacent dock provides a berth for the large cruise ships that call at Key West. Don't miss the sunset-watching ritual held every evening *(weather permitting)* on **Mallory Square Dock** *(behind Mallory Square, follow Fitzpatrick St. through parking lot to dock).* Here, locals and visitors gather to view the spectacular Key West **sunset★★**, described by John James Audubon as "a blaze of refulgent glory (that) streams through the portals of the west." During the winter tourist season *(late Nov-late Mar)*, awaiting sunset becomes a fête of sorts, with mimes, jugglers, fire-eaters, and trained dogs entertaining audiences along the dock.

Shipwreck Historeum – *1 Whitehead St. in Mallory Sq. Open year-round daily 9:45am-4:45pm. $8.* ✱ ♿ *305-292-8990. www.shipwreckhistoreum.com.* The feel of a 19C dockside warehouse is re-created here. Following a video on the early wreckers of Key West, actors recount the thrills and dangers of the wrecking business. Visitors can roam two floors of exhibits of items salvaged from the 1856 wreck of a square-rigged packet. From the second floor, climb the lookout tower for a 360° **view★** of the·island.

Key West Aquarium – ▨ *Wall St. Open year-round daily 10am-6pm. $8.* ♿ ☎ *305-296-2051. www.keywestaquarium.com.* Founded in 1935, this was the Keys' first tourist attraction. Wall tanks here display a variety of denizens from local waters, such as pufferfish, grouper, angelfish and spiny lobsters. A touch tank allows tactile encounters with starfish, conchs, anemones and other sea creatures. At the rear of the building, a large **shark pen** harbors the gliding forms of a variety of sharks. Rays and barracudas occupy an outside pool.

Return to Front St. and continue west past the intersection with Whitehead St.

Recognizable by its distinctive arched bays, the old **Coast Guard Building** *(219 Front St.)* served as the first naval storehouse in 1856. The town's oldest government edifice and the oldest masonry building in the Keys now holds the shops of Clinton Square Market. Adjacent to the building, the imposing brick Romanesque Revival **US Customs House/Post Office** (1891) now houses the Key West Museum of Art and History.

Key West Museum of Art and History (M) – *281 Front St. Open year-round daily 9am-6pm. $8.* ☎ *305-295-7337.* This small museum focuses on Keys heritage and area artists. Although the permanent collection is limited, rotating exhibits, such as a retrospective of paintings by Tennessee Williams or a survey of local Caribbean-style folk art, are often notable.

A **Civil War memorial (1)** honoring Union soldiers occupies the small greensward called Clinton Place *(Greene and Whitehead Sts.).*

Cross Front onto Greene St.

★ **Mel Fisher Maritime Heritage Society** – *200 Greene St., in raised brick plaza diagonally across from Customs House. Open year-round daily 9:30am-5pm. $6.75.* ♿ ▯ *($2/hr).* ☎ *305-294-2633. www.melfisher.org.* Housed in a former Navy building, the museum recounts the story of the discovery of the *Nuestra Señora de Atocha*, a Spanish galleon that sank in the Florida Straits in 1622, by **Mel Fisher**. The don of modern treasure hunters, Fisher, who died in 1998, spent 16 years and lost a son in his unswerving pursuit of the wreck. In 1985 Fisher's crew found their prize on the ocean floor, the total spoils valued at more than $400 million. A video details the 1985 discovery of *Atocha's* mother lode; displays on the first floor feature some of the fabulous gold, silver, gems and other artifacts recovered from the dive site. The second floor is devoted to special exhibits and traveling shows.

Cross Whitehead St.

★ **Audubon House** – *205 Whitehead St., across from Mel Fisher's museum. Open year-round daily 9:30am-5pm. $8.50.* ♿ ☎ *305-294-2116. www.audubon-house.com.* Capt. John Huling Geiger built this gracious Neoclassical house in the 1840s. Its restoration by Key West native Mitchell Wolfson in 1960 sparked the island's preservation movement. Wolfson dedicated the house to America's premiere ornithologist, **John James Audubon**, who visited Key West in 1832 while working on his authoritative volume *Birds of America*. Decorated in 19C period furnishings, the house is notable for its fine collection of 28 original **Audubon engravings** and for its lovely tropical **garden**. Noteworthy also is a rare collection of porcelain birds by British artist Dorothy Doughty.

Dylan Kibler/Mel Fisher Maritime Heritage Society

Artifacts from Mel Fisher's Museum

Peppers of Key West
See map. 602 Greene St., ☎ 305-295-9333. Warm climates traditionally breed hot foods, and many of the fuels that feed the fire are featured at this small, engaging store and tasting shop. The hottest chiles on earth are native to the Caribbean (*habaneros* and Scotch bonnets) and are the key ingredient in the famous West Indies jerk meat marinades. At Peppers, you'll find a comprehensive array of hot sauces, salsas, marinades and spice mixes (many made in Florida). A session at the tasting bar (crackers and water are supplied) will bring tears to even the most experienced —or should we say, seasoned—chile-heads.

Continue one block south on Whitehead St.

A plaque identifies **Kelly's Caribbean Bar & Grill (A)** *(corner of Whitehead and Caroline Sts.)* as Airways or Pigeon House, because it hosted the first corporate offices of Pan American Airways. In October 1927, the airline launched the first commercial flight from Key West to Havana, made by a Fokker Tri-motor F-7. The name "Pigeon House" derives from the fact that Pan Am sent carrier pigeons along in earlier flights to carry messages should an emergency occur en route. The pigeons actually roosted in this building (moved from its original location at the north end of Duval Street), now owned by actress Kelly McGillis.

Cross Whitehead and enter the gates to the Truman Annex, a 44-acre private condominium development on the grounds of the former naval station. Continue for one block and turn left on Front St.

Harry S Truman Little White House Museum – *111 Front St. in Truman Annex. Entrance near Hilton Hotel at the presidential gates on Whitehead St.. Open year-round daily 9am-5pm. $8. ☎ 305-294-9911. www.trumanlittlewhitehouse.com.* This large, unpretentious white clapboard house, the favorite retreat of America's 33rd president, **Harry S Truman (1884-1972), gives a rare glimpse of the personality and private life of the man the press called "an uncommon common man." Built in 1890 as a duplex for the paymaster of Key West's naval station, the unadorned dwelling, with wooden jalousies, was first visited by Truman in 1946 (his physician had persuaded him to take a respite from official duties). Prior to Truman, Thomas Edison had lived here while working on his depth charge for the Navy during World War I.

Truman found the casual atmosphere and warm climate of Key West relaxing. Over his next seven years in office, he spent 175 days of "working vacations" at his "Little White House." He ran the country from the desk that still sits in a corner of the living room. Indeed, Truman came to relish his time in Key West, declaring it his favorite place in the world—aside from his boyhood home, a farm near Independence, Missouri.

Tours of the house begin with a 10min video detailing the time Truman spent here. The house is furnished much the way it was during the Truman era, with most of the pieces chosen by Miami decorator Haygood Lassiter in 1948. Truman's personal **desk** can be seen in his bedroom upstairs.

Return to Kelly's at the corner of Whitehead and Caroline Sts., and continue east on Caroline.

*Heritage House Museum and Robert Frost Cottage (B) – *410 Caroline St. Visit by guided tour (30min) only. year-round daily 10am-4pm. $6. ☎ 305-296-3573. www.heritagehousemuseum.org.* Much of Key West's 19C and 20C history is embedded in this pastel-green Classical Revival Conch mansion. Built by Capt. George Carey, the house (c.1834) was purchased and restored by Jessie Porter Newton in 1934. A fifth-generation Key Wester and granddaughter of Dr. Joseph Porter, Miss Jessie, as she was known, figured prominently in local literary and preservationist circles. Her home's eclectic furnishings reflect her travels to Europe and the mid-20C island lifestyle of the literati. Many items from her collection of antiques and museum-quality artifacts were gifts from ships' captains who brought them back from the South Pacific, Malaysia and the Orient.

In the rear garden sits tiny **Robert Frost Cottage** *(not open to the public)* where the poet spent 15 winters between 1945 and 1960. In the garden, visitors listen to a recorded reading of Frost's poem *The Gift Outright*, which was read at President John F. Kennedy's inauguration.

Continue to the corner of Caroline and Duval Sts.

The stately 1838 **Joseph Porter House (C)** *(429 Caroline St.)*, now an art gallery, belonged to the prominent Porter family for eight generations. Extensively remodeled after Dr. Joseph Porter and his wife took possession of it in 1896, the house today represents a mélange of Second Empire, Victorian and Italianate elements. Dr. Porter—born here in 1847—was later named the state's first public health officer and recognized as one of the country's foremost authorities on sanitation and yellow fever.

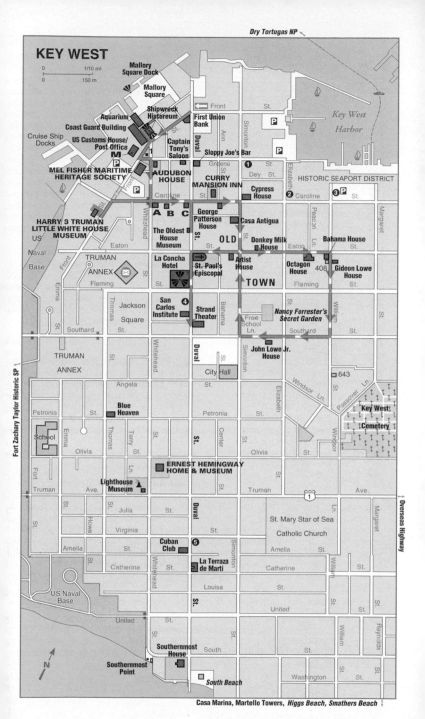

Turn right on Duval St. and walk half a block.

The Oldest House Museum – *322 Duval St. Open year-round daily 10am-4pm. $5. ☎ 305-294-9502.* Considered the oldest house in Key West, this small, two-story clapboard residence—formerly known as The Wrecker's Museum—was built c.1829 on Whitehead Street, then moved here in 1832. Its 19C furnishings, which include fine Meissen tea and chocolate pots, reflect the comfortable lifestyle of wrecker Capt. Francis Watlington, who lived here until the late 1800s. Spacious grounds in the rear hold a cookhouse and pavilion with more exhibits relating to the wrecking industry.

Return to Caroline St., turn right and walk east for half a block.

Key West Key Lime Pie Company
See map. 701 Caroline St.
☎ *305-294-6567.* The quintessential dish of the Florida Keys was reputedly made first at Curry Mansion in Key West and has been the subject of much legend, amendment and competition ever since. Most, if not all, restaurants in Key West offer it for dessert; numberless delis and small grocery stores package their own versions; and an annual competition sponsored by a local radio station declares the city's best. Most versions are based on a graham-cracker crust, which holds a key lime custard topped with meringue or chiffon; many are over-sweetened for sophisticated palates, obliterating the bitter/tart tang that is unique to the limes. This Old Town store devotes itself solely to the dessert. Here you can get not only pie, lime juice and key lime expertise, but an exquisite chocolate-covered version that's indulgent to a degree, perfectly befitting the Key West ethos.

★**Curry Mansion Inn** – *511 Caroline St. Open year-round daily 10am-5pm. $5.* ♿ ☎ *305-294-5349. www.curry mansion.com.* William Curry, a self-made millionaire and mayor of Key West, built the rear of this rambling, white Victorian mansion before his death in 1896. His son Milton greatly expanded the house at the turn of the century, adding elaborate reception rooms and bedrooms to the front. Now an inn, the mansion retains its belle-epoque grandeur. Visitors can take a self-guided tour of the house, which offers the only publicly accessible **widow's walk** *(third floor)* in Key West. After your tour, relax on the wide, shady veranda.

Built around 1889, the elegant white frame **George Patterson House** *(across from Curry Mansion at 522 Caroline St.; not open to the public)* features gables, porches and galleries adorned by delicate spindlework—all characteristic elements of the Queen Anne style.

Continue to the corner of Caroline and Simonton Sts.

Distinctive for its unpainted, weathered cypress exterior, the 1887 **Cypress House** *(601 Caroline St.)* was originally owned by the Kemp family, Bahamians who are credited with introducing the sponge industry to Key West. The low facade and simple lines of this private inn typify Bahamian architecture.

Turn right on Simonton St. and continue half a block.

Casa Antigua – *314 Simonton St. Courtyard garden open Nov-May daily 10am-6pm. Rest of the year daily 11am-7pm. Closed Thanksgiving Day & Dec 25. $2.* ♿ ☎ *305-296-3887.* The first incarnation of this square, beige Mediterranean Revival structure with brown balconies was the Trev-Mor Hotel, one of the island's earliest hotels (1919). The first floor held the Trevor and Morris Ford dealership (note the garages at street level). Ernest Hemingway spent several weeks in an apartment here on his first trip to Key West in 1928; while there he worked on his novel *A Farewell to Arms.* Extensively rebuilt after a fire in 1975, the building now houses a Caribbean crafts shop and boasts a tropical garden out back.

Walk half a block up Simonton to Eaton St., then left on Eaton for half a block.

Donkey Milk House – *613 Eaton St. Not open to the public.* This 1866 Neoclassical structure acquired its unusual name from the donkey-drawn milk carts that pulled into the alleyway behind it in the mid-19C. In 1886 it was home to Peter A. ("Dynamite") Williams, the US marshal famous for halting a fire that same year by using dynamite to divert the flames.

Continue east on Eaton St. and cross Elizabeth St.

One of Old Town's best-known homes, the unique **Octagon House** *(712 Eaton St.)* was built in 1885 by Richard Peacon, who opened Key West's first supermarket. Renovated by acclaimed interior designer Angelo Donghia in the 1970s, the house was also briefly owned by clothing designer Calvin Klein.

Continue on Eaton St. to the corner of William St.

Bahama House – *730 Eaton St. Not open to the public.* Originally constructed on the island of Abaco, this symmetrical white pine structure was disassembled and brought to Key West by schooner in 1847 as the home of Bahamian shipbuilder John Bartlum. Its wide airy verandas on both stories, louvered windows and doors and low-ceilinged interior rooms typify Bahamian architecture. Exterior siding incorporates boards of different widths. Note these same features on the house next door *(408 William St.),* which was transported from Green Turtle Cay.

Turn right on William St.

Note the temple form of the c.1866 **Gideon Lowe House** *(409 William St.),* a fine example of the Classical Revival style.

Walk two blocks south on William to Southard St. and turn right. Continue west 1.5 blocks.

Built of heart pine and Honduran mahogany, the 1855 **John Lowe Jr. House** *(620 Southard St.)* was constructed with wooden pegs, mortise-and-tenon joints and square timbers. The second story was added later, creating a Classical Revival house tempered by Bahamian influences. Its widow's walk—one of the few remaining on the island—was once used to sight downed ships offshore by the house's first owner, wrecker John Lowe Jr.

Continue to intersection of Simonton St. and turn right; walk one-half block north and turn right on Free School Ln. to a small gate at its end.

Nancy Forrester's Secret Garden – *1 Free School Ln. Open year-round daily 10am-5pm. $6.* ☎ *305-294-0015.* Owner-artist Nancy Forrester has devoted more than a quarter-century to creating her personal one-acre tropical oasis amid the hubbub of downtown Key West, opening it to the public in 1994. Today the lush botanical garden enamors nature lovers who wander its winding paths among ferns, heliconias and orchids, beneath a canopy of century-old hardwood trees—Spanish limes, sapodillas, gumbo-limbos—and a collection of rare palms. Visitors can pause to meet the many caged tropical birds the artist has adopted, including several talking birds.

③ Reef Relief
See map. 201 William St. ☎ *305-294-3100.* This small store and information center is a treasure house of knowledge about the endangered tropical environment that surrounds the Keys and Key West. Numerous natural history books, pamphlets and broadsides explain the issues and challenges besetting the region—such as the effort to install sewage treatment systems in many of the Keys—and the unique landscapes and creatures that advocates are trying to preserve. The fact that visitors and residents alike must be reminded not to damage the reefs, bays and waters of south Florida is an unfortunate commentary on the prevailing state of affairs. However, Reef Relief pursues a friendly, low-key approach to the challenge.

Return to Simonton St. and turn right. Continue 1.5 blocks north and turn left on Eaton St.

Key West surgeon Thomas Osgood Otto built the lavender Queen Anne **Artist House** *(534 Eaton St.)*, which is distinguished by its octagonal turret. Now a guest house, the two-story 1887 structure features wraparound verandas ornamented with slender balusters and delicate corner brackets.

Continue west to corner of Eaton and Duval St.

St. Paul's Episcopal Church – *401 Duval St. Open year-round Mon-Sat 9am-5pm, Sun 7am-5pm.* ♿ ▯ ☎ *305-296-5142. www.stpaulskw.org.* Oldest church in the Florida diocese, St. Paul's was established in 1832. The current white Spanish Colonial building (1919), with its imposing belltower, is the fourth church on the site. Vaulted wooden ceilings inside are designed to resemble inverted ships' hulls.

Turn left and walk south on Duval St.

Since its opening in 1926, Duval Street's highest landmark building has been **La Concha Hotel** *(no. 430)*. The six-story, pink concrete hotel (now a Crowne Plaza property) has housed such luminaries as Tennessee Williams, who wrote *Summer and Smoke* here in the mid-1940s. Late in the afternoon, stop by the hotel's rooftop bar, **Top of La Concha**, for a drink and a panoramic **view**★ of the island and its surrounding waters.

Duval Street

© Eric P. Lucas

> **4 Margaritaville Cafe**
> *See map. 500 Duval St.* ☎ 305-292-1435. This popular cafe and its adjacent souvenir shop is owned by singer Jimmy Buffett, who got his start playing in Key West bars. Treat yourself to a "cheeseburger in paradise" or go next door, where you can purchase a variety of souvenir items inspired by Buffett's song lyrics, including his famous "lost shaker of salt."

Cross Fleming St. to the 500 block of Duval St.

San Carlos Institute – *516 Duval St. Open year-round Tue-Sun 11am-5pm. Closed Jan 1, Easter Sunday, Dec 25. $3 contribution requested.* ♿ ☎ *305-294-3887.* This imposing Spanish Colonial structure was built in 1924, but its roots date back to 1871. Founded as a social club and school by Cuban exiles during the Ten Years' War, the nonprofit institute was named for Seminario San Carlos, a famed learning center in Cuba where Father Felix Varela planted the seeds of Cuba's independence movement (a bronze likeness of the priest stands in the lobby of the Key West site).

The present building, the third on this site, serves as school, museum, library, art gallery and theater. Two floors of exhibits relate to Cuba's fight for independence from Spain. Displays on the ground floor focus on **José Martí**, organizer of the second effort for Cuban independence, who often spoke here. Interior walls are lined with blue majolica tiles that were imported from Spain; floors incorporate checkered Cuban mosaics.

Across the street from the San Carlos Institute, note the pastel ornamented facade of the former **Strand Theater** *(527 Duval St.)*, a 1930 movie palace restored in 1993. It now houses Ripley's Believe It or Not Odditorium.

> **5 Flamingo Crossing**
> *See map. 1107 Duval St.* ☎ *305-296-6124.* Take a refreshing break from sightseeing at this popular purveyor of warm-weather treats. All the ice cream and sorbet here is made by hand in the back. Naturally, the focus is on tropical flavors such as mango, key lime (tantalizingly and properly bitter) and coconut. Also on the menu is an array of frozen yogurt, fruit smoothies and tropical blended drinks. You can sit inside in the air-conditioned interior, but the elevated patio offers an excellent vantage on the Duval Street scene.

A half-dozen blocks up Duval Street are two additional sites that relate to Cuban history. The **Cuban Club** *(1108 Duval)* is a two-story, white frame replica (1989) of the Key West headquarters of Sociedad Cuba, established in 1900 to offer education, medical care and social activities to the Cuban émigré community. Fire destroyed the original building in 1983; the present incarnation, which incorporates the original columns, turrets and facade pediment, houses shops and condominium units.

Nearby, **La Terraza de Martí** (locally known as "La-te-da") restaurant *(1125 Duval St.)* occupies the former home (1892) of cigar manufacturer Teodoro Pérez. From its second-floor balcony, the leader of the Cuban Revolutionary Party, José Martí, frequently exhorted his countrymen to action.

ADDITIONAL SIGHTS

Fort Zachary Taylor Historic State Park – *Enter through gatehouse to Truman Annex at the west end of Southard St. Open year-round daily 8am-dusk. $4/vehicle plus 50¢/person.* 🅿 ☎ *305-292-6713. www.fttaylor.com.* Remains of the three-story, trapezoidal 19C brick fort started in 1845 (but never completed) form the centerpiece of this 87-acre park overlooking the Atlantic Ocean. During the Civil War, some 800 Union soldiers were quartered here, but they saw no significant action. Today you can walk along vestiges of the fort's 5ft-thick battlements and visit the small **museum** that showcases artillery once employed here.

Nearby, a pleasant wooded grove edges a narrow, somewhat rocky Atlantic **beach** affording opportunities for swimming, fishing and snorkeling.

★★ **Ernest Hemingway Home and Museum** – *907 Whitehead St. Open year-round daily 9am-5pm. $9.* ☎ *305-294-1136. www.hemingwayhome.com.* Half-hidden amid lush vegetation, the gracious stucco house enjoys renown as the place where Key West's legendary resident, novelist Ernest Hemingway, spent his most productive years.

Built by wealthy merchant Asa Tift in 1851, this one-of-a-kind house is made of coral rock mined on the property and covered with stucco. Tift brought the French Colonial-style cast-iron pillars, verandas and balusters from New Orleans. Full-length double-paned arched windows open like doors to catch island breezes. Sparsely decorated rooms contain period pieces, some of which belonged to the family. In Hemingway's bedroom, notice the **ceramic cat** made for "Papa" by Pablo Picasso

A wooden catwalk once connected the master bedroom to Hemingway's **studio**, a pleasant room above the carriage house where he wrote such classics as *Death in the Afternoon*, *For Whom the Bell Tolls* and *To Have and Have Not*. (The character of Freddy in the latter novel is modeled after Joe Russell, the late owner of Sloppy Joe's Bar.) The attractive grounds contain a large **swimming pool**—the first one built on the island. Commissioned by Pauline in the 1930s while Hemingway was off covering the Spanish Civil War, the $20,000 pool infuriated "Papa" when he returned. He reportedly railed at Pauline, declaring that she had spent his last cent, and threw a penny on the ground to emphasize his point. His wife had the coin embedded in the cement by the pool where it remains to this day.

Hemingway with Trophy (c.1935)

Hemingway Collection/J.F. Kennedy Library, Boston

Key West Lighthouse Museum – *938 Whitehead St., across from Hemingway House. Open year-round daily 9:30am-5pm. Closed Dec 25. $6.* 🅿 ☎ *305-294-0012.* Built in 1846 and decommissioned in 1969, this white-brick lighthouse now offers a sweeping **view** of the island from atop its 90ft tower. A **lightkeeper's quarters** on the grounds, panelled in gleaming Dade County pine, displays lighthouse lenses, military artifacts and period rooms re-creating the lifestyle of early 20C light keepers.

Key West Cemetery – *Margaret St. and Passover Ln.* ♿ *Guided tours ☎ 305-292-6829.* Monuments to Key West's past can be found among the 35,000-plus headstones, which date to 1847 when the earlier cemetery near the south coast

---

■ The Making of "Papa"

Ernest Hemingway (1899-1961) first visited Key West in 1928 with his second wife, Pauline. He had already achieved literary fame with the 1926 publication of *The Sun Also Rises*, and was returning to the US after years of living in Europe. After a brief stay in Cuba, the couple arrived in Key West, where a new Ford was to have been waiting for them to drive north. However, shipment of the car was delayed, giving the Hemingways time to become acquainted with the island Ernest dubbed "the St. Tropez of the poor."

For three subsequent winters they returned here, then in 1931 purchased a large but run-down house, which Pauline described at the time as a "miserable wreck." They renovated the structure and Hemingway lived there until his marriage ended in 1939; Pauline remained in the house and continued to be a prominent member of Key West society until her death in 1951.

It was during his Key West years that Hemingway cultivated his machismo "Papa" image, spending his days writing, fishing and drinking with a coterie of locals he called the "Key West Mob." His legend continues to infuse many corners of the island and is the impetus behind the annual **Hemingway Days** festival. Held in conjunction with the writer's birthday (July 21), the week-long event features look-alike contests, arm wrestling and several other "Papa"-like activities.

Other Hemingway landmarks include **Sloppy Joe's Bar** *(201 Duval St.)*, a cavernous local pub that was "Papa's" favorite hangout. **Captain Tony's Saloon** *(428 Greene St.)* housed the original Sloppy Joe's bar from 1933 to 1937. Hemingway attended cockfights and boxing matches in the two-story, blue clapboard Conch cottage called **Blue Heaven** *(729 Thomas St.)*. A former brothel, it now contains a cafe *(see Address Book)* and artists' studios.

was washed out by a hurricane. A bronze sailor surveys marble markers co memorating seamen lost in the 1898 sinking of the *USS Maine*. Another p contains an arch inscribed *A Los Martires de Cuba* ("to the Cuban Martyrs"), the who died in the 1868-78 insurrection against Spain.

East Martello Museum – *3501 S. Roosevelt Blvd. Open year-round daily 9:30a 5pm. Closed Dec 25. $6.* ♿ ☎ *305-296-3913*. The names of this brick tower a its counterpart, West Martello Tower, derive from a type of impregnable cylindric tower first built in Corsica in the Middle Ages. Begun in 1862 as back-up fort cations to nearby Union stronghold Fort Zachary Taylor, the East Martello Tow was never completed. Yellow fever, labor strikes and wartime exigencies delay the work, and in 1873 building ceased on the unfinished battlements.

Today, remains of the East tower house the **Key West Art & Historical Society** Historical exhibits range from ancient Indians through the sinking of the *USS Ma* to local 20C literary figures (including seven Pulitzer Prize winners, Ern Hemingway and Tennessee Williams among them). The art gallery hosts spec exhibits, notably, the "junkyard sculpture" of late Key West folk artist **Stanley Pap** folk art by local Cuban painter **Mario Sanchez**; and the famous **portrait of Hemingw** by WPA artist Erik Smith.

Broad, man-made **Smathers Beach**—the largest on the island—stretches for 2 along South Roosevelt Boulevard.

■ A Key to Limes

When you think of a lime, you probably picture a dark green, seedless Persian lime, a hybrid of the fruit that originated in Southeast Asia. Indigenous to Malaysia, limes were introduced to the western Mediterranean region by returning crusaders in the 12C and 13C. Christopher Columbus brought limes on his second voyage (1493) to the New World, where the tree rapidly took root throughout the Caribbean and spread to Florida and Central America. Before Hurricane Andrew hit in 1992, 90 percent of the limes grown in the US were from Florida.

Florida's signature dessert, key lime pie, depends on the biting acerbic juice of the key lime *(Citrus aurantifolia)*. First planted in the Florida Keys by botanist Henry Perrine in the 1830s, this small, yellowish, seed-filled citrus fruit can be found growing on thorny trees in backyards throughout the Keys.

West Martello Tower – *White St. and Atlantic Blvd., on Higgs Memorial Bea Open year-round Tue-Sat 9:30am-3pm. Closed major holidays.* ♿ ♿ ☎ *305-2 3210*. Companion to East Martello Tower, this Civil War citadel served as a look tower during the Spanish-American War. Its brick ruins are now edged in trop plantings maintained by the Key West Garden Club.

Adjacent to the tower, **Higgs Beach** (also called Monroe County Beach) is anot popular local spot on the Atlantic for swimming and sunbathing.

Southernmost House – *1400 Duval St. Not open to the public*. This rambli cream-colored brick Queen Anne manse with pale green trim (built in 1899 Judge J. Vining Harris) claims to be the southernmost house in the continental Anchoring the south end of Duval Street, the elegant structure exemplifies Queen Anne style in Key West: Its variation of color, shape, texture and emb lishment have been modified to suit both local tastes and climate.

Small **South Beach** lies across from the house. Around the corner *(west end of So St.)*, a large red, black and yellow buoy marks what it claims is the **Southernm Point** in the lower 48 states. (In fact, the true southernmost point extends from restricted naval base just to the west.) In front of the buoy, sidewalk vendors ha a variety of "southernmost" seashells and trinkets.

EXCURSION *Map p 66*

★**Dry Tortugas National Park** – *69mi southwest of Key West. Accessible only plane or boat. Open year-round dawn-dusk.* ⚠ ☎ *305-242-7700. No concessi available on the island*. Encompassing 100sq mi in the Gulf of Mexico, the p protects the small cluster of reef islands called the Dry Tortugas, west of the Flo Keys. One of these, 10-acre Garden Key, is the site of **Fort Jefferson**, the larg coastal stronghold built by the US in the 19C. Sitting in the middle of a windsw nowhere, this vast brick fort echoes with its own past. Park waters offer g opportunities for wreck-diving, snorkeling and fishing *(information available fr visitor center at fort)*.

Spanish explorer Ponce de León named these islands *Las Tortugas* ("The Turtle when he explored them in 1513. (The anglicized addition of the word "Dry" re to the islands' lack of fresh water.) They remained Spanish possessions until Flo

Access: By Plane departs from Key West International Airport year-round daily. One-way 40min: half day $179/person, full day $305/person, camping trip $329/person. Advance reservations required. ▢ For details, contact Seaplanes of Key West: ☎ 305-294-0709 or 800-950-2359; www.seaplanesofkeywest.com.

By Boat: departs from Historic Seaport at end of Margaret St. year-round daily 8am (check in time:7:30am), returns to Key West by 5:30pm. One-way 2hrs 15min. Commentary. $109 incl. breakfast and lunch. Reservations recommended. ♿ ▢ ($8) Yankee Fleet: ☎ 305-294-7009 or 800-634-0939; www.yankeefleet.com.

came under US control in 1821. Recognizing the importance the Tortugas could play in keeping shipping channels open between the Atlantic and the Gulf of Mexico, American military strategists recommended locating a fort here; construction of Fort Jefferson began in 1846.

Inside the visitor orientation area, a film details the fort's history. Parade grounds inside the walls hold remnants of a cavernous magazine, soldiers' barracks and officers' quarters. A self-guided walk leads through the arched casemates and up onto the battlement wall, where a lighthouse, no longer functioning, still stands. From this vantage point, there's a lovely **view**★★ of the fort and nearby Bush and Loggerhead keys. (The former supports a boisterous colony of terns.) The top of the surrounding moat also serves as a walking path, and a palm-fringed white-sand snorkeling **beach** lies on the island's west side.

■ From Prison to Park

Sixteen million bricks were used to form the perimeter walls, which measure 50ft high and 8ft thick. The weight of the structure eventually caused the walls of the ill-fated fort to sink into its unstable base of sand. By the time the Civil War broke out, the brick hexagon was only two-thirds completed.

Though soldiers never fired at an enemy from Fort Jefferson, it did serve as a prison for Union deserters during the Civil War. In 1865 **Dr. Samuel Mudd** was interned here as a co-conspirator in President Lincoln's assassination. (Mudd unwittingly set the broken leg of Lincoln's fleeing assassin, John Wilkes Booth, without realizing Booth's identity.) During a yellow fever epidemic in 1867, Mudd unstintingly treated the prison's victims of the disease. His efforts won him a pardon from President Andrew Johnson and he was released in early 1869. Yellow fever struck the citadel again in the early 1870s, and four years later it was finally abandoned. Proclaimed a national monument in 1935, the fort was changed to national park status in 1992 in order to protect the nearby coral reef and the shipwrecks that are now popular dive sites.

R. Gould

Fort Jefferson

Nature Coast

Great Blue Heron – © Lynn M. Stone

The section of Gulf Coast stretching from the Suwannee River, near Florida Panhandle, down to Hernando County, above Tampa, is often called the "re Florida" because so much of the area has remained undeveloped. While ancie burial grounds indicate the region was inhabited as early as 500 BC by Indians of t Deptford culture, this coast remained a wilderness well into the 18C, when Spani soldiers made an occasional appearance.

In 1835 a quiet woodland setting near Bushnell saw a skirmish that helped preci tate the Second Seminole War. On December 28, **Maj. Francis Dade** and a command some 100 soldiers were en route from Fort Brooke (Tampa) to provide relief units Fort King (Ocala) when they were ambushed by Seminole Indians. Dade and most his men were killed. Today the **Dade Battlefield Historic State Park** *(off Rte. 301, 1mi sou of Bushnell)* commemorates this battle with an annual reenactment the last weeke in December *(for information: ☎ 352-793-4781)*.

After the US government began forcing Seminoles out of Florida to Oklahoma res vations in the 1830s, white settlers established inland plantations, growing sugar ca and Sea Island cotton. During the Civil War, several salt furnaces operated along t Gulf Coast supplying salt to the Confederate army. These plants were considered important to the war effort that workers were exempted from military duty. Follow the war, homesteaders began to arrive. Eventually commercial fishing and lumb industries thrived as fish caught in local waters were transported to wholesale dealers in Cedar Key by sailing sloop, and cedar trees were harvested and shipped to Crystal River and Cedar Key to be carved into pencils. A few of the Gulf settlements began attracting northern visitors to large hotels and sportsmen's lodges. Visitors arrived in Ocala by train, then made the final journey to the coast by horse and buggy.

The area's quiet, natural beauty—which captivated landscape artists Winslow Homer and George Inness in the late 19C—still entices visitors today. While the main north-south artery, US-19/98, can be as congested as any Florida highway, a turn west will invariably lead to an unspoiled coastal hamlet such as Suwannee, Yankeetown or Pine Island. An abundance of wildlife, including alligators, manatees, armadillos and bald eagles, makes its home in and around the region's wetlands, hammocks and crystal-clear, spring-fed rivers. Area restaurants are widely known for local seafood delicacies, including redfish, Gulf shrimp, oysters and stone crab.

CEDAR KEY

Population 790

Map p 91

Tourist Information: www.cedarkey.org ☎ 352-543-5600

Occupying Way Key, the largest (about 1.5mi long) in a cluster of low-lying islands 3mi off the mainland (and the only one linked by bridge), this historic Gulf Coast town supports a mix of commercial fishermen, artists and weekenders, many of them from Tallahassee and Gainesville. The pace is slow in the down-home hamlet of tin-roofed porches and weathered piers with views of bayou and bay. Most activity centers on the three-block stretch of Second (Main) Street and the "Big Dock" *(off A and C Sts.)*, lined with gift shops and seafood restaurants.

Cedar Keys National Wildlife Refuge, a group of 12 beach-rimmed islets—nesting areas for pelicans, ospreys, white ibis and hundreds of other species of birds—lies 5mi offshore *(boat trips depart from city marina year-round daily 11am-dusk; round-trip 1hr 30min; commentary; $12;* ♿ 🅿 *Island Hopper ☎ 352-543-5904).*

The 1860 completion of the first trans-Florida railroad, linking Cedar Key on the Gulf with Fernandina Beach on the east coast, put the town on the map. Real boom times came in the 1870s and 80s when a commercial seafood industry thrived and regular steamer service operated to New Orleans, Tampa, Key West and Havana, Cuba; many of the hip-roofed tabby buildings on Second Street are former hotels and saloons dating from this era. Lumbering was also a mainstay until an 1896 hurricane destroyed two sawmills where cedar (lightweight and easy to cut without splitting) was processed for northern pencil manufacturers. Today there are fewer than 1,000 year-round residents and more than half the houses are owned by out-of-towners. Tourism is on the rise, however, and the seafood industry is regenerating, thanks to new small-scale aquatic breeding farms for clams and oysters, whose once-flourishing beds were exhausted in the 1930s.

Cedar Key Dock at Sunrise

SIGHTS

Cedar Key Historical Society Museum – *609 2nd St., at Rte. 24. Open daily Nov-Apr Mon-Sat 11am-5pm, Sun 2pm-5pm. Rest of the year Mon-Thu & Sun 2pm-5pm, Fri & Sat 11am-5pm. $1. & ☎ 352-543-5549.* A picturesque two-story tabby structure, built in 1871 as one of the first private residences on the island, houses the small but comprehensive museum. Highlighted by an extensive collection of **19C photographs**, displays focus on Cedar Key's history as a major US sponge exchange and center for commercial oystering, fishing and turtling. There are also artifacts from the Eagle Pencil Co. and Eberhart Faber sawmills once located here, along with beautifully crafted brushes and brooms from a local palm-fiber factory that operated in the area from 1910 to 1952.

Cedar Key Museum State Park – *12231 S.W. 166 Court (1.5mi from town center). Open year-round Thu-Mon 9am-5pm. Closed Dec 25. $1. & ☎ 352-543-5350.* Opened in 1962, this one-story brick museum contains a remarkable collection of **Florida shells** and glassware assembled by the late St. Clair Whitman, a local resident and self-taught naturalist. Additional exhibits trace Cedar Key history through Indian and other artifacts. Outside stands Whitman's late-19C red-shingled Victorian home, which was moved from its original site on Goose Cove and awaits restoration.

© Lynn M. Stone

Manatee Springs State Park

EXCURSION

Manatee Springs State Park – *34mi north near Chiefland. Take Rte. 24 east for 9mi; turn left on Rte. 345. At Chiefland, take US-19/98 north to Rte. 320 west and follow to park entrance. Park hrs & fees p 350. Canoe rentals. △ ✗ & ☑ ☎ 352-493-6072.* Feeding into a sparkling run, Manatee Springs forms the center piece of this 2,000-acre nature preserve. An area for swimming is roped off at the crystal-clear head waters. Nearby, a board walk *(.25mi)* zigzags alongside the run, passing through a swamp lush with cypress, gum, ash and maple trees. Along with bald eagles and various wading birds, alligators can be spotted and perhaps an occasional wintering manatee along the walk, which ends at an **observation deck** on the Suwannee River.

CRYSTAL RIVER

Population 3,485
Map opposite
Tourist Information: www.citruscountychamber.com ☏ 352-795-3149

The 7mi waterway that gives Crystal River its name was known until the mid-19C as "Weewahiiaca," from two Creek words meaning "clear water." Of the 30 natural springs feeding the river, 28 form headwaters at **Kings Bay**, considered one of the county's most important **manatee sanctuaries★**, harboring some 200 of the gentle sea cows each winter. A premier area for boating, fishing, scuba diving, snorkeling and underwater photography, Kings Bay also forms the focal point of **Crystal River National Wildlife Refuge** which encompasses nine small, undeveloped bay islands *(accessible by boat only; for information check with local dive operators or refuge office ☏ 352-563-2088)*.

As the only area in Florida where people may swim and interact directly with manatees, Kings Bay is exceedingly popular with nature lovers. Numerous local dive shops offer boat, snorkeling and scuba rentals, along with guided boat tours of the river and bay. *Best time to see manatees is January through March. Recreational water-use regulations—including strict boat speed limits—are enforced to protect the manatees.*

SIGHT

Crystal River Archaeological State Park – *3400 N. Museum Point Rd., 2mi north of town center. Park hrs & fees p 350.* ♿ 🅿 *☏ 352-795-3817.* It is believed that this 14-acre prehistoric ceremonial site was established by Indians of the Deptford culture (500 BC to AD 300), who lived in small villages on nearby islands and came to the mainland to bury their dead. Members of the Weedon Island culture used the site from about AD 300 to 1300. Why they left is a mystery.

At the entrance a **visitor center** *(open year-round daily 9am-5pm)* offers a display of ancient arrowheads and tools and an interpretive video. Outside, a path *(.5mi)* leads past two midden mounds of discarded oyster shells, three burial mounds and two temple mounds. Along the trail, you will pass two mysterious **ceremonial stones**, or stelae, more commonly associated with Central American groups and rare to North America. The stones were placed here around AD 440, possibly as markers for the summer and winter solstice.

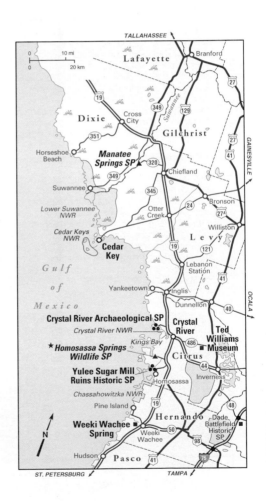

EXCURSIONS

★ **Homosassa Springs Wildlife State Park** – *7mi south in Homosassa. Take US-19/98 south to Rte. 490; turn right on Rte. 490 and follow signs to park at 9225 W. Fishbowl Dr. Open year-round daily 9am-5:30pm. $7.95.* 🍴 ♿ 🅿 ☏ *352-628-2311 or 352-628-5343. www.homosassasprings.org. Visitors can park on Rte. 19 and take an interpretive boat ride (included in admission fee; 20min; commentary)* *along Pepper Creek. Parking is also available on Fishbowl Dr. across from the park's west entrance.* This 45ft-deep natural spring forming the headwaters of the Homosassa River provides a **sanctuary for rehabilitating manatees** scheduled for release back to the wild after recovering from boating accidents. Those too seriously injured to survive in the wild are allowed to stay here. An underwater observatory permits a close-hand look at the manatees, paddling lazily through schools of speckled trout, redfish, jack crevalle and snook. The 185-acre park is also a refuge for injured and orphaned bobcats, Florida black bear, the endangered American crocodile, alligators,

■ Florida's Gentle Giant

With its clumsy, gray-brown, sausage-shaped body, gentle nature and doleful expression, the West Indian manatee *(Trichechus manatus)* is one of the most beloved members of Florida's extensive and varied family of wildlife. This curious beast is a marine mammal, but is unrelated to the whale, seal or dolphin. Its closest relative is, in fact, the elephant, although the manatee's two front flippers contain the same bones (arranged differently) as the human hand. Manatees use their undulating tails to propel themselves forward; flippers function as rudders. Females normally begin breeding when they're about seven years of age. After a 13-month gestation period, a cow typically gives birth to one calf; a newborn manatee weighs about 66 pounds.

The herbivorous manatee has earned the sobriquet "sea cow," given its habit of browsing on aquatic vegetation—consuming as much as 100 pounds per day. On such a diet, an adult manatee can measure up to 13ft long and weigh more than 3,000 pounds. Manatees frequent rivers, estuaries, bays and canals. While these animals once flourished, it is estimated that only about 2,000 of them survive in the US. All now reside in the southeast, traveling to the Carolinas and Louisiana in summer, and spending winter in Florida's warm spring-fed rivers, which maintain a constant temperature of 72°F-74°F. (Manatees cannot survive for extended periods in water colder than 68°F.)

Manatees have no natural enemies, but development of the state's coastal areas has diminished feeding grounds, forcing the slow-moving mammals into boating areas where they often become tangled in fishing lines and injured or killed in collisions. Indeed, boat strikes currently rank as the leading human-related cause of manatee mortality in Florida. In 1973 manatees were listed as an endangered species; to further protect them, the entire State of Florida was established as a manatee sanctuary in 1978. Among the best spots for **viewing** manatees in their natural habitat are Homosassa Springs State Wildlife Park and Kings Bay *(see map)*. Manatee season officially runs from November 15 to March 15, but the best viewing time is generally January through March. To adopt a manatee, contact **Save the Manatee Club** *(☎ 800-432-5646)*; funds go toward education, research and lobbying efforts.

Manatees at Crystal River

© Mark J. Thomas/DPA, Inc.

river otters and birds of prey. Be sure to attend one of the manatee programs *(daily 10:45am, 1pm, 3:15pm)* and educational wildlife encounters *(daily 11:30am, 1:45pm)*.

Yulee Sugar Mill Ruins Historic State Park – *10mi southwest on Rte. 490 in Homosassa. Park hrs & fees p 350.* ▯ ☏ *352-795-3817.* Partially restored limestone ruins survive as the last remnant of a 5,100-acre sugar plantation called Margarita and owned by **David Levy Yulee**. Founder of the first trans-Florida railroad, Yulee was later elected the first US senator from Florida. The mill began operation in 1851 and supplied sugar and its by-product, molasses, to Confederate troops during the Civil War. In 1864 Union troops burned the plantation, but the mill was spared; the cast-iron boiler, steam engine and processing kettles remain intact.

Ted Williams Museum and Hitters Hall of Fame – *11mi east near Hernando. Take Rte. 486 east toward Hernando; museum is located 3.5mi west of Hernando at the entrance to Villages of Citrus Hills, 2455 N. Citrus Hills Blvd. Open year-round Tue-Sun 10am-4pm. Closed major holidays. $5.* ♿ ▯ ☏ *352-527-6566.* The extensive collection of memorabilia housed here pays tribute to baseball great **Ted Williams** (b. 1918), who played for the Boston Red Sox between 1939 and 1960 before retiring and moving to Florida to pursue his other love: fishing. During his illustrious career, the left-fielder batted .344 (the sixth-highest average in history) while stroking 521 home runs. The diamond-shaped museum, dedicated in 1994, includes a theater with bleacher seats that shows a 45min film of Williams discussing his choice of the top 20 hitters of all time. These players, including Babe Ruth, Lou Gehrig, Joe DiMaggio, Ty Cobb, Willie Mays and Mickey Mantle, are honored in the Hitters Hall of Fame.

Weeki Wachee Spring – *21mi south at the intersection of Rte. 50 and US-19 in Weeki Wachee. Open year-round daily 10am-5:30pm. $15.95.* ✕ ♿ ▯ ☏ *352-596-2062. www.weekiwachee.com.* Designed around a freshwater spring, the multi-theme park is best known for an underwater theater where local "mermaids" have performed in the crystal-clear water since 1946. In addition to an exotic bird show, a wilderness river cruise *(30min)* and a petting zoo, the park operates one of the largest raptor rehabilitation centers in Florida. Successful graduates include eagles, hawks, falcons and vultures that swoop and dive daily in the Birds of Prey show.

Visitors can swim in Weeki Wachee Spring at **Buccaneer Bay**, the only natural-spring water park in the state *(open Mar-Aug daily; weekends only Sept)*. Three water slides, bumper boats, a beach, lagoon, rope swings and a volleyball court provide hours of entertainment.

North Central Florida

Thoroughbred Farm, Ocala – © Mark J. Barrett

A magnet for biking, fishing and canoeing enthusiasts, this largely rural area—running across the peninsula from Alachua, Marion and Lake counties in the west to Volusia and Seminole counties in the east—is one of remarkable natural beauty. A gently rolling terrain of open pasture and shady back roads distinguishes the region, which is perhaps best known for its darkly mysterious rivers, freshwater springs, complex strings of lakes (the Tsala Apopka chain alone contains seven) and the 430,000-acre **Ocala National Forest**.

Before white settlers arrived in the mid-19C, Timucuan and then Seminole Indians made their homes here. Many of the lakes and rivers (Withlacoochee and Ocklawaha, for example) retain their Seminole names. During the period of British occupation (1763-83), the St. Johns River in the east was the site of several sugar-cane and indigo plantations. After the Civil War, settlers began taking advantage of the Armed Occupation Act, which provided free 160-acre tracts of land to homesteaders in Florida. Before the development of the railroad in the 1870s and 80s, most early settlers were farmers who grew citrus and raised cattle.

With a strategic location on the St. Johns River, Sanford became an important supply center for the central Florida interior, receiving goods by paddle wheeler from Jacksonville. Steamboats also ferried supplies down the Silver River to Silver Springs, from where they were transported to surrounding settlements by wagon.

By the 1870s, commercial citrus cultivation accounted for myriad small boomtowns that appeared across central Florida, shipping produce through Gainesville and Ocala. Although the great freeze of 1894-95 spelled doom for many small outposts, well-preserved Victorian architecture in McIntosh, Windsor, Waldo and Mount Dora still recalls the glory days. In 1889 phosphate mining became a mainstay of the Ocala area until World War I cut off the predominantly European market. Agriculture supported the eastern counties, where cool lake breezes and good soil conditions proved ideal for commercial nurseries and vegetable farms.

While retirees and tourism now bolster the area's economy, central Florida continues to earn most of its revenue from agriculture, boosted by light manufacturing. Although the citrus industry was hit hard again by bad freezes in the early 1980s, citrus remains an important local crop. Tiny mom-and-pop fruit stands abound on back roads; be sure to stop for a jar of homemade marmalade or orange-blossom honey.

GAINESVILLE

Population 95,447
Map below
Tourist Information: www.visitgainesville.net ☎ 352-374-5231

A friendly college-town atmosphere pervades Gainesville, home to the University of Florida. The busy 2,000-acre campus lies primarily to the west of US-441, the main north-south thoroughfare. The historic downtown area, Courthouse Square and quiet residential streets lined with loblolly pines and live oaks occupy the east side of town. Gainesville was laid out in 1853 as the new seat of Alachua County, replacing Newnansville farther north. Some say the name Gainesville (originally spelled without the final "E") came from a campaign to gain enough votes from the reluctant Newnansville citizens to support the new location; others argue the town was named for **Edmund Gaines**, a prominent US general who fought in the Seminole Wars.

In the late 19C, Gainesville thrived as a shipping center for citrus, strawberries, phosphate and lumber. Local revenues now depend largely on the university. Despite suburban sprawl, some 700 buildings are preserved in five historic districts. Notable among the turn-of-the-last-century structures in the **Northeast Historic District** is **Thomas Center** *(302 N.E. 6th Ave.)*. Built in 1910, the elegant Mediterranean Revival-style house was remodeled as a hotel in 1928 and is now a cultural center.

SIGHTS

Courthouse Square – *S.E. 1st St. and University Ave.* Brick-paved streets, wide boulevards and early 20C commercial buildings—some housing pleasant outdoor cafes—help maintain the character of Gainesville's old downtown. A local landmark, the **clock tower** contains the original clock from the second (1885) Gainesville courthouse, demolished in 1959. The grand Beaux-Arts style 1909 post office building fronted by a two-story Corinthian portico, is now home to the **Hippodrome State Theater**.

University of Florida – *S.W. 13th St. between University Ave. and S.W. Archer Rd. Campus map and parking information available at Main Entrance information booth, US-441 (S.W. 13th St.) and S.W. 2nd Ave.* Located on 2,000 acres, this is Florida's oldest and largest university, consolidated in 1906 from several state educational facilities (including Florida Agricultural College in Lake City). The university admitted only men until 1947, when about 600 women joined the student body of 9,000. Today, with some 43,000 students, 16 colleges and four graduate schools, the University of Florida ranks among the country's 10 largest universities. The campus includes several early 20C Collegiate-Gothic-style buildings (now part of a historic district), a teaching hospital, an 84,000-seat football stadium (the Gators are a perennial national title contender), two museums and the 81-acre Lake Alice Wildlife Preserve.

★ **Samuel P. Harn Museum of Art** – *S.W. 34th St. and Hull Rd. Open year-round Tue-Fri 11am-5pm, Sat 10am-5pm, Sun 1pm-5pm. Closed major holidays.* ♿ 🅿 ☎ *352-392-9826. www.arts.ufl.edu/harn.* Opened in 1990, the Harn Museum is the state's first major art museum on a college campus. Some 35,000 objects assembled at the University of Florida over the last several decades—previously stored in attics and closets—are now consolidated in the striking 62,000sq ft post-Modern building, distinguished by roof pyramids and a three-story glass atrium. Periodic shows draw on the permanent collection, which includes strong holdings in **early 20C American art**; the **tribal art** of West Africa and Papua New Guinea; Asian sculpture and painting; and pre-Columbian pottery. The museum also features exhibits by contemporary artists—both established and emerging.

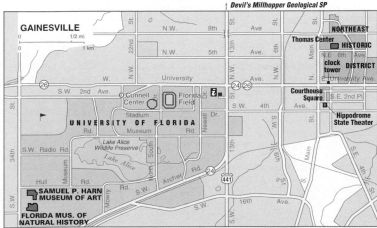

★**Florida Museum of Natural History** – *S.W. 34th St. and Hull Rd., adjacent to Harn Musem of Art. Open year-round Mon-Sat 10am-5pm, Sun & holidays 1pm-5pm. Closed Thanksgiving Day & Dec 25.* & 🅿 ☏ *352-846-2000. www.flmnh.ufl.edu.* This official state repository for Florida's natural history collection houses the museum's departments of Natural Sciences and Anthropology and the largest **research collection** of fossil and modern invertebrates, vertebrates and plants in the South. The museum's two main facilities on the university campus are Dickinson Hall *(not open to the public)*, which serves as the repository, and Powell Hall, the education and exhibition center. Here in Powell Hall, the emphasis is on Florida and Caribbean natural history. Displays explore **Florida environments**, such as the ecosystems of a coral reef, a savanna, and temperate and tropical hammocks. The Northwest Florida exhibit features a full-size limestone cave. Windows into Natural History allows visitors to investigate the state's plants and insects using computers, microscopes, observation chambers and other scientific equipment. Another gallery is devoted to Florida fossils and a fourth to the flora and fauna of South Florida. Classrooms, a gift shop and a large gallery of changing exhibits are also housed in Powell Hall.

★**Devil's Millhopper Geological State Park** – *4732 Millhopper Rd., off N.W. 53rd Ave./Rte. 232. Park hrs & fees p 350.* ☏ *352-955-2008. Ranger-led walks Sat 10am. Insect repellent recommended.* Stop at visitor center for a 5min orientation video; then take the winding staircase to the bottom of the dramatic **sinkhole** known as Devil's Millhopper, after an Indian legend that told of the devil hurling human bodies into its depths. Here, watered by burbling falls and supported by cool, below-grade temperatures, thrives plant life similar to that of Appalachia. Mosses and liverworts hold moisture, allowing larger plants to grow. Among these, needle palms—rare for northern Florida—grow here because the sinkhole rarely experiences freezing temperatures.

Measuring 120ft deep and 500ft wide, this depression was probably formed in two stages. Sinkholes are created as rainwater seeping into limestone substrata forms an underground cavern; eventually the cavern roof collapses, leaving a deep cavity. The first collapse of Devil's Millhopper occurred as many as 14,000 years ago and the second about 1,000 years ago, resulting in a funnel-like shape similar to that of a corn hopper (a device used to feed corn into a grist mill).

Fred Bear Museum – *Fred Bear Dr., just west of I-75 off S.W. Archer Rd/Rte. 24. Open year-round daily 10am-6pm. Closed Jan 1, Easter Sunday, Thanksgiving Day, Dec 25. $5.* & 🅿 ☏ *352-376-2411.* A tribute to its namesake, the late bow-hunter and founder of Bear Archery, the museum presents a large collection of archery artifacts as well as Bear's trophies. A variety of mounted beasts, including grizzly bears, moose and tigers, lines the walls of the second-floor gallery. The self-guided tour includes taped explanations of how Bear and others bagged some of these trophies. You can glimpse the production area of Bear Archery products through windows along one side of the second floor.

Kanapaha Botanical Gardens – *4700 S.W. 58 Dr., off S.W. Archer Rd./Rte. 24, 1.5mi west of I-75. Summer months offer the best color. Open year-round Mon-Tue & Fri 9am-5pm, Wed & weekends 9am-dusk. Closed Dec 25. $3.* & 🅿 ☏ *352-372-4981. www.hammock.ifas.ufl.edu.kanapaha.* There is a lighthearted, almost wild feeling to this 62-acre garden maintained by the North Florida Botanical Society. Visitors may wander along a 1.5mi paved walkway that dips in and out of fern cobbles and palm hammocks, passing through flower beds, an herb garden and an occasional vine-draped trellis. Florida's largest collection of **bamboo** species is found here (some plants grow 2in/hr during the spring season). A water lily pond nestles in a cove of Lake Kanapaha.

EXCURSIONS *Map p 99*

★**Paynes Prairie Preserve State Park** – *10mi south on US-441 in Micanopy. Park hrs & fees p 350.* △ & 🅿 ☏ *352-466-3397. www.afn.org/~pprairie.* Named for King Payne, an 18C Seminole leader, this park ranks as one of Florida's most important natural sites. The irregularly shaped basin, measuring 8.5mi at its widest point, was formed as the terrain settled over a sinking limestone bed that periodically fills with water. A **visitor center** *(2mi from entrance at end of Park Dr.)* and nearby observation tower *(follow short path in front of visitor center)* both offer a sweeping **view** over **Paynes Prairie**, now a marsh where wild Spanish horses (reintroduced in 1985) roam freely. During the late 1600s, the prairie was the site of the largest cattle ranch in Spanish Florida. In the late 19C, the area became a lake with a busy steamboat route until the water drained abruptly, leaving one boat stranded. The 22,000-acre preserve today boasts a rich cross-section of Florida habitats, including swamps, ponds, pine flatwoods and hammocks woven with over 25mi of hiking trails. Sandhill cranes, bald eagles and other wildlife winter here.

Micanopy – *10mi south on US-441. Most shops are open daily 10am-5pm.* An antiques center with a sleepy, unspoiled air, this tiny village was founded in 1821 as the first permanent white settlement in what is now Alachua County. The town was originally called Wanton but was renamed in 1834 for a powerful Seminole chief who once ruled this territory. Enormous live oaks shade the main street, Cholokka Boulevard; shops, housed in early 20C commercial buildings, overflow with vintage china, collectibles, clothing and books. The **Micanopy Historical Society Museum** *(Cholokka Blvd. and Bay St; open year-round daily 1pm-4pm; $2;* & **⌿** ☎ *352-466-3200; www.co.alachua.fl.us)* explains the town's past through historical photographs and artifacts.

★**Marjorie Kinnan Rawlings Historic State Park** – *17mi south in Cross Creek. Take Rte. 20 east 9mi to Rte. 325; follow Rte. 325 south 8mi to Cross Creek. Site is just south of town on right. Grounds open year-round daily 9am-5pm.* & *Visit house by guided tour (45min) only, Oct-Jul Thu-Sun 10am-4pm (every hour, limited to 10 people). Closed Jan 1, Thanksgiving Day, Dec 25. $3.* **⌿** ☎ *352-466-3672.* Well-known for her affectionate portrayals of life in backwoods Florida, author **Marjorie Kinnan Rawlings** (1896-1953) owned this rambling Cracker-style house and 72-acre grounds from 1928 until her death. Among the many original furnishings is the writing table, on the front porch, where Rawlings wrote her Pulitzer Prize-winning book, *The Yearling* (1938), and a subsequent novel *Cross Creek* (1942). Both novels were later made into popular films. The house sits in a citrus grove dominated by a magnificent magnolia tree. Just across the road, a leaf-carpeted path makes a short loop *(.25mi)* through a hardwood hammock of wild palms, oaks, sweet gums, hickories and hollies.

OCALA★

Population 45,943
Map p 99
Tourist Information: www.ocalacc.com ☎ 352-629-8051

Centered in the rolling green countryside of Marion County, Ocala is synonymous with horses. The "Lexington of the South," as it has been dubbed, contains some 400 farms for Arabians, Clydesdales, thoroughbreds and quarter horses, and ranks high as a training and breeding center. Each February the city hosts the month-long **Horse Shows in the Sun** that feature hunting and jumping competitions. Agriculture and a booming cattle industry (the largest in Florida), along with a constant influx of northern retirees, make Marion one of the fastest-growing counties in America.

A US military outpost known as Fort King was established here in 1827 and served as headquarters for central Florida during the Seminole wars. Settlers arrived in the 1840s, and by the late 19C Ocala had become a major shipping center for phosphate and citrus fruits. A number of Victorian and Queen Anne-style houses from that era are preserved in the 55-block **Ocala Historic District** *(centered on Fort King St. between Watula Ave. and 13th St.).*

A natural pastureland owing to the underlying limestone aquifer that waters it, Marion County is now home to some 450, or 75 percent, of Florida's thoroughbred breeding and training facilities. These facilities have produced 41 North American champions and six Kentucky Derby winners. *For a view of the countryside farms, resplendent in rolling pasture and magnificent live oaks, drive south of the city on S.W. 27th Ave. (Rte. 475A) or S.E. 3rd Ave. (Rte. 475). For tours of thoroughbred farms, contact Ocala Marion County Chamber of Commerce (☎ 352-629-8051; www.ocalacc.com).*

SIGHTS

★**Appleton Museum of Art** – *4333 N.E. Silver Springs Blvd. Open year-round daily 10am-6pm. Closed Jan 1 & Dec 25. $6.* ✗ & **⌿** ☎ *352-236-7100. www.appletonmuseum.org.* A dramatic axial sculpture fountain enlivens the approach to this elegant two-story Neoclassical structure clad in travertine marble. In 1986 Chicago industrialist Arthur I. Appleton (owner of a thoroughbred breeding and training facility in Ocala) donated funds to build the museum on 44 acres of land donated by the city of Ocala. Today the 67,000 sq ft museum, land and art collection are jointly owned by the Florida State University Foundation and the Central Florida Community College Foundation.

First-floor galleries frame a central courtyard and feature Classical and Egyptian antiquities, West African sculpture, pre-Columbian pottery, and an extensive display of **Asian art**, including lovely jades, porcelains and Tibetan bronzes. The upper level is devoted primarily to traveling exhibits. The museum also mounts several temporary shows throughout the year. A new wing houses the permanent collection of European and North American academic art, classrooms and a library.

★**Silver Springs** – **Kids** *5656 E. Silver Springs Blvd./Rte. 40 (1.5mi east of Appleton Museum). Open Feb-Labor Day daily 10am-5pm. Rest of the year Thu-Sun 10am-5pm. $31.95 (includes all rides and shows).* ✗ & **⌿** *($5)* ⩜ *boat rides and Jeep*

Glass-Bottom Boat Tour of Silver Springs

Safari. ☏ *352-236-2121. www.silversprings.com.* A subtropical hammock surrounding 50 natural springs at the head of the Silver River sets the scene for this 350-acre multitheme nature park. Together the waters form the largest **artesian spring** in the world, producing about 5,000 gallons per second (which would fill an Olympic-size swimming pool in two minutes). Timucuan Indians worshipped the sparkling waters as the "shrine of the water gods." Visitors here began arriving by steamboat as early as the 1860s—making Silver Springs the oldest attraction in Florida.

The 25-min **Glass-Bottom Boat Rides** provide a clear view of the underwater world of the main spring, including several caverns (the deepest is 81ft) that contain fossilized bones of Pleistocene animals. Waters here are so pure (98 percent) that they have been the setting for Tarzan movies and the James Bond film *Moonraker.* The **Lost River Voyage** *(25min)* stops at an animal rehabilitation post for eagles and other birds and animals. The popular 15-min **Jeep Safari** travels through a natural habitat site, where vultures, egrets, armadillos, rhesus monkeys and Amazonian two-toed sloths (which eat, sleep, mate and give birth while upside down) roam free. Next to Jeep Safari, visitors can feed giraffes, llamas, pygmy goats and baby deer at **Doolittle's Petting Zoo**. Enclosures along the boardwalk trail of **Ross Allen Island** hold alligators, crocodiles, flamingos and giant tortoises. Be sure to see the three animal shows offered several times a day. From the island, you can catch the **Jungle Cruise** *(30 min)* down the Fort King Waterway past an open-air zoo of exotic animals.

Adjoining Silver Springs, **Wild Waters** 🎟, a nine-acre water park *(on Rte. 40)* features a 450,000-gallon wave pool, eight flumes with water sleds and a miniature golf course *(open Apr-Sept daily 10am-7pm; $21.95;* ✗ ♿ 🅿 ☏ *352-236-2121).*

Discovery Science Center – 🎟 *50 S. Magnolia Ave. Open year-round Tue-Fri 9am-4pm, Sat 10am-4pm. Closed major holidays. $3.50.* ♿ 🅿 ☏ *352-620-2555.* While the center's focus is on children, visitors of any age can easily become caught up in interactive exhibits designed to explain such scientific phenomena as light, sound, gravity, motion and space. Perhaps most intriguing are the **holusions**, images formed by random patterns that trick the eye into seeing a three-dimensional image.

EXCURSIONS

Don Garlits' Museums – *10mi south of city center. Take Exit 67 off I-75 and go east on Rte. 484; take first right on Rte. 457A. Museum entrance is on right at 13700 S.W. 16th Ave. Open year-round daily 9am-5pm. Closed Dec 25. $8; $1. combination ticket.* ♿ 🅿 ☏ *352-245-8661. www.garlits.com.* Champion drag racer and Marion County resident "Big Daddy" Don Garlits—the first to break 200mph—founded his **Museum of Drag Racing** in 1976. Drag racing is a one-on-one quarter-mile competition in which drivers accelerate custom dragsters from a dead stop and race in a straight line; it differs from stock-car competitions, where drivers race on a circular track using autos that are custom-built to resemble street models. (Stock cars originally were built entirely from stock parts). The plain, single-story

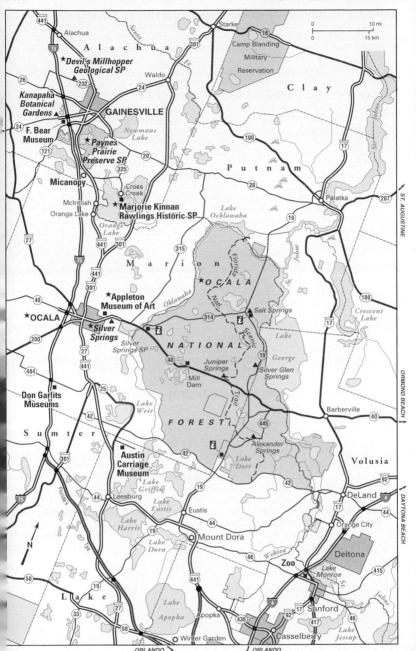

building is packed with trophies, vintage gas tanks and an excellent collection of antique autos and engines with mind-boggling capacities for torque and horse-power. Garlits' first dragster (1954)—a car so ugly that *Hot Rod Magazine* wouldn't even print a picture of it—is housed here, as is "Swamp Rat I," his first world-record-setting dragster, and many of the 33 subsequent models in that series. Prized stock cars and dragsters complete the displays. In an adjacent building, the **Antique Car Museum** exhibits a collection of some 100 classic automo-biles, including many Fords from the 1930s and '40s.

★**Ocala National Forest** – *11mi east of Ocala. Enter at Highway 40 Visitor Center, 10863 E. Rte. 40; 2.5mi east of Silver Springs. Open year-round daily 9am-5pm. Closed Dec 25. △ ▣ ☏ 352-236-0288. Two additional visitor centers serve the forest: Salt Springs to the north (14100 N. Rte. 19); and Pittman to the south (45621 Rte. 19) near Lake Dorr. Each offers maps, forest-related exhibits and a bookstore.* Established in 1908, Ocala National Forest is the oldest national forest east of the Mississippi. Locally known as "Big Scrub" for its predominance of scrub sand pine and oaks, the forest encompasses some 383,000 acres of wetlands, timber, scrub, hiking trails and freshwater lakes and springs. It stretches about 60mi from southern Marion County up to Lake Ocklawaha. To the west lies the Ocklawaha River; the St. Johns River and Lake George mark the eastern boundary. The Florida National Scenic Trail cuts through the forest north to south. Other trails varying in length *(.5mi to 7mi)* are available to hikers.

Freshwater Springs – *Open mid-May-mid-Sept daily 8am-8pm. Rest of the year daily 8am-dusk. $3.* △ 🄿 *(no camping at Silver Glen;* ☎ *352-236-0288).* Some of central Florida's most beautiful natural springs grace the forest. Picturesque **Juniper Springs** *(17mi east of visitor center on Rte. 40; canoe rental;* ☎ *352-625-2808)* features a palm-fringed swimming area, enclosed in the 1930s by the Civilian Conservation Corps, and a short nature trail through subtropical foliage and past bubbling spring "boils." The 7mi trip down Juniper Creek through the Juniper Prairie Wilderness is a particularly popular canoe run. Clear waters draw boaters, snorkelers and scuba divers to **Alexander Springs** *(10mi southeast of Juniper Springs on Rte. 445).* The combination of fresh water and salt water flowing into the head-spring at **Salt Springs** *(junction of Rte. 19 and Rte. 314; boat & canoe rentals;* ☎ *352-685-2255)* creates differences in salinity at different depths, causing objects viewed underwater to appear unusually distorted. Popular with snorkelers, **Silver Glen Springs** is surrounded by ancient Indian shell mounds *(8mi north of junction of Rte. 19 and Rte. 40).*

Florida National Scenic Trail – *Within the forest, primary access points to the trail are the Clearwater Lake Recreation Area (Rte. 42), Alexander Springs (Rte. 445), Farles Lake (Forest Rd. 595-1), Juniper Springs (Rte. 40), Hopkins Prairie (Forest Rd. 88-C near Lake Kerr), Lake Delancy (Forest Rd. 75-2) and the Rodman Recreation Area on Lake Ocklawaha. Both day and overnight hikes are permitted. Florida Trail Assn.:* ☎ *352-378-8823 or 800-343-1882. www.florida-trail.org.* Offering more than 300mi of hiking in Florida, this is one of eight National Scenic Trails in the country and will eventually run the length of the state (more than 1,000mi are currently completed, but sections are missing). A 67mi stretch of the scenic trail threads through Ocala National Forest. The north/south route, marked by orange-colored blazes, winds through scrub pine, live oak and juniper stands; skirts lakes and springs; and traverses cypress and gum swamps via well-maintained boardwalks.

Austin Carriage Museum – *23mi southeast of Ocala. Take US-441 south 13mi to Rte. 42; go east 4mi to Weirsdale, south 2mi on Rte. 25, then east 1.4mi to museum entrance at 3000 Marion County Rd. Visit by guided tour (1hr 30min, only, Mon-Fri 1pm-5pm. $10 contribution requested.* ♿ 🄿 ☎ *352-750-5500 www.continentalacres.com.* Tucked away at the edge of Ocala National Forest, this museum boasts the largest private collection of antique horse-drawn carriages in the country. More than 75 of them from the late 19C and early 20C have been restored to near-mint condition with tufted velvet and leather upholstery, shiny brass ornaments and working lamps. They include a Tour Neau Sociable, one of only three models of this US-made pleasure carriage still intact; a hunting carriage with a dog compartment; and a carriage used by MGM Studios in 1930s movies.

★**Marjorie Kinnan Rawlings Historic State Park** – *20mi north in Cross Creek, 4.5mi west of US-301 on Rte. 325. Description p 97.*

Northeast Coast

ANDREW JACKSON
After Whom Jacksonville Was Named
1822

Though motorists once raced through this corner on their way south, more and more travelers are discovering the myriad charms of the 125-mile strand from Fernandina Beach to Daytona Beach. Long heralded for historic St. Augustine and boisterous Daytona Beach, northeast Florida also claims its own sea islands (the southern part of Georgia's famous chain). The city limits of Jacksonville take in the greatest area of any US city.

Though Spanish sailor-explorer **Ponce de León** landed in northeast Florida in 1513 and "claimed" it for Spain, such bravado amounted to little more than planting a flag on the moon. Real ownership required permanent settlement, and this was not achieved until St. Augustine was founded in 1565, preceding Jamestown, Virginia, by 42 years. The 600 original settlers barely held on under the onslaught of diseases, hurricanes and attacks by Indians and English mariners. To defend themselves they constructed a massive fort, Castillo de San Marcos, which now draws thousands of visitors annually.

Except for a brief British occupation (1763-83), St. Augustine remained Spanish for the next 256 years until Spain handed Florida over to the US in 1821. Jacksonville was founded soon afterward, 30mi north on the banks of the St. Johns River, and rose to prominence as a port and tourist town. By the end of the 19C, however, Jacksonville's days as Florida's premier destination were over, thanks largely to Henry Flagler's Florida East Coast Railway, which opened up St. Augustine and other sunny spots farther south. In modern times, Jacksonville has carried the banner of industry and commerce while St. Augustine has exploited its image as a bastion of history. Another magnet for tourists in this region, particularly during college and university students' Spring Break, is the relative newcomer Daytona Beach.

Travelers to Jacksonville today will find a modern, skyscraping metropolis that beckons with art museums, a landscaped riverwalk and nearby beaches. Scars of drug-associated crime are evident in the downtown area, but city leaders have initiated bold new revitalization projects, including the acquisition of a professional football team, the Jacksonville Jaguars. St. Augustine, on the other hand, cossets tourists at almost every turn with red-tile roofs, quaint courtyards of 17C coquina buildings, quiet lanes lined by mossy trees and charming B&Bs. To the south, fast-growing Flagler County still maintains an undiscovered feel while offering several worthwhile attractions along A1A.

DAYTONA BEACH

Population 64,112
Map below
Tourist Information: www.daytonabeach.com ☎ 386-255-0415 or 800-854-1234

Gateway to a 23mi stretch of hard, wide beach⚓⚓, this sun-worshippers' sanctuary is known for stock-car races. Spring Break crowds and drives on the beach. From February to April, the streets and beaches teem with racers, motorcyclists, racing fans and college students. Visitors in need of a day off from the beach can find a number of cultural attractions highlighting the area's prehistoric and pioneer past.

In the late 18C and early 19C, planters settled in the area and then left. Indigo, rice and sugar cane plantations failed because of raids during the second Spanish occupation (1783-1819) and because the brutal Second Seminole War (1835-1842) demoralized the landowners. The town was laid out in the early 1870s on the site of an abandoned plantation. The railroad's arrival in the 1880s and an influx of wealthy vacationers 12mi north in Ormond Beach launched the Daytona area. However, it was auto racing that altered the city's course and provided its most distinguishing feature. The introduction of I-95 in the early 1970s pulled the town's commerce west. Soon the downtown deteriorated, but refurbishment began in 1982. The city's efforts paid off six years later when downtown Daytona Beach was placed on the National Register of Historic Places. Today eight million annual visitors make tourism the city's dominant industry.

Recently, sections of the beach have become no-car zones *(see Speed City below)*. As part of a $200 million redevelopment project, a beachside parking garage and several hundred first-class hotel rooms have been added. Two new high-rise replacement bridges connect the mainland with the beach, the one extending US-92 (International Speedway Boulevard) to the beach. Projected to open in 2002, Ocean Walk Village, part of a new condominium-hotel resort, will include beachside stores, restaurants, a water park and sports/entertainment and convention facilities that promise new life for the Main Street area.

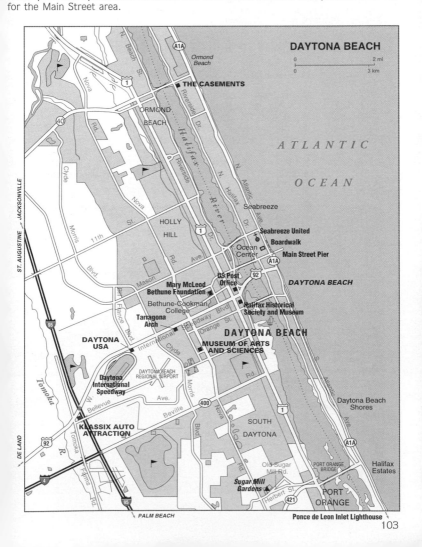

■ Speed City

Begun here in 1902, the sport of auto racing continued on the beach until the late 1950s, when a track was built. Early racers, including Barney Oldfield, Sir Malcolm Campbell and Sir Henry Seagrave, regularly set speed records on the beach; speeds leapt from 57mph in 1902 to an incredible 275mph in 1935. Several major formula and stock-car races are now held at the **Daytona International Speedway**, including the famous **Daytona 500** in February. March brings thousands of rumbling motorcycles for Bike Week, followed by flocks of students for the annual rite of Spring Break. The tradition of driving on the beach continues to the present day. *For a $5 fee, motorists may cruise a designated stretch of the 23mi strand—driving no more than 10mph—or they may park, set up an umbrella and join the suntan set, which clusters around Main Street Pier and the Boardwalk amusement area.*

SIGHTS

Start your tour at the ocean and travel west.

Boardwalk and Main Street Pier – 🔲 A 20ft-wide concrete walkway with benches and telescopes, Boardwalk extends three blocks north from Main St. to Ora St. WPA workers constructed the promenade and 4,500-seat coquina-rock bandshell in the 1930s. The 1,000ft-long pier dates from 1925, when it replaced the 1900 original that was destroyed by fire. Tourists young and old gravitate to this area in all seasons, encountering a seaside bazaar of video arcades and fishing rentals, as well as the popular Space Needle *($2)* and sky lift *($3)* rides *(mid-May-Sept daily 11am-midnight; rest of the year daily 11am-9pm; combination ticket $4;* ☎ *386-253-1212)*. Dominating the skyline near the pier, the sprawling stepped structure, built in 1989, houses a resort hotel.

Halifax Historical Society and Museum – *252 S. Beach St. (3 blocks south of US-92). Open year-round Tue-Sat 10am-4pm. Closed Thanksgiving weekend & Dec 25-Jan1. $3.* ♿ ☎ *386-255-6976. www.halifaxhistorical.org.* Located in the Beaux-Arts Merchants Bank building (1910), this museum houses a 1938 model of the Boardwalk and murals of such landmarks as the Ponce de León Inlet Lighthouse. Noted Florida landscape artist Don J. Emery, who designed the 1926 Spanish-style **Tarragona Arch** *(W. International Speedway Blvd. and Tarragona Way)*, and his son painted the murals in 1947. The museum also keeps Native American artifacts and auto racing memorabilia, as well as an extensive collection of 19C postcards.

The Spanish Renaissance-style **US post office** at 220 N. Beach St. (1932, Harry M. Griffin) features a terra-cotta roof and gargoyles. Griffin also designed the Mission-style **Seabreeze United Church** in 1930 *(501 N. Wild Olive Ave.)*.

Daytona Beach

★**Museum of Arts and Sciences** – *1040 Museum Blvd. (off Nova Rd., .7mi south of US-92W). Open year-round Tue-Fri 9am-4pm, weekends noon-5pm. Closed major holidays. $5.* & ▯ ☎ *386-255-0285. www.moas.org.* Located on Tuscawilla Preserve, the museum offers fine permanent exhibits of pre-Castro Cuban art, American paintings and decorative art, and African ritual pieces. Furniture, portraiture and landscape paintings from the colonial period to the turn of the century are found in the **American gallery**★★. On display are Chippendale chairs (c.1780), a Hepplewhite desk (c.1800), paintings by Albert Durand and Gilbert Stuart, silver, pewter and glasswork.

A gift of former Cuban president Fulgencio Batista, the **Cuban art** collection chronicles life in Cuba from 1759 to 1959. The gallery devoted to **African art** presents 165 masks, totems and other objects from 30 different cultures.

The sciences are represented by a prehistory wing that showcases a 130,000 yr-old giant ground sloth **skeleton**, found several miles south of the museum. Temporary exhibits and an outdoor display of modern sculpture round out the museum's holdings. A 22,000sq ft wing showcasing Americana opened in the fall of 2001.

Mary McLeod Bethune Foundation – *640 Mary McLeod Bethune Blvd. (on the campus of Bethune-Cookman College). Open year-round Mon-Fri 9am-4pm.* ▯ ☎ *386-255-1401. www.bethune.cookman.edu.* Educator **Mary McLeod Bethune** (1875-1955), daughter of a freed slave, lived in this two-story white clapboard house from 1914 to 1955. She established Florida's first black girls' school here in 1904 and later became an advisor to five US presidents and served in FDR's administration. The house was the state's first site to honor an African American. Bethune's furnishings, awards, letters and other mementos are displayed inside.

★**Daytona USA** – *1801 W. International Speedway Blvd. (1mi east of I-95). Open year-round daily 9am-7pm. Closed Dec 25. $16.* ✗ & ▯ ☎ *386-947-6800. www.daytonausa.com.* Built in 1959 to move auto racing off the beach, **Daytona International Speedway** hosts eight major annual car and motorcycle races in February, March, July and October. The rest of the year was fairly quiet until this interactive motor-sports center replaced the former visitor center in July 1996. Visitors now can computer-design and video-test their own NASCAR stock cars, change a race car's tires in a timed pit-stop competition, broadcast a race finish from a sound booth and interview famous racers like Jeff Gordon and Dale Jarrett via laser-disc technology. A 14min movie, *The Daytona 500*, puts viewers in the midst of the adrenaline-pumped highlight of the speedway's race year—traveling at a simulated 190mph. New in 2001, NASCAR simulators that combine motion, video projection and sound let visitors experience the sensation of championship racing: guests hop inside, buckle up and accelerate to more than 200 mph. Half-hour guided **speedway tours** *($6)* take visitors to the pits, the infield (jammed with campers during race events) and around the 2.5mi track, with its 31° banked turns *(weather and track schedule permitting).* Adventurous entrants in the Richard Petty Driving Experience, named for one of NASCAR racing's all-time champions, are treated to a high-speed, three-lap stock-car ride around the Daytona track *($105; must be 16 years of age or older).*

★**Klassix Auto Attraction** – *2909 W. International Speedway Blvd. Turn left on Tomoka Farms Rd. (first light west of I-95 overpass); take first left on Bellevue Ave. and immediate left into museum. Open year-round daily 9am-6pm. $8.50.* & ☎ *386-252-3800. www.klassixauto.com.* This classic-car-lover's dream, which opened in early 1994, makes a convincing case for the glamour of sports cars. Relive the 1950s in a life-size diner with carhops, a drive-in theater and a vintage garage. The second floor, comprising nearly half of the facility's 54,000sq ft space, features many Corvettes—from their inception in 1953 to the present. Other displays include the *Batmobile* from the television show. Some 120 vintage vehicles and motorcycles are set amid neon signs, videos presenting a streamlined history of racing, and period music. All this, plus a real ice-cream parlor, makes Klassix a fun stop even for nonenthusiasts.

■ Bike Week

Each year in early March some 350,000 bikers roll into Daytona Beach on their Harleys and Hondas for 10 days of races, swap meets and parties, known collectively as Bike Week. Festivities culminate with the **Daytona 200**, a superbike championship race first run in 1942 on Daytona's wide sands. Today the International Speedway hosts the event, which attracts motorcycle-racing fans from around the world. For information about accommodations and events, call the Daytona Beach Area Convention and Visitors Bureau *(☎ 800-854-1234; www.daytonabeach.com)* and ask for the *Bike Week Pocket Guide.*

EXCURSIONS *Map p 103*

★**The Casements** – *5mi north in Ormond Beach at 25 Riverside Dr. Take US-1 north to Granada Ave. Turn right (east) and cross Ormond Bridge. Turn right onto Riverside Dr. Open year-round Mon-Thu 9am-9pm, Fri 9am-5pm, Sat 9am-noon. Closed major holidays.* ⅙ 🅿 ☎ *386-676-3216.* Now a cultural and civic center, this gracious 1912 mansion named for its many casement windows was the winter home of oil tycoon **John D. Rockefeller** (1839-1937) from 1918 until his death. Rockefeller entertained various celebrities here, including Will Rogers, Harvey Firestone and racer Sir Malcolm Campbell. In the decades after Rockefeller's death, the house went through several incarnations, becoming a women's junior college, a retirement home and an apartment hotel. Vandals partially destroyed it in the early 1970s, after which the city bought the house for $500,000 and began to restore it.

Tours *(Mon-Fri 10am-2:30pm)* take visitors through the second-floor Rockefeller room, which contains the tycoon's grand mirror and desk. The third floor houses a collection of Boy Scout memorabilia. From here, an octagonal stained-glass skylight casts a beam down to the first floor. A two-acre grassy garden across the street offers fine views of the river. The Casements also presents lectures, concerts and exhibits.

Sugar Mill Gardens – *5mi south in Port Orange. Take US-1 south and continue 5mi. Turn right (west) onto Herbert St. (1 block north of Rte. 421/Old Dunlawton Rd.); follow Herbert St. 1mi and turn right on Old Sugar Mill Rd. Entrance on left. Open year-round daily dawn-dusk.* ⅙ 🅿 ☎ *386-767-1735.* Ruins of a 19C sugar plantation are preserved in the 12-acre county park. Started by Patrick Dean of the Bahamas, the mill was partially destroyed—and Dean was slain—by Indians in 1836 during the Second Seminole War. During the mill's heyday, juice was extracted from sugar cane by crushing it between steam-powered rollers. This process yielded sticky brown sugar and its liquid by-product, molasses. A pleasant trail completely shaded by live oaks leads to the ruins along informal gardens and past concrete prehistoric beasts, the remains of a dinosaur park that operated here in the 1950s.

★**Ponce de León Inlet Lighthouse** – *11mi south of US-92 in Ponce Inlet. Take A1A (which becomes Atlantic Ave.) south to Beach St. Turn right on Beach, continue .3mi to Peninsula Ave. and turn left; lighthouse is .2mi farther on left. Open May-Aug daily 10am-9pm. Rest of the year daily 10am-5pm. Closed Dec 25. $4.* 🅿 ☎ *386-761-1821. www.ponceinlet.org.* First lit in 1887, this 175ft red beacon never missed a night of operation until 1970, when expenses forced the government to move to a nearby Coast Guard station. Restoration began in 1972 and the light was relit 10 years later. Today visitors here find one of the most complete restored light stations in Florida. Several keepers' cottages and outbuildings display nautical memorabilia, maps, photographs and model ships. A new lens exhibit building contains an 1860 first-order Fresnel lens retired from the Cape Canaveral Lighthouse. Visitors may climb the 203 steps of the original light tower for a breathtaking 360-degree **view**★★ of the ocean and inland waterway.

JACKSONVILLE★

Population 735,617
Map pp 114-115
Tourist Information: www.jaxcvb.com ☎ 904-798-9111 or 800-733-2668

The largest city in the US—in terms of area—extends over 840sq mi in Florida's northeastern corner, anchored by the north-flowing St. Johns River. In recent decades numerous revitalization projects, such as the transformation of the old Union Station into the **Prime F. Osborn Convention Center**, and the expansion of **Alltel Stadium** (formerly known as the Gator Bowl) have helped offset urban blight. Broad beaches aside, other city offerings include museums of art and science, charming historic neighborhoods a zoo and newly developed waterfront.

Jacksonville was founded in 1822, named to honor Gen. Andrew Jackson, then provisional governor of Florida. During the Civil War, the city was sacked repeatedly by both armies. The most decisive battle fought in Florida took place 45mi west of Jacksonville in Olustee, when, in February 1864, Confederate troops defeated Union forces. Volunteers reenact that skirmish each February at **Olustee Battlefield Historic State Park** *(off US-90, 14mi east of Lake City).*

Following the war, noted author **Harriet Beecher Stowe** purchased a house just south of Jacksonville in 1867. The year 1901 lives in infamy in Jacksonville's history: that year a devastating fire destroyed much of downtown. By 1910, the city had become the winter headquarters of the fledgling motion-picture industry; such popular stars as comic actor Oliver Hardy began their careers here.

■ The Beaches *Map p 116*

Kathryn Abbey Hanna Park – *500 Wonderwood Dr.; on A1A, south of Mayport Naval Station.* A distinctly sylvan atmosphere lures visitors to this 450-acre oceanfront park. Named in memory of Florida historian and educator Kathryn Abbey Hanna, the park boasts a splendid white-sand **beach** minus the intrusive urban backdrop. Scenic hiking and biking trails lace the park.

Jacksonville Beaches – *East of downtown via Rte. 90/Beach Blvd. or Rte.10/Atlantic Blvd.* Linked by Route A1A, three towns line the shore, north to south: Atlantic Beach, Neptune Beach and Jacksonville Beach, all from the turn of the 19C (as you head north, houses show more of the traditional Shingle style). **Atlantic Beach**, most affluent of the beach towns, contains a small, but increasingly chic shopping district with several locally popular restaurant/bars. **Neptune Beach** is almost entirely residential. **Jacksonville Beach** is a blue-collar community turning upscale after almost a two-decade-long building moratorium. Its new downtown plaza is centered on a 7,000-seat amphitheater, the site, each spring, of one of America's largest blues festivals. The best beach restaurants are found at Jacksonville Beach *(see Address Book)*. A concrete boardwalk edges the beachfront between Fourth Avenue and the lifeguard station. At Fifth Avenue South, a long fishing pier juts into the ocean.

Ponte Vedra Beach – *From A1A south, bear left on Ponte Vedra Blvd.* Ranging along the coast south of Jacksonville Beach, this wealthy residential and resort community is home to some of the nation's most prestigious professional tennis organizations. From its headquarters in Ponte Vedra Beach, the Association of Tennis Professionals oversees nearly 70 tournaments in 31 countries; the Tournament Players Club is also located here.

In the second half of the 20C, the **Port of Jacksonville**, extending along the St. Johns River between its main facilities at Talleyrand Docks and Blount Island, took its place among the Southeast's most important deepwater ports. Florida's three principal rail systems—CSX, Norfolk Southern and Florida East Coast—established headquarters here. Skyscrapers, notably Gulf Life Tower on the river's southbank (1967; now South Trust Bank) and Independent Square on the north bank, rose along the downtown skyline.

Jacksonville Today – Thanks to a 1968 referendum that merged the governments of Jacksonville and Duval County, Jacksonville now ranks as the largest metropolitan region (in terms of area) in the US. In recent decades, many sections of the city have fallen victim to serious urban blight; public and private efforts to grapple with the problem have set numerous revitalization projects in motion. One example is the transformation of the old Union Station passenger terminal into the **Prime F. Osborn Convention Center**. The 1993 decision of the National Football League to locate a professional franchise in Jacksonville sparked expansion and improvements to the **Jacksonville Municipal Stadium** (formerly known as the Gator Bowl) and surrounding areas; the Jacksonville Jaguars played their first regular-season home game in September 1995.

DOWNTOWN

Shopping, entertainment spots, offices and a newly constructed hotel crowd the north side of the St. Johns River; the south bank offers strolls along a boardwalk or museum-browsing. Two transportation services worth the ride link both sides of the river: the 2.5mi Skyway people mover and privately operated water taxis, allowing access to both banks without the annoyance of reparking the car. Water taxis also provide transportation to the stadium on game weekends.

North of the River

★**Jacksonville Landing** – *2 Independent Dr.* ☎ *904-353-1188.* This two-level, horseshoe-shaped building was completed in 1987 as an early part of the downtown's revitalization. With its upscale boutiques and eateries, Jacksonville Landing is one of the signature "festival marketplaces," like Boston's Faneuil Hall. After shopping, amble along the broad concrete walkways bordering the river for views of the opposite bank. When completed, the walkway will extend a full mile west to the **Cummer Museum**, creating a pedestrian link between the cultural center and the skyscrapers of downtown.

PRACTICAL INFORMATION ....Area Code: 904

Getting There – **Jacksonville International Airport (JIA)**: 15mi north of city; *(information:* ☎ *741-4902).* Transportation to downtown via taxi *($22).* Rental car agencies *(p 343)* located at airport. Amtrak **train** station: 3570 Clifford Ln. *(☎ 800-872-7245; www.amtrak.com).* Greyhound **bus** station: 10 N. Pearl St. *(☎ 800-231-2222; www.greyhound.com).*

Getting Around – Local **bus service** is provided by Jacksonville Transit Authority (JTA) *(year-round daily; 75¢ to city, $1.50 to beaches; schedules and route information* ☎ *630-3100).* **Skyway Express monorail** travels between the Convention Center, Jefferson St., Hemming Plaza, Omni Hotel, San Marco and Florida Community College Jacksonville *(year-round Mon-Thu 6:30am-7:30pm, Fri 6:30am-10pm & Sat 10am-10pm; every 4min; 35¢;* ▣*).* **Water taxi** departs from docks at Riverwalk and Jacksonville Landing *(year-round Sun-Thu 11am-9pm, Fri & Sat 11am-11pm; runs continuously; one-way 10min; $2;* ♿ ▣*)* Bass Marine **Taxi** *(*☎ *730 -8685).* Downtown metered **parking**: 50¢/hr.

Visitor Information – **Jacksonville and the Beaches Convention and Visitors Bureau**, 201 E. Adams St., Jacksonville 32202, *(open year-round Mon-Fri 8am-5pm;* ☎ *798-9111 or 800-733-2668; www.jaxcvb.com).* **Visitor Center**, 2 Independent Dr. in Jacksonville Landing, provides information on shopping, entertainment, festivals and recreation, *(open Mon-Sat 10am-8pm, Sun 12:30pm-5:30pm;* ♿ ☎ *791-4305). .*

Accommodations – Area *Visitors Guide* including lodging directory available (free) from Jacksonville and the Beaches Convention and Visitors Bureau. Accommodations range from hotels *($80-$150)* to motels *($35-$75)* and bed-and-breakfast inns *($75-$180).* Campgrounds and RV parks are also available in the area. *Rates quoted are average prices per night for a double room and are subject to seasonal variations.*

Sightseeing – By **riverboat cruise** *(round-trip 2hr 30min; commentary; lunch $22; dinner $33).* For schedules and reservations, call **River Cruises** ☎ 396-2333.

Shopping – **Shops of Historic Avondale**: designer boutiques, antiques, restaurants; **Jacksonville Landing**: specialty shops, restaurants and entertainment *(☎ 353-1188);* **Avenue Mall**: department stores, 110 specialty stores, eateries *(☎ 363-3060).*

Entertainment – Consult the arts and entertainment section of the *Times-Union* (Fridays) and *Travelhost* publication for schedules of cultural events. **Jacksonville Symphony Orchestra** schedules Broadway shows and plays *(☎ 355-2787);* **Theatre Jacksonville**: drama, comedy and musicals *(☎ 396-4425).* **Times-Union Center for the Performing Arts** *(information:* ☎ *633-6110).* Free **concerts** at Jacksonville Landing, Center Courtyard *(☎ 353-1188).* For arts and sporting events tickets contact **Ticketmaster** *(☎ 353-3309; www.ticketmaster.com).*

Sports and Recreation – The area's **beaches** offer swimming, surfing, boating and fishing. Boat rentals available at area marinas. **Spectator sports**: **Jacksonville Jaguars** (NFL) at Alltel Stadium ☎ 633-2000. **Jacksonville Suns** at Wolfson Baseball Park ☎ 358-2846. Many area **golf** clubs welcome visitors: Champions Club at Julington Creek *(☎ 287-4653);* Mill Cove Golf Club *(☎ 646-4653);* Jacksonville Beach Golf Course *(☎ 247-6184).* **Fishing** information is available in the *Visitors Guide* or visit www.jaxcvb.com for information on deep-sea fishing.

ADDRESS BOOK

For a legend of price listings for hotels and restaurants, see p 76.

Staying in Jacksonville and the Northeast Coast

The Lodge & Club – *607 Ponte Vedra Blvd., Ponte Vedra Beach.* ✗ ♿ ▣ ⚓ ☎ *904-273-9500 or 800-234-4304. www.pvresorts.com. 66 rooms.* **$$$$$** Pampering à la nearby Ponte Vedra Inn & Club prevails at this seafront sister resort. Attentive service and a full recreational menu are the order of the day at the sprawling Mediterranean-style complex, complete with belvedere towers, red barrel-tile roofs and Palladian windows. Custom-furnished quarters (all extra-large and oceanfront) in tints of teal or bone hold cushioned reading nooks, terry robes, personal safes and private patios; some have vaulted ceilings. Big, brightly tiled bathrooms house Jacuzzi or Roman tubs and separate showers. A multi-lane lap pool dominates the fitness center, and golf and tennis are available nearby.

Amelia Island Williams House – *103 S. 9th St., Fernandina Beach.* ♿ ▣ ☎ *904-277-2328 or 800-414-9258. www.williamshouse.com. 8 rooms.* **$$$** Edging Fernandina's historic district, this 1856 mansion (the town's oldest) was once owned by a surveyor for the firm of Lawrence Washington, George's brother and by descendants of England's King Henry I and the *Mayflower* Pilgrims. Behind a fleur-de-lis fence of iron, museumlike interiors show off furnishings that belonged to Napoleon III and the last emperor of China. The B&B's themed guest rooms (such as Italianate, Chinese and Victorian) revel in 17C Japanese block prints, brocaded bed linens, marble-topped tables or other lavish appointments. Generous bathrooms boast claw-foot or Jacuzzi tubs. Breakfasts are equally grand.

Casa Monica Hotel – *95 Cordova St., St. Augustine.* ✗ ♿ 🅿 ⌕ ☎ *904-827-1888 or 800-648-1888. www.casamonica.com. 138 rooms.* **$$$** Downtown's newly resurrected Medieval-style fort was built in 1888 as a winter getaway for America's top-tier families. Its regal features—towers and arches, hand-painted tiles, iron poster beds—will make you think you've landed in Moorish Spain. Decorated with plush velvets and tapestry fabrics in papal jewel tones, accommodations are fitted with amenities suitable for a modern-day king. Enjoy a designer martini and live music *(jazz Fri and Sat nights)* in the hotel's neoned **Cobalt Lounge**.

Florida House Inn – *20 and 22 S. 3rd St., Fernandina Beach.* ✗ 🅿 ☎ *904-261-3300 or 800-258-3301. www.floridahouse.com. 15 rooms.* **$$$** The pulse of Fernandina's historic district quickened when this hotel was restored room by room in 1991. It's the oldest continuously operated lodging in Florida. Porches upstairs and down connect the inn's two component houses, the first dating from 1856, the second from 1882. Christmas-colored exteriors anticipate the conviviality of the plaid bar and family-style dining room within. Brawny antiques fill guest rooms, small to spacious, 10 with working fireplaces. Complimentary continental and customized breakfasts can be enjoyed on the garden patio.

St. Francis Inn – *279 Saint George St., St. Augustine.* 🅿 ⌕ ☎ *904-824-6068 or 800-824-6062. www.stfrancisinn.com. 17 rooms.* **$$$** In America's ancient city, no place pulsates with more warmth than this three-story, vine-covered inn on a cobblestone lane. An artesian fountain bubbles in the brick patio; the placid pool beckons swimmers just beyond. Built as a trapezoid devoid of right angles, the house dates from 1791. Rough plastered ceilings, dark open beams and flickering fireplaces mark the public space, laid out with oriental rugs. Soft quilts, fringed lamps and vintage photos adorn the guest rooms. The inn's trencherman breakfasts might include "piggy pudding" (rich pastry over sausage), herbed egg-and-tomato pie or blueberry cobbler.

The White Orchid – *1104 S. Oceanshore Blvd., Flagler Beach.* ♿ 🅿 ⌕ ☎ *386-439-4944 or 800-423-1477. www.whiteorchidinn.com. 8 rooms.* **$$$** Here, in one of Florida's last residentially scaled beach towns, professional restaurateurs keen on accent and ambience operate an airy, Deco-styled B&B on the shore road bordering the ocean. Savvy settings create a cool, uncluttered look in guest rooms that highlight distinctive features: the milky sheen of curved walls in glass brick, a red phone against a cobalt-blue couch and tony Oriental touches like a lacquer panel and live orchid in the bathroom. During happy hour (actually two hours), guests enjoy wine by the pool. Mornings bring freshly cooked breakfasts stylishly served in a big bay-windowed space, best suited for dolphin sightings.

Cabana Colony Cottages – *2435 S. Atlantic Ave., Daytona Beach Shores.* ♿ 🅿 ⌕ ☎ *386-252-1892 or 800-293-0653. www.daytonashoreline.com. 12 rooms.* **$$** It's easy to remember why you came to Florida when you stay at these dwellings directly by the sea. They date from 1927 and feel like places to play: there are free beach chairs, barbecue grills and videos you can take to your room. Outside and in, the cottages are painted in cool white and pastels and furnished in wicker, with seashell motifs and area rugs on tile. Some one-bedroom, some two, each has its own fully equipped kitchen that families especially love—and, yes, there's a guest laundry.

House On Cherry Street – *1844 Cherry St., Jacksonville.* 🅿 ☎ *904-384-1999. www.1bbweb.com. 4 rooms.* **$$** Near downtown (where Cherry Street ends at the mile-wide St. Johns River) this two-story brick house, embraced within historic Riverside, dates from Jacksonville's renewal after the great fire of 1901. The 14ft-ceilinged foyer, parlor, porch and dining room occupy the downstairs; guest rooms sit above, most with river views, and all furnished with solid antiques. Throughout are collections of clocks, duck decoys, American coverlets, and Oriental rugs on oak and pine floors. Breakfast served inside or on the porch is continental midweek, full on weekends.

Riverview Hotel – *103 Flagler Ave., New Smyrna Beach.* ✗ ♿ 🅿 ⌕ ☎ *386-428-5858 or 800-945-7416. www.riverviewhotel.com. 18 rooms, 1 cottage.* **$$** Dowager of Flagler Avenue, this 1885 hotel lately gave in to the street's playful style, its exterior now painted pink, its gingerbread renewed and canopies freshened. Today the three-story survivor at the foot of the draw-

bridge fits in with the shops of windsocks and casual wear leading to the beach:
Riverview's lobby is itself a busy gift store. Wicker, paddle fans, antique
armoires and floral spreads on reproduction four-posters create a tropical mood
in the guest rooms. Lodgers enjoy expanded continental breakfasts beneath the
palms by the pool. Seafood pasta, beef Wellington and the catch of the day are
served at **Riverview Restaurant**, the hotel's brick-walled hub of food and drink
overlooking the Intracoastal Waterway.

Dining in Jacksonville and the Northeast Coast

Beech Street Grill – *801 Beech St., Fernandina Beach.* ♿ ☎ *904-277-3662.*
www.beechstreetgrill.com. **$$$ Florida**. Since the Grill's opening in 1990, vaca-
tioners especially have flocked to this art-filled, two-story sea captain's house
built 101 years earlier, drawn as much by the refined interiors as the food.
Chippendale-style balustrades, marble mantels and fireplace facades set the
scene for signature dishes such as macadamia-nut-encrusted grouper with
curried citrus glaze, and Parmesan-encased red snapper with mustard-basil
cream. Many blackboard specials daily. *Dinner only.*

La Crepe en Haut – *142 E. Granada Blvd., Ormond Beach.* ☎ *386-673-1999.*
$$$ French. Graced with ornamental art, upholstered oval-back chairs and tex-
tured carpets, four warmly lit rooms, belle-epoque style, ensconce patrons at
this pricey, celebrity-favored haunt. The menu is rooted in French gastronomy
(the appetizers alone are astounding), while nightly specials satisfy more contemporary tastes with offerings like richly herbed seafood pasta, grouper with
risotto, baked salmon with almonds, and salads of arugula and Sonoma greens.
The restaurant cum bistro/bar is housed (since 1979) upstairs within a tree-
filled gallery of shops.

Matthew's – *2107 Hendricks Ave., Jacksonville.* ♿ ☎ *904-396-9922.*
www.matthewsatsanmarco.com. **$$$ New American**. South of the river in stylish
San Marco, five chefs in white and five waiters in black perform balletic moves
within the open kitchen and a dining room that seats a mere 55. Walls of bur-
nished blond wood rise high above Jacksonville's influentials, who feast on Kobe
beef carpaccio, yellowtail snapper, or seared duck breast with foie gras ordered
from nightly changing menus. Alternatively, a five-course chef's tasting meal is
available. Patio dining depends on the weather. *Dinner only.*

Who's On Fourth – *22 S. 4th St., Fernandina Beach.* ♿ ☎ *904-261-7700.*
$$$ Seafood. Enter through a vine-covered arch and a corridor of movie-star mug
shots—notably of Abbot and Costello, whose famed routine "Who's on First?"
inspired the restaurant's name. The setting inside is quiet: 15 tables in a boxy
space conspicuously devoid of art. But the buzz in the box, much favored by
locals, goes on cocktail-party style, accompanied by live, soft guitar music.
Choices from the limited, but well-executed menu include customized vegetarian
dishes; veal with prosciutto over fettuccine; and grilled New York strip with shi-
itake demi-glace. Patio dining is available seasonally. *Dinner only.*

Cortessés Bistro – *172 San Marco Ave., St. Augustine.* ♿ ☎ *904-825-6775.*
$$ Continental. Intimate rooms with hardwood floors, clothed tables and fresh
flowers exude Old World charm at this bustling, Euro-style bistro. Blue Plate
specials share menu space with pasta primavera, Minorcan fish stew (lobster,
scallops and shrimp in stock, topped with romesco sauce) and veal Oscar. The
baci fudge tart typifies Cortessés' tempting desserts. Patrons may dine outside
in the greenery-garnished patio or sample late-night fare and live jazz in the
Flamingo Room bar.

Creekside Dinery – *160 Nix Boatyard Rd., St. Augustine.* ♿ ☎ *904-829-6113.*
$$ Low Country. It's hard to believe that a busy highway is only a quarter-mile
away from this rustic floorboarded house, set beside a misty marsh and sur-
rounded by tall oaks. Beer-battered shrimp, oak-planked grouper and broiled
seafood platters spice up the spacious, informal setting. Tiki torches discourage
the no-see-ums on the outdoor deck, but if you're not comfortable, retreat
inside, or to the screened-in porch for a table over the water. "Dainty Diners'
portions are available. Live music entertains patrons Wednesday through
Sunday. *Dinner only.*

First Street Grille – *807 N. 1st St., Jacksonville Beach.* ♿ ☎ *904-246-6555.*
$$ Seafood. Tiered seating rising behind big windows supplies most lunch and
dinner guests with views of the ocean at one of Jacksonville's best, yet sur-
prisingly affordable, beachside restaurants. Etched-glass dividers and white
tablecloths nod towards formality but dress is casual here. Favorite dishes
include sautéed red snapper, bayou shrimp, and roast rack of lamb. In warm
weather, choose the outdoor deck for access to the beach scene. A combo sets
up on weekends between the Tiki Bar and deck, and on Sundays there's an à
la carte brunch.

Lighthouse Landing – *4940 S. Peninsula Dr., Ponce Inlet.*   *904-761-9271.* **$$ Seafood.** Folks at this land's-end locale have lived off the sea since 1846. The pace here is permanently slow, so you'll want to work on a beer and soak up the Old Florida atmosphere at a weathered plank table while waiting for your order of oysters, shrimp or crab. Long past its working days, the skiff *Genevieve* sails on as an inside bar. Of the quirky signs that decorate the restaurant's walls, perhaps the best reads: "Today's soup, cream of yesterday's special." Ponce de León Inlet Light *(p 106)* rises across the dirt road.

Jacksonville Landing

Gwen Cannon/MICHELIN

Florida Theatre – *128 E. Forsyth St. Performances year-round. Access during non-performance times by appointment only.*   *Box office*   *904-355-2787. www.ftjax.com.* This historic Mediterranean Revival building (1927) is a survivor of America's era of opulent movie palaces. The theater closed as a movie house in 1980, but was renovated and reopened in 1983 as a performing-arts center hosting concerts, lectures and films. The lobby whimsically re-creates a Moorish courtyard by night, with side balconies and deep blue ceilings.

Jacksonville Museum of Modern Art (JMoMA) – *333 N. Laura St. Preview gallery open year-round Tue-Fri 11am-2pm.*   *904-366-6911. www.jmoma.org.* In 2001 the museum, founded in 1924 as the Fine Arts Society, relocated downtown to historic Hemming Plaza adjacent to Jacksonville's City Hall. Known as JMoMA, the museum occupies five floors in the former Western Union building (1931) designed by local architects Marsh & Saxelbye. Renovation begun in 2000 is expected to be completed for full opening in the fall of 2002 and will include a museum store and cafe. Works by local and Florida artists are featured at this regional museum. Pre-Columbian artifacts and artworks by Alexander Calder, Ellsworth Kelly and Helen Frankenthaler highlight the permanent collection.

Ritz Theatre & LaVilla Museum – *829 N. Davis St. Open year-round Tue-Fri 10am-6pm, Sat 10am-2pm, Sun 2pm-5pm. Closed major holidays. $4.*   *904-632-5555.* This theater, museum and gallery celebrate one of the richest African-American communities of the bygone South. LaVilla first flourished as an antebellum plantation, and during Reconstruction as an independent, largely black-governed municipality, before annexation by the city of Jacksonville. The 20C heyday of this "Harlem of the South" derived largely from a dynamic mix of entre-preneurs, the working class and professionals, including the songwriting Johnson brothers, James Weldon and J. Rosamond, whose tunes and theater productions played in New York and elsewhere. Their story is featured in the museum. Art exhibits and concerts are part of the schedule of events at the Ritz.

Springfield Historic District – *Bounded by Hogan's Creek to the south, Boulevard to the west, 12th St. north and Ionia St. east.* This neighborhood just north of downtown is enjoying a revival after almost a century of decline. In the late 19C, Springfield emerged as a popular resort area, later becoming a center for military training during the Spanish-American War. The area bloomed after the fire of 1901: houses went up in the Classic, Colonial Revival, Eastlake and Queen Anne styles, with 3,000sq ft properties neighboring cozy bungalows. Henry John Klutho,

111

an architect who designed many Jacksonville buildings after the fire, briefly operated a movie studio here. However, suburbanization following WWII led to the
district's decline. Its renewal began in the mid-1980s when one square mile was
listed on the National Register of Historic Places. Today a newly diversified, largely
African-American neighborhood is reaping recent investments, yielding a mix of
rehabilitated residences and locally owned stores and restaurants, though still with
aspects of blight. Landmark at the southwest edge of the district is **Bethel Baptist
Institutional Church** *(215 Bethel Baptist St.)*, a massive yellow brick structure, dominated by its bell tower.

★**Riverside/Avondale Historic District** – *Bounded by the St. Johns River on the
south and by I-10 and I-95 on the north.* Jacksonville's showcase neighborhoods
reveal a variety of architectural styles: Mediterranean Revival, Art Deco, Queen
Anne, Colonial Revival, Georgian, Shingle, Tudor, Prairie and Bungalow. Developed
after the great fire of 1901, both Riverside and Avondale enjoyed a long heyday
as Jacksonville's most desirable addresses. Several houses in this district were
designed by Henry John Klutho, who favored the Prairie style. The entire area was
placed on the National Register of Historic Places in 1985.

■ The Great Fire

On the afternoon of May 3, 1901, a fire broke out at the Cleveland Fibre
Factory near downtown. A deadly gusting wind carried sparks to the dry
wood and pitch rooftops of nearby buildings, and within an hour the city
erupted in flames. The conflagration consumed most of downtown and
many residential areas. The worst disaster in Jacksonville's history, the fire
nevertheless provided the city with an opportunity to transform itself.
Architects and artisans flocked here, and a new downtown rose quickly
from the ashes. Newspaperman H.L. Mencken, who had covered the fire
for the *Baltimore Morning Herald*, reported that Jacksonville's population
more than doubled in the decade following the fire.

Riverside Avenue between Memorial Park and Van Wert Street is the backbone of
the historic area; streets between here and the river retain the most elegant, best-
preserved houses. **Memorial Park** *(1600 block of Riverside Ave.)*, recently
rehabilitated and now a focal point for community events, was designed by
Frederick Law Olmsted to commemorate Florida's World War I veterans. Nearby
Five Points *(intersection of Park, Margaret and Lomax Sts.)* offers offbeat shopping
and dining in an eclectic, historic setting, popular with youth.
Drive down **St. Johns Avenue** for a pleasant passage beneath enormous live oak trees.

Some of the largest, most elaborate
mansions survive along this broad thoroughfare. The avenue passes the **Shops of
Historic Avondale** *(St. Johns Ave. at Ingle-
side)*, an assemblage of upscale boutiques and restaurants established in the
1920s.

Well worth a look is the looming **Riverside
Baptist Church**★ *(intersection of Park and
King Sts.)*, a massive Mediterranean Re-
vival edifice conceived by celebrated
Florida architect Addison Mizner.

★★**Cummer Museum of Art and
Gardens** – *829 Riverside Ave., at Post
St. Open year-round Tue & Thu 10am-
9pm; Wed, Fri & Sat 10am-5pm; Su
noon-5pm. Closed major holidays. $6.
&. ☐ ☎ 904-356-6857. www.cum-
mer.org.* This elegant museum holds
broad collection of European and American art and decorative arts. With its remarkable **riverfront setting** and interactive
arts education center, the Cummer
boasts a reputation as one of Florida's
best small art museums.

Jacksonville residents Arthur and Ninah
Cummer constructed a grand residence
on the Riverside estate that belonged to
his father, lumber baron Wellington W.
Cummer. Ninah planted formal gardens

❶ Heartworks Gallery & Cafe
*Map p 114. 820 Lomax St.
in Five Points ☎ 904-355-
6210.* After a morning at
the Cummer Museum, drive
around the corner for lunch
in colorful Five Points. The
nondescript facade of this
cafe belies its laid-back pace
and funky interior, where a
gallery of artistic
concoctions leads to an
equally eclectic eating space.
Along with daily board
specials, the carrot dog
(organic carrot on Dijon
bun) with twice-baked
hazelnut potatoes; black
bean chili salad; and other
creations are offered with
healthy tickers in mind. The
hummus pita (with
sunflower seeds, sprouts
and feta) is especially
heartwarming. A stroll along
shop-lined Park Street
should provide the requisite
post-meal exercise.

and decorated the house with fine art. After her death the mansion and its art treasures were converted to a museum, as her will stipulated. In the 1960s the house was demolished and a new museum structure erected on the site, but the original Italian and English formal gardens were retained, as was the mahogany-paneled Tudor Room. Through acquisitions and gifts, the collection has expanded to more than 4,000 works.

Begin in the concourse gallery to the left of the entrance foyer. By proceeding clockwise through galleries around an open courtyard, visitors witness a progression of works from classical antiquity to the 20C. Two galleries facing the garden *(nos. 5 and 6)* are reserved for temporary exhibits.

After viewing pre-Columbian, Egyptian and ancient Roman artifacts in the concourse gallery, proceed through galleries 1 to 4 to see oil and tempera Gothic and Renaissance panels, and Renaissance, Baroque and Mannerist oil paintings. Highlights include *Madonna and Child* (c.1400) by Antonio Gaddi, woodcuts by Albrecht Dürer, and works by Cranach the Elder, Giorgio Vasari, Salomon van Ruysdael and Peter Paul Rubens.

The Wark collection of **early Meissen porcelain** occupies gallery 7 *(across the court-yard)* and includes some 750 pieces of tableware dating from 1710-50, the first 40 years of European porcelain production. During this period, the factory in Meissen, Germany, was the first and only manufacturer of true, hard-paste white porcelain outside China. Don't miss the two complete 18C tea services, one owned by Marie, the last Queen of Hannover; and a dinner service owned by Elizabeth, Empress of Russia.

American art appears in galleries 8 and 9, the centerpiece of the latter being Thomas Moran's monumental *Ponce de León in Florida* (1878), a recent acquisition. Paintings by Winslow Homer, Thomas Sully and George Inness figure among the other fine landscapes and portraits on view. A luminous trio of works by William-Adolphe Bouguereau highlights 19C European paintings in gallery 10, while gallery 11 offers selections from European and American Impressionism and contemporary art.

The concourse gallery leads to **Art Connections** Kids, the

Horoldt Saucer, Meissen (c.1725)

Cummer Museum, Jacksonville

center where colorful, free-standing displays interpret aspects of art education. Formal Italian and English **gardens** behind the museum offer pergola-shaded paths among meticulously maintained greens and hedges, statuary and reflecting pools. Beyond the grounds rolls the St. Johns River.

South of the River

Riverwalk – The broad expanse of boardwalk extending a mile along the south bank across from downtown draws joggers, strollers and noontime lunchers by day, meanderers by evening, and fun-loving revelers during several annual festivals. The walk offers some of the best views of the river and the north bank, with Jacksonville Landing framed by gleaming office towers. Lovers of seafaring lore will enjoy the **Jacksonville Maritime Museum** (**M**¹), a small collection of artifacts presenting the city's maritime history *(1015 Museum Cir., Unit #2, at foot of Main St. Bridge; open year-round Mon-Thu 10:30am-3pm, Fri & Sat 10:30am-5pm, Sun 1pm-5pm; closed Jan 1, Dec 25;* & 🅿 ☎ *904-398-9011; www.jaxmarmus.com).* The **Jacksonville Historical Center** (**M**²) likewise presents the city's past from pioneer days to the present through artifacts, photographs and panel displays *(next door to Maritime Museum; open year-round daily noon-5pm;* & ☎ *904-398-4301).* Just west of the Main Street bridge lies Friendship Park, established in 1965; the geyserlike **fountain** at its center shoots jets of water high into the air.

★ **Museum of Science and History and Planetarium** – Kids *1025 Museum Cir. Open year-round Mon-Fri 10am-5pm, Sat 10am-6pm, Sun 1pm-6pm. Closed major holidays. $6.* & 🅿 ☎ *904-396-7062. www.jacksonvillemuseum.com.* History is adventure and science is fun at this hands-on museum near the foot of Main Street Bridge. Exhibits designed for all ages explore natural and physical sciences, regional natural history and North Florida's past.

113

The first floor reveals the mysteries of chemistry, physics and biology. **Atlantic Tails** studies threatened marine mammals in northeast Florida waters. **Living World** houses creatures from water, land and air, while the conservation-oriented **Hixon Courtyard** displays a landscaped floral garden. Highlighting the upper-level, **Currents of Time: A History of Jacksonville and Northeast Florida** begins around 10,000 BC and continues to the turn of the 21C, featuring music of each period; note especially the chant-and-response that anticipates jazz. Be sure to see the Civil War steamship sunk by a Confederate "torpedo" in 1864 in the St. Johns River.

The Alexander Brest Planetarium boasts a state-of-the-art sound system. Multimedia shows are held daily *(fee included in admission price; check at ticket office for show times)*.

ADDITIONAL SIGHTS

Map p 116

Jacksonville Zoo – [Kids] *8605 Zoo Pkwy. From downtown, drive north on I-95 to Hecksher Dr./Exit 124. Turn right and continue .5mi to zoo. Open year-round daily 9am-5pm. Closed Thanksgiving Day and Dec 25. $6.50.* ✗ ⴲ ⴲ ⴲ *904-757-4463. www.jaxzoo.org.* With some 750 reptiles, birds and mammals thriving on its 73-acre site on the Trout River, this zoo ranks as a leader in botanical and zoological conservation; more than six endangered species have been successfully bred here. A highlight is the **African veldt**, where a boardwalk crosses a 16-acre grassy enclosure, home to lions, ostriches and gazelles. **Seronera Overlook** puts visitors face-to-face with elephants keeping cool in a 275,000gal pool; an adjacent reptile house displays venomous snakes. At the **Great Apes of the World**, only a thin pane of Plexiglas separates viewers from western lowland gorillas, chimpanzees and other primates. **Wild Florida** features Florida's wetlands and its denizens such as alligators, bobcats and flamingos; be sure to take the bog walk. In the petting zoo at **Okavango Village**, a re-created fishing community in southwest Africa, kids encounter pygmy goats and miniature horses. Footsore visitors can hop aboard the **Okavango Railroad** *(runs every half-hour; round-trip 30min; $5).* Plans call for completion of a Latin American animals exhibit by 2004.

Anheuser-Busch Brewery – *111 Busch Dr. From downtown Jacksonville, drive north on I-95 to Busch Ave. east/Exit 125 and follow signs. Open year-round Mon-Sat 9am-4pm. Closed major holidays.* ⴲ ⴲ ⴲ *904-696-8373. www.budweiser tours.com. If under 18 years of age, must be accompanied by an adult.* Fresh, yeasty aromas fill the air at this massive brewery north of downtown. Inside, a self-guided tour introduces the brewing and bottling processes and tells the long and colorful company history. In business since 1852, Anheuser-Busch Companies, Inc., operates numerous popular Florida theme parks, including SeaWorld, Cypress Gardens and Busch Gardens.

Alexander Brest Museum – *2800 University Blvd. N., on Jacksonville University campus. Use north entrance to campus and bear left; follow signs to museum. Open year-round Mon-Fri 9am-5pm, Sat noon-5pm. Closed university holidays.* ⴲ ⴲ ⴲ *904-744-3950.* A modest yet significant collection of decorative arts and pre-Columbian artifacts occupies four galleries of the Phillips Fine Arts Building. Most of the collection was acquired by Jacksonville engineer and businessman Alexander Brest, whose construction firm built much of the city's early road network. Be sure to see the **Tiffany and Steuben glass** and selected pieces of **Boehm porcelain** and intricately carved European and 17C-19C oriental **ivories**. The small wood-frame **cottage** just behind the Phillips building was occupied during the mid-1880s by English composer **Frederick Delius**, who settled in nearby Solano Grove while trying to establish himself as an orange grower. The cottage was moved here from Solano Grove in 1961.

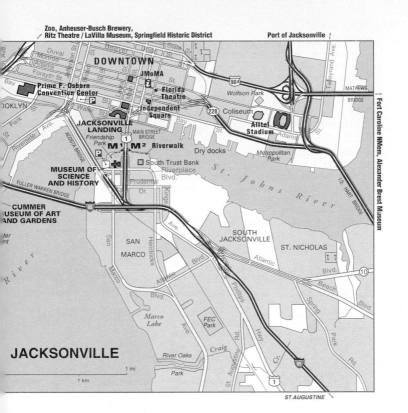

Zoo, Anheuser-Busch Brewery,
Ritz Theatre / LaVilla Museum, Springfield Historic District   Port of Jacksonville

DOWNTOWN

Duval
Monroe
Adams
Forsyth St.

JMoMA

Prime F. Osbern
Convention Center

Florida
Theatre

Wolfson Park

Independent
Square

JACKSONVILLE
LANDING

Coliseum

Friendship
Park

Riverwalk

Alltel
Stadium

MAIN STREET
BRIDGE

Dry docks

Metropolitan
Park

South Trust Bank
Riverplace
Blvd.

MUSEUM OF
SCIENCE
AND HISTORY

St. Johns River

CUMMER
MUSEUM OF ART
AND GARDENS

SOUTH
JACKSONVILLE

ST. NICHOLAS

SAN
MARCO

Marco
Lake

FEC
Park

River Oaks
Park

Craig

JACKSONVILLE

1 mi
1 km

ST. AUGUSTINE

Fort Caroline NMem, Alexander Brest Museum

★**Fort Caroline National Memorial** – *12713 Fort Caroline Rd. 13mi from downtown
via Rte. 10A/115 east. Turn left (north) on Monument Rd. and follow signs to park.
Open year-round daily 9am-5pm. Closed Dec 25.* ♿ 🅿 ☎ *904-641-7155. Insect
repellent recommended.* This replicated fort on the south bank of the St. Johns
River depicts what the original fort may have looked like. The fate of Fort Caroline
mirrors the fate of 16C French attempts to gain sovereignty in the New World.

■ **A Somber Tale**

Fort Caroline was established in 1564 by some 300 Huguenots who arrived
from France under the command of René de Laudonnière. On board was
Jacques Le Moyne, a French artist assigned to document the expedition. They
erected a triangular wooden fort some 5mi upriver. Starvation was rampant
that spring of 1565. Disheartened, the French were preparing to abandon
the colony when Huguenot mariner **Jean Ribault** arrived with fresh supply
ships from France. He brought disturbing news: the Spanish king was
sending an armada under the command of Pedro Menéndez de Avilés to
attack the French settlement. The Spanish arrived shortly after Ribault, but
the confrontation proved inconclusive. Determined to attack the Spanish
before they could return, Ribault set sail, only to be swept far south of his
goal by hurricane winds.

After establishing a beachhead at St. Augustine, Menéndez marched north
to Fort Caroline and slaughtered the French, sparing women and children.
The 50-some men who escaped, de Laudonnière and Le Moyne among
them, returned to France. Menéndez garrisoned Fort Caroline and returned
to St. Augustine.

The Spanish hastened to forestall Ribault and his men, who had been seen
making their way up the coast on foot in two separate columns. Eventually
they met a party of Frenchmen south of St. Augustine. Unarmed and
starving, the French surrendered but were killed by Menéndez' soldiers.
The second French column, Ribault among them, were similarly dispatched.
Thereafter, the inlet, beach and river were known by the name *matanzas*
(Spanish for "place of slaughters"). Fort Caroline (renamed San Matéo)
remained a Spanish stronghold until 1568, when a Frenchman on a mission
of revenge burned the fort to the ground, killing all of its occupants. The
Spanish rebuilt the fort, only to abandon it the following year.

115

Begin at the visitor center, where displays recount the story of the fort and of the French attempts to establish a stronghold in the New World. Artifacts on display include period weapons, tools, armor and Timucuan Indian artifacts.

From the visitor center, a short path leads to the reconstructed fort. The present version, erected in 1964, is based on the drawings of the artist Le Moyne, and is estimated to be about two-thirds the size of the original. The actual site of Fort Caroline is believed to have been on a river plain that was eroded away by tides after the river channel was dredged in the 1880s. A monument to Jean Ribault marks a scenic overlook on the St. Johns River, .5mi east of the park entrance.

Naval Station Mayport – *On Mayport Rd., 15mi from downtown. Take Atlantic Blvd. (Rte. 10) east to Mayport Rd. (A1A) and turn left; follow signs to entrance gate.* Commissioned in 1942, this bustling 3,409-acre military base at the mouth of the St. Johns River ranks among the largest naval installations in the US.

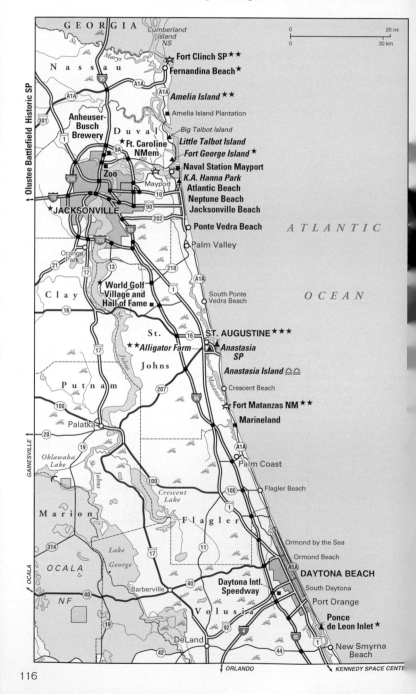

Mayport is home base to five squadrons of Light Airborne Multipurpose System Mark III helicopters and 23 ships, including destroyers, frigates, guided-missile cruisers and an aircraft carrier. Through Mayport's weekend **Visit Ship** program, one vessel is made accessible for guided tours *(vessels change weekly; visit by 1hr guided tour only, year-round Sat 10am-4pm, Sun 1pm-4pm; ☎ 904-270-6289)*. A brick lighthouse, erected in 1859, sits on the property *(not open to the public)*. The historic fishing village of **Mayport** *(west of naval base via A1A)* offers rough charm in its narrow streets, shrimping vessels and "shrimp shacks" that serve up bounteous portions of fresh crustaceans. A1A crosses the St. Johns River via car ferry from Mayport landing to Fort George Island *(operates year-round daily 6:20am-10pm every half hour; one-way 10min; $2.75/car and driver, 50¢/person; St. Johns River Ferry Service & ☎ 904-241-9969)*.

THE SEA ISLANDS *Map p 116*

*Fort George Island

20mi northeast of Jacksonville. From downtown take I-95 7mi north to Exit 124 (Heckscher Dr. east). Continue east 15mi to Fort George Rd. and turn left.

Though this lush sea island bordering St. Johns River to the north holds stories from every phase of Florida's human history, Fort George Island bears few marks of its long occupation. Timucuan Indians lived here for 3,500 years before the French—and later the Spanish—laid claim to Florida. Mission San Juan del Puerto (for which the river was named) was founded here in 1587 by Spanish monks. It is thought that a fort established by British Gen. James Oglethorpe was located near the island's center, though no traces remain.

During the 1760s, the island flourished as a profitable plantation. Today the land seems to be returning to wilderness: Timucuan shell middens lie concealed beneath dense overgrowth; elegant Sabal palms lining the avenue to Kingsley Plantation are nearly dwarfed by surrounding evergreens; and tall stands of pampas grass flourish on the fairways of the deserted Ribault Club, once an exclusive golf resort. The plantation, along with Fort Caroline, lies on land protected by the 46,000-acre Timucuan Ecological and Historical Preserve.

★**Kingsley Plantation** – *11676 Palmetto Ave. From Fort George Rd. turn left onto unpaved Palmetto Ave. and continue 2mi to plantation. Open year-round daily 9am-5pm. Closed Dec 25. ▣ ☎ 904-251-3537. Insect repellent recommended. Information desk located at the main house.* The oldest remaining plantation house in the state, and best-preserved example of the plantation system that flourished in Florida's Territorial Period, lies at the end of a peaceful, forested road. Kingsley Plantation originally formed part of a land grant given by the governor of Spain to John McQueen, who in the 1790s erected the stately house that sits today near a sleepy marsh. The property was sold in 1817 to Zephaniah Kingsley, a wealthy member of the Florida Territory's Second Legislative Council. Convinced that the viability of Florida's plantations depended on slavery, Kingsley advocated a "task system" that allowed slaves to attend to family needs. A maverick for his time, he married an African woman and provided for her and their four children. An important producer of Sea Island cotton, the plantation passed through several hands, including Kingsley's nephew, before being acquired by the state in 1955.

Begin at the **main house**, where interpretive displays examine the Sea Island cotton industry and the life of Zephaniah Kingsley and his nephew. Exhibits in the adjacent kitchen building recall the life of slaves at the plantation. Ruins of 23 of the original 32 slave cabins—built of tabby, a compound of lime, sand and shells—stand in a semicircle near the entrance to the plantation site.

If you stay on Fort George Road instead of turning off for the plantation, **Fort George Island State Cultural Site** *(open daily year-round; & ☎ 904-251-2320)* offers a 4.4mi loop drive around the island with 28 numbered signposts marking points of historic interest *(self-guided tour booklets available at the Old Ribault Club, 1.5mi from entrance on right)*.

Little Talbot Island *Just east of Fort George Island via A1A.*

Sheltering Fort George Island from the Atlantic's force, this 2,500-acre barrier island has remained free of development save for the facilities of **Little Talbot Island State Park**. Occupying the entire island, the park offers miles of pristine, white-sand beaches≈, as well as a hiking trail (4.1mi) through live oaks and hollies in the hardwood hammock on the island's west side *(park hrs & fees p 350 ; & ▣ ☎ 904-251-2320)*.

On neighboring **Big Talbot Island** *(just northwest of Little Talbot Island via A1A)*, large sections of the hammock are developed as private residences.

★★Amelia Island *42mi northeast of Jacksonville via A1A.*

Vacationers flock to this 13.5mi barrier island in Florida's northeasternmost corner. Named by Gen. James Oglethorpe after Princess Amelia (daughter of King George II of England), the island lies across St. Marys River from Georgia's Cumberland Island. Virgin beaches, salt marshes and hardwood forests attract nature lovers, while golf courses, championship tennis facilities and the resort amenities of exclusive **Amelia Island Plantation** and **The Ritz-Carlton, Amelia Island** lure sybaritic visitors. In the town of Fernandina Beach, the Centre Street Historic District holds boutiques, specialty shops and impressive Victorian houses. Despite its popularity, the island seems sparsely inhabited throughout the year.

MMMmm is for Magna's
103 Centre Street. ☎ *904-321-0404.* You'll probably agree that the perfect remedy for the overexertions of sightseeing can be found at this upscale salon. A full complement of services is available at Magna's—from pedicures and facials to manicures and massage. If you have only a few minutes, opt for the Chair Massage at $1 per 60 seconds. If you can spare an hour, go for the Classic Swedish Ultimate massage *($75)* or the Body Wrap with Foot Massage *($90)*. The latter pampering offers a choice of thermal-blanket wraps; you might want to try the Tranquillity Moisture Cocoon or the Sea Salt Body Polish.

★**Fernandina Beach** – *On the north end of Amelia Island. Follow A1A north and turn left on Atlantic Ave., which becomes Centre St.* Named for Ferdinand, consort to Queen Isabella of Spain, the town was established in the late 18C, thriving as a port on the border between Spanish Florida and the US; smugglers routed clandestine goods through here when Thomas Jefferson's Embargo Act of 1807 closed US ports to foreign shipping.

As president of the Florida Railroad Co., Sen. **David Yulee** (1810-1886) persuaded residents to move the town south from its swampy site to its present location, where goods could easily be transferred from rail to cargo steamer. After the Civil War, Fernandina experienced a "Golden Age" of growth as shipping increased and tourists came to enjoy Florida's salubrious climate.

The **Old Fernandina Depot** (1899) now houses the chamber of commerce where walking-tour maps of the historic district are available *(102 Centre St. open year-round Mon-Fri 9am-5pm, Sa 10am-2pm;* & ▯ ☎ *904-261-3248).*

Shrimp Boats along Fernandina Docks

★**Centre Street Historic District** – *Centre St. between 11th St. and Front St., bounded on the north and south by Escambia and Elm Sts.* Fernandina's principal east-west artery dead-ends at the waterfront overlooking the Amelia River. The street lies at the heart of a 50-square-block National Historic District filled with 450-plus structures built between 1857 and 1910. The heaviest concentrations of historic buildings lie along North Sixth and South Seventh streets, and Centre Street itself. Most prominent is the brick **Nassau County Courthouse** *(Centre St. at 5th St.),* an eye-catching Victorian structure (1891). Don't miss **Tabby House** *(northwest corner of 7th and Ash Sts.)*, built in 1885 of tabby and Portland cement. The 1895 **Bailey House** *(opposite Tabby House)* sports the towers and fish-scale exterior paneling typical of Queen Anne style. **Fairbanks House** *(S. 7th and Cedar Sts.)* is a stunning Italianate pile (1885). Also worth seeing is eclectic **Villa las Palmas** *(315 Alachua St.)*, a cedar-shingled residence dating from 1910.

Amelia Island Museum of History – *233 S. 3rd St., 3 blocks south of Centre St. Visit by guided tour only, year-round Mon-Sat 11am & 2pm. $4. Library and 2nd floor open year-round Mon-Fri 10am-5pm. Closed major holidays.* ▣ ☏ *904-261-7378.* Lovingly refurbished, the former county jail today guards local history. A departure from traditional museums, this "oral-history museum" features unlabeled artifacts and maps. Information is provided by docents who regale visitors with the story of Amelia Island. Tours proceed at a leisurely pace through display rooms; a reference room stocked with historical information, maps and architectural documents is open to visitors. The museum operates architectural and historical walking tours of sections of Fernandina Beach and Centre Street *(2hr guided walking tour departs from Old Depot at the foot of Centre St. year-round Mon-Sat; reservations required; $10).*

★★**Fort Clinch State Park** – *2601 Atlantic Ave. Park entrance just west of A1A. Park hrs & fees p 350.* ⚠ ▣ *Fort open year-round daily 9am-5pm; $2.* ⚠ ▣ ☏ *904-277-7274.* This splendid expanse offers access to a wide beach, a fishing pier and nature trails; its centerpiece is a well-preserved brick fort. Separated from Georgia by the St. Marys River, Fort Clinch was established in the late 1840s to protect Cumberland Sound, gateway to Fernandina Harbor, and named for Gen. Duncan Lamont Clinch, a hero of the Seminole Wars.

Fort construction was incomplete when the Civil War began in 1861; Confederate troops took Fort Clinch easily. The following year, the Georgia and South Carolina sea islands fell into Union hands, leaving Florida in isolation; the Confederates quickly withdrew. By the late 1860s, the fort's brick and masonry walls were vulnerable to heavier shot from newly invented rifle-barreled cannons. The federal government deactivated the obsolete fort in 1867, maintaining it without a garrison except briefly during the Spanish-American War. Fort Clinch opened in 1938 as one of Florida's first state parks.

Displays in the visitor center outline US government defense systems prior to the 1840s and detail the construction of Fort Clinch. From the center, a short path leads to the fort, its massive pentagonal walls interrupted only by a wooden drawbridge. Visitors are free to roam the impressive four-acre interior, exploring rooms, bomb-proof shelters and officers' quarters, or to climb the ramparts for a **view** of Cumberland Island across the river. Rangers in period dress offer daily living-history demonstrations, illustrating the life of soldiers billeted here.

Bookstore Browsing

Amelia Island's historic downtown holds a variety of shops and galleries of interest to serious shoppers or to simply the window variety. Two Centre Street bookstores contain a treasury of tomes about local lore and history as well as readings on the region and Florida itself. In the heat of midday or after a meal, stroll into **Books Plus** *(107 Centre St.; ☏ 904-261-0303)*, a spacious repository of the latest fiction, mystery stories, travel guides and children's books, to name a few of the store's many categories. There's also a selection of singular greeting cards, stationery and journals. Then amble on to **The Book Loft** *(214 Centre St.; ☏ 904-261-8991)* to check out this intimate booknook's shelf contents. You may find biographies of famous Floridians, expertise on the state's fauna or stories about pirates among the thousands of new and used titles here. Staff members at both stores are friendly and helpful.

ST. AUGUSTINE★★★

Population 11,592
Map p 121
Tourist Information: www.visitoldcity.com ☎ 904-829-1711 or 800-653-2489

The oldest continuously occupied European settlement in the US (from 1565) lies on Florida's east coast, 33mi south of Jacksonville. Situated on a finger of land extending south from the mainland, between the Matanzas River on the east and the San Sebastián River on the west, historic St. Augustine mingles humble, one-story 18C structures with architectural showpieces from the 19C, cheek-by-jowl with 20C tourist attractions. The city's time-burnished flavor is captured in narrow, cobbled lanes lined with red-roofed buildings of pale coquina, many of them survivors of the 18C.

Historical Notes

European Tug of War – In 1565 Spanish ships commanded by **Pedro Menéndez de Avilés** dropped anchor near the present-day harbor. Menéndez' mission was to overpower "heretical" French Huguenots at Fort Caroline, who claimed the territory as their own, and to establish two cities as footholds of the Spanish empire. About 600 settlers set about building a fort between the Matanzas and San Sebastián rivers. The new colony was named St. Augustine in honor of the patron saint of Avilés, Menéndez' hometown. Ill-equipped to raise food, settlers plundered the stored harvests of the Indians. In retaliation, the natives drove colonists from their homes to their flimsy wooden fort. In 1587 St. Augustine became the capital of Spanish Florida. Subsequent years brought peace in concert with the success of Franciscan missionary efforts among the Timucuans. Beginning in 1565, a chain of about 100 **missions** grew northward along the coast, but had disappeared by the early 18C, victims of British raids and the elements.

■ Henry Morrison Flagler

The son of an itinerant Presbyterian minister, Flagler (1830-1913) was born in Hopewell, New York. At age 14, sick of school, he set out to Ohio to make his fortune. There he landed a job in a general store for $5 a month, and soon developed a knack for salesmanship. Eventually Henry entered into partnership with his friend, wealthy industrialist John D. Rockefeller. Their oil refinery, incorporated in 1870 as Standard Oil Co., established huge fortunes for the two influential men.

Henry M. Flagler (c.1905)

Henry Morrison Flagler Museum Archives

Flagler visited Florida in 1877 on the advice of doctors treating his invalid wife, Mary. Widowed by 1883, Flagler honeymooned in St. Augustine with his second wife—Mary's former nurse, Ida Alice Shourds. The businessman shrewdly observed that while its agreeable climate drew wealthy winter visitors, the city offered few amenities. Two years later, Flagler had hatched a plan to erect a luxury hotel and transform St. Augustine into a resort rivaling France's Riviera. His plan involved improving the railway to link the city with the populous centers of the Eastern seaboard. Flagler's massive **Ponce de Leon Hotel**, its less elegant counterpart the Hotel Alcazar, and the Casa Monica Hotel, a large property that he purchased, formed the basis of St. Augustine's heyday as Florida's premier resort destination. The oil magnate eventually acquired additional rail lines to found Florida East Coast Railway, extending south from Daytona to Miami via Palm Beach. Divorced and married a third time (his second wife had lapsed into incurable insanity), Flagler spent the rest of his life developing resorts in south Florida. Upon his death, his remains were interred at St. Augustine's **Memorial Presbyterian Church★**, a lavishly appointed Renaissance-style edifice (1889, Carrère and Hastings) commissioned by Flagler to commemorate his daughter, who died of complications from childbirth.

uropean challenge to Spain's sovereignty grew imminent in 1670 when England bunded the Carolina colony, with its capital at Charles Town some 275mi north. St. ugustine's governor began construction of a massive stone fort, Castillo de San Marcos. eposits of **coquina** had been discovered on nearby Anastasia Island; created by sedi-entation of seashells, the water-soaked stone proved an ideal material with which to uild a permanent fortification. In 1702 British troops tried unsuccessfully to penetrate e fortress walls. In 1740 the forces of British general **James Oglethorpe**, who had founded settlement at the Savannah River in 1733, marched on St. Augustine; they were later orced to retreat when Spanish reinforcements arrived from Cuba. However St. ugustine became British territory when Spain relinquished Florida to England by the **eaty of Paris** in exchange for Cuba, which had been captured by the British.

ritish St. Augustine – Following the transfer of land, nearly 3,000 Spanish citizens ailed from Florida to Cuba and the West Indies. The British settlers built roads, bunded public schools and erected buildings in St. Augustine. During the American evolution, the city became a training ground for forces preparing to defend Florida.

1783 the British governor received word that Florida was to be transferred back Spain under the new Treaty of Paris, by which Great Britain formally acknowledged merican independence.

121

Americanization – Only a handful of those Spanish settlers who had evacuated 20 years earlier chose to return. Instead, St. Augustine was peopled by a hodgepodge of Spanish, English, American, Minorcan, Italian, Greek, Swiss, German, French and Scottish settlers, slaves, free blacks and Seminole Indians. As trade with the American states to the north increased, St. Augustine's Spanish culture declined.

The American states to the north grew more populous and their residents became hungrier for territory. Upon ratification of the **Adams-Onís Treaty** in 1821 by which Spain ceded Florida to the US, the American flag rose over the Castillo.

The end of the Civil War brought an improved rail line to the city, but it was the resumption of the tourist trade—and the arrival of H.M. Flagler in particular—that spurred St. Augustine's economic recovery after the war.

SIGHTS

Begin your visit at the city's modern **visitor center**, where knowledgeable staff will answer questions, make reservations and offer discount tickets to many area attractions. This is also a good place to obtain tickets for the privately owned **sightseeing trains** that tour the city throughout the day, stopping at points of interest. A small theater here screens a dramatization of St. Augustine's founding.

Practical Information ....Area Code: 904

Getting There – Jacksonville International Airport (JIA): 52mi north of St. Augustine via US-1 *(information: ☎ 741-4902)*. **Transportation to St. Augustine** *(advance reservations required)*: East Coast Transportation *($70/1-3 people; ☎ 246-3741)*, or Dial-a-Ride *($55/1-2 people; ☎ 829-0880)*. Rental car agencies *(p 343)* located at airport. Nearest Amtrak **train** station is in Palatka *(☎ 800-872-7245; www.amtrak.com)*. Greyhound **bus** station: 1000 Malaga St. *(☎ 800-231-2222; www.greyhound.com)*.

Getting Around – Visitors are encouraged to park in the Visitor Information Center parking lot. Parking regulations are strictly enforced; yellow curbs indicate no-parking zones.

Visitor Information – St. Johns County Visitors and Convention Bureau, 88 Riberia St., Suite 400, St. Augustine 32084 *(☎ 829-1711 or 800-653-2489; www.visitoldcity.com)*. City of St. Augustine Visitor Information Center, 10 Castillo Dr., near San Marco Ave. *(open Apr-May daily 8:30am-6:30pm, Jun-Labor Day daily 8:30am-6:30pm; rest of the year daily 8:30am-5:30pm; ✗ ♿ ⊡ [$3]; ☎ 825-1000)* . These organizations provide information on shopping, entertainment, festivals and recreation.

Accommodations – Area visitors **lodging directory** available *(free)* from St. Johns County Visitors and Convention Bureau. Accommodations range from **hotels** *($110-$245)* to **motels** *($55-$125)* and **bed-and-breakfast inns** *($100-$225)*. KOA **campground**: St. Augustine Beach *(☎ 471-3113)*; RV and camping at Indian Forest Campground *(☎ 824-3574)*. Rates quoted are average prices per night for a double room and are subject to seasonal variations. See *St. Augustine lodgings in Jacksonville Address Book*.

Sightseeing – Narrated **trolley tours** of historical district offer on-and-off privileges *(depart from Old Jail complex year-round daily 8:30am-5pm; every 15-20min; call for schedule and admission fees; ☎ 829-3800)*. Sightseeing **trains** depart from eight different stations and stop at attractions, shops and restaurants; tickets valid for three consecutive days *(depart from 170 San Marco Ave. and 7 other stations year-round daily 8:30am-5pm; every 15-20min; $12; package tours from $22-$62; ♿ ☎ 829-6545)*. Guided **walking tours** of Old St. Augustine *(year-round daily 8pm; $5)*, Ancient CityTours *(☎ 797-5604)*. **Horse-drawn carriage tours** *(year-round daily 8:30am-11pm; round-trip 1hr; $15 with a $50 minimum)* by St. Augustine Transfer Co. *(☎ 829-2818)*. Scenic **cruises** leave from Municipal Marina *(year-round daily 11am-4:30pm, extended hours during summer months, additional cruises mid-May-mid-Oct; round-trip 1hr 15min; $9.50; ♿ ⊡ ☎ 824-1806)*.

Sports and Recreation – St. Augustine Beach pier and the lighthouse pier offer excellent **fishing**; bait and tackle shop at 442 Ocean Vista Ave. Some area **golf** clubs welcome visitors: St. Augustine Shores Golf Club *(☎ 794-GOLF)*; St. Johns County Golf Course *(☎ 825-4900)*.

Shopping: St. George Street in the historic district *(☎ 829-1711)*; **Lightner Antique Mall** *(☎ 824-2874)*; **St. Augustine Outlet Center** with more than 90 factory outlet stores *(☎ 825-1555)*. **Belz Factory Outlet World** around 75 outlet stores *(☎ 826-1311)*.

Castillo and St. George Street

After a visit to the Castillo, a meander down **St. George Street** offers the best exposure to St. Augustine's past and present. This backbone of the old city retains its historic flavor despite an abundance of gift and souvenir shops, restaurants and other establishments catering to tourists. Many of these businesses occupy restored 18C buildings. St. George Street is closed to vehicular traffic between the Old City Gate *(north end of St. George St. at intersection with Orange St.)* and the **Plaza de la Constitución** *(bounded by St. George, King and Charlotte Sts. and Cathedral Pl.)*, a broad space laid out as a parade ground by Governor Mendez de Canzo about 1600.

St. George Street

★★**Castillo de San Marcos National Monument** – *1 S. Castillo Dr. at Orange St. Open year-round daily 8:45am-4:45pm. Closed Dec 25. $4. Cannon firings and reenactments: call for schedules.* ▣*(25¢/hr)* ☎ *904-829-6506. www.nps.gov/casa. Repairs and renovation starting spring 2001 may necessitate temporary closure of the site.* Defender of St. Augustine since the beginning of the 18C, the oldest masonry fort in the US overlooks Matanzas Bay at the northern boundary of the old city. The Castillo withstood every enemy attack that beset it and today ranks among the best-preserved examples of Spanish Colonial fortifications in the New World.

■ A Fortress of Stone

The increasing threat from English, Dutch and French forces convinced Spanish officials in Madrid that St. Augustine needed a permanent stone fortification. By 1671 rafts had begun ferrying blocks of coquina to the site from quarry pits on Anastasia Island. Construction continued fitfully, but by 1695 the Castillo was largely complete. Four-sided, with pointed triangular bastions at each corner, the structure boasted 12ft-thick outer walls broken only by an iron portcullis. The outwardly sloping lower walls were designed to counter artillery fire. A wooden drawbridge traversed a broad moat. During the 18C, barrel-vaulted rooms were added. A coquina ravelin was erected beyond the drawbridge, and an earthen embankment, or glacis, rose outside the moat.

By 1702 the fort had proven its worth, sheltering St. Augustine's residents within its walls as English troops sacked the town. England saw the Spanish fort as a threat to land it claimed in Georgia. In 1740 English warships under Gen. James Oglethorpe bombarded the fort for 27 days. Their cannonballs sank into the soft coquina walls, however, and did little damage. The Castillo was handed over to British authority in 1763, when Florida was transferred from Spain to Great Britain. Renamed Fort St. Mark and fortified during the American Revolution, the structure was recovered by Spain at the close of the war. In 1821 the Spanish flag was lowered here for the last time as Spain ceded Florida to the US. The Castillo, renamed Fort Marion for Revolutionary War commander Francis Marion (the legendary "Swamp Fox"), served as a military prison until the early 20C. In 1924 it was designated a national monument.

Castillo de San Marcos

Begin your visit by attending a ranger talk *(20-30min; daily from 10am every ho on the hour)* in the interior courtyard. Other rooms contain displays describing fo history. Don't miss the presentation of ordnance used at the fort; from this displa you must stoop to enter a low passageway leading to the powder magazine de in the northeast bastion. A long stairway ascends to the **gundeck**, outfitted wi some of the Castillo's original cannons and mortars. A panoramic **view** from he demonstrates the ease with which sentries could monitor an intruder's approac

Old City Gate – *North end of St. George St.* This handsome pair of coquina pilla supported a gate that served as the only entrance to the city through the Cu Line, a wood-and-earthwork fortification erected after the English attacked it 1702. The wall extended from the Castillo to the San Sebastián River. The prese coquina structures were built in 1808.

★**St. Photios National Greek Orthodox Shrine** – *41 St. George St. Open yea round daily 9am-5pm. Closed major holidays.* ♿ ☎ *904-829-8205.* The on national shrine of the Greek Orthodox Archdiocese of North and South Ameri occupies Avero House, an unassuming white historical residence. Dedicated in 197 to the first Greek settlers in the New World, the shrine honors St. Photios, t Ecumenical Patriarch of the Greek Orthodox Church. In 1768 nearly 2,000 Greek Minorcans, Corsicans and Italians left their troubled homelands for life in the Ne World. When living conditions at their New Smyrna colony (75mi south of S Augustine) became unbearable, the surviving settlers fled north in 1777 and esta lished a center for worship in the former Avero residence. The Greek Orthod Church purchased it in 1966.

Spanish Quarter Village

Exhibits tell the story of New Smyrna colony and the role of its survivors in the development of St. Augustine. In the shrine chapel, candles illuminate 30 **frescoes**, executed in the Byzantine style and depicting Christian saints and scenes from the life of Christ Jesus.

★**Spanish Quarter Village** – *33 St. George St. Open year-round daily 9am-5pm. Closed Dec 25. $6.50.* ☎ *904-825-6830.* Behind a low wall fronting St. George Street, this living-history museum re-creates the latter years of the city's first Spanish period. Within, eight structures have been rebuilt in accordance with research by the Historic St. Augustine Preservation Board.

After entering through Florencia House, visitors may walk the grassy "streets" of St. Augustine c.1740. The dwellings of a foot soldier, an artillery sergeant and a cavalryman emphasize variations in wealth, rank and status of soldiers based at the Castillo. A smithy works in the restored **blacksmith shop**, while costumed interpreters demonstrate activities of 18C life. One of the fine restored historic residences, **Mesa-Sanchez House** (**A**) began as a one-room coquina house built for the family of a shoreguard stationed at the Castillo *(visit by guided tour only)*. Guides recount the house's history as a residence, boardinghouse, barbershop, store and restaurant. Of special interest is a large display of kitchen tools.

★**Peña-Peck House** – *143 St. George St. Visit by guided tour (30min) only, year-round Mon-Sat 10am-4:30pm, Sun noon-4pm. Closed major holidays. $4.50.* ☎ *904-829-5064.* Erected in the 1740s as the residence of St. Augustine's royal treasurer, this gracious two-story edifice began as a simple, U-shaped building similar to those found throughout the city in the first Spanish period. It was renovated in the late 1830s by Dr. Seth Peck, a New Englander, for use as a medical office; a second story was added to accommodate the doctor's family. The house remained in the Peck family until 1931, when it was willed to the city by Dr. Peck's granddaughter. Today the Women's Exchange offers guided tours of the house, which is partly furnished with Peck family heirlooms.

★★**Cathedral-Basilica of St. Augustine** – *North side of Plaza de la Constitución. Open year-round daily 7am-5pm.* ♿ ☎ *904-824-2806. www.thefirstparish.org.* The scalloped facade and tower mark the home of the parish of St. Augustine, considered to have been founded in 1565, and therefore ranking as the oldest Catholic parish in the nation. The parish church was abandoned and relocated numerous times throughout the 18C. Not until 1793 did diocesan authorities commission a permanent structure of coquina north of the plaza. An 1887 fire destroyed all but the walls and facade. Noted architect James Renwick—who was visiting St. Augustine at the time of the fire—aided in the reconstruction. The cathedral was designated a Minor Basilica in 1976.

Inside, massive decorated timbers support the lofty ceiling above floors of colorful Cuban tile. A large, ornamental reredos of gold and white wood, incorporating the marble altar table from the original church, highlights the sanctuary.

King Street

★**Government House Museum** (**B**) – *48 King St. Open year-round daily 9am-5pm. Closed Dec 25. $2.50.* ♿ ☎ *904-825-6830.* A stately, two-story masonry edifice, Government House retained its official purpose throughout nearly 400 years of existence. The first construction on the site appeared in 1599. St. Augustine's governor stipulated that a parade ground be laid out surrounded by governmental buildings, among them his own residence. The house subsequently became the official governor's residence. A crumbling hulk by 1687, it was rebuilt of more durable coquina, but succumbed to fire during the British attack in 1702. Rebuilt by 1713, it was renovated in 1759 and again in the late 18C. After 1821 the US government used the structure as a courthouse, post office and civil services building. Today Government House serves as a museum and headquarters of the Historic St. Augustine Preservation Board.

Inside, a small museum provides a comprehensive look at the development of St. Augustine. Colorful displays describe the cultural collage of settlers during various periods of history and present aspects of life in the new settlement, including commerce, social structure, architecture and entertainment.

★**Flagler College** – *74 King St. Guided tours (30min) May-Aug & Christmas school break daily 10am-4pm; $4.* ♿ ☎ *904-829-6481. www.flagler.edu.* Formerly the Ponce de Leon Hotel, this grand edifice was the cornerstone of Henry Flagler's master plan to transform St. Augustine (and with it, much of Florida) into an American resort destination. The Spanish Renaissance building today houses the residence facilities, dining room and lecture halls of Flagler College.

Interior accessible by guided tour only. A handsome bronze statue of Henry Flagler stands before the arched main entrance leading into an arcaded courtyard. Tours begin in the Main Hall beneath an 84ft rotunda richly decorated with gold leaf and Maynard murals. The oak wainscoting, leaded-glass windows and whimsical, lion's-head light fixtures in the **dining room** are all original. Some of the most prominent

■ Florida's Ponce de Leon Hotel

Henry Flagler determined that his hotel would be a grand, permanent structure, reflecting the city's Spanish architectural heritage. Villa Zorayda offered the model: cast-in-place concrete construction. Flagler hired Thomas Hastings and John M. Carrère, an inexperienced team of young architects (Flagler's friendship with Hastings' father may have influenced his choice) who went on to an illustrious career, designing the New York Public Library. Working alongside were Bernard Maybeck (then in the early stages of his career) and Louis Comfort Tiffany. The interior decoration of the Ponce de Leon was Tiffany's first significant commission.

The architects produced the nation's first major building employing poured-concrete construction. It was embellished with Medieval, Moorish, Mediterranean and Victorian elements; most prominent are its Renaissance overtones. The twin bell towers remain today a distinctive feature of St. Augustine's skyline. Terra-cotta ornamentation adorns the gray concrete walls and palm trees flourish on the grounds. Decorated with Austrian crystal chandeliers crafted by Tiffany and dramatic murals painted by American artist George W. Maynard, the hotel opened for business in January 1888.

The Ponce de Leon fared well only a few years; economic downturns and competition curtailed the flow of vacationers. During World War II, the building was leased to the US Coast Guard. It reopened after the war but its days as a resort hotel were numbered. In 1967 the hotel ceased operation and the building was converted into the private liberal-arts college it houses today.

1 Second Read Books
See map. 51 Cordova St. ☎ *904-829-0334.* Forgot to bring a paperback along on your travels? Or just finished one and need new reading material? Then stop in at this small bookshop adjacent to Flagler College to peruse the selection of used hard- and softback fiction and nonfiction at bargain prices. Owned by two former teachers, six-year-old Second Read stocks a variety of titles of contemporary interest. Mysteries, science fiction, novels and cookbooks share shelf space with books on self-help and spirituality, women's studies and religion. The bookstore's purchase of pre-owned books depends upon their quality and topical appeal; payment is made in the form of store credit or cash.

figures of the early 20C, including presidents Warren Harding, Theodore Roosevelt and William McKinley, sat in these dining-room chairs.

★★ **Lightner Museum** – *75 King St., across from Flagler College. Open year-round daily 9am-5pm. Closed Dec 25. $6* ☎ *904-824-2874. www.lightnermuseum.org.* Echoing the Spanish flavor of Flagler College rises the massive bulk of Flagler's former Hotel Alcazar (1888). Today the corridors and rooms where guests once trod house a diverse assortment of decorative arts and collectibles, including an array of art glass. Sciences, natural and human, are the focus of exhibits on the first level; weights and scales, mineral collections and drafting tools are presented as if in a Victorian-era exhibition hall. Don't miss the steam engine created of blown glass. Antique instruments occupy the music room, and late-19C objects are displayed in a section outfitted as a Victorian village. The main baths *(second level)* house Lightner's extensive collection of **art glass**. From Bohemian to Bristol to spatter and spangle, the handsomely displayed pieces are grouped largely by type, style and manufacturer. Works by Louis Comfort Tiffany, as well as Wedgwood, Meissen, majolica and lusterware glass and porcelain are featured.

Intricately carved 19C furniture from India, samplers stitched in the 18C, and an Art Nouveau parlor suite number among the pieces in Lightner's decorative arts collection *(third level)*.

Zorayda Castle – *83 King St.* A glimpse of Moorish Spain in downtown St. Augustine, this compact, two-story concrete "castle," with its contrasting plain and richly ornamented surfaces, scalloped archways and square corner tower, was a radical departure from the city's primarily wood and coquina construction when it was built in 1883. Boston entrepreneur Franklin W. Smith commissioned Villa Zorayda, as he called it, in admiration for the Alhambra in Granada, Spain; the building was intended to replicate a wing of that 12C castle at one-tenth scale. St. Augustine's first poured-concrete structure, the villa served as the inspiration for Flagler's Ponce de Leon Hotel.

■ The Hotel Alcazar

Henry Flagler commissioned this hotel as a comfortable, yet less luxurious alternative to the Ponce de Leon Hotel. Designed by Carrère and Hastings, the poured-concrete structure boasted shops and a casino annex with a large swimming pool, ballroom, bowling alley, billiards room and a gymnasium and spa—including Russian (dry) and Turkish (steam) baths. To Flagler's surprise, guests preferred the relaxed atmosphere of the Alcazar to the more formal Ponce de Leon, and the hotel soon outstripped its neighbor in popularity. The same economic factors that slowed business at the Ponce de Leon also proved the Alcazar's undoing. The hotel closed its doors for good in 1937.

In 1946, empty and forlorn, the building was purchased by Otto C. Lightner, a Chicago publisher. Following his own credo that "everyone can be a collector of something," Lightner had amassed a rather indiscriminate collection of objects and decorative arts. By 1947 the vast assemblage had been installed in the corridors of Hotel Alcazar. Financial difficulties plagued operations, but local citizens kept the museum alive; today it occupies the former spa and gymnasium. The casino and ballroom have been restored to their original condition; an antiques mall and cafe occupy the drained basin of the pool.

Lightner Museum, The Hotel Alcazar

South of the Plaza

Spanish Military Hospital – *Aviles St., just off the Plaza de la Constitución. Open year-round Mon-Sat 10am-4:30pm, Sun noon-4:30pm. Closed Dec 25. $2.50. ☎ 904-827-0807.* Originally a stable, the simple rose-colored building is a reconstruction of the apothecary wing of St. Augustine's military hospital. Acquired by the Spanish government in 1791, it served as the main hospital after 1818. Razed in 1880, it was reconstructed in 1967 by the Historic St. Augustine Preservation Board, which operates it as a museum. Inside, a bed-filled ward and several rooms paint a picture of medical care in the late 18C, from dried herbs to the rudimentary surgical implements of the day. Copies of the c.1790 *reglamentos*—rules governing the operation of hospitals and the educational requirements of doctors and apothecaries—are posted on the walls.

★**Ximenez-Fatio House** – *20 Aviles St. Visit by guided tour only, year-round Mon & Thu-Sat 11am-4pm, Sun 1pm-4pm. ☎ 904-829-3575.* This two-story coquina residence offers a look at the way early St. Augustine buildings were expanded and adapted for various uses. Operated as a boardinghouse for most of the 19C, the structure was built in 1798 by Spanish merchant Andrés Ximenez as his residence and general store. Under a later owner, the establishment thrived as St. Augustine's most popular inn from the mid-19C to the late 19C, when competition from Henry Flagler's hotels slowed business.

> **2 Denoel French Pastry**
> *See map. 212 Charlotte St.,* ☎ *904-829-3974.* Take a break from sightseeing at this European-style lunch room and bakery on colorful Charlotte Street, just around the corner from the Spanish Military Hospital. Patrons come for mid-morning, made-on-the-premises French pastries to complement an espresso or cafe au lait. Otherwise they order sandwiches of Black Forest ham or Genoa salami, among other choices, on home-baked croissants or French bread. Soups du jour and tomatoes stuffed with shrimp or chicken salad are added attractions. A fixture among city merchants, the Denoels have been baking here in St. Augustine since 1966.

Today the house is restored to reflect the period between 1830 and 1850; individual rooms are appointed as if to accommodate various 19C boarders. Research commissioned by the National Society of the Colonial Dames of America (current owners of the property) authenticates the paint color and other decorative treatments. Objects unearthed in archaeological digs at the site are displayed throughout the house.

★**Old St. Augustine Village** – *250 St. George St. (entrance on Bridge St.). Open year-round daily 9am-5pm. Closed Thanksgiving Day, Dec 24-25. $7.* ♿ ☎ *904-823-9722. www.old-staug-village.com.* Nine historic houses, dating from 1790 to 1910, occupy a full city block *(bounded by St. George, Bridge and Cordova Sts. and St. Joseph Convent)* that was part of the original 16C walled colonial town. Five are currently open to the public, along with gardens and courtyards. Famous residents and visitors included Prince Achille Murat, nephew of Napoleon Bonaparte; John James Audubon; Mark Twain; and Greta Garbo. The block was acquired for preservation by a St. Augustine resident who donated the properties to the Museum of Arts and Sciences of Daytona Beach in 1988.

The oldest is the pink **Prince Murat House** (1790), a Spanish Colonial constructed of coquina. Contents include china that bears the Murat family cipher, Murat's father's bed from Château de Versailles near Paris and other French Empire-style furnishings. Under restoration is the Colonial Revival **William Dean Howells House** (1910) rented by the American novelist, who hosted writer Sinclair Lewis here. Exhibits in the **Star General Store** and Dow and Canova houses pertain to the French in Florida's history and Cracker culture, among other topics. Several remnants are visible: the city's Rosario Defense Line (mid-1700s); footers of the bridge across Maria Sanchez Creek; and the oldest known Catholic burial ground in the US, dating to 1597. Throughout the village, interpreters provide entertainment and information.

★★**Gonzalez-Alvarez House (The Oldest House)** – *14 St. Francis St. (between Charlotte and Marine Sts.). Visit by guided tour (30min) only, year-round daily 9am-5pm. Closed Easter Sunday, Thanksgiving Day, Dec 25. $5.* P ☎ *904-824-2872. www.oldcity.com/oldhouse.* This handsome National Historic Landmark dwelling is thought to be St. Augustine's oldest extant residential structure. Initially a flat-roofed, rectangular coquina building with tabby floors, the house was built in the early 18C for Tomás Gonzalez y Hernandez, a settler from the Canary Islands. A second story, fireplace and balcony were added when the structure housed a tavern. The Geronimo Alvarez family acquired the house in 1790 and it passed through generations before being sold in 1882. In 1918 the house was purchased by the St. Augustine Historical Society, whose members restored the structure to its 18C appearance.

The gloomy lower level, with its rugged tabby floors and exposed coquina walls, describes the spartan lifestyle of the Gonzalez family, while the upstairs reveals the relative comfort enjoyed by the Alvarez family. The mosquito-netted, four-poster bed and porcelain pitcher and washbowl in the upstairs bedroom date from Florida's Territorial Period.

Tovar House – *Adjacent to the Gonzalez-Alvarez House; same hours as above.* Formerly the residence of José Tovar, this building was purchased in 1918 by the St. Augustine Historical Society. Today its rooms house the **Museum of Florida's Army** with displays tracing the history of the army in the region. Costumed mannequins, replicated flags and muster rolls illustrate life for soldiers in Florida from 1565 to the present.

San Marco Avenue

Fountain of Youth Archaeological Park – *155 Magnolia Ave. Open year-round daily 9am-5pm. Closed Dec 25. $5.50.* ♿ ☎ *904-829-3168.* Visitors can drink from the small spring at this privately owned park, although the waters are as devoid of supernatural powers—and more sulfurous—as any water in this part of Florida. While stories proclaiming this spot as the landing site of Ponce de León his search for the fantastical fountain are the stuff of legend, the importance of the **archaeological site** here is unquestioned. In recent decades, researchers from the Smithsonian Institution in Washington, DC, and the University of Florida have uncovered artifacts and building foundations that indicate Pedro Menéndez de Avilés' presence here, as well as the probable location of the Timucuan village of Seloy, home to the Indians who welcomed Menéndez in 1565.

★**Mission de Nombre de Dios** – *San Marco Ave. and Ocean Ave. Open year-round Mon-Fri 8am-5:30pm, weekends 9am-5pm. Closed major holidays.* ▫ ☎ *904-824-2809.* A 208ft stainless-steel cross marks the approximate spot where Pedro Menéndez de Avilés and his men came ashore to take possession of Florida for Philip II of Spain in 1565. Menéndez' chaplain marked the event by celebrating Mass, thus establishing the Mission de Nombre de Dios, the first Catholic mission in the US. Nothing remains today of the original structures. The gleaming cross, erected in 1966 to commemorate the 400th anniversary of the founding of St. Augustine, looms above the placid salt marsh bordering a forest of cypress and palm trees. Paths lead to an ivy-covered chapel housing the **Shrine of Our Lady of La Leche**, originally erected here in 1613 by Spanish settlers.

★**Old Jail** – *167 San Marco Ave. Open year-round daily 8:30am-5pm. Closed Easter Sunday & Dec 25. $5.* ▫ ☎ *904-829-3800.* This dark-red Victorian building has a somber history. Erected in 1892 to serve as the St. Johns County Jail and sheriff's residence, the edifice was largely funded by Henry Flagler, eager to see the previous jail relocated from near the entrance to his Ponce de Leon Hotel. Now smartly restored, the Old Jail depicts the extent to which the lives of the sheriff and his family revolved around the care of the prisoners.

Guided tours explore the bedrooms, living room, office and kitchen of the sheriff's residence. The jailhouse itself is divided into separate sections for white, black and female prisoners and those requiring maximum security. The walls bear handcuffs, shackles and a collection of antique handguns used in crimes. Out back stand the gallows used to mete out punishment before the turn of the 19C.

Florida Heritage Museum – *167 San Marco Ave. Same hrs as Old Jail (above). $5.* ▫ ☎ *904-829-3800.* Florida and St. Augustine history is glossed over here in three small rooms through displays of objects of everyday life. The broad permanent collection includes early coins, weapons and furniture from the first Spanish period, as well as dolls, toys, quilts and Civil War artifacts. Particularly noteworthy is an exhibit on Henry Flagler that traces the Flagler family's genealogy and features a model of the Florida East Coast Railway.

Anastasia Island *Map p 116*

St. Augustine Lighthouse and Museum – *81 Lighthouse Ave. Take A1A south and turn left on Old Beach Rd., across from the Alligator Farm. Open year-round daily 9am-6pm. Closed Easter Sunday, Thanksgiving Day, Dec 25. $6.50.* ▫ ☎ *904-829-0745. www.stauglight.com.* This brick-and-iron lighthouse, painted with a black-and-white spiral, has illuminated the northern point of Anastasia Island since 1874. The current structure replaced an earlier wood-and-coquina tower that toppled into the ocean. A panoramic **view** awaits those who climb the 219 stairs to the top, where the original Fresnel lens boasts a beam distance of 19 nautical miles. The brick **lightkeeper's residence**, a Victorian structure gutted by fire in 1970, was rebuilt in 1988. Displays recount the lives of the keepers—who operated the light until its automation in 1955.

Anastasia State Park – *A1A, just south of Lighthouse Museum. Park hrs & fees p 350.* △ ▫ ☎ *904-461-2033.* Devotees of sun and sand flock to the broad, lovely **beach**⚐⚐ edging this 1,492-acre state park for some of the area's finest fishing, swimming and sunning. A protected saltwater lagoon provides excellent canoeing and windsurfing. The park's boundaries encompass dunes, salt marshes, scrublands and hammock as well as the quarries from which blocks of coquina were taken to construct Castillo de San Marcos.

EXCURSIONS *Map p 116*

★**World Golf Village and Hall of Fame** – *12mi north via I-95, exit 95-A. Open year-round daily 10am-6pm. $10 Hall of Fame; $7 IMAX; $13.50 combination ticket.* ✕ ♿ ▫ ☎ *904-940-4123 or 800-948-4746. www.wgv.com.* Opened in May 1998, this facility's centerpiece is the **Hall of Fame**, a two-story, 75,000sq ft museum that pays tribute to the greatest male and female golfers of past and present, both American and international. Crystal busts display the likenesses of 90 athletes (through 2001); visitors watch video highlights of golfers' careers at computer stations. Elsewhere, the museum inspires even non-avid golfers with 18 interactive exhibits. Visitors can play an 1880s-style putting green with hickory-shafted putters; have their swings computer-analyzed; or watch highlights of golf's greatest moments in a mini-theater.

■ Visiting a Gator Farm

Have you come all the way to Florida and not seen an alligator yet? Well, about 2,500 crocodilians live at the **St. Augustine Alligator Farm**★★ 🧒 in landscaped habitats and re-created swamps. Plan to attend the informative shows *(hourly)* in the reptile theater, where knowledgeable staff handle Florida snakes and even a white alligator. You may wonder if the alligators sunning themselves in the **main pen** are alive, since they stay immobile for long periods (they are). A special indoor exhibit, **Gomek Forever**, honors a 1,700-pound saltwater crocodile from New Guinea who was the park's star resident from 1990 until his death in 1997. Now mounted, Gomek consumed 100 pounds of nutria and chicken a week during the warm season (most crocodilians don't eat in cold weather). Don't miss the **Land of Crocodiles**, Alligator Farm's outstanding—and rare—collection of all 22 species of crocodilians that also showcases macaws and other exotic birds. The wading **bird rookery** is home to egrets, herons and wood storks during the nesting season. *A1A, 1mi south of the Bridge of Lions. Open year-round daily 9am-5pm (Jun-Aug 6pm). $14.25.* ♿ 🅿 ☎ *904-824-3337. www.alligatorfarm.com.*

Gwen Cannon/MICHELIN

Spread across 450 acres between St. Augustine and Jacksonville, the $250 million village also includes two resort hotels with two 18-hole golf courses and a 300-seat IMAX theater.

★★**Fort Matanzas National Monument** – *15mi south via A1A, on Matanzas River south of Crescent Beach. Open year-round daily 8:30am-5:30pm. Closed Dec 25.* 🅿 ☎ *904-471-0116. www.nps.gov/foma.* A 300-acre park here preserves a coquina watchtower erected in 1742 to defend Matanzas Inlet. In 1565 some 250 French Huguenot soldiers and settlers were slaughtered here by the forces of Pedro Menéndez de Avilés, thereby changing the course of Florida's history.

Soldiers in a wooden tower had maintained watch over Matanzas Inlet since 1569. If approaching ships were sighted, a runner carried the news to St. Augustine. The 1740 siege of the Castillo de San Marcos made the Spanish realize the potential for British invasion, and the need for an armed fortification here at the "back door" to St. Augustine. Piers were sunk into the marshy soil of a small barrier island at the inlet's mouth, and the coquina structure soon arose.

In the visitor center, a short film describes the turbulent history and modern restoration of Fort Matanzas. From a nearby landing, board a ferry for the trip across the Matanzas River to the fort itself. Stairs and ladders lead up to the gun balcony, from which you can explore the soldiers' and officers' quarters and the upper balcony. Back on the mainland, a nature trail leads among bayberry, live oak, saw palmetto, Spanish bayonet and red cedar trees to a plaque commemorating the site of the massacre.

Marineland – 🧒 *18mi south via A1A at 9507 Ocean Shore Blvd. Open year-round Wed-Mon 9:30am-4:30pm. Closed Dec 25. $12.* ⛺ ✗ 🅿 ☎ *904-460-1275 or 888-279-9194. www.marineland.net. Check schedules at entrance for times of shows and oceanarium feedings.* This old oceanfront park straddling A1A was conceived as an underwater film studio by a group that sought footage of marine life. Founders included Cornelius Vanderbilt Whitney, great-grandson of transportation magnate Cornelius Vanderbilt, and Ilia Tolstoy, grandson of acclaimed Russian author Leo Tolstoy. Opened in 1938, the studio quickly became a tourist attraction. Techniques for photographing dolphin behavior and recording dolphin sounds were pioneered here.

Most of the park's 3,000 resident sea dwellers swim and play in two massive oceanariums and in smaller aquariums. Dolphins swim right up to visitors at the **Top Deck** of the circular oceanarium, also the site of jumping dolphin shows. Dolphins in-training perform throughout the day at the Dolphin Stadium. Be sure to check out **Wonders of the Spring**, a 35,000-gallon freshwater aquarium featuring largemouth bass and other native Florida species. Plans call for the addition of an environmental learning center.

Orlando Area

One of the most popular tourist destinations in the US, the Orlando area in central Florida attracts some 43 million visitors annually. Best known as the home of Walt Disney World, the region also boasts the elaborate theme parks of Universal Studios, SeaWorld and a number of major corporate headquarters. The city of Orlando itself, the state's largest inland city, serves as the region's hub. Though superhighways lined with chain hotels, resort complexes, eateries and discount shopping malls now web the flat, lake-pocked subtropical landscape of this growing region, historic neighborhoods still grace the older portions of cities and towns.

As you move southwest farther into the interior, the land becomes less developed and more devoted to agriculture. The towns of Lakeland and Lake Wales sit at the heart of the state's citrus-growing region and offer a quieter, more nostalgic atmosphere, as well as a subtle change in terrain. At the southern end of the state's north-south-running Central Highlands, this area occupies a gently rolling landscape. Iron Mountain, just north of Lake Wales, is one of the peninsula's highest points at 298ft. Central Florida experienced its first influx of settlers—largely north Florida cattlemen who were attracted to the area's lush grasslands—after the end of the Second Seminole War in 1842. Forty years later, towns mushroomed along the line of Henry

Plant's **South Florida Railway**. Railroad access encouraged tourism and other economic ventures, including lumbering and a healthy naval stores industry that produced turpentine, pitch and rosin from the sap of the locally abundant longleaf pines. After a killing frost in the 1890s, citrus farmers from the northern part of the state migrated south to join the growers already in this area, and the citrus industry burgeoned.

In contrast to the wealthy winter visitors who arrived by train in the early 1900s, mid-century tourists were middle-class families traveling by car. The ever-growing pace of tourism increased exponentially in the early 1970s with the opening of Walt Disney World 20mi southwest of Orlando. The corridor stretching between the two and south to Kissimmee quickly became a commercial mecca, while the area southwest of Kissimmee has managed to maintain its traditional base in the citrus economy. Today Orlando and its environs rank among the fastest-growing metropolitan areas in the US.

KISSIMMEE

Population 47,814
Map p 133
Tourist Information: www.floridakiss.com ☎ 407-847-5000

Two distinct personalities characterize Kissimmee [pronounced kiss-SIM-ee]. A placid residential community spreading along the shores of 29sq mi Lake Tohopekaliga quietly reflects the town's historic role as a center of Florida's cattle industry. Less than a mile away, visitors throng the glittering length of US-192, which extends from downtown to Walt Disney World, giving rise to the city's moniker, the **"Gateway to Disney."**

The area was not permanently occupied until American cowmen settled here in the 1840s. After the federal government ceded overflowed lands to the states for reclamation, Pennsylvania industrialist **Hamilton Disston** purchased four million acres in the swampy Kissimmee, Caloosahatchee and Peace river valleys. He established a land company at Allendale, a tiny settlement that he renamed Kissimmee and set about dredging canals linking lakes in the region. The South Florida Railway landed its terminus at Kissimmee and the town developed as a center for shipbuilding, agriculture and transportation. Demand for beef throughout the first half of the 20C fueled the region's cattle industry.

The opening of Disney World in 1971 foretold Kissimmee's metamorphosis from farm community to tourist center. US-192 became a lively corridor of amenities designed to accommodate the flood of Disney-bound visitors. As Kissimmee's population boomed, cattle ranchers retreated south to less populous areas. Today over 4 million tourists annually flock to the putt-putt golf courses, water parks, motels, shopping centers and amusement parks that line both sides of US-192. In the evening, crowds fill "dinner shows," where meals match the theme of the accompanying live entertainment; theme run the gamut from medieval England to the Old West to gangland Chicago.

Although development pushes inexorably eastward toward the town of St. Cloud, Kissimmee's old commercial area appears as it might have in the days before Disney. Placid Lakefront Park extends along the northern shore of **Lake Tohopekaliga** a few blocks from downtown. A stroll along **Broadway Avenue** *(south of US-192 via Main St.)* reveals charming storefronts that are reminiscent of Kissimmee's late-19C days as a cattle town.

SIGHTS

Flying Tigers Warbird Restoration Air Museum – *231 N. Hoagland Blvd. From US-192 turn south on Hoagland Blvd. and follow signs. Open year-round daily 9am-5:30pm (Sun 5pm). Closed Dec 25. $8.* & 🄿 ☎ *407-933-1942. www.warbirdmuseum.com.* Less a museum than the active workshop of an organization devoted to the restoration and reconstruction of vintage World War II aircraft, this facility sits on the grounds of Kissimmee's small regional airport. Since 1972, when the organization's founder began restoring American "warbirds" to flying condition, Flying Tigers has returned some 24 planes to the air. Guided tours explore the storage hangars for an up-close look at 28 beautifully restored aircraft, and the workshops for glimpses of those under restoration. Planes commonly on view include a Boeing B-17, a P-51 Mustang, an A-4 Skyhawk and a Russian MIG 21. Planes are occasionally flight-tested *(call for schedule)* and the museum offers warbird rides.

A World of Orchids – *2501 Old Lake Wilson Rd. From I-4 take Exit 25B west and proceed west 2mi on US-192; turn left on Old Lake Wilson Rd. (Rte. 545) and continue 1mi. Open year-round daily 9:30am-4:30pm. Closed major holidays.* & 🄿 ☎ *407-396-1887. www.a-world-of-orchids.com.* The tropical conservatory landscaped with waterfalls and winding paths, contains an ever-changing rainbow of bright, flowering orchids from around the world. Hundreds of species flourish here, including several rare ones.

Splendid China – *3000 Splendid China Blvd. From I-4 take Exit 25B west and proceed west 3mi on US-192. Open year-round daily 9:30am-7pm. $28.88.* ✗ ♿ 🄿 ☎ *407-397-8820.* Laid out on a sprawling, 76-acre site just west of the entrance to Disney World, Splendid China departs from the traditional rides-and-attractions theme parks that abound in the immediate vicinity. Intended to offer the visitor a "10,000-mile journey through 5,000 years of Chinese history and culture," the park presents some 60 scale replicas of China's architectural and natural wonders in a landscaped setting. The handcrafted **replicas★**, executed at scales ranging from 1:3 to 1:15, were created using techniques and materials authentic to the original periods of construction. Chinese actors, dancers and acrobats bring to life the "Mysterious Kingdom of the Orient" *(nightly 6pm except Mon).*

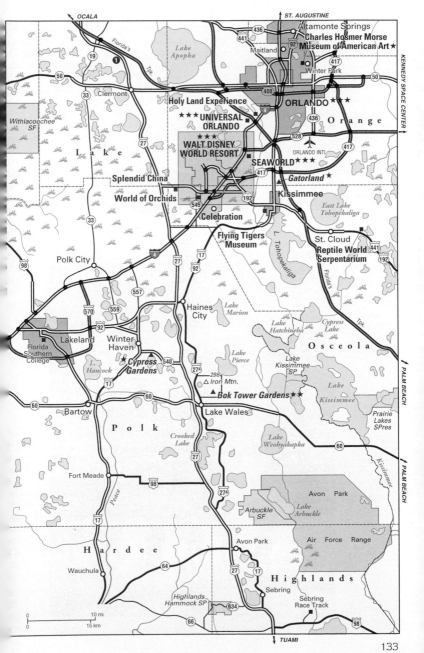

133

EXCURSIONS

★**Gatorland** – 🏠 *6mi north of Kissimmee at 14501 S. Orange Blossom Tr. (US-17/92/441). Open year-round daily 9am-7pm. $17.93.* ✗ ♿ 🅿 ☏ *407-855-5496 or 800-393-5297. www.gatorland.com.* What this animal park lacks in technological magic, it makes up for with the charm common to 1950s-era theme parks. Gatorland was founded in 1949 as a combination amusement park and alligator farm selling alligators for their meat and skins.

Gaping alligator jaws "swallow" visitors at the entrance to the gift shop. For a quick orientation, take a narrated chug around the park on the Gatorland Express. From the **observation tower**, views extend over the park and its 10-acre bird sanctuary. Plan to attend the live shows held throughout the day, particularly the "**Gator Jumparoo**," during which alligators lunge 4ft out of the water at chicken pieces dangled by handlers. At the park's south end, a rope bridge leads to a boardwalk stroll through cypress swamp forming the northern head of the Kissimmee chain of lakes, which flows from here to the Everglades, 175mi south.

Reptile World Serpentarium – *12mi east of Kissimmee at 5705 E. Irlo Bronson Memorial Hwy. (US-192). Open Oct-Aug Tue-Sun 9am-5:30pm. Closed Thanksgiving Day & Dec 25. $5.50.* ♿ ☏ *407-892-6905.* Part snake zoo, part cottage industry, this center shelters a collection of snakes and reptiles from around the world and holds a commercial snake venom business. Mambas and cobras are among some 60 types of snakes and reptiles lying in repose here; placards describe their native habitats and eating habits. Be sure to witness the daily "milking" of poisonous snakes for their venom *(noon & 3pm)*, which is processed for use in research and production of antivenin.

★**Cypress Gardens** – 🏠 *34mi south of Kissimmee. From US-192 take I-4 west 10m to US-27 south; continue 18mi. Exit at Cypress Gardens Blvd. Open year-round daily 9:30am-5pm. $32.95.* ✗ ♿ 🅿 ☏ *863-324-2111. www.cypressgardens.com.* Opened to the public in 1936, Cypress Gardens proclaims itself Florida's first, and longest continually operating, theme park.

The gardens were born in the mid-1930s when Midwest businessman Dick Pope and his wife Julie, longtime winter visitors to Florida, purchased 16 acres on Lake Eloise and hired laborers to transform virgin swampland into a tropical garden park. Today 8,000 plant varieties from 90 countries are displayed throughout the year.

Water-Ski Stunts at Cypress Gardens

Meander through the fragrant pathways of the **Botanic Gardens** edged with gardenias, bougainvillea, hibiscus and palm. A boat cruise along cypress-draped canals may be an option. The antebellum-themed **Southern Crossroads** features live-performance ice shows and the new **FloraDome**. The **Wings of Wonder** glass conservatory houses more than 1,000 colorful butterflies. Visitors can sniff herbs, vegetables, fruits and roses known to thrive in the southern US in the **Plantation Gardens**. Train buffs won't want to miss **Cypress Junction**, an elaborate model railroad exhibit. Panoramic **views** of the park and points beyond await riders of **Island in the Sky**, a revolving platform that rises 153ft. Children will enjoy the junior-size rides and games assembled at Carousel Cove. Beyond Southern Crossroads lies **Nature's Arena**, focused on **Nature's Boardwalk**, a small complex of shoreside habitat areas for deer, wallabies, capybaras and other creatures, and the **Birdwalk Aviary**, where friendly tropical birds and munjac deer freely interact with visitors. **Calling All Animals** hosts raptor and reptile shows and **Antique Radio Museum** features early sets (complete with golden-era radio programs). Scale re-creations of many of the state's best-known historic buildings highlight the **Florida Historical Railway Garden**.

Not to be missed are Cypress Gardens' trademark **water-ski shows**, executed by a resident team of 50-plus champion skiers, the highlight of which is the four-tier human pyramid.

** **Bok Tower Gardens** – *35mi south of Kissimmee. From US-192 take I-4 west 10mi to US-27 south. Take US-27 south to Burns Ave. (Rte. 17A) and follow signs to the gardens at 1151 Tower Blvd. Open year-round daily 8am-6pm. $6.* ✕ ⅙ ▯ ☎ *863-676-1408. www.boktowergardens.org.* Born in The Netherlands, **Edward William Bok** (1863-1930) worked in US publishing houses before founding his own publishing company in 1886. In 1920 his autobiography, *The Americanization of Edward Bok*, won a Pulitzer Prize. Bok decided to create a nature sanctuary as a gift to the American people. He invited Frederick Law Olmsted Jr., son of the famed creator of New York City's Central Park, to transform a sandy, pine-covered site atop Iron Mountain into a botanical haven. The 130-acre park was dedicated in 1929 at ceremonies led by President Calvin Coolidge.

Gardens and Tower – Begin at the **visitor center** *(follow signs from parking area)* to view displays on the gardens' history and an introductory film. From here, meander along bark-mulched paths amid lush stands of live oaks, conifers, palm trees and ferns. Ever-changing splashes of color are painted seasonally on this green canvas by flowering plants, among them azaleas *(in bloom Dec-Mar)* and camellias *(in bloom Nov-Mar)*. **Window by the Pond**, a small wooden hut fitted with a large plate-glass window, welcomes visitors to sit and watch the play of life unfolding in a freshwater pond. The marble **excedra**, a monumental semicircular conversation seat, marks the 298ft summit of Iron Mountain, considered the highest point in peninsular Florida. Encircled by a placid moat, the 205ft **tower** *(interior not open to the public)* of pink-and-gray-streaked Georgia marble and buff-colored coquina is the focal point of the gardens. Designed by Philadelphia architect Milton B. Medary, the Gothic Revival shaft is embellished with turquoise and brown earthenware tiles, masterfully carved sculptures and friezes, and intricately wrought ironwork. Designed in England, its **carillon** of 60 chromatically pitched bronze bells is operated by hammers from a keyboard located on the sixth level.

Pinewood – *Visit by guided tour only, mid-Sept-mid-May daily 11:30am & 1:30pm. $5.* ⅙ ☎ *863-676-1408.* This elegant estate was erected in 1931 as the winter home of Bethlehem Steel executive Charles Austin Buck. Landscape architect William Lyman Phillips, an associate in the Olmsted Brothers firm, and architect Charles Wait conceived a Mediterranean Revival design that harmonizes formal and natural gardens with tile roofs, terraces and softly shaded stucco walls. Detailed woodwork and Cuban tiles adorn the interior, furnished with 17C, 18C and 19C French, Italian and Spanish antiques. Formal gardens incorporate citrus allées that terminate in circular plantings of trees—elements common in Italian Renaissance garden design. The property was acquired by Bok Tower Gardens in 1970.

ORLANDO★★★

Population 185,951
Map p 133
Tourist Information: ☎ 407-363-5800 or www.orlandoinfo.com

Once a sleepy orange-producing area, sprawling metropolitan Orlando now ranks as one of the nation's fastest-growing cities, as well as a tourist mecca attracting 43 million visitors annually. While the rapidly expanding southwestern corridor is filled with outlet malls, hotels, restaurants and entertainment complexes, the older, lake-dotted downtown, with its historic architecture, retains the charm of early 20C Florida. To protect pioneers during the Second Seminole War, the US government established several forts in the area. The settlement that arose around **Fort Gatlin** (1838) formed the nucleus of the future city of Orlando. By the 1860s the embryonic town occupied part of a vast cotton plantation. Citrus intruded as a major crop in the 1880s when the new South Florida Railway gave local growers access to wider markets. Orlando's economy remained rooted in agriculture through the first half of the 20C until a man named Disney forever changed the face of the city.

Demographic and financial forecasters predict that, together with Walt Disney World's continual expansion, Universal Orlando's plans to triple the size of its complex, and the city's attraction as a convention center, Orlando will continue to be one of the country's fastest-growing areas well into the 21C. Orlando ranks among the top five US cities in terms of the number of conventions held per year; its 1.1 million sq ft Orange County Convention Center is currently undergoing expansion to double its present size. In addition, one of Orlando's major thoroughfares, **International Drive**, has increasingly become an attraction unto itself, lined as it is with dozens of restaurants and smaller tourist haunts.

■ The Dawn of Disney

In 1965, having secretly purchased almost 30,000 acres in Orange and Osceola counties, **Walt Disney**, animated-film wizard and creator of California's Disneyland, announced plans to build a theme park outside Orlando. Overnight, land values in the area skyrocketed; throughout the rest of the decade, development engulfed the communities to the southwest along the I-4 corridor. Walt Disney World opened to great fanfare in 1971. SeaWorld followed two years later, and Universal Studios Florida joined the local theme-park ranks in 1990. In the intervening years, metropolitan Orlando tripled its population and now boasts the largest concentration of hotel rooms in the US. The area ranks as one of the top commercial tourist destinations in the world. Service-oriented development has produced endless outlet malls, restaurants and entertainment facilities and, in turn, created more jobs: service sector employment has increased nearly 138 percent within the last decade. Local industry has burgeoned with the addition of a number of large corporations—AT&T, Westinghouse and the American Automobile Assn. among them—to old-timers Tupperware and Lockheed Martin. Even Hollywood has moved east, with both Universal and MGM-Disney studios filming dozens of movies and television shows in Orlando.

DOWNTOWN *Map p 141*

Since Orlando's incorporation in 1875, this area has been the city's administrative hub. Though it fell victim to the decay that afflicted most downtown areas in the 1960s, it has been revitalized in the last four decades, becoming a lively night spot popular both with residents and travelers. An eight-square-block core, centered on Orange Avenue and encompassing Church Street Station, is designated the **Orlando Downtown Historic District**.

Several residential historic districts surround downtown. The **Lake Cherokee District** *(south edge of downtown)* and the **Eola Heights District** *(northeast of downtown)* feature fine examples of Mediterranean, Colonial, Classical and Tudor Revival houses, as well as Art Deco structures, bungalows and substantial Victorians built between 1875 and 1930.

★**Orange Avenue** – Old Orlando's main business thoroughfare holds an eclectic mix of architecture that reflects the city's past and present. Anchoring the south end of the avenue, the classically inspired, domed **City Hall** (1992) is fronted by an expansive fountained plaza. Off the interior lobby, the **Terrace Gallery** displays changing exhibits devoted to the works of regional artists.

A block north, in the shadow of the SunTrust Center tower, is the old **First National Bank Building** (**A**) *(corner of Orange and Church Sts.)*. Now part of Valencia Community College, the 1930 structure combines Classical Revival composition with Art Deco details. **McCrory Five & Dime** *(corner of Orange and Pine Sts.)* was once the largest McCrory store in the south, but now contains a game arcade. Its streamlined, horizontal lines exemplify the 1930s Art Moderne style. Several blocks away

PRACTICAL INFORMATION ....Area Code: 904

Getting There – **Orlando International Airport (MCO)**: 7mi south of city; information booth *(open daily 7am-11pm; multilingual service;* ☎ *825-2352)*. Transportation to downtown: **limo** *($125)*; **taxi** *($25)*; 24hr-**shuttle** vans *($15)* provided by Transtar *(*☎ *856-7777)* or Mears *(*☎ *839-1570)*; **public transportation** *(Bus #11: Mon-Sat 4:45am-10:45pm, Sun 5:45am-6:45pm; bus #51: Mon-Sat 5am-8:15pm, Sun 5:15am-7:15pm)*; and hotel courtesy shuttles. **Rental car agencies** *(p 343)* are located at airport. Amtrak **train** stations: 1400 Sligh Blvd., Orlando, and 150 W. Morse Blvd., Winter Park *(*☎ *800-872-7245; www.amtrak.com)*. Greyhound **bus** station: 555 N. John Young Pkwy. *(*☎ *292-3424 or 800-231-2222; www.greyhound.com)*.

Getting Around – Local **bus service**: Lynx *(year-round daily; $1; transfers 10¢; schedule & route information:* ☎ *841-8240)*. The **Beeline** (Rte. 528), East-West Expressway and Central Florida GreeneWay are **toll roads**. Downtown **shuttle** service: Lymno *(Mon-Thu 7am-10:30pm, Fri 7am-midnight, Sat 10am-midnight, Sun 10am-10pm; every 5min)*. I-Ride **trolley system** services the International Drive area *(daily 7am-midnight; every 15 minutes; 75¢ each way;* ☎ *248-9590; www.iridetrolley.com)*. Metered downtown street parking 75¢/hr; average rate for parking garages $1/hr, $7/day. **Parking** information ☎ 246-2154.

Visitor Information – **Orlando/Orange County Convention and Visitors Bureau**, 6700 Forum Dr., Suite 100, Orlando FL 32821; **Official Visitor Center**, 8723 International Dr., Suite 101 *(open year-round daily 8am-7pm, closed Dec 25;* ☎ *363-5872; www.orlandoinfo.com)*. The **Orlando Magicard** *(free)* offers the holder savings on accommodations, attractions, dining and shopping *(information:* ☎ *800-551-0181)*. *The above organizations provide information on shopping, entertainment, festivals and recreation.*

Accommodations – Area visitors' guide including **lodging directory** available *(free)* from **Orlando/Orange County Convention and Visitors Bureau**. Many hotels offer transportation to Disney and Universal attractions. For information on accommodations within Disney parks, (see Walt Disney World entry heading). **Hotel reservation service** ☎ 800-950-0232. **Central Reservation Service** operates 24hr courtesy phones at airport *(*☎ *339-4116)*. Accommodations range from luxury **hotels** *($150-$400)* to **motels** *($55-$125)* and condominiums. **Youth Hostel**: Orlando/Kissimmee Resort *($14-$19/person; $30-$57/family)* ☎ 396-8282. **Campgrounds** and RV parks available in area. *Rates quoted are average prices per night for a double room and are subject to seasonal variations.*

Entertainment – Consult the arts and entertainment section of the *Orlando Sentinel* (Fridays), *Travelhost* and *See Orlando* publications for schedules of cultural events, attractions and restaurant information. **Bob Carr Performing Arts Center**: Orlando Opera Company, ballet, Broadway performances *(*☎ *849-2577)*; **T.D.Waterhouse Centre**: sporting events, rock concerts, circus *(*☎ *849-2020)*; **Citrus Bowl Stadium**: rock concerts, sporting events *(*☎ *849-2000)*. For arts and sporting-events tickets contact **Ticketmaster** *(*☎ *839-3900; www.ticketmaster.com)*.

Sports and Recreation – **Spectator sports**: Orlando Magic basketball (NBA), T.D. Waterhouse Centre *(*☎ *896-2442)*; Seminole **Greyhound** Park *(*☎ *699-4510)*; Orlando-Seminole **Jai Alai** Fronton *(*☎ *339-6221)*. Many area **golf clubs** allow nonmembers. Captain's Choice Golf Services, Inc. books tee times and offers transportation to most local courses *(reservations* ☎ *352-1102)*. **Public courses**: International Golf Club *(*☎ *239-6909)*; Casselberry *(*☎ *699-9310)*; Orange Lake Country Club offers golf and water sports *(*☎ *239-0000)*. **Shopping**: Belz **Factory Outlet World**, International Dr. has over 150 stores *(*☎ *354-0126)*; **Church Street Exchange**; **Park Avenue**, Winter Park.

ADDRESS BOOK

For a legend of price listings for hotels and restaurants, see p 76.

Staying in the Orlando Area

Disney's Animal Kingdom Lodge – *2901 Osceola Pkwy., Bay Lake.* ✗ ♿ ▣ ⌇ ☎ 407-934-7639. *www.disneyworld.com. 1,293 rooms.* **$$$$** When booking a reservation at this horseshoe-shaped lodge, ask for a Savanna View room, which offers vistas of Animal Kingdom's grazing animals from its private balcony. Bring binoculars and a zoom camera, because some creatures come within 30ft. Other rooms overlook the parking lot or the 9,000sq ft swimming pool. Decorated with African spears and masks, the lobby has a stream running through it and a huge mud fireplace. Enjoy breakfast in Boma-Flavors of Africa, a family restaurant, and later stop for Kenyan coffee in Victoria Falls Lounge.

Disney's Fort Wilderness Resort – *4510 Fort Wilderness Tr., Lake Buena Vista.* ✗ ♿ 🅿 ⚲ ☎ *407-824-2900. www.disneyworld.com. 406 cabins.* $$$$. *(Campsites also available $).* The ultimate in resort self-catering, this collection of log houses and cabins is complemented by campsites designed for pitching tents or hooking up trailers or mobile homes. Outdoor grills are plentiful and activities range from hay- and pony rides to volleyball, biking, fishing and basketball; youngsters especially will enjoy the petting farm. Nightlife centers on a musical review *(nightly),* where ticket holders enjoy an all-you-can-eat feast and sing-alongs.

Disney's Grand Floridian Resort & Spa – *4401 Grand Floridian Way, Lake Buena Vista.* ✗ ♿ 🅿 ⚲ ☎ *407-824-3000. www.disneyworld.com. 900 rooms.* $$$$ Disney's most luxurious property is a Victorian-era waterside complex set on 40 acres along Magic Kingdom's monorail route. The flagship resort's five-story lobby—with carved moldings, an aviary and an open-cage elevator—is topped by illuminated stained-glass domes. Elegant guest rooms feature late-19C-style woodwork and old-fashioned sink fittings. While parents are enjoying the full-service spa, kids can frolic at The Mouseketeer Club. The French-inspired menu at **Citrico's** includes entrées such as the signature braised veal shank or bouillabaise, paired with a suggested wine.

The Peabody Orlando – *9801 International Dr., Orlando.* ✗ ♿ 🅿 ⚲ ☎ *407-352-4000 or 800-PEABODY. www.peabodyorlando.com. 891 rooms.* $$$$ The eastern outpost of Memphis' original Peabody is in the Plaza International district. Potted palms, bamboo furnishings, and a two-story waterfall fill the lobby atrium. Twice a day the red carpet is rolled out for the resident ducks to march to the marble fountain. Light woods and pastels extend the hotel's tropical theme to the spacious bedrooms. Venerable **Dux** restaurant envelops diners in its signature motif—paintings of waterfowl on the walls and duck-shaped butter patties. The "haute global" cuisine includes such dishes as grilled veal chop with foie gras sauce and yellow tail snapper with artichoke and apricot chutney.

Portofino Bay Hotel – *5601 Universal Blvd., Orlando.* ✗ ♿ 🅿 ⚲ ☎ *407-503-1000 or 888-837-2273. www.universalorlando.com. 750 rooms.* $$$$ Operated by the Loews Corp. on Universal theme-park property, this colorful five-floor hotel edges a large body of water like the bayside Italian fishing village for which it is named. Tile roofs slant out over wrought-iron balconies and many rooms overlook a cobblestone piazza. Rooms are spacious, with four-poster beds, duvets, armoires and marble-accented bathrooms. Personal butlers *($100 per day)* perform tasks like unpacking and arranging local bookings. There are even manicured, Italian-style bocce-ball courts. All guests are admitted to Universal parks an hour before the general public via water taxi across the lagoon.

Eo Inn & Urban Spa – *227 N. Eola Dr., Orlando.* ✗ ♿ 🅿 ☎ *407-481-8485 or 888-481-8488. www.eoinn.com. 21 rooms.* $$$ Overlooking Lake Eola in Thornton Park and facing downtown Orlando's skyline, this upscale boutique hotel operates within a recently remodeled building built in 1923. Luxurious guest quarters are electronically equipped to serve as a workplace around the clock. New Age music and soothing sounds of forests and seashore issue forth from each room's CD player. The third floor has a rooftop terrace where guests can soak up Florida sunshine and enjoy iced beverages; continental breakfasts are served here. Open to the public, the full-service day spa is up top as well, as is a popular bakery-cafe, where locals and guests enjoy muffins and lattes.

Renaissance Orlando Resort – *6677 Sea Harbor Dr., Orlando.* ✗ ♿ 🅿 ⚲ ☎ *407-351-5555 or 800-327-6677. www.renaissancehotels.com. 778 rooms.* $$$ The exterior of the 10-floor hotel at this massive, 27-acre complex, situated close to SeaWorld and other area attractions, is architecturally uninspiring, but its interior reveals a cavernous, sunlit atrium sheltering 13,000 plants, an aviary, a waterfall and a koi-filled fish pond. Guest quarters are large, attractively done in gold, green and teak. Facilities include basketball, volleyball and lighted tennis courts. Equated with excellent seafood and sterling service, **Atlantis** satisfies bons vivants with its signature lobster bisque and offerings such as Florida grouper with honey bourbon sauce.

The Courtyard at Lake Lucerne – *211 N. Lucerne Circle East, Orlando.* ♿ 🅿 ☎ *407-648-5188 or 800-444-5289. www.orlandohistoricinn.com. 30 rooms.* $ Ringing a tropical courtyard, this complex of four historic residences (1893-1940) overlooks downtown's Lake Lucerne. Each one reflects the period of its heyday from Victorian jewel-tone fabrics and sleigh beds to offbeat Art Deco suites with kitchenettes. The oldest, the Norment-Parry Inn, served as a hotel and rehab center before being remodeled as a B&B in 1986; its six rooms are furnished with European and American antiques. Breakfast is served on the veranda of the antebellum manor that boasts three lavish Edwardian guest rooms as well as stately columns, a Tiffany-like stained-glass window and a marble fireplace.

Wonderland Inn – *3601 S. Orange Blossom Tr., Kissimmee* ♿ 🅿 ☎ *407-847-2477 or 877-847-2477. www.wonderlandinn.com. 11 rooms.* **$$** Located in Kissimmee, not far from the theme parks, this brick house with a separate cottage alongside offers relaxed, homey comfort. Brightly colored murals, flowers and birdcages are everywhere. Rooms include a refrigerator, coffeemaker and cable TV; some rooms have kitchenettes. The house lounge is a popular gathering spot for guests to have a soft drink or a glass of wine. If you like fresh-squeezed orange juice, you can pick your own oranges to go with the complimentary continental breakfast. Colombian coffee is served daily in the dining room.

Dining in the Orlando Area

Emeril's – *6000 Universal Blvd., Universal Studios CityWalk, Orlando.* ♿ ☎ *407-224-2424.* **$$$$ Cajun-Creole**. Famed New Orleans chef and TV star Emeril Lagasse arrived in Orlando with his signature "Bam!" in 1999. The place has been standing room only almost ever since. Insiders sometimes take dinner at the bar because it beats the reservations backlog. Emeril is only in town on an average of once a month, so chef Barnard Carmouche holds the fort for him, serving up Cajun-Creole specialties and toothsome sweets like chocolate souffle with Grand Marnier, fresh berries and hot chocolate sauce. In the cellar some 12,000 bottles await uncorking.

Charlie's Lobster – *8445 International Dr., Orlando.* ☎ *407-352-6929.* **$$$ Seafood**. This elegant Mercado Village restaurant prepares fresh local seafood as you like it—grilled, sautéed or broiled. Regulars know to select from the chef's daily specials, such as blackened tuna with herb hollandaise and citrus-glazed barbecued black grouper. Natural wood wainscoting and planters hanging from the 15ft ceiling create a relaxed setting. A popular dessert at Charlie's is the cheesecake with fresh berry sauce. *Dinner only.*

Chatham's Place – *7575 Dr. Phillips Blvd., Orlando.* ♿ ☎ *407-345-2992.* **$$$ Continental.** This intimate, privately owned restaurant is a comfortable change from all the city's theme-park hoopla. The smiling staff is friendly, and they do a fine job with the restaurant's signature dish, black Florida grouper slathered in pecan butter. The rack of lamb *au jus* and baked jumbo shrimp also earn raves—in fact, Chatham's routinely gets high marks from patrons.

Le Coq au Vin – *4800 S. Orange Ave., Orlando.* ☎ *407-851-6980.* **$$$ French.** This small, unpretentious restaurant serves some of the best French food in central Florida. It's the place where rival chefs dine on their days off. Louis Perrotte supervises the kitchen, while his wife Magdalena welcomes the guests. The dining spot is named for its most popular, and least expensive, dish; more daring diners opt for the braised rabbit.

Wolfgang Puck's Cafe – *Downtown Disney West Side, Lake Buena Vista.* ♿ ☎ *407-938-9653.* **$$$ International.** This isn't one restaurant, it's a quartet. There's a casual cafe and a lively sushi bar downstairs—and a quick takeaway counter next door. Upstairs is Puck's famed fine-dining establishment. Although the celebrated chef has closed his renowned Spago's in Hollywood, California, it seems as if the place has been reborn here in Orlando. Tiles and polished wood are featured in the decor. Kitchens are open, so patrons can see their signature pizzas being twirled and brick-oven-baked. Virtually every dish involves an imaginative fusion of American, Asian and European tastes and ingredients. *Dinner only in second-floor dining room.*

Harvey's Bistro – *390 N. Orange Ave., Orlando.* ☎ *407-246-6560.* **$$ American.** Comfort food with a modern slant keeps residents coming back to this stylish eatery inside downtown's Bank of America building. Hearty entrées include pot roast in rosemary-burgundy gravy and roast duck with strawberry sauce. Lighter appetites can order the day's catch. Dark-wood paneling, black-and-white marble floors, and mirror-lined walls give the buzzing dining room a chic, yet casual look.

Straub's – *5101 E. Colonial Dr., Orlando.* ♿ ☎ *407-273-9330* **$$ Seafood.** Chef/owner Rob Straub has built an international reputation with his fresh mahi mahi, Florida lobster tail, and salmon steak marinated in lime juice, spices and honey. Ask the wait staff for suggestions because they know what's fresh. All the fish is prepared to order, and insiders prefer their fish grilled or broiled, not the traditional deep-fried. *Dinner only.*

White Wolf Cafe – *1829 N. Orange Ave., Orlando.* ☎ *407-895-5590.* **$$ International.** Located in the heart of Orlando's Antique Row, this bistro is named for a dog, the owner's white German shepherd. The storefront started life as an antique shop, with a few snacks being served to bring in customers and give the local trade a place to relax. Gradually the food took over. Tables and chairs moved in, knickknacks moved out. The cuisine is international, including a few aromatic dishes from Morocco to spice up the menu.

Thai Place – *501 N. Orlando Ave., Winter Park.* & ☎ *407-644-8449.* **$ Thai.** This small restaurant is decorated with a black ceiling painted with artwork, similar to ceilings found in native Thai homes. Curries here include red, green, yellow and peanut, all made from different pastes and laced with fresh herbs and spices. Beware, though—the kitchen staff can produce some dishes that may overwhelm your palate while bringing tears to your eyes. Try the *pla lad prig* (whole fish baked with spices in red bell peppers) for a taste you won't forget. Thai spring rolls are crispier and spicier than their Chinese cousins, and they come with a tangy peanut sauce.

(nos. 37-39 Magnolia Ave.), the Queen Anne-style **Rogers Building** (c.1906) boasts a rare facade of pressed zinc panels. At the north end of downtown rises the **Barnett Bank Center** *(formerly the Du Pont Center; Orange Ave. and Livingston St.)*, a lofty, three-towered high rise topped by silver spires. Completed in 1987, the building displays works of art, including Renoir's *Washerwoman*, in its public courtyard and lobby areas.

Church Street Station

★**Church Street Station** – 🈁 *129 W. Church St. Open year-round daily 11am-1am (Fri-Sat 2am).* ✗ & 🅿 ☎ *407-422-2434. www.churchstreetstation.com.* This entertainment/shopping complex, begun in the 1970s, served as the area's rejuvenating force. The complex features brick-paved walkways, re-created storefronts and Victorian interiors. Church Street Station comprises restaurants and themed showrooms, featuring live music and dancing from country-and-western, contemporary and classic rock to Dixieland jazz. Recently, decreasing business has forced the closing of the top floor of the complex, but the new ownership may lead to a reopening. The old brick **Orlando Railroad Depot** (**B**) (1887-90), which now houses offices, typifies late-Victorian railroad design in its domed cupola and eyebrow roofline covering dormer windows. On the tracks beside it sits "**Old Duke**," a 1912 Baldwin steam locomotive.

★**Orange County Regional History Center** (**M**) – *65 E. Central Blvd. in Heritage Sq. Open year-round Mon-Sat 9am-5pm, Sun 11am-5pm. Closed major holidays. $7.* & ☎ *407-836-8500. www.thehistorycenter.org.* Housed in the former county courthouse (1927), this facility features four floors of engaging exhibits, many of them interactive, that highlight Central Florida's colorful history. Dominating the entry is the two-floor-tall orange **dome** with moving model icons from manatees to space shuttles. View the introductory video *(15 min)* in a rocking chair in the Orientation Theater. Then enter a re-created Timucuan village, settle into a Florida cowboy's saddle, walk within a mock citrus grove and see how Disney's Cinderella Castle was constructed. One of the original courtrooms is open for viewing *(third floor)*.

Lake Eola Park – *Central Blvd. and Rosalind Ave.* Downtown's best place for a pleasant stroll or quiet break, the city's most popular park offers a band shell for concerts, paddleboats, a playground and a cafe. Attractive landscaping rims the lake, as does a pathway for walking, jogging and skating. Numerous benches provide good spots to view the city skyline and the lake's fountain, which is illuminated at night.

Additional Sights

★**Orlando Museum of Art** – *2416 N. Mills Ave., in Loch Haven Park. Open year-round Tue-Sat 10am-5pm, Sun noon-5pm. Closed major holidays. $6.* ☐ ☎ *407-896-4231. www.omart.org.* Formed as a local art center in 1924, the museum doubled its gallery space in 1997. The heart of the permanent collection is rotated in four contemporary galleries. More than 600 works of **19C and 20C American art** include paintings by John Singer Sargent, George Inness, Georgia O'Keeffe, Maurice Prendergast and Gene Davis. Pre-Columbian cultures are represented by Western Mexican, Peruvian and Costa Rican pottery, jade, stone and textile artifacts dating from 1200 BC to AD 1521. An African collection features Yoruba beadwork, Asante statuary and Benin metalwork.

★**Orlando Science Center** – 🚼 *777 E. Princeton St., in Loch Haven Park. Open Jun-Aug Mon-Sat 9am-5pm (Fri & Sat 9pm), Sun noon-5pm. Rest of the year Tue-Sat 9am-5pm (Fri & Sat 9pm), Sun noon-5pm. Closed Thanksgiving Day & Dec 25. $9.50.* ✗ ☐ ☎ *407-514-2000. www.osc.org.* This cylindrical building with its four-story central atrium opened in 1997 as a museum for children and adults alike. On Level 1 *(ground floor)*, NatureWorks features lifelike dioramas of Florida

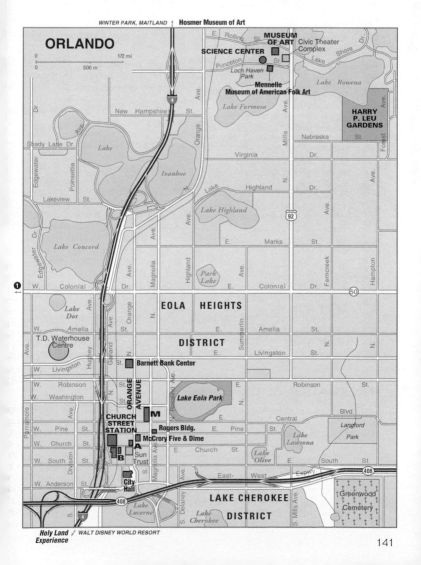

ecosystems, including cypress and mangrove swamps (with real turtles and baby alligators) and a coral reef. Level 2 is dominated by Science City, whose interactive displays relate to mathematics, physical sciences and engineering, among them a power station and a suspension bridge. On Level 3, Cosmic Tourist instructs visitors in geology and astronomy. Level 4 features human anatomy in BodyZone, and Tech Works emphasizes applied technologies, especially computer simulation and laser optics.

The center's two theaters—one for large-format films and planetarium shows, and the other for live performances and science demonstrations—are complemented by the rooftop **Crosby Observatory** *(open Fri & Sat, weather permitting)*, which houses Florida's largest refractor telescope. With 207,000sq ft of floor space, the Science Center is among the first in the country to tailor its exhibits and programs to mandated public-school science and math curricula requirements.

Between the Science Center and Museum of Art in Loch Haven Park stands **Fire Station #3**, Orange County's oldest standing firehouse (1927): The brick structure holds Orlando's original fleet of American LaFrance fire trucks, as well as 19C and 20C fire-fighting equipment.

Mennello Museum of American Folk Art – *900 E. Princeton St., diagonally opposite the Science Center. Open year-round Tue-Sat 11am-5pm, Sun noon-5pm. $4. ☎ 407-246-4278. www.mennellomuseum.com.* Installed in a restored mansion overlooking Lake Formosa, this museum is one of the country's few that showcase American folk art exclusively. Most of the gallery space is reserved for Michael and Marilyn Mennello's definitive collection of works by Maine-born artist **Earl Cunningham** (1893-1977), who painted in St. Augustine for decades. Changing exhibits of other folk art, often whimsical and humorous, and a small, well-stocked gift shop, occupy remaining rooms. Be sure to stroll the lovely grounds at the rear of the mansion.

① Lakeridge Winery & Vineyards

Map p 133. About 20mi west of Orlando. Take the East-West Expressway west to the Florida Turnpike; head north on turnpike to Exit 285 (Rte. 50 west). Follow Rte. 50 west to US-27 and go north 5.5mi to vineyard. ♿ ▯ ☎ 904-394-8627 or 800-768-9463. One of only three Florida wineries, Lakeridge was established in 1989. About 66 acres of native muscadine and Florida hybrid bunch grapes grow in the well-drained soil, where European varieties cannot survive. A guided tour includes a 14min introductory video and a view of the winery and bottling room from a second-story deck. At the end of the tour, visitors can taste the vineyard's wines. Grapes are harvested in late June and early August.

★**Harry P. Leu Gardens** – *1920 N. Forest Ave. Purchase tickets in the Garden House. Open year-round daily 9am-5pm. Closed Dec 25. $4. ♿ ▯ ☎ 407-246-2620. www.leugardens.org.* Orlando businessman and exotic-plant collector Harry P. Leu donated his house and 50-acre botanical reserve to the city in 1961. Situated along the southern shore of Lake Rowena, the gardens are renowned for their 2,000-plus **camellia collection** *(in peak bloom from Dec-mid Feb)*. Some 1,000 roses representing 250 varieties color the largest formal **rose garden** in the state *(in bloom from Mar-Jan)*. A small conservatory devoted to orchids, ferns and bromeliads stands near the southeast corner of the garden. Built as a farmhouse in 1888, the two-story white frame **Leu House Museum** was enlarged by subsequent owners—including the Leu family, who lived here from 1936 to 1961 *(visit by 30min guided tour only, daily 10am-3:30pm; closed Jul)*. The gracious Garden House opened in 1995, holds a gift shop, class rooms and meeting space.

INTERNATIONAL DRIVE *Map p 159*

Located approximately 8mi southwest of downtown Orlando, this major thoroughfare has been the focus, along with Kissimmee, of much of the city's new tourism development. Like Manhattan's Fifth Avenue or Los Angeles' Hollywood Boulevard, Orlando's International Drive has become a destination in itself, attracting many of the same visitors who frequent Disney World and Universal. I-Drive, as it is locally known, runs from Route 417 north through SeaWorld to the point where the Belz Outlet Mall meets Universal Orlando at the Florida Turnpike. Its fulcrum is the massive **Orange County Convention Center**—second largest in the country—now in the process of leapfrogging across to International Drive' other side as part of its expansion. The convention center accommodates international meetings, national conclaves, and regional and local conferences by the thousands each year, slowing I-Drive traffic to a crawl. Concentrated along a 7mi stretch are some 375 shops, 150 restaurants (including some specially themed dinner theaters) and a variety of glitzy attractions.

Below is a sampling of International Drive's offerings from north to south. For trolley service, see Practical Information.

Wet 'N Wild – Kids *6200 International Dr. Open year-round daily 10am-6pm. $29.95. ☎ 407-351-9453.* People who want to get soaking wet will find plenty of water here. You can slide into pools from high towers, aim squirt cannons at your friends and boogie-board on artificial surf, for starters.

Adreniline Heights – Kids *7400 International Dr. Open year-round daily 8am-10pm. $6 per activity. ☎ 407-963-6515.* For the upwardly mobile, this entertainment/sports complex is the place to be. There's a rock-climbing wall, a trapeze, balloons to ride in and other options. Instructors are on hand for stunt training and to help with all activities. Safety gear is provided.

Ripley's Believe It or Not Orlando Odditorium – *8201 International Dr. Open year-round daily 9am-1am. $12.95. ☎ 407-363-4418.* The items on display here are offbeat, but intriguing: a Rolls Royce made from toothpicks, a 13ft jade rickshaw, X-rays of a dog that swallowed a knife, P.T. Barnum's fake mermaid and many other strange paraphernalia.

Guinness World Records Experience – *In Mercado at 8445 International Dr. Open year-round daily 10am-11pm (Fri & Sat midnight). $12.95. ☎ 407-248-8891.* This 18,000sq ft facility specializes in EST: the smallEST, largEST, oldEST and other superlatives. Based on the world-famous book of records, this attraction holds a video-packed, trivia-laden collection of strange facts and feats. The visit ends with a motion-simulated film ride.

International Trolley & Train Museum – Kids *8990 International Dr. Open year-round daily 10am-9pm (Sun 8pm). $6.95. ☎ 407-363-9002.* Parents and children especially fascinated with toy trains will find this museum of interest. The entire room has been transformed into a world of model trains, chugging over mountains, through tunnels, over bridges and into miniature towns. Outside, a miniature railway takes visitors on a ride around the property.

The Pointe – *9101 International Dr. ☎ 407-248-2838.* This 17-acre, five-level shopping and entertainment complex houses some 60 specialty retailers, restaurants, dance clubs and other attractions. Its southern anchor is a toy store that features a giant teddy bear, spinning top and building blocks. A 20-theater cinema and a 500-seat IMAX theater are also on the premises. At The Pointe's north end is Wonder Works.

Wonder Works – Kids *9067 International Dr. Open year-round daily 9am-midnight. $15.95. ☎ 407-351-8800.* This interactive amusement center is built to resemble a three-story mansion turned upside down, as if flipped by a Caribbean windstorm. The interior is filled with lots of shoot-to-destroy video games.

EXCURSIONS *Map p 133*

Holy Land Experience – *4mi southwest of downtown Orlando. Take I-4 west to Exit 31A (Conroy Rd.). Turn right onto Vineland Rd. Entrance is on the right. Open year-round Mon-Thu 10am-5pm, Fri-Sat 9:30am-7pm, Sun noon-5pm. $17. ✗ ⴠ ▯ ☎ 407-376-2065 or 866-872-4659 (toll-free). www.theholylandexperience.com.* Among the newest attractions in Orlando (and not without controversy), this $16 million, 15-acre theme park opened early in 2001 and bills itself as a "living, Biblical museum" that focuses on a re-creation of the city of Jerusalem prior to 66 A.D. The brainchild of Marvin J. Rosenthal, head of an evangelical Christian ministry, the complex is designed to immerse visitors in the Holy Land of two millennia ago through replicated religious sites and reenactments.

Guests pass through the simulated gate of ancient Jerusalem to a series of structures containing exhibits on Judeo-Christian history. Visitors can enter the re-created Qumran Caves, where the Dead Sea Scrolls were hidden; hear a discussion about the coming of the Messiah in front of a scaled-down version of Herod's Temple; and walk into a replica of Jesus' burial site, among other experiences. Theatrical presentations and musical entertainment are provided throughout by 180 staff members attired in garb of the period. In the on-site cafe, fare based on Middle Eastern dishes is served. A 17,000sq ft scriptorium that will contain manuscripts, bibles and other artifacts is scheduled to open here in summer 2002.

★**Charles Hosmer Morse Museum of American Art** – *5mi north of downtown Orlando in Winter Park. Take I-4 north to Exit 45 (Fairbanks Ave.) Go east on Fairbanks to Park Ave. Turn left onto Park Ave. Museum is at 445 N. Park Ave. Open year-round Tue-Sat 9:30am-4pm (Fri 8pm Sept-May), Sun 1pm-4pm. Closed Jan 1,*

Wisteria Panel (c.1910), detail by Louis Comfort

Thanksgiving Day, Dec. 25. $3. ♿ 🅿 ☎ *407-645-5311. www.morsemuseum.org.*
An extensive group of works from the studios of artist **Louis Comfort Tiffany** (1848-1933) forms the centerpiece of this 4,000-piece collection of late 19C and early 20C American and European paintings, decorative and graphic arts, American art pottery, Art Nouveau jewelry and Arts and Crafts furniture. Founder Jeannette McKean named the museum after her industrialist grandfather, who retired in Winter Park. First shown at Winter Park's Rollins College in 1942, the Morse collection moved in 1995 to its present 10,000sq ft quarters, specifically designed to showcase large window panels and architectural elements.

Framed by two marble columns with capitals of Favrile glass daffodils from Tiffany's Long Island mansion, the 20ft-high Tiffany window gallery displays the exquisite **leaded windows** that he designed for the 1893 World's Columbian Exposition in Chicago. Another gallery is devoted to the **chapel interior** (1893) Tiffany created for the same exposition. Holdings include the stunning **Magnolia Window** from the Tiffany family's New York City mansion, as well as glass panels by William Morris, Frank Lloyd Wright and John Lafarge. Among the other beautifully preserved **Tiffany pieces** that occupy the majority of the museum's 19 galleries are lamps, vases, jewelry, blown glass and pottery.

The south end of Park Avenue holds the entrance to **Rollins College** *(at Holt Ave.)* a private, four-year coeducational liberal arts college founded in 1895. Take time to stroll the serene palm-studded 67-acre campus, located on the shores of Lake Virginia. The lobby of Crummer Hall displays two 1929 **Tiffany medallion windows**

SEAWORLD ORLANDO★★★

Map p 159

Tourist Information: www.seaworld.com ☏ 407-351-3600 or 800-432-1178

This 200-acre marine adventure park mixes entertainment and education in its many animal shows, touch pools and aquariums. Opened in 1973, the park is one of three SeaWorlds nationwide. Together these parks, owned by Anheuser-Busch, support the world's largest collection of marine life. In addition to its public attractions, SeaWorld actively pursues research and breeding programs, and has successfully bred killer whales (orcas). The Beached Animal Rescue and Rehabilitation Program has assisted hundreds of wild animals in distress, including manatees, dolphins and whales.

Adjacent to SeaWorld, Anheuser-Busch's **Discovery Cove**, opened in 2000, enables visitors to swim with a dolphin and other marine life.

Helpful Hints – As is the case with most Orlando attractions, the busiest periods are during summer, Christmas and spring vacations. Along with the park's rides—Kraken, Wild Arctic, and Journey to Atlantis—many of SeaWorld's most interesting attractions are shows, whose schedules are listed in the map of the park you receive when you purchase your ticket. Plan the core of your visit around scheduled show times, as the other attractions are relatively accessible throughout the day. The killer whale shows in Shamu Stadium are the most popular.

When you enter the park, you may want to ask at the Information Center about the behind-the-scenes guided tours *(60min; $7.95)* that explain the park's animal care, training and research facilities, including its Arctic and deep-sea divisions. The latest is the Adventure Express tour *(6hrs)*, an escorted tour limited to 16 people that includes reserved seats at some shows and backdoor access to some park rides *($65; advance reservations required, ☏ 800-406-2244)*. The Trainer for a Day program *(8hrs; limited to 3 guests/day 13 years & older; $349/person)* allows visitors to work alongside experts to train and care for a dolphin, anteater, birds and other animals.

VISIT

Kids *7007 SeaWorld Dr. (International Dr.). From downtown, follow I-4 west to Exit 28, then follow signs to SeaWorld. Open year-round daily 9am. Closing times vary, depending on events. $47.95.* ✗ ♿ 🅿 ⅢⅢ ☏ *407-351-3600 or 800-432-1178. www.seaworld.com.*

Roughly elliptical, SeaWorld is a maze of walkways with a large lagoon dominating its southern half. Pools and aquariums are situated throughout the park. **Marine Mammal Shows** are repeated several times daily *(check park map for times)*.

Enter through the park's six-acre gateway area with a 55ft lighthouse at its heart. The tower, painted with a stylized image of Shamu, the park's trademark killer whale, stands atop rocks in a million-gallon harbor, surrounded by sailing ships and stone sea lions. Its beacon guides nighttime visitors back to their vehicles. Adjacent ticket and guest-relations counters, restaurants and gift shops all give the area a pleasant harbor-town ambience.

SeaWorld

145

Just beyond the gateway is the **Tropical Reef**, into which are set some three dozen small aquarium tanks representing a wide variety of marine habitats and sea creatures, such as moray eels and chambered nautiluses. Behind the building is a **Tidal Pool** where visitors may touch and examine sea anemones, sea cucumbers and other marine mammals while posing questions to a naturalist. To the right of the tropical reef, a short walkway leads to the **Dolphin Nursery**, where young marine mammals are nurtured. South Seas dancers perform by the lagoon at the **Luau Terrace** in a Hawaiian-style dinner show *(check park map for luau information)*.

Key West at SeaWorld – Moving clockwise from the gateway, a short walk brings you to this quirky village, which re-creates the spirit of Florida's farthest resort outpost. Attractions include **Stingray Lagoon**, where visitors can touch the broad flat fish as they swim by; **Turtle Point**, which introduces several endangered species; and **Dolphin Cove**, where staff members are on hand to stage playful interaction with the marine mammals. Visitors can take part in a nightly sunset celebration just like the ones on Mallory Square in Key West.

Key West Dolphin Stadium – Watch dolphins leap 18ft above the water and execute full flips and triple twists during the five-times-daily show. These graceful mammals further demonstrate their learning skills as trainers dance with them and ski around the pool—each foot on the nose of a dolphin. *Those seated in the first few rows may get wet.*

Manatees: The Last Generation? – This exhibit immerses visitors in the underwater world of the famed Florida manatee. You can watch these marine giants, some weighing 1,000 pounds, from above the water and below. Narration explains how the gentle sea cow hears, sees and feels, and suggests ways that visitors can help to save the endangered species from extinction.
SeaWorld operates an ongoing manatee release program, in which orphaned or injured manatees are released into the wild (orphans are released at the age of five or six).

Journey to Atlantis – You're guaranteed to get wet—very wet—at this thrill ride. As the story goes, the mythical lost city of Atlantis has mysteriously risen from the floor of the Aegean Sea, and you're one of the first explorers. Your eight-passenger Greek fishing boat is actually a high-speed roller coaster that carries you through dark passageways haunted by evil sirens, down a nearly vertical 60ft waterfall and around a pair of S-curves into another free-falling plunge.
Continue clockwise (south) from Atlantis, which is at SeaWorld's northeastern corner.

Kraken – SeaWorld's newest roller-coaster ride is billed as Orlando's "longest, fastest, tallest, steepest and floorless." Visitors who board this ride *(you must be at least 54in tall)* are whisked to the height of a 15-story building, plunged down at speeds of 65mph and turned upside-down seven times before the ride is concluded.

Penguin Encounter – Step on the moving walkway for a ride past a frosty 30°F setting where puffins, murres and several species of penguins—including chinstrap, gentoo, rockhopper and king—reside. Through a glass-sided observation pool you can view the graceful swimming of these flightless birds.

Pacific Point Preserve – Rocky shoals of an open-air pool capture the atmosphere of the Pacific coast. Harbor and fur seals bob in the waters, sea lions lounge on rocks, and a symphony of sounds is always in progress. Best time to watch: when attendants are staging a feeding session.

Sea Lion and Otter Stadium – Sea lions Clyde and Seamore, the Abbott and Costello of the pinniped family, star as stranded buccaneers in "Clyde and Seamore Take Pirate Island." After a clever otter steals a pirate's treasure map, he enlists the help of the dynamic duo in recovering the scaly wealth. A harbor seal gets in the act and there's more visitor interaction than ever.
Stroll west from the stadium to the SeaWorld Theater. The Sky Tower is immediately to its south.

SeaWorld Theater – The 25min show presented here has little or nothing to do with the sea, but it's a family favorite. "Pets Ahoy" features the talents of 12 dogs and 18 cats—nearly all of whom were rescued from animal shelters—as well as birds, rats, three pot-bellied pigs and a one-horse stampede.

Sky Tower – For those who want a bird's-eye **view** of SeaWorld, this tower lifts passengers in a rotating chamber to the top of a 400ft shaft for a view of Orlando area attractions *($3)*. A footbridge crosses the central lagoon to attractions on its far side.
Return to your clockwise course around the lagoon.

Terrors of the Deep – At the entrance to this exhibit, a small outdoor pool houses several varieties of sharks and rays. Inside, visitors walk through an acrylic archway that tunnels through a 660,000gal aquarium. The tank's B-shaped contours were specifically designed to accommodate the swimming patterns of sharks, five different species of which glide through these waters. Smaller tanks contain beautiful but deadly lionfish, sinister barracuda and other denizens—reputedly the largest collection of "dangerous sea creatures" in the world.

Cirque de la Mer – This "Circus of the Sea" presents a 25min musical adaptation of "The Flight of the Condor," a traditional South American story. Narrated by renowned Peruvian comedian Cesar Aedo, the show blends music and dance, athletic and aerobatic feats with dramatic special effects.

Immediately south, at the **Anheuser-Busch Hospitality Center**, guests are offered free samples of the company's famous beers. A brief film, *The Color of Life*, recounts the company's role in conservation. Brawny horses that serve as the Busch mascots are pastured in the adjacent **Clydesdale Hamlet**. A festive eight-horse hitch of Clydesdales parades around the park, weather permitting *(check at Clydesdale Hamlet for times)*.

Shamu Stadium – SeaWorld's signature attraction, this water show, staged in a five-million-gallon tank, stars the renowned five-ton killer whale Shamu, along with his protégés. Guided by their trainers, the trio leaps and twirls to music in a whalesome water ballet that is simultaneously captured on an immense high-resolution video screen. Trainers also enter the water to interact with the killer whale and demonstrate some truly remarkable feats.

In the 30min show, **The Shamu Adventure**, animal expert Jack Hanna introduces the audience to Alaska's Glacier Bay, the fjords of Norway and the subantarctic Crozet Islands of the South Indian Ocean. Video footage of whales in their natural habitats points up behavior that is then mimicked in SeaWorld by Shamu and offspring. The last performance of the evening incorporates a light show, **Shamu Rocks America**, performed to rock music *(check park map for times)*. *If you don't wish to get doused with icy salt water, or if you have expensive camera or video equipment, don't sit in the first 14 rows. For the best seats during peak season, arrive 15-30min before show time.*

Orca Show at Shamu Stadium

147

Just in front of the stadium, you can see whales swimming and interacting with trainers between shows in the 1.2-million-gallon pool at **Shamu: Close Up!** This research facility fosters study of killer whale behavior as well as sponsoring a successful breeding program.

Shamu's Happy Harbor – This playground is geared to the under-10 crowd. Kids have to conquer four stories of nets to enter the park. Once there, they can shoot through tunnels, explore a submarine, cool down in water mazes, crawl through a sea of beach balls and descend slippery slides into a tropical paradise.

Wild Arctic – A virtual-reality helicopter ride takes passengers on a northern adventure, pitching and rolling over a crevassed landscape above caribou, polar bears and narwhals. After narrowly escaping an avalanche, you disembark at a mock-up of an arctic research station, featuring above- and below-water views of beluga whales as well as polar bears, walruses and harbor seals. Here visitors learn how station scientists while away the long frozen days monitoring whale creaks, whistles and clicks. *Visitors who don't want to experience the pitching and reeling of the helicopter ride can travel to Base Station Wild Arctic by simulated cross-country ski tour.*

Atlantis Bayside Stadium – The 3,800-seat water stadium, on the southwest shore of the SeaWorld lagoon, is home to a 30min stunt show, **The Intensity Games**. Taking advantage of a craze for "extreme" sports, it features a 20-member team of record-holding water skiers. Speed, strength, stamina, danger and the "big air" athleticism of world-class gymnastics are part of this fine show. Look for long-distance jumping, high-speed barefoot skiing and aerial acrobatics *(check park map for times)*.

★★DISCOVERY COVE

Kids *6000 Discovery Cove Way (International Dr.). Adjacent to SeaWorld. Open year-round daily 9am-5:30pm. $199 to swim with a dolphin (minimum age is 6 years); $109 for non-swim package (fee may be lower off season, Jan-May). Price includes lunch, parking, & 7-day SeaWorld pass. Reservations required (4-6 weeks in advance advised); admission limited to 1,000 visitors/day.* ✗ க் ▯ ☎ *877-434-7268. www.discoverycove.com.*

This newly opened 30-acre marine park, owned and operated by SeaWorld's parent company, Busch Entertainment Corp., provides visitors a one-on-one encounter with a bottlenose dolphin as well as other sea and land creatures. Opened in 2000, Discovery Cove comprises a series of neighboring pools and lagoons amid sand beaches within a tropical landscape of towering palms and thatched huts. Its dolphin population has reached 30 and on-site staff members number some 400.

Helpful Hints – Discovery Cove promotes itself as a place to spend a full day. Both the dolphin swim and non-swim packages include lunch with beverage *(bringing food or drink into the park is prohibited)*. Visitors should bring a swimsuit and leave jewelry at home. During cooler weather, wet suits are available at no cost, as are snorkeling equipment and flotation vests *(year-round)*. Sunscreen and beach chairs are also provided at no extra charge. Changing rooms have lockers and are stocked with towels.

Upon entry, those who have reserved a dolphin encounter should schedule their preferred swim time (times are allotted on a first-come, first-served basis).

One of Discovery Cove's newest attractions is the Trainer for a Day program *(8hrs limited to 3 guests/day 13 years & older; $349/person)*, wherein visitors may work alongside experts to train and care for a dolphin, anteater, birds and other animals. The program also includes swimming with a dolphin *(for details, contact Discovery Cove)*.

Visit

Upon arrival, visitors may enjoy a cup of coffee in the entry building, which resembles the clubhouse of a beach resort. After registering, guests are escorted to the equipment and changing rooms. Pathways bordered by flowers and shrubs lead to the Coral Reef, the Ray Lagoon, Aviary, Tropical River and Dolphin Lagoon *(Park maps are embedded in large stones along the way.)* Visitors may snorkel around the **coral reef** and several grottos, investigate a submerged shipwreck, and view thousands of exotic fish. Resembling the Caribbean's famed Stingray City, the watery habitat of the rays *(in which visitors may snorkel)* holds cownose and southern varieties up to 4ft in diameter. On shore, a large, net-enclosed **aviary** contains some 300 colorful birds in free flight; patrons are permitted to feed and touch the birds. Winding through the aviary, as well as the rest of the park, is the river, where visitors can swim or float along on an inner tube. Guests may also enjoy the large swimming lagoon, bordered by a sandy beach.

Making Friends with a Dolphin

For most visitors, the highlight is the 45min lecture and trainer-guided interaction with a bottlenose dolphin *(some weigh up to 600 pounds)* at Dolphin Lagoon. Guests are first briefed on the behavior and physique of the dolphin, as well as given rules for the swim experience. Then follows a brief orientation film. Swimmers are led into the water *(on average, maintained at a temperature of 75°F for the dolphins)* in groups of six or seven to become acquainted with the dolphin by touching it and viewing it up close. Each person then takes a brief, trainer-supervised **ride** by holding onto the dolphin, careful not to place hands on or near the mammal's blowhole.

UNIVERSAL ORLANDO★★★

Map p 133

Tourist Information: www.universalorlando.com ☎ 407-363-8000 or 888-322-5537

Based in Southern California, Universal Studios opened its first attraction in Florida in 1990. Since then the expanded theme park, now operated under the umbrella title of Universal Orlando, has emerged as a healthy competitor for Walt Disney World, whose massive presence lies a few miles to the south along the I-4 corridor. Visitors must use trams, buses and perhaps rental cars to move from one Disney entertainment center to another, spread out, as they are, over dozens of square miles of former orange groves. At close to 840 acres, Universal Orlando is much more compact, and utilizes an advanced level of amusement technology to make up for what it may lack in real estate.

In the past few years, Universal Studios has been taking giant steps toward head-on-head competition with Disney. Formerly a single theme park and working movie studio, the fantasy broker has expanded its focus with an impressive new theme park, **Islands of Adventure**, which opened fully in mid-1999. "Islands" is linked to **Universal Studios Florida** (the original park) with an upscale dining, entertainment and shopping complex, **Universal CityWalk**, completed in spring 1999. Also newly completed on the premises are several resort hotels, including the first-ever Hard Rock Hotel, and more studio production space, nearly tripling the size of the pre-existing Universal Studios.

Kids *1000 Universal Studios Plaza. Follow I-4 west to Exit 29B. Turn right on Hollywood Way and follow signs to Universal Studios. Open year-round daily 9am. Closing times may vary depending upon events. $50.88 Universal Studios or Islands of Adventure (2-5 day tickets available).* ✗ ⅙ 🅿 ⅢⅢ ☎ *407-363-8000. www. universalorlando.com Caution: several rides at Universal Orlando, particularly within Islands of Adventure, involve water, so it's best to visit the park knowing in advance that you will probably get wet, perhaps even soaked, and plan accordingly.*

UNIVERSAL STUDIOS FLORIDA

The original 444-acre theme park and working studio (with nine soundstages), Universal Studios Florida ranks as the largest motion picture and television facility outside Hollywood, California. Intended as a place where visitors can "ride the movies," the park bases its attractions on popular films and television shows, continuing the tradition begun in 1915 by the studio's California founder, **Carl Laemmle**, who encouraged paying visitors to stop by and watch movies being made. The Orlando site was chosen for its climate and established tourist base, and for its appeal to movie and television talent. Well-known film director-producer **Steven Spielberg**, as creative consultant, carefully designed the Florida site as an "integrated production and entertainment facility."

Since streets frequently double as movie sets, you might see a film in progress as you tour the park. You may also visit soundstages such as the one used full-time by cable television's Nickelodeon Network. Adjacent to the soundstages are 8 thrill rides, 9 different shows (several in 3-D), more than a dozen animated characters and some 16 celebrity look-alikes, who pose for photos with visitors. A brass band and the Blues Brothers provide street theater. Some two dozen shops beckon with shelves full of merchandise. There are nearly 20 restaurants, bistros, snack bars and drive-ins as well.

Helpful Hints – Arrive 30min to 1hr prior to opening time. As soon as the gates open, head for Twister, Terminator 2, Back to the Future and JAWS; then visit E.T. Adventure, FUNtastic World of Hanna-Barbera, and Kongfrontation. Plan to see shows during midday, when ride lines are longest; check the Preview of Today's Rides and Shows for scheduled times. The VIP Tour Experience gives visitors priority entrance to leading attractions *(72hr advance reservations required);* for specifics, www universalorlando.com ☎ 407-363-8295.

Visit

Below are descriptions of most of the popular attractions in counterclockwise order from the entrance.

Chrome and glass-block shops and eateries line the **Front Lot**, where such celebrity look-alikes as Laurel and Hardy, Marilyn Monroe and Charlie Chaplin might put in an appearance. Universal's reproduction of **Hollywood** (California) angles off to the right, where palms sway above such legendary landmarks as the Beverly Wilshire Hotel and Schwab's soda fountain. Among replicas of the exclusive shop fronts of Rodeo Drive lies **Lucy, A Tribute**, a gallery devoted to actress-comedian Lucille Ball memorabilia and clips from the *I Love Lucy* show, popular in the 1950s.

Terminator 2: 3-D – Arnold's back, with a vengeance, in *Battle Across Time*, the sequel to the popular Schwarzenegger film *Terminator 2: The Final Judgment*. The gripping 12min film marries stunt work, state-of-the-art special effects and in-your-face 3-D to keep viewers on the edge of their seats. At $23 million, the action movie—directed by James Cameron whose credits include the 1998 hit, *Titanic*—is said to be the most expensive footage ever shot, minute for minute.

The Gory Gruesome & Grotesque Horror Make-up Show treats audiences to a view of comical make-up artists who demonstrate the tricks of their trade. **AT&T at the Movies** is an interactive arcade where visitors can touch the technology of moviemaking.

E.T. Adventure – The magic of director Steven Spielberg's popular film is captured both in this ride and its waiting area, where visitors are guaranteed to spend time. Long lines weave through a dark, dreamy Northwest forest, scented with evergreens. E.T. has returned to Earth to obtain our assistance in healing his Green Planet, which has fallen ill. Riders hop aboard bicycles that carry them and the unforgettable extraterrestrial on an airborne adventure above an American cityscape and on to E.T.'s beloved home.

Fievel's Playland – Another tribute to a Spielberg character, this whimsical playground is based on the antics of Fievel the mouse (from the animated film *An American Tail*). Nets for climbing, tubes for exploring, and watery slides for getting wet make up this miniature world.

A Day in the Park with Barney – Colorful sets with top-flight stage effects complement songs by the beloved purple dinosaur of PBS fame and his friends, Baby Bop and B.J. The endearingly kooky Mr. Peekaboo, a human character, adds to the fun. After exiting the theater-in-the-round, the audience enters "Barney's Backyard," an educational play area.

Animal Planet Live – Pet lovers flock to this show where the screen's most lovable animal stars—Lassie, Beethoven, Mister Ed, and others—perform tricks with a live supporting cast of cats, birds and other animals.

Back To The Future: The Ride – In Universal's most popular ride, you'll heed the taped plea of Doc Brown (actor Christopher Lloyd) to help save the universe from evil villain Biff Tannen. Board a Time Vehicle for a white-knuckle flight into the Ice Age, where you'll thunder over glacial fields and free-fall into a flaming volcano. Multisensory special effects enhance the experience.

Men in Black Alien Attack – This high-tech ride is the first in history to allow two side-by-side vehicles to compete (the tabulated score is visible in each car). Riding in "training vehicles," passengers aim "alien zappers" at some 120 electronic targets that pop up along the route. Computerization generates a choice of 12 different ride endings and thousands of ride experience options.

Wild, Wild, Wild West Stunt Show – Commandeering the stage of this amphitheater, the Hopper (as in Clod) family hams it up with fancy shootin' and stuntsmanship. *Check park map for times.*

At the east end of the lagoon, small, weathered clapboard facades and street vendors re-create the New England seaside atmosphere of **Amity**, fictional setting of the 1975 movie hit *Jaws*.

JAWS – On a cruise through the waters around Amity, passengers find themselves virtually in the maw of that infamous and indestructible great white shark. Boat pilots, however, have a few tricks up their sleeves, and after some spectacular fiery clashes, all are returned safely to shore.

Along the north edge of the Lagoon lies **San Francisco**. The old Ghirardelli chocolate factory and trolley tracks running through the street leave no doubt that you've entered that city's famous Fisherman's Wharf area.

Earthquake: The Big One – The attraction begins with a behind-the-scenes look at how Charlton Heston made the movie *Earthquake* in 1974. Visitors then board a San Francisco subway for a truly ground-breaking trip, in which the earth shakes and cataclysm follows.

Beetlejuice's Graveyard Revue – In this live, camp musical revue emceed by the incorrigible Beetlejuice, Dracula, Frankenstein and his bride, and other movie monsters stomp through rock-'n-roll classics. *Check park map for times.*

The streets of **New York** capture the romantic, if somewhat decrepit, charms of the brownstones, parks and billboards of the Big Apple. At various intervals, the **Blues Brothers** stage their own outdoor show on Delancey Street. *Check map for times.*

Kongfrontation – After winding through a New York subway station with graffiti-splattered walls, passengers board cable cars for a trip above the city. With the great Kong on the loose, they're guaranteed a primate confrontation or two.

Twister! Ride It Out – An adaptation of the 1996 movie of the same name, Twister! subjects visitors to the fury of a large tornado as it rages through a rural town on the Great Plains, right down to tanker fires, broken water mains and a flying cow, just 20ft away.

Flintstones Characters and Friends

Stage 54 (Production Central) features props and sets from a recent major Universal film or television show, actually re-creating some of the film's most dramatic scenes. Six warehouse-style buildings contain working soundstages, while the centrally located **Boneyard** features such classic movie props as the dorsal fin sported by the great white shark in *Jaws*.

The FUNtastic World of Hanna-Barbera – Belying its childlike cartoon theme, this ranks as one of the park's most action-packed rides. A theater audience strapped into rollicking seats takes a simulated zoom through cartoonland, visiting the Flintstones, the Jetsons, Yogi Bear and a host of other Hanna-Barbera familiars along the way. The exit leads into a hands-on playroom filled with cartoon whimsy. *For those interested in the cartoon but not the motion, stationary seats are located at the front of the theater.*

Nickelodeon Studios Tour – *Tours operate continuously 9am-closing; first-come first-served;* ♿. The tour gives visitors a look at the two soundstages used by Nickelodeon. Even when the cameras aren't rolling, a guide explains the process of putting a show together and takes visitors past soundstages, make-up and hair departments, and dressing rooms.

UNIVERSAL'S ISLANDS OF ADVENTURE

With producer-director Steven Spielberg as creative consultant, "Islands" is recognized as a triumph of imagination. Its gateway area, Port of Entry, opened in the fall of 1998, and the grand opening of the entire theme park took place in mid 1999. Swooping roller-coaster loops tower over this 21C, high-tech amusement complex. With its eclectic architecture representing a variety of world harbor cultures, **Port of Entry** serves as a shopping and dining area as well as a departure point for Universal Orlando's man-made archipelago around a large lagoon. One of the five islands, **Seuss Landing** features whimsical characters of children's literature favorite Theodor "Dr. Seuss" Geisel. Another island called **Toon Lagoon** brings to life classic cartoon characters. Realistic dinosaurs stalk visitors at **Jurassic Park**, while high-tech thrill rides are the main attractions of **The Lost Continent** and **Marvel Super Hero Island.** Shops and restaurants, themed to match the island whereon they stand, complement the attractions while offering visitors a calming break from the hair-raising, stomach-churning thrill rides.

Visit

Port of Entry – The starting point begins here in this port town with its looming lighthouse and bustling arcade of food and beverage outlets, such as the Backwater Bar and chic shops like the Ocean Trader Market. Boats depart from here for the five themed islands that comprise the bulk of the park (though most visitors prefer to walk).

Below are highlights of each of the five islands, which are described in counter-clockwise order from the entrance.

Seuss Landing – On this island, all is linked to the famed series of children's books by Dr. Seuss. As his readers would expect, the architecture here lacks symmetry and straight lines. Mounts on the elaborate **Caro-Seuss-el** represent elephant-birds, the cowfish and other Seuss characters. For refreshments, visitors dine at the Green Eggs and Ham Cafe (where eggs are really green), or sip slurpies at the Moose Juice Goose Juice. Floppy headgear is available at the Cats, Hats & Things shop.

The Cat in the Hat – Visitors ride on 6-passenger "couches" through 18 scenes from Seuss books that include a 24ft perception-altering tunnel. Some 30 Seuss characters join the fun, among them The Cat in the Hat and Thing 1.

One Fish, Two Fish, Red Fish, Blue Fish – Visitors ride a fish, steering it to avoid squirts from a series of waterspouts and streams. All the while a rhyming riddle is broadcast to give clues on how to stay dry while rising and dropping 15ft within the orbit.

The Lost Continent – Dominated by the hills and valleys of the Dueling Dragons, this island, based on fantasy novels and movies, is of particular interest to kids. Visitors can cool off at the Frozen Desert restaurant and browse at bazaars called Treasures of Poseidon and the Dragon's Keep.

Dueling Dragons – This thrill ride is a must if you're a roller-coaster enthusiast. The coaster, with two intertwined tracks, is inverted, so that passengers' legs dangle freely. Riders climb, four abreast, onto a dragon representing Fire or another representing Ice. As the two dragons zoom through a medieval forest, they climb 125ft, side-by-side. Then Fire shoots off to the left at 60mph and Ice dives right at 55mph to complete a series of upside-down flips that involve close misses with the other dragon.

Eighth Voyage of Sinbad – An amusement, at last, where guests can sit back and watch while *others* perform daredevil feats. Legendary Sinbad sets out on a death-defying voyage, dodging water explosions and fiery dangers, including a 10ft-high circle of flames, all of which he survives.

Jurassic Park – Stephen Spielberg's technological savvy is much in evidence on this island, which is filled with dinosaur rides and scary experiences. Naturally, one of the snack spots is the Pizza Predatoria and there's a retail outlet called the Dinostore.

River Adventure – As you ride within the park, thunder and lightning split the stormy skies. The terrifying *Tyrannosaurus rex* is pursuing you closely, the beast's savage teeth coming at times within inches of your face. The only escape is down an 85ft water chute—reputedly, the longest, steepest and fastest built to date.

Pteranodon Flyers – Guests are invited to climb onto the backs of these replicated flying creatures from millions of years ago and take an aerial tour above **Camp Jurassic**, with its ancient volcano and amber mine. The flyers' wings extend 10ft on either side of the passengers.

Toon Lagoon – Here on this island comic books and film cartoons come to life, especially along **Comic Strip Lane**, home of the Pandemonium Cartoon Circus. If there's one place to eat an oversize sandwich, it has to be at Blondie's: Home of the Dagwood Sandwich, where patrons pay per the thickness of the sandwiches they make. Toon Toys and Gasoline Alley are two of the island's most visited stores.

Dudley Do-Right's Ripsaw Falls – Nell's in trouble, and the incompetent Canadian Mountie of "Rocky and Bullwinkle" fame must save her from the evil Snidely Whiplash. Visitors join the rescue, which ends with a 15ft plunge beneath a lagoon's surface, the first-ever ride below water level. Anticipate getting wet!

Popeye and Bluto's Bilge-Rat Barges – The 12 passengers on this rapid white-water raft ride get squirted by water cannon from Popeye's boat and encounter an 18ft octopus, its 12ft tentacles bulging with water. On the last stop, a boat wash, passengers are sure to get drenched.

Marvel Super Hero Island – The last island holds the attraction that garners the most enthusiasm: the Spider-Man ride. It's probably best to eat *after* going on it or on **Doctor Doom's Fearfall** or on any ride, but Captain America's Diner is a popular choice for refreshments. The Comics Shop and the Marvel Alterniverse hold myriad memorabilia.

Amazing Adventures of Spider-Man – This ride is a theme-park first: an attraction that combines moving vehicles, filmed 3-D action and special effects. As they try to help Spider-Man retrieve the stolen Statue of Liberty, riders don 3-D night-sight goggles, take a 400ft "sensory drop" into darkness, and speed around a 1.5-acre set racked with fiery battles between good and evil.

Incredible Hulk Coaster – A series of chilling swoops and loops, this ride is a close competitor with the popular Dueling Dragons. Passengers are shot out of Dr. Banner's Gamma Force Accelerator with the same G-force of an F-16 jet. They zoom from 0 to 40mph in 2 seconds, roll over 7 times and plunge underground twice, all within 2 minutes and 15 seconds.

UNIVERSAL CITYWALK

Completed in the spring of 1999, this 30-acre, two-tiered promenade of individually themed entertainment venues, hotels, restaurants and dance clubs fronts a four-acre harbor. It is connected by bridges to the entrances of Universal Studios Florida and Universal's Islands of Adventure, which are accessible only through CityWalk.

By the end of 2002, the Loews Corp. will have constructed three luxury accommodations on the grounds of Universal Orlando, adjacent to CityWalk. Opened in 1999, the brightly colored **Portofino Bay Hotel** captures the look and feel of the Italian Riviera, with fishing boats in a harbor, like its namesake town in Italy. In early 2001 the first **Hard Rock Hotel**, adorned throughout with rock-music memorabilia, made its debut, and in 2002 Loews will add the Royal Pacific Resort.

Visit

Famous names pop up everywhere in CityWalk. A paean to the Gulf Coast's vagabond minstrel, **Jimmy Buffett's Margaritaville** is a combination nightclub and restaurant featuring the requisite "cheeseburger in paradise." If you can hear the chef shouting "Bam," you're obviously in **Emeril's Restaurant Orlando**, dining on Chef Lagasse's famed Creole-style cuisine. Hoop fans tend to haunt the **NBA City** restaurant, autograph books in hand, while car buffs sip and sup at the NASCAR Cafe's bounteous buffet. CityWalk possesses the world's largest **Hard Rock Café** as well as a replica of New Orleans' celebrated watering hole, Pat O'Brien's, complete with dueling pianos and a "flaming fountain" patio.

As to music, there's plenty available in CityWalk night spots like Margaritaville and The Groove, Latin Quarter and others in addition to the 2,200-seat **Hard Rock Live** where recognized artists from around the globe perform. At **Bob Marley's**, the Jamaican home and garden of the reggae messiah have been re-created. The formidable **CityJazz** boasts the Thelonious Monk Institute of Jazz and the Down Beat Jazz Hall of Fame along with a performance theater. Within CityWalk there's also a 20-screen, 5,000-seat Cineplex Odeon theater and a bounty of specialty shops sporting offbeat and colorful wares.

WALT DISNEY WORLD® RESORT★★★

Map p 159
Tourist Information: www.disneyworld.com ☏ 407-824-4321

Truly a microcosm unto itself, this immense 29,900-acre (47sq mi) complex—about twice the size of Manhattan Island—lies 20mi southwest of downtown Orlando and encompasses four extensive theme parks (Magic Kingdom, Epcot, Disney's Animal Kingdom and Disney-MGM Studios), 28 separate resort hotels with nearly 30,000 rooms, 8 nightclubs, 3 water parks, six 18-hole golf courses, a 200-acre sports complex, numerous lakes, a zoological park and much more. First opened in 1971 with Magic Kingdom, Walt Disney World continues to grow, combining in its attractions the romantic nostalgia of the mid-20C Disney vision with the fast-paced technology of the 21C.

■ Disney's Dream Comes True

Born and raised in the Midwest, **Walter Elias Disney** (1901-1966) showed early signs of a keen imagination and an aptitude for drawing. By age 21 he had established an animation studio in Kansas City. When that failed, he headed for Hollywood, California. The Disney Brothers Studios, established by Walt and his brother Roy in 1923, scored its first popular success in 1928 with *Steamboat Willie*. The film, starring a mouse named Mickey, combined animation and the new technology of sound. Disney's first full-length animated film, *Snow White* (1937), met with instant success.

In the early 1950s, disillusioned with the tawdriness of amusement parks, Disney began planning his own. **Disneyland**, which opened in July 1955 in Anaheim, California, was destined to change the face of global amusement. Disney launched plans to open a second theme park. He wanted to acquire a far larger tract that could be buffered from the sort of commercial development that had sprung up around the 180-acre Anaheim site. His new park would create a Disney-styled world where visitors could eat, sleep and enjoy his entertainment. Walt Disney chose central Florida as the site of his new park in the mid-1960s, presumably because land was inexpensive, the climate was good, and growth was anticipated in the area. As building began, however, Disney was diagnosed with cancer; the 65-year-old cartoonist died in 1966. The immensely popular Disney concept has also been exported abroad. In 1983 Tokyo Disneyland opened, followed in 1993 by Disneyland Paris. Hong Kong Disneyland is scheduled to open in 2005.

Walt Disney envisioned his Florida property as an **Experimental Prototype Community of Tomorrow** (Epcot)—a model for future communities and a showcase of American creativity. In 1971 Magic Kingdom opened, followed in 1982 by Epcot. Seven years later, Disney-MGM Studios was added, combining a working film studio and theme park that celebrates the magic of movies. Disney's Animal Kingdom opened to the public in 1998. Orlando's Walt Disney World remains the largest Disney complex and the most visited theme park in the world.

Today, Walt Disney World Resort includes the **Walt Disney World Speedway**, which hosted its first Indy 200 race in 1996, and **BoardWalk**, a replica of a 1930s-era Atlantic-coast town, with shops, restaurants, nightclubs and a hotel. Completed in 1997 were **Disney's Wide World of Sports**, a 200-acre complex with a baseball stadium and facilities for amateur and professional sports, and the **Richard Petty Driving Experience**, a 145mph test-track adventure. **Downtown Disney**, a shopping-dining-and-nightlife complex, opened in 1998. The company even launched a brand-new Disney Cruise Line based at Port Canaveral, on the Atlantic coast. Disney's newest hotel is the 1,293-room **Animal Kingdom Lodge**, which overlooks the theme park of the same name. Planned for 2002 is Disney's Pop Century Resort, a 5,700-room hotel featuring large-scale American icons like the jukebox.

The first residents occupied their homes in 1996 in Disney's $100 million planned community called **Celebration**, located 15mi south of Magic Kingdom. Covering 4,900 acres, Celebration embodies the conglomerate's vision of the late 19C American small town. The community includes its own school, health-care facility and business district.

PRACTICAL INFORMATION ....Area Code: 407

When to Go

Walt Disney World is busiest during the summer, Christmas and spring holidays. The least crowded period falls between Thanksgiving and December 25, followed by September and October, then January. Mondays, Tuesdays and Wednesdays—except during holiday seasons—are the busiest days of the week at Magic Kingdom. Tuesdays and Wednesdays are more crowded at Epcot; attendance at Disney-MGM Studios is heaviest on Thursdays and Fridays. Sunday morning tends to be least crowded at all the parks. Due to constant updating and maintenance, some rides and eating facilities may be closed.

During the summer months *(late May-late Sept)*, temperatures range from 85°-95°F during the day, and from 68°-75°F at night. Humidity is high and afternoon thundershowers are frequent. The rest of the year, temperatures average from 75°-82°F during the day, and dip between 52°-65°F at night. Lightweight, comfortable clothing, a hat and sunscreen are suggested.

Your Visit – On the day of your visit, arrive at the park when ticket booths open, usually one hour before the scheduled opening time. With your ticket, you will receive a Walt Disney World guide, detailed map and show schedule that lists times for performances, parades and all other entertainment. Visitors staying at Walt Disney World properties can enter the parks at 7:30am on selected days (Magic Kingdom: Mon, Thu & Sat; Epcot: Tue & Fri; Disney-MGM Studios: Wed & Sun). *(For up-to-date schedules: ☎ 824-4321; www.disneyworld.com)*. All **guided tours** are limited to 15-20 people; prices are in addition to park entrance fees; advance reservations are required *(☎ 939-8687)*.

Getting There

By Air – **Orlando International Airport (MCO)**: 28mi northeast of Walt Disney World; information booth *(open daily 7am-11pm; multilingual service; ☎ 825-2352)*. **Shuttle** service to Walt Disney World *(departs from baggage claim area year round daily every 15-20min; $14/one-way, child $10)*; Mears Motor Shuttle ☎ 839-1570. **Limo** and **taxi** service is also available. **Rental car** agencies *(p 343)* are located at the airport. If **driving** from Orlando airport, take the Beeline Expressway, Route 528 west *(toll)*, then continue on I-4 west to parks.

By Car – Walt Disney World is located 20mi southwest of downtown Orlando. Take I-4 west to Exit 26B for best access to Epcot, Typhoon Lagoon, Downtown Disney and River Country. For the most direct route to Disney's Animal Kingdom, Wide World of Sports, Disney-MGM Studios and the Magic Kingdom take Exit 25B (Route 192 west) and follow signs to the various parks. Trams shuttle visitors to the main gates from pick-up areas throughout the sprawling parking lots. Note the section and row where you park; it's easy to lose track of your vehicle.

By Train or Bus – Nearest Amtrak station: 1400 Sligh Blvd., Orlando *(24mi from park; ☎ 800-872-7245; www.amtrak.com)*. Greyhound station: 555 N. John Young Pwky., Orlando *(26mi from park; ☎ 292-3424)*, and 16 N. Orlando Ave., Kissimmee *(12mi from park; ☎ 800-231-2222; www.greyhound.com)*.

General Information

Accommodations – The vast Walt Disney World Resort complex offers close to 30,000 rooms at 28 properties that include resort **hotels**, **villas**, **condominiums**, **cabins** and **campgrounds**. Rates vary depending on location, type of hotel and season; rates are lower during early Jan-mid-Feb, mid-Apr-mid-Jun and Sept-mid-Dec. Children under 18 stay free in rooms with parents. In-room baby-sitting service is available. **KinderCare** center accepts 1- to 4yr-old children. For all reservations ☎ W-DISNEY (934-7639), dial *88 from specially marked phones, or visit the Guest Relations booths at individual parks.

Outside the Disney Complex – Numerous lodgings lie within easy reach *(5-10min)* of the main entrances. Accommodations range from **luxury hotels** *($199-$350)* to moderate **hotels** *($90-$220)* and budget **motels** *($49-$65)*. Many offer free shuttle service to Disney attractions. Make reservations three to five months in advance—especially for summer and holiday stays. Information on area accommodations available from the **Orlando/Orange County Convention and Visitors Bureau** *(☎ 363-5872; www.orlandoinfo.com)*. *Rates quoted are average prices per night for a double room and are subject to seasonal variation.*

Visitor Information – For general information and to request a free Vacation Guide, contact **Walt Disney World Guest Information**, PO Box 10040, Lake Buena Vista FL 32830-0040 *(☎ 824-4321; www.disneyworld.com)*. All Walt Disney

World attractions are accessible to visitors with disabilities. All attractions are free for children under 3. **Parking:** $6. Same-day **reentry** is permitted with a valid ticket and hand stamp. Proper dress is required at all times. Baby strollers and wheelchair rentals available in limited quantities *($6)*. For most visitor services (foreign language maps, information for guests with disabilities, baby facilities, lost and found, storage lockers, banking facilities, camera centers, Disney character greetings), contact Guest Relations at individual parks: City Hall, Main Street U.S.A. at Magic Kingdom; near gift stop at Epcot; Hollywood Boulevard at Disney-MGM Studios; next to Creature Comfort at Animal Kingdom. For **lost children**, check the lost children's logbooks at Baby Care Centers or contact Guest Relations. For **medical emergencies**, contact the First Aid Centers near Guest Relations.

Admission Fees	**Adults**	**Children**
Free for children under 3 years of age.		*(ages 3-9)*
One-day/One park ticket	$48	$38

Also available are 4- to 7-day passes as is an Annual Passport (unlimited admission to all 4 parks). Check www.disneyworld.com for most current fees. **FASTPASS** is a free, computerized system to avoid waiting in lines at 19 attractions. Guests insert theme-park ticket into a turnstyle and receive a FASTPASS with a time to return. Upon return they proceed directly to the attraction through a FASTPASS entrance, with little or no wait.

Note: unless otherwise specified, admission fees for individual Disney attractions in this guide are the single adult price only (children's fees are lower); taxes are not included.

Park Hours – Each park has individual hours. In general Animal Kingdom opens at 8am, the other three theme parks open at 9am (Epcot's World Showcase opens at 11am, however) and the water parks at 10am, while closing hours vary seasonally and depending upon the day's events. *It is strongly advised that you check www.disneyworld.com or call Disney World in advance of your trip to obtain the current hours for the month in which you intend to visit.*

Getting Around – **Monorail trains, buses, ferry boats and water taxi** *(all free)* link all attractions including hotels and resorts throughout the complex. **Buses** operate approximately every 20min, starting 1hr prior to park opening until closing. Routes painted in RED are direct routes after 4pm. The only exceptions: Service to Magic Kingdom, Epcot, Disney-MGM Studios from Disney's Old Key West Resort and the Disney Institute operate on scheduled pick-up times between noon and 6pm. Service to Disney's Blizzard Beach Water Park operates on a schedule with up to a 35min interval between buses on some routes.

Eating – A wide selection of eateries punctuates the complex. Sidewalk stalls sell fresh fruit, hot dogs, ice cream and snacks; cafeterias and carryout stands accommodate diners on the run; more expensive restaurants *(lunch $14.95-$21.95/person, child $6.99; dinner $16.95-$47/person, child $7.95-$9.55)* mirror the theme of the parks in which they are located. Make reservations early in the day by contacting Guest Relations. Crowds and lines are heaviest at peak dining hours *(11:30am-2pm and 6-8pm)*. Dining at any of the Disney Resort hotels and dinner shows is open to the public; for priority-seating reservations ☎ 939-3463.

Sports and Entertainment – Enjoy a round of **golf** on one of Disney's six championship courses *($60-$170; for tee times ☎ 824-2270)*. Other recreational opportunities available to the general public and Disney Resort guests include tennis, boating, fishing, health club, swimming, waterskiing and horseback riding. **Youth Education Series** programs focus on nature, art, culture and ecology ☎ 939-2223).

A variety of live-performance stage shows are presented in the parks throughout the day. All operate on a first-come, first-served basis. For times, check the show schedule brochure; each park prints its own entertainment schedule. **Disney Character Breakfast** served daily at various resort hotels and at all four parks. Reservations can be made 60 days in advance *(☎ 939-3463)*.

Disney by Night – During the summer months and on holidays, visitors are treated nightly to an extravaganza of lights, lasers and fireworks at the three original parks. **SpectroMagic**, a stellar parade of lighted floats, makes its way down Main Street U.S.A. twice each evening; while **Fantasy in the Sky** fireworks transform the Magic Kingdom into a wonderland to the tune of "When You Wish Upon a Star." **IllumiNations** held around the lagoon at Epcot showcases a breathtaking display of lasers, fountains, music and fireworks. The Fantasmic! laser-and-water display at Disney-MGM Studios is also spectacular. Consult entertainment schedules for locations and times.

Useful Numbers   ☏

Emergency	**911**
Hotel and Dinner Show Reservations	934-7639
Walt Disney Resort Information	824-4321
Resort Dining and Recreation	939-3463
Magic Kingdom Lost and Found *(same day)*	824-4521
Epcot Center Lost and Found *(same day)*	560-6105
Disney-MGM Studios Lost and Found *(same day)*	560-3764
Animal Kingdom Lost and Found *(same day)*	938-2265
Central Lost and Found	824-4245

MAGIC KINGDOM

Kids *Take I-4 west to Exit 25B (US-192 west). Turn right on World Dr. and follow signs to entrance of park. In general open year-round daily 9am; closing times vary.*

This Florida version of the Magic Kingdom lacks some of the old-fashioned attractions and sentimental appeal preserved in the original California Disneyland. Roughly square, the 107-acre Florida park includes seven areas that radiate out from the Central Plaza in front of Cinderella Castle. Shops, eateries, attractions and costumed "cast members" (ride attendants, shopkeepers and other staff) in each area echo the dominant theme of their "land."

Helpful Hints – Magic Kingdom is the most popular—and thus crowded—of the four parks, and the most time-consuming to access. After taking a shuttle across the parking lot to the **Ticket and Transportation Center**, you board either a monorail train or a replica paddlewheeler that crosses the Seven Seas Lagoon. Thrill rides—Space Mountain, ExtraTERRORestrial Alien Encounter, Splash Mountain and Big Thunder Mountain—along with Pirates of the Caribbean tend to attract the greatest crowds; head for them first.

A guided walking tour, Keys to the Kingdom, explains the park's history and technology and takes in several rides, as well as the Diamond Horseshoe Saloon Revue *(departs from City Hall daily 8:30am, 9:30am, 10am & 1:30pm, except holidays; 4hrs; 16 years or older; $58, including lunch; reservations required theme park admission required; ☏ 407-939-8687).*

Main Street, U.S.A.

Tidy Victorian storefronts holding commercial shops re-create the milieu of an early 19C town. In designing Main Street, U.S.A., Walt Disney used a film device called forced perspective: upper stories of buildings are not as high as lower ones, giving the buildings a taller appearance. Adding to the atmosphere, a horse-drawn trolley, antique fire engine, omnibus, "horseless carriages" and jitneys carry passengers between the Town Square and Central Plaza. Minstrels often stroll the street, and the cartoon-character-filled **Disney's Share a Dream Come True Parade** wends its way down Main Street every afternoon, highlighting recent animated film successes *(check park brochure for show times)*. During evenings in peak periods (summer and Christmas holidays), the **SpectroMagic** parade fills the street with a dazzling spectacle of Disney characters. The parade is often followed by **Fantasy in the Sky**, featuring flying Tinkerbell and a fireworks display *(check brochure for show times)*.

Walt Disney World Railroad – Passengers can board steam trains that circle the park, stopping at Frontierland and Mickey's Toontown Fair. Purchased from the Mexican government, the trains were formerly used to haul sugarcane and tropical fruit.

> **1** **River Country**
> **Kids** *See map. Adjacent to Bay Lake. Take I-4 west to Exit 25B (US-92 west). Turn right on World Dr. and follow signs to park. Open May-Aug Tue-Thu & Sat 10am-6pm; rest of the year hours vary. $15.95, $13.25 children ages 3-9.* Swimsuit clad visitors slip and slide down rapids, through flumes and around a boulder-strewn "river" in Disney's six-acre answer to the local swimming hole.

Tomorrowland

Bowing to the age of technology, Walt Disney World in the mid-1990s undertook a major overhaul of Tomorrowland attractions, many of which were outdated. Rather than attempt to predict the future, Disney has opted to create a "fantasy future city," recapturing the futuristic visions of the 1920s and 30s.

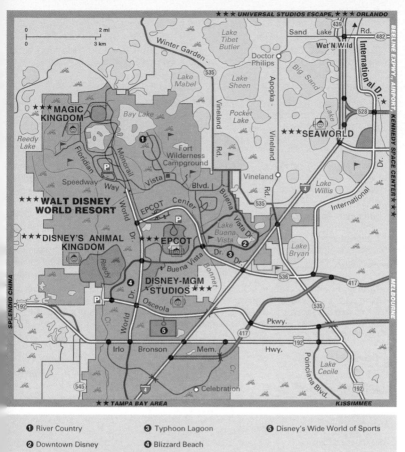

1 River Country   **3** Typhoon Lagoon   **5** Disney's Wide World of Sports

2 Downtown Disney   **4** Blizzard Beach

ExtraTERRORestrial Alien Encounter – ⅢⅢ Line up early for a truly spine-tingling 18min in this sci-fi scenario designed with the help of special-effects guru George Lucas. Inside the Interplanetary Convention Center you'll meet a maniacal corporation executive from another planet who attempts to demonstrate his new technique of intergalactic teleportation. The experiment goes awry, and a hideous alien space creature mistakenly materializes. The ensuing blitz of sound, light and other special effects in the darkened theater treats the audience to a terrifyingly realistic encounter with a carnivorous monster.

Timekeeper – Guided by a madcap robot (whose voice is supplied by comedian Robin Williams), spectators at this engrossing CircleVision 360 film *(15min)* journey through time from the age of dinosaurs to the future. Along the way you'll meet such historical figures as Mozart, Leonardo da Vinci and H.G. Wells, as the camera swoops through breathtaking scenery from around the world.

Astro Orbiter – Pilot your own orbiter through swirling planets around Tomorrowland's colorful central spire. Although popular with the younger set, the updated ride affords adults good views of the Magic Kingdom.

Carousel of Progress – Housed in a round building, the revolving theater circles four stages where life-size Audio-Animatronics® characters portray the evolution of life in an American home, from the pre-electric 19C to the computerized end of the 20C.

Buzz Lightyear's Space Ranger Spin – This "interactive space fantasy" teams visitors with characters from *Toy Story* in defending Earth's battery supply against the evil Emperor Zurg. Piloting your own XP-38 Space Cruiser equipped with twin laser cannons, you "shoot" and steer in an adventure "to infinity and beyond." As combatants fire the infrared lasers, targets spring to animated life.

Space Mountain – ⅢⅢ Since it opened in 1975, this roller coaster enclosed in a futuristic mountain has been one of Disney's most popular rides. Not for the faint of heart, Space Mountain hurtles passengers through near-darkness, plunging them into sudden, atmospheric comet showers and past faintly twinkling stars.

Tomorrowland Indy Speedway – Young and old motorists alike take the wheel of these small sports cars and maneuver them along a gently curving raceway—inset with an iron track to keep things on course. *Children must be 52in tall to drive.*

Tomorrowland Transit Authority – Hop aboard this overhead tram for a bird's-eye view of the "city of the future" as imagined by early science-fiction visionaries.

Mickey's Toontown Fair

Retaining bits and pieces of Mickey's Starland, which it has replaced, Toontown Fair occupies a relatively quiet, three-acre corner of the Kingdom. Scaled to visitors under age 10 (and their parents), the whimsical village is built of pastel-shaded, round-edged buildings with a sort of gingerbread appeal. For kids who want to meet their favorite Disney characters, this is the best place.

Toontown Hall of Fame – In effect a big Disney store with the ambience of an old-fashioned country fair tent, the Hall of Fame boasts "character greeting locations" where Goofy and Pluto, for instance, shake hands, scrawl their autographs and pose for photos all day long.

Mickey's Country House – A stroll through Mickey's cozy home gives visitors a look at the lifestyle of Disney's greatest celebrity, including a peek at his grocery list. Displayed are plaques and trophies of his years of success. A corridor leads to a soundstage and theater; Mickey himself (now in his 70s, but with a seemingly direct line to the Fountain of Youth) holds court backstage, signing autographs for admirers (except during parade times).

Minnie's Country House – Opposite Mickey's house, of course, is Minnie's quaint pink palace. It reflects a traditional role for "the fairer sex" where even the appliances seem to smile and giggle. Across the lane are **Donald Duck's Boat**, the *Miss Daisy*, which lures youngsters to climb through its tunnels and up its stairs; and a child-size roller coaster, **The Barnstormer at Goofy's Wiseacre Farm**.

Fantasyland

With the fairy-tale air of an old European village, the original Fantasyland in California was Walt Disney's personal favorite. While this version lacks some of the quaintness of the original, it still ranks as the most popular area in all Walt Disney World. Adults with a taste for whimsy are captivated by its old-fashioned magic, as are young children who have seen the Disney classics through rerelease and on videotape. Live shows are held periodically at the **Castle Forecourt Stage** and a **Fantasyland Pavilion.** Merlin the Wizard also appears in front of Cinderella's Carousel for a **Sword in the Stone** presentation *(check park brochure for show times)*.

Cinderella Castle – Of all the castles in Disney theme parks worldwide, this 189ft high Gothic extravaganza, ornamented with its turrets, towers, gold spires and leaded-glass windows, is the largest. It was inspired by one of the 19C castles built in Bavaria by King Ludwig II. Though the interior is not an attraction but a restaurant, the arched entrance through the castle gate is inlaid with detailed mosaic depicting the rags-to-riches story of Cinderella.

Cinderella's Golden Carousel – Many of the mounts on this merry-go-round are hand-painted antiques. A band organ plays Disney tunes as horses gallop beneath a canopy painted with scenes from the Disney movie *Cinderella*.

Legend of the Lion King – In this 15min condensation of the popular animated film, life-size stick puppets mouth lines prerecorded by the original voice talent of James Earl Jones, Jeremy Irons and others.

It's a Small World – This cross-cultural fantasy was conceived for the 1964 World's Fair and embodies an idealized view of international brotherhood. Boarding small boats, visitors float past 500 Audio-Animatronics® children and animals representing nearly 100 nations, all singing the repetitive theme song.

Dumbo, the Flying Elephant – Longtime favorite with small visitors, the carnival-style ride allows passengers to make their individual Dumbos soar up and down by manipulating a knob in front of the seat.

Mad Tea Party – This updated version of the old teacup favorite looks like a modern tilt-a-whirl with cup-and-saucer conveyances. Passengers control the amount of spin by turning a wheel in the center of each cup.

Ariel's Grotto – A cast member dressed as *The Little Mermaid* poses for photos in a concrete sea cave as little girls line up with their dads to await their turns. Little boys are more amused tiptoeing around an unpredictably spouting fountain outside the cave.

Disney Animated Classics – Fantasyland lauds Disney's early celluloid successes with several enclosed or "dark" rides. Based on animated feature films, these rides whisk visitors past Audio-Animatronics® figures and scenes that unfold the movie's plot

■ **Tips for Visiting Walt Disney World**

See popular attractions early, during a parade or late in the day.

Eat lunch or dinner during non-peak hours (before 11:30am or after 2pm and from 4pm-6pm or after 8pm).

Choose a restaurant that takes priority-seating reservations.

See a show or browse in the shops in the afternoon when many rides have long lines.

Best places to see the fireworks at Epcot: Matsu No Ma lounge in the Japan pavilion; the patio of the Rose & Crown in the United Kingdom pavilion; and Cantina de San Angel in the Mexico pavilion.

In **The Many Adventures of Winnie the Pooh**, passengers in "hunny pot" vehicles journey through a storybook page and into the Hundred Acre Wood to meet Pooh, Tigger and the other beloved characters. **Snow White's Adventures** takes visitors from the Seven Dwarfs' cozy cottage to an encounter with the Wicked Queen and on to a happy ending. Riders aboard the pirate-ship gondolas of **Peter Pan's Flight** float out of the Darling children's bedroom above a charming, fiber-optic version of night-time London. Soon after, passengers are plunged into Never Never Land, where Captain Hook, Smee and the Lost Boys await in their galleon.

Liberty Square

A celebration of America, Liberty Square re-creates a brick and clapboard colonial town set around a central square. Cast from the same mold as the revered original, a Liberty Bell sits in the center of the square. The 130-year-plus live oak designated as the site's "liberty tree" was discovered on the Disney property and carefully transplanted to this location.

Haunted Mansion – ⅲ Hosts of ghosts and ghouls spook the creepy mansion that looms ominously along the shore of the Rivers of America. From the "stretch-room," where heights and dimensions are not what they appear, visitors board small black "doom buggies" for a spine-tingling trip among holographic images and haunting, if humorous, special effects.

Hall of Presidents – This impressive multimedia production begins with an unabashedly patriotic film on the history of the Constitution, then blossoms into an Audio-Animatronics® tour de force in which all 43 US Presidents appear on stage for a roll call and, of course, a few speeches.

Liberty Belle Riverboat – A three-decker, ginger-bread-trimmed stern-wheeler, the *Liberty Belle*, plies the Rivers of America, past Audio-Animatronics® animals, an old-time trapper and an Indian village.

Frontierland

The Old West lives on in the wooden walkways, country stores and saloon of this frontier town. On many afternoons, gunslingers take to the rooftops for a rambunctious shoot-out. The **Diamond Horseshoe Saloon Revue**, a dance hall-style show, is performed several times daily in the Golden Horseshoe Saloon at the edge of Liberty Square. At **Country Bear Jamboree**, a winsome troupe of Audio-Animatronics® "Bear-itones" sings, tells jokes and generally delights crowds with their down-home performances *(check park brochure for show times)*.

© Disney Enterprises, Inc.

Big Thunder Mountain Railroad

2 Downtown Disney
See map. Take I-4 west to Exit 27. Turn north onto Rte. 535.; left at first light on Hotel Plaza Blvd. Entrance to Marketplace at intersection of Hotel Plaza Blvd. and Buena Vista Dr.; Pleasure Island and West Side extend west along Buena Vista Dr. ✂ ♿ P ☎ *407-824-4321.* This shopping and entertainment district on the southern shore of Lake Buena Vista is the most adult-oriented of any Disney attraction. Parents and children browse the shops of Marketplace by daylight, but after the sun goes down, the restaurants, nightclubs and theaters of Pleasure Island and West Side take center stage.

Marketplace – Kids *Open 8:30am-11pm.* This complex boasts an overwhelming assemblage of Disney character collectibles, along with resort wear. At the LEGO Imagination Center, visitors are awed by gargantuan, detailed structures built from the tiny plastic Danish bricks.

Pleasure Island – *Open 10:30am-2am; free until 7pm ($19.81). Must be 18yrs or older unless accompanied by a parent. BET Soundstage™ Club and Mannequins Dance Palace require proof of 21 years of age.* Eight nightclubs and a commercial theater offer late-night entertainment in a "warehouse" setting, ranging from rock 'n roll, Top 40, rhythm-and-blues, jazz and comedy to a fireworks display that concludes each evening. At the Adventurers Club, "members" parody a British travelers' fraternity. Adjacent to Pleasure Island stands the globe-shaped, celebrity-owned Planet Hollywood restaurant.

West Side – *Open 10:30am-2am; free admission.* At 66 acres the largest of the three Downtown Disney areas, West Side includes two restaurant-nightclubs, Bongos Cuban Cafe and the House of Blues; a Cirque du Soleil theater; a five-story interactive "virtual-reality" entertainment center called DisneyQuest; and a 24-plex cinema.

Splash Mountain – IIIII Riders board dark dugouts for a languid float through swamps and bayous inside Splash Mountain, as Br'er Rabbit, Br'er Fox and other characters from the 1946 Disney classic *Song of the South* serenade passing boats. At the mountaintop awaits one of the biggest thrills in the Magic Kingdom: a 52ft flume that hurls dugouts down a 47-degree slope to a monstrous soaking splash.

Big Thunder Mountain Railroad – This runaway train pulls out of an old mining town, then gathers steam as it roller-coasters through and around a red-rock mountain, negotiates a terrain of hoodoos, caves and canyons, and even plunges down through a dark, rickety mine shaft.

Tom Sawyer Island – Log rafts carry energetic explorers across the Rivers of America to Tom's island, where they can wander through Injun Joe's cave, the stockaded Fort Sam Clemens, a swinging footbridge, a tree house and more.

Adventureland

An eclectic mix of Polynesian, Moorish French Colonial and Spanish Colonial architecture establishes an exotic atmosphere here.

Enchanted Tiki Room – The 10min show presented here—"Under New Management"—introduces brash birds Iago (from Disney's *Aladdin*) and Zazu (from *The Lion King*) as the new landlords of the Tiki Room. When they offend the resident tiki gods, however they find themselves in big trouble. A cast of Audio-Animatronics® birds and orchids hold their own in this funny fantastical show that blends several choreographed musical numbers.

Magic Carpets of Aladdin – Adventureland's newest attraction, the magic carpets take four passengers each on a ride around a mammoth Genie lamp, while riders try to avoid water squirted from camels. On the ground, the **Agrabah Bazaar** and the Zanzibar Trading Company beckon visitors with a wealth of marketplace offerings.

Swiss Family Tree House – Visitors can climb through the sprawling, 80ft artificial banyan tree that re-creates the arboreal home of the indefatigable Swiss Family Robinson. This famous family originated in the 19C novel of Johann David Wyss, and was later immortalized in a Disney film.

Pirates of the Caribbean – IIIII Considered among the most popular amusement park rides ever created, this piratical adventure embodies the spirit of Disney at its best. Boarding boats, visitors weave through a darkened swamp before entering a Caribbean village raided by pirates. There the crafts drift past a series of sets peopled by lifelike buccaneers, pigs, parrots and more. (Disney designers used their own faces as models for the pirates' features.)

Jungle Cruise – Passengers on this nostalgic Disney favorite float down a jungle river that combines features of Africa, Asia and South America. Beware of mechanized crocodiles, hippos and elephants that pop up along the way past ruins overgrown with lush foliage. Boat pilots spice up the trip with pun-laced dialogue. Nearby, you'll find **Shrunken Ned's Junior Jungle Boats**, a remote-controlled attraction.

EPCOT

Kids *Take I-4 west to Exit 26B; go west on Epcot Center Dr. and follow signs to park entrance on left. In general open year-round daily 9am; closing times vary. World Showcase open daily 11am (10pm during summer months).* $$$$.

The daunting 260-acre Epcot is divided into two distinct areas: Future World, housing pavilions devoted to technology and ingenuity, and World Showcase, where the culture and architecture of 11 nations are represented. The Land and Living Seas pavilions function as working research centers as well as attractions. Coming to Future World in 2003 will be **Mission: SPACE**, a simulated astronaut adventure where guests will experience weightlessness and other effects of outer space.

Future World

Eight large pavilions here encircle the 180ft-high faceted geosphere that has come to symbolize Epcot. The 16-million-pound structure is supported by pylons sunk 100ft into the ground. Sponsored by major American corporations, pavilions here house rides, interactive display areas and films, all saluting humankind's ingenious technological achievements.

Spaceship Earth – Spiral up 18 stories in a time-machine vehicle inside Epcot's giant landmark sphere, where you'll ride past animated scenes depicting the history of human communication from prehistoric tribes to present-day technology. On the way down, you'll have a "satellite's view" of Earth. Back on the ground, take a film-simulated "ride" along the information highway and explore an ever-changing floorful of interactive simulations and video games that illustrate state-of-the-art communications technology in the **Global Neighborhood**.

Innoventions – Two facing crescent-shaped buildings behind Spaceship Earth showcase some of the world's newest inventions. Virtual keyboards, computer chips that learn, and a virtual reality tour of St. Peter's Basilica in Rome are just some of the ideas presented at **Innoventions West**. Across the plaza at **Innoventions East**, you'll find the latest developments in "smart-home" technology, auto design and the information superhighway. Most of the displays are interactive, entertaining even as they educate.

The Living Seas – Essentially a 5.7-million-gallon aquarium, this old-fashioned crowd-pleaser, with waves lapping its exterior, begins with a short film on the sea, then proceeds to the **Caribbean Coral Reef Ride**, a tram that moves through an acrylic cylinder in the world's largest man-made saltwater aquarium. After the ride, visitors board an elevator down to **Sea Base Alpha**, a prototype undersea research facility. Here you'll learn about ocean ecosystems and watch an array of marine life, including dolphins, sharks and manatees, cavort in large modular tanks. *Certified divers may enjoy a scuba adventure called Dive Quest (3hrs; $140; reservations ☎ 407-939-8687).*

© Robert Holmes

Spaceship Earth and Monorail

Test Track – Presented by General Motors, this attraction invites guests to buckle up to experience the spirals and speeds that experimental cars endure, including road handling, impact-testing and suspension checks.

The Land – Setting the tone for the ecological theme of this enormous working greenhouse, a plaque outside the entrance contains a quote by the late, renowned scientist René Dubos, who called the earth "a garden to be cultivated." Inside, the **Living With the Land** boat ride transports visitors, accompanied by a live narrator, through a simulated rain forest, desert and prairie before emerging into the pavilion's greenhouse gardens. Here scientists experiment on a variety of herbs, vegetables and other plants to perfect growing methods and to develop new hybrids. Horticulture enthusiasts may wish to take the **Harvest Tour**, a 45min guided walk through the greenhouses. *Sign up for tours outside "Food Rocks" on the first floor.* In the **Harvest Theater**, characters from Disney's 1994 animated film *The Lion King* act out an environmental fable entitled *The Circle of Life*. Audio-Animatronics® bands, such as The Peach Boys and Pita Gabriel, sing the praises of good nutrition in the musical **Food Rocks** show *(15min)*. An extensive food court occupies much of the interior of this building.

© Disney Enterprises, Inc.

Honey, I Shrunk the Audience

Imagination! – Inside lopsided glass pyramids, visitors are guided by an Audio-Animatronics® chairman of the "Imagination Institute" and his sidekick on a fantastic journey through the potential of human imagination presented by the film company, Kodak. At journey's end, riders can exercise their own imaginations in **Image Works-The Kodak "What If" Labs**, an interactive treasure house of high-tech gizmos—ranging from an electronic symphony and paintbrush to electronic Stepping Stones, which play music and create light when you step on them. Next door in the Imagination Institute, you'll don 3-D glasses to watch the rollicking, laugh-packed multisensory experience **Honey, I Shrunk the Audience** *(20min)*.

Wonders of Life – Informative films, multimedia shows and interactive exhibits in **Fitness Playground** explore health and the human body inside this geodesic dome. **Body Wars** ride reigns as one of Epcot's few thrillers. In a flight simulator, passengers are "shot" into the human body for a mad dash through the circulatory system. **The Making of Me** is an entertaining and sensitive film on human reproduction. In the multimedia presentation **Cranium Command** *(15min)*, Buzzy, an Audio-Animatronics® robot appears against a film backdrop that traces a day in the life of a 12yr-old boy.

Universe of Energy – Here a pyramidal roof winks with 80,000 photovoltaic cells that produce solar energy to power the ride within. **Ellen's Energy Adventure**, starring comedienne Ellen DeGeneres, is a multi-dimensional journey that explores where energy has come from and where it may be going. Bill Nye, the Science Guy, takes Ellen on a trip all the way back to the Big Bang to explain the origin of fossil fuels. They get a fright in the Jurassic era when confronted by lifelike Audio-Animatronics® **dinosaurs**. By the time they return to the late 20C, everyone has a greater grasp of the world's current energy needs.

World Showcase

The 1.3mi promenade at World Showcase circles a 40-acre lagoon and passes the pavilions of 11 different countries. Each pavilion—staffed by nationals of the country it represents—reflects the architecture, foods, crafts, costumes and traditions of that culture. Live performers are often on hand to play music or demonstrate other artistic endeavors specific to their native land. Some pavilions also feature rides or films.

A variety of live stage shows are held at **America Gardens Theatre by the Shore** *(in front of the American Adventure pavilion)*. In the evenings, World Showcase lagoon and pavilions become the setting for **IllumiNations**, an extravaganza of laser lights, music, fountains, and fireworks *(check park brochure for show times)*.

Mexico – Both the dynamism of current-day Mexico and the dignity of its past are evident here. A lush tropical garden leads the way to a small-scale reproduction of a Mayan pyramid, housing a gallery of **pre-Columbian artifacts**. Beyond the gallery lies a colorful colonial plaza, where vendors sell Mexican wares. At the far edge of the plaza runs **El Rio del Tiempo**. Passengers on this boat ride drift down the River of Time through a history of Mexico, from smoking volcanoes to the modern landscapes of Mexico City.

Norway – Norway re-creates a small cobblestone plaza lined with a mix of traditional and medieval architectural styles. One-room **Stave Church,** a replica of a 12C house of worship, contains changing exhibits on Norwegian topics. **Maelstrom**, the pavilion's major attraction, plunges riders through treacherous northern seas.

> **3 Typhoon Lagoon**
> *See map. Take I-4 west to Exit 26B. Go west on Epcot Center Dr. and turn right on Buena Vista Dr. Follow signs to park entrance on right. In general open daily 10am-5pm (extended closing hours in summer); closed Sun & Mon in winter. Best to call for hours. $29.95, $21.73 children ages 3-9.* ☎ *407-824-4321.* Four times the size of River Country, Typhoon Lagoon claims to be "the ultimate water park." Water slides, rapids and snorkeling compete here with the site's highlight: an immense wave pool pounded by 4ft surf.

China – The red and gold opulence of Beijing's Temple of Heaven (replicated at half size) overlooks a Chinese garden here, where koi shimmer through a pond crossed by elegant walkways. The interior houses an ornamented Hall of Prayer for Good Harvest; a **museum** that features changing exhibits of Chinese art; and a CircleVision 360 Theater, where the vastness of China is portrayed in the film **Wonders of China: Land of Beauty, Land of Time**. A narrow street angling off from the temple is fronted by the facade of a house, school and shops.

Germany – A facade modeled after the Eltz and Stahleck castles backdrops cobblestone St. Georgesplatz, a square named for its prominent statue of St. George and the Dragon. Small buildings reflecting the turreted structures of a German village surround the plaza, and a traditional glockenspiel chimes the hour. Buildings contain shops and a capacious *biergarten*-style restaurant whose popular dinner show serves up oom-pah entertainment. East of the pavilion, an outdoor model railway re-creates Germany's "Romantic Road" between Füssen and Würzburg.

Italy – A certain desultory elegance permeates this plaza, where reproductions—the elaborate Doge's Palace, and a brick campanile topped with a sculpted angel—re-create Venice's Piazza San Marco. Antiqued facades, an open-air market, and a Bernini-inspired fountain *(rear of plaza)* add to the *dolce vita* atmosphere. Classical musicians often perform here. Facing the pavilion on the lakefront is a Venetian gondola landing missing only the gondolier.

American Adventure – Prominently situated at the midpoint of World Showcase, a five-story brick building serves as the host pavilion. Several major colonial landmarks inspire its architecture: Independence Hall in Philadelphia, Boston's Old State House and Thomas Jefferson's Monticello in Charlottesville, Virginia. The highlight here is **The American Adventure**, a state-of-the-art multimedia show *(25min)* narrated by startlingly lifelike Audio-Animatronics® versions of Ben Franklin and Mark Twain. The pair comment sagaciously on the show's retrospective of great moments and figures in American history.

Japan – Landscaped with peaceful water and rock gardens and perfectly placed evergreens, this pavilion captures the contemplative serenity of traditional Japan. Its prominent bright blue, five-story pagoda is based on the 8C Horyuji Temple in Nara. At the rear, a re-creation of an 18C feudal castle houses changing exhibits of **Japanese art**. Visitors can purchase an array of Japanese items in Mitsukoshi Department Store, a venerable mercantile institution dating to the 17C, housed in a reproduction of Kyoto's 8C Gosho Imperial Palace. World Showcase Lagoon is perfectly framed by the pavilion's red torii, a Japanese gateway commonly built at the entrance to a Shinto shrine.

Morocco – Elaborate tilework and carvings crafted by Moroccan artisans under the patronage of the King of Morocco create a faithful and detailed representation of the sights, smells and sounds of this North African country. Fronted by a replica of Marrakech's famous Koutoubia Minaret, the pavilion is divided into a new and old medina, or city. Beyond the fountain of the new city's plaza lies the **Royal Gallery**, which houses changing displays of Moroccan art in its exquisitely ornamented interior. The narrow, exotic casbah opens onto a formal Moroccan restaurant and a bevy of shops.

France – Capturing the romantic atmosphere of turn-of-the-century Paris, the main street is lined with mansard-roofed buildings. Even the Eiffel Tower stands here, at one-tenth its actual size. A second street re-creates a provincial village scene, complete with shops and an authentic French restaurant. A 17C parterre garden is a nice place to sip a glass of imported wine. As an added treat, the whole of France fills five screens in the film **Impressions de France** *(20min)*, a compelling scenic tour of the country. Lest you forget this is Disney, however, the Hunchback of Nôtre Dame and Esmeralda, his love, occasionally sign autographs here.

United Kingdom – Hundreds of years of British architecture—from a 15C brick home to the 16C thatched-roof cottage of Anne Hathaway (Shakespeare's wife) to a 19C English garden—are represented along a brick-paved street. Specialty shops and a pub that serves British-brewed ales complete the scene. You may find Beatles impersonators regaling listeners with Fab Four hits from the pub's courtyard.

Canada – Celebrating Canada's cultural diversity, the pavilion features a model of a 19C French chateau-style hotel, totem poles and a longhouse, as well as a log trading post. Landscapes here vary from a replica of Victoria's famous Butchart Gardens to a re-created Rocky Mountain gorge. In the CircleVision 360 theater, the film **O Canada!** surrounds the audience in spectacular scenery.

DISNEY'S ANIMAL KINGDOM

Kids *Take I-4 west to Exit 25B. Go west on US-192, right (north) on World Dr. and left (west) on Osceola Pkwy., then follow signs to parking plaza. In general open year-round daily 8am; closing times vary.*

Disney's newest theme park is devoted to the natural world: animals living and extinct, as well as creatures of the imagination. Geographically the largest park, Animal Kingdom has placed 1,000 animals (of 200 species) and four million plants (of 3,000 species) on more than 500 acres of land. Whimsy meets stark reality here, as visitors can move from colorful pageants to a re-created African savanna and villages, and can even watch veterinary surgeons at work. No matter that dinosaurs graze, dragons lurk and many animals and insects speak—this is Disney at its best.

Although animal-rights activists have expressed concern for the welfare of park denizens, Animal Kingdom delivers an unabashedly conservationist message. Visitors can meet with animal behavior experts, monitor animal-care facilities and learn about the depletion of world rain forests and grasslands. Mock research stations offer a glimpse of field observation procedures.

Helpful Hints – Animal Kingdom extends in four directions from its hub, the **Tree of Life**, in the heart of Discovery Island. The two most favorite attractions, Kilimanjaro Safaris and Dinosaur, are at opposite ends of the park; head first to one or the other to beat the crowds. Two popular live shows, "Festival of the Lion King" and "Tarzan Rocks!" are presented in large, open-air amphitheaters. You'll also find long lines for the 3-D film **It's Tough to Be a Bug** beneath the Tree of Life. As you head toward Discovery Island from Animal Kingdom's main gateway, you'll first pass through **The Oasis**, a lush botanical garden whose grottoes are inhabited by brightly colored macaws, miniature deer, iguanas, tree kangaroos and other unusual animals. Discovery Island occupies a man-made riverine island; footbridges link it to the other segments of the park. If you think of The Oasis as being a 6 o'clock from this axis, you will find DinoLand U.S.A. at 4 o'clock, Camp Minnie-Mickey at 8 o'clock, Africa at 10 o'clock and Asia at 2 o'clock. Rafiki's Planet Watch is reached by train from Africa.

Various shows, parades and musical performances are scheduled throughout the day in Animal Kingdom. You can obtain a schedule along with the park map you're given at the entrance.

Discovery Island

Fashioned as a tropical artists' colony, Discovery Island is home to roving world musicians, puppeteers and storytellers as well as resident experts in fine arts and crafts.

Tree of Life – This park centerpiece is a giant (145ft) man-made tree of unidentifiable classification, into whose 50ft-wide trunk and 8,000 branches are intricately carved 325 images of mammals, birds, reptiles, amphibians and insects. Adapted from Disney's animated feature *The Lion King*, it celebrates all creatures in the song "The Circle of Life." The tree is visible from points throughout the park. At its foot, birds and small animals revel in pools and meadow-like plots

It's Tough to Be a Bug – ⅢⅢ A delightful cast of animated insects and arachnids—crickets, beetles, bees, ants, spiders and the like—express the harsh "reality" of their lives in a 430-seat theater beneath the "roots" of the Tree of Life. Meanwhile, the audience, wearing 3-D glasses, experiences such special effects as termite sneezes (you'll get wet), stinkbug emissions and a cloud of pesticide (actually fog).

Camp Minnie-Mickey

Resembling an Adirondack summer camp with its pine-and-oak buildings and picnic shelters, this is the perfect place for younger children to interact with favorite Disney characters. "Green rooms"—jungle and forest canopies—act as greeting areas where Mickey Mouse and friends, Winnie the Pooh, and characters from *The Lion King* and *The Jungle Book* sign autographs for their visitors. There are two live-performance venues *(check park brochure for show times)*.

Festival of the Lion King – *30 min.* This splashy show presents 50 performers in bright African tribal garb or animal costumes, singing, dancing and doing aerial acrobatics on (or above) four giant rolling stages to melodies like "Hakuna Matata" and "The Circle of Life." Toward the end of the show, Simba (the Lion King) himself, assisted by Pumba (the warthog) and Timon (the meerkat), leads the audience in a chorus of "The Lion Sleeps Tonight." The show is held in a hexagonal open-sided, roofed pavilion with seating for 1,000.

Grandma Willow's Grove – *12min.* "Pocahontas and Her Forest Friends" is the name of the musical presented in this amphitheater, named for its resident talking tree. Guided by the ancient willow's wisdom, Indian maiden Pocahontas (another animated Disney star) learns the only animal that can save all the forests and their inhabitants is—you guessed it—humans.

4 Blizzard Beach

🄺🄸🄳🅂 *See map. Just west of World Dr., adjacent to Disney's All-Star Resorts. Take I-4 west to Exit 25B. Turn right on World Dr.; then left on Buena Vista Dr. and follow signs. In general open daily 10am-5pm, with extended hours in summer; closed Fri & Sat in winter. Best to call in advance for hrs. $29.95.* ⅢⅢ ☎ *407-824-4321.* This star in the constellation of Disney attractions entertains visitors with slides and rides in a tropical lagoon framed by snow-capped mountains. At Blizzard Beach you can ride tubes down a twisting series of falls, race on mats down an eight-lane sluiceway, and experience a 120ft drop at 55mph on Summit Plummet. *Arrive early to avoid long lines, which can last an hour or more for a 20-second slide. Towels and lockers are available for rent.*

Blizzard Beach

© Disney Enterprises, Inc.

Kilimanjaro Safari

Africa

While Disney excels at homogenizing exotic cultures, real or imagined, the river port of **Harambe** may be its best effort yet. Shop owners peddle their wares from marketplace stalls in this authentic representation of a coastal Kenyan community. White-coral walls and reed-thatched roofs typify the Arab-influenced architecture.

Kilimanjaro Safaris – ⅢⅢ These "backcountry" journeys are Animal Kingdom's leading attraction. The staging point for the journeys is at the far end of Harambe village. The entrance line winds through a warehouse of safari gear in the shadow of a giant baobab tree. Open-sided all-terrain trucks carry 32 passengers at a time down a rutted and twisting dirt road, across river fords and through tropical forests, to the grasslands of the Serengeti Plain. Assisted by a bush pilot-game warden (who flies ahead as a wildlife spotter), travelers look for rhinoceroses, elephants, lions, cheetahs, zebras, giraffes, baboons, various gazelles and antelopes, and other residents of the savanna. These animals are all real but much of the rest of the journey is fantasy.

Pangani Forest Exploration Trail – This self-guided trail through a bamboo jungle affords close-up views (through crystal-clear acrylic windows) of two troops of lowland gorillas, some of whom seem to thrive on the attention; several hippopotamuses, easily viewed swimming underwater from a bi-level viewing area, and nearly three dozen species of exotic birds beneath a canopy of trees in an enclosed aviary. A re-created wildlife research station includes maps and computerized exhibits, as well as a display of the cutaway burrows of rare naked mole rats, a creature that never sees the light of day.

Rafiki's Planet Watch

To reach Rafiki's Planet Watch, visitors must board the Wildlife Express—a 190 colonial-style, narrow-gauge steam train—from Harambe's East African Depot. Upon arrival at Planet Watch, it's a 100yd walk through a jungle of lush vegetation to the central building.

An off-the-beaten-path facility, this is Disney's best statement of eco-consciousness. In addition to animal-care facilities (which visitors can monitor through surveillance cameras) and a children's petting zoo ("The Affection Section"), there are interactive demonstrations and high-tech exhibits of animal behavior and of conservation work being performed around the world. One particularly poignant "exhibit" in a darkened sound booth warns of the destruction of the planet's rain forests.

Visitors are able to look through a window on an operating room where veterinarians perform surgical procedures on park animals.

Asia

The fictional kingdom of Anadapus, a rural Asian village set within rain forest vegetation, is home to the **Maharajah Jungle Trek**, a walking tour that winds past decaying temple ruins. Visitors might glimpse Bengal tigers, Komodo dragons and other animals that roaming freely without apparent barriers from guests or from one another. **Kali River Rapids** is a whitewater thrill ride through the foaming rapids of the Clakrandi River.

Flights of Wonder – The avian talents of falcons, macaws, ibis and other birds are featured in this free-flying show at the Caravan Stage. The story line features a treasure-seeking youth and a wise, if mythological, phoenix.

DinoLand U.S.A.

This theme area has the greatest appeal to the elementary-school set. It is constructed to resemble a research camp from which a paleontological dig is taking place. The supposed discoveries of DinoLand's pseudo-paleontologists are shown at the **Fossil Preparation Lab** (now exhibiting bones of a 50ft *Tyrannosaurus rex* as they are cleaned and studied by staff from the Field Museum in Chicago).

Meanwhile, research notes from the scientists accompany displays along the **Cretaceous Trail**. You'll find plants (cycads, palms, ferns) and animals (turtles, lizards, beetles) that survived the calamity, 65 million years ago, believed to have ended the age of dinosaurs. You may even spot a nest of fossilized dinosaur eggs. Nearby is **The Boneyard**, a playground of slides, rope bridges, tunnels and caves that mimics a fossil park.

Dinosaur – Visitors who board a 12-passenger "Time Rover" are sent by a deranged scientist back to late-Cretaceous times to bring home a living dinosaur, just before an asteroid threatening all life strikes the planet. Along their tilting, twisting, bumpy route, they dodge Audio-Animatronics® dinosaurs and plunge through total darkness before narrowly escaping meteoric disaster and returning home, mission accomplished.

Tarzan Rocks! – *30min.* Seemingly out of place in DinoLand, this entertaining musical show at Theater in the Wild is inspired by Disney's animated feature film *Tarzan*. A stylized fusion of rock-music spectacle with aerial stunts and in-line skating action, this high-energy concert re-creates the mood of the film.

★★★DISNEY-MGM STUDIOS

Kids *Take I-4 west to Exit 26B. Go west on Epcot Center Dr. and turn left on Buena Vista Dr. Follow signs to studio entrance on left. Alternate access via Exit 25B (US-192 west); turn right on World Dr. and follow signs to entrance on right. In general open year-round daily 9am; closing times vary.* ⊪.

This theme park/studio celebrates the magic of filmmaking, from animation and stuntsmanship to adventure and romance. Art Deco architecture throughout the 154-acre site re-creates the look of Hollywood, California in its 1930s and 40s heyday. Sophisticated techniques coupled with a playful, fun-loving style characterize the attractions, which include rides, film performances and live shows—often with audience volunteers—that provide behind-the-scenes explanations of moviemaking. As a working studio, Disney-MGM produces scores of television shows and Disney animated films.

The least crowded of the four parks, this one also has a more compact design that makes visiting easy. As in all the parks, thrill rides and newest attractions tend to have the longest lines; experience the Twilight Zone Tower of Terror and Star Tours first.

Lined with palm trees and sleek, low-slung Art Deco-style buildings filled with commercial shops, **Hollywood Boulevard** opens onto a central plaza by a lush red-and-gold, pagoda-roofed replica of Mann's Chinese Theater in Los Angeles. The latter's forecourt is set with footprints of famous folk and Disney stars.

A 25min evening show, **Fantasmic!**, complete with Disney music, animation and special laser effects, is presented in a 6,900-seat amphitheater.

The 360-degree twists and turns of the high-speed **Rock 'n' Roller Coaster** are amplified by a synchronized rock soundtrack by Aerosmith resonating from speakers in each vehicle.

The Great Movie Ride – *22min.* Housed in the model of Mann's Chinese Theater, this ride takes you on an unforgettable trip through the great movie classics. A tram with a live guide moves you through a multimedia show that includes everything from clips of classic Disney films to a western shoot-out where you're caught in the crossfire between the real and the imaginary.

Sunset Boulevard – For a glimpse of the glamorous Hollywood of the 1930s, walk down this palm-lined street set with its Mediterranean Revival facades, antique autos, fruit vendors in Depression-era garb, and the swing music of Glenn Miller playing from hidden speakers. You may even be caught in the middle of an impromptu street skit. At a neon-lit movie palace, Mickey and other Disney characters sign autographs and pose for photographs.

Beauty and the Beast – **Live on Stage** – A rousing live stage version *(20min)* of the Disney motion picture features lip-synching cups and pots as well as a costumed chorus singing and dancing their way through the film's highlights *(check park brochure for show times)*.

© Disney Enterprises, Inc.

Twilight Zone Tower of Terror

Twilight Zone Tower of Terror – At the end of Sunset Boulevard looms the wonderfully decayed Hollywood Tower Hotel, where guests enter a world of illusion. Incorporating part of an episode from the popular television series *The Twilight Zone* (1959-1965), this 10min thrill ride transports visitors back in time to a stormy night when a group of guests mysteriously disappeared from the hotel. Laser technology and convincing architectural details—cobblestone walkways, vine-covered trellises and iron gates—enhance the effects. The ride culminates in a series of drops, including a 13-story plunge in the old service elevator.

Voyage of The Little Mermaid – *17min.* This musical stage show is based on the 1989 Disney animated hit *The Little Mermaid*. Special effects, such as the dark and misty undersea feel of the theater, enhance the experience.

Studios Backlot Tour – *35min.* Boarding a tram, visitors snake through back lots and boneyards of the working studio, past a prop and costume warehouse and a street lined with the facades of houses used in motion pictures and television shows. The tour takes in George of the Jungle's treehouse and The American Film Institute Showcase before it climaxes in **Catastrophe Canyon**, where it seems the whole show could be derailed by a deluge.

Who Wants To Be a Millionaire-Play It! – Guests get an opportunity to hop into the hot seat at this newest attraction at Disney-MGM Studios. Based on the popular television game show of recent times, this live, interactive show is staged in a detailed re-creation of the New York City set.

Backstage Pass – *30min.* A behind-the-scenes walking tour past soundstages and postproduction suites is led by a guide who explains the inner workings of filmmaking. The tour includes visits to the re-created sets of hit television shows "Home Improvement" and "Who Wants to Be a Millionaire."

The Magic of Disney Animation – Visitors on this walking tour of a **working animation studio** get a glimpse of what Disney does best. Beginning in a gallery that displays Disney's Oscar trophies and animated clips from Disney classics, the tour introduces animation with a short film featuring news anchor Walter Cronkite and comedian Robin Williams as pre-taped guides. Visitors then walk through viewing galleries above the studio, where they can observe various stages of the animation process being applied to an upcoming Disney movie. The tour ends with a 10min film that highlights scenes from Disney's animated hits.

Along **New York Street**, building facades use forced perspective to fool the eye into believing that the skyscraping vista of the Empire State Building and other towers are looming large at the end of the street. Several musical and theatrical shows are presented here.

Backlot Theater – *32min.* "Disney's The Hunchback of Notre Dame: A Musical Adventure" is the show featured in this theater. Lively gypsies give the hit movie a live-action spin with elaborate stage sets, puppetry and special effects.

"Honey, I Shrunk the Kids" Movie Set Adventure – Youngsters are dwarfed by enormous blades of grass and insects in the fantastical playground, where everything is made to be climbed on, slid through and touched.

Jim Henson's Muppet© Vision 3D – *25min.* After visiting a reproduction of the Muppet set, visitors watch a funny film featuring the late Henson's winsome stars and some startlingly realistic 3-D and other special effects.

Star Tours – *10min.* This popular, futuristic thrill ride was jointly conceived by Walt Disney "Imagineers" and Star Wars creator George Lucas. Led by Star Wars droids C3PO and R2D2, travelers board a StarSpeeder for a voyage to the Moon of Endor. Through the large "window" in their craft, space travelers experience excellent special effects during their simulated high-speed voyage.

⑤ Disney's Wide World of Sports
See map. Take I-4 west to Exit 25B. Turn right on World Dr., right again on Osceola Pkwy. at first interchange, and follow signs. Open daily 10am-5pm. For admission fee: www.disneyworldsports.com. ☎ 407-824-4321.
This 200-acre complex has professional-caliber facilities for more than 30 competitive sports, including baseball, basketball, bicycle racing, soccer, tennis and track and field. Numerous championship amateur and pro events are scheduled here; the Atlanta Braves major league baseball team make their spring-training home at the complex's 7,500-seat stadium.

Indiana Jones Epic Stunt Spectacular – *30min.* Re-creating scenes from the adventure-packed Indiana Jones movies, a riveting and humorous show is staged in this 2,200-seat, open-air amphitheater. Members of the audience are chosen to participate as extras, while the cast and crew enact awesome stunts—complete with a variety of pyrotechnics—and the show's host explains the techniques behind them.

Sounds Dangerous Starring Drew Carey – Television's Drew Carey stars in "Undercover Live" featuring a binaural audio soundtrack.

Fringing Echo Lake, **Lakeside Circle** is replete with such "California Crazy" architecture as an ice-cream booth in the shape of Gertie—a dinosaur derived from a 1914 cartoon by Windsor McKay—and a Spanish galleon housing a restaurant. Palms edge the lake and a cheerful fountain festoons its center.

The Panhandle

Beach at Seaside – Gwen Cannon/MICHELIN

Squeezed between Georgia, Alabama and the Gulf of Mexico, the Panhandle extends 200mi westward from the Florida peninsula in a band 30mi to 100mi wide. This region lies far enough north to trumpet a summer tourist season and far enough west to be in a different time zone from the rest of Florida (Central Time Zone begins at the Apalachicola River, 45mi west of Tallahassee). Rolling hills clad with pines and hardwoods mark the region. The state's highest point (345ft) is tucked up against Alabama. In personality the Panhandle more closely resembles its Deep South neighbors, Georgia and Alabama, than it does Florida's fast-paced Atlantic coast, though Destin 50mi east of Pensacola, challenges any place in the state for rapid, upscale change.

For 7,000 years mound-building tribes lived in the region and took a good living from the sea. Spanish explorers gained toeholds here in 1528 and 1539 at St. Marks and again in 1559, when Don **Tristán de Luna** established a short-lived settlement at Pensacola six years before the founding of St. Augustine. Spain failed to rediscover northwest Florida until the late 17C. It jockeyed with France for control of Pensacola Bay for nearly half a century. Settlement in the vicinity of Panama City began only in the late 19C, although France had established a fort in the area in 1717 and the British attempted settlement during their possession of West and East Florida (1763-1783). Spain again held the Florida Territories until 1819, before capitulating to American expansionist demands. Soon thereafter, Tallahassee sprang to life as the seat of Florida government. Throughout the 19C, the Panhandle's deepwater ports exported the bounty of the region's waters and forests. Inland plantations grew cotton and sugar; pine forests hummed with sawmills; and the Gulf yielded remarkable numbers of fish. More recently, large military installations like Eglin Air Force Base and the Pensacola Naval Air Station have pumped money into the region, and a burgeoning tourist trade has lined the coast from Pensacola to Panama City with resorts and retirement homes. Fortunately, the **Gulf Islands National Seashore** protects large chunks of wild beach and dune environment.

Visitors to the Panhandle today are rewarded with gorgeous beaches, an emerald sea teeming with fish, well-preserved historic towns and true Southern hospitality. Although the area's renowned white-sand beaches took a pounding in October 1995 from Hurricane Opal—the worst storm to hit this coast in 30 years—most of the dunes, beaches, smaller coast roads and beachfront accommodations were restored within a year thereafter.

APALACHICOLA★

Population 2,334
Map p 177
Tourist information: www.apalachicola.com ☎ 850-653-9419

Occupying the tip of a spit of land where the Apalachicola River empties into the Gulf of Mexico, Apalachicola (a Creek word meaning "land beyond") is a serene little fishing community. Within the last decade, tourists have begun to discover the excellent deep-sea fishing and laid-back lifestyle in this formerly isolated section of Florida, a factor which has helped to diversify the economy of the former single-industry town.

Apalachicola was once the third-busiest port on the Gulf (eclipsed only by New Orleans, Louisiana, and Mobile, Alabama), the destination for crops of wealthy north Florida and south Georgia cotton planters during the 1830s and 40s. There, the fiber was sold to a factor, or cotton broker, and shipped to New York, Boston or Europe. Prosperous brokers built impressive houses, some of which still grace Apalachicola's quiet streets. By the 1920s, rails had replaced shipping as the country's major means of transportation; Apalachicola, a port with no railroad, sank into obscurity.

The city's location on an estuary has long dictated its economy; fishing and oystering remain the town's major industries. The Apalachicola basin boasts one of the country's largest **oyster nurseries**, producing more than three-fourths of Florida's annual crop—about 1,500 tons of oyster meat—as well as more than half its shellfish.

SIGHTS

★**Historic Downtown** – *Walking-tour maps available at the Chamber of Commerce (99 Market St.).* Water Street served as Apalachicola's commercial hub in the 1830s. The best example of a surviving **cotton warehouse** stands at the corner of Water Street and Avenue E; here cotton was compressed and readied for shipment. Just up the street *(corner of Ave. E and Commerce St.)* is the **Sponge Exchange** (c.1838), where harvested sponges were cleaned and sold. Although the sponge trade here never approached that of Tarpon Springs, the industry employed more than 10 percent of the town's population at its zenith.

One of the city's best examples of Greek Revival antebellum architecture is the white porticoed **Raney House** *(128 Market St.)* built by merchant David Raney in 1838. The restored Victorian **Gibson Inn** *(corner of Ave. C and Market St.)*, whose wide wraparound veranda commands a view of the bay, still accommodates overnight guests, as it has for nearly 100 years. A number of other early houses, like those along Avenue E, represent various architectural styles, including Greek Revival and Victorian *(houses are not open to the public, but are indicated on the walking-tour map)*.

John Gorrie State Museum – *6th St. & Ave. D. Open year-round Thu-Mon 9am-5pm. Closed Jan 1, Thanksgiving Day, Dec 25. $1.* 🕭 🅿 ☎ *850-653-9347.* Exhibits in this one-room structure chronicle the career of Apalachicola physician **John Gorrie** (1803-1855), inventor of an artificial refrigeration process. To cool his yellow-fever patients' rooms, he devised a machine that used cool air to chill brine; the cold brine was then used to freeze fresh water. A replica is on view (the actual patented model resides in the National Museum of American History at the Smithsonian Institution in Washington, DC.). Gorrie is buried across Sixth Street on a plot of land known as Gorrie Square.

Trinity Episcopal Church – *6th St. and Ave. D, at Gorrie Square. Open year-round Mon-Fri 8am-noon, weekends 8am-5pm.* 🕭 ☎ *850-653-9550.* Organized in 1835, Trinity is one of the oldest churches in North Florida. Dr. Gorrie was among its founders. The white pine Greek Revival church was built in 1839 in upstate New York, then taken apart and shipped piece-by-piece to Apalachicola, where congregation members re-assembled the structure using wooden pegs. Inside, note the original organ and pews (c.1840), as well as the unusual hand-stenciled ceiling.

Chestnut Street Cemetery – *Between 6th and 8th Sts. on Ave. E.* Laden with moss-draped live oaks, the burial ground dates to before 1831 and contains the graves of yellow-fever victims; Confederate soldiers, seven of whom fought at Gettysburg as part of the Florida Brigade; shipwrecked sailors; and ordinary citizens. Noted botanist Alvin Wentworth Chapman, who moved to Apalachicola to study Southern flora, is also buried here.

Lafayette Park – *West end of Ave. A.* This shaded park, replete with gnarled oaks and azaleas, is perched on a high bluff overlooking Apalachicola Bay. Brick walkways crisscross the landscape, leading to a replica turn-of-the-last-century gazebo in the center. Take the boardwalk on the south end to the overlook for an expansive **view** of the bay. A marker identifies the estuary as one of world's most productive oyster beds.

EXCURSION

⌂ **St. George Island** – *6mi east of Apalachicola. Take US-98 east 4mi to Eastpoint. Turn right on causeway (Rte. 300) and follow it to island.* This relatively undeveloped barrier island, for years accessible only by boat, retains a rich history as a pirate's hideout, Indian campground and playground for late-19C vacationers. Its forests provided a resource for the early turpentine industry (scars can still be seen on the island's slash pines). Some 25mi long, St. George is the largest of three barrier islands off the coast of Franklin County—and the only one connected by causeway to the mainland. Completion of the causeway in 1965 spurred construction of vacation homes in the middle and west end. The east end and Cape St. George at the western tip are preserved as state lands. Today the white-sand beaches are popular with locals for a weekend getaway.

Barrier islands Isle de Chien or **Dog Island**, east of Apalachicola, and **St. Vincent Island**, 9mi west, protect the mainland from high winds and hurricanes. In 1948 two millionaire brothers purchased St. Vincent and populated it with exotic animals. Now owned by the US Fish and Wildlife Service, the 12,358-acre St. Vincent National Wildlife Refuge provides sanctuary for endangered plants and animals, including bald eagles, loggerhead sea turtles, indigo snakes and gopher tortoises, as well as 180 species of birds. Red wolves are bred here for reintroduction into the wild. The refuge is only open for day use *(park hrs & fees p 350; ferry service from Indian Pass; look for signs along Rte. 30 west of Apalachicola; St. Vincent Island Shuttle* ☎ *850-229-1065).*

★★ **Dr. Julian G. Bruce St. George Island State Park** – *East end of St. George Island. Follow Rte. 300 to park entrance. Park hrs & fees p 350.* △ ᕦ �‖ ☎ *850-927-2111.* High dunes dotted with sea oats and sparkling white **beaches**⌂ characterize this 1,900-acre park, named in honor of a local dentist active in Apalachicola's civic affairs. Its beaches consistently rank among the top in the US. Largely uninhabited until the late 19C, St. George Island sacrificed much of its pine forests to the turpentine industry. Although the land was acquired in 1963, the park was not opened to the public until 1980.

Boardwalks and hiking trails thread the salt marshes, pine forests and oak hammocks, where osprey, snowy plovers and diamondback terrapins number among the abundant wildlife that finds habitat here. Bay and Gulf waters harbor flounder, redfish, sea trout and shellfish. Although pleasant in all seasons, the park is at its best in early spring and late fall when there is a respite from the intense summer heat.

FORT WALTON BEACH

Population 19,973
Map p 176
Tourist information: www.destin-fwb.com ☎ 850-244-8191 or 800-322-3319

Located on the Gulf coast 40mi east of Pensacola, this beach town began as a Confederate installation in 1861. After **Eglin Air Force Base**—one of the world's largest air bases—tourism generates the most revenue, from some 2.5 million annual visitors who savor the quartz sand beaches and sumptuous seafood.

Walton Guards (named for George Walton, acting governor of Territorial Florida) garrisoned the fort, which was abandoned when the Confederates left Pensacola to fight farther north. After the war, one of the original guards, John Thomas Brooks, founded Brooks Landing at the old Indian mound where the guards had camped. Fort Walton Beach grew from this settlement.

Eglin Air Force Base began in the early 1930s as a golf course owned by a wealthy innkeeper who donated 4,160 acres of land to the government for a bombing and gunnery range. Today the 720sq mi base boasts unique testing facilities and ranges, and ranks as the county's leading source of revenue.

SIGHTS

Gulfarium – 🄺🄸🄳🅂 *1010 Miracle Strip Pkwy. (1mi east of town on US-98). Open mid-May-mid-Sept daily 9am-6pm. Rest of the year daily 9am-4pm. Closed Thanksgiving Day, Dec 25. $14.* ᕦ �‖ ☎ *850-243-9046. www.gulfarium.org.* For 40 years this marine-life attraction has entertained area beach enthusiasts. Trained dolphins leap 20ft into the air and perform other amazing stunts. Scuba divers handle sharks, stingrays and moray eels. Other exhibits showcase sea lions, tropical birds and fish. Gulfarium rescues stranded turtles and birds and, in conjunction with the University of West Florida, conducts research that uses dolphins to coax responses from autistic children.

Indian Temple Mound Museum – *139 Miracle Strip Pkwy. (US-98). Open Jun-Aug Mon-Sat 9am-4:30pm, Sun 12:30pm-4:30pm. Rest of the year Mon-Fri 11am-4pm, Sat 9am-4pm. Closed Jan 1 & Dec 25. $2* ‖ ☎ *850-833-9595. www.fwb.org.* It may be surprising to find a 15ft-high earth mound rising from the flat commercial strip of Fort Walton Beach. Indians built the mound as a ceremonial center about 600 years ago. A replica log-and-thatch temple tops the mound, and the adjacent long, low building houses a collection of Native American artifacts found within a 40mi radius. In addition to authentic pottery, bone and stone tools, and spear points, the museum presents replicas of ancient Indian crafts.

Air Force Armament Museum – *6mi north of US-98, on Rte. 85 (east side) just past interchange with Rte. 189. Open year-round daily 9:30am-4:30pm. Closed Jan 1, Thanksgiving Day, Dec 25 & federal holidays. &. 🖪 ☎ 850-882-4062. www.eglin. af.mil/sponsor/museum.htm.* Dedicated to the display of Air Force weapons, this spacious facility satisfies civilians' curiosity about the world's most advanced defense system. Outside stand more than 20 aircraft and missiles including a B-17, B-52, SR-71 Blackbird, and Mace and Hound-dog missiles. Two floors of indoor exhibits chronicle air weaponry from World War I to Desert Storm. Among the highlights are the **Weapons Display Vault**, with its impressive glass cases full of antique and modern guns; a sobering POW exhibit; and an innocent-looking replica of "Fat Man"—the atom bomb that exploded over Nagasaki in 1945, instantly annihilating 45,000 people.

EXCURSIONS

Destin – *8mi east of Fort Walton Beach via US-98.* Destin is Florida's largest and most upscale Gulf Coast resort city north of Naples. Today this once-sleepy fishing village shimmers with high-rise condominiums and boutiques as well as requisite beach shops. The city claims the largest charter sportfishing fleet in Florida and Destin's dining scene repeatedly draws the attention of *Wine Spectator* and *Florida Trend* magazines. The area's quartz sand beaches rank among America's best.

Fred Gannon Rocky Bayou State Park – *16mi northeast in Niceville. From US-98, take Rte. 85 north 12mi to Rte. 20. Go east on Rte. 20 about 3mi to park. Park hrs & fees p 350.* △ &. ☎ 850-833-9144. For a non-beach nature outing, try this secluded little park nestled against an arm of Choctawhatchee Bay. Named for an Air Force colonel who helped establish the park in the mid-1960s, Rocky Bayou encompasses 357 acres of sand pine forest with hiking trails and campsites. Anglers may try their luck with both freshwater and saltwater fish. The former frequent Rocky Creek; the latter inhabit the bay.

■ Destin's Destiny

Tourist information: ☎ *850-651-7131 or 800-322-3319. www.destin-fwb.com.* Contrary to what some may think, the city's name doesn't play on the notion of destiny but comes from its founding fisherman. Leonard Destin arrived from New London, Connecticut, sometime just before 1840. He and others who followed discovered what came to be the town's motto, "The luckiest fishing village in the world." The Gulf Stream passes so close off-shore that abundant gamefish can be landed within clear sight of the beach. The city's emergence from a small fishing community has, in fact, come quickly. At least initially, it stemmed more from outside occurrences than from intention. Two events in the mid-1930s cast the town's future. In 1936 a bridge went up that connected Destin with Fort Walton Beach. Soon after, the first tourists began arriving: they were called "visiting fishermen." After locals finished seining in the morning, they took visitors sportfishing in the afternoon. At about the same time, a local landowner donated land to the government that gave rise to Eglin Air Force Base north across Choctawhatchee Bay. Eglin accounts for more than 100,000 jobs, many of them high-paying, drawing talent from all over America. Expensive subdivisions went up; colleges were constructed. Indicative of demand, Okaloosa-Walton Community College opened in 1963 and is today the largest of Florida's 28 two-year colleges, with 16,000 students. Its new $20 million arts center provides the surrounding community with traveling Broadway shows, musical performances and art exhibits.
The worldly lifestyle attracted many south Floridians seeking alternatives to their region's big-city problems. Two new north-south bridges were built across the bay. Inexpensive beachfront was snapped up for development. County residents, and then vacationers, came looking for upscale leisure by the beach. In a twinkling, the beach shanties and mom-and-pop motels gave way to swank condominiums, posh restaurants and high-end shops. Construction cranes still are everywhere. Roads can't accommodate traffic. There's often congestion and, at least for old-timers, a sense that maybe Destin hasn't been all that lucky after all. Promoters now call this area of Fort Walton Beach and Destin the **Emerald Coast** for its shimmery green gulf waters. Vacationers call it paradise.

INLAND PANHANDLE★

Map below

Tourist information: ☏ 850-892-3191

A little-known region of the state, the Inland Panhandle has been left in the dust of progressive Florida. Visitors to the Panhandle today will notice a world of difference between the sprawling coastal cities, with their more transient military- and tourism-related populations, and the small, sparsely populated inland towns that have changed little over past decades. Farming and forest products support the economy of this region, where some of Florida's more distinct geological features—hills, cliffs, sink-holes, caverns—are found. Just west of the state's capital, **Apalachicola National Forest** extends through parts of Leon, Liberty and Wakulla counties.

Like its Deep South neighbors, the Inland Panhandle was tamed by large plantation owners. Cotton, sugar and tobacco were shipped from Georgia and Alabama through Florida on the Apalachicola River to the Gulf of Mexico. Interspersed among the plantations were, and still are, backwaters of poor whites and blacks hopeful that economic development will bring better living conditions.

SIGHTS *(organized from west to east)*

Blackwater River State Park – *7720 Bridge Rd., Holt. Take Exit 10 off I-10, and follow Rte. 87 north to US-90. Take US-90 east 5.6mi to sign; turn left and go 3mi to park. Park hrs & fees p 350.* △ ♿ 🅿 ☏ *850-983-5363.* This 590-acre park centers on a 2mi stretch of the Blackwater River, a tannin-stained, sandy-bottomed waterway with inviting white sandbars. Part of the designated **Florida Canoe Trail**, the river slides past forests of oak, red maple and tupelo intermingling with meadows of wire grass and gallberry. Denizens of the park include white-tailed deer, turkeys and bobcats. A short hiking trail meanders through the expanse.

De Funiak Springs – *80mi east of Pensacola. Take Exit 13 off I-10 and turn left (north) on Rte. 331; turn right at the second traffic light on Live Oak St., which dead-ends at Circle Dr. www.defuniaksprings.com.* Named in 1882 for the chief engineer on the Louisville & Nashville Railroad, this former train station became a town of wealth when the New York Chautauqua association chose it as the winter home for its cultural and educational symposia. Though the Chautauqua programs officially ended in 1928, De Funiak Springs continues to host annual cultural activities, and many graceful turn-of-the-19C homes attest to the halcyon period of the town's history.

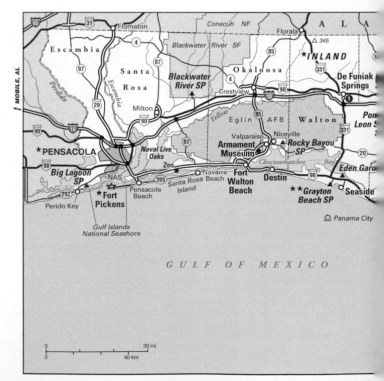

★**Circle Drive** – *The Chamber of Commerce (Circle Dr. and West Ave., next door to library) offers brochures of a walking or driving tour around Circle Dr.* Rimming the town's spring-fed lake, this 1mi loop proceeds beneath ancient live oaks and magnolias and passes house after house of historical and architectural note. Built in 1886, the **Walton-De Funiak Library** *(100 Circle Dr.)* contains a small collection of swords and other weaponry dating as far back as AD 1100. When Frederick De Funiak, the town's namesake, ignored a request for a donation to the library, the Ladies' Library Assn. removed his name from the sign over the entrance. To this day the sign reads simply, "Library."

Next door, the white wooden **Chautauqua Hall of Brotherhood** houses the Walton County Chamber of Commerce. Across the street, **St. Agatha's Episcopal Church** (1896) boasts beautifully preserved stained-glass windows. The three-story Victorian at no. 188, with its fanciful trim and twin turrets, is noteworthy as is the 1904 **Tharpe House** *(no. 262)*, with its large double verandas. Note also the c.1888 "Dream Cottage" *(no. 404)* built for Wallace Bruce, former US consul to Scotland and the house at no. 550 (1907), with its magnificent balconied portico.

Ponce de Leon Springs State Park – *On Rte. 181A, Ponce de Leon. Take Exit 15 off I-10; follow Rte. 81 north and turn right on US-90. Park is .5mi south of US-90. Park hrs & fees p 350.* ◨ ☎ 850-836-4281. A rock-and-concrete **pool★**, built around a spring flowing with emerald-green water, forms the centerpiece of this site, named for the explorer

❶ Chautauqua Winery
Map p 176. Intersection of I-10 and US-331. ☎ *850-892-5887.* The showcase grapevines topping the hill above the junction of these two highways are sure attention-getters. Adjacent to them sits an attractive structure that serves as a visitor/orientation center and gift shop for the wine-producing enterprise. Established in the mid-1980s, this regionally famous winery has won numerous awards for its sweet wines made from local muscadine grapes. The vineyards (located 12mi north) annually produce 400,000 pounds of grapes, which are made into wine here at this location along the busy interstate. Stop by to watch a 4min video on the wine-making process and view the stainless-steel fermenting tanks through a glass booth. Visitors are also treated to free tasting samples.

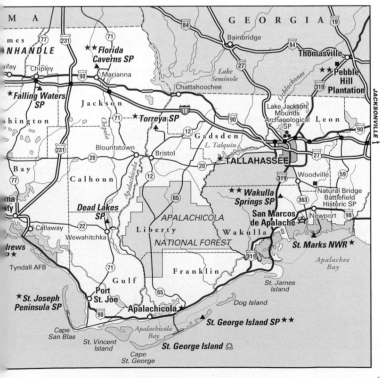

associated with the legendary fountain of youth. The refreshing 68°F water is just right for swimming on a hot day. Twenty developed acres of the 443-acre park offer picnic facilities and two walking trails *(.4mi each)* winding through a flood-plain forest of moss-draped cypresses. Anglers cast the creeks for largemouth bass, catfish, chain pickerel and panfish.

★**Falling Waters State Park** – *Off Rte. 77 south of Chipley. Take Exit 18 off I-10 and follow Rte. 77 south 1mi; turn left on Rte. 77A and continue 1mi to park. Park hrs & fees p 350.* ⚠ 🅿 ☎ *850-638-6130.* Here you'll see a rare stream-fed **waterfall** that plunges into a 100ft-deep sinkhole. A wooden platform provides a good vantage point for peering into the abyss; where the water ends up remains a mystery. A short boardwalk trail encircles other sinkholes, all formed long ago by the seepage of rainwater into the ground's porous limestone. Over the years, the area's natural resources have been tapped several times: the famous waterfall powered a grist mill during the Civil War; a legal whiskey distillery operated here around 1880; and in 1919, wildcatters drilled down 3,900ft trying to find oil. Three short nature trails *(.8mi total)* wind past these sites and through a hard-wood hammock and a pine forest flecked with wildflowers.

★★**Florida Caverns State Park** – *On Rte. 166, 2.6mi north of Marianna. Park hrs & fees p 350. Caverns visit by guided tour (1hr) only, year-round daily 9:30am-4:30pm. Closed Thanksgiving Day & Dec 25. $5.* ⚠ 🅿 ☎ *850-482-9598.* Limestone caves (featuring Florida's only tourable cavern) show off a remarkable variety of subterranean architecture comparable to some of the largest caves in the country. These caverns formed 40 to 60 million years ago when the level of an underground stream dropped, leaving a cavity in the earth. Bizarre creations result from slow drips of acidic water into the cave. Tours begin with a 15min movie in the **visitor center**, then move to a nearby cave, made accessible to the public by the Civilian Conservation Corps in 1938. Lights illumine stalagmites (that grow from the floor), stalactites (that hang from the ceiling), soda straws, columns, rim-stones, flowstones and draperies. *Guides request that you not touch the fragile formations, since oil from skin can damage them.*

★**Torreya State Park** – *Off Rte. 12 in Rock Bluff, 13mi north of Bristol. Take Exit 25 south off I-10; follow Rte. 12 south 11mi; turn right on Rte. 1641 and continue 7mi to park. Park hrs & fees p 350.* ⚠ 🅿 ☎ *850-643-2674.* The 150ft-high **bluffs** here afford views of the Apalachicola River and the thick forests beyond. Torreya trees—a rare species of conifer *(Torreya taxifolia)*—grow only on these bluffs. A 7mi loop trail threads through the forest and along the ridge. Perched at the edge of the bluff, the two-story white clapboard **Gregory House**, built in 1849 by planter Jason Gregory, affords visitors a glimpse of plantation life on the river. Daily tours describe the period antiques inside and recount local history *(visit by 1hr guided tour only, year-round Mon-Fri 10am, weekends & major holidays 10am, 2pm & 4pm; $1; time zone is Eastern).* From the front lawn, the **river view** glows with a luminous beauty, especially in the golden light of an autumn sunset.

Bottomlands of Torreya State Park

Population 36,417
Map p 177
Tourist Information: www.panamacitydowntown.com and www.800pcbeach.com
☎ 850-233-6503 or 800-722-3224

Bordered on three sides by bays, Panama City ranks second to Pensacola as the Panhandle's leading port. Visitors ignore the no-nonsense industrial corridors of the city and head directly for **Panama City Beach**⌂, a 20mi stretch of sugar-white sand bordering turquoise Gulf waters. Stretching mile after mile along the main drag are high-rise condominiums, inexpensive motels, hot-dog and ice-cream stands, water parks and miniature golf courses. Miracle Strip Amusement Park *(12000 Front Beach Rd.)* has attracted thrill-seekers for more than 30 years.

Although Spanish sailors explored the area in the early 16C, it was the English who established a permanent village here in 1765. Despite the building boom that has altered the face of Panama City Beach in recent decades, much natural beauty remains. Popular area sports include golfing, snorkeling, diving and game fishing.

Two downtown districts are also worthwhile, linked by a trackless trolley *(50¢-$1)*. Shops, restaurants and art galleries line **Harrison Avenue** *(from 6th St. south to Government)*, recently refurbished with wide landscaped sidewalks, and its vicinity. The Visual Arts Center of Northwest Florida *(19 E. 4th St.; ☎ 850-769-4451)* showcases and sells regional art. Renewal of the historic **St. Andrews** district *(west of Harrison St. along St. Andrews Blvd. between 10th & 12th Sts.)*, which dates from 1827, remains incomplete but its persistent shopkeepers supply the odd music store, gallery and coffee shop along with a few restaurants to make the district worth a visit.

SIGHTS

★St. Andrews State Park *– 4607 State Park Ln. (east end of Panama City Beach). Park hrs & fees p 350.* △ ὅ ▯ ☎ *850-233-5140.* A lovely refuge of fine sand beaches and freshwater marsh, pine flatwoods and sand pine scrub, this park occupies land on either side of the entrance channel to St. Andrews Bay. Fishing piers and jetties extend into Grand Lagoon and the Gulf of Mexico, where flounder, trout, dolphin, bluefish, bonito, redfish and Spanish mackerel abound. Jetties form protected pools perfect for swimming and snorkeling.

A nature trail *(.6mi)* wends past a reconstructed Cracker turpentine still, a two-story wood-and-brick structure typifying those that operated in Bay County into the 1930s. Charts and diagrams outline the distillation process.

Shell Island *– Accessible by boat only. Departs Jetty Dive Store at St. Andrews State Park Feb-Oct daily 9am-5pm (on the half-hour). One-way 5min. Commentary. $9.50 (snorkeling $17.95).* ▯ *Captain Blacks* ☎ *850-233-0197. Shell Island has no facilities of any kind, nor any shade; plan accordingly.* Created in the 1930s by the dredging of the channel, this unspoiled barrier island measures 7mi long and .5mi wide. Most of the island is owned by the park, with Tyndall Air Force Base and a few private owners holding the remainder. Here visitors will discover a gorgeous strand of aquamarine water and squeaky white sand, backed by a scrub-covered dune ridge. For best shell finds, walk away from the tip of the island, where visitors tend to cluster, and wade a few feet into the surf.

Gulf World Marine Park *–* 🏫 *15412 Front Beach Rd. Open Jun-Aug daily 9am-4pm. Rest of the year daily 9am-2pm. Closed Thanksgiving Day & Dec 25. $17.56.* ὅ ▯ ☎ *850-234-5271. www.gulfworldmarinepark.com.* This popular marine attraction features a new 2,000-seat dolphin stadium and a large tropical garden that is climate controlled. Some 25 exhibits and shows throughout the day include performing parrots, scuba demonstrations and sea lion acrobatics. Visitors may interact with dolphins in the water and pet stingrays that have had their barbs removed. The park is part of a regional network established to rescue stranded sea animals.

Museum of Man in the Sea *– 17314 Panama City Beach Pkwy. (on US-98, .25mi west of Rte. 79). Open year-round daily 9am-5pm. Closed Jan 1, Thanksgiving Day, Dec 25. $5.* ὅ ▯ ☎ *850-235-4101.* Recognizable by its outdoor display of large submersibles, this small facility traces the history of diving. Run by the Institute of Diving, the museum offers chronologically arranged exhibits, starting with dioramas of 17C divers who salvaged wrecked vessels using diving bells. Among other displays are diving suits, fish tanks, and artifacts from the Union transport ship *Maple Leaf*, which sank near Jacksonville in 1864. Photographs and videos explain the work of underwater archaeologists on wrecks off the Florida coast, including the *Maple Leaf*, the *Urca de Lima* (1715) and the *Atocha* (1622).

EXCURSIONS

Eden Gardens State Park – *32mi northwest in Point Washington. From Panama City, take US-98 west 31mi to Rte. C-395. Go north 1mi to park entrance. Gardens open year-round daily 8am-dusk. $2/vehicle.* ♿ 📷 ☎ *850-231-4214.* Built of yellow heart-pine by lumberman William Henry Wesley in 1895, the stately Greek Revival **house** features wraparound porches on two levels *(visit by 40min guided tour only, year-round Thu-Mon 9am-4pm; $1.50)*. House tours inventory the large collection of antiques—especially Louis XVI furniture—amassed by Eden's final private owner, New York journalist Lois Maxon. Pieces include an 1820 carved rosewood canopy bed, a Chippendale mahogany bedside table, English chandeliers and a Louis XVI mirror. A sloping lawn surrounds the house and ancient oaks are hung with Spanish moss. Visitors may picnic at the 200 lumber mill site on picturesque Tucker Bayou.

FABS
2236 Rte. 30A in Seaside.
☎ *850-231-5636*
or 888-231-6662.
www.fabsflorida.com.
Few women can resist the *fabulous* luxury swimwear and lingerie adorning the windows of this small boutique in Seaside. Enter via the vine-covered latticework and find yourself being handed a glass of ice tea or wine, with nibbles, while you ahhh and admire. Tempting—and pricey—nightgowns, undergarments and leisurewear in ever-so-pale pastels and loaded with lace; the softest of bathrobes; sturdy straw hats; and exotic swimsuits with matching coverups tug on even the most ardent wallet-hugging browsers in this wall-to-wall fantasy of femme fatale fashion.

Seaside – *35mi west of Panama City on US-98A along Rte. 30A.* Located off US-98 midway between Panama City Beach and Fort Walton Beach, the tiny town of Seaside reflects the nostalgic vision of developer **Robert S. Davis**, who remembered the area in simpler times. After only 20 years, his award-winning planned community, platted in 1981 by Miami architects Andres Duany and Elizabeth Plater-Zyberk, approaches build out. More than 400 cottages, shops and restaurants in Easter-egg pastels huddle together on 80 acres. Drawn from the East Coast's vernacular architecture, elements such as picket fences, widow's walks, latticework balconies, fanciful parapets, and steep-pitched roofs with deep overhangs conform to Davis' architectural guidelines. Although owners are free to hire their own architects, the community building code requires they use only pre-World War II materials (i.e., tin roofs and wood siding).

The resulting variety of frame vernacular designs suggests a beach town of Key West ilk, but the newness of the place lends it the aura of a Hollywood set. Indeed, as "Seahaven," it was the focus of the popular 1998 movie, *The Truman Show* (Star Jim Carrey's Natchez Street "home" is known locally as the Truman House).

Seaside

■ The White Beaches of the Panhandle

What makes the Panhandle coast beaches so white? According to Florida International University's Dr. Stephen Leatherman, director of the International Hurricane Center in Miami and popularly known as "Dr. Beach" for his ratings of America's leisure beaches, quartz is responsible for the color and texture of these sands. Whereas most beaches contain multiple minerals, the Panhandle's shores are composed of nearly pure quartz. Eons ago, sediments eroded from the Appalachian Mountains and washed down to the Gulf of Mexico. Waves pummeled these sediments, grinding up the minerals and eventually washing most of them away, leaving quartz to color the sands. The Panhandle's beaches stay so sparkling white because the area's rivers flow over limestone on their way into the Gulf; since limestone does not produce sediment, no impurities are introduced into the pristine sand.

To maintain the community atmosphere, only residents and guests may drive on the brick side streets *(golf carts are popular transport)*. Seaside has been featured in *Architectural Digest* and has won accolades from several organizations, the American Institute of Architects and Progressive Architecture among them. It has inspired similar developments in Florida, including knockoffs that trade on the style without re-creating the pedestrian-friendly community that Davis envisioned.

★★**Grayton Beach State Park** – *1.5mi west of Seaside on Rte. 30A. Open year-round daily 8am-dusk. $3.25/vehicle.* △ ㅎ ☎ *850-231-4210*. This small park harbors a gorgeous 1mi strand of shoreline that has been rated one of the country's top 10 beaches by the University of Maryland's Laboratory for Coastal Research. However, a rash of new development, rising numbers of seasonal residents and visitors, and substantial loss of dunes to recent hurricane activity have compromised the character of the beach and its namesake hamlet. Though not as wide as some area beaches, Grayton offers plenty of room for exploring or just swimming and sunning. A lovely nature loop *(1mi)* penetrates a tunnel of dwarf live oaks and emerges out past the dunes and pine flats on a trail lined with wild daisies, goldenrod and saw palmetto.

PENSACOLA★

Population 56,255
Map p 176
Tourist Information: www.visitpensacola.com and www.pensacolabeach.com
☎ 850-434-1234 or 800-874-1234

Hugging the western shore of Pensacola Bay and well protected by Santa Rosa Island and Perdido Key, Pensacola remains the Panhandle's leading port. To the southwest, **Pensacola Naval Air Station** has become a major contributor to the city's economy. At the other end of town, the University of West Florida lends a youthful vibrancy, and a new airport, completed in 1990, has welcomed more than two million business travelers and vacationers, many of whom slip off to **Pensacola Beach** and the Gulf Islands National Seashore.

Spanish conquistadors visited Pensacola Bay as early as 1516; permanent settlement was established in 1698. For decades thereafter, the Spanish, French and British played tug of war with Pensacola. In 1781, Spain recaptured the town from the British, rechristening English streets with such names as Salamanca and Tarragona. When the British and Americans warred in 1812, Spain let the British use Pensacola as a base from which to incite Indians to fight the Americans. Andrew Jackson stormed into town in 1814 and ran the Brits off. In 1821 Spain ceded Pensacola to the US as part of the Florida purchase.

Three months before the Civil War, Confederates seized forts at Pensacola. Union forces entrenched themselves at Fort Pickens and in October 1861, exchanged fire with Confederates across the bay. By 1862 southern troops had conceded Pensacola. Since then, only the flag of the US has flown over the "City of Five Flags."

DOWNTOWN

★**Seville Historic District** – Concentrated between Tarragona and Florida Blanca streets and Garden and Main, Seville is the oldest of the three contiguous historic districts, brimming with frame vernacular, Victorian and Creole houses, many converted to law offices, restaurants and shops. Streets here were platted by the British in 1765 and renamed by the Spanish. *Purchase tickets for Historic Pensacola Village at the visitor center (Tivoli House, 205 E. Zaragoza St.) or at T.T. Wentworth Jr. Florida State Museum (330 S. Jefferson St.). Village open year-*

Practical Information..Area Code: 850

Getting There – **Pensacola Regional Airport (PNS)**: 3mi northeast of city; domestic flights ☎ 436-5000. Transportation to downtown: **taxi** *($9)* and hotel courtesy **shuttles**. **Rental car agencies** *(p 343)* located at airport. Amtrak **train** station: 980 E. Heinberg St. *(☎ 800-872-7245; www.amtrak.com)*. Greyhound **bus** station: 505 W. Burgess Rd. *(☎ 800-231-2222; www.greyhound.com)*.

Getting Around – Local **bus service**: Escambia County Transit System *(☎ 595-3228)*. The city's trackless **trolley** runs every 7-15min *($1)*; *(schedule ☎ 595-3228 ext. 30)*. Downtown historic district is best explored on foot. Downtown metered parking available *(25¢/hr)*.

Visitor Information – **Pensacola Convention and Visitor Center**, 1401 E. Gregory St., Pensacola FL 32501 *(open year-round daily 8am-5pm; ☎ 434-1234 or 800-874-1234)*; **Pensacola Beach Visitor Center**, 735 Pensacola Beach Blvd. *(open year-round daily 9am-5pm; ☎ 932-1500 or 800-635-4803 www.pensacolabeach.com)*. *These organizations provide information on shopping, entertainment, festivals and recreation.*

Accommodations – Area visitors' guide including **lodging directory** available *(free)* from Pensacola Convention and Visitor Center. Accommodations offered include **hotels** *($65-$190)*, **motels** *($40-$90)* and **condominiums** *(rates lower in winter)*. **Campgrounds** and RV parks are also available. Coastal **camping**: Big Lagoon State Park *(☎ 492-1595)*; Fort Pickens, Gulf Islands National Seashore *(☎ 934-2622 or 800-365-2267)*. *Rates quoted are average prices per night for a double room and are subject to seasonal variations.*

Shopping – Palafox Historic District and Seville Historic District.

Entertainment – Consult the arts and entertainment section of the *Pensacola News Journal* (Fridays) for schedules of cultural events. **Pensacola Civic Center**: concerts, shows and sporting events *(☎ 432-0800)*. **Saenger Theatre**: Broadway shows, plays and symphony concerts *(☎ 444-7686; for advance tickets, contact Ticketmaster: ☎ 434-7444, www.ticketmaster.com)*.

Sports and Recreation – The **Moors Golf Club** *(open to public; ☎ 995-4653)*. **Pensacola Greyhound Track** *(year-round; ☎ 455-8595)*. **Canoeing trips**: *(4mi-11mi)* Adventures Unlimited *(☎ 623-6197)*.

round Tue-Sat 10am-4pm; closed major holidays; $6; ▯ ☎ 850-595-5985 www.historicpensacola.org. Price includes guided tours of Old Christ Church, Lavalle and Dorr houses (tours depart from Tivoli House) and admission to the museums of Commerce and Industry, the Wentworth Museum, Julee Cottage and Quina and Barkley houses.

Museum of Commerce – *Tarragona and Zaragoza Sts.* Contained in this masonry warehouse is a turn-of-the-19C streetscape, complete with wooden sidewalks, dim street lamps, walk-in barbershop, leather and harness shop, music store and others.

Seville Historic District

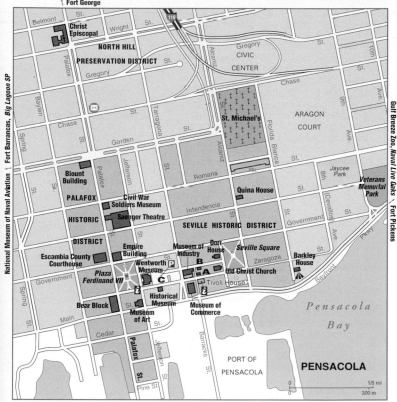

Museum of Industry – *200 E. Zaragoza St. (opposite Museum of Commerce)*. A late 19C warehouse showcases the industries that fueled Pensacola's early growth—brick making, forestry, shipping and fishing. Clay from local bluffs was fired into bricks. Huge forests of pine, oak, cedar and cypress were harvested for lumber, as well as rosin, pitch and turpentine. And the area was once known as the "red snapper capital of the world." Among the informative exhibits are a replica brick kiln, lumber machinery and an old fishing boat.

Julee Cottage (**A**) – *210 E. Zaragoza St. (next door to Museum of Industry)*. Completed in 1808, this saltbox dwelling is one of the oldest extant houses in the city. Owned by Julee Panton, a free black woman, the house originally sat five blocks to the west. Much of the original cypress framework has been lost, but some ceiling timbers and pegged framing remain. In the re-created interior, the lives of free blacks in colonial Florida are traced.

Lavalle House (**B**) – *205 E. Church St. (across courtyard from Julee Cottage). Visit by guided tour (1hr) only, year-round Tue-Sat 11am & 1pm.* The 1805 French Creole home was built by brick maker and builder Charles Lavalle. Brick piers elevated the house, and windows on all sides allowed cross ventilation. Bright interior and exterior color schemes typify the Creole style. Inside, where four rooms display 1820s furnishings, the ochre and yellow walls mimic the colors of local clays.

Old Christ Church – *Adams and Zaragoza Sts. Visit by guided tour only, year-round Tue-Sat 11am & 1pm.* This white-washed brick church, built in 1832, serves as a museum and special events hall. The Union army used it as a barracks and hospital; it later served as a public library and home to the Pensacola Historical Museum. The church sits opposite pleasant **Seville Square**, a park with overhanging live oaks, where the Spanish built a fortified outpost in the 1750s.

Dorr House – *Church and Adams Sts. Visit by guided tour only, year-round Tue-Sat 11am & 1pm.* An example of gracious living in the 19C, this 1871 Greek Revival house was built by Clara Barkley Dorr, widow of lumber tycoon Eben Dorr and daughter of merchant George Barkley. The restrained elegance of the pale yellow exterior gives way to a more luxurious style within. Big bay windows with lace curtains and the unusual **jib windows**—the lower halves of which open out like doors—lend a light, airy feel. Heart-pine floors, sliding pocket doors, and a roomy kitchen bespeak the residents' refined lifestyle. Period antiques grace the rooms.

Quina House – *204 S. Alcaniz St. (one block north of Seville Square).* This simple wood-frame cottage was built in the early 1800s by Italian native Desiderio Quina in the Creole style. Slaves constructed the 1.5-story house on brick piers, using native pine, cypress and oak. The separate kitchen was later attached to the rear of the main house. Interior appointments include an 1840 mahogany-laminated buffet, a maple wood bed, finger-pine kitchen floors, and a mid-19C Chinese Chippendale cabinet.

Barkley House – *Florida Blanca and Zaragoza Sts.* Wealthy Pensacola merchant George Barkley erected the grand bayfront house in the 1820s for his wife, and here they raised nine children. The wide gallery porch and dormer windows represent Creole architectural influences, while the central-hall floor plan borrows from American tradition. Sometimes called a "high house" because of its elevated first floor, the home commands a splendid **view** of Pensacola Bay.

St. Michael's Cemetery – *Alcaniz and Chase Sts.* Established on land deeded as burial ground by the King of Spain in 1806, this plot contains many noteworthy examples of monumental sculpture. Early town settlers, as well as priests, political leaders and slaves are buried here. Among the nearly 3,000 graves are many raised tombs, similar to those found in New Orleans.

★**Palafox Historic District** – Just west of the Seville Historic District *(along Palafox St. from Garden St. to Pine St.)*, **Palafox Street**, the commercial spine of Pensacola since the late 19C, retains the look of earlier days. Though fires and hurricanes have destroyed some of the old buildings, many remain intact and others have been restored. The 1907 Beaux-Arts **Blount Building** *(Garden and Palafox Sts.)* boasts impressive terra-cotta arches and copper cornices. One block south, the Spanish Baroque **Saenger Theatre** (1925) was the venue for vaudeville acts and Hollywood features; it now offers Broadway plays and concerts. Continuing south on Palafox you encounter the massive **Escambia County Courthouse** *(at Government St.)*, a Renaissance Revival structure dating from 1887. And just across the street (east side) looms the 10-story **Empire Building** (1909), also known as Seville Tower.

On the other side of Government Street lies a peaceful park of live oaks and magnolias, **Plaza Ferdinand VII**. Its central location has made the plaza a site of important events: Spanish Governor Callava handed over West Florida to Andrew Jackson here in 1821. Across Palafox Street, the colorful ironwork balconies and ornate arches of the two-story **Bear Block** (1892) once ornamented the wholesale grocery of Lewis Bear Company. South of Main Street, toward the wharves, was the haunt of sailors, longshoremen and streetwalkers. These 60 acres here are landfill made from ships' ballast.

Civil War Soldiers Museum – *108 S. Palafox Pl. Open year-round Tue-Sat 10am-4:30pm. Closed Jan 1, Thanksgiving Day, Dec 25. $5. & www.cwmuseum.org ☎ 850-469-1900.* A wonderful variety of artifacts, maps, documents, paintings and photographs here retell the story of the Civil War's major campaigns. Life-size dioramas portray the gore of a Confederate field hospital and the austerity of a Union camp. A short film *(23min)* recounts the Civil War history of Pensacola.

T.T. Wentworth Jr. Florida State Museum – *330 S. Jefferson St. Open year-round Tue-Sat 10am-4pm. Closed major holidays. $6 admission ticket also includes Historic Pensacola Village. & www.historicpensacola.org. ☎ 850-595-5985.* Completed in 1908 as the City Hall, this substantial Renaissance Revival building features a triple-arched entrance, four red-tiled towers and a second-story arcade. The first two floors house the eclectic collection of local realtor Theodore Thomas Wentworth, who started collecting in 1906 at age 8. Among the grab bag of items found here are mounted animals, antlers, license plates, old radios and antique Coke machines. A hands-on area 🄺 for children occupies the third floor.

In the plaza behind the museum, visitors may view the **Colonial Archaeological Trail** (), an in-progress excavation that has unearthed evidence of Spanish, British and American forts built between 1752 and 1821 *(visit during daylight hours; site not lit at night)*.

Pensacola Historical Museum – *115 E. Zaragoza St. Open Apr-Sept Mon-Sat 9am-4:30pm. Rest of the year Mon-Sat 10am-4:30pm. Closed major holidays. $ & ☎ 850-433-1559.* Lodged in the Arbona Building (c.1882), this informative museum—operated since 1960 by the Pensacola Historical Society—provides an overview of Pensacola's complex past. Exhibits are organized by a quartet of themes, each presented more or less chronologically: native Indian presence, multicultural influence, maritime past and military heritage. The two-story brick building was erected by Spanish immigrant Eugene Arbona, who operated a saloon here. (His family lived on the second floor.)

Pensacola Museum of Art – *407 S. Jefferson St., 1 block south of T.T. Wentworth Museum. Open year-round Tue-Fri 10am-5pm, Sat 10am-4pm. Closed major holidays. $2. & ☎ 850-432-6247. www.artsnwfl.org/pma.* This yellow stucco Mediterranean Revival structure (1908) served as the city jail until the 1950s. Iron cell gates now close on classrooms of young art students. The museum's permanent collection of Steuben and Tiffany glass pieces, and 20C American works on paper is augmented by annual traveling exhibits.

ADDITIONAL SIGHTS

Veterans Memorial Park – *9th Ave. and Bayfront Pkwy. Open daily year-round.* ♿ ☎ *850-433-8200.* Set between the newly developed Aragon neighborhood and beautiful Pensacola Bay, this manicured little park possesses a 256ft black granite wall with the engraved names of all 58,217 Americans who died in the Vietnam War. A small-scale replica of the Vietnam Veterans' Memorial in Washington, DC, the memorial is accompanied by a computer that provides data about the veterans and helps friends and relatives locate their loved ones' names on the wall.

North Hill Preservation District – *Bordered by Blount, Wright, Palafox and A Sts.* Just northwest of the Palafox Historic District lies the 50-block North Hill neighborhood, a gathering of Victorian houses built at the turn of the 19C for Pensacola's upper middle class. Architectural styles represent Queen Anne, Neoclassical, Mediterranean Revival and Tudor Revival. Massive Spanish Colonial-style **Christ Episcopal Church** (1902) squats at Palafox and Wright streets. It boasts a copper dome rising 64ft and stained glass taken from the Old Christ Church on Seville Square. The corner of Palafox and LaRua Streets was the site of **Fort George**, the largest of three forts built by the British in 1778. A small park here displays a re-created section of the battlement. One block north in Lee Square, the oblong park in the middle of Palafox, a 50ft-high **obelisk** honors the Confederacy.

★★**National Museum of Naval Aviation** – *Located at the US Naval Air Station, 8.5mi from downtown. Take Garden St./US-98 west (which becomes Navy Blvd./Rte. 295). Stay on Rte. 295 south and follow signs to museum. Open year-round daily 9am-5pm. Closed Jan 1, Thanksgiving Day, Dec 25.* ♿ 🅿 ☎ *850-453-2389, flight deck:* ☎ *850-453-2025. www.naval-air.org.* More than 150 aircraft and nearly 300,000sq ft of exhibit space make this one of the largest air and space museums in the world. Among the many highlights are a sleek fleet of the Blue Angels' A-4 Skyhawks suspended in diamond formation in a seven-story glass-and-steel atrium; a replica World War II aircraft carrier equipped with such fighters as the Corsair, Hellcat and Avenger; a replica World War II airship; hands-on trainer cockpits; a Stearman biplane flown by former president George H. Bush; and a motion-based flight simulator *($3)*. A new 9,000sq ft **Flight Adventure Deck** promotes understanding of basic principles of flight through simulators and interactive displays, including several wind tunnels. Videos, flight gear and outdoor exhibits round out the museum's offerings.

Blue Angels' A-4 Skyhawks

Courtesy Pensacola Convention & Visitor Center

The IMAX theater *($5.50)* presents the museum's signature film *The Magic of Flight*. In the entrance hall is the striking **Spirit of Naval Aviation Monument**, representing pilots in flight gear from five conflicts since World War I.

Fort Barrancas – *Located at the US Naval Air Station, 8.5mi from downtown. Take Garden St./US-98 west (which becomes Navy Blvd./Rte. 295). Stay on Rte. 295 south and follow signs to fort. Open Apr-Oct daily 9:30am-4:45pm. Rest of the year daily 10:30am-4pm. Closed Dec 25.* 🅿 ☎ *850-934-2600. www.nps.gov/guis.* One of four forts built in the first half of the 19C to protect Pensacola Bay—now administered by **Gulf Islands National Seashore**—Fort Barrancas perches on a bluff (or *barranca* in Spanish) providing a fine view of the bay and barrier islands. The Spanish recognized the strategic importance of this location and built a fortification here in 1698. The present fort was constructed by some 60 slaves between 1839 and 1844. Only during the Civil War did the fort see any fighting, and then briefly. Until 1947 the fort was used for artillery training. Visitors may take a self-guided tour through cavernous gallery passageways; note the arched brickwork.

Another fort, the **Advanced Redoubt** *(.2mi north on Taylor Rd.)*, was built to protect the navy yard from an inland invasion. The self-guided tour here takes you from the point of view of an attacker—over parapets, around a dry moat, up to the drawbridge—to show how suicidal an attempted assault would be. Prickly sand spurs now constitute the fort's main defense. *Wear high-top shoes.*

SCENIC DRIVE *15mi. Map p 176*

Route 399 from Pensacola Beach east to Navarre Beach.

Traversing an undeveloped section of **Santa Rosa Island**, this lovely route offers unspoiled views of the Gulf of Mexico on one side and the Intracoastal Waterway on the other. Though the first few miles pass the shops and condos of Pensacola Beach, the road soon enters a quiet strand with vistas of a pale green sea broken by rolling dunes of sea oats and wildflowers. Along this stretch you'll find many public beach access points. After 6.5mi you enter the Santa Rosa area of the Gulf Islands National Seashore. The next beach access does not occur for several more miles. The drive ends at the low-key hamlet of Navarre Beach.

EXCURSIONS *Map p 176*

Naval Live Oaks Reserve – *1801 Gulf Breeze Pkwy. 8mi southeast via US-98. Cross Three-Mile Bridge into Gulf Breeze (6mi from downtown) and head east 2mi. Open year-round daily 8am-5:30pm. Closed Dec 25.* ♿ 🅿 ☎ *850-934-2600. www.nps.gov/guis.* Headquarters for the **Gulf Islands National Seashore**, this 1,300-acre preserve encompasses land set aside by President John Quincy Adams in 1829 as a federal tree farm to supply timber for warships. Dense, disease-resistant live oaks that thrived in coastal areas were ideal for building ships. Displays in the visitor center demonstrate methods and materials of early shipbuilding, and interpretive trails meander to Pensacola Bay and Santa Rosa Sound through a peaceful forest of pines and majestic live oaks bearded with Spanish moss.

The national seashore, which stretches sporadically westward 150mi from Fort Walton Beach, Florida, to Gulfport, Mississippi, includes several beach parks—among them Rosamond Johnson Beach on Perdido Key, southwest of Pensacola, and Santa Rosa Island Beach to the southeast—as well as forts Pickens and Barrancas, the Advanced Redoubt and battery ruins on Perdido Key.

Big Lagoon State Park – *13mi southwest at intersection of Rtes. 293 and 292A. Take US-98 west to Gulf Beach Hwy. (Rte. 292). Turn south on Rte. 293 and follow signs. Park hrs & fees p 350.* ⚠ ♿ 🅿 ☎ *850-492-1595.* Spreading on 698 acres alongside Big Lagoon, this aromatic haven of pines and evergreen oaks, saw palmetto and rosemary harbors a wealth of mammals and waterbirds. Trails lead back along a tidal marsh and out to the lagoon. The park road curves through a pine forest open to views of the water and ends 2.5mi later at a boardwalk punctuated by picnic pavilions. A short walk takes you to a 40ft observation tower that affords excellent views of Perdido Key, the Gulf and lagoon, and herons wading in the sun-dappled shallows.

★**Fort Pickens** – *17.6mi southwest on Santa Rosa Island. Cross Three-Mile Bridge into Gulf Breeze and continue on Rte. 399 to Santa Rosa Island. Turn right (west) on Fort Pickens Rd. and follow it 9mi to fort on western tip of island. Open Apr-Oct daily 9:30am-4:45pm. Rest of the year daily 8:30am-4pm. Closed Dec 25. $6/vehicle.* ⚠ ♿ 🅿 ☎ *850-934-2600. www.nps.gov/guis.* Largest of the forts erected to defend Pensacola Bay and the navy yard, this colossal bastion was a triumph of coastal defense when it was built by slave labor in 1834, yet ironically was obsolete by the 1860s. During the Civil War, new technology such as rifled cannon and armored warships rendered a brick fort defenseless. Visitors will discover both the original fort and the changes it underwent during its 118 years of service: a dynamited wall, a concrete gun battery (1898) dividing the parade ground, a filled-in moat, and quarters that once housed Apache prisoner **Geronimo**. A parcel of Gulf Islands National Seashore, Fort Pickens also maintains a visitor center, museum and auditorium, large campground, fishing pier and two self-guided nature trails.

Gulf Breeze Zoo – 🅺ids *17mi east in Gulf Breeze. Take US-98 east 11mi to 5701 Gulf Breeze Pkwy. (entrance on south side). Open year-round daily 9am-5pm. Closed Thanksgiving Day & Dec 25. $9.95.* 🍴 ♿ 🅿 ☎ *850-932-2229. www.the zoo.com.* Among more than 700 animals are representatives of several endangered species, including gibbons, ring-tailed lemurs and scimitar-horned oryx. The **lowland gorilla enclosure** and the petting zoo rate as perennial favorites, as does the 20min train ride through a 30-acre open range that provides a home for more than 100 animals, such as the pygmy hippopotamus and the alligator.

PORT ST. JOE

Population 3,644
Map p 177
Tourist Information: www.gulfcountybusiness.com ☎ 850-227-1223

The 36mi separating this rural county seat from Panama City seem like as many years. Its remoteness from centers of tourism (and consequent lack of economic benefit) qualifies this sleepy shore as the poster child for what's promotionally called "Florida's Forgotten Coast." The site of the state's first constitutional convention, this little town boasts a museum that commemorates a defining moment in Florida's emergence from territory to statehood. If you approach Port St. Joe on US-98, a defunct paper mill (west side of town), once the area's largest employer, breaks the lovely views of palm- and pine-lined St. Joseph Bay and distant **Cape San Blas**. Angling into the Gulf of Mexico, the cape flashes a jewel of a state park for those who make the 20mi drive from Port St. Joe. Popular area sports include skin diving, charter fishing and swimming in the Gulf waters.

In 1996 Port St. Joe lost its only significant private-sector employer when the paper mill shut down. Now throughout Florida's northwest, the St. Joe Co., the county's largest landowner, is converting its pine forests to sites for home construction. The town and the mill have a certain appeal as almost museumlike anomalies in a state experiencing prosperity nearly everywhere else. A new downtown marina is a hopeful sign.

Port St. Joe is otherwise the market town for vacationers along St. Joseph Peninsula, popular because of its cottages and motels, and its proximity to Wewahitchka *(22mi north)*, the center of tupelo honey production featured in the movie *Ulee's Gold* with Peter Fonda, and to **St. Vincent Island**, where a national wildlife refuge affords protection for threatened species *(ferry service 10mi east of Port St. Joe; ☎ 850-229-1065; see Apalachicola chapter)*.

Fruit Stand near Port St. Joe

SIGHT

Constitution Convention State Museum – *200 Allen Memorial Way; .5mi north of US-98. Open year-round Thu-Mon 9am-noon & 1pm-5pm. Closed Jan 1, Thanksgiving Day, Dec 25. $1.* ♿ 🅿 ☎ *850-229-8029.* The informative little museum commemorates Florida's first constitutional convention. On this site in late 1838, delegates from the Territory's counties met to draft a state constitution. St. Joseph (as Port St. Joe was called) was then a booming town; a yellow fever epidemic and a hurricane in the early 1840s nearly wiped it off the map. Exhibits detail area and state history, and a replica convention meeting room features automated mannequins who deliver a 3min program.

EXCURSIONS *Map p 177*

★**St. Joseph Peninsula State Park** – *20mi southwest of Port St. Joe. Take US-98 east and bear right on Rte. 30A; continue 7mi and turn right on Rte. 30E. Follow Rte. 30E 8mi to park entrance. Park hrs & fees p 350.* ♿ 🅿 ☎ *850-227-1327.* Occupying the end of a narrow peninsula, this gorgeous 2,516-acre park offers 8mi of white sand **beach** on the Gulf of Mexico and another 8mi along St. Joseph

Bay. It was ranked in 1998 in *USA Today* as the nation's third best beach, after two in Hawaii. Indians once gathered shellfish from the bay's shallow water. During World War II, US Army forces trained here. Now these pristine beaches and quiet forests attract anglers, campers and beach-lovers. Bird-watchers have recorded more than 200 species, including endangered peregrine falcons. In the fall, Monarch butterflies stop here during their migration south to Mexico.

Dead Lakes State Park – *25mi northeast in Wewahitchka. Follow Rte. 71 north through Wewahitchka; continue 2mi north to park entrance (east side). Park hrs & fees p 350.* △ ♿ 🅿 ☎ *850-639-2702.* A natural lake, formed when the Apalachicola and Chipola rivers flooded 12,000 acres of cypress swamp, is preserved here. Dead trees give the lake an eerie aspect but do not deter fishermen, who find the lake alive with freshwater fish. Two short trails wind through a swamp and a longleaf pine woodland.

TALLAHASSEE★
Population 150,624
Map p 177
Tourist Information: www.seetallahassee.com ☎ 850-413-9200 or 800-628-2866

Set amid rolling hills some 12mi from the Georgia state line and 20mi from the Gulf of Mexico, Florida's capital city was considered a sleepy southern town—despite the presence of Florida State University (FSU) and Florida Agricultural and Mechanical University (Florida A&M)—until its explosive development in the 1970s and 80s. Today Tallahassee is primarily a center of government, which (including the universities) employs nearly half the local workforce. Despite the city's recent growth, its moss-draped live oaks, abundant azaleas, and gracious old houses of its historic core bespeak the charm of the Old South.

Historical Notes

From Mounds to Missions – Members of the Mississippian culture peopled the shores of Lake Jackson as early as AD 1000. Evidence of their existence survives in three earth temple mounds at **Lake Jackson Mounds Archaeological State Park** *(1313 Crowder Rd.)*. By the time European explorers arrived in the 16C, the area was dominated by the Apalachee, an agricultural Mississippian tribe with established villages throughout northwest Florida.

In 1528 Spaniard Pánfilo de Narváez led an unsuccessful gold-seeking expedition to Apalachee country. De Soto and his men camped in the area during the winter of 1539-40; a historical marker recalls the event at the **Hernando de Soto State Archaeological Site** *(1022 DeSoto Park Dr.)*. By 1675 Franciscan friars had constructed seven missions near the modern capital; **San Luis de Talimali** eventually served as the provincial seat for more than 40 Apalachee villages. Missions endured until the 18C, when most were destroyed by British soldiers and Seminoles during Queen Anne's War (1702-1713). Apalachees who were not killed in the conflict fled to other areas, opening the way for Seminoles to migrate into the region from Georgia (Tallahassee is a Seminole Indian word meaning "old fields".)

Birth of a Capital – Under Spanish rule, Florida was divided into two provinces, East and West Florida, with capitals at St. Augustine and Pensacola, 400mi apart and connected only by rough trails. After the US acquired the two Floridas from Spain in 1821, Tallahassee, halfway between the two capitals, was chosen as the site of the permanent seat of government. Work began on a capitol in 1826, but financial difficulties prevented its completion. Thirteen years later, Congress appropriated $20,000 and a brick and mortar edifice was erected in 1845, the year Florida gained statehood.

As early settlers usurped the land, hostilities with the Seminoles continued until most of the Indians were relocated after 1858. When the Civil War broke out, Tallahassee was the largest town in northcentral Florida, with much of its success attributable to the cotton industry. It became the only Confederate capital east of the Mississippi to remain uncaptured. Today a monument at **Natural Bridge Battlefield Historic State Park** commemorates the battle *(reenacted every March)* in which Union troops were repulsed *(Natural Bridge Rd., off Rte. 363, 6mi east of Woodville)*.

DOWNTOWN *Map p 183*
A walking-tour guide is available from the visitor center (106 E. Jefferson St.)

Downtown Tallahassee sprouted up around a four-block quadrant bounded by Capitol Square, Adams and Monroe streets and Park Avenue. The 200ft clearing designed to protect the city from Indian attack now contains a seven-block-long linear park.

PRACTICAL INFORMATION ....Area Code: 850

Getting There

By Air – Tallahassee Regional Airport **(TLH)**: 5mi southwest of city; domestic flights
(☎ 891-7800). Transportation to downtown: **taxi** ($12) and hotel courtesy
shuttles. **Rental car agencies** (p 353) are located at airport.

By Train and Bus – Amtrak **train** station: 91812 Railroad Ave. (☎ 800-872-
7245; www.amtrak.com). Greyhound **bus** station: 112 W. Tennessee St.
(☎ 800-231-2222; www.greyhound.com).

Getting Around

Walking-tour maps of downtown historic districts available (free) from
Tallahassee Area Convention and Visitor Bureau. Local **bus** service: Taltran ($1;
free transfers). Free transportation around downtown on **Old Town Trolley Tour**
(year-round Mon-Fri 7am-6pm; every 20min; ☎ 891-5200). Metered parking
available downtown (25¢/hr).

General Information

Visitor Information – **Tallahassee Area Visitor Information Center**, 106 E. Jefferson
St., Tallahassee FL 32301 (open year-round Mon-Fri 8am-5pm, Sat 9am-1pm;
☎ 413-9200).; **Tallahassee Chamber of Commerce**, 100 N. Duval St., Tallahassee FL
32302 (Mon-Fri 8am-5pm; ☎ 224-8116). These organizations provide information on shopping, entertainment, festivals and recreation.

Accommodations – Area visitors' guide including **lodging directory** available (free)
from **Tallahassee Area Visitor Information Center**. Accommodations offered include
hotels ($65-$100) and **motels** ($45-$70). Rustic and RV **camping**: Tallahassee East
KOA Kampground (☎ 997-3890). Rates quoted are average prices per night
for a double room and are subject to seasonal variations.

Shopping: **Historic downtown** (E. Park Ave. and the Capitol); the town of Havana
(on US-27, 12mi north of city) is known for its antique shops.

Entertainment – Consult the arts and entertainment section of the Tallahassee
Democrat (Fridays) for schedules of cultural events. **Florida State University**: year-
round concerts, recitals and opera; for schedules and ticket information:
☎ 644-4774. **Tallahassee Symphony Orchestra** (☎ 644-6500).

Sports and Recreation – **Florida State University** athletic events (☎ 644-1830);
Florida A&M University athletic events (☎ 599-3141); **Tallahassee Tiger Sharks** professional ice hockey, home games (Oct-Apr; ☎ 224-4625). Seminole **Golf** Course
(open to public); ☎ 644-2582. **Whippoorwill Sportsman's Lodge** offers fishing,
boating and camping (☎ 875-2605). You can go crabbing, hiking, fishing and
bird-watching at **St. Marks National Wildlife Refuge** (☎ 925-6121). **Wakulla Springs
State Park** features nature trails and river cruises (☎ 922-3633). Gulf beaches
are located about 70mi south of Tallahassee.

ADDRESS BOOK

For a legend of price listings for hotels and restaurants, see p 76.

Staying in Tallahassee and the Panhandle

Beachfront Cottages in Seaside – 2311 E. Hwy. 30A, Seaside. 🅿 ☎ 850-
231-2294 or 888-732-7433. www.seaside.fl.com. 12 units. $$$$ Modeled on
a guesthouse designed by Thomas Jefferson for Monticello, these cozy one-
bedroom cottages are first-rate for Gulf-front location. Exteriors are
cream-colored board; rooms inside (including a kitchen) are theatrical, sleek
and angular, warmed by exceptional lighting, colorful fabrics and art.
Hammocks and Jacuzzis with privacy curtains occupy decks that face the water.
Rental rates include a bottle of wine, bicycles, morning paper and house-
keeping.

Henderson Park Inn – 2700 Scenic Hwy. (Rte. 98E), Destin. 🍴 ⛵ 🅿 🏊
☎ 850-654-0400 or 800-336-4853. www.hendersonparkinn.com. 36 rooms.
$$$ Set apart by its namesake park from the hurly-burly of high-rise Destin,
the inn, though only a decade old, sports a shingled exterior that evokes cot-
tages at Cape May, NJ, or Newport, RI. The two three-story buildings front
either the pool or beach. Most rooms are luxuriously large, done in soft seashell
tones, with ceiling fan, three-way lamps and French doors to a balcony or
porch; amenities include Jacuzzi, microwave and small refrigerator.
Complimentary buffet breakfast is served in the stylish lobby restaurant that
features contemporary American fare.

Coombs House Inn – *80 6th St., Apalachicola.* ♿ □ ☎ 850-653-2785 *www.coombshouseinn.com. 18 rooms.* $$$ People lodge here four or five nights, even though the location is miles from the beach. The inn is too inviting the town too unmarred by development, the area beaches too compelling not to stay. Lofty in age, the two houses—one a lumber baron's pride—that make up the inn date from early 1900. Lofty, too, are the cypress-beamed interiors with hand-carved antiques, rich chintzes and hand-colored prints. Innkeeping is warm, yet thoroughly professional; breakfasts are extravagant and fun amid fellow boarders. Porches are equipped with ceiling fans and rocking chairs.

Governors Inn – *209 S. Adams St., Tallahassee.* □ *(free valet)* ☎ 850-681-6855 *or 800-342-7717. 41 rooms.* $$$ Arched and understated, the exterior of this hotel resembles a high-end jewelry store. A briefcase-toss from the capitol, the inn supplies the catbird seat downtown. Two 19C shops were gutted to house the hotel, skylights installed and rooms furnished with plantation-style reproductions, including finial-topped four-poster beds. Filled by lobbyists during the spring legislative session, Governors offers expanded continental breakfasts and evening cocktails and snacks in the clubby lounge. The weekend package for two, with dinner coupon, is a good value.

Patrones – *307 Defuniak St., Grayton Beach.* □ ☎ 850-231-1606. *www.city directory.com/patrones. 5 units.* $$$ Secluded within a compound of arty shops beside freshwater Western Lake, these piney lodgings rate as one of Florida's best vacation buys. Spaces are all one of a kind, laid-back and comfortable with porches and kitchens. Most coveted is the boathouse cottage, directly beside the lake. Otherwise opt for upstairs quarters, where views are better and stays are quieter than downstairs. Restaurants and a sugar-soft beach are an easy walk away.

Marsh House – *205 Cevallos, Pensacola.* ♿ □ ☎ 850-433-4866. *www.dotsta .net/biz/marsh. 3 rooms.* $$ Forget croaking frogs. This house borders a historic district and takes its name from the original owners. Though the two-story structure is new—high-pillared upstairs and down with picket-lined porches for rockers and swings—its design neatly blends with its spruced-up, older neighbors. The contemporary guest rooms, all opening to the second-level veranda, are pleasantly themed: for Alaska, sleigh beds and mural with cooling Northern landscape; for Florida, wicker and pastels; and for Louisiana, warm tones velvety and plush. Guests enjoy a bottle of wine upon arrival, an expanded continental breakfast, a hot tub and laundry.

New World Landing – *600 S. Palafox St., Pensacola.* ♿ □ ☎ 850-432-411 *or 800-258-1103. www.newworldlanding.com. 15 rooms.* $$ Pride of Pensacola, this inn celebrates the port city's nearly 450 years of European settlement. An old warehouse in the seaport district—close to Seville Square shops and restaurants—was converted to house the low-scaled, two-story structure some 15 years ago. It is so solidly built that even street-facing corner rooms admit no sound. All guest quarters are large and distinctively furnished with art and artifacts. Uncommon value includes a complimentary continental breakfast.

Killearn Country Club & Inn – *100 Tyron Circle, Tallahassee.* ✃ ♿ □ ☎ 850-893-2186 *or 800-476-4101. www.killearncountryclub.com. 34 rooms.* $ Offering an exceptional deal in the wooded hills of the city's prime residential area, less than 10mi northeast of downtown, the inn features rooms on two stories. Though they're basic motel style—dated and plain—guest rooms are comfortable and equipped with wet bars. What appeals is the setting, the recreational options and the low cost of the lodgings. The pool is Olympic size and there are 8 tennis courts. Affordable golf packages provide unlimited play for two on the 27-hole PGA tournament-quality course.

Dining in Tallahassee and the Panhandle

Criolla's – *170 E. Hwy. 30A, Grayton Beach.* ♿ ☎ 850-267-126 *www.criollas.com.* $$$$ **Creole.** Criolla's creative chef superbly adapts Caribbean taste to contemporary comfort in cuisine and decor within these four intimate dining rooms. Trayed ceilings hung with paddle fans evoke Jamaican style. Murals, posters, kitschy blown glass and tableware are all boldly colorful. Guests easily lapse into Antillean moods while dining on Caribe-style redfish with curried crawfish, bacon-wrapped grilled swordfish, or charred grouper with seafood-filled coconut. *Dinner only.*

Jackson's – *282 S. Palafox St., Pensacola.* ♿ ☎ 850-469-9898. *www. jacksonsrestaurant.com.* $$$$ **Continental.** One of Florida's finest dining spots, this newcomer is housed in a Civil War-era building across from the park where Andrew Jackson accepted Florida from Spain. Behind French doors is a sleek contemporary setting: blond tongue-in-groove and brick walls, a chandelier of Daliesque boughs dangling from the ceiling. Opt for the braised veal shanks, the pan-seared bourbon strip steak or grilled grouper, all generously served. Before 6pm, prix-fixe dinners cost half the evening tariff. *Dinner only.*

Marina Cafe – *404 Hwy. 98E, Destin.* ♿ ☎ *850-837-7960. www. marinacafe.com.* **$$$$ New American.** Gone are the seafood shacks that long characterized the fishing village of Destin. Glossy dining vaults mark the new high-rise resort city. Marina Cafe is one of its glories, super-high ceilinged and tiered for views of yacht anchorage that will knock your Guccis off. Moet & Chandon can be ordered by the glass, though most prefer a bottle to accompany coconut-ginger skewered gulf shrimp, rotisserie duck, or prime filet mignon; everything is à la carte. The big carousel-shaped bar marks the entry. Dockside tables are usually an option. *Dinner only.*

Bud & Alley's – *2236 E. Hwy. 30A, Seaside.* ♿ ☎ *850-231-5900. www.seaside.com.* **$$$ Mediterranean.** Raining cats and dogs? Abandon the informal roof deck—a favorite for tapas and drinks—but maintain the mood by retreating to the beamed dining rooms below (named for Seaside developer's dog and a restaurant partner's cat). Tee shirts and shorts are accepted despite white-linen service. Favored dishes include Basque-style seafood stew; a mixed grill of fish, sausage and filet mignon; and eggplant-spinach lasagna. Music is provided nightly in summer. *Dinner only.*

Capt. Anderson's Restaurant – *5551 N. Lagoon Dr., Panama City.* ♿ ☎ *850-234-2225. www.captandersons.com.* **$$$ Seafood.** This pride of the Panhandle can serve 2,000 diners a night without a single bad meal. They've been at it since 1967, up from 4,000sq ft to some 40,000 now, located dockside where guests start arriving at 4pm to see the fleet come in. Three rooms festooned with nets, upside-down dories and dive suits can hold 620 hungry souls; others may prefer the Dockside Bar. Top menu items are the Gulf shrimp and crabmeat casserole au gratin, whole fresh Gulf flounder, and churrasco steak. *Dinner only.*

Chez Pierre – *1215 Thomasville Rd., Tallahassee.* ♿ ☎ *850-222-0936. www.chezpierre.com.* **$$$ French.** This big, two-story, rose-colored house full of whimsical French art and provincial furniture dishes up worldly cuisine amid the "y'all" style of regional politics (depending on traffic, the restaurant is a 10-minute drive from the capitol). Pierre's is a magnet for both high-rolling lobbyists and vacationers indulging in a small splurge. Tournedos of beef, roasted duckling, and slow-cooked lamb chops epitomize the classic French fare. Keep in mind Sunday brunch, seasonal outdoor dining and weekend music.

Owl Cafe – *15 Ave. D, Apalachicola.* ♿ ☎ *850-653-9888.* **$$ Seafood.** At the Owl, people, food and ambience all celebrate this old seafaring town. Plank floors, high tin ceilings, paddle fans and proud homage to Apalachicola in Richard Bickel's black and white photos (on permanent display) suit a sophisticated, informal crowd. They dine from a select menu that features a half-dozen pastas with seafood; black grouper fillet with artichoke hearts; and jambalaya of chicken, shrimp and sausage. Close to all downtown lodgings, the cafe is only a block from the quiet Apalachicola River, where fishing boats anchor for the night.

Hopkins House – *900 N. Spring St., Pensacola.* ♿ ☎ *850-438-3979. www.pensacolanewsjournal.com/dining.* **$ Southern.** Not to be missed among 40 blocks of fashionable residences from the turn of the last century is this legend in the North Hills Preservation District. Transformed into a boarding house by "Ma" Hopkins in 1949, Number 900 has for years served only please-pass-the-platters country cooking, three meals a day most of the week. The popular dining rooms hold big checkered-cloth tables. While waiting for a table, you'll work up an appetite on the wraparound porch along with anybody who's anybody in town.

Although most of the major commercial activity has moved to suburban malls, a focal point of the modern downtown is **Adams Street Commons**, a block-long, brick-paved section *(between Pensacola St. and College Ave.)*. This serpentine thoroughfare, lined with restaurants and offices, creates a pleasant lunchtime retreat for local business people. The two-story brick building with ornamental ironwork on the northeast corner of Pensacola and Adams Streets was formerly **Gallie's Hall** (c.1874), the city's first opera house. On the other side of City Hall sits the modern **Mary Brogan Museum of Art and Science (MOAS)** 🧒, which opened in 1999 and features three floors of interactive exhibits as well as permanent and rotating works of art *(350 S. Duval St.; ☎ 850-513-0700; www.thebrogan.org)*.

★ **Capitol Complex** – *400 S. Monroe St., at Apalachee Pkwy*. Crowning Tallahassee's downtown is the Capitol Complex. The restored 1845 Capitol and the modern 1978 Capitol juxtaposed here symbolize Florida's evolution.

★ **Old Capitol** – *Open year-round Mon-Fri 9am-4:30pm, Sat 10am-4:30pm, Sun & holidays noon-4:30pm. Closed Thanksgiving Day & Dec 25.* ♿ ☐ ☎ *850-487-1902. www.dos.state.fl.us/dhr/museum*. This white stucco Neoclassical building, with its elegant columned portico and gray-trimmed pediment, ornaments the plain concrete structure that rises behind it. Constructed near the site of a log cabin that held the Florida's first legislative meeting in 1824, the original Capitol has undergone major transformations such as the doubling of usable space. Its 1970s restoration required demolishing 80 percent of the structure. Frank P. Milburn's 1902 design features a handsome lantern-crowned dome and bas-reliefs of the state seal on the front and back pediments. Red-striped window awnings shade the interior from the summer sun as they did at the turn of the 19C. Inside, a grand central staircase divides the rotunda, which is topped by a multicolored **art-glass dome.**

Since 1982 the Old Capitol has served as a museum. A self-guided tour directs visitors to the **Old Supreme Court Chamber** and to early-20C governor William Jennings office suite on the first floor. The second floor features the former **House and Senate Chambers**. Historical exhibits, including a collection of reproductions of the state's constitutions, fill the rooms between the chambers.

Capitol Complex

Directly across Monroe Street from the Old Capitol, the twin marble columns of the **Vietnam Memorial** *(corner of Apalachee Pkwy. and S. Monroe St.)* honor more than 300,000 Floridians who served in the Vietnam War.

New Capitol – *Open year-round Mon-Fri 8am-5pm. Closed major holidays.* 🍴 ♿ ☎ *850-488-6167. Guided tours available: call for hours.* This 22-story concrete tower, flanked by two domed four-story wings, looms 307ft above the original Capitol. Built by Edward Durell Stone (architect of the Kennedy Center in Washington, DC) in 1978 to provide needed space for governmental chambers and state offices, the New Capitol ranks as Tallahassee's tallest building. Guided tours take in the Heritage Chapel, which features an altarpiece illustrating the Creation; the **House of Representatives and Senate chambers** *(open to the public when Legislature is in session, each Feb and Mar)*, which anchor the building at either end; and the rotunda containing the marble and bronze Great Seal of Florida. Atop the skyscraper's 22nd floor, an observation deck affords unique sweeping **views**★ of the city and its surroundings. Original artworks, including a pair of murals portraying symbols of the state's environment *(Plaza level)*, and a permanent collection of paintings by Florida artists *(outside the House Chamber)*, are displayed throughout the building.

Union Bank Building – *219 Apalachee Pkwy., at Calhoun St. Open year-round Mon-Fri 9am-4pm.* ♿ ☎ *850-561-2603*. This unusual little edifice (c.1841), the oldest surviving bank building in Florida, housed one of Tallahassee's first banks. Union Bank lasted just two years before its 1843 failure, which has been variously attributed to a poor cotton crop, the Seminole Wars and financial mismanagement

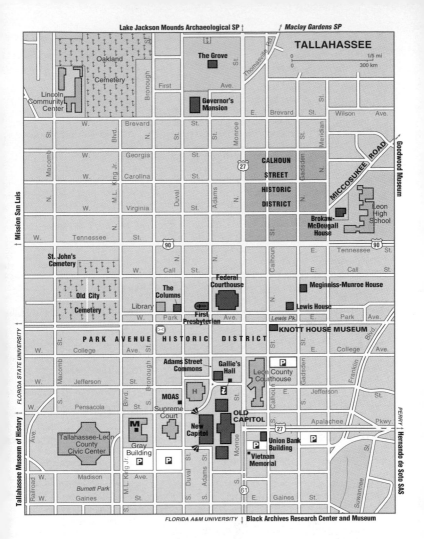

Originally located on South Adams Street, the blue stucco structure, marked by three fanlights on the facade, saw incarnations as a bank for freed slaves, a shoe factory and a dance studio before being moved to its present location in 1971. Restored to its 1841 appearance and furnished with period antiques, the bank opened to the public as a museum in 1984. Today the building houses an overflow collection from the Black Archives Research Center, although one room is devoted to memorabilia from its days as a bank.

★Park Avenue Historic District – *District runs along a seven-block section of Park Ave. bounded by Macomb St., Meridian Rd. and Call St.* In 1830 this mixed-use neighborhood, now composed of commercial, residential and religious buildings and bisected by parks, formed the northern boundary of Tallahassee. Adjoining downtown, Park Avenue—whose name was changed from McCarthy Street in 1905 at the request of one of the district's wealthy matrons—became a prestigious address. Although the Greek Revival style predominates, other styles of architecture are represented, including Victorian and Classical Revival. Anchored on the west by the city's two oldest cemeteries, the district spreads eastward to the vernacular 1854 **Meginniss-Munroe House** *(125 N. Gadsden St.)*, now the LeMoyne Art Foundation, a local gallery that hosts traveling art exhibits.

Lewis House – *316 E. Park Ave. Open year-round Mon-Fri 10am-3pm. Closed one week in September and major holidays.* ♿ 🅿 ☎ *850-224-6048. www.fccmh.org.* The 2.5-story, Southern vernacular frame house (c.1845) with its turret bay window was built for Charles Dyke, a well-known Florida editor. From 1850 to 1993 it remained in the hands of the Benjamin C. Lewis family, whose members included prominent Tallahassee bankers. It currently houses the headquarters of the Florida Council for Community Mental Health. Eastlake-style oak paneling and decorative spoolwork adorn the conference room and various fireplace mantels inside the house; coffered ceilings cover the front and back parlors.

★**Knott House Museum** – *301 E. Park Ave. Visit by guided tour (1hr) only, year-round Wed-Fri 1pm-4pm, Sat 10am-4pm. Closed Jan 1, Thanksgiving Day, Dec 24-25.* ♿ ☎ *850-922-2459. www.dos.state.fl.us.* In the waning months of the Civil War, this two-story wood Classical Revival residence (c.1843) served as the headquarters of Union general Edward McCook, who read the **Emancipation Proclamation** from its front steps on May 20, 1865. It was home to former state treasurer William Knott and his family and earned the sobriquet, "The House That Rhymes," because of Mrs. Knott's propensity to write poems that she attached with satin ribbons to her furniture. Now a museum, the house has been restored to its appearance in 1928—the year the Knotts added the portico. A mahogany staircase leads to the second floor, where a bedroom has been converted into a gallery for local history exhibits.

Federal Courthouse – *110 W. Park Ave., at corner of Monroe St. Open year-round Mon-Fri 8:30am-5pm. Closed major holidays* ♿. Dedicated in 1939 by US Treasury Secretary Henry Morganthau, the imposing Georgia marble Classical Revival courthouse (1936, Eric Kebbon) is notable as Tallahassee's most significant Works Progress Administration (WPA) project. The building, which once served as the city's post office, contains murals depicting milestones in Florida history. A $20 million annex of glass and marble was completed in 1998.

First Presbyterian Church – *110 N. Adams St. To view the sanctuary, inquire at church office next door.* This prim, white Greek Revival church (1838) reigns as the oldest sanctuary in continuous use in Florida. The structure, which provided early settlers refuge from Indian attacks, has undergone four renovations over the years. White paneling and wainscoting and a simple wooden communion table decorate the austere interior.

The Columns – *100 N. Duval St. Open to the public only as offices of the Tallahassee Chamber of Commerce.* Tallahassee's oldest house within the original city limits was built by banker William "Money" Williams in 1830. This stately brick Greek Revival structure, with its two-story pedimented entrance portico, served as Williams' Bank of Florida office as well as his home. Moved from its original site across the street in 1975, The Columns now houses the Chamber of Commerce. The building's interior still contains its original pine floors, door facings and windows; the exterior was recently restored to its turn-of-the-19C appearance.

Old City Cemetery – *Entrance on M.L. King Jr. Blvd. between Park Ave. and Call Sts. Walking-tour brochure available at entrance.* ☎ *850-222-7100.* Live oaks, azaleas and camellias dot the landscape of Tallahassee's oldest public cemetery, authorized in 1829 by the Territorial Legislative Council and acquired by the city in 1840. Markers ranging from flat marble slabs to elaborate carved monuments in the 11 acre plot bear witness to the city's earliest history. Slaves, free men, Confederate and Union soldiers, and victims of the 1841 yellow fever epidemic are among those buried here.

St. John's Cemetery – *Entrance on Call St. between Macomb and M.L. King Jr. Blvd.* ♿ ☎ *850-222-2636.* Adjacent to the Old City Cemetery and graced by native flowers, palmettos and oaks, this graveyard was established in 1840 to serve parishioners of St. John's Episcopal Church. Twin stone obelisks mark the grave of Prince Achille Murat, nephew of Napoleon Bonaparte, and his wife, Princess Catherine. Two former Florida governors, David S. Walker (1865-1868) and William Bloxham (1881-1885; 1897-1901), are also interred here.

Calhoun Street Historic District – *District lies along and adjacent to Calhoun St., bounded by Tennessee, Georgia and Meridian Sts.* This area was laid out in 1825 as the "North Addition" to the city. Called "Gold Dust Street" in the mid-19C because it counted so many prominent Tallahassee citizens among its residents, Calhoun Street still boasts a number of elegant town homes from the period. Greek Revival, Victorian and Bungalow are among the architectural styles represented. The only house open to the public in this district is the **Brokaw-McDougall House** *(329 N. Meridian; open year-round Mon-Fri 9am-3pm; closed major holidays;* 🅿 ☎ *850-891-3900).* Graced with an elegant portico and crowned by an Italianate cupola, this two-story ochre frame structure (c.1856) originally belonged to a livery stable owner. The second floor now houses offices of the Historic Tallahassee Preservation Board, but visitors are welcome to walk through first-floor rooms to appreciate the 14ft ceilings and period furnishings. Outside, gravel paths lace restored formal 19C gardens that were first laid out in the early 1850s.

Florida Governor's Mansion – *700 N. Adams St., 1mi north of Capitol Complex. Visit by guided tour (45min) only. Mar-mid-May Mon, Wed & Fri 10am-noon. Call for Dec holidays.* ♿ 🅿 ☎ *850-488-4661.* Patterned after Andrew Jackson's antebellum home near Nashville, Tennessee, this Neoclassical residence has housed Florida's governors since 1957, when it was built on the site of the 1907 mansion (Jackson was Florida's first territorial governor). A beveled-glass window inscribed with the state seal crowns the front door; six Corinthian columns flank the entrance.

Tours include the state dining room, reception room, guest bedroom, Florida Room and garden. Dentil crown molding and Italian marble floors distinguish the entrance hall; 18C English antiques furnish the public rooms. Note the original paintings on loan from the John and Mable Ringling collection, including two Audubon prints, and an Austrian brass clock (c.1820) from the Marquis de Lafayette's nephew. The dining room holds an impressive silver collection from the decommissioned battleship *Florida*. Guests exit by way of a formal brick-walled English garden. Next door, you can glimpse **The Grove**, a brick antebellum house built for Territorial Governor Richard Keith Call in 1825 and still in the hands of his family.

ADDITIONAL SIGHTS

★ **Museum of Florida History** (**M**) – *500 S. Bronough St. In the R.A. Gray building, two blocks west of Capitol Complex; entrance on basement level. Open year-round Mon-Fri 9am-4:30pm, Sat 10am-4:30pm, Sun & holidays noon-4:30pm. Closed Thanksgiving Day & Dec 25.* ⏃ 🅿 ☎ *850-488-1673. www.flheritage.com.* Occupying the ground floor of the state archives building, exhibits such as a re-created Confederate campsite and a 1926 Florida farmhouse kitchen recount the state's history from prehistoric times to the 20C. Of particular interest is a 12,000-year-old **mastodon skeleton** discovered in Wakulla Springs in 1930. A replica citrus packing house (c.1920) illustrates the importance of the citrus industry to the state's economy, while panels of early photographs detail the contribution made by the lumber industry. Highlighting the waterways display is a reproduction of the forward portion of the steamboat *Hiawatha*, which plied the Oklawaha River in the early 1900s.

Black Archives Research Center and Museum – *On the campus of Florida A&M University. Open year-round Mon-Fri 9am-4pm. Closed major holidays.* ⏃ 🅿 ☎ *850-599-3020.* Housed in the Greek Revival Carnegie Library (1907), the eclectic group of artifacts and papers held here witness the black presence in southern, national and international history. Several small rooms, opened to the public in 1977, display a collection of items ranging from Zairean ivory carvings to a Ku Klux Klan robe. Among the museum archives are the original copy of the 1864 National Anti-Slavery Standard and a collection of rare recordings of famous black musicians.

★ **Maclay Gardens State Park** – *3540 Thomasville Rd. Gardens on left, .5mi north of Capitol Circle. Open year-round daily 8am-dusk. $3.25/vehicle.* ⏃ ☎ *850-487-4556.* This 28-acre garden was created by New York financier Alfred B. Maclay in 1923 and donated to the state of Florida by his widow 30 years later. Maclay planned his garden around winter and spring—the seasons he stayed here. In winter more than 100 varieties of **camellias** burst into bloom; in spring azaleas, dogwood, wisteria, mountain laurel and magnolias festoon the grounds. The single-story **Maclay House**, formerly a hunting lodge (c.1905), contains family furnishings and exhibits relating the evolution of garden design in Europe *(open Jan-Apr daily 9am-5pm; $3)*. South of the house, a formal flower garden boasts a 500ft-long allée with a reflecting pool that looks out over Lake Hall. This surprise **view**, one of several in the gardens, was a popular device in garden design of the 1920s.

★ **Mission San Luis** – *2020 W. Mission Rd. From downtown, take Tennessee St. west past Florida State University; turn right on White Dr. and right again on Mission Rd. Open year-round Tue-Sun 10am-4pm. Closed Thanksgiving Day & Dec 25.* ⏃ 🅿 ☎ *850-487-3711. www.flheritage.com.* The Spanish mission village (c.1656) and fort (c.1696) established by Franciscan friars was the largest of their Florida missions. Here the Spaniards and Apalachee Indians lived together for 50 years. In its heyday, San Luis boasted a population of 1,500 and comprised a fort, an Apalachee council house, a church, Spanish-style residences and a large central plaza. Threatened by British attack, San Luis residents abandoned their village and fort in 1704, setting the complex afire as they fled.

The **visitor center** contains scale models of the Apalachee council house and fort, and Spanish and Apalachee artifacts found on the property. A reconstructed colonist's

● **Aristotle's Coffee Garage**
1935 W. Tennessee St.
☎ *850-222-6922.* On your way to or from Mission San Luis, stop for a break at this converted brick garage, popular with students. Surprisingly spic and span inside and out for a college hangout, Aristotle's offers exotic coffees and teas, tempting pastries and cakes, cushy couches and a mix of tables and chairs (often occupied by students with open textbooks) within airy, funky surroundings. If it's close to lunchtime, you may want to order a sandwich here from the garage's limited selection. A few gift items like coffee mugs are for sale and there's a small front patio with outdoor seating as well.

home (known as the Spanish House), the mission church (c.1680), the friary and Apalachee chief's house and council house (c.1660) may be visited (the fort site is being excavated). Throughout the site, costumed interpreters demonstrate period crafts and activities.

★**Tallahassee Museum of History and Natural Science** – Kids *3945 Museum Dr. Take Capitol Circle S.W. to Orange Ave., turn right on Rankin Ave.; continue .3 mi to where Rankin dead-ends into Museum Dr. Open year-round Mon-Sat 9am-5pm, Sun 12:30pm-5pm. Closed major holidays. $6.50.* ╳ ♿ 🅿 ☏ *850-576-1636. www.tallahasseemuseum.org.* This museum, set on 52 wooded acres near the airport, was created to acquaint visitors with North Florida history and wildlife. Follow the boardwalk through a cypress swamp to a natural-habitat **zoo** featuring indigenous animals such as river otters, white-tailed deer and Florida panthers. **Big Bend Farm** comprises a 19C Cracker farmhouse, church and schoolhouse, which were relocated to this site. Near the visitor center sits **Bellevue**, the modest log house (1841) of Catherine Murat, widow of Prince Achille Murat. This nephew of Napoleon Bonaparte came to America in the early 19C and established a planta-tion near Tallahassee, where he met and married Catherine Daingerfield Willis, great-grandniece of George Washington. The residence was moved to the museum in 1967.

★**Canopy Roads** – *Driving guide available from visitor center.* Shaded by an airy vault of moss-draped live oak branches, five specially designated historic roads—Old St. Augustine, Old Bainbridge, Meridian, Centerville and Miccosukee—fan out from Tallahassee. During the 1980s, as development encroached, preservationists became concerned about the future of these thoroughfares. Consequently, they are now protected by county ordinance. Although most of the roads still maintain their rural Old South character, part of the bordering landholdings have been sold off to developers, and local traffic has increased.

Old St. Augustine Road – The oldest of the canopy roads dates to the 1600s when known as the Royal Road, it linked St. Augustine with the missions in Leon County. During the British occupation, it was called King's Highway. Later it was renamed Bellamy Road, because Leon County landholder John Bellamy's slaves were used in the 1820s to extend the highway to Pensacola. Today Old St. Augustine con-tains cool stretches of dense canopy from Capitol Circle to Williams Road.

Old Bainbridge Road (Route 361) – Originally a Native American trail, Old Bainbridge served as a major thoroughfare for Leon County's early Spanish inhabitants. A Spanish mission once occupied the plot that now forms the right-of-way where Old Bainbridge crosses I-10; several Spanish *rancheros* were also located along this stretch of road.

Meridian Road (Route 155) – This route runs due north from its starting point at the **prime meridian line** from which all land surveys in the state of Florida were conducted *(corner of Meridian Rd. and Bloxham St.)* beginning in 1824. Although the road starts in the city, the canopied portion doesn't begin until the route crosses I-10. From there, Meridian leads to US-319 in Grady County, Georgia, terminating near Pebble Hill Plantation.

Canopy Road

Centerville Road (Route 151) – Thought to have been established in the 1820s as an avenue linking area plantations to the capital city, Centerville Road also begins in Tallahassee, but the canopied portion is limited to the section east of Capitol Circle. From there it winds along a shaded 17mi course, passing through the tiny community of Chemonie Crossing and ending at Miccosukee. On the way, the **Old Pisgah United Methodist Church** *(Old Pisgah Church Rd., 7.6mi north of Capitol Circle)*, a simple wooden structure built in 1858, exemplifies early frontier church design.

Miccosukee Road (Route 146) – In the 1700s this former footpath led to Miccosukee, an Indian village located in the same spot as its modern namesake. In the 1850s plantation owners carted bales of cotton on this road to markets in Tallahassee. Today vast acres of plantation woodland still line picturesque Miccosukee Road. The remains of one of these plantations can be visited *(below)*.

★**Goodwood Museum & Gardens** – *1600 Miccosukee Rd. Visit by guided tour (45min) only, year-round Thu-Fri 10am-4pm. $5.* ▯ ☏ *850-877-4202. www.good woodmuseum.org.* Set back from heavily trafficked Miccosukee Road, these buildings and grounds remaining from a 2,400-acre plantation offer quiet respite amid bustling suburbia. Now being restored after years of deterioration, the Main House, along with several outbuildings, has witnessed a succession of owners and some 150 years of regional history.

Hardy Croom, a lawyer and planter from North Carolina, amassed the estate in the early 1830s. After his death, his brother Bryan Croom completed the main house in the 1840s. During the early 20C, a new owner transformed its Italianate exterior into the Colonial Revival style the residence displays today. Purchased in 1925 by state senator William Hodges, an avid horticulturist, Goodwood soon became the center of Tallahassee's social life, and remained so until 1978, upon the death of his wife. Restored as a house museum, Goodwood is owned and maintained by a private foundation and serves as a setting for luncheons, teas and other community events.

Fronted by a columned portico, the two-story stucco **Main House** is topped by an eight-sided, windowed cupola; the interior of the house boasts the first frescoes in Florida. The Old Kitchen serves as a visitor center and gift shop. A five-room cottage, Rough House, now a tearoom, was built to function as the pool cabana. The c.1911 swimming pool has been renovated as a reflecting pool. Other outbuildings are slated for reuse: a one-time roller-skating rink as an outdoor performance space; the Carriage House as a meeting hall; and the woodshed as an artifact restoration shop.

The 19-acre grounds have been restored to approximate features of the estate's gardens in the 1920s.

EXCURSIONS *Map p 177*

★★**Wakulla Springs State Park** – *16mi south in Wakulla Springs. Take Rte. 61/319 south from Capitol Circle; follow left fork and continue 8mi on Rte. 61; turn left on Rte. 267. Entrance on right. Park hrs & fees p 350. All boat tours depart from dock. River Cruise Wildlife Tour: daily 9:45am-5pm; round-trip 45min; commentary; $4.50. Glass-Bottom Boat Cruise (water conditions permitting): daily 11am-3pm; round-trip 45min; commentary; $4.50.* ✗ ⬥ ▯ ☏ *850-224-5950.* Set amid lush vegetation in rural Wakulla County, one of the world's largest and deepest springs forms the centerpiece of this 2,900-acre park. Reputed to have been discovered by Spanish explorer Ponce de León around 1521, the spring was home to paleo-Indians over 10,000 years ago. In 1935 Ed Ball, an heir to the Du Pont fortune and owner of sizable timber interests in north Florida, purchased the spring and its surrounding acreage. After his death, the property was acquired by the State of Florida and opened as a state park in 1986.

Known by indigenous peoples as "mysterious water," this underground spring pumps some 400,000 gallons of crystal-clear water per minute into the Wakulla River. The source of the spring's waters, which maintain a constant year-round temperature of 70°F, remains a secret. Although divers have plumbed to depths of 360ft, the spring's source has never been reached.

To cruise this river is to travel back in time. Longleaf pine, beech and cypress trees dripping with Spanish moss surround the river; alligators, turtles and a wealth of waterbirds call its shores home. This primeval atmosphere provided the jungle setting for a number of films, including *Tarzan* movies (late 1930s to early 1940s), *Creature from the Black Lagoon* (1954) and *Airport '77*.

On the banks of the river, a stucco Mission-style guest lodge (c.1937) features a hand-painted cypress ceiling, imported Spanish tiles and Tennessee marble floors in the lobby. Nature trails within the park wind through a variety of plant communities, including old-growth floodplain swamps and longleaf pine forests.

Turtles Sunning at Wakulla Springs State Park

★**St. Marks Lighthouse and National Wildlife Refuge** – *23mi south in Newport.*
Take Rte. 363 south to Wakulla and turn left on Rte. 267; continue to US-98 and
turn left. Travel 3mi on US-98 and turn right on Rte. 59 to park entrance. Open
May-Sept daily 6am-9pm. Oct-Apr daily 6am-7pm. $4/vehicle. & 🅿 ✆ *850-925-*
6121. http://saintmarks.fws.gov. This 40mi, 67,000-acre parcel encompasses one
of Florida's oldest lighthouses, a nature museum, wildlife preserve and recreation
area. The **visitor center** *(open year-round Mon-Fri 8:15am-4pm, weekends 10am-*
5pm; closed major holidays) introduces the refuge via a video *(15min)* and several
shadowbox exhibits detailing area history and wildlife. Constructed in 1829 of limestone bricks taken from the ruins of nearby San Marcos de Apalache, the **lighthouse**
(7mi south of nature center) remains in use today. A wooden observation tower
affords opportunities to watch some of the park's 300 species of birds and the
Monarch butterflies who migrate here in late October.

San Marcos de Apalache – *26mi south in St. Marks. Take Rte. 363 to St. Marks.*
Turn right on Old Fort Rd. and follow to end. 🅿 Located at the confluence of the
Wakulla and St. Marks rivers 5mi from the Gulf of Mexico, San Marcos marks the
construction site of Spain's first North American ships, a feat of Pánfilo de Narváez
and his troops. Because of its river proximity, San Marcos was also the site of early
Spanish forts and subsequent English and Confederate ramparts. The first for
(c.1679) was burned by pirates in 1682. Thirty-six years later, the Spanish constructed a second wooden fort here; they began work on a third—this one
stone—in 1739. In 1857 a federal marine hospital was constructed on the site
using stones from the Spanish bombproof. During the Civil War, Confederate soldiers refurbished San Marcos, renaming it Fort Ward. After a four-year blockade
by Union gunboats, the Confederate army surrendered the fort in 1865.
Today a windowless concrete **museum**, built on the hospital's foundation, contains
exhibits detailing the site's history *(open year-round Thu-Mon 9am-5pm; closed*
Jan 1, Thanksgiving Day & Dec 25; $1; ✆ *850-922-6007).* A self-guided walking
tour *(pamphlet available in the museum)* leads visitors along the banks of the
Wakulla River past the limestone outlines of the fort's north and west walls and
the Spanish bombproof, as well as around the large, wooded hill that served as
powder magazine for Confederate soldiers.

EXCURSION TO THOMASVILLE, GA *25mi northeast via US-319*
(Thomasville Rd.). Map p 177.

Situated in a 300,000-acre area around the Florida/Georgia border between
Tallahassee and Thomasville is the greatest concentration of original plantations in
the US. The majority of these sites are now private estates. Pebble Hill Plantation
in Thomasville, is one of only 3 of 71 existing antebellum estates open to the public
(Goodwood and Melhana are the other two). Vast acres of pine forests join the
two cities along Route 319.
By the 1840s Thomasville was a cotton town. After the Civil War, the town pro-
moted its climate and elevation as tonics for healthy living, attracting moneyed
northerners in great numbers by rail. Grand hotels were quickly erected to house
them, and Thomasville prospered as a winter resort well into the early 1900s.
Wealthy industrialists converted the cotton plantations into private hunting preserves for their seasonal residences.

Today this community of 20,000 is a thriving Main Street City (designated in 1982) with a revitalized downtown, a large medical complex, several parks, and a variety of accommodations and attractions for a steady stream of tourists. Hunting is still popular in the area: although much of the land is privately owned, a few facilities, such as **Myrtlewood Hunting Plantation,** are open to the public for hunting, sporting clay, and fishing *(16947 Hwy. 188; guides & overnight lodging available; ☎ 229-228-6232).*

Downtown – Colorful Broad Street is flanked by spruced-up storefronts housing restaurants, home furnishings and gift shops, a sporting goods store and many other businesses. Located in the basement of an attractive brick building is the city's **visitor center** *(135 N. Broad St.; ☎ 229-227-7099; www.thomasvillega.com).* Wide Dawson Street holds several handsome dwellings, including the **Lapham-Patterson House** (1885), distinguished by its lack of right angles to facilitate air flow; the original owner, a survivor of the Great Chicago Fire of 1871, suffered from lung damage *(626 Dawson St.; visit by 1hr guided tour year-round Tue-Sat 9am-4pm, Sun 2pm-4pm; $4; ☎ 229-225-4004).*

★★**Pebble Hill Plantation** – *5mi south of downtown on US-319; entrance on right. House visit by guided tour (2hrs) only, Oct-Aug Tue-Sat 10am-5pm, Sun 1pm-5pm. Closed Jan 1, Thanksgiving Day & Dec 24-25. $7; grounds $3.* ☂ ☐ ☎ *229-226-2344. www.pebblehill.com.* Venerable live oaks shade the lane that winds up to the graceful white-brick manor house on this 3,000-acre plantation. Purchased by Ohio industrialist Howard Hanna in 1896, Pebble Hill was a working farm owned by Hanna's granddaughter Elisabeth (Miss Pansy) Ireland Poe. The original house (1827) was virtually rebuilt in 1936 by Abram Garfield (son of President James Garfield) after most of the original structure burned to the ground. Pebble Hill remained in the Hanna family until Miss Pansy died in 1978. For many years, the plantation was a private retreat for wealthy northerners who came south during the winter to hunt quail; the site was opened to the public in 1983. Virtually all the furnishings are original to the house.

A free-standing mahogany staircase dominates the foyer of this 42-room mansion. English wallpaper, Hanna family antiques and early **Audubon prints** number among the treasures found here. The intimate **Indian Room** holds an intriguing collection of arrowheads, spears, guns (note the rifle-base lamp), scrimshaw and other artifacts. Filled with overstuffed furniture, the informal **Drawing Room** at the east entrance connects to the house by way of a glassed-in loggia. The room's focal point is a wraparound mural by Palm Beach artist J. Clinton Shepherd depicting wildlife native to the region. Outside, a formal garden with brick walkways connects beds of azaleas, camellias and annuals.

The **ticket house** and photographic exhibits detailing the family's and estate's history are in the plantation's former cow barn, which once housed a prize Jersey herd. All of the barns and stables—handsome brick buildings with green shutters—are modeled after designs by Thomas Jefferson. Among the 17 outbuildings are a bath-house built to resemble Noah's ark, a log cabin school where plantation children were tutored, and a guest cottage.

Pebble Hill Plantation

■ Melhana: The Grand Plantation

Approaching the inn from the lengthy entrance road lined with moss-draped oaks and expansive pasture, visitors feel a heightened sense of anticipation. The opportunity to overnight at a Southern plantation is rare. Yet guests have done just that since 1997, when Charles and Fran Lewis opened their formidable estate after restoring it to late-19C opulence. Amid immaculately manicured grounds, complete with parterre gardens, magnolia trees and a goldfish pond, peacocks stroll and roosters crow. A **Percheron-drawn carriage** awaits beneath the porte cochere, ready to tour guests around the 50-acre resort. Afternoon tea

is served in the spacious **Hanna Room**, paneled in magnolia wood. Nightly, a chef-prepared, seven-course menu emphasizes local ingredients in Southern fare such as wild mushroom strudel with Alabama goat cheese, Savannah-style crab cakes, pork roulade stuffed with sausage cornbread, and pecan-crusted rack of lamb with squash soufflé *(the restaurant is open to nonguests year-round daily 6pm-10pm; reservations required)*. Complimentary gourmet breakfasts are equally lavish. Housed in the antebellum manor and in converted outbuildings, the 38 suites and rooms are all lavishly appointed, most with floral bedspreads and draperies, antique furnishings and four-poster or iron beds. Generous bathrooms feature mirror-paneled walls, showers and Jacuzzi tubs. Bounteous with tropical plants, the terrarium-style **pool house** holds a sizable swimming pool, dressing cabanas, fireplace and sitting area. Guests may also use the

Gwen Cannon/MICHELIN

fitness center and play tennis and croquet. The serene setting and attentive service from a caring staff infuse one's stay throughout with gracious Southern hospitality indeed. *Located 4mi south of Thomasville off US-319 at 301 Showboat Lane, the resort is open year-round (guided tours daily 10am & 1pm; $10; 24hr advance reservations required).* ☎ *229-226-2290 or 888-920-3030. www.melhana.com.*

Returning to Tallahassee, the most scenic route is via Meridian Road *(Rte. 155 exit Pebble Hill and turn right on US-319; go 4.7mi. south and turn right or Meridian Rd.)*, one of Leon County's designated canopy roads. The route passes the privately owned inn **Susina** *(1420 Meridian Rd.)*, an antebellum plantation house built by Thomasville architect John Wind, who also designed an earlier version of Pebble Hill.

South Florida

Aeral View of Miami Beach – Bill Staley/Tony Stone Images

Florida's most heavily developed strip extends along the Atlantic in a 70mi-long megalopolis from Miami to West Palm Beach. Called the Gold Coast, this region packs in some of the state's most valuable real estate, from the multimillion-dollar compounds of Palm Beach to the high-rise condos of Miami Beach. Here in the urban backdrop to America's sandbox, people drive fast, work hard, and take the big business of tourism seriously. The majority of South Florida's residents live on a swath of land some five to ten miles wide; just to the west lie the nearly unpopulated expanses of the Everglades.

Before the arrival of the first European explorers, South Florida was inhabited by Tequesta Indians. These hunter-gatherers subsisted on a diet of fish, clams, manatee and turtle meat, and flour made from the roots of the coontie, a palm-like tropical plant that grew wild throughout the region.

During his initial explorations in 1513, Ponce de León sailed into Biscayne Bay, but there was no real effort to colonize Indian territory until Pedro Menéndez de Avilés turned his sights to South Florida—ideally situated to control the Florida Straits—after founding St. Augustine in 1565. After failing to establish a permanent settlement and mission here in 1567, the Europeans retreated.

The area became an established tourist mecca in the 1890s when **Henry Flagler** tamed the frontier with his famous **Florida East Coast Railway**, extending the line from St. Augustine to Palm Beach and then later to Miami and the Keys. In-between towns like Fort Lauderdale and Boca Raton, already settled by vegetable and fruit farmers, did not attain full resort status until the 1920s. Synonymous with warm sunshine and fresh oranges, southeast Florida has throughout this century attracted hordes of visitors from points north to its year-round warm weather, clear blue water and elegant resorts.

Whether your tastes take you to the posh shops of Palm Beach's Worth Avenue, to the art museums of West Palm Beach, to Miami Beach's bright parade of world-class Art Deco architecture, to Fort Lauderdale's famous beach, or to Miami's cultural melting pot of eateries, festivals and languages, South Florida promises to keep you entertained.

BOCA RATON★

Population 74,764
Map p 204
Tourist Information: www.bocaratonchamber.com ☎ 561-395-4433

Early mapmakers mistook the area for a similar site near Miami's Biscayne Bay and called it by the same Spanish name, *Boca Ratone* (popularly translated as "mouth of the rat"). Situated halfway between Fort Lauderdale and West Palm Beach, sun-soaked Boca Raton has catered to the well-heeled for more than 70 years. This clean, prosperous community, whose 2mi stretch of public beaches is warmed by Gulf Stream waters flowing only 200 yards offshore, still attracts monied visitors.

However, tourism—which swells the city's population by 10 percent in the winter season—gave way to high-tech industry as Boca's largest source of commercial revenue when more than a dozen major companies, including IBM and Sony, initiated operations here. Sony has since moved out of Boca Raton, but the legacy of IBM, though the company's presence has been downsized, remains: a skilled labor pool and a technological infrastructure, which have helped attract communications and health-care companies, among others. The town also boasts well-kept parks, year-round professional theater, golf, fishing, and winter polo matches. A city ordinance requires all new commercial buildings to meet the strict standards of Boca's architectural board.

■ Mizner's Magic

In 1925 Addison Mizner's corporation began construction of a hotel that would draw hundreds of rich and famous visitors. The open arcades and pastel pink walls of the Mediterranean Revival-style Cloister Inn (now Boca Raton Resort and Club) rose from the coastal swampland in just six months. The flamboyant architect envisioned an entire city with landscaped gardens and promenades, world-class theaters and a huge cathedral. Work on his grandiose plan was well underway when the Florida real-estate bubble burst. Even so, by the end of 1925 Mizner had sold $11 million worth of lots.

The Cloister Inn remains a testament to Mizner's vision, as does **Camino Real**, a 160ft-wide avenue once divided by a canal on which gondolas ferried the Cloister's guests from the inn to the beach. Another surviving Mizner structure, the **Administration Building** *(2 E. Camino Real, at intersection of Dixie Hwy.)*, modeled after El Greco's home in Toledo, Spain, now houses a popular restaurant. After decades of uninspired building, the Mediterranean style has returned with **Mizner Park** *(400 N. Federal Hwy., between Palmetto Park Rd. and Glades Rd.)*, a pink stucco shopping/office/apartment complex (1991) distinguished by its airy arcades, fountains and courtyards.

SIGHTS

Old Floresta – *Bounded by W. Palmetto Park Rd., Periwinkle St., N.W. 9th Ave. and N.W. 7th Ave.* Drive down Aurelia, Azalea, Hibiscus or Oleander streets for a glimpse at one of Boca's oldest neighborhoods. Designed by Addison Mizner for his executives in 1925, Old Floresta still boasts 29 original houses characterized by red barrel-tile roofs and light-colored stucco walls. Large palm and banyan trees shade these quiet, pleasant streets.

Boca Raton Historical Society – *70 N. Federal Hwy. Open year-round Tue-Fri 10am-4pm. Closed Dec 25-Jan 2.* & 🅿 ☎ *561-395-4154. Self-guided city tour map available; reservations for Boca Raton Resort & Club tour can be made here.* Identifiable by its gilded dome, the elegant **Old Town Hall**★ was originally designed by Addison Mizner as Boca Raton's first municipal edifice. Mizner began construction in 1926, but after his financial collapse, the project was completed a year later by William E. Alsmeyer of Delray Beach. The finished building, fashioned with beams and paneling of pecky cypress (a porous wood resistant to termites) and pine floors, housed city officials and the fire and police departments until 1983. The first-floor library now contains archives, photographs and Mizner artifacts and a gift shop occupies the old fire bay. A time line of Boca's history is permanently on display.

★**International Museum of Cartoon Art** – 🄺🄸🄳🅂 *201 Plaza Real. Open year-round Tue-Sat 10am-6pm, Sun noon-6pm. Closed Thanksgiving Day, Dec 25. $6.* & ☎ *561-391-2200. www.cartoon.org. At press time, the museum's future was in jeopardy; it may have closed in the interim.* At the south end of the stylish Mizner Park shopping complex stands this two-story, 50,000sq ft, Mediterranean Revival-style showplace, opened in March 1996. Only a small portion of the museum's archival collection—containing more than 160,000 original works on paper, and more than 1,000 hours of animated films—can be exhibited at any one time, however.

Here you'll find an original 19C newspaper tear sheet of Richard F. Outcault's "The Yellow Kid," generally regarded as the first comic strip, as well as other comic strips, comic books, gag and editorial cartoons. Also here is the **Hearst Cartoon Hall of Fame**, begun in 1975. "Beetle Bailey" creator Mort Walker is regarded as the museum's founder.

★**Boca Raton Museum of Art** – *501 Plaza Real, in Mizner Park. Open year-round Tue-Sat 10am-5pm (Wed & Fri 9pm), Sun noon-5pm. Closed major holidays. $8.* ✗ ♿ ᴾ ☏ *561-392-2500. www.bocamuseum.org.* Formerly located in the Old Floresta section of Boca Raton, the museum recently moved to this newly constructed 44,000sq ft space (2001). A modern take on the Mediterranean Revival style, the pink pastel, two-story structure includes a children's education center, meeting facilities, an auditorium and a cafe; a sculpture garden graces the grounds. The museum anchors a 5.7-acre site slated for development as a cultural center, which, in addition to the already completed outdoor amphitheater, will feature a concert hall.

Expanding on a collection donated in 1989 by Dr. and Mrs. John J. Mayers, the museum's permanent collection *(2nd floor)* includes late-19C and early-20C works by such modern masters as Matisse, Degas, Picasso and Klee as well as pre-Columbian and African art and contemporary works. The first floor is reserved for temporary exhibits that are rotated seasonally.

FEC Railway Station – *747 S. Dixie Hwy. Not open to the public.* To enhance the town's appeal for guests arriving on the Florida East Coast Railway, Boca Raton Club owner Clarence Geist commissioned this graceful structure (1930) with its arched loggias, spiral columns and roof of interlocking sienna tiles. When passenger service was discontinued in 1963, the station rapidly fell victim to decay and vandalism. The local historical society rallied the community to save it, and—thanks to a donation from the Count and Countess deHoernle, whose name it bears—the station now enhances an otherwise bland commercial stretch. A 1930 steam locomotive and other railroad cars sit on special sidings outside the building.

★**Boca Raton Resort & Club** – *501 E. Camino Real.* ♿ ☏ *561-395-3000. www.bocaresort.com. Visit by guided tour (1hr 30min) only, year-round Tue 1:30pm; $5; reservations required through Boca Raton Historical Society ☏ 561-395-6766. Otherwise, open only to hotel guests (see Miami Address Book) and club members.* The world-class hotel that put Boca Raton on the map began life as the Cloister Inn, a 100-room Mediterranean Revival-style inn completed in 1926.

Architect Addison Mizner, fueled with his success in Palm Beach, pushed himself to a higher creative level than ever before, even forming his own corporation to finance the work. Though Mizner went bankrupt a year after the hotel opened, the Cloister Inn continued to attract well-heeled patrons as it still does today.

The original part of the hotel remains as the **east wing** *(right side of the palm-lined driveway leading to the hotel)*, decorated with pecky cypress beams and 15C Spanish furniture. On the wing's first floor, gilt columns and a soaring ceiling distinguish the Cathedral Dining Room. Note the scrupulous attention to ornamental detail throughout the grand lobby and other public areas.

Outside, espaliered bougainvillea climbs the wall beside Romanesque arches, while a loggia and cloister open onto a central courtyard whose fountains are accented with bright Spanish and Portuguese tiles. A 1929 addition—300 rooms in two wings—by the new owner, Indiana utilities millionaire Clarence Geist, created the hotel's present horseshoe shape. Arthur Vining Davis, founder of the Arvida Company, bought the hotel in 1969 and added the 300ft pink tower.

★**Red Reef Park** – *1400 N. Ocean Blvd. (A1A), 1 mi north of Palmetto Park Rd.* ▤ ☏ *561-393-7974.* A densely vegetated dune, a boardwalk and a pleasant beach for swimming, fishing and snorkeling over an artificial reef occupy the east side of this 67-acre park. The west side contains the **Gumbo Limbo Nature Center** 🄺🄸🄳🄢, a 20-acre swatch of tropical hammock preserved in its natural state. A small but inviting **visitor center** *(open year-round Mon-Sat 9am-4pm, Sun noon-4pm; closed major holidays;* & *; ☏ 561-338-1473; www.fau.edu/gumbo)* displays live snakes, tanks of living corals and crustaceans, and a shell collection. Large outdoor salt-water tanks allow visitors an up-close look at anemones, urchins, loggerhead turtles and other marine life. An informative boardwalk trail (.3mi) winds through a tropical hammock and mangrove wetland, past strangler fig trees, paradise trees, and the red-bark gumbo-limbo. A 40ft observation tower clears the forest canopy, providing ocean views.

Spanish River Park – *Map p 202. 3001 N. Ocean Blvd./A1A. Entrance on west side, just north of Gumbo Limbo Nature Center. Open year-round daily 8am-dusk. $8/vehicle, $10/vehicle weekends.* & ▤ ☏ *561-393-7815.* Taking its name from a shallow freshwater stream that coursed along its western edge before the creation of the Intracoastal Waterway, the park provides oceanfront as well as coastal woodlands recreation. A nature trail *(.25mi)* beside the lagoon provides a pleasant stroll through the forest.

Boca Raton Resort & Club

Katie Deits/© CAMERA GRAPHICS

EXCURSIONS *Map p 202*

★**Morikami Museum and Japanese Gardens** – *12mi northwest of Boca Raton. Take I-95 north to Linton Blvd. and go west 3.5mi; turn south on Jog Rd. and continue 1.5mi to park at 4000 Morikami Park Rd. Open year-round Tue-Sun 10am-5pm. $7.* ✗ & ▤ ☏ *561-495-0233. www.morikami.org.* Begun on a 200-acre parcel donated to Palm Beach County by prosperous pineapple farmer George Sukeji Morikami, this museum, opened in 1977, pays homage to Japanese culture. Morikami immigrated here from Japan in the early 1900s to join the Yamato

Colony, a Japanese agricultural community on the southern edge of Delray Beach. Begin at the white stucco **museum exhibition building**, whose oriental architectural overtones are accented inside by dark wood trim and shoji screens. In the Seishin-an Tea House adjacent to the lobby, visitors can watch an authentic Japanese **tea ceremony** *(third Sat of every month at noon, 1pm, 2pm & 3pm; $3/person)*. A lakeside walk away lies **Yamato-kan★**, inspired by a Japanese imperial villa. The rooms include a bath and bedroom, both serenely furnished like a traditional Japanese home. Other rooms hold interactive displays, as well as a permanent exhibit on the Yamato Colony. *In accordance with Japanese custom, visitors must remove their shoes before entering; paper slippers are provided.* Some 16 acres of gardens typifying traditional Japanese styles from the 9C to the 20C feature traditional koi ponds, waterfalls and a **bonsai garden**. The museum sponsors four **annual festivals:** the Japanese New Year *(Jan)*; Hatsume Fair *(Feb)*, celebrating the advent of spring; Children's Day *(Apr)*; and Bon Festival *(Aug)*, featuring Japanese folk music, dancing and a sunset lantern-floating ceremony.

Courtesy Morikami Museum

Tea Ceremony

★Arthur R. Marshall Loxahatchee National Wildlife Refuge – *8mi west of Boca Raton, on US-441. Take I-95 to Rte. 806/Atlantic Ave. west to US-441; go north on US-441 3mi to refuge entrance. Open year-round daily 6am-dusk. $5/vehicle* 🅿 ☎ *561-734-8303. http://loxahatchee.fws.gov.* Encompassing 147,000 acres of freshwater habitats unique to the Everglades, this refuge provides a home to more than 18,000 alligators and numerous species of birds and other wildlife, including the endangered snail kite and wood stork. The visitor center *(open mid-Oct-Apr daily 9am-4pm, weekends til 4:30pm; rest of the year Wed-Fri 9am-4pm, weekends til 4:30pm; closed Dec 25)* contains dioramas and exhibits on local ecology. Behind the center a boardwalk *(.4 mi)* snakes back into a bald cypress swamp. Reptiles flourish here, as do a variety of ferns and colorful bromeliads and trees, some streaked with the red baton rouge lichen. Another trail *(.8 mi)* marked with interpretive signs circles a freshwater impoundment past an observation tower. Canoeists can take a 5.5mi loop trail into the refuge, which is surrounded by a 57mi-long canal and levee that stores water for area residents.

FORT LAUDERDALE★

Population 152,397

Map p 209

Tourist Information: www.sunny.org ☎ 954-765-4466 or 800-227-8669

Fort Lauderdale lies a mere 23mi north of Miami and covers 30sq mi—the largest city of sprawling Broward County. Straddling 300mi of natural and artificial waterways, this "Venice of America" is a boater's paradise with 40,000-plus registered yachts, many of which are moored at the Radisson **Bahia Mar Yacht Basin** on the Atlantic Intracoastal Waterway. Second among Florida's busiest ports, **Port Everglades** handles some 23 million tons of cargo each year and ranks as the world's third largest cruise port (Miami is first) with close to three million people departing annually for Caribbean ports of call.

The area's first residents were Tequesta natives, followed by the Spanish in the 16C and, by the early 1800s, the Seminoles, who cohabited peacefully with area settlers until the Second Seminole War. Major William Lauderdale and his detachment built a army fort atop a series of Tequesta Indian mounds here in 1838; the city that grew up around it inherited the name of the fort's commanding officer. In 1896 Henry Flagler's Florida East Coast Railway entered Fort Lauderdale en route to Miami, catalyzing the development of a busy agricultural community. Florida governor **Napoleon Bonaparte Broward** (for whom the county is named) spearheaded a state-sponsored program of Everglades reclamation, or drainage, in 1906, beginning at the south fork of the New River.

Like Miami to the south, Fort Lauderdale today is also undergoing a dramatic makeover, with new luxury hotel development and the enlargement of major infrastructure. Completed in fall 2001, a significant expansion to the county convention center increased the facility to 230,000sq ft. Nearby, the 17th Street Causeway bridge has been transformed with new bike lanes, improved traffic flow and 55ft-high vantage points for pedestrians. To handle increasing passenger volume, the regional airport is undergoing a billion dollar expansion that will double the size of its terminals, lengthen runways and add parking space.

The Strip

DOWNTOWN

Fort Lauderdale's downtown has undergone a dramatic face-lift in the last dozen years, especially with the creation of the **Arts and Sciences District**. This district—bounded by E. Broward Boulevard on the north, the New River on the south, and S.E. Third and S.W. Seventh avenues on the east and west, respectively—encompasses the Museum of Art, the Museum of Discovery and Science and the Broward Center for the Performing Arts *(201 S.W. 5th Ave.; ☎ 462-0222)*. The latter, a contemporary complex on the river's north bank, brings world-class performances to the city. The Broward Center anchors the western terminus of **Riverwalk**, a tree-lined bricked esplanade that stretches along the north and south banks of the New River. Just east of downtown, trendy **Las Olas Boulevard** boasts a wide variety of shops, galleries and outdoor cafes *(between S.E. 6th and 11th Aves.)*.

■ The Strip

Lauderdale's famed **Strip★** of beach, which stretches for 2mi along Atlantic Boulevard *(on A1A, from Sunrise Blvd. to Bahia Mar Yacht Basin)* had become known in the 1950s not only for its beauty but as the destination for thousands of college students—from all over the US—who flocked there each year during Spring Break. Fort Lauderdale reigned for some 30 years as the mecca of Spring Break bacchanalia—celebrated in the film *Where the Boys Are* (1960). In the mid-1980s, city officials began actively discouraging the legions of collegiate visitors from adopting local beaches as a springtime playground. Fort Lauderdale Beach is now quiescent, with families and older visitors making up its predominant elements.

The Strip, which fell into a state of seediness in recent decades, has been enlivened by an ambitious beach redevelopment program that has attracted new businesses and added a $26 million beachfront promenade. Having shed its image as the capital of springtime frivolity, Fort Lauderdale, with its diversified economy—tourism generates $4.2 billion annually—and growing cultural offerings, now ranks among America's most attractive and liveable mid-size cities.

★**Stranahan House** – *335 S.E. 6th Ave., .2mi south of Las Olas Blvd. just above New River Tunnel. Open Oct-Jun Wed-Sat 10am-4pm, Sun 1pm-4pm. Jul-Aug Wed-Fri 10am-4pm. Closed major holidays. $5.* ☐ ☎ *954-524-4736. www.stranahanhouse.com.* Airy and elegant, the two-story frame house skirted by wide verandas is Broward County's oldest building, and its most popular historical site. It was built on the banks of the New River in 1901 by **Frank Stranahan**, the area's first permanent white settler, who came to the area in 1893 from Ohio to operate a ferry on the New River.

Practical Information .... Area Code: 954

Getting There – Fort Lauderdale/Hollywood International Airport (FLL): 4mi south of city *(information: ☎ 359-1200)*. Transportation to downtown: Airport Express **shuttle** *($11-18; ☎ 561-8888)*; **taxi** *($14)* and hotel courtesy shuttles. **Rental car agencies** *(p 353)* located at airport. Train service to Palm Beach and Miami by Tri-Rail *(☎ 800-874-7245)*. Amtrak **train** station: 200 S.W. 21st Terr. *(☎ 800-872-7245; www.amtrak.com)*. Greyhound **bus** station: 515 N.E. 3rd St. *(☎ 800-231-2222; www.greyhound.com)*.

Getting Around – Local **bus service**: Broward County Mass Transit (BCT) *($1; information: ☎ 357-8400)*. **Downtown shuttle** between Courthouse and BCT Terminal *(year-round Mon-Fri 7:30am-6pm, every 10min)* and the TMAX Express *(year-round Fri-Sat 6pm-1pm; ☎ 761-3543)*. **Water taxi** along Intracoastal Waterway and New River *(year-round daily 10am-1:30am; $7.50; ☎ 467-6677)*. Metered **parking** *(25¢/hr)* along Andrews Ave. near the hospital and Las Olas Blvd.

Visitor Information – **Greater Fort Lauderdale Convention and Visitors Bureau**, 1850 Eller Dr., Suite 303, Fort Lauderdale FL 33316 *(open year-round Mon-Fri 8:30am-5pm; ☎ 765-4466 or 800-227-8669; www.sunny.org)*. **Greater Fort Lauderdale Chamber of Commerce**, 512 N.E. 3rd Ave., Fort Lauderdale FL 33301 *(open year-round Mon-Fri 8:30am-5pm; ☎ 462-6000)*. *These organizations provide information on shopping, entertainment, festivals and recreation.*

Accommodations – **Area vacation planner** including lodging directory available *(free)* from **Greater Fort Lauderdale Convention and Visitors Bureau**. Accommodations range from luxury **hotels** and **spa resorts** *($175 and up)* to moderate **inns** and **motels** *($100-$175)* and superior small **lodgings** *($50-$100)*. Youth **hostel** *($20; ☎ 567-7275)*. Campgrounds and RV parks available. *Rates quoted are average prices per night for a double room and are subject to seasonal variations.*

Entertainment – Consult the arts and entertainment section of the *Sun Sentinel* (Fridays) and *Travelhost* magazine, or the 24hr hotline ☎ 357-5700, for schedules of cultural events. **Broward Center for the Performing Arts** *(☎ 462-0222)*; **Sunrise Musical Theater** *(☎ 741-7300)*. For tickets: **Ticketmaster** *(☎ 523-3309; www.ticketmaster.com)*.

Sports and Recreation – Boating, windsurfing, snorkeling, diving and sunbathing at area beaches. For information on recreation and area parks ☎ 563-PARK. **Cruise ships** depart from Port Everglades. **Fishing** piers: Fisherman's Wharf *(☎ 943-1488)*; Anglin's Fishing Pier *(☎ 491-9403)*. Carolina **Golf** Club *(☎ 753-4000)*, Jacaranda Golf Club *(☎ 472-5836)* and Diplomat Country Club *(☎ 457-2000)* welcome nonmembers. **Shopping:** downtown on Las Olas Blvd.; Galleria Mall, Sunrise Blvd.; Swap Shop, 3291 W. Sunrise Blvd. (shopping and entertainment) *(☎ 791-7927)*; Sawgrass Mills, 12801 W. Sunrise Blvd. (outlet mall) *(☎ 846-2350)*.

This graceful example of Florida pioneer architecture is located on the site of the trading post Stranahan originally set up to serve settlers and Seminoles. In 1906 Stranahan converted the 2,000sq ft structure into a home for himself and his new wife, Ivy Cromartie. After Frank's death, Ivy remained in the house until her death in 1971. In the early 1980s the home was restored to its 1915 appearance and furnished with period pieces, several of which belonged to the Stranahans. The interior boasts double-beaded wall paneling expertly crafted from Dade County pine.

★ **Museum of Art, Fort Lauderdale (MoA)** – *1 E. Las Olas Blvd. Open year-round Tue-Sat 10am-5pm, Sun noon-5pm. Closed major holidays. $10.* ✗ ♿ ▯ ☎ *954 525-5500. www.museumofart.org.* Edward Larrabee Barnes designed this three-story white structure (1986) on a prominent corner near the New River, a part of the city's downtown revitalization. Opened in 2001, a new two-story wing designed by Oscar Vago adds 10,000sq ft of exhibit space. The museum comprises over 5,000 pieces ranging from a sizable collection of paintings by American Impressionist **William Glackens** to works by Pop artist Andy Warhol. It is also known for its collection of **CoBrA art★★**—the largest assemblage in the US.
Born in Paris in 1948, the CoBrA movement consisted of Expressionists from **Co**penhagen, **Br**ussels and **A**msterdam who drew their inspiration from folk art and children's drawings. Pierre Alechinsky, Christian Dotremont, Karel Appel and Carl Henning Pedersen are among the movement's best-known artists. Pan-African, pre-Columbian, Native American and a growing collection of contemporary Cuban art round out the museum's holdings.

Old Fort Lauderdale Museum of History (**M¹**) – *231 S.W. 2nd Ave. Open year-round Tue-Sun noon-5pm. Closed Jan 1, Jul 4, Dec 25. $5.* & ☎ *954-463-4431. www.oldfortlauderdale.org.* Housed in the 1905 **New River Inn**, this facility chronicles the city's past from its founding to the present day. Changing exhibits focus on specific aspects of local history. The museum is operated by the Fort Lauderdale Historical Society, which also maintains a research library nearby *(219 S.W. 2nd Ave.).*

The building housing the research library forms part of the **Historic Village Complex** *(bounded by S.W. 2nd St., N.W. 1st Ave., Broward Blvd. and the New River)*, containing several vernacular early-20C structures. The 1904 **Bryan Homes** *(301 and 303 N.W. New River Dr.)* have been connected and converted into the River House restaurant and the New River Inn. All three properties were owned by the Bryan family, who were among the city's first settlers. Broward County's oldest hotel, the inn was constructed using hollow concrete blocks made with local sand by Fort Lauderdale's first builder, Edwin King. The Dade County pine **King-Cromartie House** *(229 S.W. 2nd Ave.)*, built in 1907 on New River Drive, was moved via river barge to its present site in 1971 *(2hr guided tours of the house Sat 1pm, 2pm & 3pm; contact the museum for details).*

** **Museum of Discovery and Science** – 〔Kids〕 *401 S.W. 2nd St., 1 block south of Broward Blvd. Open year-round Mon-Sat 10am-5pm, Sun noon-6pm. Closed Thanksgiving Day & Dec 25. $12.50 combo ticket (for museum and IMAX theater).* & ▣ *($3)* ☎ *954-467-6637. www.mods.org.* Opened in 1992, this slick $32 million facility attracts people of all ages. The three-story museum acquaints visitors with a variety of scientific fields ranging from ecology to physics—beginning with the fantastic **gravity clock** in the atrium. Florida EcoScapes dominates the first floor: live trees and native plants form the setting for examples of local flora and fauna, including a colorful coral reef, an underground cave and a walk-in beehive. A children's discovery center features interactive exhibits and a play area.

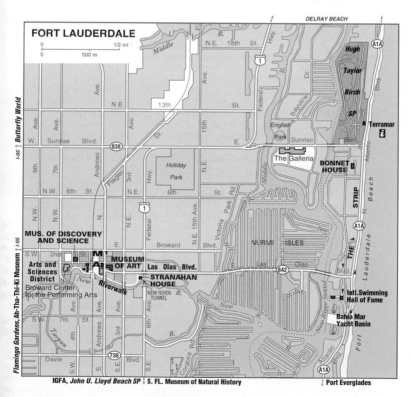

On the second floor the exhibit Gizmo City gives visitors an opportunity to play virtual volleyball and surf the Internet. Other highlights include the **Manned Maneuvering Unit** ride and **Space Base**, a flight simulator that re-creates a trip to the moon. Newly opened ExploraZone features some 30 exhibits that focus on the marvels of science. Downstairs, an IMAX theater shows a variety of 2D and 3D films such as *Dolphins* and *Cyberworld* on a five-story-high screen *(year-round; call for show times* ☎ *954-463-IMAX).*

ADDITIONAL SIGHTS

International Swimming Hall of Fame – *1 Hall of Fame Dr., off A1A. Open year-round Mon-Fri 9am-7pm, weekends 9am-5pm. Closed Thanksgiving Day & Dec 25. $3.* ♿ ☎ *954-462-6536.* This museum and aquatic complex, built in 1965 and updated with a $13 million renovation in 1990, centers on two 10-lane, 50m Olympic pools, the site of international, national and regional swimming, diving and water-polo competitions. Above the gift shop, a 10,000sq ft **exhibition hall** is dedicated to the sports of swimming, diving, water polo and synchronized swimming. Descriptive panels, photographs and memorabilia illustrate the history of each sport and its inclusion in the Olympics. Visitors can access biographies of famous international aquatic athletes on a touch screen.

Hugh Taylor Birch State Park – *3109 E. Sunrise Blvd. and A1A. Park hrs & fees p 362.* △ ♿ 🅿 ☎ *954-564-4521.* The original property on which the park lies was purchased for $1 per acre by Chicago attorney Hugh Taylor Birch, who came south in 1893 in search of respite from city life. Donated for use as a state park in 1942, the 180-acre site rests on a barrier island between the Atlantic Ocean and the Intracoastal Waterway. Ringed today by urban development, the park extends along 1.5mi of beachfront and includes a lagoon system, mangrove swamps and hardwood hammocks. Birch's former home, Terramar (c.1940), now houses the **Terramar Visitor Center** *(open year-round weekends & holidays 10am-5pm).*

★**Bonnet House** – *900 N. Birch Rd. Visit by guided tour (1hr 15min) only, early Oct-mid-Aug Wed-Fri 10am-1:30pm, weekends noon-2:30pm. $9.* 🅿 ☎ *954-563-5393. www.bonnethouse.com.* Nestled on a 35-acre wooded oasis, this two-story coral rock and Dade County pine house reflects the talent of its architect, Chicago muralist **Frederic Clay Bartlett** (1873-1953). Avid art collectors, Bartlett and his first wife, Helen, purchased an impressive group of paintings on their travels. After Helen's death in 1925, Frederic donated 24 works by post-Impressionist masters, including Georges Seurat's *A Sunday On La Grande Jatte,* to the Art Institute of Chicago in his wife's memory *(see Michelin THE GREEN GUIDE Chicago).*

Six years later, Bartlett married Evelyn Fortune Lilly. An artist, Evelyn encouraged her husband to add touches of whimsy, such as an aviary, the marine mural on the ceiling of the south loggia, and the fanciful shell inlay in the north loggia, to their winter residence. After Frederic's death, Evelyn continued to winter here. Having no heirs, she deeded the property to the Florida Trust for Historic Preservation in 1983.

A lagoon rimmed with stately Royal palms fronts Bartlett's 1920 interpretation of a plantation house with its wrought-iron balustrades from New Orleans—a design that he intended as a reaction against the craze for Mediterranean Revival architecture that Addison Mizner was perpetuating in Palm Beach. Named for the yellow Bonnet lilies that still bloom at the south end of the lagoon, the 30-room structure contains the family's eclectic collection of furnishings and objets d'art. The **music room** showcases an 1871 square Steinway piano and a delicately carved marble bust of *The Veiled Lady* by Italian sculptor Giuseppe Croff. Evelyn's realistic portraits and still-life paintings hang in the former guest wing.

The first building on the estate, Bartlett's **studio**, with its high beamed ceiling and two-story north window, displays his works as well as those he collected. Also on the grounds are the tiny, round shell museum and adjoining orchid house.

EXCURSIONS *Map p 202*

John U. Lloyd Beach State Park – *4mi south in Dania Beach. 1mi north of intersection of Dania Beach Blvd. and A1A at 6503 N. Ocean Dr. Park hrs & fees p. 262.* 🍴 ♿ 🅿 ☎ *954-923-2833.* Named after the man who was Broward County's district attorney for more than 30 years, this 251-acre park at the northern end of a narrow, elongated barrier island affords great views, uncrowded beaches and quiet forests. The 11,500ft-long **beach** is dotted with shaded picnic sites and sea turtle nesting areas, and extends northward to a paved fishing jetty. Whiskey Creek, a mangrove-lined tidal waterway, divides the park along its length and harbors manatees and abundant bird life. A hardwood forest and man-made wetland fill the park's interior. A self-guided walk traverses the hammock.

South Florida Museum of Natural History – 🄺🄸🄳🅂 *6mi south in Dania Beach. From Las Olas Blvd., take US-1 south to museum entrance on S.E. 4th Terrace (.5mi south of Stirling Rd.). Open year-round Tue-Fri 10am-4pm, Sat 10am-6pm, Sun noon-6pm. Closed Jan 1, Thanksgiving Day, Dec 25. $9.95.* ♿ 🅿 ☎ *954-925-7770. www.gravesmuseum.org.* Exhibits in this two-story building chronicle range of archaeological periods including ancient Egypt and Florida's early history and geology.

The first gallery contains an 8ft 7in-long **quartz crystal** weighing 6,600 pounds, as well as Florida fossil shells. Guarded by a giant statue of Neptune, the **Maritime Gallery** simulates an underwater environment, showcasing artifacts recovered from shipwrecks

Exhibits on South America highlight Peruvian and Columbian pottery, sculpture and jewelry; note the extensive collection of **miniature vessels** dating from AD 1100-1450. Other galleries feature a Turkish Mugla house and a replica of King Tut's tomb. A new Asian exhibit showcases Far East culture and history; and the most recent acquisition, a raptor skeleton, is being billed as "a missing link in dinosaur-bird evolution."

★**IGFA World Fishing Hall of Fame & Museum** – 12mi *south in Dania Beach. From Las Olas Blvd., take I-95 south to Griffin Rd., then west to Anglers Ave. Turn left and continue to center's entrance at 300 Gulf Stream Way in Sportsman's Park. Open year-round daily 10am-6pm. Closed Thanksgiving Day & Dec 25. $4.99. ☒ & ☐ ☎ 954-922-4212, 800-422-4665. www.igfa.org.* The large metallic fish anchoring this three-story, 60,000sq ft facility clearly identifies the headquarters of IGFA. More than 60 years ago, the **International Game Fish Assn**. was formed to keep records and establish rules of ethics for the sport of game fishing. Expanded roles now include conservation and education. Six museum galleries, a children's discovery room, library, museum store, cafe and offices, as well as the hall of fame, and an outdoor marina and 3.5-acre wetlands make up the complex. Visitors may first view an introductory film *(18min)* in the orientation theater. In the Fishing Hall of Fame, life-size mounts of record catches dangle from the ceiling, flags indicate member nations and displays tout the feats of recreational fishing. Museum highlights include the Legacy Gallery, which celebrates famed anglers like Ernest Hemingway, IGFA's first vice president; and the **Catch Gallery**, where visitors may reel in a marlin or bass via virtual reality.

Adjacent to IGFA on the grounds of the park is Bass Pro Shops Outdoor World.

★**Butterfly World** – 10mi *north in Coconut Creek. Take I-95 north to Sample Rd.; continue west 4mi to 3600 W. Sample Rd.; enter at Tradewinds Park, on left. Open year-round Mon-Sat 9am-5pm, Sun 1pm-5pm. Closed Thanksgiving Day & Dec 25. $12.95 ☒ & ☐ ☎ 954-977-4400. www.butterflyworld.com.* Tucked away in a county recreational park, Butterfly World offers a pleasant walk through a screened-in aviary landscaped with waterfalls and bright blooms to resemble a tropical rain forest. Inside, some 2,000 rainbow-colored butterflies flit around, vying with the flowers in beauty. Outside the aviary, a rose garden and vine-covered arbor surround a small pond, attracting local species of the order Lepidoptera. A small pavilion here contains mounted specimens of exotic insects and butterflies from around the world.

© Barry Barker/Odyssey/Chicago

Young Visitors Enjoy Butterfly World

Flamingo Gardens – 16.5mi *west in Davie. Take I-595 west to Flamingo Rd.; continue 3mi south to entrance on left at 3750 Flamingo Rd. Open Oct-May daily 9:30am-5:30pm. Rest of the year Tue-Sun 9:30am-5:30pm. $12. ☒ & ☐ ☎ 954-473-2955.* Lush tropical plantings grace the grounds of the former citrus plantation owned by Floyd and Jane Wray. After Floyd's death in 1959, Jane set up a foundation to develop botanical gardens here in memory of her late husband. Today paved paths traverse a mosaic of tropical plants and a narrated tram tour *(25min; $3)* takes visitors through a wetlands area and part of the original citrus grove. The Wrays' original home, furnished with period pieces, operates as a museum *(open year-round daily 11am-5pm)*. Displays of alligators, crocodiles and birds of prey, a walk-through aviary and daily wildlife encounters *(12:30pm, 1:30pm & 2:30pm)* add to the fun.

Ah-Tha-Thi-Ki Museum – *65mi west of Fort Lauderdale via I-75. Take I-75 west to Rte. 833 (Exit 14); turn north 17mi to Big Cypress Seminole Indian Reservation. Open year-round Tue-Sun 9am-5pm. $6.* ♿ 📷 ☎ *954-792-0745 or 863-902-1113. www.seminoletribe.com/museum.* The name of this $12 million museum, opened in 1997 by the Seminole Indians, means "a place to learn, a place to remember." Upon arrival, visitors view a 17min orientation movie on the Seminoles' 300-year history in Florida. The 5,000sq ft exhibit hall presents a series of dioramas and displays illustrating tribal customs and beliefs, including such artifacts as traditional jewelry, clothing, weapons and musical instruments—some on loan from the Smithsonian Institution. Students of culture can learn more about the Seminoles through interactive computer technology; there's also a reference library and a folklore theater.

Outside the museum building, signs along a 1.5mi boardwalk identify native medicinal and other plants. About halfway along its route stands a "living village" of chickee homes where members of the Seminole tribe can be seen cooking and creating such traditional crafts as wood carvings, handmade dolls and basketry. Ritual ceremonies and dancing may be performed on special occasions *(call ahead for information)*.

MIAMI★★★

Population 362,470

Map p 214

Tourist Information: www.tropicoolmiami.com ☎ 305-539-3000 or 800-933-8448

Renowned for its tantalizing tropical landscape of blue sky, aqua waters and fabulous white beaches, Miami is one of the most popular resort destinations in the US. Each year some ten million visitors from around the world pour into Greater Miami. In this winter playground they enjoy golf, tennis, yachting, deep-sea fishing, scuba diving, a lively nightlife and sunshine. Because of its key position on the Florida Straits near the southeast tip of the state, Miami boasts the world's largest cruise port, accommodating nearly 3.5 million passengers annually to and from the Caribbean and South America.

Geographical Notes

Physical Features – Greater Miami embraces all of Miami-Dade County along with numerous islands, including Miami Beach, a long, narrow barrier island located 2.5mi off the mainland between Biscayne Bay and the Atlantic Ocean. Primarily flat, the topography averages only 10ft above sea level, with a narrow limestone ridge (5mi across at its widest point) running north-south along the coast. Mangrove swamps and hardwood hammocks that once bordered the ridge are now gone, but the region retains lush vegetation such as bougainvillea, banyan trees, poincianas and palms. Until the early 20C, the Everglades were an unbroken wilderness in this region, stretching almost to Biscayne Bay. The Glades met the limestone ridge near the modern inter-section of N.W. 32nd Avenue and 18th Terrace, creating a waterfall that in turn formed the headwaters of the 4mi-long Miami River. In 1909 the falls were cut off from the main body of the river when the man-made Miami River Canal was dredged in order to drain water from the Everglades.

To the east of downtown lies 39mi-long Biscayne Bay. Seven causeways link the main-land to Miami Beach, while an eighth, Rickenbacker Causeway, brings auto traffic to Virginia Key and Key Biscayne, situated to the south.

Composition – Sprawling along the coast, the 2,400sq mi Miami metropolitan area—stretching from Aventura, at the north border of Miami-Dade County, south to Homestead—is actually a collection of 30 municipalities that lend the city a complex persona at once urbane and small-town. The actual City of Miami consists of the 1.5sq mi downtown district at the mouth of the river as well as several other communities that are annexed to the city but retain strong characters of their own. Among these are Coconut Grove and Coral Gables. Most of the county comprises densely populated business and residential sections, but southern Miami-Dade County remains largely agricultural.

In 2000 the population of Miami-Dade County reached more than 2.25 million people, with nearly one-fifth of them living in the City of Miami—making it Florida's largest in terms of population. About half of the residents are Latino, with Caucasians and African Americans making up the bulk of the other half of the population. As a result, distinct ethnic communities exist, most notably Little Havana, just west of downtown; Little Haiti, west of Biscayne Boulevard below 79th Street; and the African-American neigh-borhoods of Overtown, Liberty City and Brownsville. Even as this ethnic diversity has led to tense confrontations, the mix is precisely what makes Miami so interesting.

Historical Notes

Early Explorers – Pedro Menéndez de Avilés came ashore here in 1566. In 1567 additional Spanish colonists, led by a Jesuit priest, arrived to found a Catholic mission, which was short-lived. During the next century and a half, the native Tequesta pop-ulation was reduced by disease and by wars with the Creek Indians. When Florida became a British Colony in 1763 at the end of the French and Indian War, the remaining Tequestas accompanied the retreating Spanish to Cuba.

By the mid-1830s a handful of pioneers had settled in the area, then dominated by a 2,500-acre sugarcane plantation. Early settlements were obliterated by Indians in the early stages of the Second Seminole War, however. The US Government estab-lished **Fort Dallas** on the north side of the Miami River in 1838. When the Second Seminole War ended in 1842, William English, nephew of the plantation's owner, platted a town on the south side of the river. His name for the new town, Miami, is thought to derive from an Indian word meaning "sweet water."

The Mother of Miami – By the late 19C, **William and Mary Brickell** and **Julia Tuttle** were the two major landholders in the area. Brickell, a native of Steubenville, Ohio, bought part of the William English tract on the south side of the Miami River in 1870 and opened a store. By 1880 the Brickell family owned all of the prime bayfront land south to Coconut Grove.

Meanwhile, Julia Tuttle's campaign to put the fledgling town on the map earned the widow from Cleveland the title "Mother of Miami." She sought the help of **Henry Flagler** and his Florida East Coast Railway (FEC). In exchange for riparian rights and half of

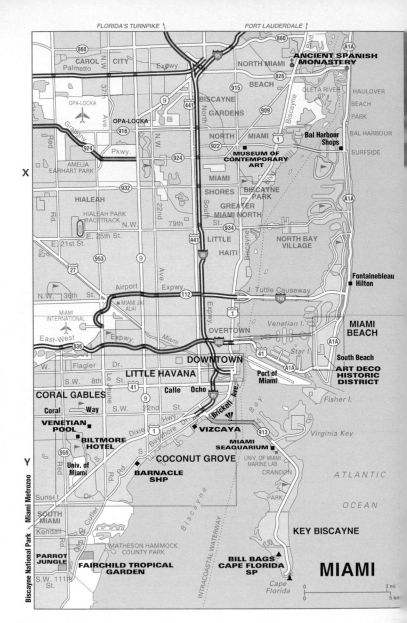

Tuttle's land, the entrepreneur laid out streets, supplied the town with water and elec tricity, financed a channel across the bay and donated land for community buildings. In April 1896, the first train chugged into the village of 300 citizens, which was inco porated three months later. The following year the grand **Royal Palm Hotel** opened on the old Fort Dallas site, complete with swimming pool, elevators and a park wit coconut palms. Unfortunately, Flagler's hotel fell victim to the 1926 hurricane an was demolished several years later.

Boom, Bust and Recovery – While growth corresponded directly to the developmen of the FEC and the federal highway system, a number of developers lured buyers wit the promise of something new and different: Carl Fisher's Miami Beach; Georg Merrick's planned Mediterranean paradise, Coral Gables, complete with man-mad canals and costumed gondoliers imported from Italy; and the North Miami-Dade deve opments of Hialeah and Miami Springs, created by James Bright and Glen Curti beginning in the early 1920s.

Whole towns were created from the ground up. Curtiss' 1926 design for **Opa-Loc** (*north of the airport*) featured buildings (*some still standing*) inspired by *The On Thousand and One Tales from the Arabian Nights*. The mid-1920s marked the begin ning of the end, however. Anti-Florida propaganda and tax investigations had alread put a damper on investment by 1925, when a Miami cargo embargo—forced by backlog of unloaded steamship and railroad freight—severely affected the state economy. A deadly hurricane in 1926 dealt the final blow.

214

While Florida's troubles may have preceded the 1929 crash, the state's economy was also among the first in the country to revive. Ironically, Prohibition helped. Eager for tourists, officials generally turned a blind eye to illegal gambling and to rumrunners who smuggled liquor in from the Bahamas. In 1931 the state legalized pari-mutuel betting. Tourists from the North poured in. Joining them were thousands of Latin American travelers arriving by sea plane.

In wartime, chic Miami Beach hotels were transformed into military barracks; the area's beaches became drill fields. In 1942 the US Navy moved its Gulf Sea Frontier headquarters to Miami. More than 50,000 Navy recruits were trained at the Sub-Chaser School opened at the Port of Miami. During the war, Miami International Airport was established at the original Pan Am base at N.W. 36th Street, where World War I flying ace **Eddie Rickenbacker** had helped start Eastern Airlines several years earlier. At the end of the war servicemen flowed into the city to take advantage of inexpensive housing and educational opportunities offered by the University of Miami under the G.I. Bill.

Growing Pains – Miami was a logical destination for exiles fleeing Fidel Castro's new government in the aftermath of Communist revolution in Cuba in 1959. Beginning in 1965, a series of airlifts bringing families from Cuba to Miami increased the Cuban refugee population to 400,000. For the most part, Miamians embraced the exiles. Tensions mounted, however, when more jobs started going to Cubans than to locals. The socioeconomic climate further deteriorated when the 1980 Mariel boatlift from Cuba dumped some 125,000 refugees, including criminals released from Cuban prisons, onto Miami streets.

That same year, a violent riot broke out in Liberty City when four white policemen were acquitted by an all-white jury in the beating death of a black insurance salesman. The three-day clash left 19 dead and caused more than $50 million in damages. Much of the Anglo population began to flee.

By the mid-1980s, the national recession had hit Miami hard. Banks foreclosed on unfinished condos, shopping malls stood half-rented and the new billion-dollar Metrorail ran virtually empty. For a time it appeared the only people profiting in the faded resort were the "Cocaine Cowboys"—from illegal drug smuggling.

Modern Multicultural Metropolis – The popular television show, *Miami Vice* (1984-1989), helped Miami's comeback, giving the city's pink stucco and palm trees, and even its seamy side, an allure. A more tangible economic boost came from a new free trade center (now **World Trade Center** Miami) established in the early 1980s. The 40,000-seat-capacity convention center in Miami Beach has hosted political conventions and attracts international trade shows. The city is known as the site of the annual **Orange Bowl Parade** *(held on New Year's Eve)* and is home to four major professional sports teams.

Downtown, innovative office towers compose the dramatic city skyline, while the Miami-Dade Cultural Center has done much to polish Miami's cultural image. Future plans call for the creation of a museum park to hold a new science center, a world-class park and an art museum. Construction of a new performing arts center in the vicinity is also anticipated.

The **Port of Miami**, the world's busiest cruise harbor, serves as a shipping hub for agricultural produce as well. Despite the income generated by the port and by international trade, however, Miami counts tourism as its top industry.

Fall 1994 marked a new influx of refugees preceding the return of Haiti's President Jean-Bertrand Aristide to power at the end of the year. Around the same time, Fidel Castro sanctioned the emigration of Cuban citizens, presumably to force negotiations on the US trade embargo. In just a few weeks, thousands of refugees fled Havana on makeshift rafts. In the meantime, thousands more were detained at the US naval base in Guantanamo (on the eastern tip of Cuba), as well as in Panama. The refusal by US officials to let the refugees—many of them children—travel on to America provoked heated demonstrations and highly vocal rebukes from Miami's Cuban exile community. In 1994 President Clinton ended America's open-door policy and set a quota on the number of Cubans immigrating to the US. No doubt, Miami will continue to struggle with its multifaceted image as it continues to reinvent itself.

DOWNTOWN *Map p 224*

A vibrant 1.5sq mi quarter surrounded on three sides by the warm waters of Biscayne Bay and the Miami River, Miami's downtown exudes the bustling atmosphere of a Latin city. Here retailers purveying their wares—electronic goods, jewelry, clothing and fragrances—in Spanish and Portuguese draw visitors from Cuba, Puerto Rico and Latin America. The site of the city's first wooden commercial structures now features a dense array of government and office buildings in a host of architectural styles including Neoclassical, Art Deco, Mediterranean Revival and the stark contemporary design of the skyscrapers that illuminate Miami's night skyline. The commercial area built by Henry Flagler was incorporated as the City of Miami in July 1896. On Christmas night of that year, a fire devoured most of the small downtown. Vulnerable frontier buildings were quickly replaced with new masonry

PRACTICAL INFORMATION...............................Area Code: 305

Getting There

By Air – **Miami International Airport (MIA)**: 7mi northwest of downtown; international and domestic flights (☎ 876-7000). Multilingual Information Service, Concourse B, D and G (open daily 11am-10pm), Concourse E (open daily year-round). Transportation to downtown: **SuperShuttle** ($12; ☎ 871-2000), **taxi** ($18-$21), **Metrobus** and hotel courtesy **shuttles. Rental car agencies** (p 343) located near airport.

By Train and Bus – Amtrak **train** station: 8303 N.W. 37th Ave. (information: ☎ 835-1221; reservations ☎ 800-872-7245; www.amtrak.com). Greyhound **bus:** Miami International Airport; 4111 N.W. 27th St. and 700 Biscayne Blvd.; Miami Beach: 7101 Harding Ave. (reservations: ☎ 800-231-2222; www.greyhound.com).

Getting Around

By Public Transportation – Miami-Dade Transit Agency operates a public transit system connecting Greater Miami and beaches via Metrorail, Metromover and buses. **Metrorail** trains serve downtown Miami extending northwest to Hialeah and south to Kendall (daily 6am-midnight; every 20min, every 5min during peak hours; $1.25 each way, exact change only; free transfers to Metromover). **Metromover** elevated rail system links the Brickell Ave. and Omni areas, and loops around downtown (daily 6am-midnight; every 2min; 25¢). Metrorail connections at Government Center and Brickell stations, with limited nearby public parking ($2/day, free on weekends). **Metrobus** operates countywide (Mon-Fri 4:30am-2am, weekend hours vary; $1.25 each way, exact change only; bus-to-rail transfers 25¢). Schedules and route information ☎ 770-3131. Disabled visitors ☎ 263-5400.

Tri-Rail provides **commuter rail** service between West Palm Beach and Greater Miami connecting to Metrorail (Mon-Fri 4:30am-8pm, Sat 6:45am-10pm, Sun 6:45am-8pm; $3.50-$9.25 round-trip depending on zones traveled). For schedules and route information: ☎ 800-TRI-RAIL, www.tri-rail.com.

By Car – Miami is laid out on a grid: the intersection of Flagler St. and Miami Ave. divides the city into four quadrants: southwest, northwest, southeast and northeast. Avenues and courts run north-south; streets and terraces run east-

west. **Speed limit** within city: 25mph unless otherwise posted. Signs with the orange "Follow the Sun" symbol (right) direct visitors to major tourist destinations (maps available at airport and from car rental agencies). Downtown metered **parking:** $1.25/hr. Parking lot: $2 for first hour, $1.25 each additional half hour. For information, contact the Miami Parking Authority (Mon-Fri 7:30am-5:30pm ☎ 373-6789; www.miamiparking.com).

By Taxi – Metro Taxi (☎ 888-8888), Flamingo Taxi (☎ 885-7000); Yellow Cab (☎ 444-4444).

General Information

Visitor Information – **Greater Miami Convention and Visitors Bureau**, 701 Brickell Ave., Suite 2700, Miami FL 33131 (open year-round Mon-Fri 8:30am-5pm ☎ 539-3000 or 800-283-2707;www.tropicoolmiami.com). **Miami Beach Visitor Information Center**, 1920 Meridian Ave., Miami Beach FL 33139 (open year-round Mon-Fri 9am-6pm, weekends 10am-4pm; ☎ 672-1270; www.ci.miami-beach.fl.us). These organizations provide information on shopping, entertainment, festivals and recreation.

Accommodations – Area visitors guide including **lodging directory** available (free) from the **Greater Miami Convention and Visitors Bureau**. **Reservation service:** Greater Miami Hotel Assn. (☎ 531-3553 or 800-531-3553). **Central Reservation Service** (☎ 274-6832 or 800-950-0232) operates 24hr courtesy phones at airport. Accommodations range from downtown **hotels** ($150-$250), luxury beachfront hotels ($200 and up) to economy **motels** ($50-$100). Miami Beach International Youth **Hostel** ($42-$72; ☎ 534-2988). Rates quoted are average prices per night for a double room and are subject to seasonal variations.

PRACTICAL INFORMATION ....Area Code: 305

Local Press – Daily news: *Miami Herald*; entertainment section *Weekend* (Friday). Spanish editions: *El Nuevo Herald* and *Diario Las Americas*. Periodicals: *Miami New Times*, *Travelhost* and *Miami Today* (weekly).

Sightseeing – For sightseeing tours, consult the *Greater Miami & the Beaches Vacation Planner* available from the Greater Miami Convention and Visitors Bureau. Daily **cruises** around Greater Miami and Fort Lauderdale operate from Bayside Marina and the docks at 24th St. and Collins Ave. Miami Beach Art Deco Historic District **walking and bike tours** (☎ 672-2014; www.mdpl.org). Dr. Paul George's Historic Tours—including Little Havana—are sponsored by the Historical Museum of Southern Florida *(Oct-Jun; boat tours, dinner in Coral Gables, gallery tours and walking tours;* ☎ *375-1625; www.historical-museum.org)*.

Shopping – **Downtown:** Omni International Mall and shopping district, Bayside Marketplace. **Coconut Grove:** CocoWalk, Streets of Mayfair. **Miami Beach:** Lincoln Road Mall. **North Miami Beach:** Bal Harbour Shops. Aventura: Aventura Mall. **South Miami-Dade:** Dadeland Mall, Dolphin Mall, The Shops at Sunset Place.

Entertainment – Consult the arts and entertainment section of local newspapers for schedules of cultural events and addresses of theaters and concert halls. To purchase tickets, contact the box office or **Ticketmaster** *(☎ 358-5885; www.ticketmaster.com.)*

Venue	Performances	Tickets ☎
American Airlines Arena	Touring shows and sporting events	358-5885
Miami-Dade County Auditorium	Florida Grand Opera, Concert Association of Florida, visiting ensembles	358-5885
Colony Theater	Ballet Flamenco La Rosa, Off-Broadway, theater, dance, comedy, concerts, film festivals	674-1026
Jackie Gleason Theater	Miami City Ballet, touring shows and concerts	358-5885
Gusman Center for the Performing Arts	Florida Philharmonic Orchestra, Miami International Film Festival, concerts and plays by touring companies	372-0925
Coconut Grove Playhouse	Plays	442-4000

Sports and Recreation – **Tennis** courts are plentiful; some area hotels offer tennis instruction and clinics. For further information contact Miami-Dade Parks and Recreation Department *(☎ 755-7800)*. Public **golf** courses: Miami Springs Golf Course *(☎ 805-5182)*; Normandy Shores Golf Course *(☎ 868-6502)*; Key Biscayne Golf Course *(☎ 361-9129)*.

Spectator Sports: Thoroughbred racing at Calder Race Course, 21001 N.W. 27th Ave. *(year-round Thu-Mon 12:30pm;* ☎ *625-1311; www.calderracecourse.com)*; Hialeah Park, 2200 E. 4th Ave. *(simulcast races year-round; live racing mid-Mar-late May;* ☎ *885-8000; www.hialeahpark.com)*; Gulfstream Park, 901 S. Federal Hwy., Hallandale *(Jan-mid-Mar Wed-Mon;* ☎ *931-7223; www.gulf-treampark.com)*.

Greyhound racing at Flagler Greyhound Track, 401 N.W. 38th Court *(year-round daily;* ☎ *649-3000)*. **Miami Jai Alai** , 3500 N.W. 37th Ave at N.W. 36th St. *(Wed, Fri-Sat 7pm; www.decoweb.com/jai-alai* ☎ *633-6400; www.miamijai-alai.com)*. **Miami Dolphins** (NFL) *(☎ 620-2578)*; **University of Miami Hurricanes** sporting events ☎ *284-2263)*; **Miami Heat** (NBA) *(☎ 577-4328)*; **Florida Marlins** (MLB) *(☎ 626-7400)*. Purchase tickets for major sporting events at the box office or through Ticketmaster *(above)*.

Useful Numbers ☎

Police/Ambulance/Fire	**911**
Police (non-emergency)	579-6111
Beach Patrol, City of Miami Beach	673-7711
Dental Referral (24hrs)	667-3647
24-hour Pharmacy: Walgreens, 12295 N. Biscayne Blvd.	893-6860
Main Post Office, 2200 N.W. 72nd Ave.	639-4280
South Beach Post Office, 1300 Washington Ave.	800-275-8777
Weather (recorded)	229-4522
Hurricane Information	229-4470

ADDRESS BOOK

For a legend of price listings for hotels and restaurants, see p 76.

Staying in the Miami Area and South Florida

The Breakers – *1 S. County Rd., Palm Beach.* ⅄ ⅙ ▯ ⅃ ☏ *561-655-6611 or 888-273-2537. www.thebreakers.com. 572 rooms.* $$$$$ A Palm Beach icon, this 1926 mega-resort takes its cue from Italy's Renaissance palazzos. Twin belvedere towers recall Rome's Villa Medici and the nymph fountain at the entrance resembles the one at Florence's Boboli Gardens. The regal lobby's hand-painted, vaulted ceiling recalls the Palazzo Carega in Genoa. Luxurious guest rooms are done in light woods, seaside colors and tobacco-leaf prints. The beach is private, of course. The four-acre site holds two golf courses, 21 tennis courts, 11 restaurants, an outdoor spa and shopping arcade.

Delano – *1685 Collins Ave., Miami Beach.* ⅄ ⅙ ▯ ⅃ ☏ *305-672-2000 or 800-555-5001. wwwianschragerhotels.com. 238 rooms.* $$$$$ South Beach's minimalist trend started with Philippe Starck's redo of New York hotelier Ian Schrager's 1947 beachside oasis named for Franklin Delano Roosevelt. Billowing white curtains—no doors—give access to the lobby, where large, overstuffed Alice-in-Wonderland chairs are installed. More curtains separate lounge areas sparsely clad with antiques, bric-a-brac, and artworks by Dalí and Man Ray. Plush, white-on-white guest quarters boast top amenities and fresh flowers. Delano's "simple-chic" decor and rooftop spa have recently lured such famous guests as Demi Moore. A favored celebrity haunt, Delano's **Blue Door** restaurant, once co-owned by pop star Madonna, serves memorable dishes like sea bass in a brown butter sauce with hearts of palm.

Biltmore Hotel – *1200 Anastasia Ave., Coral Gables.* ⅄ ⅙ ▯ ⅃ ☏ *305-445-1926 or 800-727-1926. www.biltmorehotel.com. 280 rooms.* $$$$ This massive National Historic Landmark in Coral Gables looks like a misplaced Spanish palace. Its wedding-cake shape is topped by a 300ft tower modeled after the Cathedral of Seville's Giralda tower. Vaulted hand-painted ceilings, palm-filled courtyards and balustraded balconies are just some of the features that have attracted presidents, royalty and movie stars here since 1926. Then there's the 1.25-million-gallon pool and personalized service. Well-appointed guest rooms include feather beds, easy chairs and private safes. Famed for its lavish Sunday champagne brunch—served outdoors in a tropical setting—the hotel boasts an immaculate 18-hole golf course as well.

Boca Raton Resort & Club – *501 E. Camino Real.* ⅄ ⅙ ▯ ⅃ ☏ *561-35-3000 or 888-491-2622. www.bocaresort.com. 960 rooms.* $$$$ Grand dame of Boca Raton, this exclusive property was designed by Addison Mizner in 1926 as the Cloister Inn. Successive additions retained the graceful blend of Spanish, Italian and Moorish styles, helping to create a well-landscaped, self-contained paradise, to which entry is rigidly guarded. The height of luxury, lodgings can be reserved in the Cloisters (the original building), the modern 27-story tower, the oceanfront beach club or at spacious one- or two-bedroom golf villas. Ten dining spots, two lounges, three golf courses, a private beach, and a wide spectrum of recreational activities and sybaritic pamperings round out the offerings.

The Chesterfield – *363 Cocoanut Row, Palm Beach.* ⅄ ⅙ ▯ ⅃ ☏ *561-659-5800. www.redcarnationhotels.com. 53 rooms.* $$$$ Located around the corner from Worth Avenue, this posh, white stucco property, accented with red-and-white striped awnings, embodies Lord Chesterfield's dictum, "Anything worth doing is worth doing well"—the quote the hotel places on its brochures. The intimate hostelry has sheltered such illustrious personages as Oscar de la Renta, Catherine Deneuve and Margaret Thatcher; it continues to cater to an upscale clientele with amenities like fresh fruit in the lobby, terry robes and sachets in rooms and a gourmet basket upon arrival. Guest quarters sport a singular decor, spacious closets and marble bathrooms. Enjoy the clubby library, poolside cabana, lunch in the courtyard and a drink or dinner in the Leopard Lounge.

The Hotel – *801 Collins Ave., Miami Beach.* ⅄ ⅙ ▯ ⅃ ☏ *305-531-2222 or 877-843-4683. www.thehotelofsouthbeach.com. 52 rooms.* $$$$ Todd Oldham designed nearly everything in this renovated Art-Deco gem (1936) off South Beach's famous Ocean Drive. A huge mirror-shaped tile mosaic and velveteen couches—block-patterned in rose, green, and gold—pick up flecks of color from the lobby's original terrazzo floor. Blue and neon-green cottons and pale wood furniture brighten the bedrooms. Bask in the sun at the new Mediterranean-style rooftop pool and reserve a table at **Wish**, the indoor-outdoor restaurant that serves up creative fish dishes and other specialties. Celebrity sightings are probable.

Sea View Hotel – *9909 Collins Ave. Bal Harbour.* ⚑ ☎ *305-866-4441 or 800-447-1010. www.seaview-hotel.com. 100 rooms.* **$$$$** A beachfront jewel, this swank Euro-styled boutique hotel was built in 1947 as one of Bal Harbour's first high rises. Remarkably spacious, designer-appointed guest quarters show off rich fabrics, wicker chairs, glass-topped metal tables and solid pine armoires. Walk-in closets, mini-refrigerators and marble-floored bathrooms are added amenities. Cozy cabanas rim the Olympic-size pool that overlooks the Atlantic. On-site services include a beauty salon, fitness center and restaurant. Guests are given a *pasaporte* with discount coupons for a spree at the Bal Harbour Shops, a five-minute walk away.

Hotel Place St. Michel – *162 Alcazar Ave. Coral Gables.* ☎ *305-444-1666 or 800-848-hotel. www.hotelplacestmichel.com. 27 rooms.* **$$$** Nestled within Coral Gables' walker-friendly downtown, this two-story European-style bed-and-breakfast inn appeals especially to those from abroad and those with a passion for antiques. The parquet-floored reception area and adjoining sitting room are reminiscent of homey Continental inns. The subdued, Old World-style decor of each guest room typically features floral bedspreads and matching curtains. Amenities include fresh fruit upon arrival, evening turn-down with French chocolates, complimentary continental breakfast and morning newspaper. Favored by locals, **Restaurant St. Michel** offers a variety of French dishes, wild game, elaborate desserts and an extensive wine list.

The Pillars – *111 N. Birch Rd., Fort Lauderdale.* ☎ *954-467-9639 or 800-800-7666. www.pillarshotel.com. 23 rooms.* **$$$** Bordering the busy Intracoastal Waterway, this upscale urban oasis cultivates British Colonial cachet in decor and personal attention. The front door opens onto hardwood floors and an intimate sitting area dressed in red-striped and neon-green fabrics. Adjoining is a small library, complete with grand piano and shelves of books and videos. Carpeted in leopard print, a curved staircase leads to upper-level guest quarters. Rooms are smartly appointed with floral bedspreads, armoires and plantation shutters. Pool and patio overlook the water, with its continuous parade of yachts.

A Little Inn By The Sea – *4546 El Mar Dr., Lauderdale-By-The-Sea.* ☎ *954-772-2450 or 800-492-0311. www.alittleinn.com. 29 units.* **$$** Fronting 300ft of private beach, this Mediterranean-style bed-and-breakfast inn is centrally located in a seaside village just north of Fort Lauderdale. Family-run, it's reminiscent of Old Florida in the 1950s. Furnished in wicker, the breezy, three-floor lobby includes a 10ft fountain. A tropical, brick-covered courtyard overlooks the pool, barbecue area and beach. There's even an adults-only rooftop patio for sunning au naturel. Rooms and suites are done in floral patterns. A continental breakfast buffet is served in the lobby. Beach chaises and bikes are complimentary to guests.

Miami River Inn – *118 S.W. South River Dr. Miami.* ☎ *305-325-0045 or 800-468-3589. www.miamiriverinn.com. 40 rooms.* **$$** Listed on the National Register of Historic Places, this downtown bed-and-breakfast inn was completed in 1910. Located on the Miami River's west bank, just steps from Little Havana, the gated compound is also within walking distance of Brickell Avenue.

Nightlife along Ocean Drive

Painted pale yellow with olive trim, the inn serves as a tropical oasis of soaring palms and native plants amid Miami's bustling downtown. Refurbished rooms, most with hardwood floors, are appointed with period antiques and feature spacious baths. Two cottages have a living room and fireplace. Complimentary continental breakfast, with homemade muffins, can be savored outdoors.

The Clay Hotel (Hostelling International Miami Beach) – *1438 Washington Ave., South Beach.* ✗ ☎ *305-534-2988 or 800-379-2529. www.clayhotel.com. 120 private rooms, 220 dorm beds.* $ Located on a bustling commercial corner just steps from colorful Espanola Way, this high-occupancy hostel offers good value for your lodging budget. Sporting a strawberry-hued exterior with striped awnings, the three-story Art Deco building is rich in history: it was home to Al Capone's gambling ring in the 1930s, Desi Arnaz' rumba craze in the '50s, and the filming of the pilot for *Miami Vice*. Wood-carved French doors and terra-cotta floors beckon weary guests, many laden with backpacks. Rooms with private baths offer air conditioning, mini-refrigerators, TV, and phones with voice mail. Luggage storage, laundry facilities, fax and computer services are available on-site.

Dining in the Miami Area and South Florida

Café L'Europe – *331 S. County Rd., Palm Beach.* ♿ ☎ *561-655-4020. www.cafeleurope.com.* **$$$$ Continental**. French doors, beveled brick, mahogany paneling and gleaming brass lend an air of refinement to this tony venue. Fresh floral bouquets and colorful place settings add panache. Epitomizing *la belle vie* Palm Beach style, L'Europe serves more than 5,000 ounces of caviar each year. Favorites among the Austrian- and Asian-influenced cuisine include sweetbread and poached pear; pan-seared ahi tuna sashimi; Wiener schnitzel; and the house signature dessert: apple pancake with seasonal fruit compote. There's a formal dining room, a Euro-style bistro, and a piano bar featuring jazz on weekends. The 40-seat wine room holds a redwood-paneled wine locker.

The Forge – *432 Arthur Godfrey Rd. (41st St. & Royal Palm Ave.), Miami Beach.* ☎ *305-538-8533.* ♿ **$$$$ Continental**. There's no sign on the exterior of this ornate building, but the beefy valets and sleek cars curbside are clues to the clientele. Thick carpet, plush sofas, stained glass, tapestries and art adorn the restaurant's brick-walled interior. Soft piano music and candlelight add romantic air. The aromas of oak-fired grilled steak and roast duck augur a fine dining experience; especially mouth-watering is the Grand Marnier soufflé. Regular customers store their cigars in a giant humidor within their own private locker. Wednesday is disco night at this retro restaurant, noted for frequent sightings of celebrities, politicos and athletes.

La Vieille Maison – *770 E. Palmetto Park Rd., Boca Raton.* ☎ *561-391-6701.* **$$$$ French**. Bon vivants especially will enjoy the atmosphere of the Impressionist art- and antique-filled house, constructed in 1928. Seven separate rooms, awash in the colors of Provence, offer intimate dining in a setting reminiscent of a French country manor. Signature delights include Maine lobster bisque, medallions of lamb with rosemary, beef with bearnaise, and venison loin with a Beaujolais sauce. For the finale, try the French apple tart topped with freshly whipped cream. A small courtyard provides outdoor seating if there's a wait.

Mark's Las Olas – *1032 Las Olas Blvd., Fort Lauderdale.* ♿ ☎ *954-463-1000. www.chefmark.com.* **$$$$ New American**. Chef-owner Mark Militello's trend-setting cuisine continues to draw a well-heeled, noisy crowd to his much-frequented downtown restaurant, open since 1994. Warm wood floors, stone accents, suede benches and walls sponged with Mediterranean color create an inviting setting. Memorable appetizers include the Maine lobster brûlee with truffled potatoes. Oak rotisserie entrées are a house specialty, as are the pumpkin ravioli, and mango Scotch-bonnet barbecued pork T-bone. Devoted people-watchers, and those preferring quiet conversation, will enjoy dining outside on the metal tables and chairs.

Norman's – *21 Almeria Ave., Coral Gables.* ☎ *305-446-6767. www.norman .com.* **$$$$ International**. Chef Norman Van Aken's nationally acclaimed "New World" cuisine highlights the city's Latin American, Caribbean and Asian tastes. Amid its elegant setting, the Coral Gables' haunt offers dishes like Turks and Caicos cracked-conch chowder with saffron and toasted coconut, Vietnamese soft spring rolls filled with seared tuna, and truffle oil-infused Argentinian beef tenderloin over creamy potato hash with roasted peppers. Tantalizing aromas issue forth from the wood-burning ovens of the open kitchen, which provide patrons with plenty of lively cooking theater.

Cap's Place – *2765 N.E. 28th Court in Lighthouse Point, north of Pompano Beach. Turn east at US-1 & N.E. 24th St. and follow signs to Cap's Place Dock, adjacent to Lighthouse Point Yacht Basin & Marina. From there it's a 10min boat ride.* ☎ *954-941-0418. www.capsplace.com.* **$$$ Seafood.** Listed on the National Register of Historic Places, this restaurant/bar is rustic, rich in history, and fun, especially for families. In the 1920s founder Cap Knight relocated several wooden shacks, floating them on a barge up the Intracoastal Waterway from Miami to Cap's Island, north of Pompano Beach. Back then, the place was a gambling casino and rum-running joint. Celebrity diners have included Winston Churchill, the Vanderbilts and the Rockefellers, Errol Flynn and George Harrison. Memorable are the house-smoked fish dip, the hearts of palm salad, homemade rolls and key lime pie.

Joe's Stone Crab – *11 Washington Ave., Miami Beach.* ♿ ☎ *305-673-0365 or 800-780-2722. www.joesstonecrab.com. Open mid-Oct–mid-May.* **$$$ Seafood.** Located at the southern end of Miami Beach, this high-energy eatery has been a legend since 1913, when founder Joe Weiss began serving the succulent rust-colored crustaceans whose claws contain meat that rivals lobster for sweetness. Caught mainly off Florida's Gulf Coast between October and May, stone crabs possess the ability to grow new claws within 12 to 18 months (fishermen take only the claws, since they contain the crab's only edible meat). Medium- to jumbo-size stone crab claws are conveniently cracked open and served chilled with the house mustard sauce. Sides—coleslaw and creamed spinach—are big enough for two. Expect to line up for dinner, but if you're too hungry to wait, order from Joe's adjacent take-out counter and have a surf-side picnic.

Mai-Kai – *3599 N. Federal Hwy., Fort Lauderdale.* ♿ ☎ *954-563-3272 or 800-262-4524. www.mai-kai.com.* **$$$ Polynesian.** Popular for its dinner show, Mai-Kai has been attracting tourists and locals since 1956. Its South Seas appearance—thatched roofs, tiki torches, tropical palms and cascading waterfalls—seems out of place alongside a six-lane thoroughfare. Entering the fenced "village" via a wood-plank bridge, patrons can order one of 50 specialty drinks in a dimly-lit saloon that resembles a wrecked ship. Served in intimate dining rooms or on the garden patio, exotic dishes include lobster Bora Bora, roast duck Mai-Kai, filet mignon Madagascar and coconut curry bouillabaisse. Standard American fare is also available. But what most people come for are the Tahitian dances performed by the curvy dancers and muscular musicians of the Islander Revue troupe *(nightly except Mon; extra cost)*.

El Rancho Grande – *1626 Pennsylvania Ave., Miami Beach* ☎ *305-673-0480.* **$$ Mexican.** Located just off lively Lincoln Road Mall, this family-owned dining spot, dressed inside and out in bold primary colors, has the feel of a roomy cantina. Sombreros, sarapes and other South of the Border accents decorate the walls; square wooden tables and solid chairs accommodate diners. The extensive menu offers standard Mexican dishes and sides, presented in a variety of combinations. For a sampling of several flavors, try the *plato Mexicano*, a hearty assemblage of marinated pork, chicken enchilada, *chile relleno* (green pepper stuffed with cheese), beef burrito, refried beans and rice. Margaritas and Mexican beer are also available.

Versailles Restaurant – *3555 S.W. 8th St., Little Havana.* ♿ ☎ *305-444-0240.* **$$ Cuban.** Near the western perimeter of Little Havana lies one of the quarter's most prominent attractions. Local transplants get their fix of home cooking at Versailles. In this large dining spot you can enjoy ultra-sweet *café Cubano* from a stand-up counter inside or outside. Amid a swirl of fast-paced conversations, hearty Cuban sandwiches and heaping plates of food from a magazine-size menu are served inside the main dining room. Most rib-sticking dishes, such as roast pork and grilled *palomilla* steak with garlic and onions, come with generous portions of black beans and white rice. Specialties include *ropa vieja* (shredded beef in a tomato-based sauce) and *plátanos verdes* (fried green plantains). Finish your meal with flan, a type of custard akin to crème caramel.

The Floridian Restaurant – *1410 E. Las Olas Blvd., Fort Lauderdale.* ☎ *954-463-4041.* **$ American.** Inexpensive, tasty food and generous portions are what make "the Flo" popular among Las Olas insiders. It's always busy at this upscale diner-style eatery, where dining rooms are cheery with poster-lined red, green or blue walls. Allow 5min to read the encyclopedic menu that includes peanut-butter-chip muffins; 17 types of burgers; Mexican meatloaf; and a "Fat Cat" breakfast of strip steak, eggs, grits, toast and Dom Perignon for two. Another caloric dish ("the mess!") is heavenly hash, topped off with chocolate cake. No one leaves hungry.

Hamburger Heaven – *314 S. County Rd., Palm Beach.* ☎ *561-655-5277* **$ American**. A Palm Beach institution since 1945, this old-fashioned diner boasts the "world's greatest hamburgers" and more. At the counter of the always-packed place, diamond- and Gucci-clad millionaires are often seated next to construction workers. Red fabric booths along the wall offer more space for dining. Breakfast fare, soups, salads and cold or grilled sandwiches, as well as burgers, fill the straightforward menu. Take your pick of hamburger toppers from jalapeño peppers, onions, smoked bacon and cheese to sauerkraut, avocado, mushrooms or homemade chili.

Tiffany's – *22 N.E. 15th St., Homestead.* ♿ ☎ *305-246-0022.* **$ American**. Located about 3mi west of the Florida Turnpike in the Shoppes of Tiffany Square, this Victorian-style eatery provides a pleasant alternative to fast-food breakfasts and lunches, especially if you're traveling to the Everglades or the Keys. Grandmotherly accents—handmade wreaths, crocheted curtains, simple pine tables—create a cozy country setting. Menu offerings like Georgia pecan waffles, stuffed Homestead tomatoes, and onion soup make the stop worthwhile. Specials might include a grilled portabello mushroom sandwich. Desserts are homemade: try the three-layered strawberry cake or the German-chocolate version.

Tobacco Road – *626 S. Miami Ave., Miami.* ☎ *305-374-1198. www.tobacco-road.com.* **$ American**. This neighborhood bar, one block west of Brickell Avenue in downtown Miami, holds the oldest liquor license in the county. During Prohibition, "The Road" was a speakeasy, frequented by the likes of Al Capone. During World War II, its licenses were revoked on charges of indecent behavior. Regentrified today, Tobacco Road attracts a mix of downtown yuppies, lawyers, students and bikers. It's known for offering some of Miami's best live music nightly; Blues singers B.B. King and Koko Taylor have played here. Daily dinner specials include lobster, but the after-midnight steak specials are the real deal.

structures that adhered to a vernacular style of architecture. The downtown's best example of vernacular storefront architecture is the 1914 Chaille Block (Miami Ave. between N.W. 4th and N.W. 5th Sts.), which was recently incorporated into the facade of the new federal prison. By World War I, new hotels and stores incorporated open walkways beneath a second-floor veranda, an architectural style clearly suited to the subtropics. Several such structures remain, notably the 1912 Waddel Building (24-36 N. Miami Ave.).

It was not until the late 1960s that the downtown reached its apex as a retailing, business and entertainment district. In recent years, the revivified quarter has welcomed a large cluster of contemporary high-rise hotels and office buildings including **International Place** (1985, I.M. Pei & Partners) a 47-story tiered tower (*100 S.E. 1st St.*) lit nightly by colored lights, and the 55-story **First Union Financial Center** (1984, Edward Bassett Skidmore, Owings & Merrill), the tallest building in South Florida (*200 S. Biscayne Blvd.*). The spread of downtown south of the Miami River along Brickell Avenue has resulted in the emergence of that area—once lined with the homes of Miami's richest citizens—as an international financial district containing numerous Latin American and Caribbean banks and law firms. Miami currently boasts international bank offices as well as multinational corporations.

© Bill Wisser

Metromover at International Place

Sights

★**Miami-Dade Cultural Center** – *101 W. Flagler St. ☎ 305-375-1072.* A complex of three Mediterranean Revival buildings—the Miami Art Museum, the Historical Museum of Southern Florida and the fortress-like Miami-Dade Public Library—the center rests atop an elevated 33,000sq ft tiled plaza that illustrates architect Philip Johnson's design for a cultural oasis above the busy downtown streets.

★**Miami Art Museum** (**A**) – *Open year-round Tue-Fri 10am-5pm, weekends noon-5pm. Closed major holidays. $5. ♿ P ☎ 305-375-3000. www.miamiartmuseum.org.* Dedicated to presenting international art of the post-World War II era, with an emphasis on art of the Americas, the museum stages several major shows a year in its two levels of gallery spaces and auditorium. The permanent collection, a small selection of which is displayed on a rotating basis, includes 50 works by such noted contemporary artists as Christo, Alexander Calder, Jasper Johns, Robert Rauschenberg, Marcel Duchamp and Rufino Tamayo. Exhibits of new work change four times a year. Raymond Duchamp-Villon's black marble sculpture *Cheval Majeur* stands near the museum's entrance.

★★**Historical Museum of Southern Florida** (**B**) – *Open year-round Mon-Sat 10am-5pm, Sun noon-5pm. Closed Jan 1, Thanksgiving Day, Dec 25. $5. ♿ P ☎ 305-375-1492. www.historical-museum.org.* The Historical Assn. of Southern Florida and its museum represent the region's most important historical organization and facility. Housed on the museum's second floor, the permanent exhibit "Tropical Dreams: A People's History of South Florida" recounts the area's colorful past. The wealth of artifacts and mixed-media presentations include an early Tequesta Indian settlement, treasures from sunken Spanish galleons, a Conch house from the heyday of Key West's sponge trade and a 1923 trolley car. The first floor contains a gallery for temporary exhibits focusing on Miami history and folklife, and a research library with an extensive collection of books, maps and historical photographs.

US Federal Courthouse – *301 N. Miami Ave. ♿ P ☎ 305-536-4548.* Designed in 1931 by Phineas Paist and Harold D. Steward as a courthouse and post office, this three-story keystone Neoclassical gem now serves only the former function. Denman Fink's mural, *Law Guides Florida's Progress* (1940), a whimsical look at the wide array of peoples and occupations in the Sunshine State, decorates the central courtroom on the second floor. The building also contains a lovely Moorish courtyard.

Alfred I. Du Pont Building – *169 E. Flagler St.* This Depression Moderne edifice (1939, Marsh and Saxelbye) was built as the headquarters of the Florida National Bank, which was controlled at the time by the Du Pont family. On the exterior, 16 stories of polished limestone rise above the first level of black granite. During World War II, the US Navy appropriated a portion of this building for its local offices. After the war, the structure reestablished itself as one of downtown's most prominent professional addresses. Today it houses the offices of a national bank.

Claude and Mildred Pepper Bayfront Park – *Biscayne Blvd. between N.E. 4th and S.E. 2nd Sts.* Known locally as Bayfront Park, the 32-acre greensward was dredged from bay bottom in the mid-1920s. A popular venue for many decades, the park fell into disuse in the 1970s. Isamu Noguchi, famed Japanese landscape architect, planned the park's $30 million face-lift in the late 1980s. Noguchi's design incorporates (from south to north) his sculptures—the *Challenger Memorial* (**1**) and *Slide Mantra* (**2**) for children—as well as a prominent fountain, a broad bayside promenade, a laser light tower (**3**) and a large amphitheater. These elements have helped restore the park's popularity.

★**Bayside Marketplace** – *401 Biscayne Blvd. Open year-round Mon-Sat 10am, Sun 11am; closing hrs vary. ☎ 305-377-4091. www.baysidemarketplace.com.* Linked to the north side of Bayfront Park via sidewalk, this complex, composed of several buildings connected by plazas and open-air walkways, sits on the northeastern edge of downtown Miami overlooking the turquoise waters of Biscayne Bay. Completed in 1987 at a cost of $68 million, Bayside and its profusion of boutiques, eateries and entertainment sprawls over 235,000sq ft of space. The lower level teems with vendors hawking ethnic wares and local souvenirs; the upper level is devoted to mainstream chain stores. Distinguishable from the waterfront by the giant yellow guitar atop the resident Hard Rock Cafe, the marketplace lures visitors with its beguiling ambience and vibrant nightlife. Cruises on Biscayne Bay are available on a wide variety of vessels berthed near Bayside's northern pavilion.

Freedom Tower – *600 Biscayne Blvd.* One of Miami-Dade County's most striking buildings, the tower sits on the northern edge of downtown. Designed by the famed New York architectural firm of Schultze and Weaver, whose credits also include the Biltmore in Coral Gables and The Breakers in Palm Beach, the Spanish Renaissance Revival building consists of a three-story base that buttresses a slim 12-story tower. At the top is a cupola inspired by the 16C Giralda Tower in Seville, Spain.

The 1925 structure housed the *Miami News*, the city's first newspaper, for more than 30 years before it was transformed into a federal processing center for Cuban refugees in 1962. As a symbol of liberation for the Cuban community, it was renamed "Freedom Tower." After the federal government closed the center in the mid-1970s, it stood vacant for several years and fell into disrepair. In the late 1980s, the tower was restored to its original splendor. In 1997 it was purchased by the family of exiled Cuban revolutionary leader Jorge Mas Canosa, with plans to build a museum of Cuban refugee history and culture here *(museum is scheduled to open spring 2002)*.

Brickell Avenue – *Also map p 214.* Named for a wealthy pioneering family who owned bayfront land south of the Miami River, Brickell Avenue is a broad, four-lane street—divided by a tree-shaded median—that parallels the contours of nearby Biscayne Bay for its entire 2mi length south of downtown. By the early 1900s, elegant estates began to spring up along the street, leading to its sobriquet "**Millionaires' Row**." Artist Louis Comfort Tiffany, Miami Beach developer Carl Fisher and politician William Jennings Bryan were among prominent residents; Chicago entrepreneur James Deering erected his palatial Villa Vizcaya at its southern end. In the 1970s and 1980s, high-rise condominiums and modern office buildings began to replace the mansions. Soon an international financial center had emerged along Miami's new "Wall Street." Signature residential high rises include **The Palace** *(no. 1541)*, recognizable by the striking stepped wing emanating from its east side; **The Imperial** *(no. 1627)*, with its red veneer, square windows and sloping roof, and **The Atlantis** *(no. 2025)*, whose much-photographed "skycourt" consists of a 37ft square-shaped hole punched out of its central massing. This open-air cube contains a winding staircase and a live palm tree. Each of these structures was designed by Arquitectonica, a local firm famous for its innovative, quirky designs and stunning use of color. Sitting between The Palace and The Imperial is the 28-story **Villa Regina** *(no. 1581)*, a condominium notable for its vivid color scheme, a product of the imaginative palette of Israeli artist Yacov Agam.

LITTLE HAVANA *Map p 233*

Immediately east of downtown, a 3.3sq mi section of Miami bounded by the Miami River (east), S.W. 37th Avenue (west), N.W. Seventh Street (north) and Coral Way (south) represents one of the city's most lively and exotic neighborhoods. Along **Calle Ocho**, or Eighth Street—Little Havana's main thoroughfare—sidewalk vendors hawk a variety of wares and ubiquitous stand-up *cafeterias* dispense tiny cups of dense black *café Cubano*. A bewildering array of small businesses, including the diminutive botanicas that sell religious paraphernalia for practitioners of *Santería*, a form of voodoo, cater to a Latin clientele. English is rarely spoken.

■ A Haven for Refugees

Ever since Cubans fleeing the Castro regime began pouring into the area in 1959, Little Havana has remained a magnet for refugees from a variety of Spanish-speaking nations. By the late 1920s, Eastern Europeans had moved into the quarter, reaching their peak population in the early 1950s. Thereafter many residents relocated and the old neighborhood declined. By the mid-1950s, Hispanics occupied the quarter, paving the way for the subsequent Cuban influx that reached flood proportions after the US commenced its "Freedom Flights" in 1965. The large concentration of Cubans in the quarter prompted its sobriquet, "Little Havana." Southwest Eighth Street, alternately known as Highway 41 and Tamiami Trail, became the district's most important commercial thoroughfare. Densely populated Little Havana is largely an immigrant community with a preponderance of young Latin American families and elderly residents. Although Nicaraguans count among the thousands of Hispanics who call Little Havana home, the sector remains the political nerve center of the influential Cuban exile colony. Refugees still seek sanctuary here, where virtually everyone speaks Spanish, and housing—although limited—is inexpensive.

Cuban history is remembered in places such as **José Martí Park** *(351 S.W. 4th St.)*. Named for the apostle of Cuban independence (José Martí, 1853-1895), the park overlooks the western bank of the Miami River.

One of the quarter's most famous landmarks is the **Orange Bowl** *(1501 N.W. 3rd St.)*, a sports arena in the northern sector that was built in increments and completed in 1979. Many college and professional football games have been played in the venerable stadium.

Each year on the second Sunday in March, Little Havana hosts the most popular of all Hispanic-oriented events, the **Calle Ocho Open House**. This gala street party, the culmination of a week-long Lenten festival known as Carnaval Miami, attracts in excess of one million revelers to a 2-mi-long portion of Eighth Street.

Sights

Visit the following sights beginning at S.W. 32nd Ave. and S.W. 8th St., and work your way east. Note that at S.W. 26th Ave., Calle Ocho becomes a one-way thoroughfare heading east. Metered parking is available on both sides of S.W. 8th St.

Woodlawn Park Cemetery – *3260 S.W. 8th St.* Miami's largest and one of its oldest (1913) burial spots, Woodlawn Park is the final resting place for thousands of Cuban refugees. The somber black marble wall commemorates the "Unknown Cuban Freedom Fighter" killed in the Bay of Pigs invasion in 1961. Two former exiled Cuban presidents, as well as Anastasio Somoza, longtime dictator of Nicaragua, are interred here.

1 Nicaragua Bakery
Map p 233. 1169 S.W. 8th St. ✗ ☎ *305-285-0239.* One of the most successful Nicaraguan businesses in Little Havana lies two blocks east of Memorial Plaza. Sample delicacies such as *tres leches* (three-milks cake), *torta des pasas* (raisin cake) and *torta de mantequilla* (butter cake) along with a steaming demitasse of *café Cubano*.

2 El Crédito Cigar Factory
Map p 233. 1106 S.W. 8th St. ☎ *305-858-4162.* In 1969 the El Crédito company, which began in Havana in 1907, opened in Miami. The largest hand-rolled cigar factory in Miami-Dade County now produces more than one million cigars annually. Celebrities Bill Cosby and Robert Goulet have been counted among its customers. Descendants of the founding Carillo family owned and operated the business until only recently, when it was purchased by New Jersey-based General Cigar. Visitors can watch the cigar-making process through glass windows looking into the factory.

Latin Quarter – So designated by the City of Miami in the late 1970s to promote the district as a tourist attraction, the quarter stretches along Calle Ocho between S.W. 17th and S.W. 12th avenues. (The north-south portion of the quarter reaches from N.W. First to S.W. Ninth streets.) Here quaint street lamps rise above brick sidewalks set with stars bearing the names of an international array of prominent Hispanic entertainers, including Julio Iglesias and Gloria Estefan.

Máximo Gómez Park – *Southeast corner of S.W. 15th Ave.* For a glimpse of local color drop by this tiny plaza, named for the Dominican Republic-born Chief of the Cuban Liberating Army and known locally as Domino Park. As they have been doing since the early 1960s, Cubans, primarily elderly men, assemble here daily for spirited games of dominoes (introduced to the hemisphere by the Spanish), chess, cards and checkers.

Cuban Memorial Plaza (**A**) – *In the median of S.W. 13th Ave./Cuban Memorial Blvd. and S.W. 8th St.* A hexagonal marble monument topped by a flickering eternal torch decorates this small square. Created in 1971 to honor those members of Brigade 2506 who lost their lives in the aborted invasion of Cuba in April 1961, the plaza now serves as a rallying point for political demonstrations.

Teatro Martí – *420 S.W. 8th Ave., at southwest corner of S.W. 4th St.* Several blocks southwest of the Miami River Inn is Teatro Martí, one of Little Havana's oldest (founded in 1963) and the most important of the quarter's four theaters for film and live presentations. The theater is housed in the Riverside Commercial Building, built by the Ku Klux Klan as its headquarters in 1926.

Templo Adventista del Septimo Dia (**B**) – *862 S.W. 4th St. at corner of 9th Ave.* Built in 1925 by the Seventh Day Adventist Church, this stucco structure exemplifies Mission-style architecture erected by the Spanish in many parts of their colonial empire. Today the congregation is largely Nicaraguan.

Dominoes Game at Máximo Gómez Park

Warner House – *111 S.W. 5th Ave.* This Neoclassical mansion was built in 191 by the Warner family, who lived there and also used it as a venue for a successful floral business. Fully restored, it now houses the Archaeological and Historical Conservancy, among other occupants.

Located one block east of Warner House, the **Miami River Inn** (**C**) *(118 S.W. Sout River Dr.),* comprises several restored early 20C buildings that now function as bed-and-breakfast inn *(see Address Book).*

★★CORAL GABLES *Map p 232*

Grandest and most successful of South Florida's boomtime developments, Cora Gables covers a 12.5sq mi area just southwest of downtown Miami. The area bounded roughly by S.W. 57th Avenue (Red Road) on the west, S.W. 37th Avenu (Douglas Road) on the east, S.W. Eighth Street (US-41) on the north and S.W 72nd Street (Sunset Drive) on the south, and embraces a 6mi bayside stretc running south along Old Cutler Road. While largely residential, this city within city also boasts the **University of Miami** campus, several golf courses and some of th area's finest Mediterranean Revival architecture and mature tropical landscapin

Sights

To visit downtown, park on Miracle Mile (Coral Way) or Ponce de Leon Blv (metered parking) and walk. Giralda Ave. between Ponce de Leon Blvd. and Galian St. is notable for its trendy restaurants, Aragon Ave. for its specialty shops. Oth sights in Coral Gables are best reached by car. Street names in residential sectio

■ The City Beautiful

By 1921 **George Merrick** (1886-1942) had purchased 3,000 acres of undeveloped scrubland to form a comprehensively planned community in which
buildings, streets, public plazas and utilities—discreetly out of sight—were
conceived as a unified whole. Broad boulevards, formal entrances, sculpture and parklike landscaping associated with European cities were
important components. Introduced to America at the 1893 World's
Columbian Exposition in Chicago, such features were integral to the influential "City Beautiful" movement that swept the country following the
exposition. Merrick assembled a team of top engineers, planners and
designers. Among them were landscape architect **Frank Button**, artist **Denman
Fink** (Merrick's uncle), and architects **H. George Fink**, **Phineas Paist** and **Walter
DeGarmo**, the first registered architect in Florida. The prevailing style was
Mediterranean Revival, a popular early 20C design featuring elements such as
clay roof tiles, small towers, wrought ironwork, breezy courtyards and
loggias.

Beginning in 1925, several small thematic villages designed to reflect the
architecture of China, Italy, South Africa, France and the antebellum South
added a theatrical touch to Merrick's fantasy city. Years in advance of
zoning laws, Merrick segregated business, manufacturing and public services into specific areas. Street lighting and fire alarms ensured safety.
Luxury hotels, an exotic swimming pool, a country club and playing fields
offered recreation. Churches and schools—including the first buildings of
the University of Miami—met religious and educational needs.

Merrick's real genius lay in promotion. He opened sales offices in Atlanta
and Chicago, operated 86 buses to haul in prospective buyers, and
managed a sales force of 3,000. Hawkers included **Edward "Doc" Dammers**,
the city's first mayor, who sold lots from a horse-drawn wagon. A bril-
liantly devised series of canals (linking the landlocked community to
Biscayne Bay) enabled Merrick to advertise waterfront property—the
"Miami Riviera"—in his development. By 1924 $7 million worth of lots in
the new community had been sold. The next year Merrick's development
received its charter, becoming the City of Coral Gables.

*of Coral Gables are painted on whitewashed concrete markers and placed at
corners, low to the ground. A free Coral Gables driving-tour map is available at
the City Hall (405 Biltmore Way) information desk. Coral Gables Chamber of
Commerce is another source of information: ☎ 305-446-1657, www.gables
chamber.org.*

Coral Way – This busy thoroughfare is the main east-west artery in downtown
Coral Gables. The four-block section between Douglas and LeJeune roads has been
renamed **Miracle Mile** (really a half-mile). Shops range from discount stores to chic
boutiques. Fronted by Corinthian columns, the two-story, coral-colored 1926
Colonnade Building *(no. 169)* features a baroque, Spanish-inspired arched entrance
topped by spires. Used as a training center for World War II pilots and as real-
estate offices, the building now holds a restaurant. Walk inside to view the marble
interior of the 75ft-high **rotunda**, connected to the Omni Colonnade Hotel tower
built just north of the Colonnade Building in 1985.

Miracle Mile terminates at **City Hall** *(405 Biltmore Way)*. Designed by Phineas Paist
and Denman Fink, this coral-rock monument topped by a three-tiered tower cost
$200,000 to build in 1927. The curved, colonnaded front bay is slightly skewed
so the building aligns with angled Biltmore Way.

Coral Gables Merrick House – *907 Coral Way. Visit by guided tour (45min) only, year-
round Wed & Sun 1pm-4pm. Closed major holidays. Grounds are open daily
year-round. $2. ⚒ 🅿 ☎ 305-460-5361.* George Merrick's two-story boyhood
home was added in 1906 to the modest frame cabin that existed on the land
Merrick's father purchased in 1899. Designed by Merrick's mother, Althea, the
house features indigenous oolite limestone (coral rock) and Dade County pine and
adapts New England architecture to the area's subtropical climate. The homestead—and later Merrick's planned community—was named for the structure's
coral-rock construction and distinctive gabled roof. In 1976 the City of Coral Gables
acquired the house and restored it. The interior is appointed with period and
Merrick family furnishings, including the Baldwin grand player piano owned by
Althea Merrick; surrounding gardens contain trees from the family's original plantation.

Houses along Coral Way between Toledo and Madrid streets represent a variety of
interpretations of the area's Mediterranean Revival architecture. Three doors west
of Coral Gables Merrick House is **Poinciana Place** *(937 Coral Way)*, the home George
Merrick built in 1916 for his new wife. Coral Gables' first mayor, Edward "Doc"

Dammers, originally lived at 1141 Coral Way. Architect H. George Fink designed the one-story, rock **Casa Azul** *(1254 Coral Way)*, distinguishable by its blue glazed-tile roof, for himself in 1924.

★★Biltmore Hotel – *1200 Anastasia Ave. Guided tour (30min), year-round Sun 1:30pm, 2:30pm & 3:30pm.* ✗ ♿ 🄿 ☎ *305-445-1926 or 800-727-1926. www.biltmorehotel.com.* Recently restored and reopened, the Biltmore was inaugurated in 1926 as South

Coral Gables Congregational Church

Florida's premier winter resort. This massive tile-roofed "wedding cake" boasted a Mediterranean Revival design by the prestigious New York architectural firm of Schultze and Weaver (designers of the Waldorf-Astoria Hotel in New York City) and formed the centerpiece of Coral Gables' 1,600-acre "Country Club Section." The 300ft-high tower with triple cupola—inspired by the 16C Giralda tower of the Cathedral of Seville, Spain—can be seen from miles around.

Remarkably, the 280-room extravaganza went up in just 11 months. The cost was $10 million; $1 million alone was spent on decorating the **lobby** with custom-loomed carpets, Italian marble and Spanish tiles. In addition to a clubhouse modeled after an Italian Renaissance palazzo, there were two 18-hole golf courses, miles of bridle paths, 20 tennis courts, a polo field and a 1.25-million-gallon **pool**. While guests preferring fresh water frolicked here, Italian gondoliers ferried saltwater bathers down a canal to the beach on nearby Biscayne Bay.

Venetian Pool

In its heyday, the Biltmore attracted Hollywood stars such as Bing Crosby, Judy Garland and Ginger Rogers, as well as welcoming well-heeled Northerners who checked in for the entire winter season. (For their convenience, prominent brokerage firms interspersed branch offices among the beauty parlors and shops set around the central open-air courtyard.) After the crash, the Biltmore fell on hard times and from 1942 to 1968 served as a hospital, first for the Army, then for the Veterans' Administration. Ceilings were dropped, windows blocked and the marvelous pool filled with concrete.

Visit – Two separate restoration efforts—one completed in 1987, the other in 1992—restored not only the pool but also elegant ballrooms and the second-story lobby, with travertine marble columns running the length of the room. Hand-painted with gold stars, the 45ft-high groined and vaulted ceiling was refurbished by 35 ecclesiastical restorers. Its former glory fully reclaimed, the hotel is now the setting for elegant weddings, fashion photography and major motion pictures.

Directly opposite the hotel is the 1924 **Coral Gables Congregational Church** *(3010 DeSoto Blvd.)*, built on land donated by George Merrick in memory of his father, Solomon Merrick, a Congregational minister who served at Plymouth Church in Coconut Grove. With its arcaded loggias, arched bell tower and ornate baroque entry, the yellow stucco building is an excellent example of Spanish Colonial architecture and was the first church in Florida to be named to the National Register of Historic Places *(open year-round daily by appointment only; & ▯ ☎ 305-448-7421)*.

★★Venetian Pool – *2701 DeSoto Blvd. Open Jun-Aug daily Mon-Fri 11am-7:30pm, weekends & holidays 10am-4:30pm. Rest of the year Tue-Sun 10am-4:30pm. $5. ✗ & ▯ ☎ 305-460-5356.* A limestone quarry that supplied building materials for the area's early homes formed the base of this whimsical municipal pool. Working in tandem in 1922, artist Denman Fink and architect Phineas Paist concocted a fanciful design incorporating a casino, towers, striped light poles (inspired by those lining Venice's Grand Canal) and footbridges that crossed the free-form swimming area. The pool is drained each night and refilled with water from underground artesian wells. Today the renovated Venetian Pool, ornamented with waterfalls and pocked with rock caves, provides a unique recreational venue for Coral Gables residents and visitors.

Entrances – Designed to set Coral Gables apart from surrounding areas, grand drive-through entrances also welcomed visitors with suitable pomp—much in the spirit of the triumphal arches of Spanish cities like Seville and Toledo. Only four of eight planned entries were built. The 1922 **Granada Entrance** *(Granada Blvd. and Tamiami Tr.)* was the first. Of rough-cut coral rock, this 300ft-long gateway boasts a 40ft-high arch and flanking pergolas. **Commercial Entrance** *(Alhambra Circle, Madeira Ave. and Douglas Rd.)*, completed in 1923, is dominated by a 600ft curved coral-rock wall and archway marking the approach to the business section of the

Gables. Costing nearly $1 million, the 1925 **Douglas Entrance** *(Tamiami Tr. and Douglas Rd.)*, called *La Puerta del Sol* (Gate of the Sun), was designed with a series of arcades and complexes to suggest a Spanish town square. Smaller than originally planned, it nevertheless included a 90ft clock tower, grand arch, shops, galleries, apartments and a lavish ballroom. (Renovated, it now houses offices.) Equally elaborate is the **Country Club Prado Entrance** *(Country Club Prado and Tamiami Tr.)*. This 1927 gateway of stuccoed concrete occupies a 240ft length of grassy median at the end of a tree-shaded boulevard. Recalling an Italian Renaissance garden, the symmetrical layout incorporates 20 masonry pillars topped with classical urns and pedestal fountains at both ends of a reflecting pool.

Plazas – Intended to break the predictable grid of house lots, 14 plazas were also created for Coral Gables. Many served as European-style traffic circles, highlighted by fountains, such as the elaborate tiered pedestal supporting an obelisk at **DeSoto Plaza** *(Sevilla Ave. and Granada and DeSoto Blvds.)*.

Another notable landscape feature is the Coral Gables **Water Tower** *(Alhambra Circle, Ferdinand St. and Greenway Ct.)*. Disguised as a lighthouse, this decorative landmark was actually a utility, providing water to the city until 1931. The tower has been restored to its original color and design.

★**Lowe Art Museum** – *1301 Stanford Dr., on University of Miami campus. Take US-1 (S. Dixie Hwy.) south to Stanford Dr.; turn right on Stanford and pass under Metrorail; museum is second building on right. Open year-round Tue-Wed & Fri-Sat 10am-5pm, Thu noon-7pm, Sun noon-5pm. Closed Jan 1 & Dec 25. $5.* ⅊ 🅿 ☎ *305-284-3535. www.lowemuseum.org.* Named for Joe and Emily Lowe, wealthy New Yorkers who donated the funds for the building, the museum was initiated by Miami citizens who wanted to create a space where traveling exhibits could be displayed. Opened in 1952, the museum now showcases a permanent collection of some 8,000 works. Housed in a high-ceilinged one-story structure, expanded in 1996 to 38,600sq ft, this diverse assemblage highlights objects from the pre-Columbian and Greco-Roman periods, Renaissance and Baroque paintings, European masters and 19C-20C American paintings, Native American textiles and jewelry, and African and Asian art. Annual special exhibits complement the permanent collection.

Begin to the left of the spacious, glass-fronted lobby in Bermont Hall, which contains Picasso pottery and American paintings. Pass through a Greco-Roman Antiquities gallery to the Kress Collection of **Renaissance and Baroque art** to see works (14C-17C) by Tintoretto, della Robbia, Guardi, Isenbrandt and Jordaens. The Beaux-Arts Gallery features 19C-20C European and American works; exhibits are rotated twice a year, but always include examples from the museum's important collections of Frank Stella and Roy Lichtenstein paintings.

Off a central garden, several smaller galleries include masks, sculpture, ceramics and beadwork from Africa, Asia and the Americas. A fine **Native American collection** of textiles, baskets and pottery from the Southeast, Southwest and Northwest cultural areas occupies the Barton Gallery. The Green galleries and halls at the rear of the museum showcase contemporary art and changing exhibits.

③ GameWorks

🅺🆂 *See map. 5701 Sunset Dr. in The Shops at Sunset Place.* ☎ *305-667-4263. After 10pm, children under 18 must be accompanied by parent or legal guardian. www.gameworks.com.* At this 31,000sq ft. combination interactive arcade and indoor theme park, noise and flashing lights abound. Attractions include Jurassic Park-The Lost World dinosaur encounters (while you're seated roller-coaster style), simulated Indy 500 and Daytona racing, and the Big Win Zone where prizes are gadgets and stuffed animals. Some games incorporate "vertical reality" technology, wherein free-fall is simulated through mechanical seating and a 24ft-tall screen. The on-site Gameworks Grill serves burgers, pizza, meatloaf dinners and other American fare, while the Arena Bar caters to grown-ups. Don't be surprised if the place is particularly crowded on rainy days. *Other locations in Fort Lauderdale and Ybor City.*

★★**Fairchild Tropical Garden** – *Map p 214. 10901 Old Cutler Rd., 10mi south of downtown. Open year-round daily 9:30am-4:30pm. Tram tours (40min) Mon-Fri 10am-3pm on the hr, weekends 10am-4pm on the hr. Closed Dec 25. $8.* 🍴 ⅊ 🅿 ☎ *305-667-1651. www.fairchildgarden.org.* Set on 83 well-tended acres studded with a series of 12 man-made lakes, the largest botanical garden in the continental US boasts more than 2,500 species of plants and trees from around the world. The gardens, named for plant explorer David Fairchild, opened in 1938. Plant here are grouped by families and arranged in spaces that vary from narrow allées to open beds. A tram tour takes visitors past a sampling of the garden's flora, including 500 species of **palms** and a group of rare **cycads**, a species that dates from the Cretaceous period some 100 million years ago. Tropical vegetation is maintained in a steamy greenhouse; a separate garden nurtures endangered botanical species. The **Gate House Museum of Plant Exploration**, housed in a limestone cottage built in 1939 by the Civilian Conservation Corps, holds interpretive displays that tell the story of botanists (including Fairchild himself) who comb the earth seeking unusual plants. A 2-acre rain forest is under development and a display on the vegetation of the Caribbean is planned. Fairchild's own private estate, **The Kampong**, can be visited in nearby Coconut Grove.

★**Parrot Jungle and Gardens** – 🆔 *Map p 214. 11000 S.W. 57th Ave. Open year-round daily 9:30am-6pm. $15.95.* ✗ ♿ 🅿 ☎ *305-666-7834. www.parrot jungle.com.* A rainbow of vividly colored macaws perched inside the entrance greets visitors to this first-generation Miami tourist attraction, which opened its doors in 1936. The site is home to more than 1,100 exotic birds, including some 80 pink flamingos that frequent **Flamingo Lake**. Within the park, a path winds through lush tropical gardens and a walk-through aviary, past banana trees, orchids, bromeliads and a banyan tree that shades nearly an acre of land. In the amphitheater, trained macaws and cockatoos perform such feats as riding a bicycle across a tightrope and roller skating *(trained-bird shows and wildlife shows are presented 4 times daily; consult schedule for times)*.

By early 2003, Parrot Jungle plans to move to a new site on Watson Island, in Biscayne Bay east of downtown Miami via US-41 (MacArthur Causeway). Blueprints for the new 18-acre, $47-million park include an Everglades exhibit, a children's petting zoo, baby bird and plant nurseries, a 500-seat theater, two amphitheaters, jungle trails and aviaries.

★★COCONUT GROVE *Map pp 232-233*

Lush foliage and banyan trees enhance the tropical feeling of this picturesque village stretching 4mi south of Rickenbacker Causeway along Biscayne Bay. The oldest community in the Miami area, Coconut Grove retains a strong sense of history in its quiet residential neighborhoods, where many of the vine-covered bungalows and Mediterranean-style estates date to the early 20C. By contrast, trendy bars and cafes make the downtown one of Miami's liveliest entertainment spots. Pulsing with activity at night and on weekends, the Grove is also widely known for its Saturday farmers' market and colorful fairs occurring throughout the year. Among the most notable are the **Arts Festival** (late Feb); the **Goombay Festival** (early Jun), a celebration of Bahamian culture; and the **King Mango Strut** (late Dec), a zany parade. Completed in 1987, the $14 million, city-operated **Dinner Key Marina** provides some 600 boat slips complete with electricity, telephone and cable-television hookups. A preservation movement that actively opposes development reflects a continued effort to maintain the distinctive identity of this historic community.

■ The Grove

Cocoanut Grove (spelled with an "a" until 1919) owes its name to Horace Porter, a Connecticut doctor who started a short-lived coconut plantation here in 1873. In 1882 Charles and Isabella Peacock open a hotel called Bay View House (later Peacock Inn); the fashionable hostelry established a sense of social cachet and attracted many winter visitors who returned to build houses of their own.

By 1890 Cocoanut Grove had become the largest town on the south Florida mainland, boasting the first school, library and yacht club in the region. On the west side of town a sizable black Bahamian community took root. These settlers supported themselves by salvaging shipwrecks, manufacturing coontie starch, and working in the local construction and service industries. By the early 20C, estates on the eastern and southern bayfront had become a prime winter address for society figures and affluent industrialists like James Deering. Artists, academics and writers—including Robert Frost—affiliated with the Winter Institute of Literature at the University of Miami were drawn to the town's intellectual community. Alexander Graham Bell and Charles Lindbergh were frequent visitors.

Although Coconut Grove was annexed by the City of Miami in the summer of 1925, the village has not lost its independent character and bohemian flair.

Sights

To fully enjoy this area, reserve a day to see Vizcaya and the nearby Miami Museum of Science and Space Transit Planetarium, and a second day to explore Coconut Grove proper. To shop in the village and tour The Barnacle, park on Grand Ave. or Main Hwy. (metered parking) and walk. Other sights are best visited by car. Tourist information: Coconut Grove Chamber of Commerce ☎ 305-444-7270; www. coconutgrove.com.

★★**Vizcaya** – *3251 S. Miami Ave. Open year-round daily 9:30am-5pm (gardens 5:30pm). Closed Dec 25. $10. ✗ ♿ 🅿 ☎ 305-250-9133. Guided tour covers first-floor rooms. After the tour, visitors are free to visit the second-floor rooms and stroll through the gardens.* Overlooking the calm, blue waters of Biscayne Bay, this ornate Italian Renaissance-style villa and formal gardens embody the fantasy winter retreat of their builder, **James Deering** (1859-1925). The 35-acre estate was raised from a Florida hardwood hammock in 1916. Deering's Vizcaya (a Basque word meaning "elevated place") required 1,000 workers, $15 million and over two years to complete. On Christmas Day

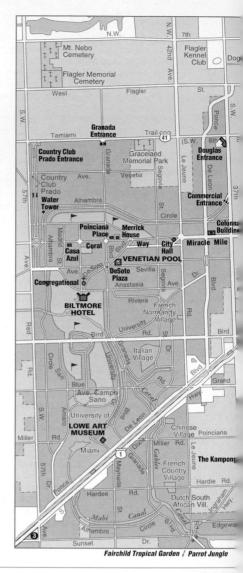

Fairchild Tropical Garden / Parrot Jungle

■ The Men Behind the Mansion

The second son of William Deering, developer of the Deering harvester machine, James joined the family's Illinois-based farm machinery business after graduating from Northwestern University and Massachusetts Institute of Technology. When his company merged with McCormick Harvester Co. in 1902, Deering became vice president of the newly formed International Harvester Co. Like many of the Sunshine State's illustrious snowbirds, ill health first brought Deering to Florida.

In 1912 Deering purchased 180 acres of Miami shoreline. Craving privacy, Deering envisioned a "homey" cottage on the banks of Biscayne Bay. His decorator and art advisor, Paul Chalfin, had grander ideas. A graduate of the École des Beaux-Arts in Paris and former curator at the Boston Museum of Fine Arts, Chalfin accompanied Deering to Europe, where the two men combed old European castles and Italian villas for treasures to fill the house—which had yet to be built. By the time they returned, Deering had amassed such a collection that he realized his house would have to be designed to fit its furnishings instead of the other way around.

For this job, Chalfin hired New York architect F. Burrall Hoffman Jr. Inspired by 15C and 16C villas in the Venetian countryside, Hoffman's design resulted in a triumphal merging of Italian Renaissance style with Florida's tropical landscape. Two floors of rooms surround a central courtyard (now roofed to protect the priceless art within from heat and humidity). An airy loggia follows three sides of the ground floor; second-floor rooms open onto galleries overlooking the courtyard.

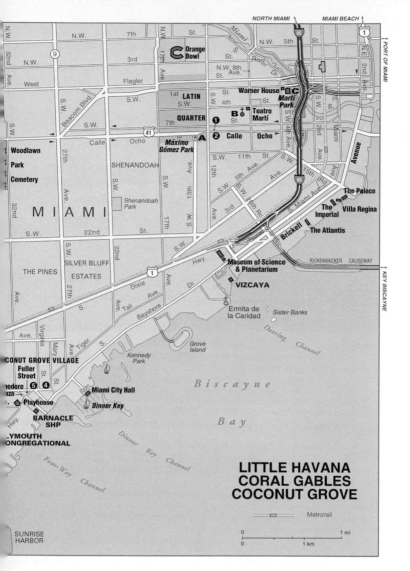

1916, Deering moved into his new 70-room mansion. Deering, who never married, lived at Vizcaya until his death in 1925. The following year, the house and gardens were badly ravaged by the legendary 1926 hurricane. The Deering family hired Paul Chalfin in 1934 to renovate the house and replant the gardens in preparation for opening the house as a museum. But public interest in Vizcaya waned, and in 1945 the family sold 130 acres to the Catholic Church to build a hospital complex. Deering's estate remained in the hands of his heirs—his brother's children—until 1952, when Dade County purchased the villa and its remaining 35 acres for $1 million.

The 34 rooms open to the public incorporate elements of four major styles: Renaissance, Baroque, Rococo and Neoclassical. The Neoclassical **entrance** hall contains hand-blocked c.1814 wallpaper from the Paris workshop of Joseph Dufour. Three pairs of 1C AD Roman marble columns adorn the **Renaissance Hall.** The walls and ceiling of the Italian Rococo **Music Room** are covered with canvas panels hand-painted with a fanciful marine theme. Overlooking the gardens, the **Tea Room** is actually an enclosed loggia, featuring a 17C Nubian marble mantelpiece and a modeled ceiling with Neoclassical motifs. The room's stained-glass wall displays Vizcaya's emblematic sea horse and caravel.

Reclusive Deering lived in a suite of rooms on the second floor. His elegant sitting room and bedroom incorporate elements from the Neoclassical and Adam styles. Also of note is the second-floor **dining room**, whose walls are covered by murals of nautical theme.

The **East Loggia,** with its striking colored-marble floor, opens onto the terrace that fronts the bay. Just off the terrace sits the **Stone Barge,** an ornamental Venetian-style breakwater where Deering once tied his luxurious 80ft yacht, Nepenthe. The barge is embellished with sculpture by A. Stirling Calder (father of renowned 20C sculptor Alexander Calder) and bordered by striped replicas of Venetian gondola poles.

Bayside View of Vizcaya

More than 10 acres of formal gardens flank the south side of the house. Colombian-born architect Diego Suarez planned the fan-shaped Italian hill garden with its curvilinear parterres. Here tropical plants replace their European counterparts (i.e., clipped jasmine hedges substitute for traditional boxwood). The garden's central axis draws the eye up a water stairway to a two-room baroque casino, or garden house, set on an artificial hill. Semicircular pools and domed stone gazebos define the garden's east-west axis.

The farm section of the estate is located across South Miami Avenue from the villa. Residences for members of Vizcaya's managerial staff were located here, as were stables, a dairy and poultry house. A $10 million restoration of 11 buildings at the Farm Village is currently underway.

Miami Museum of Science & Space Transit Planetarium – *3280 S. Miami Ave., across from Vizcaya. Open year-round daily 10am-6pm. Closed Thanksgiving Day & Dec 25. $10.* ♿ ⚑ ☏ *305-646-4200. www.miamisci.org.* Housed in a Mediterranean-style building decorated with arches and barrel tiles, the museum features over 150 exhibits that allow visitors to touch objects, climb a rock wall and dig for fossils while learning about everything from gravity to mastodon teeth. Out back, the Wildlife Center—which doubles as a rehabilitation facility for birds of prey—displays wood storks, tortoises, pythons and boa constrictors. The adjacent planetarium offers astronomy and laser shows.

In the next decade, expansion plans call for a proposed Science Center of the Americas, in association with the Smithsonian Institution, to be constructed on a four-acre site in downtown Miami, pending adequate funding.

Miami City Hall – 3500 Pan American Dr. (off S. Bayshore Dr.). Located on **Dinner Key**, a small island attached to the mainland by landfill, this two-story Streamline Moderne gem with a flat roof and glass-block windows was designed in 1933 as the seaplane terminal for Pan American Airways. (Note the roofline frieze of winged globes, rising suns and eagles.) In the peak years of the late 1930s, flights left for 32 foreign countries and some 50,000 passengers per year passed through making this the largest international port of entry in the US. (Charles Lindbergh was one of the early pilots.) The terminal originally featured a second-story restaurant and promenade deck. Watching the spectacle of large flying clipper ships taking off and landing in Biscayne Bay—tended by ground crews clad in bathing suits—was a popular weekend pastime. The last flight left Dinner Key in 1945 and the building has served as the city hall since 1954.

★**Coconut Grove Village** – *Centered on the intersection of Grand Ave. and Mai. Hwy.* Once a sleepy village with a single grocery store, the downtown has undergone several transformations in recent decades. Galleries, coffeehouses and head shops abounded in the 1960s, replaced in the '70s by tony boutiques stocked with Gucci handbags. Today sidewalk cafes and clothing shops cater to the under-40 crowd, attracting local students, professionals and tourists alike. Cultural offbeat are now a relatively rare sight, but don't be surprised to encounter occasional gangs of leather-clad bikers roaring through the village on weekends.

A mélange of high-end shops and boutiques appealing to "Generation X" clientele fill **Streets of Mayfair** and **CocoWalk**. Cafes line **Commodore Plaza** and the north end of Main Highway, while interesting boutiques are tucked into **Fuller Street**.

At the south end of town is the 1926 **Coconut Grove Playhouse** *(3500 Main Hwy.)*. Twisted columns flank the Moorish-style entry of the substantial three-story corner building, originally a movie house. Current offerings in the 1,100-seat theater and more intimate cabaret room include experimental dramas as well as Broadway-bound musicals and plays. *For information on performances* ☎ *305-442-2662.*

★★**Barnacle State Historic Park** – *3485 Main Hwy. Open year-round Fri-Mon 9am-4pm. Interior of house by guided tour (1hr) only. Closed Jan 1, Thanksgiving Day & Dec 25. $1.* ☎ *305-448-9445. www.gate.net/barnacle.* This five-acre bayfront site preserves one of the last patches of tropical hardwood hammock in Coconut Grove, along with the 1891 home of **Ralph Middleton Munroe**. An accomplished sailor and yacht designer, Munroe came here in 1877 on a sailing trip and returned four years later to stay. In 1886 he purchased 40 acres for $400. To frame his new house, Munroe used lumber salvaged from a shipwreck. Nicknamed "The Barnacle" for its octagonal center that tapers to a small open-air vent, the five-room, hip-roofed structure features a Bahamian design well-suited to the Grove's tropical climate. A veranda covers two sides of the square structure, providing shade and catching prevailing breezes; the cupola atop the hipped roof draws hot air up through the central octagonal room inside. In 1908 Munroe enlarged the single-story house by jacking it up and adding a new ground floor in concrete underneath.

Virtually unchanged since Munroe's day, the house remained in the family until the 1970s and still contains the original furnishings. The 1926 **boathouse**, showcasing Munroe's shipbuilding tools, is also open to visitors. Moored just offshore is a replica of the *Egret*, a shallow-draft sailboat called a sharpie, ideal for navigating the bay waters. Munroe designed the original 28ft *Egret* himself.

④ Streets of Mayfair
Map p 233. Grand Ave. between Virginia and Mary Sts. ☎ *305-448-1700.* A Borders bookstore anchors the corner of this complex, a colorful array of high-end shops, restaurants and movie theaters that occupies an entire block on Grand Avenue. The vine-draped, pink and white concrete extravaganza was designed in 1979 by Grove architect Kenneth Treister (whose work includes the Holocaust Memorial in Miami Beach) and originally housed boutiques reportedly used to launder South American drug money. Be sure to explore the interior courtyard *(enter from Virginia St.)*, reminiscent of the style of architect Antonio Gaudí in Barcelona. Treister adorned this courtyard with lush greenery, multilevel walkways, tiled fountains and striking copper bird sculptures.

⑤ CocoWalk
Map p 233. 3015 Grand Ave. on the west side of Virginia St. ☎ *305-444-0777.* Opened in 1991, the U-shaped ensemble of bars, chain stores, clubs and movie theaters embraces an open plaza with a central cupola-topped pavilion. Pink stucco and three levels of loggias and balconies give the mall a cheerful tropical air. Stop in Café Tu Tu Tango to try the restaurant's tapas-style offerings and view the cafe's array of works by local artists at the same time.

Charles Avenue – Once called Evangelist Street for its many churches, this quiet road runs west through the oldest black community on mainland Florida. Known as Kebo, the area was settled in the 1880s by Bahamians who came north by way of Key West. These pioneers helped northern settlers cultivate tropical greenery in the village and brought many of the seeds for the soursops, sugar apples and Barbados cherries that thrive here today. The avenue is notable for its early 20C **shotgun houses**. A drive west to the corner of Douglas Road brings you to one of the first cemeteries in South Florida, used since 1906. Note the unusual two-headed images on the Bahamian gravestones.

Farther down Douglas Road, just south of Main Highway, is **The Kampong** *(4013 Douglas Rd.; visit by appointment only second Sat of each month; $10;* ☎ *305-442-7169; www.ntbg.org)*, botanist David Fairchild's private estate and garden. Fairchild first introduced soybeans and many exotic fruits to North American soil; the original plantings are in this garden.

★**Plymouth Congregational Church** – *3429 Devon Rd. Visit by appointment only. Open Sun for church service only.* ⟨⟩ ☐ ☎ *305-444-6521.* This 1917 Spanish Colonial-style church was modeled after a 16C mission in Mexico, recalled by the

CocoWalk

broad facade with symmetrical bell towers flanking a curving roof parapet. Of loca oolitic limestone, the building and massive cloister walls were reportedly built by a single Spanish mason using nothing more than a hatchet and a plumb line. The walnut door (c.1600) is thought to be from a monastery in the Pyrenees moun tains. Tucked into the charming banyan-shaded grounds are a small meditatior garden, a rose garden and a tropical cloister garden.

Moved from its original site near the Peacock Inn, the one-room **schoolhouse** at the north end of the property dates back to 1887 *(open by appointment only)*. Buil of lumber from a salvaged shipwreck, it initially housed a Sunday school run by Isabella Peacock. In 1889 it became the first public school in what is now Miami Dade County. The bell is original.

KEY BISCAYNE *Map p 214*

Locals enjoy the 7mi-long barrier island, located 2mi south of downtown Miam as a haven for water sports and bicycling and as a residential neighborhood. Firs named Santa Marta by Ponce de León in 1513, Key Biscayne caught the public' attention when President Richard Nixon bought a vacation home here in the 1970s It is now an affluent community boasting luxury accommodations, fine restaurant and some of the state's prettiest beaches.

In 1825 the Cape Florida Lighthouse was erected at the tip of the key to guid ships safely through the Florida Channel. In the early 1900s, Dr. Willian J. Matheson dredged a yacht basin and planted thousands of coconut trees The Rickenbacker Causeway opened in 1947 with a then-pricey 25-cent toll *(no $1)* and linked Miami to the island across Biscayne Bay. Key Biscayne experience a construction surge in the 1960s and high rises sprang up next to working-clas residential neighborhoods.

Today residents of Key Biscayne—now its own incorporated city—enjoy a slov pace bolstered by a small but thriving commercial center. The southern end ceded to two popular beachfront parks, Crandon and Bill Baggs. Head west o the causeway toward Miami for spectacular **views★** of downtown and its comme cial artery, Brickell Avenue. *Tourist information: Key Biscayne Chamber c Commerce ☎ 305-361-5207, www.keybiscaynechamber.org.*

Sights

★**Miami Seaquarium** – Kids *4400 Rickenbacker Causeway, 5mi east of the Ke Biscayne tollbooth. Open year-round daily 9:30am-6pm. $24.45. ✗ ₺ ▯ ☎ 30. 361-5705. www.miamiseaquarium.com.* In its late 1950s heyday, this 37-ac marine-life park served as the set for the TV series *Flipper* and home to its sta a dolphin. Today, shows are offered daily *(see brochure for times)*. Lolita, the fiv ton star of the **killer whale show**, draws the largest crowds with her graceful leap Nearby, visitors can watch fish and sharks being hand-fed by divers in a reef tan A new wildlife exhibit, Crocodile Flats, opened in 2000, housing some two-doze Nile crocodiles. The main building provides two levels to view some 10,000 var eties of aquatic life. At the back of the park, sharks swim in an open-air chann that is crossed by several bridges. The world's first controlled manatee breedir program—a joint effort with the University of Miami marine lab next door—also takes place here. In the planning stages is a $17.5 million complex to house four temperature-controlled pools and a new stadium for spectators.

★**Bill Baggs Cape Florida State Park** – *1200 S. Crandon Blvd., 7mi from Key Biscayne tollbooth. Park hrs & fees p 350.* ⚠ ✕ 🅿 ☎ *305-361-5811.* A mile of Biscayne Bay beachfront attracts locals to this secluded 412-acre park on the south end of Key Biscayne. Additionally, a new 74-acre wetlands area has been created. The park owes its name to the newspaper editor of the now-defunct *Miami News*, who encouraged the land's preservation. The original 95ft-high brick **Cape Florida Lighthouse** was constructed in 1825; tours of the keeper's quarters and kitchen follow presentation of a 14min video *(visit by 1hr guided tour only—arrive 30min early; Thu-Mon 10am & 1pm; $2)*. During the Seminole War in 1836, Indians set fire to the structure. In 1846, engineers rebuilt the tower and, in 1855, raised it 30ft. The light was destroyed again in 1861—this time by Confederate sympathizers. Relit after the war, the beacon operated until 1878 when it was replaced by the Iron Fowey Rock Lighthouse set in the reef some 7mi southeast of Cape Florida. The light is operational again, serving as a navigational aid. The hardwood hammock bordering the beach has been replanted with such native species as sea grape trees and wax myrtle. A bicycle trail loops through the park, and a 1.5mi nature trail weaves through an adjacent 63-acre resurrected wetland.

GREATER MIAMI NORTH *Map p 214*

During the boom years of the 1920s, planned subdivisions, including Morningside, El Portal and Miami Shores, were developed as theme communities, often featuring Spanish or Mediterranean Revival-style architecture. Many of the other new North Miami communities stood unfinished after the bottom fell out of the real-estate market in 1926.

Today Greater Miami North is largely residential, a mix of luxury apartment houses, modern suburban developments and remnants of the older, established neighborhoods. The fashionable district of Aventura, just north of Lehman Causeway, comprises luxury resorts and the upscale **Aventura Mall**, containing fine shops and department stores.

Sights

★**Museum of Contemporary Art** – *770 N.E. 125th St., North Miami. Open year-round Tue-Sat 11am-5pm, Sun noon-5pm. Closed major holidays. $5.* ♿ 🅿 ☎ *305-893-6211. www.mocanomi.org.* Architect Charles Gwathmey combined cubes and cylinders in designing the simple but elegant 23,000sq ft building on palm-studded grounds within the North Miami civic complex. Joan Lehman—wife of Congressman Bill Lehman and a sculptor in her own right—was the leading financial sponsor of the museum, which opened in 1996. Shown on a rotating basis, the more than 350-piece permanent collection includes works by Jasper Johns, Roy Lichtenstein, Robert Rauschenberg and other well-recognized artists, but also contains mixed media installations, kinetic sculpture and videos by artists such as Dennis Oppenheim and Martin Kersels. Changing exhibits feature other artists like French sculptor Annette Messager, Brazilian performance artist Tunga and American pop artist Keith Haring.

★★**Ancient Spanish Monastery** – *16711 W. Dixie Hwy., North Miami Beach. Take Biscayne Blvd. (US-1) north to N. Miami Beach Blvd. Turn left, then right on W. Dixie Hwy. Open year-round Mon-Sat 9am-5pm, Sun 1:30pm-5pm. Closed major holidays. $5.* ♿ 🅿 ☎ *305-945-1461. www.spanishmonastery.org.* Nestled on a woodsy site, the Cloisters of St. Bernard of Clairvaux provides an in-depth look at a 12C monastery. This superb example of early Gothic architecture, named for the influential leader of the Cistercian Monks, was completed in the Spanish province

---

■ A Giant Jigsaw Puzzle

Shipped in hay in numbered boxes, the stones were quarantined by US officials (hoof-and-mouth disease had broken out in Segovia). The hay was destroyed and the haphazardly repacked stones were left in crates for over 25 years. After Hearst's death in 1951, two South Florida developers bought the stones, hoping to reconstruct the cloisters as a tourist attraction.

All 36,000 stones—some weighing 3,000 pounds—were spread over the 20-acre site. Allan Carswell, a renowned stone mason, was hired to supervise the process of fitting the stones together, using photographs that Hearst had taken of the intact monastery. Nineteen months and $1.5 million later, the reconstructed cloisters opened in 1954, only to be sold in 1964. The complex now houses an Episcopal church.

of Segovia in 1141. Nearly eight centuries later it was disassembled and moved to the US by **William Randolph Hearst** *(see box p 237)*. A wealthy American newspaperman and collector extraordinaire, Hearst purchased the monastery in 1925, planning to reconstruct his "greatest art treasure" on the grounds of San Simeon, his lavish California estate *(see Michelin THE GREEN GUIDE California)*, but his plans went awry.

Visitors enter the Ancient Spanish Monastery, as it is locally known, through a 200-pound wrought-iron gate crowned with the Latin inscription meaning "These Sacred Cistercian Walls." On the southern perimeter of the lush side garden stands the entrance to a long cloister. The top of its portal is adorned with the figure of Mary, the mother of Christ, encircled by angels. A series of ribbed arches form the cloister's vault; tile now covers the floors that once consisted of small stones.

The **Chapel of St. Bernard de Clairvaux**, which served as the monks' refectory, occupies the first corridor; the small iron bell at the entrance once called the brothers to meals. Above the altar, two circular stained-glass windows, depicting scenes from the Book of Revelation written by St. John, are as old as the monastery. They represent two of only three known **telescopic windows** in existence (so-named for the three rings of receding frames that encase the windows, creating a telescopic effect). In the middle of the complex stands a **prayer well** composed of elements of an AD 1C Roman temple.

A life-size statue of King Alfonso VIII stands at the end of the first corridor; diagonally across the courtyard is a statue of his grandfather, King Alfonso VII of Castile and Leon, under whose auspices the monastery was initially built. Located midway along the second corridor, the **Chapter House** formed part of the original monastery. The medieval pink-limestone, Gothic-style altar (at the corner past the Chapter House) was carved in Cannes, France. Ten corbels along the cloister walls—part of Hearst's art collection—portray shields of 12C Segovia noble and royal families who pledged their allegiance to both the Catholic Church and the Spanish king.

SOUTH MIAMI-DADE COUNTY *Map p 202*

Isolated by the marshy fringes of the Everglades, the southern portion of Miami-Dade County (below Coral Reef Drive) was among the last parts of Florida to be settled and remains a separate community in both spirit and appearance. While the fast-growing region has its share of tract housing and new shopping malls, its rural western section is still dominated by produce farms, lime groves and tropical plant nurseries, preserving a distinctive small-town feel virtually nonexistent elsewhere in the Miami area.

Development came with the southern expansion of the Florida East Coast Railway from Miami in the early 1900s. Homestead, now the largest city in South Miami-Dade, was named in 1904 when flat railcars full of building materials labeled "homestead country" arrived at the end of the line. The region's fertile soil, produced by draining the swampy Glades, proved ideal for beans, tomatoes, avocados and other cash crops. By the 1950s South Miami-Dade was one of the top vegetable-producing areas in the US.

Its agricultural economy was devastated in 1992, when Hurricane Andrew spent its full fury in and around Homestead. Recovery was aided by the $7.9 billion Hurricane Relief Bill, the largest federal disaster package of loans and grants in US history. Funds provided a face-lift to **Homestead's Old Downtown** *(38mi southwest of downtown Miami)*, the historic business district where recently restored early-20C storefronts lining Krome Avenue recapture the original character of this former railroad town.

Sights

★★ **Miami Metrozoo** – [Kids] *12400 S.W. 152nd St. 18mi from downtown Miami. Take Florida's Turnpike south to Exit 16. Go west on S.W. 152nd St. and follow signs to zoo. Open year-round daily 9:30am-5:30pm (admission gates close at 4pm). Narrated tram ride ($2) tours the zoo and offers behind-the-scenes glimpse of hatcheries and breeding pens. $8.95* ✕ ♿ ▯ ☎ *305-251-0400. www.miami metrozoo.com.* The best way to see the zoo is to wander at your own pace along the 3mi loop trail that winds through the park. An elevated monorail also makes regular runs around the grounds, offering its riders a bird's-eye view of the animal habitats.

Occupying 290 acres of landscaped park, this popular cageless zoo specializes in tropical species adaptable to South Florida's hot climate. Some 900 reptiles, birds and mammals—primarily from Asia, Africa and Australia—are showcased. Camouflaged moats and other inconspicuous barriers separate zoo visitors from the animals, who roam freely in natural habitats.

Among the highlights are an affectionate band of **lowland gorillas** (a walk-in viewing cave permits a close-up look) and a group of stunning **Bengal tigers**, whose habitat

Bengal Tiger at Metrozoo

© Stephen Frink

features a replica of Cambodia's 13C Angkor Wat ruins. Animal feedings and wildlife shows occur throughout the day *(check brochure for times)*. **PAWS**, a children's petting zoo, is also a popular attraction. Part of a recent $3 million expansion, Dr. Wilde's World holds a children's playground and exhibit area, complete with frogs, snakes and spiders. The tropical free-flight aviary housing some 300 Asian birds is being rebuilt after suffering hurricane destruction in 1992 *(projected reopening is 2003)*.

Gold Coast Railroad Museum – *12450 S.W. 152nd St., across the road from Metrozoo. Open year-round Mon-Fri 11am-3pm, Sat 11am-4pm. Closed major holidays. $5.* 🅿 ☏ *305-253-0063. www.goldcoast-railroad.org.* A self-guided tour of this museum's grounds reveals numerous historic, renovated railroad cars, including the *California Zephyr*. A highlight is the Pullman car *Ferdinand Magellan*, used by presidents Franklin Roosevelt, Harry Truman, Dwight Eisenhower and Ronald Reagan. A collection of train parts and related memorabilia are also on display.

★**Coral Castle** – *28655 S. Dixie Hwy., 30mi south of Miami (2mi north of Homestead). Open year-round daily 9am-6pm (Fri & Sat 8pm). Closed Dec 25. $9.75.* ♿ 🅿 ☏ *305-248-6344. www.coralcastle.com.* Shrouded with an air of mystery concerning its construction, this three-acre mansion and monolithic sculpture garden was crafted of more than 1,100 tons of coral rock (oolitic limestone) beginning in 1918. Ed Leedskalnin, a 5ft-tall, 110-pound Latvian immigrant, took 20 years to create the sculptures, reportedly without using any mechanical equipment. To escape the invasion of a new subdivision, reclusive Leedskalnin moved the carvings a distance of 10mi to their present site in 1936. Coral Castle has been listed on the National Register of Historic Places since 1984.

Be sure to see the movable **Nine-Ton Gate**; Polaris Telescope, a 25ft-high, 30-ton rock telescope aimed toward the North Star; the 20ft-long Florida Table, carved in the shape of the state and surrounded by 10,000-pound coral rock chairs; and the two-story tower where Leedskalnin lived in spartan quarters upstairs and labored with crude tools in the room below.

★**Biscayne National Park** – *East end of N. Canal Dr. (S.W. 328th St.) in Homestead. 38mi south of downtown Miami. Take Florida Turnpike south to Exit 2 (Campbell Dr.). Drive east to Kingman Road, then south to S.W. 328th St. (N. Canal Dr.). Turn east again and travel 6mi to Dante Fascell Visitor Center (open year-round daily 8:30am-5pm; closed Dec 25). Park grounds open year-round daily 8am-5:30pm. Closed Dec 25.* △ ♿ 🅿 ☏ *305-230-7275. www.nps.gov/bisc.* The largest marine park in the US was established in 1980 to help protect a 275sq mi area of coastal wetlands, mangrove shorelines, coral reefs and 32 small barrier islands (keys). The protected waters stretch 26mi south from Key Biscayne to Card Sound near Key Largo, running between the coastline and the underwater continental shelf.

Star attractions are the **reefs★★★**, located about 10mi offshore. Here warm Gulf Stream currents nurture some 50 species of living coral that create a hospitable environment for loggerhead turtles, spiny lobsters, sponges and flamboyant tropical fish, including the brilliant rock beauty and parrot fish.

Biscayne's **Dante Fascell Visitor Center** at Convoy Point features life-size dioramas of the park's habitat areas. Three videos—an overview, a park history and the effects of 1992's Hurricane Andrew—are shown in a theater. Interpretive exhibits are displayed along a short bayside walking trail from which fishing is permitted. Canoe rentals are available for bay excursions. A dive shop offers scuba and snorkeling rentals for visitors venturing to the Atlantic reefs, which are accessible only by boat.

Weather permitting, park-sponsored reef trips leave from the visitor center. A glass-bottom boat tour (daily 10am; round-trip 3hrs; $19.95), snorkeling trip (daily 1:30pm & Mon-Thu 10am; round-trip 3hrs; $29.95; bring swimsuit and towel; gear and snorkeling vests provided) and scuba-diving excursion (Fri-Sun 8:30am; round-trip 4hrs 30min) are offered. Reservations recommended for all boat excursions; Biscayne National Underwater Park Inc. ☎ 305-230-1100; www.nps.gov/bisc.

In winter (when mosquitoes are less numerous), boat transportation is offered with reservations to Elliott Key, 7mi offshore. Camping and nature walks are available on the island. To bird-watch or explore estuaries along the main coast, you can rent a canoe at the visitor center at Convoy Point.

Fruit & Spice Park – *24801 S.W. 187th Ave. at S.W. 248th St. in Homestead. 27mi southwest of downtown Miami. Open year-round daily 10am-5pm. Closed Dec 25. $3.50.* ♿ 🅿 ☎ *305-247-5727.* Opened in 1944, this unusual tropical park rebounded from Hurricane Andrew with a flourish. Hundreds of varieties of exotic fruit and nut trees, vegetables, herbs and spices have been replanted in geographical theme areas across its 32 acres, with mango and avocado orchards among the most interesting groves. There also are such striking specimens as the Panama candle tree, named for its long yellow fruit. Future plans call for the creation of rice paddies and a small lake circled by a motorized tram. An interesting gift shop offers an array of delicacies, including canned jackfruit, lychee, sugarcane and palm nuts. Workshops on tropical plants and edible oddities are offered weekly.

MIAMI BEACH★★★

Population 87,933
Map p 244
Tourist Information: www.ci.miami-beach.fl.us ☎ 305-673-7400

Touted as one of the country's great tropical paradises, Miami Beach is justifiably famed for its fabulous palm-studded shoreline, eccentric architecture and colorful local residents. Built on dreams and speculation, this is an island in perpetual transition, where the atmosphere can shift from shabby to chic in a single block. Despite stubborn pockets of poverty, many faded neighborhoods are staging comebacks. The rejuvenated Art Deco Historic District, with its fashionable clubs and boutiques, draws its share of domestic and international visitors.

Geographical Notes

A separate community from Miami, the City of Miami Beach occupies a narrow barrier island (7mi long and 1.5mi wide) 2.5mi off the mainland, along with 16 islets scattered in Biscayne Bay. Dredging and land-fill have reconfigured the main island, where mangrove swamps once covered the entire area west of present-day Washington Avenue. Fisher Island, located at the southern tip, was created in 1905 when the Government Cut shipping channel sliced through to link Biscayne Bay with the Atlantic. The famous **South Beach** area *(below 23rd St.)* and **Art Deco District** are reached directly by MacArthur Causeway, which passes the exclusive residential neighborhoods on man-made Star, Palm and Hibiscus Islands, and offers a great view of the enormous cruise ships that dock in the Port of Miami.

Historical Notes

In 1912 New Jersey horticulturist **John C. Collins** formed the Miami Beach Improvement Co. to raise capital for a trans-bay bridge. When funds ran short, **Carl Fisher**—an Indiana automobile magnate who built the Indianapolis Speedway in 1909—stepped in with a loan. In return Fisher received 200 acres from the ocean to the bay south of the 2.5mi Collins Bridge (now the Venetian Causeway).
Two Miami bank presidents, brothers **John and James Lummus**, laid out their first subdivision, offering small lots and modest bungalows. Fisher founded his own realty company and ensured a steady stream of sunseekers to his higher-priced tropical paradise by financing a paved road from Chicago to Miami; his famed **Dixie Highway** opened to great fanfare in 1915. That same year, Collins, Fisher and the Lummuses merged their companies and soon afterwards incorporated their land as the City of Miami Beach.
By 1921 five luxury hotels provided lodging for those who could afford it. By day polo grounds, golf courses and tennis courts offered diversion. At night locals flocked to the gambling and bootleg liquor operations hidden in the back rooms of nightclubs, hoping to catch a glimpse of **Al Capone**, the notorious Chicago gangster who bought a house on Palm Island in 1928.
The end followed the crash. The area boomed again in the late 1930s due to a resurgence of tourism. In 1936 alone, some 36 hotels and 110 apartment houses were built in the new Art Deco style in South Miami Beach.
Around 1947, gangsters began buying up estates north of 23rd Street, breaking the zoning code in order to build big hotels. Miami's "Gold Coast" strip enjoyed its heyday in the 1950s and '60s, when hotels like the famous Fontainebleau flourished, then slipped into an economic decline that left many faded resorts in its wake.

★★ART DECO HISTORIC DISTRICT *Map p 244*

Listed on the National Register of Historic Places in 1979, this enclave of small-scale Art Deco hotels and apartment houses dating from the late 1920s to the early 1940s amounts to the largest concentration of architecture of its kind in the world. The official district measures about one square mile and is roughly bounded by the Atlantic Ocean on the east, Lenox Avenue on the west, Sixth Street on the south and Dade Boulevard along the Collins Canal to the north. People-watching is a prime pastime here in SoBe (local slang for South Beach), now a magnet for fashion models, designers and assorted glitterati. The real stars, however, are the buildings themselves.

Architectural Heritage – As new investment focused on north Miami Beach after World War II, the south grew increasingly shabby and economic decline was firmly entrenched by the 1960s. In 1966, however, a retrospective of the International Exposition of Modern Decorative and Industrial Arts held in Paris in 1925 sparked a renewed interest in the Art Deco style. (The term "Art Deco" was coined at this time.)
A decade later, **Barbara Baer Capitman** and **Leonard Horowitz**, two local design professionals, formed the Miami Design Preservation League to identify significant architecture in Miami Beach. The area's ensuing 1979 designation as a National

Marlin Hotel, Collins Avenue

Register Historic District was remarkable in that the roughly 800 Art Deco build-ings included were only about 40 years old—and not of an age typically considered historic. Following the 1980 Mariel boatlift, when hundreds of Cuban prisoners were shunted off to South Beach, much of the established population fled and the Art Deco buildings—regarded as tacky and outdated—began to crumble.

Fueled by the efforts of Capitman and Horowitz, preservation of the Deco District began in earnest in the 1980s and continues to this day. Because National Regis-ter listing does not prevent demolition, several exceptional buildings have been lost

■ Art Deco Style Defined

The Art Deco Historic District is especially remarkable for its continuity of architectural scale and style. This occurred because South Beach of the 1930s was redeveloped rapidly over a short period by a relatively small group of like-minded designers—most notably architects **L. Murray Dixon**, **Henry Hohauser**, **Albert Anis**, **Robert Swartburg** and **Roy France**. Although the majority of structures in the district illustrate Art Deco designs, about a third were built in the Mediterranean Revival style. The 1930 **Casa Casuarina** *(1114 Ocean Dr.)*—renovated as the grand palazzo-style home of the late clothing designer Gianni Versace—is one of the best remaining examples *(the mansion is slated to open as an ultra-luxury suite hotel in 2002)*.

Derived from the minimalist **International Style** that originated in post-World War I Europe, Art Deco used decorative stylized elements to embellish simple, massive forms. Reveling in its own sun-washed locale, Miami Deco went a step further, incorporating flamingos, herons, palm trees and other evocative tropical motifs into exuberant door grills, bas-relief plaques, murals and etched windows of frosted glass. The timing of these joyful designs—accented with neon and brightly colored trim—was ideal. Concrete-block buildings were relatively cheap to construct and allowed the new South Beach designers (many of whom were trained as engineers) to experiment with machine-age design.

to new development. Exterior changes and paint colors of new construction are, however, subject to approval by a local review board. The current trend for bright tropical hues is somewhat controversial, as the original Art Deco buildings were painted white and trimmed in primary colors.

Many Art Deco buildings in the Historic District, exemplified by **1244 Ocean Drive** (originally the Leslie hotel, 1937, Albert Anis) *(currently under renovation)* and **650 Ocean Drive** (formerly the Imperial hotel, 1939, L. Murray Dixon, but now part of the Park Central Hotel), tend to have an angular look, with symmetrical, stepped-back facades and strong vertical banding and bas-relief decoration. The 11-story St. Moritz *(1565 Collins Ave.)*, designed by Roy France in 1939, stretches upward with a soaring tower that houses elevators and mechanical works.

In contrast to the angularity of these Deco structures, the later **Streamline Moderne style** featured aerodynamic imagery; horizontal racing stripes and wraparound corners reflected a fascination with speed and motion fostered by contemporary advances in transportation and industrial design. In an unabashed imitation of an ocean liner, for example, a building might gain portholes, periscope-like air ducts and tubular railings, as seen in the 1930s **Beach Patrol Station** *(1001 Ocean Dr.)* designed by Robert Taylor. The patrol station now forms the rear facade of the **Oceanfront Auditorium**, which was added in the 1950s.

1 Deco Memorabilia
See map. If you're fond of all things Deco, or if you simply want to support a worthy cause, stop in at the beachfront shop run by the **Miami Design Preservation League** *(1001 Ocean Dr. at 10th St; ☎ 305-672-2014; www.mdpl.org).* Inside you'll find a bounty of arty souvenirs promoting the historic district as well as Miami Beach: hotel-shaped mugs with palm-tree handles, fake flamingoes, Art Deco posters, photo postcards, picture frames, coffee-table books, model cars and toys, bakelite jewelry, journals and notecards, writing pens and logo-laden ball caps and t-shirts. A recent expansion has added sales space, particularly for a sizable stock of books. Proceeds go to the League's ongoing preservation and publicity efforts. The store also serves as a welcome center and departure point for the League's many guided tours of the area. The volunteer staff can answer most questions about the district, so don't be hesitant to pose a question.

Sights

South Beach is best navigated by foot. Parking is by meter (quarters only) with a strictly enforced 2hr limit. The Miami Design Preservation League (MDPL) offers walking tours that depart from the Art Deco Welcome Center (near Oceanfront Auditorium), 1001 Ocean Dr. (year-round Thu 6:30pm & Sat 10:30am; 1hr 30min; $10) ☎ 305-672-2014, www.mdpl.org. MDPL bike tours depart from Miami Beach Bicycle Center, 6015th St. (year-round on 3rd Sun of each month 10:30am; 1hr 30min; $10 & $10 bike rental). An annual Art Deco Weekend, featuring special programs and lectures, is held in South Beach in January.

★★**Ocean Drive** – Along this lively north-south boulevard bordering the Atlantic Ocean beats the heart of the SoBe scene. By day locals and tourists nosh at shaded sidewalk cafes, while scantily clad youths streak by on in-line skates and willowy models pose for fashion shoots. At night vivid neon signs beckon revelers to some of Miami's hottest bars and dance clubs. Across the street lies fabulous **Ocean Beach**⚐⚐, refurbished and widened as part of a multimillion-dollar city project in 1982. **Lummus Park**, a magnet for teenage skaters and elderly dog-walkers alike, runs along the beach from 1st to 15th Streets. Located in the park is the nautically inspired Oceanfront Auditorium, which houses the **Art Deco Welcome Center**, an information center *(1001 Ocean Dr., ☎ 305-531-3484)* stocked with books and souvenirs. Recently the center opened a research/interpretation space on the lower level of Oceanfront Auditorium for an indepth look at the Art Deco Historic District.

The park offers a great **view**★ of Ocean Drive and its pastel parade of Art Deco hotels. The seven-story, blue-tinted **Park Central** *(no. 640)*, designed by Henry Hohauser in 1937, displays the characteristic symmetrical facade with vertical banding, steel corner windows (designed to maximize breezes in pre-air-conditioning days) and shaded central entrance. Notable for its horizontal racing stripes and futuristic double-faced tower, the yellow-and-blue-painted **Breakwater** *(no. 940)* shares a pool with the 1935 **Edison**. This Hohauser building *(no. 960)* designed with a ground-floor arcade, arched windows and three-story twisted colonnette, recalls the area's earlier Mediterranean Revival architecture.

Bal Harbour Shops, Fontainebleau Hilton

Miami City Ballet

BASS MUSEUM OF ART

COLLINS

Library

PARK

Plymouth

Collins Park Hotel

N. Bay Rd.

Bayshore Golf Course

N. Meridian Ave.

Prairie Ave.

Dade Ave.

Canal

Center Dr.

Blvd.

23rd St.

22nd St.

21st St.

20th St.

Sunset Dr.

Alton Rd.

Michigan Ave.

Collins Ave.

HOLOCAUST MEMORIAL

Miami Beach Convention Center

19th St.

18th St.

VENETIAN CAUSEWAY

Ave. Rd.

Dade Ave.

Ave.

Ave.

Convention

Jackie Gleason Theater of the Performing Arts

COLLINS AVENUE

OCEAN BEACH

City Hall

18th St.

17th St.

17th

St.

Ritz Plaza

Delano

National

Alton

Lincoln

Jefferson

Meridian

La.

17th

James Ave.

COLLINS

Sterling Building

Lincoln Theatre

West

Lincoln   Road   Mall

Lincoln   Rd.

Colony Theater

Artcenter South Florida

16th

St.

16th St.

ART   DECO

Ave.

Ave.

Ave.

Washington

SOUTH

15th

SOUTH

Lenox

Michigan

St.

Espanola   Way

ESPANOLA WAY

A1A

15th St.

OCEAN

14th St.

14th   Pl.

School

DRIVE

Flamingo Park

Meridian

14th St.

Euclid

US Post Office

Ave.

Cavalier

13th St.

Pennsylvania

13th St.

St.

Cardozo

Carlyle

12th St.

Tennis Stadium

Drexel

12th St.

P

1244

The Tides

HISTORIC

PGL

Old City Hall

11th St.

BEACH

Casa Casuarina

11th St.

Ave. Rd.

11th St.

10th St.

THE WOLFSONIAN-FIU

Ave.

Oceanfront Auditorium

10th St.

Edison

Breakwater

9th St.

9th St.

8th St.

The Blackstone

Washington

Collins

OCEAN

Lummus

BEACH

West Alton

7th St.

A1A

DISTRICT

Lenox

Michigan

Ave.

Ave.

6th St.

P

650

Park Central

5th St.

41

4th St.

OCEAN

3rd St.

School

Euclid

Ave.

SOUTH POINTE

Sanford L. Ziff Jewish Museum

ATLANTIC

OCEAN

MACARTHUR CAUSEWAY

Jefferson

Meridian

Washington

2nd St.

Collins

Ocean Front Park

Ocean

1st

Alton Rd.

Miami Beach Marina

Biscayne   St.

South Pointe Tower

South Pointe Park

SOUTH BEACH

Art Deco Building

0   1/5 mi
0   300 m

244

Among the first hotels to be restored in South Beach were a now-famous quartet: the former Leslie (1937, Albert Anis) at no. **1244**; the **Carlyle** (1941, Kiehnel and Elliott) at no. **1250**; the **Cardozo** (1939, Henry Hohauser) at no. 1300, now owned by singer Gloria Estefan; and the **Cavalier** (1936, Roy France) next door at no. **1320**. Among the latest to be renovated is **The Tides** (1936, L. Murray Dixon) at no. **1220**, owned by music-industry impresario Chris Blackwell. This 11-story hotel is the tallest on Ocean Drive.

Sanford L. Ziff Jewish Museum of Florida – *301 Washington Ave. Open year-round Tue-Sun 10am-5pm. Closed Jewish holidays. $5.* ♿ ☏ *305-672-5044. www.jewish museum .com.* Housed in the restored, copper-domed Beth Jacob Orthodox Synagogue (1936, Henry Hohauser), this cultural institution opened in 1995 to display art and artifacts relating to more than 230 years of Jewish history in the Sun-

Cafes Along Ocean Drive

© Robert Holmes

shine State. A 10-year study of Jews in Florida led to some 10,000 artifacts, photographs and mementos being combined in the MOSAIC exhibit, which became the museum's core collection in 1996. In addition, related temporary exhibits rotate three times a year.

Light streams into the large domed room through eight colorful stained-glass windows. At the eastern end stands a marble ark, crowned by a carved Torah supported by lions. A continuously running video illustrates the struggles and achievements encountered by Jews since they first landed on the Florida coast with Ponce de León to escape persecution in Spain.

★★ **The Wolfsonian-FIU** – *1001 Washington Ave. Open year-round Mon-Tue & Thu-Sat 11am-6pm (Thu 9pm), Sun noon-5pm. Closed major holidays. $5.* ♿ ☏ *305-531-1001. www.wolfsonian.org.* The seven-story Washington Storage Co. building (1927, Robertson and Patterson), distinguished by an elaborate gold-colored Moorish relief facade of cast concrete, once stored clothing and furniture during summer months, when most apartments were vacant. Now owned and operated by Florida International University, it houses a museum and research center that oversees the Mitchell Wolfson Collection: more than 70,000 pieces of American and European (mainly British, German, Italian and Dutch) art and design dating from 1885 to 1945. Rare books, graphics, political and propaganda artworks, architectural models, sculpture, glass, ceramics and furniture are included in the collection.

A **fountain** made from a glazed terra-cotta window grille from a 1929 movie theater dominates the lobby. The fifth floor is devoted to the permanent collection; about 300 works are displayed at any one time, illustrating how design has been used to help people adjust to the modern world. Focal points include design reform movements, urbanism, industrial design, transportation, world's fairs, advertising and political propaganda. Temporary exhibits occupy the sixth and seventh floors. The lower floors house museum administration and student study areas.

Washington Avenue – A busy commercial thoroughfare encompassing chic restaurants and trendy dance clubs as well as ethnic markets and Cuban coffee shops, Washington Avenue features several public buildings of note. The grand, eight-story, Mediterranean-inspired **Old City Hall** *(no. 1130)* was designed by Martin Luther Hampton in 1927, before the Deco wave swept Miami Beach. The **US Post Office** *(no. 1300)* dates from 1939. Stripped of exterior ornament, the building displays the angular lines, glass-block window treatment and somewhat harsh overall modernist look widely adopted for Works Project Administration (WPA) structures of the 1930s—a style sometimes called Depression Moderne. Lined with cast brass lockboxes, the central **rotunda** features a 1940 mural by Charles Hardman depicting vignettes from Florida history.

Planned as an artists' colony in the 1920s, **Espanola Way**★ *(between Washington and Drexel Aves.)* breathes fresh air into an otherwise shabby area. This gas-lit enclave, with its movie backdrop ensemble of Mediterranean Revival buildings decorated in coral-colored stucco and hand-painted tiles, features cozy courtyards, pink sidewalks and chic boutiques offering such apparel as sequined bikinis.

Lincoln Road Mall – *On Lincoln Rd. between Washington Ave. and Alton Rd.* ☎ *305-534-9857*. This lively, lengthy pedestrian mall abounds with trendy shops, galleries and restaurants that border a central planted thoroughfare of tiled fountains and coral rock pools. Lincoln Road is the oldest commercial street on the island, laid out in 1915 by Carl Fisher. The area staged a second comeback after it was relandscaped and closed to traffic by Morris Lapidus (a set designer-turned-architect, who designed the Fontainebleau Hotel) in the 1960s, only to be deserted in the 1970s. After a $16-million face-lift, its latest transition is complete. Shops—specializing in antiques, jewelry, books and designer clothing—and galleries improve in quality as you go west of Drexel Avenue *(most shops don't open until 11am)*. There are plenty of restaurants, serving a wide variety of cuisine; several offer alfresco dining and an opportunity for serious people-watching.

Originally a cinema, the 1935 Deco **Lincoln Theatre** *(nos. 555-541)* now hosts the New World Symphony, composed of promising music school graduates *(concerts Oct-May; for schedule: ☎ 305-673-3331)*. Visitors are welcome at the **Artcenter South Florida** *(nos. 800-810)*, a warren of exhibit areas and studio space for photographers, ceramic artists, painters, jewelry designers and printmakers. *(Other Artcenter buildings are at 924 Lincoln Rd., 1035-43 Lincoln Rd., 1655-59 Lenox Ave. and 1632 Pennsylvania Ave.)* Across the street the two-story **Sterling Building** *(no. 927)* dominates the streetfront with an undulating wall of tile-studded stucco and glass block. Across the mall at the corner of Lenox Avenue, the refurbished 1934 **Colony Theater** *(no. 1040)* presents plays, concerts and cultural programs *(for schedule: ☎ 305-674-1026)*.

Jackie Gleason Theater of the Performing Arts – *1700 Washington Ave. For performance information: ☎ 305-673-7300*. This confection of peach-colored concrete and glass block (1951, Pancoast, Hohauser and Dixon) was remodeled by Morris Lapidus in 1976, and originally hosted comedian Jackie Gleason's popular television series from 1964 to 1970. The 3,000-seat theater now stages Broadway shows and ballets. Look for Roy Lichtenstein's red-and-white-striped **Mermaid** (**1**) on the south lawn *(fronting 17th St.)*. Set into plaques on the adjacent yard, cement footprints of such celebrities as Chita Rivera, Julie Andrews and *Miami Vice* star Don Johnson form the Walk of the Stars.

★**Holocaust Memorial** – *Nos. 1933-1945 Meridian Ave.* ♿ 🅿 ☎ *305-538-1663*. Set in and around a tranquil lily pond, this memorial (dedicated in 1990) leads visitors through a circular plaza of pale pink Jerusalem stone designed as a series of outdoor passages. Names inscribed on the walls are a simple but chilling reminder of lives lost to the Nazis during World War II. The centerpiece is Kenneth Treister's *Sculpture of Love and Anguish*, which comprises several bronze vignettes and a giant 42ft-high outstretched arm symbolizing the last reach of a dying person. Miami artist and architect Treister also designed the Streets of Mayfair shopping complex in Coconut Grove.

Collins Park – *Between 21st and 22nd Aves. next to the ocean*. The area around Collins Park is the site of the first lots sold by John Collins to finance his bridge project in 1912. Modernist hotels replaced older buildings in the 1930s. The futuristic tower fin on the restored **Plymouth** *(33621st St.)*, designed by Anton Skislewicz in 1940, characterizes designs inspired by the space-age pylon featured at the 1939 World's Fair. The lobby mural by Ramon Chatov shows scantily clothed figures cavorting on the beach. (The Plymouth is now the residential home of the New World Symphony.) A grassy plaza and rounded glass-block entrance front the **Collins Park Hotel** *(2000 Park Ave., under renovation)*. Designed in 1939 by Henry Hohauser, this marvel combines Art Deco zigzag motifs with the curving walls and portholes characteristic of the Moderne style.

Collins Park is being expanded to include a cultural campus, under the development of noted architect Robert A.M. Stern. Part of the campus is the newly completed, three-story administrative building/ballet school *(2200 Liberty Ave.)* for the **Miami City Ballet** designed by Arquitectonica; passersby can watch *(weekends 10am-6pm)* the dancers practice their pliés and pas-de-deuxs behind huge glass windows. Plans call for the removal of the current library and the building of a new regional library to be designed by Stern, with completion projected for 2003. The recently expanded Bass Museum of Art is also part of the Collins Park Cultural Center.

★**Bass Museum of Art** – *2121 Park Ave.* ♿ ☎ *305-673-7530. www.bassmuseum.org. The museum is undergoing renovation; call for exhibit schedule.* This regional museum maintains a permanent collection of more than 3,000 works, encompassing European, American, Asian and contemporary art. Its European holdings are particularly rich in religious artifacts and French and Flemish tapestries.

The original landmark Art Deco structure (1930, Russell Pancoast) of oolitic limestone decorated with Mayan motifs was designed as the centerpiece of a nine-acre park given to the city in 1920 by developer John Collins. First used as both a library and art center, the building was renamed in 1964 when Austrian-born New York entrepreneur John Bass donated his art collection to the city of Miami Beach. A recently completed first-phase expansion by Japanese architect **Arata Isozaki**, who designed Team Disney near Orlando, increased the museum's size to 37,000sq ft, adding new gallery space, an enlarged museum shop, a courtyard and cafe *(a gala opening is planned for mid-2002; completion of phase two is scheduled for 2003).* Surrounded by a reflecting pool, an outdoor sculpture terrace is tucked amid the exposed columns of the raised main gallery. The latter, a white-stucco rectangular block, admits natural light through a panel of clerestory windows.

Upon reopening, the Bass will display European paintings, furnishings, altarpieces, sculpture and other works spanning the 15C to 21C. Highlights will include art by such masters as Peter Paul Rubens and Sandro Botticelli as well as 19C tapestries by Louis-Marie Baader. The main upstairs gallery will be devoted to temporary displays.

★**Collins Avenue** – Although Collins Avenue is now one of the main traffic arteries in Miami Beach, it originally knew a more affluent lifestyle, catering to pedestrians with juice bars and small boutiques. Between 16th and 23rd Streets, hotels climb to 10 stories, the maximum height allowed; below 16th they may rise higher. Among the stars from the 1940s are the **National** *(no. 1677)* by Roy France; Robert Swartburg's **Delano** *(no. 1685)*, renovated in 1995 but still recognizable by its finned spaceship tower; and the **Ritz Plaza** *(no. 1701, under renovation)* by L. Murray Dixon. With their squared, stepped-back facades and quirky central towers, these local landmarks resemble a trio of oversized party-goers dressed in giant overcoats and jaunty hats. For the best view, walk west two blocks on 17th Street and look east.

Driving north on Collins you will encounter a 13,000sq ft **mural** *(at 44th St.)* bearing the trompe-l'œil image of a triumphal arch framing the **Fontainebleau Hilton** Resort and Towers, by noted muralist Richard Haas. The real Fontainebleau is just around the corner *(no. 4441)* on the 20-acre site of the former Harvey Firestone estate. This 1,200-room extravaganza (1954) is the work of Morris Lapidus, who dubbed it "modern French Château Style." The hotel fronts a beachside boardwalk (monitored by beach-patrol joggers) stretching 24 blocks from 23rd to 47th Streets.

To the north and west lie the exclusive residential areas of Middle Beach and Bal Harbour Village, a complex of high-rise condos and resorts. **Bal Harbour Shops** *(no. 9700)* is a mecca of high-fashion stores and boutiques including Tiffany & Company, Louis Vuitton, Cartier and Neiman Marcus.

 Samba Room
See map. 1501 Collins Ave. at 15th St. ☎ *305-672-6223.* Starting to sag during a night on the town? Step inside this snazzy Cuban bar and Latin cafe for some shoulder-shaking, toe-tapping Samba sounds while you revive with a cup of high-octane Cuban coffee or a Café de Brazil (a press pot of strong black Brazilian coffee). Samba Java is also on the menu: an iced coffee concoction of coconut, cinnamon and black rum. Perhaps a rich dessert to supply a sugar rush? Choose the *flan con canela* (orange-cinnamon spiced flan) or the *pastel caliente* (Ancho chile-chocolate flourless cake). The place stays open until 2am and features Latin and world rhythms shows from time to time. You may find yourself spending the rest of the evening here. *Locations in Ft. Lauderdale and West Palm Beach as well.*

PALM BEACH★★★

Population 10,468
Map p 250
Tourist Information: www.palmbeaches.com ☎ 561-655-3282

Occupying the northern part of a 16mi-long subtropical barrier island, this strip of real estate harbors one of the highest concentrations of multimillion-dollar mansions in the world. Though it has been a refuge for the rich for more than a century, Palm Beach attracts streams of tourists—particularly in winter—who venture across one of the bridges from the mainland to sample fine restaurants, stay in world-class hotels, shop along Worth Avenue and ogle the elegant estates bordering the ocean.

Historical Notes

From Coconuts to Palms – When a Spanish schooner aptly named *La Providencia* wrecked off this coast in 1879, the area's few settlers happily inherited a windfall cargo of coconuts. They planted the spoils and met with surprising success: a flourishing grove of some 20,000 coconut palms.

This lush, tropical-looking shoreline caught the eye of Henry M. Flagler as he was scouting out a site for a new resort town. In Palm Beach Flagler claimed to have found "a veritable Paradise."

In the 1890s, Palm Beach had its first taste of the kind of development that would characterize the area for decades to come. Flagler's Royal Poinciana Hotel, now gone, opened in 1894 (the year his railroad came to town) with 540 rooms and the claim that it was the world's largest wooden structure. Flagler's indelible mark on the town is most apparent in two remaining buildings: The Breakers hotel and Whitehall, his former Palm Beach home (now the Flagler Museum).

■ High Society Architecture

The growth of Palm Beach owes much to the aquaintance of two men: Paris Singer, son of the sewing-machine magnate, and architect **Addison Mizner** (1872-1933). They met in Palm Beach, where both men had come in 1918 to convalesce. Singer's interest in architecture and Mizner's wit and bonhomie made for a quick friendship, and soon Singer was financing Mizner's bold ideas. Born into a prominent California family, Mizner at age 16 had traveled to Central America, where his father was serving as a diplomat. He later attended classes at the University of Salamanca in Spain and, though he never earned a degree, he began trading on his big talent and personality. His early exposure to Spanish culture showed in the country homes he designed in New York, where he practiced for 14 years before coming to Palm Beach.

By the time Mizner and Singer went to work, Palm Beach was already a posh resort for the wealthy. Thus when their first project, a veteran's hospital, failed to attract enough patients, they simply converted the building into the exclusive Everglades Club, of which Singer was the sole owner. Mizner was then hired by the reigning social queen, Eva Stotesbury (wife of Philadelphia banker Edward Stotesbury), to build a lavish 32-room mansion. This and similar commissions for palatial homes occupied Mizner—now Florida's foremost society architect—throughout the early 1920s, until he began his projects in Boca Raton.

Mizner and other Palm Beach architects took their inspiration from Spanish colonial manor houses and Italian Renaissance villas and palaces, developing or importing the necessary craftsmen, ceramic kilns and materials. To create an antique feeling, Mizner purposely chipped stone carvings, blackened ceilings with soot, and punctured furniture with fake wormholes. His style —broadly known as Mediterranean Revival and characterized by pastel pink stucco walls, red-tile roofs and breezy loggias with fanciful embellishments—is now considered authentic Palm Beach style and is still imitated by modern architects.

The spectacular building boom of the late 1910s and early '20s left the town utterly changed. Early wooden seaside cottages and hotels were replaced by baronial mansions, giving Palm Beach its present look. Known as the "winter Newport" (for the Rhode Island retreat of the rich and famous), Palm Beach boasted restaurants, shops, clubs, hotels and villas, all tailored to the tastes of the wealthiest people on both sides of the Atlantic—the Vanderbilts, the Rockefellers, the Duke and Duchess of Windsor. When Florida real-estate speculation caved in on itself and the Depression gripped the country in the late 1920s, Palm Beach society continued to enjoy a luxurious lifestyle; the rich merely became less ostentatious.

Bastion of Elegance – While World War II brought air bases and new construction to the mainland of Palm Beach County, it also brought German U-boats to the coast. At least 12 Allied ships were torpedoed off the coast of Florida in 1942, including several oil tankers that exploded within sight of Palm Beach. Residents responded with fundraisers and other volunteer activities as well as nighttime blackouts to impede the Germans from spotting US ships.

After the war, Palm Beach society became less formal and the season extended well beyond winter, with many residents making permanent homes on the island. Among the elite who have owned property here today are Donald Trump, Estée Lauder and Jimmy Buffett. Today Palm Beach remains a picture-perfect island of palm-lined thoroughfares, immaculately clean streets and opulent houses where the only signs of activity are the perpetually busy gardeners. Visitors to this small, well-to-do city will find shopkeepers and restaurateurs congenial, prices high and architectural beauty widespread.

DRIVING TOUR 7.5mi

Start at Southern Blvd. and Ocean Blvd. (A1A) and head north. The speed limit is 35mph, though most people drive at a lower speed.

This drive begins along the Atlantic, offering expansive **views**★★ of the ocean on the right and large, elegant houses on the left. The first mansion, partially hidden by walls and a massive gate, is **Mar-a-Lago** (1927, Joseph Urban and Marion Syms Wyeth), so-named ("sea to lake") because it extends from the Atlantic to Lake Worth. Widely considered the grandest residence in Palm Beach, this 188-room Moorish fantasy, built for cereal heiress Marjorie Merriweather Post, has been owned in recent years by Donald Trump; it is now a private social club.

Drive north 2.6mi on Ocean Blvd. and turn left at dead end on Barton Ave. Park beside church on Barton Ave. or on Via Bethesda, one street to the north.

★★**Episcopal Church of Bethesda-by-the-Sea** – *141 S. County Rd. Open year-round daily 8am-5pm. Closed major holidays.* ⚊ 🅿 ☏ *561-655-4554.* Built in the Gothic Revival style in 1927, this graceful structure of cast stone was designed by Hiss and Weeks of New York. It features a prominent bell tower and notable ornamentations, including sculptures of the four Evangelists standing in niches in the main entrance archway.

Inside, the nave sweeps upward to wooden rafters and forward to a blue stained-glass window above the altar. Called the **Te Deum Window**, the three lancets *(from left to right)* depict the apostles St. Peter and St. Paul, the risen Christ, and martyred saints Stephen and Catherine. The white limestone reredos at the high altar shows, in the left panel, Jesus healing the paralytic at the pool of Bethesda. In the south transept hangs a 17C **Madonna and Child** by Spanish painter Esteban Murillo and a suspended model ship. The nautical motif continues in the north aisle windows, which portray biblical sea scenes. A cloister to the left of the entrance leads to a courtyard and then to the **Cluett Memorial Gardens**, a small formal garden with fountains, a gazebo and cruciform parterres.

Continue .3mi north on County Rd.

★★**The Breakers** – *1 S. County Rd. Visit by guided tour (1hr) only, year-round Wed 3pm; meet in main lobby. $10. Reservations suggested.* 🍴 ⚊ ☏ *561-655-6611 or 800-273-2537. www.thebreakers.com.* When Henry Flagler's famous hotel burned for the second time in 1925, his heirs put up $6 million, hired the best architects, imported 75 artisans from Italy, and employed 1,200 craftsmen to construct a palatial hotel. Eleven and a half months later, the new Breakers was complete.

The hotel roughly follows an H-shaped layout and features twin two-tiered belvedere towers with open arches, a colonnaded porte cochere and exterior relief panels. The lobby runs the entire 200ft length of the center section (the cross in the "H") with an 18ft vaulted ceiling. From the lobby extends a lush courtyard with fountains and a sunken garden. The **Mediterranean Ballroom** boasts a hand-painted ceiling; this room is often used for charity balls, some with tickets priced at $650 and higher. From the walls of another room hang 15C and 16C **Flemish tapestries**. Behind the lobby, the Florentine dining room extends half the length of a football field; above one section of the room, a domed ceiling is painted with frescoes and Italian pastoral scenes.

Continue .3mi north to the southeast corner of Sunrise Ave.

Paramount Building – *139 N. County Rd.* This yellow building with green awnings, distinguished by its central entranceway and tall pointed arch, dates from 1927 when it opened as a 1,028-seat movie palace. Joseph Urban, set designer for the Ziegfeld Follies and architect to Austrian Emperor Franz Josef, designed the theater, reportedly drawing the plans on a tablecloth in a Manhattan restaurant. Live performers included Charlie Chaplin, W.C. Fields and Glenn Miller. Women patrons wore so much jewelry that the semicircle of box seats was dubbed the "diamond horseshoe," and season tickets sold for as much as $1,000 apiece. Closed in 1980, the building changed hands several times and the theater has been replaced by galleries, shops and offices.

Cross N. County Rd.

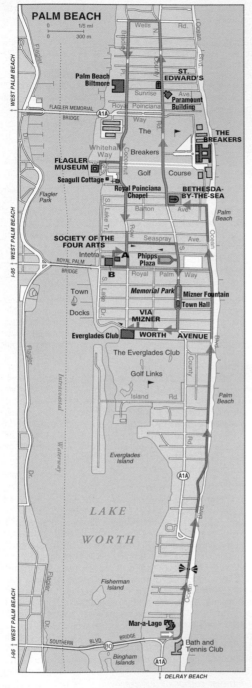

PALM BEACH

★Saint Edward's Church – *144 N. County Rd. Open year-round Mon-Fri 7am-4pm, Sat 7am-7pm, Sun 6:30am-1pm.* ♿ 🅿 ☎ *561-832-0400. www.st-edward.com.* Distinguished by elaborate decoration inside and out, this Roman Catholic church (1926) features a baroque entrance of cast stone, a belfry and a red-tile roof. In the narthex, spiral marble pillars and carved wooden gates lead into a vast sanctuary vaulted with a 65ft hand-painted coffered ceiling. The main altar was carved from a single piece of Carrara marble and measures 28ft by 15ft. Eight clerestory windows on either side of the nave represent scenes from the life of the Virgin Mary. Cloister windows on the north depict eight parables, those on the south eight miracles. Other windows were donated by such illustrious patrons as the Hearsts and the Kennedys, who worshipped here in the early 1960s.

Continue north .6mi on County Rd. and turn left onto Wells Rd. and left again on Bradley Pl.

Seven blocks down on the right stands the **Palm Beach Biltmore** (*Bradley Pl. and Sunrise Ave.*), a 1927 resort hotel that closed in 1970. Purchased that year by insurance tycoon John D. MacArthur for $1.5 million and sold seven years later for $5.3 million, the building now houses luxury condominiums.

Proceed two blocks farther south and cross Royal Poinciana Way. Continue south on Cocoanut Row (the continuation of Bradley Pl.) and take the first right onto Whitehall Way.

★★Flagler Museum – *White hall Way. Open year-round Tue-Sat 10am-5pm, Sun noon-5pm. Closed Jan 1, Thanksgiving Day, Dec 25. $8* 🅿 ☎ *561-655-2833. www.flagler.org.* Florida railroad magnate and Standard Oil partner **Henry Morrison Flagler** built Whitehall, this 55-room Gilded Age mansion overlooking Lake Worth, in 1901 as a wedding gift for his third wife, Mary Lily Kenan. Prominent architects John M. Carrère and Thomas Hastings, designers of the New York Public Library, built Whitehall in just 18 months at a cost of $2.5 million. After Flagler's death in 1913, the house remained in the family until 1925, when it reopened as the Whitehall Hotel, sporting the ungainly addition of a 10-story tower. When the hotel's finances ebbed in 1959, Jean Flagler Mathews, Henry's granddaughter, saved the family home from demolition by turning it into a historic house museum, which opened in 1960.

Louis XVI Salon, Whitehall

© Paul Rocheleau

The mansion has been restored to its Flagler-era appearance with many of the original furnishings. A formally landscaped walkway leads to a two-story veranda that spans the front of the house; lower wings on either side create the illusion of great length. **Marble Hall** is a 110ft-by-40ft imitation of a Roman villa's atrium, decorated in seven different shades of polished marble. Its opulent appointments include Louis XIV gold armchairs covered in silk velvet; a massive marble-top table; a 9ft rosewood clock; and the masterful oval ceiling mural by Italian artist Benvenuti, entitled *Crowning of Knowledge*, in homage to formal education (of which Flagler received little).

Just off the entrance hall to the south, the Italian Renaissance Library displays the original red-velvet wall covering. Next door, the **Louis XIV Music Room** is hung with Baccarat chandeliers and paintings by such 18C masters as Gainsborough and Romney; the 24-rank organ was played regularly by the resident organist.

The **ballroom** features gilt mirrors, crystal chandeliers, damask draperies and bronze fixtures hung with crystal grapes, pears and Florida bananas. In the Elizabethan Breakfast Room, guests were expected to arrive promptly at 9am. The adjoining **Francis I Dining Room**, with its carved walnut woodwork and coffered plaster ceiling, saw a procession of royalty, wealth and fame with names such as Rockefeller, Astor and Vanderbilt. After dinner, ladies withdrew to the elegant **Louis XVI Salon**.

The second floor contains the Rococo-style **master suite** dressed in yellow watered-silk damask, Mrs. Flagler's sitting room, and 14 guest suites, each decorated in a different style.

In the central outdoor courtyard, arched loggias define the north and south walls; in the middle, a marble Venus poses above four lecherous satyrs. Flagler's private railroad car, "Rambler," stands on the south lawn. Visitors may walk through the car to see its sumptuous sleeping berths and kitchen area.

On the lawn, the gray wood **Royal Poinciana Chapel** *(60 Cocoanut Row, just south of the museum)* was built by Flagler in 1896 for use by guests at his Royal Poinciana Hotel. Moved to Whitehall's grounds when Cocoanut Row was installed, the non-denominational church features a Classical clapboard facade topped by a square carillon tower and set with Georgian arched windows. Behind the chapel stands the oldest extant house in Palm Beach, **Seagull Cottage** *(not open to the public)*. In 1893 Flagler bought this Queen Anne-style cottage, built by Denver railroad entrepreneur Robert McCormick in 1886, and used it as his winter home until the completion of Whitehall. It now serves as the chapel's parish house.

Drive south .7mi and turn right on Royal Palm Way; take first right into Four Arts Plaza.

★**Society of the Four Arts** – *Four Arts Plaza.* ☎ *561-655-7226. www.fourarts.org.* Organized in 1936 to foster an appreciation for art, music, literature and drama, the Society of the Four Arts retained the services of Swiss architect Maurice Fatio to design an appropriate building. Fatio's elegantly restrained Italianate edifice now houses the **Gioconda and Joseph King Library** (**A**) *(east end of mall)*, containing more than 40,000 volumes for community use *(open Nov-Apr Mon-Fri 10am-5pm, Sat 9am-1pm; rest of the year Mon-Fri 10am-5pm; ♿ 🅿)*. The walls of the entrance loggia display canvas murals of the four arts for which the society was named. The walkway and entrance floor are made of coquina rock cut from the Florida seacoast.

In the late 1940s the society began looking for additional space for a gallery and theater. Across the street to the west stood a vacant building that Addison Mizner and his assistant, Lester Liesler, had designed in 1928. Originally a nightclub known for its asymmetrical features, this handsome structure caught the eye of prominent architect John Volk, who suggested that the society purchase it. In 1947 he went to work, transforming halls into galleries, enclosing the courtyard, converting the bar into executive offices, and creating a 716-seat theater. The resulting **Esther B. O'Keeffe Gallery Building** (**B**) provides space for exhibits, films, lectures and concerts *(open Dec-mid-Apr Mon-Sat 10am-5pm, Sun 2pm-5pm; closed major holidays; $3 contribution requested; &).*

At the west end of the grassy, palm-lined mall behind the gallery stands Isamu Noguchi's compelling pyramid, *Intetra*. Near the library, intimate **gardens** feature a Chinese rock garden, a rose garden and tranquil, fern-rimmed pools. At the entrance to the adjoining **Philip Hulitar Sculpture Garden**, Edward Hoffman's bronze, *Reaching*, gracefully evokes the mother-and-child bond. Named for the noted fashion designer, this lovely greensward boasts sculpture by renowned 20C artists, among them Henry Mitchell and Anna Hyatt Huntington.

Cross Four Arts Plaza (north) and turn right on Seaview Ave. Take first left on Cocoanut Row, then right on Seaspray and right on N. County Rd. Take second right into Phipps Plaza.

Phipps Plaza – *On N. County Rd. between Seaview Ave. and Royal Palm Way.* Planned by affluent resident socialite John S. Phipps, this peaceful Old-World cul-de-sac is a smooth mix of residential and commercial properties. The leading Florida architects of the 1920s—Addison Mizner, Maurice Fatio and Marion Syms Wyeth—contributed to the streetscape, which blends Mediterranean and Bermudan styles. Distinctive features include belfries and walls covered with tiles taken from old buildings in Cuba, ornate iron gates, winding staircases and a densely planted central park of ficus and yucca, frangipani and golden shower trees. Phipps Plaza became the town's first designated historic district in 1979.

Turn right on County Rd. and continue 3 blocks south.

Town Hall – *360 S. County Rd., between Australian and Chilian Aves.* Designed by Harvey and Clarke in 1924, this attractive building originally consisted of two separate edifices joined by a courtyard. Architect John Volk connected the two in 1965 to provide more office space for a growing city. Beige stucco walls rise to a barrel-tile roof crowned by an enclosed bell tower. On the north side of Town Hall, **Mizner Fountain** splashes into three basins upheld by heroic rearing horses. Addison Mizner designed the fountain and surrounding **Memorial Park**, an oasis in the middle of busy County Road, which features cut coral-stone pavement and plantings that flank the narrow pool leading from the fountain.

Continue two blocks south of Town Hall and turn right on Worth Ave.

Worth Avenue – *Between Ocean Blvd. and Cocoanut Row.* The East Coast's answer to Rodeo Drive in Beverly Hills, California, this charming street acts as a magnet for well-heeled tourists and residents, as well as the merely curious, who come to eat, shop, browse and ogle the merchandise. Though named for a colonel in the Seminole Wars, the avenue really measures worth in simple terms: money. Here the island's palmiest boutiques stand shoulder to shoulder and read like names from a shopper's Who's Who: Cartier, Ralph Lauren, Liz Claiborne, Charles Jourdan, Saks Fifth Avenue, Giorgio's. In between are galleries, cafes and specialty shops.

© Al Messerschmidt

Worth Avenue

Worth Avenue's mélange of styles succeeds in creating a picturesque street with a decidedly European flair. Addison Mizner designed many of the connecting two-story villas along the street in 1924, as well as the delightful vias, or alleyways, that thread off the main road into charming little courtyards of tile-work fountains and hanging flower baskets. Among these, **Via Mizner★** stands out for its labyrinthine passages and pastel walls of yellow, pink and aqua. Mizner's own four-story apartment dominates the skyline here. At the west end of the street stands his first Florida commission, the three-story **Everglades Club** *(no. 356)*—an exclusive gathering place that started life as a convalescent home for veterans of World War I. Its design blends features of Venetian, Spanish and Moorish architecture.

In spite of Worth Avenue's high-toned commercialism, visitors can buy a reasonably priced meal at a courtyard restaurant or simply stroll the bougainvillea-studded sidewalks and watch the people: chic women heavily bejeweled, men in straw boaters stepping from late-model Mercedes and convertible BMWs, slim models showing off the newest fashions, shoppers burdened with precious purchases, and the young and old with dog in tow.

WEST PALM BEACH★

Population 82,103
Map p 254
Tourist Information: www.palmbeachfl.com ☎ 561-233-3000 or 800-833-5433

Hugging the inland side of Lake Worth, this center of commerce and industry remains, to some degree, in the shadow of its glamorous parent, Palm Beach. Although it has outstripped the resort island in size, population and skyline, West Palm Beach is still viewed as a commercial suburb. Nevertheless, the city offers its own attractions, including one of Florida's finest art museums.

West Palm first attracted workers who came to build the grand hotels on Palm Beach. In 1893, under the direction of Henry Flagler, surveyors laid out a town site and named streets in alphabetical order—Althea, Banyan, Clematis, Datura, etc. While vice flourished, many civic organizations—churches, public utilities and schools—brought cohesiveness to the community. By 1909 West Palm Beach attained the county seat and propelled itself into a booming era of construction that lasted through the 1980s. West Palm Beach is experiencing a resurgence in construction. Newcomer **CityPlace**, a tony $550 million shopping, entertainment, residential and business complex, spans 55 acres east of I-95. Nearby, a 330,000sq ft convention center is scheduled to open in spring 2003. A trolley *(free)* connects CityPlace to downtown's redeveloped Clematis Street, filled with trendy shops and eateries.

Along **Flagler Drive** high-rise banks and office buildings contrast with such Palm Beach landmarks as The Breakers and Whitehall visible across Lake Worth. The **Old Northwood** neighborhood *(bounded by Flagler Dr. and Broadway Ave., 25th and 36th Sts.)* contains a number of Spanish-style homes dating from the 1920s.

The city serves as the area's transportation hub: an international airport and the restored Mediterranean Revival **Seaboard Air Line Railway Station** *(201 S. Tamarind Ave.)*, built in 1925 by Harvey and Clarke, service a burgeoning population. Two major thoroughfares (US-1 and I-95) cut through West Palm Beach, and Florida's Turnpike runs just west.

SIGHTS

★★**Norton Museum of Art** – *1451 S. Olive Ave. Open Nov-Mar Mon-Sat 10am-5pm, Sun 1pm-5pm. Rest of the year Tue-Sat 10am-5pm, Sun 1pm-5pm. Closed major holidays. $6. ✗ ㋡ ▯ ☎ 561-832-5196. www.norton.org.* Founded in 1941 by steel tycoon **Ralph H. Norton** (1875-1953), this gallery boasts a spectrum of some 4,000 pieces. In its permanent holdings, special emphasis is placed on 19C-20C American and European works and Chinese art from 1700 BC to the early 1900s. Marion Syms Wyeth, co-architect of Mar-a-Lago, designed the original museum, a modest white building along classical lines, trimmed with Alabama limestone. An expansion in 1997 more than doubled the museum's size (Centerbrook Architects). Norton began collecting art in 1921, educating himself by attending art shows in Chicago, New York and Pittsburgh. In 1939 the semi-retired Norton, who wintered with his wife in West Palm Beach, offered his art collection to The Society of the Four Arts in nearby Palm Beach. When they delayed making a decision, he purchased a city block near his house and commissioned the Norton Museum to "preserve for the future the beautiful things of the past."

The permanent collection includes a group of **French Impressionist** and **post-Impressionist** paintings by such notables as Cézanne, Matisse, Monet, Renoir, Gauguin and Picasso. Gauguin's *Agony In The Garden* (1889), a self-portrait of the artist as Christ, and Picasso's *The Red Foulard* number among the best-known works. Twentieth-century **American art** forms a significant part of the permanent holdings. Works by Hopper, O'Keeffe, Rauschenberg, Warhol and Pollock figure prominently. The museum's renowned **Chinese collection** comprises archaic jade tomb carvings from as early as the 3rd millennium BC and ritual bronzes from the Shang (c.1450-1100 BC) and Western Zhou (c.1100-771 BC) dynasties. Ceramics and Buddhist sculpture, some from the Tang period (AD 618-906), round out this collection.

A number of traveling exhibits rotate through the museum each year and musical and educational programs are presented.

Ann Norton Sculpture Gardens – *253 Barcelona Rd., north corner of Flagler Dr. Open Oct-May Wed-Sun 11am-4pm. Closed major holidays. $5.* ♿ ℗ ☏ *561-832-5328. http://realpages.com/sites/annnorton.* This former residence of gallery founder Ralph Norton has been converted to a display grounds for his second wife's sculpture. **Ann Weaver Norton** (1905-1982) came to the area in 1942 as the Norton School of Art's first instructor in sculpture. The two-story house (1925) was remodeled in the mid-1930s by Marion Syms Wyeth, who added the wrought-iron balcony and first-floor bay windows. The house now contains more than 100 of Ann Norton's sculptures and hosts frequent shows of local artists' work. In the garden, a walking trail leads past nine of Norton's monumental brick and granite **abstract megaliths**, designed to suggest Tibetan shrines, mythical beasts and totemic figures. An outstanding collection of palms—representing over 300 varieties—also graces the property.

Palm Beach Zoo at Dreher Park – [Kids] *1301 Summit Blvd., just east of I-95, accessible from Southern Blvd. or Forest Hill Blvd. exits. Open year-round daily 9am-5pm. Closed Thanksgiving Day. $6.* ✗ ♿ ℗ ☏ *561-533-0887. www.palmbeachzoo.org.* Set on 23 acres adjacent to I-95, this small zoo is home to more than 400 animals representing 128 different species. Outstanding among the 22 endangered and threatened species are the white Bengal tiger, Florida panther and golden lion tamarin. None of the animals displayed here were captured in the wild—some were borrowed from other zoos, some were donated, and others were placed here by wildlife officials. A short boardwalk nature trail *(.25mi)* leads through lush tropical foliage.

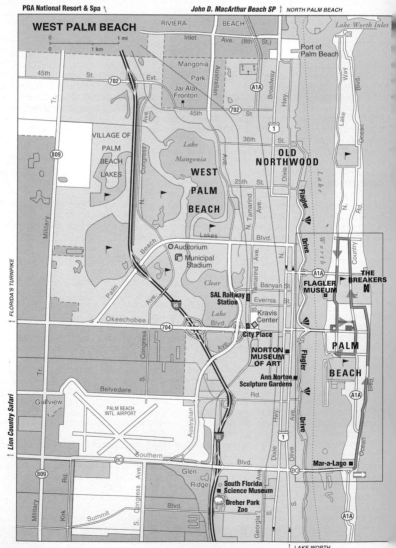

South Florida Science Museum – 📺 *4801 Dreher Trail North, just north of the zoo. Open year-round daily 10am-5pm (Fri 10pm). Closed Thanksgiving Day & Dec 25. $6 (additional $2 for planetarium shows, $4 extra for laser light shows). & 🖬 ☎ 561-832-1988. www.sfsm.org.* A mastodon skeleton in the front hall greets visitors to this single-story museum. Found in central Palm Beach County in 1967 by a work crew, most of the original mastodon bones were destroyed or looted, but enough remained for paleontologists to reconstruct the entire creature. At some of the 28 different interactive exhibits visitors can test their senses, create frozen shadows and learn about electricity. Local flora and fauna are explored in a native plant center and aquarium room; another room is dedicated to temporary exhibits. The observatory, planetarium and laser shows are perennial favorites.

EXCURSIONS *Map p 202*

★**John D. MacArthur Beach State Park** – *9mi north of Palm Beach, on Singer Island. Take US-1 north 4mi to Riviera Beach; turn right on Rte. 708 (Heron Blvd.), which becomes A1A. Follow A1A north 5mi to park entrance. Park hrs & fees p 350. & ☎ 561-624-6952.* Named for the eccentric insurance baron who donated a portion of his valuable property on Singer Island, this natural haven encompasses 760 acres of mangrove estuary and pristine beach.
The weathered wood **nature center** contains exhibits and a video *(15min)* explains the ecosystem of a barrier island *(open year-round Wed-Mon 9am-5pm; &)*. Just outside, the Butterfly Garden Trail offers a peaceful stroll among native flowers and the butterflies they attract; beside the parking lot, the Satinleaf Trail *(.5mi)* loops through a hardwood forest that supports tropical trees such as the mastic and strangler fig. A 1,600ft wooden bridge across Lake Worth Cove *(accessible by foot or tram)* provides wonderful **views**★ of the mangrove estuary and its birdlife—150 species, mainly waterfowl but also songbirds and raptors, have been identified here. A dense coastal hammock anchors the east end of the bridge, where vistors may continue on to a wide beach littered only with brown sargassum. Undeveloped Munyon Island (formerly the site of a resort hotel; now part of the park) is accessible only by boat.

★★**Lion Country Safari** – 📺 *16mi west of I-95 on Southern Blvd. (Exit 50); turn right at sign and continue 2mi to entrance. Open year-round daily 9:30am-4:30pm. $15.50. △ ✕ & 🖬 ☎ 561-793-1084. www.lioncountrysafari.com. Pets and convertibles not allowed (air-conditioned sedans available for rent).* Visitors drive an 8mi road through the park and must remain in their cars with windows closed. Billing itself as North America's first cageless zoo, this 500-acre, drive-through game preserve opened in 1967. The road loops through seven simulated African, Asian and North American habitats, taking visitors past more than 1,300 animals of 131 different species.

The first section, **Lake Nakaru**, features such exotics as the lowland tapir from South America, the white-handed gibbon and the Australian emu. The **Great Plains** includes bison and Dall sheep. Lions roam the **Gorongosa Reserve**, separated from other animals who represent their natural prey. Though easily visible, lions are apt to be asleep. The **Kalahari Bushveldt** features antelope of southwest Africa, and on the **Serengeti Plain** visitors can spot waterbuck, wildebeest and the African ostrich. The world's largest bird, the ostrich has a reputation for pecking at windshields. African elephants, an endangered species, live within a large enclosure in this section. Water buffalo may be seen in the **Gir Forest**. Finally, the **Wankie National Park** holds giraffes, zebras, rhinoceroses and chimpanzees. One of the continent's most successful chimp populations inhabits several little islands, each family segregated from the others because they cannot swim. Several generations, led by a dominant male, inhabit each island, which is furnished with wooden platforms and vine-like ropes.

An amusement park near the entrance offers boat and carousel rides, animal demonstrations, miniature golf, a petting zoo and a short nature trail.

For Golf Lovers
Sports lovers will have a field day at **PGA National Resort and Spa** *(400 Ave of the Champions in Palm Beach Gardens; ☎ 561-627-2000 or 800-633-9150; www.pga-resorts.com).* Billed as the "largest complex in the Western Hemisphere," the resort features five 18-hole tournament courses on 2,300 acres of manicured fairways, as well as a croquet complex. The resort also serves as national headquarters for the Professional Golfers of America and home to the PGA National Croquet Club. There are 339 guest rooms, 65 cottages, eight restaurants and lounges, 19 tennis courts and a 26-acre lake. Rooms are decorated in light yellow, cream, blue and green, with marble foyers, teak furnishings, high poster beds and overstuffed chairs. For nonsporting types or weary athletes, the spa includes an outdoor mineral pool with Dead Sea healing waters and stone therapy.

Southwest Coast

Courtyard, Ringling Museum of Art, Sarasota – © David R. Frazier

S tretching 120mi along the Gulf of Mexico from Bradenton down to Naples, southwest Florida presents a mirror image of the state's Atlantic Coast, but in softer tones. As on the east coast, major highways trace the shoreline, linking cities of gleaming white high rises that face the sea; but this side enjoys a calmer pace, smaller cities and waters that lap more gently on the shore. And on this coast the sun sets into the sea in a pageant of colors.

Though Ponce de León and other 16C Spanish explorers sailed along this shore, they concentrated their attentions for the most part on Tampa Bay and left the southwest coast to the Calusa Indians. White settlement, which commenced in the mid-1800s, proceeded in fits and starts until the turn of the 19C, when development solidified into a leisurely pace. While Tampa and the east coast were booming with railroads and buildings, the southwest remained agricultural. Fishing villages and a handful of scattered tourist hotels attracted those with a penchant for adventure and the resources to make an excursion by boat. By the late 1920s, though, the area was coming into its own: **John Ringling**, who had begun developing some of the islands near Sarasota, started wintering his famous circus here in 1927, the same year the Seaboard Air Line Railway finally reached Naples.

Charting a steady course of progress up to the present, southwest Florida now faces many of the same dilemmas looming in other parts of the state. Most of its coast is already developed to capacity, and a largely sophisticated and environmentally aware population is working to control the rampant growth of past decades. Large tracts of land on Sanibel and other barrier islands have been preserved for shorebirds and other wildlife; citizens are realizing the need for long-term planning in an area where tourism ranks as the top industry and the beach is its greatest asset. Recent beach replenishment projects—with sand pumped up from offshore or trucked in from elsewhere—have taken place in Naples, Venice, Bonita Beach, Marco Island, Longboat Key and Captiva Island.

For tourists the Southwest Coast continues to hold many charms. From the cultural enticements of Sarasota and the sparkling beaches and excellent resorts of the barrier islands, to the fossilized sharks' teeth buried in Venice's sands and the fashionable shops and restaurants in Naples, this diverse region offers visitors a corner of paradise.

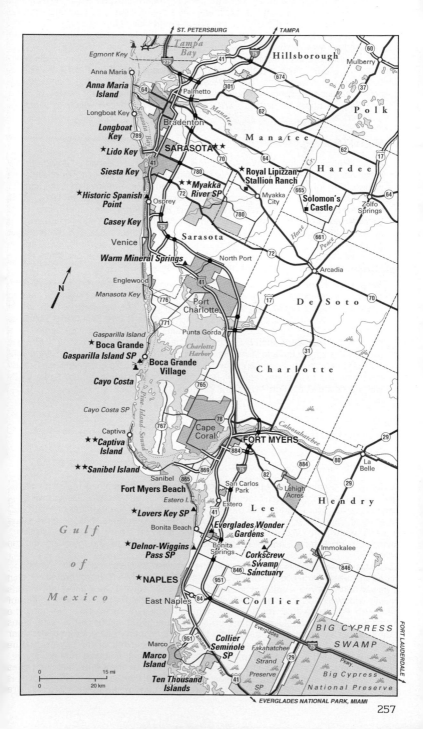

BOCA GRANDE★

Map p 257
Tourist Information: www.leeislandcoast.com ☎ 941-338-3500 or 800-237-6444

This charming village of sun-splashed houses and pastel-colored shops perches at the southern end of 7mi-long **Gasparilla Island**, separated from the mainland by a 2mi toll bridge and causeway. Spanish for "big mouth," Boca Grande refers to the pass that opens to Charlotte Harbor, one of the state's deepest natural inlets. Visitors will find here an unhurried island with natural beauty to rival the more well-known Sanibel and Captiva Islands to the south.

Making a good living from the sea, the Calusa Indians knew of Gasparilla's charms more than 1,000 years ago. By the late 1870s, Cuban and Spanish fishermen had established a fishing ranch on the north end. With the discovery of phosphate on the mainland in 1885, port Boca Grande became a worldwide shipping center. The completion of the Northern Railroad in 1907 facilitated the transport of phosphate, and also created an avenue south for wealthy northerners.

Already known as a **tarpon-fishing** mecca, Boca Grande soon grew into an actual town with streets, a post office and the stately 1912 **Gasparilla Inn** *(500 Palm Ave.)*, which continues to welcome guests. Today vacationers seek respite on the island's lovely peaceful beaches and fishermen continue to cast their lines in the waters of Boca Grande Pass in hopes of netting *Tarpon atlanticus*—which can weigh as much as 300 pounds apiece.

SIGHTS

Boca Grande Village – *Located on the south end of Gasparilla Island; follow Gasparilla Rd. south to Park St.* This charming hamlet merits a couple of hours to wander through its quaint shops, sample its restaurants, and stroll past the handful of restored early 20C buildings that make up its center. Planted in 1914, stout trees form a dark tunnel over locally famous **Banyan Street**; the white-frame 1910 **United Methodist Church** *(Gilchrist Ave. and Third St.)* still holds Sunday services. The railroad quit running here when the causeway opened in 1958, but the old **depot** *(Park Ave. and Fourth St.)* was restored in the 1970s into a plaza of shops, offices and a restaurant. Around the corner on Third Street, the former **San Marco Theatre** (1926) now holds a restaurant and yet more shops.

Gasparilla Island State Park – *On the southern end of island; follow Gulf Blvd. south of village. Park hrs & fees p 350.* 🅿 ☎ *941-964-0375.* Five separate parking lots allow access to the sparkling white beach here. At the southern tip of the island, a picnic area surrounds the two-story, white-frame **Boca Grande Lighthouse** *(follow Gulf Blvd. south to Belcher Rd.).* Built in 1890, the beacon served as a navigational aid at the mouth of Charlotte Harbor until 1966. Relit in 1986, the tower holds a museum and visitor center *(open Sept-Jul Wed-Sun 10am-4pm; contribution requested).* From here you can see Cayo Costa across breezy Boca Grande Pass, and the twin green tanks of Boca's oil-transfer station, where tankers off-load oil destined for Fort Myers and other points.

FORT MYERS

Population 48,208
Map pp 260-261
Tourist Information: www.leeislandcoast.com ☎ 941-338-3500 or 800-237-6444

A city of royal palms and tropical flowers, Fort Myers curves along the shore of the gentle Caloosahatchee River. Though development in recent decades has sprawled the urban area out past I-75 and into the jam-packed adjoining communities of North Fort Myers and Cape Coral, a renewed downtown offers restaurants, historic houses and a scenic waterfront *(for guided walking tours, see Fort Myers Historical Museum).* Just south on Estero Island, **Fort Myers Beach** is the center of the local sun-and-fun scene.

Fort Myers was established when relations between settlers and Native Americans flared up after the Second Seminole War. In 1885 Fort Myers incorporated, elected a mayor and received a visitor who would become the town's most important citizen. Newly widowed and in poor health, inventor **Thomas Alva Edison** traveled from New Jersey to Florida to look for a winter home in which to recuperate. He bought a 14-acre estate in Fort Myers and set up shop. An active member of the community, Edison imported royal palms from Cuba to line his property along **McGregor Boulevard**. The city took up where Edison left off, and now some 14mi of the city's signature avenue are edged with stately palms. The publicity that followed America's most famous inventor gave a tangential boost to Fort Myers; by the 1920s building boom, the city was off and running. Like most of southwest Florida, the economy of Fort Myers balances today on three legs: tourism, construction and agriculture.

SIGHTS

★★Edison Ford Winter Estates – *2350 McGregor Blvd. Open year-round Mon-Sat 9am-5:30pm, Sun noon-5:30pm. Closed Thanksgiving Day & Dec 25. $12.* 🖶 ☎ *941-334-3614. www.edison-ford-estate.com.* Situated on the Caloosahatchee River, this complex holds the winter homes and tropical gardens of inventor **Thomas Edison** (1847-1931) and automaker **Henry Ford** (1863-1947). Edison bought his property in 1885 and designed two connecting cottages, some of the first pre-fabricated houses in the country. In his laboratory and botanical gardens, he perfected the incandescent light bulb, the phonograph, the moving-picture camera and projector and the storage battery.

In 1896 Edison met a young man named Henry Ford. Edison encouraged Ford, who was then working in the Edison Illuminating Co. in Detroit, to follow his dream of building cars. The men became friends, and in 1916 Ford bought an adjacent house to be near his mentor. The two went camping in the Everglades and shared thought-provoking conversations, though Ford was very private and Edison nearly deaf. After Edison died, Ford never again wintered in Fort Myers, saying he could not bear to be there without his friend. Today Edison's home and the winter cottage of his billionaire buddy draw thousands of visitors a year.

Edison's Home – ♿ The star attraction here, Edison's spacious house, "Seminole Lodge," nestles in an Eden of tropical flowers and trees, odd hybrids and towering bamboo—all part of the botanical gardens the inventor used for his experiments. Tours wend along garden paths and enter the double house (as the two connected structures are called), inviting with its 14ft verandas furnished with wicker chairs and porch swings. French doors provide cross ventilation and access to the dining, living and other rooms. All are appointed the way Edison's second wife, Mina Miller Edison, left them when she died in 1947.

Ford's Home – Ford bought the "Mangoes" (1911), a relatively modest cottage, for $20,000 in 1916. The two-story frame house is furnished with pieces of the period—English walnut chairs and table, Belgian tablecloths, Wedgwood china. Tours take in the pantry, kitchen, dining room, living room and guest and employee bedrooms. Outside, a garage houses vintage Ford automobiles. A paved path connects the properties, curving by the river where Ford and Edison used to fish.

Edison Laboratory – Outfitted with test tubes and glass beakers, Edison's lab served as a testing ground for the inventor's experiments—including his work on domestic rubber production. The storage battery drove Edison to 9,000 failed experiments. After 41,000 additional tests, the battery was finally ready for patenting and marketing.

The adjacent **Edison Museum** houses six rooms filled with thousands of items, including more than 200 Edison phonographs—his favorite invention. Positioned at the end of the house tour, this museum documenting the life's work of one of the country's greatest geniuses is almost overwhelming in its scope.

Just outside the laboratory, the **banyan tree** that tire magnate Harvey Firestone brought back from India for Edison in 1925 has grown to measure some 400ft around its myriad trunks, and ranks as the world's third largest banyan.

© Michele & Tom Grimm/Tony Stone Images

Edison's Laboratory

★**Burroughs Home** – *2505 1st St. at Fowler St. Visit by guided tour (45min) only, mid-Oct-mid-May Tue-Fri 11am-3pm. $6. Free parking at Ramada Inn (one block south on 1st St.).* ☎ *941-332-6125.* This handsome 1901 Georgian Revival house was built by a Montana cattle baron and purchased in 1918 by Midwestern banker and cattleman Nelson T. Burroughs. His daughter bequeathed the house to the City of Fort Myers in 1978. Royal palms and other lush plantings grace the lawn of the two-story house, and a wraparound porch collects cool river breezes. Once the city's largest residence, the house features Florida pine floors, a mahogany fireplace, a winding staircase and original furnishings. On the engaging tour, costumed docents play the roles of the Burroughs' sisters, transporting visitors back to the turn of the 19C, when the family entertained such local leading lights as the Thomas Edisons and the Henry Fords.

Fort Myers Historical Museum (**M¹**) – *2300 Peck St., at Jackson St. Open year-round Tue-Sat 9am-4pm. Closed major holidays. $6.* ♿ 🅿 ☎ *941-332-5955. Walking tours of historic downtown conducted Jan-May Wed 10am.* Housed in a 1924 railroad depot, a summary of local history offers exhibits on the Calusa and Seminole Indians, Spanish explorers and white settlers. Among the

FORT MYERS SANIBEL CAPTIVA

> **❶ Shell Factory**
> *See map. 2787 US-41, north of Littleton Rd. in North Fort Myers.* ☎ *941-995-2141. www.shellfactory.com.* If you're tired of sifting through piles of shells on Sanibel and Captiva Islands, this store gives you the easy way out. Bins and bins of shells from many countries fill the huge warehouse space, along with shell jewelry, shell lamps and a multitude of other souvenirs. Just inside the entrance, glass cases hold a collection of labeled seashells from around the world. The factory has expanded to offer a wildlife sanctuary for exotic animals, a petting zoo, miniature golf, bumper boats and a gallery of African art.

indoor displays are a saber-toothed cat skeleton found in central Florida (only some of the bones are original), a model of Fort Myers in 1850, and collections of Carnival glass and Depression glass (inexpensive colored glass made between 1929 and 1941, now considered a collector's item). Outside stands the **Esperanza**, an 84ft private railcar—the longest and one of the last built by George Pullman. Visitors may walk through the 1930s car and observe the luxurious stateroom fitted with Cuban mahogany and brass, ice-cooled air-conditioning ducts, call buttons for summoning the porter, and a tiny kitchen for preparing large meals. On the other side of the museum sits a replica of a vernacular Cracker house.

Calusa Nature Center and Planetarium – 🄺 *3450 Ortiz Ave. Open year-round Mon-Sat 9am-5pm, Sun 11am-5pm. $4.* ♿ 🅿 ☎ *941-275-3435. www.calusanature.com.* This facility offers a pleasant diversion for children and adults. Live turtles, fish and snakes head the indoor exhibits; outside stands an

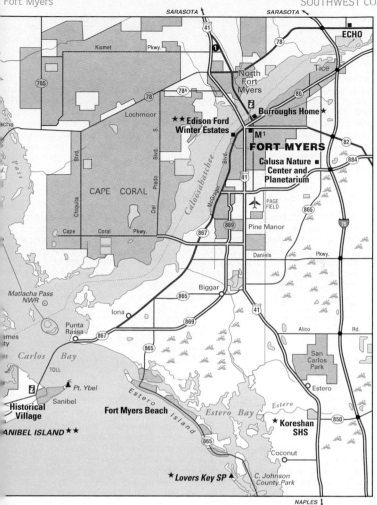

aviary for injured raptors, while a separate enclosure holds a bobcat. Three miles of interpretive boardwalk trails weave through hammocks of pine and cypress frequented by raccoons, otters, lizards and other animals. At the end of one trail sits a replica of a Seminole village and an exhibit detailing an earlier people, the Calusa. Also on the grounds is the **planetarium**, which presents star shows *(call for times; $3;* ☎ *941-275-3183).*

EXCURSIONS

ECHO – *10mi east in N. Fort Myers. Take I-75 north to Exit 26; (Rte. 78 East/Bayshore Rd.); continue 1mi east on Rte. 78 to 17391 Durrance Rd. Visit by guided tour (1hr 30min) only, Tue, Fri & Sat 10am. Closed major holidays.* 🅿 ☎ *941-543-3246. www.echonet.org.* Dedicated to helping people feed themselves, the Educational Concerns for Hunger Organization was founded in the 1970s to assist farmers in Haiti. The 40-acre site serves as a laboratory of farming techniques for the Third World. Volunteers and employees tend the urban roof and tropical lowland gardens as well as gardens grown in car tires. On tours, visitors learn how ideas developed here help feed people all over the globe. ECHO's seed bank and informational network connect gardeners, missionaries and farmers throughout the world. Also on location are special breeds of animals, a research library and gift shop.

★**Koreshan State Historic Site** – *16mi south in Estero. Take US-41 south; turn right on Corkscrew Rd. and follow it to park. Park hrs & fees p 350.* ⚠ 🅿 ☎ *941-992-0311.* This 305-acre site preserves 12 buildings from a late-19C religious community founded along the Estero River in 1893 by New York physician Cyrus Teed. Calling himself "Koresh" (Hebrew for Cyrus), Teed and his followers began constructing their "New Jerusalem," which they believed would eventually accommodate 10 million people. Though industrious, the religious order, 250 members at its peak, declined after Teed's death in 1908; their vow of celibacy virtually ensured the group's extinction. The last four members deeded part of their land to the State in 1961. A self-guided tour includes the grand art hall, planetary court, and founder's house.

★**Lovers Key State Park** – *30mi south on Lovers Key. Take I-75 south to Exit 18 and turn right on Bonita Beach Rd., which becomes Estero Blvd.; continue 11mi to park entrance at 8700 Estero Blvd. Park hrs & fees p 350.* 🅿 ☎ *941-463-4588. Canoe, kayak, rod & reel, bicycle rentals.* Occupying a gorgeous stretch of undeveloped barrier island, Lovers Key encompasses 712 acres of tidal lagoons, mangrove estuary and white-sand beach. Among the wildlife to be spotted are roseate spoonbills, egrets, alligators and endangered West Indian manatees. A boardwalk to the beach crosses two peaceful lagoons, where fishermen cast for trout, redfish and snook.

■ Estero Bay Nature Tours

Canoe or kayak the backbay estuaries on a naturalist-guided tour departing from **Lovers Key State Park** to discover the rich ecosystems of the area, or sign up for a guided paddle trip to Mound Key and hike to native American shell mounds. Pontoon cruises for novice anglers *(equipment provided)* or for leisurely viewing of the backbay are also offered along with overnight paddling excursions. If you prefer to "do it yourself," the park rents canoes and kayaks (including sea kayaks), as well as rod and reels on an hourly, half-day or full-day basis. Call for fees, schedules and reservations. ☎ *941-765-1880.*

NAPLES★

Population 20,976
Map p 264
Tourist Information: www.classicflorida.com ☎ 941-597-8001 or 800-688-3600

Just west of Big Cypress Swamp and north of the Everglades, Naples marks the edge of civilization at the southwest end of Florida. This small-scale Palm Beach is characterized by fine restaurants and hotels, upscale shops, the 1,200-seat Philharmonic Center for the Arts, more than 40 golf courses and 9mi of sun-drenched beaches. Many vacationers sample the archipelago to the south known as the **Ten Thousand Islands**; at the chain's northern extreme, **Marco Island** offers the resort life on one end and an old maritime village called Goodland on the other.

Impressed by the area's dazzling beaches and subtropical foliage, Walter S. Haldeman owner of the *Louisville Courier-Journal*, created the Naples Town Improvement Co. in 1887 (the city's name probably derives from early comparisons with Naples, Italy). The company built the Naples Hotel and the Pier, but overextended itself and went out of business.

Accessible only by boat or ox cart, the town attracted well-to-do families and reclusive millionaires who erected impressive estates along the beach. Real prosperity for Naples had to wait until the 1920s, with the arrival of the railroad and the completion of the Tamiami Trail in 1928—the latter financed largely by local landowner **Barron G. Collier** (1873-1939), a wealthy Memphis businessman who owned 1 million acres of royal palm hammock in the area. Today his namesake Collier County remains the richest county in Florida: the average annual personal income, in 1999, was $44,862. Recent census data shows Naples as one of the fastest-growing greater metropolitan areas, with a 65 percent increase between 1990 and 2000 to some 250,000 residents.

SIGHTS *Map p 264*

★**Scenic Drive** – *6mi. Follow Mooring Line Dr. (north of downtown, off US-41) south as it becomes Gulf Shore Blvd.; turn left on 19th Ave. and travel 1 block t Gordon Dr.; turn right and follow to dead end at Gordon Pass.* Driving south o Gulf Shore Boulevard, you pass some of the finest houses in Naples, with the larger more modern houses situated along the last 2.5mi of Gordon Drive. Built in 1888 the 600ft wooden **Naples Pier** *(at 12th Ave. S.)* harkens to the days when vaca tioners disembarked at this point. On the opposite side of the boulevard on 12t Avenue, **Palm Cottage** *(no. 137)*, constructed of tabby mortar (burnt seashells), among the oldest residences in Naples and serves as headquarters for Collie County Historical Society *(visit by 30min guided tour only, Oct-May Mon-Fri 1pm 3:30pm; rest of the year hrs vary; closed major holidays; $5;* ☎ *941-261-8164).* Tours of the two-story structure outline area history.

Bayfront Place Along Naples Bay

★**Lowdermilk Park** – *1405 Gulf Shore Blvd. N.* This beachfront park, with its tidy landscaping and well-patrolled parking area, shows neat and orderly Naples at its best. A groomed volleyball court, clean picnic area and snack bar, and pristine 1,000ft beach attract strollers, sunbathers and windsurfers. Only the non native, red-splotch-faced Muscovy ducks seem to be out of place.

★**Old Naples** – *5th Ave. S. and 3rd St. S.* The historic downtown offers chic shops and restaurants that open onto palm-lined streets, as well as shaded courtyards perfect for sipping tea or coffee. Galleries along **Third Street South**, particularly near

① Tin City
See map. East end of 5th Ave. S. at Goodlette Rd. ☐ A crowded cluster of shops and eateries resides along the harbor in a tin-roofed emporium that functioned as an oyster-processing plant in the 1920s. More than 40 stores here offer items ranging from scrimshaw to Hawaiian shirts. Some of the restaurants afford outdoor dining along Naples Bay.

Broad Avenue, sell original paintings, sculpture, prints and glass objects. For other shops, stroll down **Fifth Avenue South** between Third and Ninth streets.

■ Shopping the Souths

While Naples offers several shopping hubs, two attractive districts in particular, in downtown Naples, offer a treasure box of buyers' bounty. **Fifth Avenue South** is lined end to end *(9th St. to 3rd St.)* with palm trees and compelling boutiques, galleries, cafes, restaurants, antique and jewelry stores—many of them independently owned and noticeably individual in merchandise, including beach accessories, men's and women's resort wear (lots of pastels, of course), paintings and prints, local artwork and crafts (especially from shells), fine jewelry and footwear. Take a lunch break at, say, **Yabba** *(no. 711)* with a seafood salad or Caribbean grill. Or head for **Anabelle's** *(no. 494)* for your choice of Asian-influenced food downstairs, French-inspired cuisine upstairs. Dusk brings a leisurely street-festival atmosphere: patio dining along the avenue, outdoor entertainment (1940s-style crooning, Elvis impersonations, dance-school tap, keyboard solos, etc.) and the inevitable window-browsing *(some stores extend hours Thu-Sat)*. That same festive air pervades evenings along **Third Street South** *(between Broad Ave. & 14th Ave. S.)*, a power-shopper's paradise in daytime, offering 100 upscale retail outlets, many of them stocking heavyweight designer fashions and expensive baubles. Interior furnishings, fine art and antiques, a wealth of women's fashions and accessories, jewelry, books, stationery, garden and gift items beckon passers-by. Order a beverage or bite to eat outdoors at **Tommy Bahama's Tropical Cafe** *(no. 1220)* or indoors at **Terra** *(no.1300, on 13th)*. Street-corner boxes hold take-one map directories of all the Third's merchants, including those in the step-up Mediterranean-style promenade called **The Plaza**.

Across Fifth Avenue stands the Mediterranean-style **Naples Depot** *(1051 5th Ave. S.)*, built in 1927 as the southern terminus of Seaboard Air Line Railway's west coast line and now an office complex. A caboose and boxcar beside the depot contain shops.

Caribbean Gardens – Kids *1590 Goodlette-Frank Rd. (just south of Golden Gate Pkwy.). Open year-round daily 9:30am-5:30pm. Closed Easter Sunday, Thanksgiving Day, Dec 25. $14.95. ✗ ☐ ☎ 941-262-5409. www.caribbeangardens.com.* Exotic trees and animals inhabit the 52-acre garden park that began as a botanical collection in 1919. Visitors stroll among such trees as gumbo-limbo, jacaranda and Hong Kong orchid while viewing alligators, zebras, tigers and birds. The high point is a **boat ride** in an island-dotted pond that gives visitors a close look at agile primates, including the white-handed gibbon *(departs daily 10am-4:30pm; round-trip 20min)*. Animal lectures and shows add to the fun.

Naples Nature Center – *1450 Merrihue Dr., off 14th Ave. N. (adjacent to Caribbean Gardens). Open year-round Mon-Sat 9am-4:30pm. $7.50. ☐ ☎ 941-262-0304. www.conservancy.org.* A modern educational facility, this 15-acre preserve boasts hands-on displays, live snakes and other exhibits on southwest Florida's various ecosystems. Outside, a boardwalk trail loops through a mangrove swamp and past a wildlife rehabilitation center, where injured pelicans and other birds take therapeutic swims. A boat ride on the Gordon River is included in the admission fee, and canoes and kayaks are available for rent.

Teddy Bear Museum – Kids *2511 Pine Ridge Rd. near Airport-Pulling Rd. Open Dec-Apr Mon, Wed-Sat 10am-5pm, Sun 1pm-5pm. Rest of the year Wed-Sat 10am-5pm, Sun 1pm-5pm. Closed major holidays. $6. ☐ ☎ 941-598-2711. www.teddymuseum.com.* In this unusual museum, opened in 1990, you'll see more than 4,000 endearing bears. Special display areas showcase antique bears (dating back to 1903) and bears from around the world. Poohs, Paddingtons, grizzlies, soldier and sailor bears, Victorian bears, boardroom bears, and hosts of miniatures manifest the infinite variety of the time-honored teddy.

★**Naples Museum of Art** – *5833 Pelican Bay Blvd., adjacent to Philharmonic Center for the Arts. Open Oct-mid-Jul Tue-Sat 10am-4pm, Sun noon-4pm. Closed major holidays. $6. ☐ ☎ 941-597-1900. www.naples philcenter.org.* Art and architecture are suitably matched in this striking three-story showpiece adorning the

Philharmonic campus. Opened fall 2000, the $11 million, 15-gallery museum showcases temporary exhibits and a permanent collection of ancient Chinese and 20C American art. Visitors enter a massive granite portico via 16ft metal gates designed by Albert Paley and step into an outdoor sculpture court. Note therein Philip Jackson's tall bronze figures titled *The Sentinels*. Inside the domed conservatory, a stunning 30ft red glass chandelier by **Dale Chihuly** serves as an eye-catching centerpiece. His electrifying 35ft Icicle Chandelier dangles from the lobby's skylight. Permanently displayed on the first floor is the Gow Collection of Ancient Chinese Art spanning 450BC to the 19C, including a rare model of a manor compound (Han dynasty) and a silver Tibetan oboe (14-15C). On the second floor, selections of American art from 1900 to 1955 include works by Jackson Pollock and Marsden Hartley.

EXCURSIONS *Map p 257*

★**Delnor-Wiggins Pass State Park** – *West end of Bluebill Ave., off US-41. Park hrs & fees p 350.* ⚅ ▯ ☎ *941-597-6196.* If you want a break from crowded Lowdermilk Park and Vanderbilt Beach, Delnor-Wiggins is the place to go. Punctuating the heavily developed shoreline north of Naples, this delightful park offers more than a mile of unspoiled beach backed by sea grapes, sea oats, cabbage palms and mangroves. Through Wiggins Pass, at the park's north end, the Cocohatchee River finds its outlet to the sea. Also at this end, a 30ft observation tower clears the jungle canopy to provide glimpses of the Gulf of Mexico and its backwaters.

Everglades Wonder Gardens – 🆕 *14mi north in Bonita Springs. Take US-41 north and turn right (east) on Bus US-41; entrance is 1mi north of Bonita Beach Rd. Open year-round daily 9am-5pm. Closed Dec 25. $12.* ⚅ ▯ ☎ *941-992-2591.* Reminiscent of bygone Florida tourism, this 60-year-old attraction exhibits some 2,000 species of plants and animals from Florida, Asia, and Central and South America. Included are crocodiles, alligators, panthers and flamingoes housed in 1930s animal enclosures set amid lush gardens.

Corkscrew Swamp Sanctuary – *30mi northeast of Naples. Take US-41 north 9mi to Rte. 846/Immokalee Rd.; turn right (east) on Rte. 846 and continue 18mi. Turn left on Sanctuary Rd. and follow it to park entrance. Open mid-Apr-Sept daily 7am-7:30pm. Rest of the year daily 7am-5:30pm. $8.* ⚅ ▯ ☎ *941-348-9151. www.audubon.org/local/sanctuary.* Off the beaten path but well worth the visit, the country's largest stand of virgin cypress occupies this 11,000-acre tract owned by the National Audubon Society. A 2.25mi boardwalk trail begins in pine flatwoods and snakes through dense saw palmetto to a cypress swamp marked by soaring 500-year-old bald cypress trees. Visitors here may see alligators, endangered wood storks, tropical orchids and swamp lilies.

Collier-Seminole State Park – *17mi southeast on US-41. Park hrs & fees p 350.* △ ⚅ ▯ ☎ *941-394-3397.* This 6,400-acre preserve boasts a wide diversity of plants and wildlife. Tennessee advertising magnate Barron Collier donated some of his land and in 1947 the State created the park. Rare royal palms flourish in this tropical hammock, and mangrove and cypress swamps, salt marshes and pine flatwoods create an unusually variegated landscape. A 6.5mi trail offers occasional glimpses of wood storks, bald eagles, black bears and Florida panthers; the boardwalk trail *(.9mi)* loops to a viewing platform. Boat tours follow the scenic Blackwater River *(depart from concession stand year-round daily 9:30am-4pm; round-trip 1hr; commentary; $8.50;* ⚅ ▯ *Collier-Seminole State Park Boat Tours* ☎ *941-642-8898).*

On the way in, notice the monstrous **walking dredge** just off the road (on right). Used in the 1920s to construct the Tamiami Trail that stretches from Tampa to Miami, this specialized machine trudged through countless miles of soupy swamp and mud-thick glades.

SANIBEL AND CAPTIVA ISLANDS★★

Population 6,064 (Sanibel City)

Map pp 260-261

Tourist Information: www.sanibel-captiva.org ☎ 941-472-1080 or 800-850-4170

Long known as a paradise for shelling, these popular barrier islands, connected by causeways to each other and to the mainland, form a 20mi arc into the Gulf of Mexico 23mi southwest of downtown Fort Myers. Though the winter season brings a steady stream of traffic, the pockets of tranquillity and beauty that exist on these islands merit the drive over.

Spanish navigators who first discovered Sanibel and Captiva in the 16C never settled here, leaving the islands to the Calusa Indians.

Pioneers attempted to settle Sanibel as early as 1833. Development proceeded slowly up to 1963 when the causeway was built, at which time the floodgates opened to tourism. In 1995 more than three million vehicles crossed the bridge. Conservation

---

■ **Naming the Islands**

Sometime between the 16C and the 18C, the Spanish labeled the islands *Puerto de Nivel del Sur* ("port of the south plain") and *Boca del Cautivo* ("captives' entrance"). Over the years these names became corrupted to Sanibel and Captiva. Pirate lore maintains that buccaneers kept the loveliest of women prisoners on the smaller northern isle, hence its name. Since many of these legends are inextricably tangled with early 20C real-estate hype, the more likely original captive was a Spaniard named Juan Ortiz, kidnapped by the Calusa in 1528.

Practical Information .... Area Code: 941

Getting There – **Southwest Florida International Airport (RSW)**: in Fort Myers, 26mi east of islands; international and domestic flights; *(information: ☎ 768-4381; www.swfia.com)*. Transportation to Sanibel/Captiva: airport **shuttle** *($35-$55; reservations: ☎ 466-3236 or 800-566-0007)*; **taxi** *($40-$60)*. Visitor booth in baggage claim area *(open daily; hrs. vary seasonally)* ☎ 768-4374. **Rental car agencies** *(p 343)* located at airport and in Fort Myers. Nearest Amtrak **train** station is in Tampa, with Greyhound/Trailways **bus** connection to Fort Myers *(☎ 800-872-7245 or 800-231-2222)*. **Major access roads**: I-75, US-41 and Route 869 south to Sanibel Causeway; $3 toll in-bound.

Getting Around – Adventures in Paradise Trolley narrated sightseeing tour of Sanibel and Captiva departs from 21 different boarding stations in Sanibel *(Mon-Fri 10am-noon; $15; 2hrs; ☎ 472-8443)*. Sanibel **Taxi** *(☎ 472-4160)*; Sanibel **Limo** Service *(☎ 472-8888)*. No public transportation available on the islands. Best way to get around is by bicycle on the islands' 25mi of bike paths. **Bicycle rental shops**: Bike Route ☎ *(472-1955)*; Finnimore's Cycle Shop *(☎ 472-5577)*; Billy's Rentals *(☎ 472-5248)*; Yolo Watersports *(☎ 472-1296)*.

Visitor Information – **Lee County Visitor and Convention Bureau**, 2180 W. First St., Fort Myers FL 33901 *(open Mon-Fri 8am-5pm)* ☎ 338-3500 or 800-237-6444; **Sanibel-Captiva Islands Chamber of Commerce**, 1159 Causeway Rd., Sanibel FL 33957 *(open Mon-Sat 9am-7pm, Sun 10am-5pm)*, www.sanibel-captiva.org, ☎ 472-1080. *These organizations provide information on shopping, entertainment, festivals and recreation.*

Accommodations – Area visitors' guide including lodging directory available *(free)* from **Lee County Visitor and Convention Bureau**. Advance reservations are strongly suggested in season *(Dec-Apr)* and during Jul-Aug. Accommodations range from **hotels** and resorts *($185-$900)* to inns and **motels** *($129-$200)* and small **guest houses** *($100-$300)* within easy walking distance to beaches. Weekly and monthly rentals of condominiums and **apartments** available through local rental and real-estate agencies. **Camping**: Periwinkle Trailer Park (tents and RVs) *(☎ 472-1433)*. Camping is permitted only in specified campgrounds. Cayo Costa State Park accessible by boat only: hiking, shelling, camping, bicycle rental; for cabin reservations Barrier Island GEO Park *(☎ 964-0375)*. *Rates quoted are average prices per night for a double room and are subject to seasonal variations.*

Sports and Recreation – Most **beaches** have public access and restrooms. Parking at Sanibel beaches *(7am-7pm; 75¢/hr, free other times)*; at Captiva beaches parking is free. Driving on beaches is prohibited. Water sports include swimming, boating, sailing, canoeing, saltwater and freshwater fishing. The islands are accessible by Intracoastal Waterway. Major **bike** path runs from Lighthouse Point to Blind Pass at western end of island. **Nature tours** (canoe/kayak) and fishing excursions, boat and bicycle rentals in J.N. "Ding" Darling National Wildlife Refuge: Tarpon Bay Recreation *(☎ 472-8900)*. Wildlife and sunset **cruises**: Captiva Cruises *(daily 4pm-5:30pm & sunset; $17.50; ☎ 472-5300)*. **Snorkeling** and **dolphin-watching** excursions: Captain Bob's Shelling & Dolphin Watch *(daily excursions; 5hrs; $50; reservations required; ☎ 472-0982)*. For **shelling**

cruises, *see p 269*. **Golf**: Beachview Golf Club *(☎ 472-2626)*; Dunes Golf & Tennis Club *(☎ 472-2535)*; both clubs allow non-members.

Entertainment – Consult the *Sunny Day Guide* and Sanibel-Captiva Islands Chamber of Commerce publication available locally *(free)* for schedules of activities, dining and local events. **J. Howard Wood Theatre**: theater and plays *(Nov-May)* ☎ 472-0006); **Old Schoolhouse Theater**: musicals *(Nov-May)* and light theater *(summer)* *(☎ 472-6862)*.

groups rallied to protect their island from unchecked development. One notewortl result of their efforts, the J.N. "Ding" Darling National Wildlife Refuge, preserves mor than one-third of Sanibel's total acreage.
The main thoroughfares (Periwinkle Way and Sanibel-Captiva Road) today pass tony bo tique-and-restaurant complexes on Sanibel's south end, then traverse a long stretch bayside wilderness before crossing to Captiva for the 3.5mi drive to the end. Traffic mov at a leisurely pace. Though occasionally affording a view of the sea, the road most tunnels through the dense greenery shielding tasteful resorts and expensive houses.

Enjoying Sanibel Beach

SIGHTS

Bailey-Matthews Shell Museum (M²) – *3075 Sanibel-Captiva Rd. Open year-round Tue-Sun 10am-4pm. Closed major holidays. $5.* & 🅿 ☎ *941-395-2233. www.shellmuseum.org.* A must for conchologists, this attractive stucco building—opened in 1995—houses a reference collection of some two million shells. In the main exhibit hall, displays range from the geographic location of shells worldwide to the variety of mollusks that can be found on Sanibel and Captiva Islands. The role of shells in tribal art, medicine and as a food source is also explored.

Sanibel Historical Village and Museum – *950 Dunlop Rd., off Periwinkle Way in the government complex. Visit by guided tour (1hr) only, Dec-Apr Wed-Sat 10am-4pm, Sun 1pm-4pm. Rest of the year Wed-Sat 10am-1pm. $3.* & 🅿 ☎ *941-472-4648.* Set up as a pioneer village, the local history museum features a 1913 Cracker house with a dining room, parlor and kitchen furnished to depict early island life. Additional rooms contain fossil and shell displays, Spanish shipwreck artifacts and 2,000-year-old remains of the Calusa Indian culture. Other buildings on the site include a tea room, the 1926 Sanibel post office and Bailey's General Store. This store, which functioned as the hub of the community until the early 1960s, was moved here in 1993 from its original site near the causeway.

Sanibel-Captiva Conservation Foundation – *3333 Sanibel-Captiva Rd. (1mi southeast of J.N. "Ding" Darling Refuge entrance). Open late Nov-Easter Mon-Fri 8:30am-4pm, Sat 10am-3pm. Rest of the year Mon-Fri 8:30am-3pm. Closed major holidays. $3.* 🅿 ☎ *941-472-2329. www.sccf.org.* This 247-acre site surrounds a nature center containing a touch tank and informative displays on wetlands ecology. Out front is a native plant nursery; behind the center, nearly 5mi of boardwalk trails wind through wetland and upland habitats. One walk *(.3mi)* leads to a 30ft observation tower that provides fine **views** of the Sanibel River, the forest canopy, and possibly a pair of roosting ospreys or other birds. The foundation, which owns 1,800 acres in the barrier islands, works to preserve natural resources; its programs include land acquisition, habitat management, environmental education, landscaping for wildlife and sea-turtle research.

★**J.N. "Ding" Darling National Wildlife Refuge** – *1 Wildlife Dr., off Sanibel-Captiva Rd. Open Nov-Apr daily 9am-5pm. Rest of the year daily 9am-4pm. Closed major holidays.* & 🅿 ☎ *941-472-1100. www.dingdarling.org.* A showcase of barrier island wildlife abounds here in canals, inlets, mangrove swamps and upland forests. Begin at the **visitor center**, where you can acquaint yourself with the 6,300-acre refuge and its natural history through displays and videos. Jay Norwood Darling, for whom the refuge is named, owned a cottage on Captiva, and for 25 years-until his death in 1962 at age 86, he championed conservation causes on the islands. Best known as a Pulitzer Prize-winning political cartoonist, Darling also directed the US Biological Survey under President Franklin Roosevelt. Many motorists choose to take the one-way, unpaved **Wildlife Drive** *(4mi)*, which offers virtually guaranteed sightings of water birds and other animals, including the alligator *(speed limit 15mph; $5/vehicle, exact change required)*.
A 20ft observation tower *(on left, about halfway along the drive)* allows **views** of herons, egrets, roseate spoonbills, ospreys and others. For best bird-watching, visit

267

near dawn, at sunset or at low tide, when the mud flats are exposed. Near the end of the drive, the **Shell Mound Trail** *(.3mi; parking on left)* loops through lush vegetation over an ancient Calusa shell mound.

Those who want a closer look at local flora and fauna can hike the refuge's 4mi of interpretive trails, or paddle the 6mi of marked canoe courses. *Canoes, bicycles and fishing equipment are available for rent. Guided canoe and kayak excursions depart from north end of Tarpon Bay Rd. year-round daily; round-trip 2hrs; $20; reservations required. Tram tours depart from Tarpon Bay Feb-Mar (rest of the year from visitor center) Sat-Thu; round-trip 2hrs; commentary; $8. ☆ ❚ For tour schedules, contact Tarpon Bay Recreation ☎ 941-472-8900. www.tarponbay.com.*

Sanibel Lighthouse – *Point Ybel, east tip of Sanibel Island. Not open to the public.* Bureaucratic snafus kept Sanibel in the dark for more than 50 years from the time islanders first petitioned for a lighthouse. Finally erected in 1884, the 98ft ironwork beacon still guides mariners. The light and keeper's quarters, listed on the National Register of Historic Places, are the oldest buildings on Sanibel. The lighthouse stands between parking areas that provide access to a bayside fishing pier and beach.

Chapel by the Sea – *Take Sanibel-Captiva Rd. to north end of Captiva; turn left on Wiles Dr. and follow to end; turn left into church parking lot.* Built as a county school in 1901, this tiny white clapboard church offers quiet respite from sun and sea. The building was purchased by the Methodists in 1921 as a mission church, but because of a scarcity of local followers the chapel gradually became interdenominational. An adjacent **cemetery**, holding the remains of early settlers, skirts the beach under a canopy of Sabal palm, sea grape and gumbo-limbo trees.

EXCURSIONS

Cayo Costa – *Accessible by boat only. Departs from South Seas Resort on Captiva Nov-May Tue-Sat 10am, returns from Cayo Costa 4pm. One-way 1hr. Reservations required. $35. ❚ Captiva Cruises ☎ 941-472-5300. www.captivacruises.com.* Used as a quarantine station for tall ships in the early 1800s, Cayo Costa (Spanish for "key by the coast") is now owned by the state park department. Thus protected from development, the 1,600-acre island maintains its pre-European appearance, dense with palmetto brush and pine forests. **Cayo Costa State Park** occupies the north part of the island *(open year-round daily 8am-dusk; $2; guided tours offered every 3rd Sat of the month, call for schedule; △ ☎ 941-964-0375)* Visitors may hike or bike the 5mi of developed inland trails, or stroll the deserted shell-strewn beach and watch pelicans and dolphins at play. In summer, loggerhead turtles come to the island's shores to lay their eggs.

Cabbage Key – *Accessible by boat only. Departs from South Seas Resort on Captiva year-round daily 10:30am, returns from Cabbage Key 3:30pm. One-way 1h. 15min. Commentary. Reservations required. $27.50. ❚ Captiva Cruises ☎ 941-472-5300. www.captivacruises.com.* To visit this tiny island in Pine Island Sound is to travel back to the earliest days of Florida tourism. Its dominant building is the weathered **Cabbage Key Inn** (1938), built on a Calusa Indian shell mound as winter residence for the son of mystery writer Mary Roberts Rinehart. In the early

■ Shelling: Doin' the Sanibel Stoop

Dubbed *Costa de Carocles* ("Coast of Seashells") by 16C Spanish explorers, Sanibel and Captiva beaches continue to harvest a staggering number and variety of colorful shells. The islands' unusual east-west orientation intersects with the junction of gulf currents, acting as a natural catchment for the more than 200 species of mollusks that inhabit the Gulf of Mexico's shallow continental shelf.

One of the more popular pastimes here is the "Sanibel stoop," the bent-over posture assumed by serious conchologists, or shell collectors. For best finds, arrive an hour before low tide; tides are especially low at new and full moons. Two days after a northwesterly wind is the optimum time to discover the largest assortment churned up on the beach from deep waters. Common among the myriad shells found here are calico scallops, kitten's paws, turkey wings, lightning whelks, fighting conchs and

Calico Scallop

Fighting Con

Lion's Paw Scallop

Coquin

Flame A

1940s, a subsequent owner turned the house into an inn. Some 25,000 dollar bills, signed by patrons, hang from the ceiling of the restaurant, which serves good, simple fare. In this unpretentious setting, occasional celebrities such as Arnold Schwarzenegger and Jimmy Buffett blend in with tourists and fishermen. After lunch, you can take a half-mile nature trail through a dense understory of mangroves, strangler figs and sea grapes. A 30ft water tower provides a **view** of the surrounding islands.

SARASOTA★★

Population 52,715

Map p 277

Tourist Information: www.sarasotafl.org ☎ 941-957-1877 or 800-522-9799

Lying on the Gulf Coast just south of Bradenton, Sarasota offers one of Florida's best-balanced menus of attractions. Here you'll find the official art museum of Florida, a host of cultural and sports activities, two shopping districts that rival the swankest in Palm Beach, restaurants catering to all palates and budgets, and a 35mi stretch of superb beach. In addition to tourism, Sarasota's economy rides on information technology, health care and financial services to provide for the area's many monied retirees.

Historical Notes

The bulk of the area's pioneers began arriving in the late 1860s, enticed by free land offered by the federal government. In 1885 a boatload of Scottish settlers quickly set about building a community. The town elected as its first mayor, in 1902, the son of a Scottish nobleman, and the builder of one of the country's first golf courses in Sarasota. Another influential city father, **John Ringling** bought a house in Sarasota in 1912. For several years Ringling traveled with his famous **Ringling Bros. and Barnum & Bailey Circus**. Involved in local real estate in 1917, he poured much of his time and money into the area, even serving as chamber of commerce president. Thanks to Ringling, the barrier islands—once his personal property—are now linked by causeway to the mainland. In 1927 he moved the circus' winter headquarters to Sarasota, providing a much-needed injection to the local economy. Visitors paid 25 cents to watch rehearsals, with proceeds going to charity. That same year, Ringling and his wife began construction of a grand Italian Renaissance-style residence to house their growing collection of paintings. In the late 1940s Arthur Vining Davis' Arvida Corp. changed Lido, St. Armands, Longboat and other keys into bastions of high-toned houses, shops and resorts. Neighborhoods like **Indian Beach**, just south of the Ringling Museum, showcase older houses (some on the National Register of Historic Places) in styles ranging from Mediterranean Revival to simple Craftsman bungalows.

The Ringling complex, the adjacent **Florida State University Center for the Performing Arts** and the purple shell-shaped **Van Wezel Performing Arts Hall** cover the cultural spectrum, presenting art, music, dance and theater. Other options include the Sarasota Ballet, Sarasota Opera Association, Florida West Coast Symphony, and a number of small theaters and annual film festivals. Baseball enthusiasts can watch the Cincinnati Reds and Pittsburgh Pirates play spring exhibition games in the area *(see Spectator Sports)*.

Junonia

tiny coquina clams. Rare finds include the prized brown-speckled junonia, lion's paw and Scotch bonnet. *Taking live shellfish, sand dollars, sea stars and sea urchins is prohibited by state law; violators are subject to a $500 fine and 60 days in jail for a first offense. Local Sanibel ordinances prohibit taking any live shells.*

Kitten's Paw

Lovely Bowman's Beach *(3mi north of "Ding" Darling Refuge entrance; turn left on Bowman's Beach Rd.; parking 7am-7pm, 75¢/hr)* and Turner Beach *(at Blind Pass between the islands; limited parking)* are popular starting places for beginning shellers. For those wishing to venture a bit farther afield, a number of shelling excursions are available: Captain Bob's Shelling & Dolphin Watch cruises depart from Punta Rassa boat ramp *(year-round daily; round-trip 5hrs; $50; reservations required ☎ 472-0982)*; Fuery's Shelling Charters depart from 'Tween Waters Marina on Captiva Island *(year-round daily; round-trip 3hrs; $150 for up to 4 people; reservations required ☎ 466-3649)*; Captiva Cruises depart from Bayside Marina, on the north end of Captiva *(year-round daily 9am & 1pm; round-trip 3hrs; $35; reservations required ☎ 472-5300)*.

Lightning Whelk

's Eye Moon Snail

PRACTICAL INFORMATION..................Area Code: 941

Getting There and Getting Around

By Air – Sarasota Bradenton International Airport **(SRQ)**: 3mi north of city; *(information: ☎ 359-5200)*. Transportation to downtown: Regal **Limo** *(☎ 351-2547)* and West Coast Executive Sedan *(☎ 355-9645)*, 24hr reservations suggested *($12)*; and taxi *($10)*. **Amtrak** bus connection to Tampa leaves from 1995 Main St. (next to movie complex) *(☎ 800-872-7245; www.amtrak.com)*. Greyhound **bus** station: 575 N. Washington Blvd. *(☎ 800-231-2222; www.greyhound.com)*.

By Bus – Local **bus service**: Sarasota County Area Transit *(Mon-Sat 5:30am-7pm; 50¢)*; for bus schedule and route information ☎ 951-5851. Free **trolley** takes in Downtown Art District, St. Armands Circle, Lido Beach and Ringling Museum; for schedule and boarding locations ☎ 951-5851.

By Car – Rental car agencies *(p 343)* are located at airport. Downtown metered **parking** *(25¢/hr)* and free on-street parking is available.

By Taxi – Yellow Cab *(☎ 748-4800)*; Diplomat *(☎ 365-8600)*.

General Information

Visitor Information – **Sarasota Convention and Visitors Bureau**, 665 N. US-41, Sarasota FL 34236 *(open year-round Mon-Sat 9am-5pm; ☎ 957-1877 or 800-522-9799, www.sarasotafl.org)*. This organization provides information on shopping, entertainment, festivals and recreation.

Accommodations – Area visitors' guide including lodging directory available *(free)* from Sarasota Convention and Visitors Bureau. Accommodations range from luxury **hotels** and resorts *($150-$800)* to moderate **motels** *($60-$100)* and **bed-and-breakfast inns** *($75-$150)*. Rates quoted are average prices per night for a double room and are subject to seasonal variations.

Entertainment – Consult the arts and entertainment section of the *Sarasota Herald-Tribune* (Fridays) or **INFOline** *(☎ 953-4636)* for schedules of cultural events. **Van Wezel Performing Arts Hall** *(☎ 953-3366)*; **Florida State University Center for the Performing Arts** *(☎ 351-8000)*; **Sarasota Opera House** *(☎ 953-7030)*.

Sports and Recreation – Golf: Forest Lake Country Club ☎ 922-1312; Bobby Jones Golf Club ☎ 365-4653. **Sailing** charters *($30-$55/person)* and sunset cruises *($35)*, Enterprise *(☎ 951-1833)*; sailboat (reservations required) and jet-ski rentals, O'Leary's Sarasota Sailing School *(☎ 953-7505)*.

Shopping: St. Armands Circle *(☎ 388-1554)*; **Southgate Plaza** *(☎ 955-0900)*, US-41 and Bee Ridge; **Sarasota Outlet Center**, Exit 40 off I-75 North; **Gulf Coast Factory Shops**, Ellenton, Exit 43 off I-75 North.

ADDRESS BOOK

For a legend of price listings for hotels and restaurants, see p 76.

Staying in Sarasota and Southwest Florida

The Registry – *475 Seagate Dr., Naples.* ⚒ ♿ 🅿 🛎 ☎ *941-597-3232 or 800-247-9810. www.registryhotels.com. 474 rooms.* **$$$$$** Clam Pass Park wildlife preserve serves as the 23-acre backyard for this luxury gulfside resort. A board walk behind the glass-enclosed lobby leads through a forest of towering mangroves—inhabited by blue herons, bald eagles, and pelicans—to the beach. Palm-print fabrics, oak paneling and light-wood furnishings set the resort's tropical mood. **Club Zanzibar**, with its large dance floor, is hot nightspot.

Sanibel Harbour Resort & Spa – *17260 Harbour Pointe Dr., Fort Myers* ⚒ ♿ 🅿 🛎 ☎ *941-466-4000 or 800-767-7777. www.sanibel-resort.com. 34 rooms, 70 condos.* **$$$$$** Anchoring the western edge of a private peninsula along San Carlos Bay, this modern mega-resort includes three hotel/condominium high rises, a 40,000sq ft spa/fitness center, fishing pier and marina, six swimming pools, three restaurants and a berth for its private yacht. The state-of-the-art tennis facilities have hosted two Davis Cup tournaments. Rooms boast a private balcony, bathrobes and Internet access. Dining choices range from spa cuisine to dinner cruises and Sunday brunch aboard the 100ft yacht.

Bokeelia Tarpon Inn – *8241 Main St., Bokeelia (map p 260).* ♿ 🅿 ☎ *941-283-8961. www.tarponinn.com. 5 rooms.* **$$$$** It's worth heading off the beaten path to this ultra-luxury B&B, reminiscent of the days when millionaire Barron Collier came to the area to fish. Built on the shore of Charlotte Harbor, the 1914 house still lures renowned anglers and those seeking seclusion. The handsome living room has hardwood floors, an original fireplace, Indonesian furnishings and a rack of wines, from which guests help themselves. The Chart Room sports a fly-tying bench and rod-and-reel adorned walls. Overlooking the water, the second-story screened porch is a coveted spot. Guests can tour the island in the inn's golf cart and fish from a nearby pier (fishing guides can be reserved in advance).

Hotel Escalante – *290 Fifth Ave. S., Naples.* ♿ ⓟ ⌇ ☏ *941-659-3466 or 877-485-3466. www.hotelescalante.com. 71 rooms.* **$$$$** Encased in lush foliage, this Mediterranean-style complex seems more a sprawling private villa than a public hotel. Yet the sumptuous escape sits just around the corner from the splashy shops of fashionable Fifth Avenue, and only blocks from the beach. Generous, ground-level guest quarters include mahogany armoires, ceiling fans, sizable closets, spacious bathrooms, and French doors opening onto a garden or poolside patio. Complimentary continental breakfasts, a liberally stocked library, and a frangipani-filled footpath encircling the retreat make for a special stay.

Resort at Longboat Key Club – *301 Gulf of Mexico Dr., Longboat Key.* ✗ ♿ ⓟ ⌇ ☏ *941-383-8821 or 800-237-8821. www.longboatkeyclub.com. 232 rooms.* **$$$$** Hidden from public view behind a guard gate, this exclusive 410-acre Gulf Coast resort sits on a beach of sugary white sand. Long a choice for refuge-seeking celebrities, it's also a golfer's delight: 45 holes divided between two courses. Tennis is served up on 38 courts of two tennis centers. Extra-spacious rooms and suites with kitchens are furnished in tropical prints; large balconies afford views of the sea. Yoga and massage are offered in the fitness center, and bicycles, aqua cycles, sea kayaks and snorkeling equipment are on hand for guests.

Crescent House B&B – *459 Beach Rd., Siesta Key.* ♿ ⓟ ⌇ ☏ *941-346-0857. www.crescenthouse.com. 4 rooms.* **$$$** Steps away from Crescent Beach (part of Siesta Beach, one of Florida's finest), this comfortable vacation spot abounds in Caribbean colors, ceiling fans and original wood floors. Guest quarters are furnished with four-poster beds and some with Jacuzzis. Two rooms have private baths; two share a bath. The cozy parlor proffers shelves of books and the pool patio hosts continental-plus breakfasts alfresco. From here, it's an easy walk to the restaurants and shops of Siesta Village.

The Cypress – *621 Gulfstream Ave. S., Sarasota.* ♿ ⓟ ☏ *941-955-4683. www.bbonline.com/fl/cypress. 4 rooms.* **$$$** Built of cypress wood in 1940, this compact, two-story B&B is a surprising downtown find, nestled as it is within an oasis of green across from the city sailboat anchorage. Dressed in art and antiques, intimate common rooms brim with seashells, old books and musical instruments. Themed guest rooms, furnished with French mansion beds, plantation armoires and hardwood floors, overlook the bay or garden. Served in a sunny, bayside space, breakfasts are gourmet extravaganzas featuring fresh squeezed orange juice, granola and French toast. Main Street shops and the marina are a short walk away.

Jensen's Twin Palms Resort – *15107 Captiva Dr., Captiva Island.* ♿ ⓟ ⌇ ☏ *941-472-5800. www.jensen-captiva.com. 14 units.* **$$$** Perhaps the most laid-back place this side of Key West, Jensen's counts cottages, coconut palms (more than 50) and beach proximity among its alluring assets. The resort sits right on the waters of Pine Island Sound, where lucky observers might spot manatees, dolphins and otters. The modest Old Florida cottages (and apartments) come with screened porches and kitchen facilities. Guests can hop aboard Jensen's water taxi to explore the outer islands or rent a boat at the marina.

Sunshine Island Inn – *642 East Gulf Dr., Sanibel Island.* ♿ ⓟ ⌇ ☏ *941-395-2500. www.sunshineislandinn.com. 5 rooms.* **$$$** This small, pastel-shaded inn is known for its enduring hospitality and comfort. Guest rooms are light and cheery, each with an efficiency or full kitchen and sliding door to the pool area. The on-site laundry facilities and barbecue grill for guests are extra amenities that appeal especially to families. The inn is located in a quiet neighborhood across the street from the beach and a short bicycle ride away from the fishing pier and lighthouse.

Tween Waters Inn – *15951 Captiva Rd., Captiva Island.* ✗ ♿ ⓟ ⌇ ☏ *941-472-5161or 800-223-5865. www.tween-waters.com. 163 rooms.* **$$$** Framed by the gentle gulf surf and calming waters of Pine Island Sound, this timeless, self-contained resort keeps customers coming back for its recreational options and relaxed, Old Florida feel. The original beach cottages harbored the likes of Anne Morrow Lindbergh and conservationist "Ding" Darling. Those seeking contemporary space may settle into newer quarters built on stilts for great water views. Tennis clinics, an Olympic-size pool, a fitness center, and Monday night crab races in Crow's Nest restaurant keep guests well occupied. Bicycles, kayaks and canoes can be rented (a popular short paddle crosses the sound to Buck Island). Complimentary breakfast is served island style.

Uncle Henry's Marina Resort – *5800 Gasparilla Rd., Boca Grande.* ✗ ♿ ▣ ⛵ ☎ *941-964-2300. www.bocagrande.com. 18 rooms.* **$$$** Affordable accommodations on a plush island that once attracted the Astors and Vanderbilts and still seduces the rich and famous, Uncle Henry's sits on a pretty little marina that can handle yachts up to 80ft long. The Gasparilla Island lodging offers a tranquil setting with plenty of shady spots where guests can read, relax and watch boats come and go. Rooms are modest but comfy, all facing an atrium centerpiece that recalls the pirate era when buccaneer José Gaspar took over the 7mi-long barrier island. Following the golf-cart path is a fun way to explore the beaches, lighthouse and village of Boca Grande.

Tides Inn Motel – *1800 Stickney Point Rd., Sarasota.* ♿ ▣ ⛵ ☎ *941-924-7541 or 800-823-8594. www.myplanet.net/tidesinn. 12 rooms.* **$$** Ultra-clean and simply appointed, this mom-and-pop motel is a rare value. The spacious rooms are sparsely but comfortably furnished with a Florida flair. There's a large grassy backyard that's perfect for pitching horseshoes, playing shuffleboard, picnicking or plucking oranges from the trees (juicers provided). The pool area is a private, fenced-in oasis, and the famous beaches of Siesta Key lie eight blocks away, with shops, restaurants, boat rentals and a bait shop en route.

Dining in Sarasota and Southwest Florida

Beach Bistro – *6600 Gulf Dr., Holmes Beach, Anna Maria Island.* ♿ ☎ *941-778-6444. www. beachbistro.com.* **$$$$ Continental**. This tiny bistro, secreted within a motel, sits right on a white, sandy beach. The best seating faces the green waters of the Gulf of Mexico and the setting sun. Signature salads include the Tropicana (citrus, mango, kiwis, berries, roasted pecans atop baby greens with fruit frappé vinaigrette). "Lobstercargots" is a popular small plate, while Bistro bouillabaisse and Andreas "Floribbean" grouper (encrusted in toasted coconut and cashews, topped with a red pepper papaya jam) are winning entrées. Finales like bananas Foster and berry cinnamon crepes are sure to prompt a moonlit stroll on the beach. *Dinner only.*

Bistro 821 – *821 Fifth Ave. S., Naples.* ♿ ☎ *941-261-5821.* **$$$ Continental**. The interior dining space of this chic restaurant spills out onto sidewalk seating, creating a casual, open-air feeling. Facing the bar and open kitchen, one long fabric-bedecked wall booth promotes easy conversation with neighboring diners. Early Bird specials, half portions and lighter-side servings of lamb, chicken, steak, seafood (fish selections are sometimes presented *en papillote*) and pasta plates make 821 a popular dining spot. After dinner, enjoy the street festival atmosphere that prevails along Fifth Avenue *(Thu-Sat)*, where a variety of solo musicians and dance groups may be on hand to entertain.

Café on the Bay – *2630 Harbourside Dr., Longboat Key.* ♿ ☎ *941-383-0440. www.cafeonthebay.com.* **$$$ American**. Drive through the guard gate or dock your boat (Marker 15) at Longboat Key Moorings when you come to dine in this exclusive Mediterranean-styled setting of coconut palms and countless impatiens. The marina-hugging haunt hauls in the resort-casual crowd with chic-nautique interior, awash in ocean blues and assuasive aquariums. For outdoor dining, try the shady veranda, cooled by sea breezes. Café's creative menu means appetizers like tuna carpaccio and entrées such as vegetarian napoleon (warm polenta rounds layered with grilled vegetables in smoked tomato sauce), or a mixed grill of veal and ostrich medallions.

The Summerhouse – *6101 Midnight Pass Rd., Siesta Key.* ♿ ☎ *941-349-1100. www.sarasotarestaurants.com.* **$$$ Continental**. The mood here is pure romance: elegant table settings, low lighting, floor-to-ceiling windows, lots of tropical plants. The menu attests to this award-winning restaurant's inventiveness, with appetizers like roast quail grilled over lightly wilted spinach. Entrées range from grouper piccata to chargrilled venison chops topped with woodland mushrooms. Light bites are available in the second-story Treetop Lounge. The chef/proprietor is known for his cooking classes that conclude with lunch, wine and recipes. *Dinner only.*

The Veranda – *2122 Second St. (at Broadway), Fort Myers.* ♿ ☎ *941-332-2065. www.verandarestaurant.com.* **$$$ Continental**. Gracious Southern hospitality awaits patrons of this "dressy casual" restaurant, where vintage photos adorn the walls. The century-old, side-by-side houses possess a history that mixes cattlemen, a military captain, and a member of the Pulitzer publishing family. Tastes of Dixie flavor the chef's take on old favorites—appetizers like fried green-tomato salad or Southern grit cakes with pepper jack cheese and andouille sausage. Try the Southern Sampler mixed grill of fresh fish; the gulf shrimp and sea scallops with saffron fettucine; or the Bourbon Street filet medallions in a smoky sour-mash whisky sauce. After dining, request a tour of the houses, if you're so inclined.

The Dock – *845 12th Ave. S. (next to City Dock), Naples.* ♿ ☎ *941-263-9940. www.dockcraytoncove.com.* **$$ Caribbean.** Join the hullabaloo at this hive of open-air dining on the waterfront at Crayton Cove. The Old Naples institution has them waiting in line, especially on weekends, for great seafood, specialty sandwiches and "docktails." Try the daily fish fry *(3pm-6pm)* for under $10, or order Bahamian conch fritters to start and move on to Jamaican Jerk shrimp, grilled and topped with pineapple-ginger salsa. Cuban barbecued ribs brushed with sour orange *mojito*, or rum and molasses barbecued duck are other temptations from the menu. Added perks include a raw bar and Sunday brunch.

Moore's Stone Crab Restaurant – *800 Broadway, Longboat Key.* ♿ ☎ *941-383-1748 or 888-968-CRAB. www.stonecrabstoyourdoor.com.* **$$ Seafood.** A Longboat Key institution since 1967, this unpretentious, family-owned restaurant at the north end of the island offers stunning views of Sarasota Bay. Gathering stone crabs by hand in 1927 on the flats of the bay, Papa Jack Moore began the family's reputation for serving the freshest stone crabs around. The family now harvests the crustacean with its own sizable fleet. Presented as combination platters, single plates or sandwiches, the restaurant's variety of catches, from grouper to pompano, are year-round attractions.

RC Otters – *11506 Andy Rosse Lane, Captiva Island.* ♿ ☎ *941-395-1142.* **$$ American.** It's easy to feel the island spirit here in this shiplap-constructed cottage. The casual restaurant it now houses offers alfresco dining on the front porch or brick patio, and inside in intimate rooms decked with paintings by area artists. An affordable menu offers more than 200 items ranging from large, crispy salads, and sandwiches of all kinds, to lobster, ribs, steak and fish. The children's menu features some 15 kid-loving selections. Nightly entertainment usually showcases bands well-versed in Jimmy Buffett tunes.

Sharky's on the Pier – *1600 S. Harbor Dr., Venice.* ♿ ☎ *941-488-1456. www.sharkysonthepier.com.* **$$ American.** Thatched-roofed shelters and sturdy palms sprout from the spacious deck of this popular eatery, positioned to oversee all the comings and goings of anglers, surfers and sunbathers. The enclosed dining area sports dark woods, a nautical look and tables crammed with convivial crowds of seafood lovers, who come for the Macadamia grouper (with cream mango sauce), gulf shrimp, steaks and baby back ribs. Weekends and more, Sharky's hosts a variety of musical entertainment on its Tiki Deck, a great spot to watch the setting sun.

Bangkok – *4791 Swift Rd., Sarasota.* ♿ ☎ *941-922-0703.* **$ Thai.** Fresh fruits and vegetables intricately carved into bird and flower shapes, waitstaff costumed in native dress, and hand-carved teak furnishings all translate into a serene setting for enjoying authentic Thai cuisine. Favored by locals and visitors who come for the exotic flavors, beautiful presentation and pleasing prices, Bangkok excels in stir fries and spicy curries, crispy duckling and a variety of tofu dishes. The most-ordered appetizer is the flame-engulfed chicken *satay* with thick peanut sauce; the much-in-demand dessert is fried bananas. Takeouts from the restaurant make for great beach picnics.

Old Salty Dog – *1601 Ken Thompson Pkwy., City Island, Sarasota.* ♿ ☎ *941-388-4311.* **$ American.** Just across the street from Pelican Man's Bird Sanctuary, this fun spot combines an Old Florida nautical look with the ultra-casual atmosphere of boater hang-outs, while offering great views of bay traffic along New Pass. Cold beer from around the world keeps locals at the hull-shaped bar, but the real magnet is the Salty Dog: a quarter-pound hot dog dipped in beer batter, deep fried and topped with sauerkraut, sautéed onions or cheese. Traditional fish and chips, and grouper or golden snapper sandwiches can be relished inside or out on the shady wooden deck built above the water.

Yoder's – *3434 Bahia Vista St., Sarasota.* ♿ ☎ *941-955-7771. www.yoder-srestaurant.com.* **$ Amish.** Set amid Sarasota's Amish community, this homey eatery has attracted local patrons for more than 25 years. The decor is pure Pennsylvania Dutch: flowered wallpaper and an abundance of handicrafts. The menu is filled with home-cooked selections that make for bounteous breakfasts, lunches and dinners served at wallet-pleasing prices. Good choices include Mom's homemade meatloaf with Amish potato cakes or mashed potatoes, as well as thick-sliced country smoked ham with corn-fritter cakes. Yoder's pies are the talk of the town, from the requisite shoofly pie and strawberry rhubarb to the ever-popular banana cream pie and the chocolate or peanut butter versions.

THE MAINLAND

Sarasota's museums and many of its other sights are concentrated along US-41 north of downtown. Begin your exploration with the Ringling Museum and work your way south to the Downtown Art District.

★★**John and Mable Ringling Museum of Art** – *5401 Bayshore Rd. Tickets include admission to Ringling Museum, Cà d'Zan, and Circus Museum. Open year-round daily 10am-5:30pm. Closed Jan 1, Thanksgiving Day, Dec 25. $9.* ✕ ♿ ▣ ⚏ *941-359-5700. www.ringling.org. The museum is currently undergoing extensive renovation; some sections may be closed.* A treasury of European culture, this museum stands as the artistic triumph of southwest Florida. Complemented by magnificent architecture, the Ringling concentrates on paintings of the late Renaissance and Baroque periods (1550-1750), including significant works by Rubens, Van Dyck, Velazquez and Poussin. The **Baroque Collection** is considered one of the finest in the US. The 66-acre landscaped complex holds the art museum, Ringling's mansion, a gallery of circus memorabilia, the Historic Asolo Theater, and Mrs. Ringling's rose garden. A gift of John Ringling to the State in 1936, the site was designated in 1946 as the official art museum of Florida.

■ The Showman's Art

John Ringling (1866-1936), one of the founding partners of the Ringling Bros. and Barnum & Bailey Circus, first visited Sarasota in 1911, lured by reports from land speculators. The following year, he bought property north of Sarasota and built a winter home. He and his beloved wife, Mable, lived primarily in New York City at that time, and traveled abroad several times a year looking for new acts for the show. During these trips they began buying paintings, turning their passion for fine art into a dedicated connoisseurship. By the 1920s they had amassed hundreds of objets d'art, including the world's largest private collection of works by Baroque master **Peter Paul Rubens** (1577-1640).

The Ringlings soon envisioned plans for a palatial repository for their holdings. They hired architect John H. Phillips, previously known for his design work, and construction of the art museum began in 1927. Two years later, just before the museum's opening, Mable died. Ringling's fortunes declined from then until his own death, seven years later. The museum complex is his gift to Sarasota, a legacy to his adopted state.

Ringling's museum is the Greatest Show on Earth in formal attire. Where the man was quiet, his museum is flamboyant. The majestic entrance shouts its Italian-villa influence with three soaring arches crowned by a balustrade upon which stand four larger-than-life figures representing music, sculpture, architecture and painting. The museum, which opened to the public in March 1930, now welcomes more than 300,000 visitors a year.

Art Galleries – *1hr guided museum tour starts in the Rubens Galleries (galleries 1 and 2).* More than 10,000 objects (the majority acquired after Ringling's death), including 1,000 paintings, 2,500 prints and drawings, and 1,500 decorative art objects are exhibited here. Inside and out, the building displays an abundance of architectural flourishes: friezes, medallions, cartouches, wall fountains, inlaid marble mosaics and other ornamentations that Ringling found in his travels. These elements accentuate—and sometimes overshadow—the paintings.

A wing of 11 rooms, the **North Galleries** *(galleries 1-11)* offer a broad survey of late Medieval through early Baroque art of Italy and northern Europe, with emphasis on 16C and 17C Italian works. The **Rubens Galleries** center on four huge paintings (each about 15ft tall) executed by Rubens and his assistants around 1625. Part of a series called *The Triumph of the Eucharist*, the paintings were commissioned by Hapsburg Archduchess Isabella Clara Eugenia as patterns for tapestries, which to this day hang in a Carmelite convent in Madrid. The series originally included 11 paintings, although four of them were destroyed in a 1731 fire in the Archduchess' palace in Brussels. Ringling bought four in 1925; the museum acquired a fifth in 1980. These paintings, with their brilliant colors, their dramatic scenes and their breathtaking size, manifest the appeal that the Baroque period had for Ringling. The second Rubens gallery occupies a vast chamber with clerestory windows more than 30ft above the ground; the floor is of teak bought by Ringling in South America.

Continuing through this wing, you'll find numerous other Baroque masterpieces as well as fine examples from the Middle Ages and Renaissance. Among the many outstanding pieces are: Rubens' *Portrait of the Archduke Ferdinand* (1635), Lucas Cranach the Elder's visually sumptuous *Cardinal Albrecht of Brandenburg as St Jerome* (1526), Piero di Cosimo's *Building of a Palace* (1515-20) and Francesco del Cairo's mysterious *Judith with the Head of Holofernes* (c.1630).

Abraham and Melchizedek (c.1625) by Peter Paul Rubens

A graceful central **courtyard** extends 350ft out from a marble-paved bridge linking the two wings. From the bridge you can behold the formal plantings and sculpture in the elegant garden, which is lined by parallel vaulted loggias. More than 90 columns support the loggias, some of which date back to the 11C. On the other side of the bridge stretches a lovely view of Sarasota Bay.

The **South Galleries** *(galleries 12-21)* present a survey of 17C-19C European and 18C-19C American art. Found here are major works by Poussin, Vouet, Van Dyck, Jordaens and Tiepolo. The **West Galleries** *(off gallery 12)* display changing exhibits of contemporary art and house an educational area called "inner space." A nod to the museum's circus background may be seen in two American works acquired in the mid-1970s. Reginald Marsh's playful *Wonderland Circus: Sideshow, Coney Island* (1930) and Robert Henri's sensuous *Salomé* (1909) both depict early 20C performers in costume, the latter bearing the same name as Ringling's mother. Galleries 19 and 20 showcase the **decorative arts**. Furnished in the styles of Louis XV and Louis XIV, respectively, these rooms were purchased from the New York City mansion of Mrs. William Backhouse Astor. Such painted panels, gilt moldings, Chinese fans and Rococo medallions are typical of the interiors favored by American aristocrats in the late 19C.

Cà d'Zan – *May be closed for renovation; terrace open.* A paved pathway leads from the museum to Ringling's sprawling, extravagant Venetian-style palace overlooking Sarasota Bay. Ringling built the Cà d'Zan (Venetian dialect meaning "House of John") as a winter residence in 1926. The mansion, with its terra-cotta walls and red-tiled roof, its balconies and grand turret, incorporates Italian and French Renaissance, Venetian Gothic, Baroque and modern architectural elements. The west side, facing the water, glows amber in late afternoon as the sun lights up its terra-cotta walls. Inside, note the 30ft-high **court room** with painted cypress beams, the stained glass in the **tap room**, Ringling's eight-piece mahogany bedroom suite and his Siena marble bathtub. Ceiling panels in the **ballroom**, depicting dance costumes from various nations, were painted by Willy Pogany, set designer for the New York Ziegfeld Follies. Be sure to walk out on the **marble terrace** for a sweeping **view** of Sarasota Bay.

Circus Museum – 🎪 *Same hours as museum. A new building to house the Circus Museum is planned as part of the Ringling renovation.* Though not part of Ringling's original plan, this building was added as a tribute to the circus king in 1948. Ringling himself did not collect circus artifacts, but the gallery exhibits items from his era. Circus posters and photographs, antique circus wagons and calliopes, and a hodgepodge of other memorabilia depict the old days of the big top. Though somewhat static for an exhibit on the circus, the museum features worthwhile displays on tiny actor Tom Thumb and famed clown Emmett Kelly, as well as a mechanized miniature circus.

Sarasota Classic Car Museum – *5500 N. US-41; across from Ringling Museum. Open year-round daily 9am-5pm. Closed Dec 25. $8.50.* ♿ 🅿 ☎ *941-355-6228. www.sarasotacarmuseum.org.* This 50-year-old attraction boasts antique cars, musical instruments and arcade games. Over 50 classic and antique automobiles occupy one wing, including such makes as Rolls Royce, Mercedes and Pierce Arrow.

Highlighting the collection are four cars owned by circus magnate John Ringling. In the **music room** tour guides demonstrate the still-wonderful sounds of antique street organs, hurdy-gurdies and other instruments in the collection *(visit by guided tour only)*. Bring dimes and quarters for the old-fashioned arcade and pinball games.

G.WIZ – 🄺 *1001 Blvd. of the Arts. Open year-round Mon-Sat 10am-5pm, Sun 1pm-5pm. Closed major holidays. $6.* 🔥 🅿 ☎ *941-906-1851. www.gwiz.org.* The initials stand for Gulfcoast Wonder and Imagination Zone, and this hands-on facility offers good educational fun for young children. Equipped with bubblemakers, funhouse mirrors, touchable reptiles, a beehive and lots of other gear, the museum also includes a butterfly-filled habitat, a kids' lab and an outdoor science area. Annually, San Francisco's Exploratorium lends G.WIZ some 35 exhibits for display here.

Sarasota Jungle Gardens – 🄺 *3701 Bay Shore Rd. Open year-round daily 9am-5pm. Closed Dec 25. $10.* ✗ 🔥 🅿 ☎ *941-355-5305.* Envisioning an exotic botanical garden, local newspaperman David Lindsay

bought a 10-acre tract of swampland in the early 1930s, drained it and planted tropical trees and flowers imported from around the world. Brick paths wind through a dense jungle of coconut palms, viburnum, rubber trees and other fauna. Bridges cross lakes and lagoons loud with the calls of flamingos and the rush of waterfalls. An enchanting wonderland for children, the gardens also include a petting zoo and playground. Reptile and bird shows are scheduled throughout the day.

★**Downtown Art District** – *Palm & Pineapple Aves. & Main St.* Along these three streets beats the heart of downtown Sarasota. Main Street maintains the charm of old-time Sarasota, but these days it is lined with sidewalk cafes, French bakeries, art galleries, gourmet markets and chic boutiques. On Saturday mornings *(7am-noon)* a **farmers' market** at Main and Lemon streets brims with fresh flowers, herbs, vegetables and fruits, home-baked goods and garden ornaments. A stroll down Pineapple Avenue encompasses the Selby Library, with its artful mobiles and archway aquarium. One notable building, the red-tiled 1926 **Sarasota Opera House** *(one block north of Main St.)*, once hosted vaudeville acts and minstrel shows; Will Rogers, Elvis Presley and other big names performed there. Walk south to Burns Court, a tiny sidestreet of bungalow houses dating from the 1920s and a popular foreign film cinema. Pineapple Avenue is reputed as the city's antique center as well as the setting for several favored cafes with outdoor dining. One street over, Palm Avenue is lined with art galleries.

Sarasota

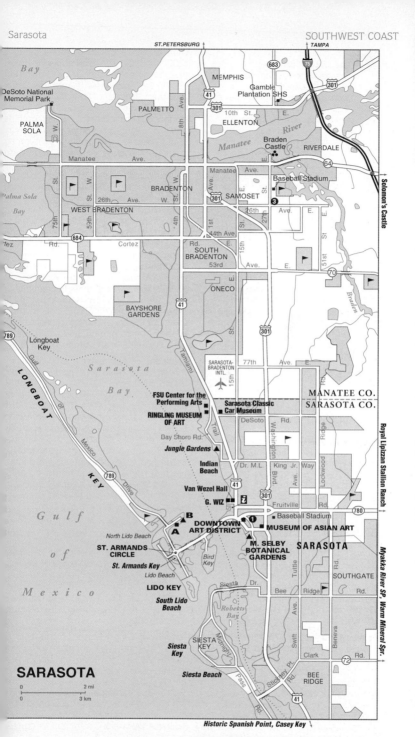

Historic Spanish Point, Casey Key

At the northern end of downtown, framed by Morrill Street and US 301, Towles Court is a full block of Caribbean-colored old Sarasota houses, transformed into galleries and artists' studios that welcome the public; its centerpiece is an imaginative sculpture garden. South of the downtown lies **Sarasota Quay** *(on US-41 at Fruitville Rd.)*, an attractive bayfront park heralded by pine arches and planted with oleander and palms. For a quiet diversion from the bustle of downtown, investigate the quay's boat docks and watch the shorebirds. At night restaurants and nightclubs pick up the pace.

★**Marie Selby Botanical Gardens** – *811 S. Palm Ave. Open year-round daily 10am-5pm. Closed Dec 25. $8.* ♿ 🅿 ☎ *941-366-5731. www.selby.org.* Occupying a nine-acre peninsula on the downtown waterfront, these lovely gardens display more

277

The Gator Club
See map. 1490 Main St.
☎ 941-366-5969. This downtown nightspot is one of Sarasota's hottest nightclubs. History buffs are drawn to the old watering hole, which opened in 1913 as a grocery store and later housed a brothel. When Prohibition ended, it debuted as Gator Bar and Grill. In the 1930s Gator was *the* hangout for circus folks in the area. Fun seekers still arrive nightly, nowadays to dance to Top 40 tunes performed by live bands. The antique mahogany bar sports a brass footrest, and the original tin ceiling holds a row of heart-shaped straw fans. Upstairs, an upscale cigar bar occupies the second floor, complete with pool tables, sofas, antiques and a large assortment of single-malt scotch. The club's name? Well, it's believed that when the place was turned into a bar, it was named for the alligators in the area.

than 20,000 tropical plants, including 6,000 orchids. The **Tropical Display House**, just beyond the entrance, is widely known for its **epiphytes** (plants that grow on other plants and take their nourishment from the air and rainfall), which include a large collection of colorful orchids and bromeliads. A paved path outside circles 20 garden areas, including the cycad collection (a class of plants that date from the age of dinosaurs), the cactus and succulent garden, the shady banyan grove and a native plant community. Here an elevated walkway takes visitors along a lush grove of palms and bamboo, past a mangrove swamp, to an idyllic **view** of Sarasota Bay, framed by a spreading pipal fig tree, known to Buddhists as the *bodhi* tree, or tree of enlightenment.

The **Mansion**, at the north end of the garden, was built as a private residence in 1935 and now hosts changing exhibits of art and photography with a botanical theme. Nearby you'll find the tropical food and medicinal plant gardens, as well as the butterfly garden, and the Tree Lab with creatures of the rainforest.

★**Museum of Asian Art** – *640 S. Washington Blvd. Open year-round Wed-Sat 11am-5pm. ☎ 941-954-7117. www. museumasianart.org. Photo ID must be left with security office.* Tranquillity and art born of the spirit of the Eastern world prevail in this small museum, reputedly the first in the southeastern US devoted exclusively to Asian art dating from the Han dynasty (206BC-220AD) to the early 20C. The newly opened museum (2000) was the brainchild of local physician/philanthropist Helga Wall-Apelt, whose numerous holdings form the permanent collection. Displayed in rotating exhibits works from China, Thailand, Cambodia, Nepal and Burma include a variety of seated Buddhas, a Cambodian sandstone sculpture of guardian lions and the Yangtze River collection of Chinese jade carvings, all effectively lit for soul-stirring viewing.

BARRIER ISLANDS

Flung out north and south along Sarasota's Gulf Coast lie several idyllic barrier islands, connected to the mainland by causeways. To the north, **Longboat Key** is a resort island, offering vacation condos and a wide variety of hotel accommodations along its 10mi of glittering sand. Directly across the causeway from downtown Sarasota lie fashionable St. Armands Key and the pleasant beach parks of Lido Key. To the south stretch the white high rises of Siesta Key and, finally, tiny residential **Casey Key**, its pastel houses tucked amid lush foliage.

Anna Maria Island – *Northwest of Sarasota; from Longboat Key, follow Gulf of Mexico Dr. north to Anna Maria Island.* This "Margaritaville" of the Gulf Coast barrier islands is coveted for its laid-back lifestyle, cottage-style residences and three fishing piers laden with water-view restaurants. Though heavily developed like most of the large barrier islands in the area, Anna Maria is worth the drive, especially for the parks on its north and south ends. Starting at the island's southwest end, attractive **Coquina Beach** provides picnic tables, ample free parking, beach cafe, playground and a wide expanse of white sand and inviting gulf water. Just south of the Route 684 causeway, **Bradenton Beach** is a quaint but energized seaside town with low-rise motels, shops and ice-cream parlors.

For a look at one of Florida's few remaining early fishing villages, drive east across the causeway to **Cortez** *(south of Cortez Rd./Rte. 684 at 119th St.).* This Manatee County Historic District contains a good sampling of vernacular structures built with local materials, one of the last working fish houses in Florida and casual waterfront restaurants.

The hub of Anna Maria Island is Holmes Beach, known for its antique shops, pancake breakfasts on the beach *p 219*, uncrowded stretches of sand and modest houses. At the northern end of the island, **Anna Maria Bayfront Park** *(northeast end of Pine Ave. at Bay Blvd.)* holds a 1,000ft expanse of shoreline running just north of City Pier. Built in 1911, the pier extends 678ft into Tampa Bay and tempts visitors with a no-frills oyster bar.

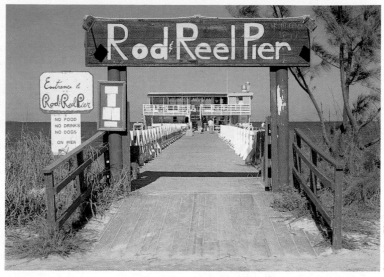

Pier at Anna Maria Island

St. Armands Key – *Located across the John Ringling Causeway from downtown Sarasota.* Named after its first homesteader, French farmer Charles St. Armand, this key began as a mangrove island rumored to have been won by John Ringling in a poker game. The majority of its 132 acres is covered by Sarasota's most famous shopping district, **St. Armands Circle★**, which owes its existence to John Ringling's vision and devotion to his wife. As Ringling explained it: "Now Mable won't have to go to Palm Beach to shop." Strategically positioned at the end of the John Ringling Causeway, the circle and the streets that radiate from it encompass more than 150 specialty shops, galleries, restaurants and businesses. The circle's hub is an oasis of palms, bougainvillea and hibiscus; around its edge, bronze plaques honor great circus performers of the past. Peak-season traffic is often bumper-to-bumper, however.

Mote Aquarium (A) – Kids *1600 Ken Thompson Pkwy., 2.2mi north of St. Armands Circle. Open year-round daily 10am-5pm. $12.* ✗ ♿ 🅿 ☎ *941-388-2451. www.mote.org.* This facility features a score of aquariums holding sea turtles, skates, moray eels and other denizens of Sarasota Bay and the Gulf of Mexico. One perennial favorite, the 135,000gal shark tank, offers both above- and below-water viewing areas. A 30ft touch tank allows visitors an opportunity to handle living sea creatures. The newest exhibit, a preserved 25ft giant squid, is the centerpiece of the mollusk section. Known for its research efforts with sharks and environmental pollutants, the Mote also operates a visitor center adjacent to its research lab and a marine mammal center across the street.

Pelican Man's Bird Sanctuary (B) – *Adjacent to Mote Aquarium. Open year-round daily 10am-5pm. Contribution*

② Cafe on the Beach
See map. 4000 Gulf Dr. in Holmes Beach. ☎ *941-778-0784.* A great way to start the day is right here on the patio at a table topped by a red and white umbrella. The cafe sits, as its name states, on the beach and attracts volleyball players, sun worshippers and the like at all three mealtimes. The all-you-can-eat pancake breakfast, served up with sausages and hot coffee, is the biggest draw, however. Folks come to watch the cooks flip flapjacks in the special screened "pancake cage"—and then enjoy the tangible results of their aerial antics.

③ Mixon Fruit Farms
See map. 2712 26th Ave. E. in Bradenton. ☎ *941-748-5829.* Set amid 350 acres of lush groves, this popular citrus outlet began life in 1939 as a roadside fruit stand. Visitors may stand on an observation platform and enjoy the hustle and bustle of the plant: 600 oranges per minute ride the conveyor belts toward a quality-control room where workers separate the good fruit from the bad. Select oranges continue on into crates for shipping or end up in the juicing room. Free samples of juice and sections of grapefruit, orange and tangerine are available in the sizable gift shop. *Open late Oct-Apr.*

© Ian Adams/DPA, Inc.

279

requested. ♿ 🅿 ☎ *941-388-4444. www.pelicanman.org.* Stroll the boardwalk here past housing for birds too disabled to return to the wild. This sanctuary rescues thousands of injured birds each year, among them herons, pelicans, ospreys, owls and cormorants. Volunteers provide information about the birds, many of which were injured by fishing lines or automobiles. A recipient of former president George H. Bush's Thousand Points of Light Award, sanctuary founder Dale Shields (a.k.a. "Pelican Man") is sometimes on hand to answer questions.

★**Lido Key** – *Just west of St. Armands Key via Ringling Causeway.* Some of the area's most prestigious real estate lies on this J-shaped barrier island, developed by John Ringling in the late 1920s. Ringling built roads and canals with the help of his circus elephants who transported timber for the causeways. A year after the key opened to the public, the Depression slowed business and the barrier islands lay quiet until the 1950s. Now posh hotels, condominiums and homes share the narrow island with popular Lido Beach, pine-fringed North Lido Beach and lovely **South Lido Beach**, flanked by an expanse of mangroves on its bay side *(1.8mi south of St. Armands Circle).*

Siesta Key – *6mi southwest of Sarasota. From downtown, take US-41 south to Siesta Dr. (Rte. 758); go west on Siesta Dr. 1mi to Siesta Key.* This popular barrier island, with its clutch of white, high-rise condominiums, is much regarded for its soft white-sand beaches. Analyzed by Harvard geologists, the fine-grained sand is millions of years old and 99 percent pure quartz (with no shell or coral content), resulting in a talcum-soft texture. **Siesta Beach** sports 2,400ft of sparkling shoreline and a seaside pavilion with a snack bar, souvenir shop and rental stand *(Beach Rd., 1mi southeast of Ocean Blvd.).*

EXCURSIONS *Map p 257*

★**Historic Spanish Point** – *8mi south in Osprey, via US-41. Open year-round Mon-Sat 9am-5pm, Sun noon-5pm. Buildings are accessible by guided tour (2hrs) only; call for hours. Closed Jan 1, Easter Sunday, Thanksgiving Day, Dec 25. $7.* 🅿 ☎ *941-966-5214. www.historicspanishpoint.org.* Jutting into scenic Little Sarasota Bay, this peaceful 30-acre site illuminates the lives of prehistoric Indians and early pioneers. Tours follow a gravel path through a landscape varying from mangrove estuary to live oak forest to formal gardens (after the tour, visitors are free to stroll the grounds on their own). The path winds past a burial mound, a packing house, a chapel and graveyard, and an archaeology dig within a 15ft-high shell midden. Called **Window to the Past**, the exhibit allows visitors to actually see the shells, bones and shards in the midden, while video footage and other displays explain the sleuth work of archaeologists. The restored gardens of former Chicago socialite Bertha Honoré Palmer, Sarasota County's leading lady in the early 1900s, are another highlight.

★★**Myakka River State Park** – *14mi east in Myakka via Rte. 72 (Clark Rd.). Park hrs & fees p 350.* △ ✂ ♿ 🅿 ☎ *941-361-6511. www.myakka.sarasota.fl.us.* One of the oldest and largest of Florida's parks, this 28,875-acre parcel stretches along the primeval Myakka River—protected by the State as a designated Wild and Scenic River—for 12mi and encompasses a wide variety of animal and plant communities. Deer and bobcat favor the palm hammocks, pine flatwoods and dry prairies, while alligators and numerous species of wading birds inhabit Upper Myakka Lake and its grassy marshes. Hiking trails traverse the park, as does a flat road suitable for bicycling. The new Canopy Walk, an 85ft-long suspension bridge, sways some 25ft high among the treetops. Popular **tram and airboat tours** give visitors a close-up look at native flora and fauna *(depart from boat basin Jan-Jun daily 10am-2:30pm, rest of the year daily 10am-1pm; no tours Dec 25; round-trip 1hr; commentary $7;* ♿ 🅿 *Myakka Wildlife Tours, Inc.* ☎ *941-365-0100). Concessionaire at the boat basin sells fishing, camping and picnicking supplies and rents boats, bicycles and canoes.*

★**Royal Lipizzan Stallion Ranch** – Kids *23mi east in Myakka City. Take Fruitville Rd (Rte. 780) east 17.5mi to Verna Rd. Turn left and continue 1.1mi to Singletary Rd. Turn right and go 4.3mi to ranch (entrance on left) at 32755. Training sessions open to the public Jan-Mar Thu & Fri 3pm, Sat 10am. Contribution requested.* ♿ 🅿 ☎ *941-322-1501.* Bred from strains of Arabian and Andalusian stallions, the so-called "aristocrats of the horse world" perform amazing feats that originated more than 300 years ago as battle maneuvers. Guests watch a free 90min outdoor training session hosted by affable, Austrian-born Col. Ottomar Herrmann. Noble Lipizzans execute difficult leaps and kicks, including the famous capriole, in which the horse jumps up and kicks his hind legs out parallel to the ground. These winter sessions prepare the troupe for a rigorous annual US tour. *Arrive early to get choice seats.*

The Springs at Warm Mineral Springs – *30mi southeast in Warm Mineral Springs. Take I-75 south to Exit 34; go 5mi south to US-41. Turn left on US-41 and continue 2.5mi to Ortiz Blvd.; turn left on Ortiz and follow 1mi to springs' entrance* *on right. Open year-round daily 9am-5pm. $10.* ✗ ⚥ 🄿 ☎ *941-426-1692. www.warmmineralsprings.com.* Indians knew of the warm mineral springs here for perhaps 10,000 years before an English hunter discovered the area in 1874. Yet it was not until the 1930s that the springs were developed for tourists. Billed to-day as a resort, Warm Mineral Springs retains the flavor of a latter-day Florida spa. Palms and lawn chairs fringe the 1.5-acre, spring-fed lake, set in a trim carpet of grass. A mostly senior clientele takes to the soothing 87°F waters and enjoys such treatments as massage, whirlpool and acupuncture.

Solomon's Castle

Map p 276. 4533 Solomon Rd. ☎ *863-494-6077. www. solomonscastle.com.* Sculptor Howard Solomon believes that "to have a house like everyone else's is to show a lack of imagination." Accordingly, he built his 12,000sq ft home in the 1970s to resemble a medieval castle, complete with turrets, stained glass and a drawbridge. Wacky and impressive, the castle and its 300 pieces of original sculpture were made entirely from discarded materials. The castle's siding, for example, incorporates shiny aluminum printing plates from a local newspaper. Visitors take a pun-filled 30min tour of the interior. A 60ft replica Spanish galleon, handmade by Solomon, contains a restaurant. Also on location are picnic tables, a gift shop and a nature trail that meanders along Horse Creek. *Open Oct-Jun.*

Space Coast

Shuttle *Atlantis* Liftoff, June 27, 1995 – Courtesy NASA

S panning some 40mi from Titusville down to Melbourne, this region experienced phenomenal growth after the birth of the space program in the late 1950s. The edge of Brevard County and its overlapping barrier islands, separated by lagoons known as the Indian River and the Banana River, are home to the thousands of people employed in the space industry, either at the Kennedy Space Center or in nearby electronics and computer companies. By contrast, the north part of the Space Coast holds one of the state's largest wilderness areas—the nearly 200,000 combined acres of Canaveral National Seashore and Merritt Island National Wildlife Refuge.

One of the earliest settlers here, Captain Douglas Dummitt, acquired land on Merritt Island in 1843. In this period just after the Second Seminole War, the Armed Occupation Act offered 160 acres to anyone who would stay for at least five years. In a jungly landscape known as Mosquito County, Dummitt began a commercial orange grove that would blossom into Florida's largest 25 years later. Here he developed his famous Indian River Oranges, which he would wrap in Spanish moss and pack in barrels for shipment by dugout to St. Augustine. Schooners relayed the delicious cargo to ports as far north as Boston. So widespread grew the fame of these oranges that czars of Russia sent ships here for them. About six million bushels are still shipped worldwide annually.

Up to World War II, most area residents made a living by fishing or raising cattle or citrus fruits. Today the space and defense industries generate the majority of the area's revenue. The service industry is second, with tourism bringing in some $650 million a year.

KENNEDY SPACE CENTER★★★

Map p 287

Tourist Information: www.kennedyspacecenter.com ☏ 321-449-4444

Protruding from Florida's Atlantic coast, this barrier island of orange groves, tidal flats and pristine beaches is home to the nation's space program. Here the world's most sophisticated technology emerges from Florida's largest east-coast wilderness. Every US rocket—from the one that carried the Explorer I satellite in 1958 to modern space shuttles—has blasted off from Merritt Island or adjoining Cape Canaveral. Opened to the public in 1966, the **Kennedy Space Center Visitor Complex** ranks as one of Florida's top attractions. More than two million visitors tour the facility each year.

Rocket launches from the beginning of the American space program up to 1964 took place exclusively at Cape Canaveral Air Force Station (called Cape Kennedy from 1963-73), located on the spit of land extending southeast from Merritt Island. The Cape had been in use by the US Air Force since 1950 as the test site for long-range guided missiles. Though both the Soviet Union and the US announced their intention in 1955 of launching artificial satellites, the Soviets took the first steps with the deployment of two Sputnik satellites in late 1957. The following year, the US launched its first satellite. In October 1958, the National Aeronautics and Space Administration (NASA) was created; its mission was the exploration of space.

Activity on the Cape accelerated after President John F. Kennedy's challenge to the nation in May 1961 "to achieve the goal, before the decade is out, of landing a man on the moon and returning him safely to Earth." The press soon declared a "space race" between the two Cold War superpowers, and NASA began buying up land on Merritt Island for its main launch facility.

NASA is currently concentrating on the **International Space Station**. A combined effort of the US, Russia, Canada, Japan and the 14 member nations of the European Space Agency, the space station requires 38 shuttle trips to carry and assemble sections to its fixed orbit 250mi above the earth. NASA's long-range plans call for a permanent lunar research base and a manned mission to Mars.

■ Missions and Moonwalks

The Mercury and Gemini missions (1961-66) accomplished several feats that captured the attention of the nation. **Alan Shepard**'s 15min ride in the cramped nose of a Redstone rocket in 1961 made him the first American in space. Early in 1962, **John Glenn** became the first US astronaut to orbit the earth. In 1965 Edward White walked in space, another first.

The new Apollo program stalled after White and fellow astronauts Gus Grissom and Roger Chaffee died in a fire on the launchpad in 1967. Following this first NASA disaster, manned missions were halted until *Apollo 7* was launched in October 1968. On July 20, 1969, **Neil Armstrong** and **Buzz Aldrin** walked on the moon, a mere eight years after Kennedy's challenge. After launching Skylab, the first US space station, the Apollo series concluded in a joint mission with a Soviet Soyuz spacecraft in 1975. NASA's answer to a reduction in funding in the late 1970s was a fleet of reusable space shuttles, which have been the centerpiece of the space program since the maiden voyage of *Columbia* in 1981. The 1986 explosion of *Challenger*, killing the entire crew of seven, concentrated national attention again on NASA. Though the flawed Hubble Space Telescope unleashed a storm of criticism, NASA regained its prestige with the spectacular in-space repair job of the telescope in December 1993.

VISIT

Visitor Complex open year-round daily 9am-dusk. Closed Dec 25 and some launch days. $24 includes all exhibits, IMAX films and KSC bus tour. Special interest tours ("Cape Canaveral: Then and Now" and "NASA Up Close") additional $20 each. ╳ ♿ 🅿 ☏ *321-449-4444. www.kennedyspacecenter.com.*

The Kennedy Space Center Visitor Complex is operated, independent of tax dollars, by a private parks services company. The complex was recently overhauled during a five-year, $130 million "redevelopment," completed in 2001. Three bus tours are offered, as well as live shows (including a face-to-face visit with an astronaut), exhibits and films. An art gallery, a children's playground, a retail shop, a cafeteria and a full-service restaurant are part of the complex.

Bus Tour – *Kennedy Space Center Tour departs year-round daily; call for schedule. 2-4hrs. Commentary, video-supplemented. Special operations or imminent shuttle launches may alter tour itineraries.* ♿ ☏ *321-449-4444.* The self-paced **Kennedy Space Center Tour** enables visitors to stop as long as they like at three restricted areas of the facility. Though the architecture is an uninspiring mix of industrial bulk and launchpad scaffolding, visitors are entertained with a recital of amazing technological facts.

PRACTICAL INFORMATION ....Area Code: 321

When to Go

The Space Coast region enjoys a mild climate with an average annual temperature of 73°F. Highs during the summer months reach into the mid-80s with frequent afternoon thunderstorms. Main tourist season for the area: October through May.

Getting There

By Air – **Melbourne International Airport (MLB)**: 35mi south of Kennedy Space Center; international, domestic and commuter flights *(information: ☎ 723-6227)*. Transportation to Kennedy Space Center: Melbourne Airport **taxi** *($85; ☎ 724-1600)*. **Rental car agencies** *(p 343)* located at airport and on US-1. Space Coast visitor information booth adjacent to baggage claim area *(☎ 952-4589)*. **Orlando International Airport (MCO)**: 37mi west of Kennedy Space Center; international, domestic and commuter flights; *(information: ☎ 407-825-2001)*. Regularly scheduled shuttle to Cocoa Beach leaves from ground level *(every two hours daily 9am-7pm; $20-$22 one-way; reservations required)*; Cocoa Beach **Shuttle** *(☎ 784-3831)*.

By Car – Kennedy Space Center is located roughly in the middle of Florida's east coast, in a region often referred to as the Space Coast. The area can be reached in about an hour's drive from most central Florida locations via Route 528 (Beeline Expressway). Sample distances from Cocoa Beach: Orlando 51mi; Jacksonville 156mi; Miami 187mi.
From Interstate I-95, exit on Route 407 East; take Route 405 (NASA Parkway) east across causeway and follow signs. Kennedy Space Center is located 6mi east of US-1 on NASA Parkway.

By Train or Bus – Nearest Amtrak **train** station is in Sanford, which is 48mi northwest of Kennedy Space Center *(☎ 323-4800 or 800-872-7245)*. Greyhound/Trailways **bus** station: 302 Main St., Cocoa *(☎ 800-231-2222)*. Local bus service: Space Coast Area Transit *(☎ 633-1878)*. Cocoa Beach **Shuttle** from area hotels to Kennedy Space Center *(pick-up 9am; return 3pm; $45/two people; ☎ 784-3831)*.

General Information

Accommodations – A wide range of hotels, motels, condominiums and campgrounds are available in Titusville, Cocoa Beach, Cocoa and Melbourne. Some offer shuttle bus service to the Kennedy Space Center. For information, contact **Florida's Space Coast Office of Tourism**, 8810 Astronaut Blvd., Cape Canaveral FL 32920 *(☎ 868-1126; www.space-coast.com)*; **Titusville Area Chamber of Commerce**, 2000 S. Washington Ave., Titusville FL 32780, *(☎ 267-3036; www.titusville.org)* or **Cocoa Beach Area Chamber of Commerce**, 400 Fortenberry Rd., Merritt Island FL 32952 *(☎ 459-2200; www.cocoabeachchamber.com)*. These organizations provide information on shopping, entertainment, festivals and recreation. Reservations for accommodations during space shuttle launches should be made well in advance. **Reservation service**: ☎ 800-USA-1969. Daily room rates range from $55-$175. Numerous campgrounds and RV parks offer full-service amenities, fishing and other recreational facilities. *Rates quoted are average prices per night for a double room and are subject to seasonal variations.*

Roving "Spaceman" at Kennedy Space Center Visitor Center

PRACTICAL INFORMATION ....Area Code: 321

Visitor Information – *Kennedy Space Center Visitor Complex: open year-round daily 9am-dusk. Closed Dec 25 and certain launch days.* ✗ ♿ 🅿 ☎ *449-4444. www.kennedyspacecenter.com.* Kennedy Space Center (KSC) is busiest between June and August and on holidays. Weekends are less crowded. Begin your visit at Information Central; here, multilingual staff provide information about the Space Center and area attractions. Arrive early; the ticket plaza is located right behind Information Central. Taking pictures is permitted; free cameras are available at the Information Counter. All exhibits are included in the admission fee. Two restaurants (The Lunch Pad and the Orbit Cafeteria) are located on the premises. Area hotel reservations can be made from the information booth located at the visitor complex. Wheelchairs and strollers are available free of charge. Call ahead for on-site kennel reservations (free). For bus tour information, see VISIT. Group tours in foreign languages are available by advance reservation; individual visitors should inquire at guest services in Information Central about foreign language tours on day of visit. A costumed "Spaceman" roams the complex from 10:30am-5:30pm for picture-taking opportunities. Movies are shown several times a day in two IMAX theaters: **IMAX 1**: *The Dream Is Alive*; **IMAX 2**: *L5: First City In Space*. Schedules vary with the season.

Shuttle Facts:

Each of the solid rocket boosters on the space shuttle contains more than one million pounds of propellant; the external tank is loaded with 500,000 gallons of liquid oxygen and liquid hydrogen. Once launched, a space shuttle in low orbit around the earth flies at about 17,500mph.

To View a Shuttle Launch – To obtain a launch schedule, visit www.kennedy-spacecenter.com. Launch viewing tickets *($34.50)* go on sale approximately six weeks prior to launch date and may be purchased on line or by phoning ☎ 449-4444. For updated launch information ☎ 867-4636 or 800-KSC-INFO (Florida only).

If you are unable to reserve a spot at KSC to watch a launch, we suggest the following alternative sites. Be sure to arrive early and make sure you have an unobstructed view to the east.

Along Canaveral National Seashore.

Along Route 402, north of Complex 39 *(see map)* in Merritt Island National Wildlife Refuge *(parts of refuge may be closed due to launch activities)*.

Along the Indian River on US-1 in Titusville between Route 528 and Route 402 *(the city permits roadside parking up to 24hrs before launch time)*.

Jetty Park *(east end of Jetty Dr.; see map)*.

Or rent a hotel room on the beach for a great vantage point.

Sports and Recreation – **Melbourne Greyhound Park** *(Mon-Sat noon & 6:30pm; Sun noon;* ☎ *259-9800).* **Airboat rides** on St. Johns River at Camp Holly *(depart year-round daily 9am-6pm; round-trip 35min; $12 (if group of 3 or more);* ♿ ☎ *723-2179),* and Lone Cabbage Fish Camp *(depart year-round daily 10am-6pm; round-trip 30min; $15;* ♿ ☎ *632-4199).* For information on other recreational activities, call tourism offices or chambers. Florida Marlins **baseball spring training** *(Mar)* in Melbourne *(*☎ *633-9200).*

Cruises	www	☎
Carnival Cruise Lines	carnival.com	800-327-7276
Disney Cruise Line	disneycruise.com	800-511-1333
Royal Caribbean Cruise Lines	royalcaribbean.com	800-327-6700

Depart for the Caribbean from Port Canaveral

Useful Numbers   ☎

	☎
Lost and Found	449-4323
First Aid	867-2776

Buses first pass the cubical, 525ft-high **Vehicle Assembly Building** (VAB) where the shuttle is assembled. As the second largest building in the world, the VAB could hold nearly four Empire State Buildings laid end-to-end. Once ready, the space shuttle inches to the pad at 1mph on the six-million-pound Crawler Transporter. At **Launch Complex 39**, visitors can climb a 60ft observation gantry and, perhaps, see a shuttle awaiting launch from another nearby complex. Shown here are a short film and exhibit on the launch procedure, a presentation that does not omit NASA's disasters.

Apollo/Saturn V Center

An excellent movie about the *Apollo 11* mission and a close-up inspection of a 363ft *Saturn V* moon rocket highlight a stop at the **Apollo/Saturn V Center**. Built of stages destined for canceled Apollo missions, the Saturn V is one of three such rockets in the world. Tours of the center include a stirring multimedia review of the Apollo series and displays of original lunar-excursion and command-service modules.

The latest addition is the **International Space Station Center**, where visitors learn about the venture that is driving the space industry in the 21C. In June 1998, the first of 38 flights from the US and Russia carried into orbit component parts for the construction of the International Space Station, a permanent orbiting scientific laboratory scheduled for completion in 2003. Eighteen countries are involved in the project. Exhibits include a movie about the station and mock-ups of its various elements, including living quarters and working space. An enclosed catwalk offers a bird's-eye view of the factory floor where module components are being processed. Concentrating on space-flight history, the special interest tour **Cape Canaveral: Then and Now** begins with a scenic 11mi drive out to Cape Canaveral. En route, visitors can glimpse shuttle facilities and the ships that salvage rocket boosters. The tour includes a visit to complexes where the first manned space flights, and more recent probes, were launched. Launch site of the first US satellite, the **Air Force Space and Missile Museum**, a 30min stop, offers an impressive array of rockets and historical artifacts displayed on the grounds and in two indoor exhibit spaces *(☎ 321-853-3246)*.

The **Rocket Garden** displays eight rockets, as well as gigantic tracking antennae and the access arm through which the *Apollo 11* crew entered their space capsule before liftoff.

IMAX 1 & 2 – *Directly behind the ticket pavilion.* Two IMAX theaters present compelling films in 70mm format throughout the day. Projected on screens more than five stories high, two **films**—*The Dream Is Alive* and (in 3-D) *L5: First City in Space*—include stunning footage shot from space. Seat-rumbling, six-channel digital stereo adds to the realistic effect.

Behind the IMAX theaters, the **Astronauts Memorial** is a moving tribute to astronauts who have made the ultimate sacrifice. Computers keep the black granite monolith tilted to the sun so that the names, engraved on panels equipped with a reflective surface, will be projected on the clouds *(names are easiest to see in the sky at sunset; weather conditions may affect visibility)*.

Just to the right of the memorial, a full-scale replica of the **Space Shuttle** *Explorer* offers visitors an idea of the relative roominess of modern space vehicles compared with the claustrophobic dimensions of pioneering spacecraft.

EXCURSION

★★ **Merritt Island National Wildlife Refuge** – *4mi east of Titusville on Rte. 402. Description p 290.*

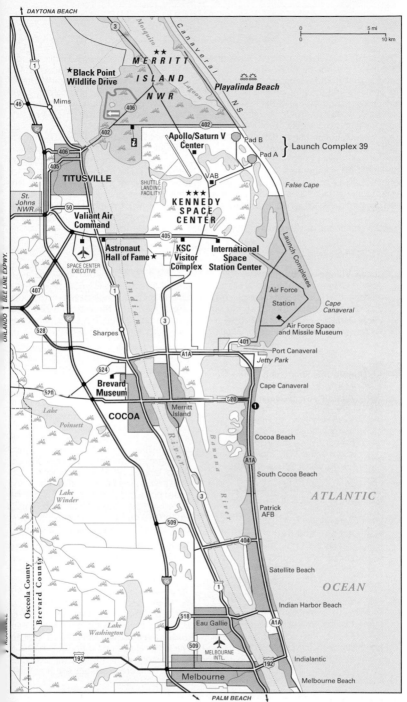

COCOA

This small coastal town might have grown faster if developer Henry Flagler, angry that he could not purchase the Plaza Hotel, had not torn out the railroad spur line serving that grand Cocoa establishment. But Cocoa had an independent spirit. One of its pioneers and premier citizens, Albert Taylor, moved here in 1886 and helped found the Brevard County State Bank—the only bank between Titusville and Key West at the time. Today the town, boosted over the last few decades by the space industry, sprawls along the Indian River yet maintains a modest population.

Due east of Cocoa across the Merritt Island Causeway (Route 520) lies the unpretentious burg of **Cocoa Beach**, where water sports and spaceflight merit nearly equal importance. Several surfing competitions are held here, and informal beach activity abounds, particularly near the 800ft Cocoa Beach Pier *(Meade Ave., off A1A)*, which offers open-air bars and live music. At the southeast corner of Port Canaveral lies **Jetty Park**, highly popular as a winter home for serious campers and also a good spot for watching rockets arc across the Atlantic. Just south of town, the missile display outside Patrick Air Force Base *(5.5mi south of Cocoa Beach on west side of A1A)* serves as another reminder of the significance of high-tech aviation to the area.

SIGHTS

★ **Cocoa Village** – *South of Rte. 520 at Brevard Ave. Brochure of the village available at Brevard Museum of History and Natural Science ☎ 321-632-1830.* For a relaxing afternoon, walk through this charming four-block, brick-paved historic district of cafes and boutiques shaded by old trees. Here, the three-story 1924 **Cocoa Village Playhouse** *(300 Brevard Ave.)*, once a venue for vaudeville acts, continues to stage a wide range of performances *(for schedules ☎ 321-636-5050)*.

❶ Ron Jon Surf Shop
Map p 287. 4151 N. Atlantic Ave. ♿ ☎ 321-799-8888. www.ronjons .com. It's hard to miss the many road signs advertising Ron Jon's as you drive south along I-95 toward Cocoa. Once you're in Cocoa Beach, it's hard to miss this gaudy two-story Art Deco surfwear palace, which has ranked as a Cocoa Beach institution since 1963.
If it's related to the beach or water sports, you'll find it in this two-acre emporium: surfboards, in-line skates, boogie boards, beachwear, bathing suits, sunglasses, surfboard wax, flip-flops and the requisite plethora of T-shirts. A "must" visit for restless kids on a rainy—or sunny—day. *Other location in Fort Lauderdale.*

Porcher House – *434 Delannoy Ave. Open year-round Mon-Fri 9am-5pm; ♿ 🅿 ☎ 321-639-3500. www. cocoafl.org.* Home to wealthy citrus growers Edward and Byrnina Porcher, the white-columned residence was built in 1916 of local coquina rock. The house was once a social center for the town's elite. Mrs. Porcher's love of bridge remains evident on the front patio, where playing-card symbols are carved into coquina blocks. After the Depression, the house was leased as a restaurant and boardinghouse. Eventually the state restored the structure, which now houses city offices on the second floor; the first floor is furnished with period pieces.

Brevard Museum of History and Natural Science – *2201 Michigan Ave. Open Oct-May Tue-Sat 10am-4pm, Sun noon-4pm. Rest of the year Tue-Sat 10am-4pm. Closed major holidays. $5. ♿ 🅿 ☎ 321-632-1830. www5.palm-net.net.* Situated on the north side of Brevard Community College, this modest museum features an exhibit on a local archaeological site and a brief overview of area history with emphasis on 19C pioneers. Temporary exhibits are presented on a regular basis.

TITUSVILLE

Population 40,670

Map p 287

Tourist Information: www.titusville.org ☎ 321-267-3036

Founded in 1873, the county seat is named for Colonel Henry Titus, a blockade runner for the Confederacy who settled here after the Civil War and built Titus House Hotel. Once a shipping point for oranges, Titusville now ties its fortunes primarily to Kennedy Space Center, which lies across the Indian River and employs some 60 percent of the local work force. The vital artery from Merritt Island to the mainland, Highway 405, is often congested with commuter and visitor traffic.

SIGHTS

★**Astronaut Hall of Fame** – *Southeast quadrant of intersection of US-1 and Rte. 405. Open year-round daily 9am-5pm (extended summer hrs). Closed Dec 25. $13.95.* ✗ ⅃ ☐ ☎ *321-269-6100. www.astronauthalloffame.com.* Honoring the first 44 US astronauts, the Hall details the accomplishments of the Mercury, Gemini and Apollo heroes in individual displays that feature not only mission gear, but also such personal items as Jim Lovell's Eagle Scout badge and Buzz Aldrin's junior-high report card. It adjoins the Astronaut Core Museum, where audiovisual and computer displays, artifacts and memorabilia, a Mercury spacecraft and the Apollo 14 lunar-command module document the history of the nation's space program. Two 10min films are shown continually: *To Explore* links the triumphs of the earliest New World adventurers to the space pioneers of present and future, while *Shuttle to Tomorrow*, shown in a space-shuttle replica outside the building, envisions future commercial space flight. In the interactive Astronaut Adventure room, visitors experience astronaut training regimens in the likes of a centrifuge machine (used for G-force training) and a shuttle-landing simulator. The museum is run by the nonprofit Mercury 7 Foundation and the US Space Camp Foundation, the latter offering year-round camp sessions in an adjoining building.

Valiant Air Command Warbird Museum – *6600 Tico Rd. (at Space Center Executive Airport, off Rte. 405, .5mi west of US-1). Open year-round daily 10am-6pm. Closed Jan 1, Thanksgiving Day, Dec 25. $9.* ⅃ ☐ ☎ *321-268-1941.* This building displays aviation memorabilia from World War I, World War II, Korea, Vietnam and Operation Desert Storm. Examples of enemy paraphernalia—a Japanese pilot's outfit, a captured swastika—and a small exhibit on women in aviation are displayed inside the building. Airplane buffs will appreciate the adjoining hangar filled with wartime aircraft. Outside the hangar sits a C-47 troop transport that took part in the D-Day invasion of Normandy.

American Space Firsts

January 31, 1958: The US launched its first earth satellite, *Explorer 1.*

May 5, 1961: The first American in space was Alan B. Shepard Jr., who completed a 15-minute suborbital flight aboard *Freedom 7.*

February 20, 1962: John Glenn Jr., aboard *Mercury,* became the first American to orbit the earth.

June 3, 1965: Edward White was the first American to walk in space when he took a 21-minute stroll outside his *Gemini 4* craft.

October 11, 1968: Frank Borman, James Lovell and William Anders completed the first manned orbits of the moon during the Apollo 8 mission.

July 20, 1969: During the Apollo 11 mission—the first manned moon launch—Neil Armstrong became the first man to walk on the moon.

July 15, 1975: Apollo 18 initiated the first cooperative international space flight; crew members Vance Brand, Thomas Stafford and Donald Slayton linked their spacecraft with the USSR's *Soyuz 19.*

April 12, 1981: The era of reusable spacecraft was inaugurated with the first space shuttle launch from Cape Canaveral.

EXCURSION

★★ Merritt Island National Wildlife Refuge – *4mi east on Rte. 402. Open year-round daily dawn-dusk. Closed 24hrs prior to space shuttle launches.* ♿ ▣ ☎ *321-861-0667. http://merrittisland.fws.gov. Roads closed south of Haulover Canal during shuttle launches.* On 140,000 acres owned by NASA, the refuge provides habitat to more than 500 animal species, including such endangered and threatened animals as the southern bald eagle, the manatee and the loggerhead sea turtle. In addition, 1,530 acres are devoted to citrus groves, some of which existed before NASA bought the land in the early 1960s. Areas open to the public *(north of Rte. 402)* offer an idea of how the Florida coast looked before the incursion of man. The **visitor center** *(on Rte. 402, 3mi east of Rte. 406)* contains informative displays on wildlife in the surrounding marshes, hardwood hammocks and pine flatwoods *(open Nov-Mar Mon-Fri 8am-4:30pm, weekends 9am-5pm; rest of the year Mon-Fri 8am-4:30pm, Sat 9am-5pm; closed federal holidays;* ♿ ▣*)*.

≏≏ Playalinda Beach – *6mi east of visitor center. No drinking water, showers or lifeguards. Clothing optional at north end.* Four miles of gorgeous unspoiled beach lies here with not a high rise in sight—except for the Vehicle Assembly Building and the two shuttle launchpads on the southern horizon. Advanced technology seems incidental here, where pelicans skim the surf and sea oats bend in gentle breezes. The beach is part of **Canaveral National Seashore**, which extends 22mi north to Apollo Beach *(accessible from A1A; open May-Oct daily 6am-8pm; rest of the year daily 6am-6pm; closed Jan 1 & Dec 25; $5/vehicle;* ♿ ▣ ☎ *321-267-1110; www.nbbd.com/godo/cns).*

★ Black Point Wildlife Drive – *Entrance 2mi west of visitor center, off Rte. 406. Stop at visitor center for self-guided driving-tour brochure. Bring binoculars.* This 7mi one-lane dirt road traverses a dike built in the 1950s to control mosquitoes. Here you'll be treated to close-up views of waterbirds and a chance to compare the different habitats associated with a shallow-water impoundment and a natural marsh. A short trail leads to an observation tower about halfway along, and several turnouts provide places to study wildlife.

Merritt Island National Wildlife Refuge

Tampa Bay Area

Tampa Skyline — © Richard Cummins/FOLIO, Inc.

Blessed with perennially fine weather and a resplendent waterfront setting, Florida's second-largest metropolitan area has carved a niche for itself as the state's west-coast capital, a destination for business travelers and vacationers alike. Tampa Bay—the state's biggest open-water estuary—is bridged by three causeways that link its two densely populated centers. On the east side of the bay sits Tampa and its soaring skyscrapers, while to the west lies the Pinellas Peninsula, site of St. Petersburg and such easygoing beach towns as Treasure Island and Clearwater. Just north, Tarpon Springs adds international flair, supporting a community of Greek sponge divers. South of St. Petersburg, the stunning **Sunshine Skyway** bridge—its mastlike yellow suspension cables (hence its name) pointing skyward—straddles the bay where it enters the Gulf of Mexico. Tampa Bay was a favorite landing site for gold-seeking Spanish explorers in the early 1500s. **Juan Ponce de León**, **Hernando de Soto** and **Pánfilo de Narváez** all sought glory and wealth in their expeditions around this wide natural harbor. After encountering hostile natives and equally inhospitable territory, the Europeans abandoned the area for nearly three centuries. By the 1820s a few settlers had made tentative homes here, with an ambition that more closely mirrored that of the natives—eking a livelihood from the sea. Unfortunately, whites and Indians came to distrust each other, and Fort Brooke was erected in 1824 to help maintain local law and order.

In the early 1880s, financier **Henry Plant** assured Tampa's future importance by connecting it via railroad to the east coast and building luxury hotels along the line. Tampa soon established a reputation as the world's cigar-manufacturing center and a significant port for the shipment of cattle, phosphate and citrus. In the meantime, St. Petersburg and other towns across the bay became known for their healthy climate, good fishing and fine beach resorts.

Today, despite the growing pains associated with any swelling metropolitan area, increasing numbers of retirees and young professionals continue to bolster the population of Hillsborough and Pinellas counties. Tampa now ranks as the 12th leading port in the US, trading in phosphate and agricultural products. Nearby, the resort-laden beach strand from St. Petersburg Beach up to Clearwater rates as west Florida's most popular. From the modern cityscape of downtown Tampa, to the attractively landscaped waterfront in St. Petersburg, to the timeless allure of the Gulf's white-sand beaches, the Tampa Bay area epitomizes Florida on the move.

291

CLEARWATER

Population 108,787

Map below

Tourist Information: www.clearwaterflorida.org ☎ 727-461-0011

Consisting primarily of a 4mi stretch of Gulf Coast barrier island, Clearwater is Tampa's beach. This popular resort, located 22mi west of Tampa, attracts each year more than a million visitors, who contribute the largest amount of revenue to the city. Vacationers cavort on the powdery sands and in the calm, sparkling waters of **Clearwater Beach**⌂, which is connected to downtown by Memorial Causeway. Although you pass through a dense commercial strip to get to the shore, once you reach it you'll find a low-key resort town that appeals to families, couples and seniors alike.

The commercial center began to develop in the late 19C after Henry Plant extended his railroad through the city and built the elegant Belleview Hotel, now the Belleview Biltmore, nearby *(see p 301)*. The c.1898 pink frame **Louis Ducros House** *(1324 S. Ft. Harrison Ave.)*, ornamented with Gothic Revival fretwork, survives as one of the few remaining structures from that period. Down the street, the Neoclassical **Pinellas County Courthouse** *(324 S. Ft. Harrison Ave.)* was hastily built in 1917 in an attempt to steal the county seat from neighboring St. Petersburg. The hefty, brick **South Ward School** *(610 S. Ft. Harrison Ave.)*, which dates back to 1906, is the county's oldest school to operate continually in one building.

SIGHTS

★**Sand Key Park** – *1060 Gulf Blvd. Park hrs & fees p 350.* ♿ ☎ 727-595-7677. Located on 65 pristine acres on a spit jutting into the Gulf of Mexico, Sand Key provides a respite from the development that crowds Clearwater Beach. This land passed through a succession of owners, including US Steel and the City of Clearwater, before Pinellas County finally bought it and opened the park in 1984. Edged with sea oats and sea grape trees, a wide, sugary sand beach forms the centerpiece of the park.

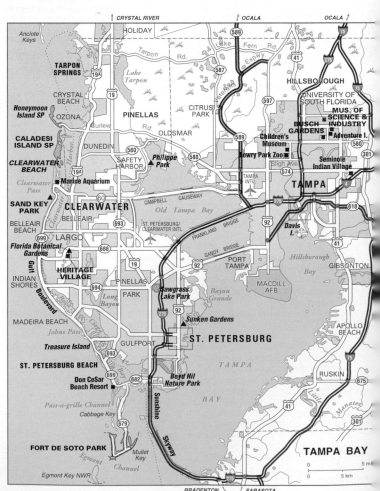

Clearwater Marine Aquarium – 🈴 *249 Windward Passage, Clearwater Beach. Open year-round Mon-Fri 9am-5pm, Sat 9am-4pm, Sun 11am-4pm. Closed major holidays. $7.75.* ♿ 🅿 ☏ *727-441-1790 or 888-239-9414. www.cm aquarium .org.* This private, nonprofit research facility is dedicated to public education and the rescue, rehabilitation and release of injured or sick marine mammals, otters and sea turtles. A 55,000-gallon mangrove seagrass pool offers visitors a close-up view of the estuary environment. A variety of sea turtles, dolphins, sharks and stingrays are also on display.

EXCURSIONS

Philippe Park – *8mi east in Safety Harbor. Take Gulf-To-Bay Blvd./Rte. 60 east to Bayshore Blvd. (last left before crossing Campbell Causeway); turn left (north) on Bayshore, which becomes Philippe Pkwy. Continue north to entrance of park at 2525 Philippe Pkwy. Park hrs & fees p 350.* ♿ 🅿 ☏ *727-464-3347.* Named for Count Odel Philippe, a French surgeon who founded Safety Harbor in 1823 and reputedly planted the area's first citrus groves, this county park occupies 122 acres of huge oak trees and sweeping green lawns that afford water views along its mile-long shoreline. The Tocobaga Indians, the last aboriginal culture to exist on Florida's central west coast, left a legacy of massive ceremonial mounds in the park. The **temple mound** *(turn left into the first parking area; mound is by the water, marked with a sign)* was the seat of the principal village of Tocobaga. When the site was excavated, archaeologists found pottery shards, bones, tools and 16C European artifacts.

★**Heritage Village** – 🈴 *8mi south in Largo. Take US-19A south to Ulmerton Rd. Turn right on Ulmerton and proceed to 125th St. Turn left; follow signs to village on left at 11909 125th St. N. Open year-round Tue-Sat 10am-4pm, Sun 1pm-4pm. Closed major holidays.* 🅿 ☏ *727-582-2123. www.co.pinellas.fl.us.* More than 20 of the county's earliest structures are displayed at this 21-acre re-created pioneer community, complete with a replica one-room schoolhouse, an early church, train depot and private homes. The oldest one, Cracker-style **McMullen-Coachman Log House**, was completed in 1852. The modest two-story **Plant-Sumner House** was built by Henry Plant in 1896 for his foreman's family. Nearby, the Victorian **Seven Gables House** (1907) is a rambling yellow structure that originally served as a bayside winter retreat for a wealthy Illinois family *(visit by 20min guided tour only)*. Also on the grounds is the Pinellas County Historical Museum, with archives and exhibits devoted to the county's past and present.

Florida Botanical Gardens – *8mi south in Largo. Take US-19A south to Ulmerton Rd. Turn right on Ulmerton and proceed to 125th St. Turn left; follow signs to Pinewood Cultural Park at 12175 125th St. N. Open year-round daily 7am-7pm.* 🅿 ☏ *727-582-2200. www.flbg.org.* Located across the bridge from Heritage Village, this 162-acre development features colorful plants arranged thematically, serene woods, a sculpture garden and an art museum. Fountains, bridges and benches highlight paths that wind past exotic and native flowers; oak, palm and fruit-bearing trees; and herb-filled courtyards and creek banks. Completed in 1999, the low-lying **Gulf Coast Museum of Art** showcases contemporary Florida and Southeastern crafts within a sunlit setting *(open Tue-Sat 10am-4pm, Thu til 7pm, Sun noon-4pm; closed major holidays; $3; ☏ 727-518-6833; www. gulfcoastmuseum.org).*

★**Caladesi Island State Park** – *9mi north on Caladesi Island. Accessible only by boat. Park hrs & fees p 350.* ♿ ☏ *727-469-5918. Ferry departs from Honeymoon Island year-round daily 10am-4:30pm; commentary; $7;* ♿ 🅿 ☏ *727-469-5942.* Situated in the Gulf of Mexico off the coast of Dunedin, Caladesi Island offers a white-sand **beach**—framed by undulating grasses—that in 1998 *USA Today* ranked among the nation's top five beaches. Benefiting from an inaccessible location that failed to attract developers, the 600-acre island survives with its native flora and fauna intact. Along the 2mi beach, visitors swim, fish, picnic, shell, stroll or explore the nature trail *(2.5mi)* through the island's interior.

Honeymoon Island State Park – *9mi north in Dunedin. Take US-19A north to Dunedin, (road becomes Broadway Bayshore Blvd.). Turn left on Dunedin Causeway Blvd./Rte. 586 and follow causeway to park. Park hrs & fees p 350.* 🅿 ☏ *727-469-5942.* In 1921 a fierce hurricane sundered this barrier island from its southern half, now called Caladesi Island. A causeway from Dunedin connects the mainland to the 385-acre park, which features a rocky beach and 208 species of plants. Once known as Hog Island (for a successful hog farm that operated on its shores), Honeymoon Island owes its present moniker to a New York developer who built 50 thatched-roof "honeymoon cottages" here in 1939. One of the last virgin slash-pine forests still standing in south Florida lies along the island's northern loop trail.

★**Tarpon Springs** – *13mi north via US-19A. See Entry Heading.*

ST. PETERSBURG★★

Population 248,232

Map below

Tourist Information: www.floridasbeach.com ✆ 727-464-7200

Lying on the west side of Tampa Bay and linked to its sister city's fast-paced commerce by three bridges, sunny St. Petersburg is Tampa on holiday. St. Petersburg ranks as Florida's fourth most populous city, with tourism-related businesses employing the most people in Pinellas County and generating some $2 billion in annual revenues. A thriving mix of young professionals, retirees and sun-seeking vacationers enjoy St. Pete's relaxed lifestyle, first-rate museums, sparkling Gulf beaches (10mi west of downtown), and almost perpetually clear skies and warm weather.

In the 1840s fishermen and settlers arrived in the area, some lured by tales of the salubrious Espirito Santo springs at Safety Harbor, discovered in the 16C by de Soto.

■ Russian, not Roulette

One of those who moved to the area for his health in the late 1870s was Detroit native **John C. Williams**, a retired Union general who purchased 1,600 waterfront acres. In 1885, an American Medical Assn. journal proposed that a "health city" be founded on the Pinellas Peninsula. The combination of warm climate, fresh air and good beaches made the Tampa/St. Petersburg area a leading candidate. Although the spa city never came into being, the peninsula's fame caught the attention of Russian speculator **Peter Demens**, who in 1888 brought his Orange Belt Railroad to John Williams' farm. Legend has it that Demens beat Williams in a lottery and earned the right to name the new city for his hometown in Russia. The original downtown laid out by Williams and Demens that year extended from Seventh Avenue South to Fifth Avenue North, and from about Ninth Street to the bay. Population lagged until 1900, when word of St. Pete's healthy climate and good fishing began to spread.

By the beginning of World War I, a second railroad connected St. Pete to Tampa, and development of the beaches had started. The Florida land boom of the 1920s elevated St. Petersburg to resort status, with 3,000 hotel rooms and a population of 60,000. Two world-class resorts were built during this decade: the Vinoy Park downtown (now the **Renaissance Vinoy Resort**) and the **Don CeSar** on the beach *(see p 301)*. Two sizable wildlife preserves lie outside the downtown core: **Boyd Hill Nature Park** *(1101 Country Club Way S.; entrance just west of 9th St. S.)* and **Sawgrass Lake Park** *(7400 25th St. N.)*, both excellent spots for bird-watching.

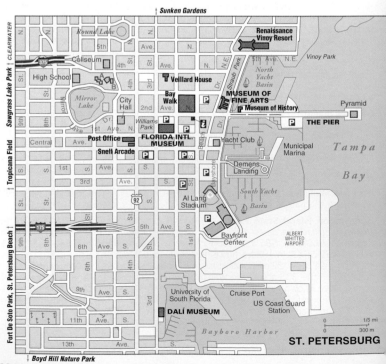

DOWNTOWN

Downtown smoothly blends old and new styles of architecture; Art Deco and Mediterranean harmonize with contemporary styles. Seven miles of landscaped waterfront parks attract visitors to the bayside to stroll the Pier, take in art museums and nearby galleries, and bask in the sun at the expansive municipal marina. The St. Petersburg Yacht Club, established more than 90 years ago, has hosted numerous international regattas.

A number of attractive structures from the early 1900s remain. Moorish-style 1926 **Snell Arcade** *(405 Central Ave.)*, with its crenellated turrets, is considered the city's best example of 1920s office architecture. Half a block north, an interior passageway leads to the open-air, Mediterranean Revival-style **post office** *(400 1st Ave. N.)*

built in 1917. St. Petersburg Public High School, erected in 1919 in the Mediterranean style, sits just off Mirror Lake *(709 Mirror Lake Dr.)*. The 1924 Coliseum *(535 4th Ave. N.)* continues to draw crowds for frequent dances. Across the street, St. Petersburg Shuffleboard Club (**A**), the largest in the world, dates to 1924; adjacent St. Petersburg Lawn Bowling Club (**B**) began in 1926, making it one of the country's oldest. **Veillard House** *(262 4th Ave. N.)*, built of rusticated stone block in 1910 for one of the city's pioneers, exemplifies a fine blend of Queen Anne and Bungalow styles.

BayWalk *(2nd & 3rd Aves. N. and 1ˢᵗ & 2ⁿᵈ Sts.)* is a recently constructed $40 million, multilevel shopping/entertainment complex packed with swank shops, restaurants and a movie theater around a tile-paved courtyard.

BayWalk

Immediately west of downtown is **Tropicana Field** *(1 Tropicana Dr.; entrance off 10th St. S. at 3rd Ave. S.)*, a 45,360-seat, covered baseball stadium where the Tampa Bay Devil Rays play their home games. To guarantee a constant 72° temperature inside the stadium, the Yale University professor who designed the field took into account such factors as humidity, air flow and atmospheric pressure within the dome.

★**Florida International Museum** – *100 2nd St. N. Open year-round Mon-Sat 10am-5pm, Sun noon-5pm. $13.95.* ✕ ⅙ ☎ *727-822-3693 or 800-777-9882. www.floridamuseum.org.* St. Pete's slick international cultural center was designed to host grand-scale traveling exhibitions from prestigious institutions around the world. A $4 million face-lift completed in 1995 modernized the 1948 structure—a former department store. Year round, the museum presents exhibits from the Smithsonian Institution, with which it is affiliated, as well as from other museums. Important shows have included "Splendors of Ancient Egypt," "Alexander The Great" and "Titanic: The Exhibition." The museum's budding permanent collection includes some 600 artifacts from President John F. Kennedy's administration and family.

★**The Pier** – *East end of 2nd Ave. N.E. Open year-round Mon-Thu 10am-9pm, Fri & Sat 10am-10pm, Sun 11am-7pm.* ✕ ⅙ 🅿 ☎ *727-821-6164. www.stpete-pier.com. Valet parking; pay parking lots & some free parking along the Pier. Free trolley rides from Pier to parking lots and to local museums.* Opened in 1973, the Pier with its modernistic upside-down pyramid, juts a quarter of a mile into Tampa Bay. The five-story structure contains an **information desk** *(open Mon-Sat 10am-8pm, Sun 11am-6pm)* and restaurants and shops on the first level, an aquarium on the second level, and a restaurant and observation deck on the top. On the third level, **Great Explorations** 🅺🅸🅳🆂, an interactive science museum, invites children to explore topics such as music making and animal care *(open year-round Mon-Sat 10am-8pm, Sun 11am-6pm; $4; ☎ 727-821-8992; www.greatexplorations.org)*. Along the Pier you'll find fishing platforms, jet-ski and sailboat rentals, and a miniature golf course.

The Pier

St. Petersburg Museum of History – *335 2ⁿᵈ Ave. N.E. Open year-round Mon-Sat 10am-5pm, Sun 1pm-5pm. Closed Jan 1, Thanksgiving Day, Dec 25. $5.* ♿ ☎ *727-894-1052. www.museumofhistoryonline.org.* Set at the foot of the Pier, this museum contains a replica of the six-cylinder Benoist airboat that made the world's first commercial flight. In 1914 Tony Jannus flew the mayor of St. Petersburg in such a plane to Tampa, 21mi northeast. Displays in the Timeline Gallery chronicle the area's history from mastodons to tourists, and include a dugout cypress canoe, a simulated 1870 general store and a replica Orange Belt Railway depot.

★★**Museum of Fine Arts** – *255 Beach Dr. N.E. Open year-round Tue-Sat 10am-5pm, Sun 1pm-5pm. Closed major holidays. $6.* ♿ 🅿 ☎ *727-896-2667. www.fine-arts.org.* Housed in an attractive Palladian-style building designed by John Volk, this museum, opened in 1965, presents a wide-ranging collection of art, from antiquities and world masterpieces to contemporary works.

All 20 galleries are located on one floor. To the left of the marble-floored Great Hall, the Acheson Gallery displays some of the museum's most notable paintings by French artists—works by Cézanne, Renoir, Monet and others. The adjacent Poynter Gallery holds a remarkable trove of early **Asian** art, including an intricate Jaina shrine (c.1600) from India. Continuing clockwise around the museum, you will encounter pre-Columbian art *(Gallery 6)* in juxtaposition with 20C American paintings *(Gallery 5)* by John Sloan, George Bellows and Georgia O'Keeffe, among others. O'Keeffe's glorious *Poppy* (1927) is considered one of the most important paintings in the entire collection. Galleries 1 through 4 offer fine examples of art from ancient Greece and Rome, the Renaissance, 18C Europe and 19C America. Of special note is the luminous collection of **Steuben glass** in Gallery 16. The back (east side) of the museum showcases two pleasant shady gardens overlooking the waterfront. The work of Antonie-Louis Barye and other sculptures grace the south garden.

★★★**Salvador Dalí Museum** – *1000 Third St. S. Open year-round Mon-Sat 9:30am-5:30pm (Thu 8pm), Sun noon-5:30pm. Closed Thanksgiving Day & Dec 25. $10 ($5 after 5pm Thu).* ♿ 🅿 ☎ *727-823-3767. www.salvadordalimuseum.org.* The world's most comprehensive collection of works by the late Spanish Surrealist resides in this single-story building located on Bayboro Harbor (just south of the Port of St. Petersburg). Searching for a repository for their vast Dalí holdings Cleveland industrialist A. Reynolds Morse and his wife, Eleanor, chose this former warehouse on the waterfront. The museum opened in 1982 after a $2 million face lift financed by the state of Florida. It has since become one of Florida's most popular art museums.

Six galleries here display pieces from the museum's collection of 95 oil paintings more than 100 watercolors and drawings, and 1,300 graphics, sculptures, photographs and objets d'art. The first gallery contains a permanent retrospective of oil paintings arranged in chronological order, starting to the left of the entrance with Dalí's childhood works (1914) and ending with his masterworks. Early paintings such as *Girl's Back* (1926), *Girl with Curls* (1926) and various self-portraits demonstrate young Dalí's talent and show the strong influence of masters from the 17C Flemish to the Impressionists and Cubists.

Between 1929 and 1940, Dalí experimented with Surrealism, often attenuating figures—as in *Archeological Reminiscence of Millet's Angelus* (1935) in order to emphasize his obsession with time, death and sex. On the south wall hang four of Dalí's masterworks, each of which took at least a year to complete. These tremendous canvases, measuring about 13ft by 10ft, were painted between 1948 and 1970. Two smaller masterworks, *Nature Morte Vivante* and *Velazquez Painting the Infanta Margarita with the Lights and Shadows of His Own Glory*, are displayed in other galleries in the museum.

ADDITIONAL SIGHTS *Map p 292*

Sunken Gardens – *1825 4th St. N. Open year-round Wed-Sun 10am-4pm. $4.* ♿ □ ☎ *727-551-3100.* Dating back to 1935, Sunken Gardens ranks as one of the area's oldest attractions. A small lake was drained here in 1903 and planted with endemic and exotic flora. Footpaths wind 15ft below street level past tropical foliage and flowering shrubs. Wildlife displays and presentations feature tropical birds and reptiles.

St. Petersburg Beach – *At the southern end of Gulf Blvd.* A resort town of nearly 10,000 residents, St. Pete Beach anchors the southern terminus of **Gulf Boulevard,** which stretches 18mi north to Clearwater, a very popular strand on Florida's Gulf coast. Though not a scenic drive, the highway does pass many beach access points sandwiched between motels and condominiums. The **beach**△ itself offers clean,

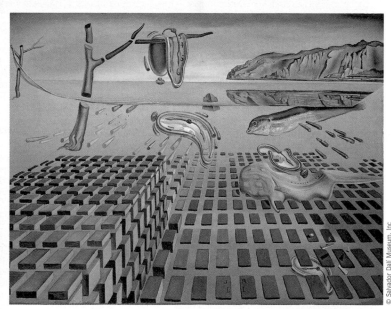

The Disintegration of the Persistence of Memory (1952-54) by Salvador Dalí

© Salvador Dalí Museum, Inc

■ Flamboyance Personified

Born and raised in a Catalonian farming village near Barcelona, **Salvador Dalí** (1904-1989) began painting at a young age. He attended the San Fernando Academy of Fine Arts in Madrid and held his first one-man show in Barcelona in 1925 at age 21. In 1929 he moved to France, where he joined the Paris Surrealist Group led by writer André Breton. Also in that year, he met Gala Eluard, his future wife and inspiration for much of his work. Surrealists eschewed convention and believed instead in the omnipotence of dreams and the suspension of conscious thought. Dalí soon became one of the movement's brash leaders, painting fantastic subjects in obsessive detail and declaring, "The difference between me and the Surrealists is that I am Surrealism." By 1940 however, Dalí had broken with the group and announced his intention to return to "Classical" painting, as embodied in the High Renaissance works of Raphael. Dalí continued executing his detailed symbolic and trompe-l'œil effects in 18 masterworks—huge canvases dealing with historical, scientific or religious themes. By the time of his death he had become as famous for his trademark handlebar mustache and publicity stunts, which often involved wild animals, as for his artistry.

white sand and gentle Gulf waters. *(Public access areas have parking pay stations; $5/day.)* The town is the setting for the historic **Don CeSar Beach Resort and Spa** *(see Tampa Address Book)*, still a home-away-from-home for the rich and/or famous. A few blocks from the hotel sits the Nancy Markhoe Gallery, a shop filled with handmade jewelry, pottery and glassworks by American craftspeople. Former president Bill Clinton made some purchases there when he was in town.

Just north, **Treasure Island** features wide, uncrowded shores. Snack bars and restrooms are available, as well as rental umbrellas, rafts and cabanas.

EXCURSION *Map p 292*

★**Fort De Soto Park** – *8mi south of St. Petersburg Beach on Mullet Key. Take Rte. 682 east and turn right on Rte. 679 (Pinellas Bayway). The park headquarters (stop for information) is 6.5mi south; fort is 2mi farther west. Park hrs & fees p 350.* △ ६ ▣ ☞ *727-582-2267. Bike, canoe and kayak rentals.* Robert E. Lee was one of four US Army engineers who in 1849 recommended a military installation for this V-shaped string of islands at the mouth of Tampa Bay. Several years later the Union took his advice, setting up a blockade on Mullet and Egmont keys. Construction of the fort began during the Spanish-American War in 1898, but the fort never saw action and it was decommissioned in 1923.

Visitors can tour the reconstructed storehouse that houses exhibits and a computerized presentation of the fort's history. Visible from here, the **Sunshine Skyway** connects Pinellas and Manatee counties. Other activities in this 1,100-acre park, located only a 15min drive from the heavily urbanized Suncoast strip, include hiking, fishing and swimming on quiet **beaches** rated among the top 10 in the US.

TAMPA★★

Population 303,447
Map p 304
Tourist Information: www.visittampabay.com ☎ 813-223-2752 or 800-448-2672

Florida's third-largest city is both port and resort. Visitors can choose from attractions ranging from the Latin accents of Ybor City to the thrill rides of Busch Gardens. Tampa's modern economy rests on business and financial services, agriculture, aquaculture, retail trade and tourism, the latter generating more than $2 billion.

Historical Notes

Exploration and Settlement – By the 16C the area was occupied by the Calusa and Timucua tribes, who subsisted on shellfish and game. Pánfilo de Narváez is credited with being the first Spanish explorer, in 1528, to see Tampa Bay. De Soto also landed briefly but continued west, never to return. When Florida became a US Territory in 1821, the government established an army post near Spanishtown Creek, a small village built by Cuban and Spanish fishermen in an area that now defines the Hyde Park neighborhood west of downtown.

■ The Other Henry

Florida's West Coast counterpart to East Coast developer Henry Flagler, **Henry Bradley Plant** (1819-1899) chose Tampa as the port for a new railroad that would connect Florida with the eastern seaboard and the West. Born to middle-class Connecticut farming parents, Plant left home at age 18 to be a jack-of-all-trades aboard a Yankee steamboat. He worked for the Adams Express Co., which shipped parcels by boat and later by railroad. When his wife's failing health forced him to spend several months near Jacksonville in 1853, Plant became manager of the company's southern region. At the onset of the Civil War in 1861, Plant organized the Southern Express Co. Beginning with the purchase of two railroads at postwar foreclosure sales, the visionary tycoon built a multimillion-dollar transportation empire that eventually included 14 railway companies and several steamship lines, and stretched from Jamaica to Boston and as far west as New Orleans and St. Louis. A number of grand hotels complemented Plant's transportation network. One of these properties was the Tampa Bay Hotel, which he began building on the banks of the Hillsborough River, west of downtown; its minarets are now city landmarks. When Plant used his influence to have the city declared a port of embarkation for US troops fighting the Spanish-American War, Tampa enjoyed international press attention. Supply trains carried food, ammunition and equipment to soldiers in Tampa; boats left the city docks piled high with goods to be shipped to Cuba. Troops camped just outside the city limits, eating at the Tampa Bay Hotel and spending their money here, much to the delight of local merchants.

Railroad transportation and a flourishing port assured Tampa's growth by attracting new businesses and commercial developers who would forever change the face of the city. One such entrepreneur was **Vicente Martínez Ybor**, who relocated his cigar business to Tampa from Key West in 1886. Ybor bought land east of downtown, where he built a factory that, after a year, produced 900,000 cigars a month. Other cigar makers soon relocated to Tampa and Spanish, Italian and Cuban workers flocked to the factories. Their community is now Tampa's historic Spanish neighborhood, Ybor City.

Cigar Box Art

Growing Pains – By the early 1900s, Tampa was exporting citrus fruit, cattle, vegetables and phosphate fertilizer on the railroads. During the Roaring Twenties' real-estate boom, Tampa developer D.P. Davis paid $3.5 million for dredgers to turn the bay bottom into a speculator's dream and promoted **Davis Islands** as "a veritable Venice at one's door." Though the islands never became a Venice, they are still considered one of Tampa's most prestigious residential areas.

The 1930s brought the Depression and the founding of the University of Tampa, which moved into the vacant Tampa Bay Hotel in 1933. In 1935 Tampa suffered a hurricane, the Labor Day monster that killed hundreds in South Florida before raking the Gulf Coast with its fury. A political storm was also brewing, with gangsters and gambling kingpins accused of corrupting city government. A spell of election outrages finally spawned a reform movement led by the city's newspaper editors.

Growth continued in the 1950s with the opening of MacDill Air Force Base, which continues to be an important source of revenue for the city. In 1958 the state selected a parcel in North Tampa as the site of the new University of South Florida. The 1,700-acre campus now has a student body of 36,000.

Tampa's many amenities and varied economy continue to attract new businesses, residents and visitors; city leaders are banking on these factors to propel the city into a new chapter of prosperity in the 21C.

DOWNTOWN *Map p 304*

The best of early Tampa's architecture survived the wrecking ball and stands today in the shadow of 30- to 40-story skyscrapers; the elegant 1915 Beaux-Arts **City Hall** *(Kennedy Blvd. and Florida Ave.)* nestles among the city's tallest buildings. The development boom of the mid-1980s included improvements like the Franklin Street Mall—a pedestrians-only brick avenue with plantings, fountains and stores extending from Cass Street to Washington—and the many sculptures and artworks that grace public spaces.

Downtown Tampa has added major entertainment centers, such as the $160 million Ice Palace arena for the city's hockey team and the $300 million **Garrison Seaport Center**, which includes the new Florida Aquarium and two cruise terminals that bring 700,000 passengers a year into the former warehouse district east of downtown. The recently opened Shops at Channelside, a $35 million-plus development, enlivens the once sleepy waterfront with restaurants, boutiques and movie theaters.

Across Beneficial Boulevard bridge from downtown, Harbour Island is a former railroad terminus that was transformed in the mid-1980s, at a $1 billion cost, into a residential and commercial complex of condominiums, office and retail space and a hotel.

★**Henry B. Plant Museum** – *401 W. Kennedy Blvd. Open Jan-Nov Tue-Sat 10am-4pm, Sun noon-4pm. Dec daily 10am-8pm. Closed major holidays. $5 ($7 in Dec).* & 🅿 ☎ *813-254-1891. www.plantmuseum.com.* The silver minarets and gold crescents atop the former **Tampa Bay Hotel**★★ have been synonymous with Tampa since the hotel's lavish opening in 1891. In 1899 Plant died of a heart attack and his hotel began to decline. Six years later, the City of Tampa bought the building, practically stealing it for $125,000; it closed as a hotel in 1930. The University of Tampa leased the building in 1933 and the city set aside the south wing of the first floor as a municipal museum. The remainder houses University of Tampa offices and classrooms. Although the architecture is spectacular, the interior has not been restored. Note domed Fletcher Lounge *(northernmost end of ground floor)*, which served as the hotel's main dining room, and the Grand Salon *(just off the lobby)*, where guests socialized. *A 14min video in the room next to the gift shop introduces the hotel.*

PRACTICAL INFORMATION .... Area Code: 941

Getting There

By Air – Tampa International Airport (TPA): 5mi west of city center *(information: ☎ 870-8700; www.tampaairport.com)*. Transportation to downtown: The **Limo** *($15; ☎ 727-572-1111)*, taxi *($16)* and hotel courtesy **shuttles**. **Rental car agencies** *(p 343)* located at airport.

By Train and Bus – Amtrak train station: 601 N. Nebraska Ave. *(☎ 800-872-7245; www.amtrak.com)*. Greyhound **bus** station: 610 E. Polk St. *(☎ 229-2174 or 800-231-2222; www.greyhound.com)*.

Getting Around

By Public Transportation – Local **bus service**: HARTline Transit System *($1.15)*. For bus schedules and route information: ☎ 254-4278, www.hartline.org. **Uptown Downtown Connector** *(Mon-Fri 6am-6pm, every 10min)*. **Suncoast Beach Trolley** from Sand Key to Pass-A-Grille *(daily 5:45am-10pm, every 30min; $1; ☎ 727-530-9911; www.psta.net)*.

By Car – Limited on-street parking; public parking garages *($1.25/hr)*.

By Taxi – United Cab *(☎ 253-2424)*; Yellow Cab *(☎ 253-0121)*.

General Information

Visitor Information – **Tampa Bay Convention and Visitors Bureau**, 400 N. Tampa St., Suite 2800, Tampa FL 33602; visitor center, corner of Ashley and Madison Sts. *(open Mon-Sat 9am-5pm; ☎ 223-2752; www.visittampabay.com)*. **Tampa Bay Visitor Center**, 3601 E. Busch Blvd. *(across from Busch Gardens; open Mon-Sat 9am-6pm, Sun 9am-2pm; ☎ 985-3601). These centers provide information or shopping, entertainment, festivals and recreation.*

Accommodations – Area visitors' guide including **lodging directory** available *(free)* from **Tampa Bay Convention and Visitors Bureau**. **Reservation service**: ☎ 800-44-TAMPA. Accommodations range from luxury **hotels** and resorts *($120-$350)* to budget **motels** *($45-$90)* and **bed-and-breakfast inns** *($80-$150). Rates quoted are average prices per night for a double room and are subject to seasonal variations.*

Local Press – Daily news: *The Tampa Tribune*; entertainment section, *Friday Extra. Travelhost, The Weekly Planet* and *See Tampa* (available free at hotels and restaurants) are handy guides to arts, entertainment and sports.

Foreign Exchange Office – American Express Travel Services, One Tampa City Center, at Franklin Street Mall and Jackson Street *(☎ 273-0310 or 800-221-7282)*.

Shopping – **Old Hyde Park Village**, W. Swann Ave. at Dakota St. *(☎ 251-3500)* **Centro Ybor**, between 7th and 9th Aves. at 16th St., Ybor City *(☎ 242-4660)* **The Shops at Channelside**, 615 Channelside Dr. *(☎ 223-4250)*; **International Plaza** West Shore Blvd. at Spruce St. (south of the airport) *(☎ 342-3790)*.

Entertainment – Consult the arts and entertainment section in the local newspaper for a schedule of cultural events and addresses of principal theaters and concert halls. **Tampa Bay Performing Arts Center** *(☎ 229-7827; www.tbpac.com)* For arts and sporting events tickets: **Ticketmaster** *(☎ 287-8844; www.ticketmaster.com)*.

Sports and Recreation – **Football**: Tampa Bay Buccaneers *(☎ 879-BUCS www.buccaneers.com)*. **Baseball**: Tampa Bay Devil Rays (St. Petersburg *(☎ 727-825-3120; www.devilray.com)*. **Hockey**: Tampa Bay Lightning *(☎ 301-6600; www.tampabaylightning.com)*. **Soccer**: Tampa Bay Mutiny *(☎ 386-2000 www.tampabaymutiny.com)*. **Thoroughbred racing**: Tampa Bay Downs *(☎ 855-4401; www.tampabaydowns.com)*. **Greyhound racing**: Tampa Greyhound Track *(☎ 932-4313; www.tampadogs.com)*. Public **golf courses**: Babe Zaharia *(☎ 631-4375)*; Rocky Point Golf *(☎ 673-4316)*.

Useful Numbers   ☎

Police/Ambulance/Fire	**91**
Traveler's Aid	273-593●
24-hour Pharmacy: Walgreen's, 2782 Henderson St.	877-436●
Weather (recorded)	645-232●

ADDRESS BOOK

For a legend of price listings for hotels and restaurants, see p 76. For information about hotel chains in Florida, see Accommodations *section at the back of this guide.*

Staying in the Tampa Bay Area

Don CeSar Beach Resort and Spa – *3400 Gulf Blvd., St. Petersburg Beach.* ✗ & ▣ ☎ *727-360-1881 or 800-282-1116. www.doncesar.com. 275 rooms.* $$$$$ This flamingo-pink sand castle—complete with turrets and bell towers—is a St. Petersburg area landmark. Carrara marble fountains and Cuban tile floors evoke the 10-story Moorish-Mediterranean style hotel's jazz-age heyday when F. Scott Fitzgerald was a regular; FDR and the New York Yankees baseball team also patronized the place in the 1920s and 30s. Elegantly designed in breezy Florida pastels and light woods, guest rooms over-look the Gulf of Mexico or Boca Ciega Bay. The tony **Maritana Grille** features a prix-fixe chef's table for small groups and wall-mounted saltwater aquariums filled with Florida species.

Renaissance Vinoy Resort – *501 Fifth Ave. N.E., St. Petersburg.* ✗ & ▣ ☎ *727-894-1000. www.renaissancehotels.com. 360 rooms.* $$$$$ Babe Ruth was among the celebrities who wintered at this opulent Mediterranean Revival 1925 landmark, considered one of St. Pete's architectural jewels. A recent ren-ovation brought the salmon color back to its exterior facade, and restored the lobby's quarry-tile floors, stenciled cypress beams and frescoed ceilings. Bedrooms are done in contemporary blond oak furnishings and muted colors. Golf, tennis and tropical gardens enhance the site. The resort's downtown loca-tion near its own marina, the Pier and shops is a plus.

Saddlebrook Resort – *5700 Saddlebrook Way, Wesley Chapel.* ✗ & ▣ ☎ *813-973-1111 or 800-729-8383. www.saddlebrookresort.com. 800 rooms.* $$$$$ *(per-person rate includes breakfast & dinner).* Nestled among 500 acres of cypress-shaded countryside, this top-notch retreat combines fine dining and spa pampering with ways to play: two 18-hole Arnold Palmer-designed golf courses and 45 clay, grass and concrete tennis courts, plus a fitness center and 7,000sq ft spa. All rooms and suites feature a balcony or patio with views of the greens, the courts or the scenic surroundings. Dining choices include the stylish **Cypress Restaurant**, known for its seafood.

Safety Harbor Resort and Spa – *105 N. Bayshore Dr., Safety Harbor.* ✗ & ▣ ☎ *727-373-3000 or 888-237-8772. www.safetyharborspa.com. 193 rooms.* $$$$ Built on springs sighted (presumably) by Pánfilo de Narváez in 1528, this historic landmark, one of the oldest US spas, is the only one in Florida with natural spring waters. Its 22-acre setting on Tampa Bay permits views of egrets, manatees and other wildlife. Indoor and outdoor pools brim with mineral water, while the 50,000sq ft spa and fitness center offers feet-to-face rejuvenation. Super-size guest rooms boast walk-through closets and large bathrooms. Spa cuisine shares the menu with pan-fried lump crabcakes and other delights in the main dining room or in the cafe.

Belleview Biltmore Resort & Spa – *25 Belleview Blvd., Clearwater.* ✗ & ▣ ☎ *727-442-6171 or 800-237-8947. www.belleviewbiltmore.com. 244 rooms.* $$$ Perched on a bluff overlooking Clearwater Bay, this sprawling, Victorian structure (1897) shelters oddly configured rooms, hidden staircases and secret trap doors. Once a retreat for the elite, the century-old haunt sports indoor and outdoor swimming pools, tennis courts, a fitness center, spa and 18-hole golf course on its 21 acres. More functional than fancy, rooms offer basic amenities and Queen Anne decor, but few high-tech touches; ceiling fans and wooden blinds recall late-19C practicality. A complimentary shuttle whisks guests to Clearwater Beach and back.

Don Vicente de Ybor Historic Inn – *1915 Republica de Cuba (9th Ave. at 14th St.), Ybor City.* ✗ & ▣ ☎ *813-241-4545. www.yborinns.com. 16 rooms.* $$ Crystal chandeliers, gilded furnishings and velvet draperies have trans-formed a former health-care center into a glitzy urban escape within Ybor City's lively Latin Quarter. Spacious suites feature draped beds, guest robes and slip-pers plus a private balcony—perfect for toasting the sunset. First owned by cigar-manufacturing entrepreneur Vicente Martinez Ybor, the two-story 1895 structure now includes a 100-seat restaurant and cigar and martini bar. The shops and restaurants of Seventh Avenue are a short walk away.

Mansion House B&B and the Courtyard on Fifth – *105 Fifth Ave. N.E., St. Petersburg.* & ▣ ☎ *727-821-9391 or 800-274-7520. www.mansion-andb.com. 13 rooms.* $$$ Cozy and casual, these two historic homes and carriage house create a comfortable covert for lodgers. Fresh flowers and hand-painted furniture add flair to guest rooms, while common areas and an outdoor pool make for pleasant places to mingle. Robes and light snacks are cheerfully provided by friendly innkeepers. Morning brings peaches-and-cream French toast, fresh fruit, yogurt and specialty cereals served in bright, adjoining breakfast rooms.

Wildlife on Easy Street – *12802 Easy St., Tampa.*   🚻 🅿 ☎ *813-920-4130. www.wildlifeoneasystreet.com. 8 cabins (overnight patrons must be at least 18 years old; per room occupancy is limited to two people).* **$$$** Sleeping quarters are small and simple but the setting—a 40-acre lakefront wildlife sanctuary— makes this lodging ideal for animal lovers. Endangered and exotic felines once rescued or retired roar behind 8ft-tall wire fences, while only feet away, guests get some shut-eye amid tiger-striped or leopard-spotted bed linens. Cabins connect to an animal habitat that places visitors within petting range of docile servals, bobcats and Siberian lynx. Coffee, muffins and juice are supplied, but in-room microwaves and small refrigerators can accommodate added provisions.

Behind the Fence B&B – *1400 Viola Dr., Brandon.* 🅿 ⚒ ☎ *813-685-8201. 3 rooms, 2 cottages.* **$$** More country than cosmopolitan in its appearance and ambience, this Cracker-style house overflows with early-American antiques, authentic Amish quilts and hand-dipped candles. The one-bedroom cottages border a large, tree-shaded backyard and swimming pool, while rooms in the two-story house overlook a quiet neighborhood. Evenings, guests gather around a fireplace for popcorn or on the back porch for lemonade. Breakfast features homemade Amish cinnamon rolls, fruit and cereal served family style.

Seahorse Cottages and Apartments – *10356 Gulf Blvd., Treasure Island.* 🅿 ☎ *727-367-2291 or 800-741-2291. www.beachdirectory.com/seahorse 11 rooms.* **$$** Tucked among the conventional motels and high-rise hotels lining Treasure Island's beachfront, these cottages offer vacationers a quaint accommodations alternative. Choices range from stand-alone cottages, some with decks and views of the beach, to second-floor apartments. The cabinlike quarters have a cozy feel and feature dark wood paneling and fully equipped kitchens. Picnic shelters, swings and beach chairs, flowering plants and palm trees enhance the common area.

Dining in the Tampa Bay Area

Bern's Steak House – *1208 Howard Ave., Tampa.*   ☎ *813-251-2421. www.bernssteakhouse.com.* **$$$ American**. Hyde Park's 40-year-old landmark and a Tampa tradition, offers meat connoisseurs six different cuts of aged US Prime beef, from chateaubriand to T-bone, served with garlic butter, soup, salad, baked potato and home-grown vegetables. The encyclopedic **wine list** boasts nearly 8,000 entries. Gilded plaster columns, red wallpaper and murals depicting French vineyards set the mood for a memorable dining experience. Order your dessert by phone in one of the many glass-encased booths upstairs. *Dinner only.*

Chateau France – *136 4th Ave. N.E., St. Petersburg.*   ☎ *727-894-7163. www.floridasecrets.com.* **$$$ French**. This early-1900s house-turned-restaurant features intimate dining on two floors and a wraparound veranda for cocktails. Bright floral wallpaper, lace curtains, wood floors and fresh roses fashion an elegant interior, where red-vested servers dote on diners' every need. Here, scallops swim in a lemon sauce, red snapper Monte Carlo is coated with spicy crabmeat, and filet mignon Roquefort is stuffed with the namesake cheese— all preludes to a finale of flaming desserts. *Dinner only.*

Hurricane Seafood Restaurant – *807 Gulf Way, St. Petesburg Beach.*   ☎ *727-360-9558. www.thehurricane.com.* **$$$ Seafood**. For nearly four decades, this popular 498-seat beachfront bar, restaurant and nightclub has been *the* spot to watch the area's signature sunsets. From the rooftop deck of the third floor, beachgoers and business types alike enjoy drinks and 360 degrees of gulf, mainland and bay. The seafood matches the view, especially the local favorite—grouper, a flaky saltwater fish served grilled, broiled, blackened or fried. After the first-floor cafe closes at 1am, the second-floor dining room becomes **Stormy's**, a late-night dance club where lights flash and fan-fueled winds whip the room to form a fake, but fearsome, hurricane.

Salt Rock Grill – *19325 Gulf Blvd., Indian Shores.*   ☎ *727-593-7625. www.saltrockgrill.com.* **$$$ American**. Oversize glass and metallic fish dangle from the ceiling, while oversize fresh fish, packed in ice and on display, await tossing on the fire at this popular waterfront eatery. Named for the local lime stone used in the restaurant's flooring, Salt Rock is famed for its wood-grilled steaks, chicken, Alaskan King Crab legs and lobster tail, served with fire-roasted vegetable kabobs. Diners overlook the intracoastal waterway from the Tiki Deck or from the main room's floor-to-ceiling windows. *Dinner only.*

SideBern's – *2208 W. Morrison Ave., Tampa.*   ☎ *813-258-2233. www.bernssteakhouse.com.* **$$$ International**. Bern's less ornate, less sedate sister restaurant buzzes and bustles as diners fill the lounge, dim sum bar and

© Jeff Greenberg/FOLIO, Inc.

Columbia Restaurant, Ybor City

main room. Sheer drapes soften the industrial-strength interior, which includes a back-lit stainless steel bar. Food here is inventive and edgy—from the coconut-curried rabbit dumpling appetizers with pineapple salsa to entrées like Thai-barbecued wild boar tenderloin. The kitchen works under the watchful eye of patrons who opt for the 18-seat chef's table. You may want to request the patio for less din while dining, since the crowd can be loud.

Columbia – *2117 E. 7th Ave., Ybor City.*   ✆ *813-248-4961. www.columbiarestaurant.com.* **$$ Spanish**. Encompassing an entire block within Tampa's historic district, Florida's oldest operating restaurant (1905), still family-owned, is a bastion of Old World charm and Spanish-Cuban cuisine. Linen tablecloths, gracious service and hand-painted tiles throughout set the scene for tapas, gazpacho and Columbia's signature paella *a la Valenciana*, the national dish of Spain. Choose a vintage label from the house cellar or try the freshly made fruit-filled sangria. Nightly *(except Sun)*, colorfully attired flamenco dancers leave patrons waving napkins and tapping their toes *(additional cost for show)*. Other locations in Clearwater Beach and St. Petersburg.

Mise en Place – *442 W. Kennedy Blvd., Tampa.*   ✆ *813-254-5373.* **$$ New American**. The city's acclaimed bistro is a trendy two-tier dining room within a 1920s building downtown, across the street from the Plant Museum. Arches and half walls separate the sprawling setting into intimate nooks where locals sup on inventive dishes such as roast chicken served with tahini-yogurt-lemon vinaigrette. Seared tuna comes in a sauce of tomato, brown butter and capers, and traditional rack of lamb is crusted with spicy mustard and pecans.

Mykonos – *628 Dodecanese Blvd., Tarpon Springs.*   ✆ *727-934-4306.* **$$ Greek**. White walls and blue accents brighten this modest, family-owned dining spot, where locals and visitors have flocked for almost a decade to enjoy authentic Greek cuisine. Baskets bulge with daily baked breads and plates overflow with Greek salad, lamb gyros and crispy *spanakotiropita* pastries. Fluent in the language, waitstaff are ready to help with tongue-twisting pronunciations of *soutzoukakia* and other specialties that issue from the open kitchen. After your meal, stroll the shops and sponge docks of this quaint riverside community.

Skipper's Smokehouse Restaurant – *910 Skipper Rd., Tampa.* ✆ *813-971-0666. www.skipperssmokehouse.com.* **$$ Seafood**. The weather-beaten walkways and overturned boats fronting this landmark restaurant belie its offshore location. Inside, the atmosphere is definitely beach style: laid back and low key. Seating is limited and the tiny **oyster bar** fills up fast, but overflow crowds can dine on alligator chili, garlic crab, and steamed mud bugs (crawfish) under the stars at outside picnic tables. Nightly, reggae, blues and zydeco musicians perform beneath the Skipperdome's thatched awning, while patrons (some shoeless) head for the outdoor dance floor.

Willie's – *1912 Main St., Brandon.*   ✆ *813-571-7630.* **$$ Seafood**. Formerly called Fat Willie's Fish Camp, this rural spot has appealed to families for generations, with its hearty seafood platters piled high with hush puppies, cole slaw and fresh fish. Alligator, Alaskan crab legs, and gulf oysters are also on the menu, but it's the catfish that keeps customers coming back. Modeled on the fish camps of the Carolinas, the 150-seat space features trophy fish and local art on its walls. Set back from the road, Willie's can be tough to find; just look for the pickup-packed parking lot. *Dinner only.*

TAMPA

PeopleMover

0   1/5 mi
0   300 m

The lush lawn of **Plant Park**, once part of the original hotel grounds, sets off the building's fanciful wood **fretwork**. Three chrysanthemum windows on the upper-most story above the portico add to the Victorian grandeur of this structure. Inside the museum, visitors glimpse what life was like for Plant's fortunate guests, lumi-naries such as Thomas Edison, Theodore Roosevelt and Babe Ruth. Brass and gilt brighten long corridors decorated with rich fabrics. Massive wooden doors open into rooms where lace draperies cascade from 11ft-high keyhole-shaped, beveled glass windows. Restored to its 1891 color scheme, the **Reading and Writing Room** contains some of its original furnishings. A fireplace at the north end is crowned with an elaborate mantel and a huge mirror. Chairs of ebonized wood with mother-of-pearl inlay hug the walls near a matching writing desk. A typical guest suite outfitted with Eastlake furniture and original electric light fixtures, and a solarium overlooking the park may also be visited.

★**Hyde Park** – *North and south of Swann Ave. between South Crosstown Expressway (Rte. 618) and Bayshore Blvd. Driving tour pamphlets available from Tampa Bay Convention and Visitors Bureau.* This district originated in the late 180 as a clutch of Cuban fishing villages and palmetto huts called Spanishtown Creek. In 1886 O.H. Platt bought and subdivided 20 acres, naming the tract for his Illinoi hometown. Tampa's wealthiest families built homes here in a wide range of archi-tectural styles. Today Queen Annes and Colonial Revivals elbow Mediterranea Revivals and eclectic bungalows. Carefully pruned yards are shaded by overhangin live oaks draped with Spanish moss. Some of the finest houses lie south of Swan between Rome Avenue and South Boulevard.

Tampa's most fashionable shopping district, **Old Hyde Park Village**, lines South Dakot and Snow avenues south of Swann Avenue. This posh development boasts chi boutiques and restaurants with outdoor dining as well as a movie theater.

Peter O. Knight House – *245 S. Hyde Park Ave. Open year-round by appointmen Closed major holidays.* ⊡ ☎ *813-259-1111.* Constructed in 1890 as a honeymoo cottage by Colonel Knight, one of Tampa's early business leaders, the house is cur rently headquarters for the Tampa Historical Society. Exhibits explain the city' cigar industry, Tampa Bay's Victorian era, the role of women in Tampa, and are shipbuilding. The Historical Society maintains a photo archive and library here.

■ The Tampa Bay Hotel

In 1890 Tampa was a grimy backwater of only 5,532 inhabitants before the Tampa Bay Hotel's architectural splendor and elegant accommodations put the city on the map. Like his competitor and former business colleague Henry Flagler, Yankee railroad magnate Henry Bradley Plant built a luxury hotel in an effort to fortify his transportation empire.

Tampa Bay Hotel

The hotel rose on a flat peninsula of citrus groves and dense woods, bounded by Hillsborough and Tampa bays; it required two years and an astounding $2.5 million to construct. Designed by New York architect John A. Wood, the five-story structure contains 500 rooms and sits upon six acres. The architect chose the then-popular Moorish Revival style, which echoed Florida's long history as a Spanish possession. Its sensational effect attracted more than 4,000 wealthy visitors a year.

Plant and his second wife, Margaret, spent another $500,000 as they traveled the world in 1889 on a buying spree for the new hotel. They scoured Europe and Asia, filling 80 railcars with fine antiques, sculpture, paintings, furniture and carpets. Some of those pieces can still be seen in the museum's permanent collection.

For years Plant's hotel—the second in Florida to have an elevator, steam heat, electric lights, telephones, running water and private baths for each suite—was the centerpiece of Tampa's social life, hosting a flurry of balls and civic events. Such world-renowned performers as French actress Sarah Bernhardt and Russian ballerina Anna Pavlova entertained audiences in the hotel's casino. In 1898 the hotel earned international fame when Plant used his influence to have Tampa declared a port of embarkation for US Army troops during the Spanish-American War.

★**Bayshore Boulevard** – Skirting the shore from the Hillsborough River to MacDill Air Force Base, this 7.2mi signature roadway provides fine **views**★ of Hillsborough Bay and the downtown skyline, and sweeps past Hyde Park, one of Tampa's oldest neighborhoods. Along the water's edge runs a landscaped sidewalk used by cyclists, skaters and pedestrians. At the north end, Bayshore passes the three-masted schooner *José Gasparilla (opposite Beach Pl.)*, named for legendary pirate José Gaspar, who once terrorized settlers along the Gulf coast. (Each February the city stages the **Gasparilla Festival**, a month-long celebration of Tampa's past.) Continuing south, the road swerves inland at Ballast Point and ends at MacDill, which served as the command center for Operation Desert Storm in 1991.

★**Tampa Theatre** – *711 Franklin St. For tours ☎ 813-274-8981. www.tampatheatre.org.* This grand 1926 movie palace, described by one historian as an "Andalusian bonbon," boasts iron entrance gates, a glazed-tile lobby and a fanciful interior blending Byzantine, Italian Renaissance, Greek Revival and other styles. Dramatic facades embellished with statuary and spiraling pillars vie for attention with the ornate proscenium arch, overhead star display and cloud machine. Year-round the 1,446-seat theater presents foreign films, concerts and special events.

Tampa Museum of Art – *600 N. Ashley Dr. Open year-round Tue-Sat 10am-5pm (Thu 8pm), Sun 1pm-5pm. Closed Jan 1, Thanksgiving Day, Dec 25. $5. ⟁ ☎ 813-274-8130. www.tampamuseum.com.* Highlights from the permanent collection of this museum include the **Classical World Gallery**, which features more than

400 Greek and Roman works. Marble sculptures, grave altars, bronze figurines and an outstanding collection of painted **Greek vases**★ offer insight into the origins of Western civilization. Also on display are modern works of sculpture and glass in the Terrace Gallery, overlooking the Hillsborough River; among the artists represented are Jacques Lipchitz, Louis Comfort Tiffany and C. Paul Jennewein. Much of the museum's exhibit space is devoted to temporary exhibits, including an annual showing of established and emerging Florida artists.

Just beside the museum, visitors will find a shady courtyard with fountains and benches, and a stairway leading to an amphitheater that provides a **view** of the striking minarets of the University of Tampa across the river.

Sacred Heart Catholic Church – *Florida Ave. at Twiggs St.* ✦ *For organ concerts* ☏ *813-229-1595. www.sacredheartfla.org.* Dedicated in 1905, this massive Romanesque stone structure features a triple-arch entrance with carved oak doors and pews, columns of Tennessee marble, stained-glass windows and a painted 14-story dome soaring above the main altar. The church was restored in 1977, after water and termite damage left the dome in danger of collapse.

★**Florida Aquarium** – Kids *701 Channelside Dr. at Garrison Seaport Center. Open year-round daily 9:30am-5pm. Closed Thanksgiving Day, Dec 25. $12.95.* ⚹ ✦ ($3) ☏ *813-273-4000. www.flaquarium.org.* Beneath a signature green glass dome, Tampa's aquatic-life facility harbors more than a million gallons of fresh and salt water. Viewing galleries are laid out in four aquatic communities. In **Wetlands**, a humid zone of cypress swamps, mangrove forests and saw grass marshes, habitats display freshwater bass, white ibis, great horned owls and other animals. The ecosystems of **Bays and Beaches** include bay bottoms, with graceful stingrays and floor-dwelling guitarfish. In the popular **Coral Reef**, colorful butterfly fish dart through forests of staghorn coral and sharks lurk in dark grottoes. One room contains a tri-panel transparent wall 14ft high and 43ft wide for the display of tropical fish of 60 species. **Sea Hunt** presents scorpion fish, the giant Pacific octopus and other residents of the deep sea.

Take the elevator to the rooftop deck where you can overlook the artificial reef and glimpse the Port of Tampa, Florida's largest port by tonnage.

★**YBOR CITY** *1.6mi from downtown Tampa. Map p 307.*

The heart of Tampa's Cuban population and the cigar capital of the world once beat within this 1sq mi historic district, now an upcoming neighborhood. Latin accents remain, even as Ybor City has been resuscitated into a trendy spot for nightlife. In 1990 it was designated one of Florida's three National Historic Landmark Districts (along with St. Augustine and Pensacola).

Historical Notes – When labor union pressures in Key West forced cigar manufacturer **Vicente Martínez Ybor** (pronounced "EE-bore") to find a new site for his operations, he chose a mosquito-infested plot of wilderness adjoining the young

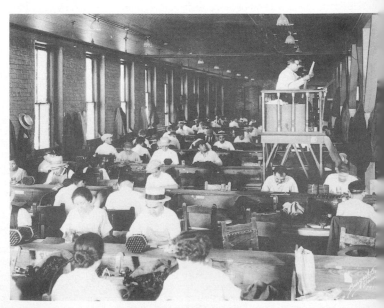

Lectore Reads to Workers at Cuesta Rey Factory (1929)

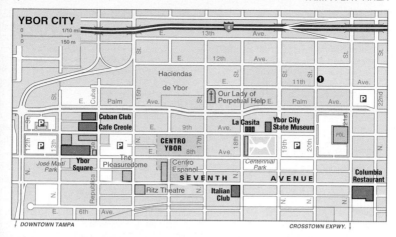

YBOR CITY

city of Tampa. The new railroad, shipping port and warm climate made this location ideal for his cigar factory, which opened in 1886 and became the largest in the world, employing over 4,000 people. Soon, the city teemed with optimistic young laborers—Cuban, Spanish, Italian and German immigrants. Spanish was the language spoken in the factory, where *lectores* read newspapers and poetry to the busy workers. Shops, restaurants, mutual-aid societies and social clubs sprang into being to serve the growing population.

In the late 1800s, Ybor City became a base of operations for the Cuban revolution. During the Spanish-American War, the US Army stationed troops here, among them Col. Teddy Roosevelt and his Rough Riders (the 1st Regiment of US Cavalry Volunteers, organized by Roosevelt during the Spanish-American War). A year after Cuba won its independence in 1898, Ybor City saw the first wave of labor strikes and unrest, as fresh immigrants—fueled by the socialist doctrines preached in their home countries—clashed with conservative Tampa business leaders.

The advent of machine-rolled cigars, the increasing popularity of cigarettes, and the beginning of the Depression spelled doom for the hand-rolled cigar industry in Ybor City.

The past decade has ushered in a resurgence of interest in Ybor City. Buildings have been renovated and historical elements spruced up as cobblestone streets, Old World street lamps and wrought-iron balconies have been installed. Now produced by machine, local cigars generate $150 million in annual sales revenue.

Sights *Map above*

Ybor City Chamber of Commerce operates a visitor center at 1800 E. 9th Ave. ☎ *813-248-3712.*

★**Seventh Avenue** – A walk along this avenue reveals some of the district's more interesting architecture. A landmark since 1905, **Columbia Restaurant** *(no. 2117; see Address Book)* is justly praised for its colorful exterior **tilework**. The three-story Neoclassical **Italian Club** *(at 18th St.)*, distinguished by its tripartite facade, has served as a center of cultural enrichment, education and financial aid to local Italians since 1894; the present structure dates from 1918. One of the largest developments in the history of Ybor City opened in 2000 between 7th and 9th Aves. at 16th St. Central Espanol, formerly a mutual-aid society that had been shuttered for years, has been renovated and reopened as the cornerstrone of **Centro Ybor**, a $45 million complex that includes restaurants, retailers, a comedy club, a high-tech entertainment center and a multi-screen movie theater set around an open air plaza. The Pleasuredome *(no. 1430)*, now an alternative dance club, occupies the building that held the city's

 Ybor City Brewing Company

Map above. 2205 N. 20th St. ☎ *813-242-9222 or 800-249-2138.* The area's first microbrewery began operation in November 1994 after a $3 million renovation of a 100-year-old cigar factory. The three-story, 36,000sq ft building now turns out 15,000 barrels of home brew a year, including the locally popular Ybor Gold, a frothy German lager; Calusa Wheat, a golden tropical ale; and Ybor Brown Ale, an Old English-style ale. Tours of the sweet-smelling facility explain the multistep brewing process and end with a sampling of the company's products.

first restaurant, where, in 1890, the Rough Riders trotted in on horseback. The avenue takes on a Mardi Gras atmosphere on Thursday, Friday and Saturday nights throughout the year, as police block traffic between 13th and 20th streets and turn Seventh into a pedestrian promenade.

Two blocks off Seventh Avenue sits the yellow brick **Cuban Club** *(2010 Avenida Republica de Cuba)*, which dates from 1917. In its heyday, the club offered its members a ballroom, library, gym, theater and medical clinic. Today the building houses a health-care organization and also hosts social events.

The nearby two-story brick **Cafe Creole** *(1320-1330 E. 9th Ave.)*, with its graceful arches, gained fame as El Pasaje, or the Cherokee Club, a rowdy hotel and restaurant that opened in 1888. In its heyday, the hotel welcomed Cuban revolutionary José Martí, presidents Teddy Roosevelt and Grover Cleveland, Sir Winston Churchill and many Florida governors.

Ybor City State Museum – *1818 9th Ave. Open year-round daily 9am-5pm. Closed Thanksgiving Day & Dec 25. $2. ㊧ ☎ 813-247-6323. Museum staff lead walking tours through the historic district from the museum (extra charge).* Housed in the 1923 yellow-brick Ferlita Bakery building, this museum outlines the development of Ybor City from frontier village to its recent renaissance. Exhibits include photographs, cigar-making tools, two commercial bread ovens and tobacco-box artwork. Guided tours of adjacent **La Casita** (1895) provide a glimpse of a typical cigarmaker's shotgun cottage.

Ybor Square – *1911 N. 13th St.* Built in 1886 by Vicente Martínez Ybor, this three-story, redbrick building once contained Ybor City's oldest and largest hand-rolled cigar factory. The remodeled complex now contains office space. From the front steps of the building, José Martí, hero of the Cuban revolution, rallied his countrymen. A small park across Eighth Avenue *(corner of 13th St. and E. 8th Ave.)* honors Martí. The park marks the original site of the home of the Pedroso family, Cubans who sheltered Martí from Spanish loyalists.

NORTH TAMPA *Map p 292*

★★ **Busch Gardens Tampa Bay** – 🎫 *3000 E. Busch Blvd. Open year-round daily 9:30am-6pm. $47.95; children 3-9 $32.95; $10.95 next-day return ticket and annual passes available. ✗ ㊧ 🅿($6) ▥ ☎ 813-987-5090 or 800-372-1797. www.buschgardens.com. Trams take visitors from parking lot to park entrance; note section and row in which you park.* In 1959 the local Busch family built a brewery just south of the University of South Florida and opened a bird sanctuary and garden on the grounds. Since then, the internationally famous zoo-amusement park with a late-19C Africa theme has become the queen of Tampa attractions. Nearly 3,000 animals roam 300 acres of tropical gardens; roller coasters and trains, music and shows add to the entertainment.

Visiting Busch Gardens – Arrive early to avoid long lines (parking areas open at 8:30am). Most popular months are Dec. and Mar-Aug; busiest days are Fri-Sun. When you purchase your ticket, you'll receive a map and guide that lists times and locations for entertainment. The daily schedule is also posted in Morocco, the first land you encounter upon entering the park. Guest Relations is located near the main entrance; staff there will exchange foreign currency at no charge. For most efficient viewing, move clockwise as you visit all 10 sections. Thrill rides like roller coasters Montu, Kumba, Python and Scorpion, and water rides Tanganyika Tidal Wave, Stanley Falls and Congo River Rapids tend to be the most popular; head for these first. Some rides are restricted by guest height, size and physical condition. Visitors may not bring coolers, food or drink into the park; a variety of eateries are scattered around the grounds. First aid is available next to the Festhaus in Timbuktu and Crown Colony's Skyride Station.

Morocco – A mosaic-tiled palace and bustling marketplace recall the romance and mystery of this section's North African inspiration. Visitors here are treated to a 36min ice show that celebrates Hollywood filmmaking. Here you will also find a bakery, an open-air dining room, and two theaters presenting musical and dance revues.

Bird Gardens – Busch's original interest, the gardens now showcase 198 exotic species. Their highlight is the **Lory Landing** aviary, a rain-forest setting in which parrots, lorikeets, hornbills and other tropical birds fly freely. Attend an unusual Bird Show featuring trained raptors and parrots, many of which fly above the audience. The theme area also includes a Flamingo Island and a koala display. Adjacent is Land of the Dragons, a play area for young children named for the nearby pen for Komodo dragons.

Stanleyville – Built to resemble an African village, the area includes the Stanley Falls Log Flume and the Tanganyika Tidal Wave, a ride that creates a huge splash as it careens down a 55ft drop. Orangutan and warthog exhibits, an orchid garden and hands-on reptile exhibit complete the attractions here. Stanleyville Theatre and Zambezi Pavilion feature live entertainment.

© Janice Travla/Tony Stone Images

The Python Roller Coaster

The Congo – Here stand some of the Southeast's most gut-wrenching roller coasters, including **Kumba**, one of the largest and fastest (60mph), which zooms riders through 7 inversions. It joins Python, a 1,200ft-long coaster with two 360-degree loops, and Congo River Rapids, a water ride. The newest is **Gwazi**, billed as Florida's first dueling, or double, wooden roller coaster, which sends guests spiraling along 7,000ft of track in two simultaneously operating trains at speeds in excess of 50mph. For the younger set there are the Ubanga-Banga bumper cars. At Claw Island, rare Bengal tigers live in a landscape similar to their native jungle habitat.

Timbuktu – In this replica of a desert trading center, you'll find the Scorpion roller coaster that drops 62ft into a 360-degree loop; and the Dolphin Theatre, starring leaping dolphins and a comical California sea lion. Arcade games line the aisles in the shopping bazaar/midway, and live shows are presented on the Festhaus stage.

Nairobi – This section features a variety of animals, including those in **Myombe Reserve**, a three-acre gorilla and chimpanzee habitat, where guests can observe primates up-close through a glass window. Asian elephants, tortoises, a petting zoo and an animal nursery are also located here. In an incongruous nod to Anheuser-Busch tradition, the international Show Jumping Hall of Fame shares space in a reptile house with snakes and lizards. From Nairobi station, the steam-powered Trans-Veldt Railroad carries visitors around the theme park in open coaches.

Crown Colony – The Victorian-style Crown Colony House hospitality center is the focal point of this part of the park. It overlooks zebras, hippos and ostriches that roam nearby Serengeti Plain. Adjacent is the **skyride** station, as well as the stables of Anheuser-Busch's famous Clydesdale horses.

Edge of Africa – This theme area comprises a short trek past habitats for such animals as baboons, hippos, lions, hyenas and meerkats. Introduced on video by noted animal handler Jack Hanna, it enables observers to get as close to large animals as acrylic panes will allow.

Serengeti Plain – From antelopes to zebras, more than 700 large African animals roam in herds on the 29-acre grassy savanna. You'll see ostriches, rhinos, giraffes, zebras and more. For viewing, take the skyride or train, but the flatbed truck tours offered by **Serengeti Safari** *($20)* enable guests to get even more up-close and personal. The newly introduced **Rhino Rally** takes passengers off-road through remote terrain and ends with a river ride aboard a washed-out pontoon bridge.

Egypt – The easternmost area of Busch Gardens holds nearly seven acres of rides, including **Montu**, a spine-tingling inverted roller coaster, as well as a replica of King Tut's tomb and shopping bazaars. **Akbar's Adventure Tours** is a simulated journey with a second-rate tour guide (as played on video by actor Martin Short) through a bustling casbah, around the pyramids and into a haunted tomb.

Take a break from the heat at **Adventure Island**, another Busch attraction across the street featuring water rides for patrons of every age *(4500 E. Bougainvillea Ave.; open late Mar-late Oct daily 10am-5pm; rest of the year hours vary; $25.95; ⚹ 🅿 $3; www.adventureisland.com; ☎ 813-987-5082).*

★★ **Museum of Science & Industry (MOSI)** – 🅺🅸🅳🆂 *4801 E. Fowler Ave. Open Jul 4-Labor Day daily 9am-7pm. Rest of the year Mon-Fri 9am-5pm, weekends 9am-7pm. Holidays noon-7pm. $13.* ⚹ ♿ 🅿 ☎ *813-987-6100. www.mosi.org.* This quintessential hands-on science museum received a $35 million face-lift in 1995

Especially for Families
A family entertainment value, the 24-acre **Lowry Park Zoo** [Kids] *(7530 N. Blvd.;* ☎ *813-932-8552; www.aza.org)* contains natural habitats for 1,600 animals, including endangered species such as the Florida panther and Sumatran tiger. West Indian manatees frolic in the Manatee and Aquatic Center, where large underwater viewing tanks put visitors nose-to-nose with these gentle giants. Kids will want to spend a couple of hours trying out the costumes, puppets and computers at the hands-on **Kid City: The Children's Museum of Tampa** [Kids] *(7550 N. Blvd.;* ☎ *813-935-8441)* just down the street from the zoo. Outside, Safety Village, a pint-size version of Tampa complete with a city hall, supermarket, bank and hospital, provides lessons in traffic safety. Children can enter many of the miniature structures to experiment with interactive exhibits.

with the addition of a starkly modern four-story, aluminum-clad wing (West Wing) designed by Arizona architect Antoine Predock. Some 450 permanent exhibits are complemented by several special exhibits each year. On the first floor, a county library offers high-tech computer games and access to the Internet. En route to the museum entrance, stop at the butterfly garden to view the brightly colored creatures and to discover how water in natural wetlands cleans itself. In the **Gulf Coast Hurricane**, visitors experience high-speed winds and learn how to prepare for tropical storms.

West Wing – The main exhibit area is housed on the second floor, where a 350-seat **IMAX Dome Theatre** presents changing films on an 82ft-high screen. Across from the theater, **Our Florida** explores the state's unique flora, fauna and geography in the context of an ordinary backyard. Highlights include a 27ft-long topographic floor map and crawl-through simulation of a gopher tortoise hole. On the third floor in **The Amazing You** exhibit, visitors see, for example, how muscles move on a bicycle-riding skeleton, and learn about nutrition at the Food for Thought Cafe. Our Place in the Universe focuses on past and future space exploration. A causeway leads to the 47-acre **Back Woods**, which includes two nature trails, a gopher tortoise habitat and several acres of wetlands.

East Wing – The **Saunders Planetarium** dominates the third floor and offers opportunities to peer into space through the museum's high-powered telescopes. At the Challenger Learning Center, visitors explore outer space through role-playing and interactive work stations.

Seminole Indian Village – *5221 N. Orient Rd. Enter through the gift shop. Open Apr-late Oct Mon-Sat 9am-5pm, Sun 10am-4pm. Rest of the year Mon-Sat 10am-6pm, Sun 10am-4pm. Closed Thanksgiving Day & Dec 25. $3.50.* ♿ 🅿 ☎ *813-620-3077.* This family-run site features thatch houses and ceremonial structures found in an actual native village. A guide explains Indian costumes and customs. Built in the shape of an eight-sided star representing the eight clans of the Seminole Nation. Built over sacred burial ground, the museum displays a variety of artifacts including jewelry, arrowheads, baskets and clothing. (The village is not affiliated with the Seminole bingo parlor adjacent to it.)

EXCURSION

Hillsborough River State Park – *20mi northeast in Thonotosassa. From downtown, take I-4 east 6mi to US-301 north (Exit 6); Follow this 14mi to park entrance on left at 15402 US-301 N. Park hrs & fees p 350. Open year-round daily 8am dusk. $3.25/vehicle.* ⚠ 🅿 ☎ *813-987-6771. www.edp.state.fl.us/parks/index .html.* Tampa's largest park covers nearly 4,000 acres of marshes, cypress swamps and pine flatwoods. Centerpiece of the park, the Hillsborough River cuts through outcroppings of Suwannee limestone and creates a series of Class II rapids *(contact Canoe Escape for 2hr or full-day canoe/kayak trips:* ☎ *813-986-2067 www.canoeescape.com).* Eight miles of marked trails, some with interpretive plaques, course along the river and through hammocks of magnolia, Sabal palm hickory and live oak. *Bring mosquito repellent in summer months.*

Across US-301 sits a reconstruction of **Fort Foster**, which served as a supply depot from 1837-38 during the Second Seminole War *(visit by 1hr guided tour only Dec-Mar daily on the hour 10am-2pm; rest of the year weekends only on the hour 10am-2pm; $2;* 🅿 ☎ *813-987-6771.)* Gen. Zachary Taylor commanded the fort briefly in 1838. During the annual Rendezvous celebration *(early Feb)*, soldiers in period uniforms interpret life in the rustic wooden fort. Tours begin just north of the ranger station at a small museum that displays Seminole War artifacts.

TARPON SPRINGS★

Population 21,003
Map p 292
Tourist Information: www.tarponsprings.com ✆ 727-937-6109

A surprising taste of the Mediterranean flavors this small town on Florida's west coast. Best known as a commercial sponging center, Tarpon Springs derives much of its character from a strong, close-knit Greek community, which fans out from the sponge docks on the Anclote River, an estuary of the Gulf of Mexico.

Arriving in 1876, the first settlers supposedly named the area Tarpon Springs for what they thought were tarpon in the mineral spring at the head of the bayou (they were mullet). Sponge beds were discovered in the area in the 1870s, and soon thereafter, the Key West commercial market moved its hub to Tarpon Springs. By the next decade, the town had developed as a winter resort and health spa. Wealthy 19C "snowbirds" built Victorian houses and bungalows around the graceful "Golden Crescent" that surrounds **Spring Bayou**. Beginning in 1905, expert sponge divers—most of whom hailed from the Dodecanese Islands near Crete—immigrated from Greece. Surpassing Key West, the Tarpon Springs sponge business peaked in the 1930s. By the late 1940s, a local blight, America's preference for synthetic sponges, and growing Mediterranean competition decimated the Florida market. In 1986, however, the Soviet nuclear-reactor disaster in Chernobyl wiped out Mediterranean beds, and Tarpon Springs became the largest natural sponge market in the world—with annual revenues of $7 million.

■ Greek Festivities

Today Greek culture maintains a tangible presence in Tarpon Springs. The longest-standing example is the **Festival of Epiphany**, celebrated here each January since the early 1900s. To commemorate the baptism of Christ at the River Jordan, a colorful contingent of children, acolytes and church dignitaries parades around Spring Bayou after a noontime Blessing of the Waters at the St. Nicholas Greek Orthodox Cathedral. The highlight occurs when the Archbishop tosses a wooden cross into the water for local youths to retrieve; the one who does so is blessed with good fortune for the coming year. Following this ritual, festivities include Greek dancing and music accompanied by mouth-watering Mediterranean food.

SIGHTS

★**Dodecanese Boulevard** – *North of Tarpon Ave., off N. Pinellas Ave./US-19A.* Running parallel to the Anclote River, this lively waterfront thoroughfare forms the commercial spine of the Greek community. While sidewalk vendors cater primarily to tourists who busily poke through bins of sponges and curios from the sea, the colorful family-run cafes and bakeries draw as many locals as out-of-towners to sample honey-soaked baklava and other Greek specialties that scent the air. Be sure to explore the side streets behind the boulevard, where the atmosphere recalls residents' homeland.

Owen Cannon/MICHELIN

Sponges for Sale on Dodecanese

Near the east end of the boulevard, working shrimp and sponge boats are tied up at the main dock. Here a **cruise★** aboard one of the traditional sponging vessels *(departs from sponge docks year-round daily 10am-4pm; does not operate Jan 6, Easter Sunday, Dec 25 and during inclement weather; round-trip 30min; commentary; $5; 🅿 [$2] St. Nicholas Boat Line ☎ 727-942-6425)* offers a demonstration of sponge harvesting. Across the street, the former **Sponge Exchange** *(no. 735)* now houses specialty shops and displays an early 20C sponge-diving boat in the plaza. The **Tarpon Springs Aquarium** *(no. 850, west end of sponge docks)* features a touch-tank swimming with stingrays and baby sand sharks *(open year-round Mon-Fri 10am-5pm, Sun noon-5pm; closed Dec 25; $4.75; ♿ 🅿 ☎ 727-938-5378)*.

St. Nicholas Greek Orthodox Cathedral – *36 N. Pinellas Ave. Open year-round Mon-Sat 9am-4pm, Sun 12:30pm-4pm. ♿ 🅿 ☎ 727-937-3277. www.epiphany city.com.* Crowned by a three-story central **rotunda** and soaring corner bell tower, this Byzantine Revival-style church of buff-colored brick was built in 1943 to accommodate the town's rapidly growing Greek Orthodox population. Site of one of the most elaborate Epiphany rituals in the US, the cathedral also draws thousands of pilgrims each year to view the glass-framed icon of St. Nicholas. The interior boasts a majestic **dome** resting on four arches, inspired by the great dome of the 6C Church of Hagia Sophia in Constantinople (Istanbul). Stained-glass windows, imported chandeliers of Czech glass and a high altar carved from Greek marble ornament the sanctuary.

Unitarian Universalist Church – *57 Read St. at Grand Blvd. Visit by guided tour (25min) only, Nov-Apr Tue-Sun 2pm-5pm. Closed major holidays. Contribution requested. 🅿 ☎ 727-937-4682.* The 1909 masonry edifice dominated by a crenellated tower showcases 11 **paintings★** by **George Inness Jr.** (1854-1926), a seasonal resident of Tarpon Springs and son of the famous American landscape painter. Characterized by vivid "living greens," dramatic shading and perspective, the works include a landscape of Spring Bayou and two religious canvases—fruits of Inness' studies with the renowned French painters of the Barbizon School near Paris—that were awarded medals in the Louvre.

Shrine of St. Michael Taxiarchis – *113 Hope St. Open year-round daily 7am-6:30pm. ♿ 🅿 ☎ 727-937-4942.* Filled with hundreds of silver icons, this tiny shrine offers an interesting glimpse of the Greek Orthodox community of Tarpon Springs. The shrine was built in 1941 by Marie Tsalichis out of gratitude to St. Michael Taxiarchis, whom Marie believed had cured her son of a tumor. Thousands of worshippers have since come to light candles, hold services and pray for miracles.

Fred Howard Park – *1700 Sunset Dr., 2mi west of downtown. ♿ 🅿 ☎ 727-943-4081.* A palm-shaded causeway leads out to this lovely island park, which features a pristine crescent of white-sand beach and an expansive view of the Gulf of Mexico. In addition to sunning and swimming, it is a favorite fishing and jogging spot.

■ Sponge Diving: A Time-Honored Trade

A primitive aquatic animal with no brain or nervous system, the natural sponge (phylum Porifera) can be found in all seas but prefers shallow, temperate waters. Living in colonies at depths ranging from several feet to 28,000ft, sponges attach to stationary objects, such as rocks and coral, on the sea floor. In shallow water these animals can be collected from a boat using a long-handled metal hook; in deeper water, divers must walk along the bottom (sponges can be harvested from depths up to 150ft) and hook the sponges by hand, walking at a 45-degree angle against the current. Attached by air hose to their boat, Tarpon Springs divers use the same type of rubberized suit, round copper helmet and iron boots introduced by the first crew of Greek spongers who arrived in 1905. Altogether, this equipment weighs 172 pounds.

After the sponges are gathered, they are cleaned and dried. The part of the sponge that consumers use is actually the animal's skeleton, which is composed of a fine meshwork of fibrous spongin—a material related to horn—that can absorb 25 times its weight in water. While there are more than 4,500 known species of natural sponges, only four with any commercial value live in the Gulf of Mexico: wool (best grade, used for car and bath sponges), yellow (household sponges), wire (packing and insulation) and grass (cosmetic sponges), in that order of quality. You will find all these for sale in Tarpon Springs, along with decorative finger sponges and loofahs—actually a land-growing member of the cucumber family.

Treasure Coast

Jupiter Inlet Lighthouse – © Richard Cummins/FOLIO, Inc.

The stretch of Florida's east coast between Jupiter in north Palm Beach County and the city of Melbourne, 100mi north, has earned the moniker "Treasure Coast" because millions of dollars worth of sunken booty has been recovered from its offshore waters. Today the area also counts lovely barrier-island beaches, nature centers, parks and museums among its riches.

In late July 1715 a fleet of Spanish galleons, laden with treasure, was driven by a hurricane onto the reefs off Florida's east coast. Eleven of these 12 ships went down beyond the barrier islands extending from St. Lucie Inlet to Sebastian Inlet. Two such treasure fleets were sent every year by Spain on a sweep of the silver and gold mines in Mexico and South America. The return route threaded the Caribbean islands, then followed the Gulf Stream up the Florida coastline.

About 700 people died in the 1715 wrecks, but of more concern to the Spanish government was the freight valued at 14 million pesos. The 1,500 survivors set up camp on the shore opposite Sebastian and, with the help of local Ais Indians, began salvaging the sunken treasure. Though most was recovered, much of the booty was soon looted by British pirates and spirited away to Jamaica. So dependent was Spain and the rest of Europe on these regular injections of precious metals and gems that an economic depression resulted from this loss.

Modern treasure hunters have determined that the galleons carried treasure not reported on ship manifests. A great deal of such undeclared cargo has been found off this coast in recent decades with the use of sophisticated technology. Pieces of eight (17C Spanish pesos) and other artifacts still occasionally wash ashore after storms churn up the ocean waters.

Settlement of the area did not occur until the late 19C, when orange and pineapple growers established permanent communities. Along with tourism, the citrus industry continues to be an economic linchpin of this relatively uncongested section of Florida's east coast.

FORT PIERCE

Population 37,516
Map p 316
Tourist Information: www.visitstluciefla.com ☎ 561-462-1535 or 800-344-8443

Located 55mi north of West Palm Beach, this midsized coastal town exists on two shores: the cluttered business district that lies along the west side of the Intracoastal Waterway, and the tranquil beaches on nearby Hutchinson Island.

Fort Pierce takes its name from the fortification built here in 1838 during the Second Seminole War by Benjamin Kendrick Pierce, brother of the 14th US president. In 1901 Fort Pierce, with a population of 300, incorporated and blossomed into a center for cattle and citrus. The city revived its role as a military outpost when it became a training base for the Navy's special amphibious teams during World War II. Cattle ranches and citrus and vegetable farms continue to prosper in the region, employing about 10 percent of the work force. Barrier-island beaches make retail and service industries economic mainstays by attracting vacationers and second-home owners. The area has also proved profitable for aquatic research. **Harbor Branch Oceanographic Institution** *(guided tours: ☎ 561-465-2400; www.hboi.edu),* established in 1971, has grown to enjoy international prominence.

From the old downtown, **Indian River Drive** *(speed limit 35mph)* travels 16mi south to Jensen Beach, offering fine views of the river and the hulking twin containers of the St. Lucie nuclear power station.

SIGHTS

★**UDT-SEAL Museum** – *3300 N. A1A, in Pepper Park (1mi north of Fort Pierce Inlet State Park). Open Jan-Apr Mon-Sat 10am-4pm, Sun noon-4pm. Rest of the year Tue-Sat 10am-4pm, Sun noon-4pm. Closed major holidays. $4.* ♿ 🅿 ☎ *561-595-5845. www.udt-sealmuseum.org.* Exhibits here vividly outline the history of the Navy SEALs (Sea, Air and Land), the elite commando units that evolved from the Underwater Demolition Teams and became famous for assisting astronauts after splashdowns. Better known as frogmen, these teams originated here in 1943 when the Navy began preparing special forces for the D-Day invasion. The museum's first section details action seen by frogmen in World War II. Another more popular exhibit relates recent events. Displays include an eerie, life-size diorama of a Viet Cong sharpening punji sticks while one of "the men with green faces," as the Viet Cong called them, emerges from the forest. In an adjoining audiovisual room, a series of films on SEAL operations runs continually.

Outside the museum, stone and metal spikes stuck into the ground represent obstacles frogmen had to remove to prepare beaches for large-scale invasions. Grounds also display boats from World War II and the Vietnam War, and more recently, an *Apollo* space capsule.

Fort Pierce Inlet State Park – *905 Shorewinds Dr. off A1A, south tip of North Hutchinson Island. Park hrs & fees p 350.* ♿ 🅿 ☎ *561-468-3985.* Lying on the north side of Fort Pierce Inlet, a scenic park preserves 340 acres of beachfront and maritime hammock. Navy frogmen trained on these beaches for the D-Day invasion of Europe, giving to one headland the name Dynamite Point. The park now is a peaceful place to surf and swim, or to picnic by the inlet and watch pleasure craft ply the aquamarine waters. A trail *(.5mi)* off the parking lot loops through a forest of live oaks, strangler figs, cabbage palms and sea grapes. Leading to the beach, four boardwalks protect the fragile dune environment and safeguard feet from sandspurs and nettles. Anglers cast for snapper, snook and other fish.

Jack Island State Preserve, a separate, 958-acre section of the park *(1.5mi north on A1A, west side of road)*, is accessible by a 300ft concrete footbridge. Actually a peninsula in the Indian River, the mangrove-covered refuge provides a nursery site for young marine animals. Raccoons, otters, ospreys, herons and other animals also make homes here. A 4.3mi trail circles the island, and a shorter one *(1mi)* leads to a 15ft observation tower offering a panoramic view of the Indian River. Other trails traverse impoundment dikes constructed to control mosquitoes.

★**St. Lucie County Historical Museum** – *414 Seaway Dr. Open year-round Tue-Sat 10am-4pm, Sun noon-4pm. Closed major holidays. $3.* 🅿 ☎ *561-462-1795.* Housed in a replica of the town's Florida East Coast Railway station, this museum renders the essence of Treasure Coast history. Exhibits start with artifacts from the Ais Indians, who occupied the area more than 2,000 years ago. The Galleon Room chronicles the 1715 treasure fleet that sank near here. The early 19C is explored in exhibits on Seminole Indians and US Army soldiers. Turn-of-the-19C storefronts and offices depict pioneer life, and an outstanding collection of photographs (1890-1920) adds realism to the displays.

The adjacent **Gardner House** (1907), a restored frame Victorian, provides a peek at life during pioneer times *(visit by guided tour only)*. The cruciform layout and 12ft ceilings helped ventilate the house, and heart pine walls repelled termites. Outside, a garage displays farm equipment and a restored 1919 fire engine. Cannons and an anchor from the 1715 Spanish galleon *Urca de Lima*, which sank in 10ft of water off Pepper Park, decorate the lawn.

Energy Encounter – 🄺🄸🄳🅂 *6501 S. A1A at Florida Power & Light Co., Jensen Beach. Entrance at Gate B on north side of plant. Open year-round Sun-Fri 10am-4pm. Closed major holidays.* ♿ 🅿 ☎ *561-468-4111 or 877-375-4386.* A perfect rainy-day activity for children, the facility offers hands-on displays that explore the worlds of electricity, nuclear power, energy conservation and environmental protection. Several presentations explain safety precautions, a comfort to visitors who stand only a few hundred feet from the plant's tremendous nuclear reactors. Manatees are occasionally spotted in the warm waters outside the plant. A boardwalk nature trail *(1mi)* traverses part of Turtle Beach.

EXCURSION

★**Mel Fisher's Treasure Museum** – *In Sebastian, about 30mi north via US-1. Museum is at 1322 US-1. Open year-round Mon-Sat 10am-5pm, Sun noon-5pm. Closed Jan 1, Easter Sunday, Thanksgiving Day, Dec 25. $5.* ♿ ☎ *561-589-9875. www.melfisher.com.* Dioramas, exhibits and artifacts here recount the search for remains of the 1715 Spanish fleet *(p 313)*. The most popular display area, the **gold room,** boasts plates, chains, crucifixes and rings, all exquisitely crafted from Peruvian gold and Mexican silver. A film provides a good introduction to the treasures housed here. A host of recovered artifacts is available for purchase in the gift shop.

HUTCHINSON ISLAND★

Map p 316

Tourist Information: www.jensenchamber.com ☎ 561-334-3444

Upon receiving a Spanish land grant in 1807, James A. Hutchinson moved his farming operations from the mainland to this 22mi-long spit of land to avoid the local Indians who had been raiding his crops and cattle. His descendants found the island's bears and wildcats as detrimental to crops and livestock as were the Indians. Through the first half of the 20C, the island stayed an uncrowded jungly strand framed by broad beaches and the pellucid Indian River.

Today condominiums, golf courses, high-rise hotels and beach cottages cover much of the island's south end to cater to a mix of visitors and part- and full-time residents. Despite this development, long, unhurried beaches remain, enticing northerners who swell the winter population to nearly 20,000 — twice its normal size. On the west side of the Jensen Beach Causeway, two local artists have carved lithe sea creatures from the stumps of dead Australian pines.

SIGHTS

★**Elliott Museum** – *825 N.E. Ocean Blvd., on east side of Stuart Causeway (A1A). Open year-round daily 10am-4pm. Closed major holidays. $6.* ♿ 🅿 ☎ *561-225-1961. www.goodnature.org.* Housed in a brick building flanked by two pink-painted wings, this repository holds an overwhelming collection of Victoriana. Harmon Elliott established the museum in memory of his inventor father, **Sterling Elliott** (1852-1922), whom Thomas Edison proclaimed "a genius."

Thirty-eight display areas, each packed with objects, document the early 1900s with toys, clothing, textiles, dolls and other items. Separate rooms re-create a period ice-cream parlor, general store, blacksmith shop and Victorian parlor. Also on exhibit are several of Elliott's clever inventions, including his knot-tying machine and 100 of his 118 US patent documents. One whole wing at the back of the museum is devoted to antique and classic automobiles; the rotating collection includes a 1903 Cadillac, a 1914 Packard touring sedan and a 1926 Bugatti.

Coastal Science Center – *890 N.E. Ocean Blvd., across from Elliott Museum. Open year-round Mon-Sat 10am-5pm, Sun noon-4pm. Closed major holidays. $6.* ♿ 🅿 ☎ *561-225-0505. www.fosusa.org.* Located on 40 acres of land that runs from A1A at Stuart Beach to the Indian River, this marine-life research facility is operated by the Florida Oceanographic Society. A slick marine-education center invites visitors to learn about the area's varied marine life through display panels, aquariums, touch tanks and computer games. Two trails *(1mi and .75mi)* explore coastal hardwood hammocks and a mangrove marsh. An observation deck and a new sting-ray touch pool are open to visitors.

★**Gilbert's Bar House of Refuge** – *301 S.E. MacArthur Blvd., 1.5mi south of A1A. Open year-round daily 10am-4pm. Closed major holidays. $4.* ♿ 🅿 ☎ *561-225-1875. www.goodnature.org.* In 1875 the US Treasury Department erected 10 "houses of refuge" along the Florida coast to aid shipwrecked sailors. Though its namesake pirate and sandbar have long since disappeared, the sole surviving restored house of refuge still stands atop a calcareous sandstone outcrop overlooking the ocean. Thirty-four rescues took place here from 1875 to World War II, when the Coast Guard turned the structure into a patrol base to guard against

attack by German submarines. The boathouse displays antique lifesaving equipment and other marine artifacts; four rooms open to the public in the green wood-frame main house contain a number of treasures, including a model ship collection.

Bathtub Reef Beach – Kids *On MacArthur Blvd., 2.3mi south of A1A.* Families with small children favor this county park, named for its shallow wading area created by an offshore reef. Constructed not by coral but by small, tube-building worms, the reef covers about 85 acres and renders the surf calm and shallow for nearly 300ft. Indigenous fauna include groupers, spider crabs, octopi and sea urchins.

JUPITER

Population 39,328

Map p 316

Tourist Information: www.jupiterfl.org ☎ 561-746-7111

Seated on the north end of the Palm Beach County coast, Jupiter offers a respite from the high energy of the Palm Beaches, yet development in recent years has placed this sprawling town firmly within the megalopolis that extends south to Fort Lauderdale and Miami.

A fort was established here in 1838 during the Seminole Wars. Fifty years later, the first train—dubbed the Celestial Railway because of its stops at Jupiter, Neptune, Venus, Mars and Juno—steamed through town. By 1895 Flagler's Florida East Coast Railway had replaced the narrow-gauge Celestial, and construction began on the Intracoastal Waterway. Jupiter grew slowly the first part of this century, its development overshadowed by Palm Beach, its chic neighbor to the south.

No longer just a city of vacation homes, Jupiter is now a thriving blend of businesses, upscale resorts, and golf and yachting communities. The 2,300-acre Abacoa development near I-95 has attracted a Florida Atlantic University honors campus and a spring-training stadium for the St. Louis Cardinals and Montreal Expos baseball teams. The area's wide public beaches and numerous reefs attract snorkelers and surfers, as well as thousands of sea turtles who make an annual pilgrimage to nest on these shores each summer.

The Jupiter Theatre *(100 E. Indiantown Rd.)*, which, in the past, presented such celebrities as Tony Bennett, Carol Channing and Rich Little, was founded by the city's most famous son, actor **Burt Reynolds**.

The Palm Beach County Tourist Information Center is located at 8020 West Indiantown Rd. in Jupiter. From I-95, take Exit 59B and go west .5mi. Open year-round daily 9am-5:30pm. Closed major holidays.

SIGHTS

Marinelife Center of Juno Beach – Kids *14200 US-1, Loggerhead Park, .25mi north of Donald Ross Rd. Open Feb-Mar Mon-Sat 10am-4pm, Sun noon-3pm. Rest of the year Tue-Sat 10am-4pm, Sun noon-3pm. Closed Jan 1, Jul 4 & Labor Day. Contribution requested.* ♿ 🅿 ☎ *561-627-8280. www.marinelife.org. Turtle walks offered in summer.* This small, low-key operation dedicated to rehabilitation, research and education started in 1983 as one woman's quest to help the area's sea turtles survive the perils of heavy beachfront development. Exhibit space feels cramped and makeshift compared to bigger-budget facilities, but this center makes up for its shortcomings with its large spirit. Scores of turtle shells, snakeskins, fish teeth, mandibles and coral are displayed in two small rooms inside the center. Knowledgeable volunteers explain how weak or injured turtles, housed in large tanks outside, are cared for until they are large enough—or well enough—to be released back into the sea. Plans are underway to build a new 12,000sq ft facility in Juno Beach Park to replace the current center.

Florida History Center and Museum – *805 N. US-1, in Burt Reynolds Park. Open year-round Tue-Fri 10am-5pm, weekends noon-5pm. Closed major holidays. $5.* ♿ 🅿 ☎ *561-747-6639.* Exhibits in this modern wood structure provide a good introduction to local maritime history. Here you'll find a Seminole dugout canoe, Spanish earthenware and pioneer fashions, as well as stories and artifacts regarding some of the area's more colorful residents: hermit pioneer "Trapper" Nelson, actor Burt Reynolds and singer Perry Como. An outdoor Seminole living-history village gives visitors insight into native culture. Traveling exhibits are presented regularly.

DuBois House – *DuBois Rd., in DuBois Park. Open Oct-Jun Wed & Sun 1pm-4pm. Contribution requested.* 🅿 ☎ *561-747-6639.* This Cracker-style house overlooking picturesque Jupiter Inlet dates from 1898 and was built on a Jeaga Indian shell mound. Two front rooms and a bedroom, furnished with family and period pieces, provide a glimpse into Florida pioneer life.

Jupiter Inlet Lighthouse – *US-1 and Rte. 707, east side of Jupiter Inlet Bridge, in Jupiter Lighthouse Park. Visit by guided tour (1hr) only, year-round Sun-Wed 10am-3:15pm. Closed major holidays. $5.* 🅿 ☎ *561-747-8380.* George Meade, commander of the Union forces at Gettysburg, designed this bright red beacon, which reigns as the county's oldest surviving structure. Southern sympathizers took out the lantern in 1861, a year after it was first lit, fearing that it illuminated their blockade runners. Since 1866 though, the lighthouse has not missed a night of operation. Standing 105ft tall, it beams a signal visible 18mi out to sea. Inside the oil house, interpretive exhibits relate local history. Visitors may climb the 105 steps to the top of the lighthouse tower for a birds-eye **view** of the surrounding area.

EXCURSION

★**Jonathan Dickinson State Park** – *7mi north of Rte. 706 on US-1. Park hrs & fees p 350.* ⚠ ▯ ☎ *561-546-2771.* English Quaker merchant Jonathan Dickinson found this area inhospitable when his barkentine, *Reformation,* wrecked on the nearby coast in 1696. Threatened, beaten and starved by the resident Indians, his group of 25 Quakers—bound from Jamaica to Pennsylvania—finally escaped, only to struggle 240mi up the coast to St. Augustine. His record of their travails provided one of the first written accounts of the southeastern Indians.

This 11,500-acre tract of land and river contains the largest piece of sand-pine scrub in southeast Florida and shelters alligators, manatees, gopher tortoises, bald eagles, scrub jays and sandhill cranes, among other unusual species. Sand-pine scrub, a rare desert-like environment of evergreen oaks and saw palmetto, covers about 20 percent of the park's acreage.

Visitors may walk the **Hobe Mountain Trail** *(.5mi)* to a high sand ridge topped by a 26ft wooden observation tower that provides a **panorama** of the flatlands, the Intracoastal Waterway, Jupiter Island, and beyond to the Atlantic. Here, from deep in the park, the landscape appears remarkably unspoiled by development. A 44-passenger tour boat plies the Loxahatchee—designated a National Wild and Scenic River—through primeval wilderness *(departs from boat dock in park year-round Wed-Sun 9am, 11am, 1pm, & 3pm; round-trip 2hrs; commentary; $12; ▯ ☎ 561-746-1466).*

JUPITER ISLAND

This scenic 16mi-long slice of once-submerged sandbar, now separated from the mainland by the Intracoastal Waterway, has for decades harbored winter homes for wealthy families. In recent years, professional athletes, including golfers Lee Trevino and Greg Norman and former Miami Dolphins quarterback Dan Marino, have bought property here. Houses occupy mostly one- and two-acre parcels, keeping population density low and real-estate value high. A hush hangs over this exclusive island, and the narrow road offers few stopping places or beach access points; bicyclists, pedestrians and motorists all proceed at a slow and measured pace.

Katie Deits/© CAMERA GRAPHICS

■ Sea Turtles

Large air-breathing reptiles of the families Dermochelyidae and Chelonidae, sea turtles inhabit all but the coldest of the earth's oceans. Five of the world's eight species of sea turtles frequent Florida waters; all are endangered, except the loggerhead *(Caretta caretta),* which is threatened. Atlantic green turtles *(Chelonia mydas),* leatherbacks and an occasional hawksbill *(Eretmochelys imbricata)* nest along the Atlantic coast of Florida between Cape Canaveral and Palm Beach. Loggerheads nest along both the Atlantic and Gulf coasts; the Kemps Ridley turtle is predominantly found in Gulf of Mexico waters.

The largest marine turtle, the leatherback *(Dermochelys coriacea),* can weigh as much as 1,300 pounds and grow to be 7ft long. The smallest, the Kemps Ridley *(Lepidochelys kempii),* measures 30in long and averages 100 pounds. Sea turtles can dive to depths of more than 3,000ft and can swim great distances, thanks to their low streamlined shell and powerful front flippers.

The longest sea turtle migration ever recorded was accomplished by a leatherback tagged in Surinam, South America. The turtle was found four months later in Ghana, Africa—over

★ Blowing Rocks Preserve – *S. Beach Rd., 1.8mi north of Jupiter Inlet. Open year-round daily 9am-4:30pm. $3.* 🅿 ☎ *561-744-6668. www.tncflorida.org. Guided walks year-round Fri & Sun 11am.* Run by The Nature Conservancy, the 73-acre refuge possesses the largest limestone outcropping on the Atlantic coast. Extending for nearly a mile along the beach, this unique rock formation contains fissures that become waterspouts during very high tides, creating dramatic plumes up to 50ft high and giving the preserve its name. West Indian manatees, great blue herons, ospreys, brown pelicans, sea turtles and other animals feed and nest among the site's four plant communities: mangrove swamp, tropical hammock, coastal strand and beach dune. Since 1985, some 60,000 native plants have been replanted and non-native species removed; as a result, 12 native animal species have returned. Tall sea-grape thickets hedge the path that runs more than a mile along the dune. A wooden pavilion beside the parking lot displays panels describing the preserve's flora, fauna and geography.

Hobe Sound National Wildlife Refuge – *2.5mi north of Bridge Rd. (entrance a dead-end of Beach Rd.). Open year-round daily dawn-dusk. $5/vehicle* 🅿 ☎ *561-546-6141. www.fws.gov.* At the north end of Jupiter Island, 735 acres of wild, unpublicized coastal habitat provide a refuge for the area's diverse animal and plant life. Refuge-sponsored turtle walks begin at the **Hobe Sound Nature Center** on the mainland *(east side of US-1, 2.3mi south of Bridge Rd.).* This separate section of the refuge comprises 232 acres of sand-pine scrub along Hobe Sound and features an informative half-mile nature walk *(open year-round Mon-Fri 9am-3pm; closed major holidays; contribution requested; ☎ 561-546-2067).*

4,000mi away. Scientists believe these reptiles navigate by means of their highly developed sense of smell and by magnetically sensitive particles in their brain that act as a natural compass.

Every two or three years, the turtles mate offshore and the female crawls up on the beach after dark to dig a nest. Here she will lay a clutch of up to 150 ping-pong-ball-size eggs. Female sea turtles find their way back to the same beaches year after year; when young turtles mature, they will likely return to the beach on which they were hatched to make their own nests. During nesting season (April to October), a single female will come ashore several times, laying from 300 to 800 eggs.

Hatchlings incubate for 54 to 57 days. After emerging from their eggs, the babies instinctively move away from the shadows and seek the brightest horizon. Glaring lights of beachfront condominiums and houses confuse the young turtles, who often head in the wrong direction, thus decreasing their chances of survival. At many beach access points, signs caution visitors to avoid turtle nesting sites and to keep lights off the beach at night during nesting season, or risk up to a $20,000 fine. It's a federal offense to touch or even to disturb a sea turtle.

During June and July, the following local organizations sponsor guided "turtle walks" on a regular basis to known nesting sites along the coast. Lucky groups may see nesting females or even tiny hatchlings. Led by a naturalist or park ranger, the walks take place after dark and can last several hours. *Bring mosquito repellent. Make reservations well in advance of your trip, as these popular walks tend to fill up quickly. Call sites by mid-April for information and reservations.*

Hobe Sound Nature Center	☎ 561-546-2067
Florida Power and Light Company	☎ 800-552-8440
Marinelife Center of Juno Beach	☎ 561-627-8280
Merritt Island National Wildlife Refuge	☎ 321-867-4077
Blowing Rocks Preserve/The Nature Conservancy	☎ 561-744-6668
Sea Turtle Preservation Society	☎ 321-676-1701
Sebastian Inlet State Park	☎ 321-984-4852
Canaveral National Seashore	☎ 321-267-1110

The Bahamas

Cable Beach (Nassau) – Cosmo Condina/Tony Stone Images

J ust 55mi off the southeast coast of Florida, this archipelago of coral islands is
sprinkled across 100,000sq mi of the Caribbean. The name Bahama derives from
the Spanish *baha mar*, meaning shallow sea, an apt description of the reef-
strewn, turquoise waters surrounding these 700-plus islands and islets, of which only
about 20 are inhabited. More than 3.5 million visitors annually—many of whom arrive
via cruise ship—are drawn to this tropical setting, most coming to Nassau or Freeport
The Bahamas' less-developed **Out Islands** (also called the Family Islands) are also gaining
popularity, particularly among sailing, fishing, snorkeling, diving and birding enthusiasts. They boast pristine beaches and residents who are easygoing and friendly. Now
serviced by commercial airlines and ships, the Out Islands include Acklins, Andros,
Bimini, Cat, Crooked, Eleuthera, Long, Mayaguana, Ragged and San Salvador islands;
the Abacos, Berry, Exuma and Inagua groups; and Rum Cay. One of the longest **coral
reefs★★★** in the world extends 140mi along the eastern edge of Andros, largest island
in the chain. A part of the British Empire since the 17C, the Bahamas are now an
independent member of the British Commonwealth.

NEW PROVIDENCE ISLAND★

Population 172,196 (including Paradise Island; 1990)
Map pp 328-329
Tourist Information: www.bahamas.com ☎ 242-322-7500

As the governmental and commercial center of the Bahamas, New Providence teems
with activity. Only 22mi long and 7mi across at its widest point, New Providence is
one of the smaller islands in the Bahamas, yet it claims more than 60 percent of the
country's total population. The island's historic heart, Nassau, still retains a traditional
British flavor, while modern resorts rise nearby.

Historical Notes

A Providential Place – Lucayan Indians had occupied the Bahamas for more than
500 years when **Christopher Columbus** arrived in the Caribbean in 1492. Scholars long
believed that Columbus's first New World landfall was on San Salvador Island at the

east edge of the Bahamas, but recent research has led to speculation that he may have landed on nearby Samana Cay instead. In any case, the land of the Bahamas was little touched by the Spanish. The same could not be said for the people. The Lucayans, enslaved by the Spanish to work mines on Hispaniola, were virtually extinct within 25 years of Columbus' arrival, victims of disease and poor treatment.

With the disappearance of the Lucayans, the Bahamas remained virtually unpopulated until the early 17C, when the Eleutherian Adventurers appeared on the scene. This band of Puritans had fled to Bermuda to escape persecution, and from there to the Caribbean. Shipwrecked off present-day Eleuthera, they established a short-lived settlement there. The group's leader, **William Sayles**, later met with better success when he discovered a fine natural harbor on another, smaller island to the west. In 1666 the Puritans established themselves on Sayles' Island. Grateful for this second chance, they rechristened the island New Providence.

The Age of Empire – At the end of the 17C, the British began to exercise control over the island when Proprietary Governor Nicholas Trott arrived. He renamed the existing settlement of Charlestown in honor of the Prince of Orange-Nassau (who would eventually reign as William III) and built Fort Nassau in 1697 on the present site of the British Colonial Beach Resort. The settlement and its harbor soon became a center for British privateers involved in plundering Spanish and French ships in the Caribbean and for wreckers salvaging vessels that had gone down on the treacherous offshore reefs. In the early 18C the island's first Royal Governor, **Woodes Rogers**, transformed the rundown, garbage-strewn town of Nassau into a "civilized place," and introduced a gridded street plan. He was also instrumental in bringing an end to piracy and in convening the first General Assembly in 1729. In the 1780s the modestly prospering island witnessed a new influx of refugees as American Loyalists (those who pledged allegiance to the British Crown) fleeing the Revolution resettled here. In 1782 the Spanish overran New Providence and occupied it for about a year before being driven out by a Loyalist militia.

Many of the Americans had brought slaves with them when they resettled on New Providence, in hopes of establishing cotton plantations. Finding the soil too poor to sustain that kind of agriculture, a number of Loyalists returned to America. They left, however, several legacies: an impressive array of English Georgian houses, two large new forts and an expanded black population. In 1838 the blacks they left behind became free men when Britain abolished all slavery within its empire. Though free, the black population of New Providence existed in a distinctly segregated society, living "over the hill" in interior enclaves such as Fox Hill, Adelaide, Gambier, and Grant's, Bain and Delancey towns.

American events continued to affect Bahamian prospects throughout the 19C and 20C. During the Civil War, a flurry of commerce gripped the island when locals and Southern sympathizers used the area as a base from which to run Northern blockades of Confederate ports.

In the 1920s American Prohibition brought further prosperity as local **rumrunners** became involved in smuggling liquor to mainland bootleggers, and American gangsters and gamblers flocked to Nassau. Interest in tourism outlasted the end of Prohibition in the 1930s, resulting in the development of Cable Beach as a resort area.

A Separate Peace – In the 1960s the island's black population grew increasingly resentful of the continued domination of politics and business by the white "Bay Street Boys," as members of the ruling United Bahamian Party were known. In 1967 the country elected its first black prime minister, **Lynden Pindling**. During the same period, tourism increasingly came to dominate the economy, as the large high-rise resorts of Paradise Island shot up, adding their modern luster to such traditional island hostelries as the mid-18C Graycliff, the now-defunct 1861 Royal Victoria, and the turn-of-the-19C British Colonial.

On July 10, 1973, the Bahamas peacefully gained their independence from Britain, with Nassau remaining the capital. Today roughly 55 percent of visitors to the Bahamas spend time here. Nassau also ranks as a regular port-of-call for some 30 cruise ships, which deliver about a million visitors to its shores annually.

★★NASSAU *Map p 324*

Long the center of the island's tourism, Nassau's historic heart beats along 25 blocks of the harbor front bordered by Bay Street on the north, Hill Street on the south, Elizabeth Avenue to the east, and West Street to the west. All aspects of the city's checkered past are reflected in the tenor of this district—from its founding by Puritans over 300 years ago to its days as a rough bailiwick of buccaneers through the eras of British Loyalists and American rumrunners, and finally into its current role as the Bahamas' banking center and a popular haven for sunseekers. Along Bay Street, countless duty-free shops cater to cruise-ship passengers, while quieter side streets shade classic pink-and-white Bahamian Colonial structures. Vestiges of formal British tradition prevail in the workings of the national government at Parliament Square and Government House.

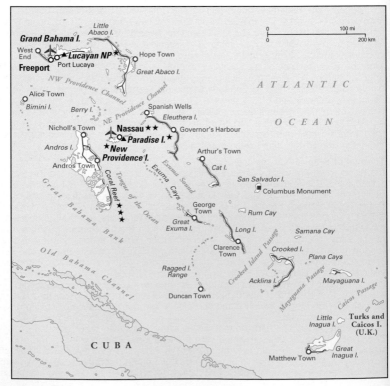

PRACTICAL INFORMATION.............................Area Code: 242

When to Go

Weather in the Bahamas is pleasant throughout the year. High season runs from mid-December through mid-April; hotel reservations should be made well in advance. During the winter months *(Nov-Feb)* temperatures average 72°F/22°C, while southern trade winds keep the islands comfortable during the summer months when temperatures average 80°F/27°C. In the rainy season *(Jun-Oct)* showers are frequent but brief.

Planning your Trip – Citizens of the US and Canada entering the Bahamas are required to present proof of citizenship (passport or birth certificate and photo ID) and a return ticket. Limit of stay: 8 months. Visitors from other countries should check with the Embassy of the Bahamas in their country before traveling. **Bahamas Tourist Office in Florida:** 19495 Biscayne Blvd., Suite 809, Aventura FL 33180 ☎ *305-932-0051 or 800-327-7678 (US).*

Getting There

By Air – Major US and international airlines fly into **Nassau International Airport** and **Freeport International Airport**. Visitor Information booths: ☎ 377-6806 (Nassau); ☎ 352-6909 (Freeport). Transportation from airports by **taxi**: Nassau International Airport to Cable Beach *($12)*, to Paradise Island *($25)*, to downtown *($18)*; Freeport International Airport to downtown *($6)*. **Bahamasair** ☎ 352-8341 provides regular service from Nassau to most of the Out Islands. **Rental car agencies** *(p 343)* are located at the airports and in downtown Nassau and Freeport.

By Boat – Cruise ships departing from Miami dock at Nassau; some make stops in Freeport. Another way to island-hop is to take the mail boat *(operating year-round; for schedules and fares contact the Ministry of Tourism or Dock Master's office, Potter's Cay Dock ☎ 393-1064).*

Getting Around

By Car and Taxi – Foremost to remember, vehicles are driven **on the left** side of the street. **Scooters** *($50/day)* and **bicycles** *($10/day)* can be rented throughout the islands. Both scooter driver and passenger must wear helmets. Unless otherwise posted, **speed limits** are generally 30mph outside city limits, 25mph within city, and 15mph in school zones. **Taxis**: Nassau ☎ 323-5111 and ☎ 323-4555; Freeport ☎ 352-6666. Small buses called "**jitneys**" are the most economical way to get around the islands *(daily dawn-dusk; 75¢; exact change required).*

General Information

Visitor Information – **Bahamas Ministry of Tourism**, PO Box N 3701, Market Plaza, Bay Street, Nassau *(☎ 322-7500; www.bahamas.com)* provides information regarding accommodations, shopping, entertainment and recreation. Visitor Relations hotline *(Mon-Fri 9am-10pm; ☎ 326-4357).*

Accommodations – Lodgings in the Bahamas range from **hotels** and resorts *($95-$575)*, and family-run **inns** *($60-$200)*, to **villas** and apartment rentals *(from $175/day for a one-bedroom)*. All hotels charge a 8%-12% room tax. *Rates quoted are average prices per night for a double room and are subject to seasonal variations.*

Foreign Exchange – The Bahamian dollar is equivalent to the US dollar. Numerous foreign banks have offices in Nassau and Freeport *(open Mon-Thu 9:30am-3pm, Fri 9:30am-5pm).*

Sports and Recreation – **Underwater expeditions** to coral reefs include half-day of instruction and reef dive *(45min)*; all-day excursion to an Out Island *(two dives and beach picnic; $135)* Nassau Scuba Centre *(☎ 362-1964; www.divenassau.com)*. Half-day **cruise** *(daily 9am-12:30pm & 12:30pm-4pm; $34)* or full-day cruise and beach barbecue *(daily; $55; snorkel gear and free pick-up at hotel included)* Barefoot Sailing Cruises *(☎ 393-0820).*

Shopping: Bay Street, downtown Nassau; **Hurricane Hole Plaza**, Paradise Island; **International Bazaar & Port Lucaya Marketplace**, Freeport. There is no sales tax charged and all goods are available duty-free.

Useful Numbers   ☎

Police/Fire	**911**	**Directory Assistance** 916	**Weather** 915

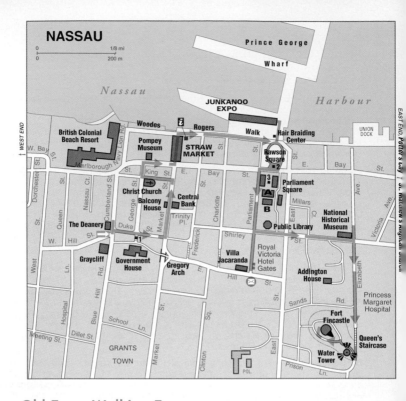

Old Town Walking Tour

Begin at the intersection of West Hill St. and Cumberland St. (which becomes Blue Hill Rd.).

Graycliff – *10 W. Hill St. (on corner of Cumberland St./Blue Hill Rd.).* One of the oldest hotels in the Bahamas, this dignified Georgian Colonial structure with its foot-thick limestone walls and two-story veranda is attributed by legend to Capt. John Howard Graysmith. The daring privateer of the schooner *Graywolf*, Graysmith is said to have built the house in the mid-18C on the site of Nassau's first Anglican church. By 1844 the building had become Nassau's first inn. During the American Civil War it served as a US officer's mess; in the mid-20C it eventually became the private home of the British peers Lord and Lady Dudley, who entertained many notable figures here, including the Duke and Duchess of Windsor and Sir Winston Churchill. Today Graycliff still operates as a fine inn and restaurant. The interior is furnished with early 20C pieces, including a Baccarat chandelier that graces the entrance hall. Outside, the cozy grounds abound in tropical foliage.

A half-block north on Cumberland Street stands **The Deanery** *(west side).* Built at the turn of the 19C as a parsonage for Christ Church, this three-story stone building with its lattice timber gallery is considered the oldest extant residence in Nassau.

Cross Cumberland St. and walk briefly south; turn left (east) on Duke St.

Broad stone steps on the street's south side lead to Government House. A statue of **Christopher Columbus (1)**, situated about halfway up the staircase, looks out over the town.

Government House – *Corner of Blue Hill Rd. and Duke St. Not open for public tours.* The stately white-columned, pink mansion now crowning Mount Fitzwilliam was built in 1932, one in a succession of official residences of Governors General dating from the 1730s. In the 1940s the **Duke and Duchess of Windsor** occupied the building during the Duke's tenure as Governor General of the Bahamas. (The Duke had reigned briefly as Edward VIII before abdicating to marry American divorcee Wallis Simpson.) On alternate Saturdays, a public **Changing of the Guard** ceremony is held here, accompanied by music provided by the Royal Bahamas Police Force Band *(year-round, every other Sat 10am).* The Governor General also hosts a **public tea party** at Government House on the last Friday of every month *(Jan-Aug 4pm-5pm; reservations and proper attire required; ☎ 242-326-5371).*

Continue east on Duke St. to the intersection with Market St.

Note the stone archway on the south end of the street. Known as **Gregory Arch**, it was built in the 1850s and served as an access point to Grant's Town, one of the traditionally black "over the hill" neighborhoods.

Turn left on Market St. and continue one block.

Small, aptly named **Balcony House** *(Market St. and Trinity Pl.; not open to the public)* is distinctive for its cantilevered balcony. Built of American cedar and over 200 years old, the house also features a staircase believed to have been part of a ship. Directly across Market Street, the **Central Bank of the Bahamas** devotes its public lobby area to changing exhibits of works by Bahamian and foreign artists.

Continue one block north on Market to King St. Turn left on King and walk west one block to George St.

Christ Church Cathedral – *George and King Sts.* Established in 1670, Christ Church was the first Anglican church in the Bahamas. The current Gothic Revival edifice with its stone buttresses and timbered, trussed interior roof was constructed in 1840 and is the fifth church on the site; the two east bays were added subsequently. It was designated the cathedral of the diocese in 1861.

Turn right on George St. and walk one block north to Bay St.

The historical **British Colonial Beach Resort** (now a Hilton property) anchors the north end of East Bay Street, former site of Fort Nassau (1695-1899). At the turn of the 19C, railroad and hotel magnate Henry Flagler built the spacious Hotel Colonial on this spot. When fire destroyed it in 1922, the government purchased the land and constructed a new hotel, later bought by Sir Harry Oakes and renamed the British Colonial.

Cross Bay St. to north side.

Pompey Museum – *Bay St., at George St. Open year-round Mon-Fri 9am-5pm. Closed major holidays. $1. ☎ 242-326-2566.* This museum devoted to the history and culture of the Bahamas occupies historic Vendue House, a well-proportioned two-story stone structure with arched bay windows. Built as a public market in the mid-18C, it served as the site of slave auctions. The current name, Pompey, derives from a rebel slave on the island of Exuma in the early 19C. In 2001 the museum was damaged by a fire at the nearby Straw Market, but was able to reopen thereafter. Exhibits trace the hardships and brutality of slave life, and the coming of emancipation. A second-story gallery features a display of the **paintings★** of local folk artist **Amos Ferguson**. Videos on Ferguson and the history and cultural traditions of the Bahamas may be viewed on request.

Continue 1 block east on Bay St.

As you walk east on Bay Street, you'll pass numerous shops selling duty-free liquors, European crystals, gems, perfumes and other merchandise.

★**Straw Market** – *Bay St. across from Market St. Open year-round Mon-Sat 7am-6pm. ♿ ☎ 242-322-7500.* Famous throughout the Caribbean, Nassau's labyrinthine Straw Market consists of a warren of small stalls where vendors, most of them women by tradition, hawk a plethora of inexpensive straw goods, T-shirts, local wood carvings and other items designed to tempt tourists. Straw-plaiting and straw work have long been done by Bahamian women, particularly on the Out Islands. Haggling with the market's vendors over the price of goods is part of the fun here. In 2001 an extensive fire burned the market to the ground; it is being rebuilt and is scheduled to reopen in fall 2002.

Walk through the market to its north, waterfront side.

© Tony Stone Images

Junkanoo Festival

Woodes Rogers Walk, named for the Bahamas first Royal Governor, leads along the dock area to shady **Rawson Square**, which is flanked by more shops and the governmental Churchill Building. A bust of **Milo Butler** (**2**) (1906-79), the first Governor General of the independent Bahamas (1973), stands at the south end of the square.

Across from the north side of the square, an open-air plaza serves as the popular **hair-braiding center**, where Bahamian women negotiate with tourists to plait their hair into tiny braids, or cornrows. Behind lies the capacious dock area of **Prince George Wharf**. Large commercial cruise ships on tour through the Caribbean dock here—some only overnight—to allow their passengers to visit Nassau.

Walk north behind Rawson Square to Prince George Wharf.

★★**Junkanoo Expo** – *Entrance faces Prince George Wharf. Open year-round daily 9am-5pm. Closed major holidays. $2. ☎ 242-356-2731. May be temporarily closed.* This former customs warehouse displays the enormous, lavishly designed costumes that enliven the annual **Junkanoo** parades. A rich Afro-Bahamian mix of traditions, Nassau's famous Junkanoo celebration revolves around a night-long parade held on December 26 (Boxing Day in England) and again on New Year's Day. Tens of thousands of spectators gather to watch the revelry, which can be heard across the island. A handful of skilled craftsmen undertake the design and building of each major costume. Sculpted of cardboard and crepe paper, costumes are embellished with bright beads and sequins and often reflect cultural or political themes, sometimes even incorporating contemporary international personalities. Winning costumes from each parade are added annually to the museum's collection and older pieces are retired. Some 30 elaborate costumes, including extra large and smaller ones, are on display. A video of past Junkanoo festivals adds the appropriate sounds and vitality to the exhibit hall.

Return to Rawson Square and cross to south side of Bay St.

Parliament Square – Governmental hub of the Bahamas, the square is centered on a **statue** (**3**) of a serenely young Queen Victoria. Three pink-and-white public buildings, built in the early 19C and modeled on the Tryon Palace in New Bern, North Carolina, flank the statue. The columned Southern Colonial structure in the middle serves as the **House of Assembly** (**A**). Behind this edifice, more pink official buildings, including the stately, colonnaded **Supreme Court** (**B**) (1921), overlook the Garden of Remembrance, a palm-shaded greensward that commemorates Bahamians who lost their lives while fighting beside the British in World Wars I and II.

Walk south up Parliament St. and cross Shirley St.

Two gateposts on the east side of Parliament Street bear the insignia of the **Royal Victoria Hotel**, once the Bahamas' most fashionable hostelry. Built in the mid-19C, the elegant building played host to Confederate blockade runners and Prohibition-era rumrunners. Fire ravaged it in 1990 and Hurricane Andrew further devastated the ruins.

Across Parliament Street, just below the intersection with East Hill Street, stands gracious **Villa Jacaranda** *(not open to the public)*, whose double galleries, shutters and stone exterior exemplify the Loyalist architectural tradition prevalent in Nassau in the mid-19C.

Walk one block north to Shirley St. and turn right (east).

The octagonal **Nassau Public Library**, on the south edge of Parliament Square *(corner of Parliament and Shirley Sts.)*, is topped by a third-floor wraparound gallery and belfry, whose bell once summoned members to openings of the House of Assembly. Originally constructed as a prison at the turn of the 18C, it became a public library in 1873.

From the library, continue east on Shirley St.

After passing the intersection *(left side)* of Millars Court, note the expansive lawn that sweeps upward to the mid-19C **Addington House**, formerly the official residence of the Anglican Bishop of Nassau and the Bahamas.

Walk east on Shirley St. to the intersection with Elizabeth St. and turn left.

National Historical Museum/Bahamas Historical Society – *Northwest corner of Shirley and Elizabeth Sts. Open Sept-June Mon-Fri 10am-4pm, Sat 10am-noon. Closed major holidays. $1. ☎ 242-322-4231. www.bahamas.net.bs/history.* Since 1976 this former hall of the Daughters of the Empire has been used by the Bahamas Historical Society to display Lucayan Indian stone tools, crockery and artifacts from the Loyalist period, old photographs and personal memorabilia.

Walk south one block along Elizabeth St.

Hewn into the rock of Bennet's Hill, the steep, 66-step **Queen's Staircase** occupies a surprisingly sylvan setting, next to a pleasant waterfall spilling over fern-draped rocks. The stairs were purportedly built by slaves in the 1790s to allow access to Fort Fincastle.

Fort Fincastle – *Located at the top of the Queen's Staircase. Open year-round daily 8am-5pm.* 🅿 ☎ *242-325-2212.* From its vantage atop the town's highest point (74ft), this small fort, shaped like a paddle wheeler, was built by Lord Dunmore in the 1790s. Though it never saw battle, the fort proved useful, serving as a lighthouse until 1817 and a signal beacon thereafter. Today the ramparts command a fine view of the waterfront and much of the island's interior.

The 126ft **water tower** adjacent to the fort was built in 1928 and is topped by a beacon light. No longer used as a water tower, it now houses an elevator that whisks visitors to an open-air observation deck with 360-degree **views★** of the island's interior and its eastern shoreline *(50¢).*

Uniphoto Picture Agency

View of Fort Fincastle and Nassau Harbour

Additional Sights
Map pp 328-329

St. Matthew's Anglican Church (**C**) – *Shirley St. west of Mackey St. Open year-round daily 9am-5pm.* ♿ ☎ *242-323-8220.* The oldest extant church structure (1802) in the Bahamas, the simple rectangular stone edifice with its Neoclassical detailing was originally referred to as the "eastern church," since it served parishioners on that side of town. A chancel, organ chamber and vestry room were added in 1887. The extensive cemetery surrounding the church contains headstones covering two centuries.

Potter's Cay (**D**) – *Just north of the intersection of E. Bay and Mackey Sts. Open year-round daily 7am-8pm.* ♿ 🅿. Located beneath the Paradise Island bridge, the stalls of this colorful marketplace feature an array of fresh fruits, vegetables and seafood. Island fishermen tie up at the dockside market to sell conch, lobster, grouper and other local specialties.

EAST END

Threaded by Eastern Road and more densely populated than the West End, the island's East End is devoted to pleasant waterfront homes and the local community of Fox Hill, which holds its own festival, Fox Hill Day, every year on the first Tuesday of August. Rocky **Yamacraw Beach** curves below McPherson's Bend at the eastern tip of the island. The drive along Eastern Road skirts the shoreline framed by elegant homes and ends at **East End Point**, where a panoramic **view** encompasses cerulean waters and offshore cays.

Fort Montagu – *East end of E. Bay St. Interior not open to public. Grounds open year-round daily.* 🅿 ☎ *242-325-2212.* Commanding the east entrance to the harbor, the small stone battlement (1742) is the oldest extant fort on the island. It was the second fort to be constructed after Fort Nassau and was intended to ward off possible attack by Spanish forces. A roadside beach on Montagu Bay stretches south from the fort.

The Retreat – *Village Rd., south of the intersection with Shirley St. and Eastern Rd. Open year-round Mon-Fri 9am-5pm. Closed holidays & Dec 25-Jan 1. $2.* 🅿 ☎ *242-393-1317.* This 11-acre botanical preserve is largely the work of Arthur and Margaret Langlois, who purchased the property in 1925. Finding that the land supported 11 kinds of palms, they set upon a 55-year endeavor of collecting other palm species worldwide and adding them to their gardens. Today the preserve features 92 genera of rare and exotic **palms★**, including species from Asia, Africa, Australia, and North and South America. Shaded paths also weave past such species as mahogany and cedar trees and orchids. In 1975 the Bahamas National Trust acquired the property; a modest but charming mid-19C Bahamian cottage on the grounds serves as the National Trust headquarters.

WEST END

Two large lakes (Killarney and Cunningham), Nassau International Airport, several private resort complexes, and a number of commercial sites lie on the sparsely settled West End of New Providence Island. After West Bay Street leaves the historic district, it hugs the coastline along the West End, affording numerous views of the azure Atlantic. When the road reaches Clifton Point, it swings southeast and heads inland.

Driving Tour

16mi. Map opposite.

From the British Colonial Hotel, head west on W. Bay St. After .5mi take the unmarked road to the left at the sign for Bahamas Medical Arts Institute. Continue .3mi to the parking area for Fort Charlotte.

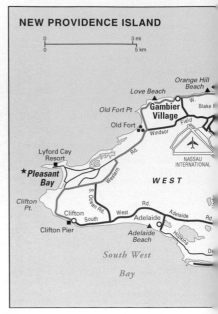

★**Fort Charlotte** (**F**) – *On Marcus Bethel Way and West Bay St. behind Clifford Park. Open year-round Mon-Sat 8am-4pm, Sun & holidays 8am-3pm. ⊡ ☎ 242-325-9186.* Built by Lord Dunmore between 1787 and 1796 during the American Loyalist period, the island's largest fortress complex actually comprises three forts: the original eastern portion, Fort Charlotte, named for George III's queen; the middle section, Fort Stanley; and the western works, Fort D'Arcy. Occupying a hill overlooking the town and harbor, the fortress was constructed of stone and armed with some 40 guns. "Dunmore's Folly," as Fort Charlotte was called, owing to the awesome expense of its construction, never saw battle and ceased to function in a military capacity in 1891. Today various casemates, living quarters and parapets are open to the public, as is a loosely re-created "pirate's torture chamber." The battlements of Fort Stanley offer a panoramic **view** of the island and western harbor.

Return to W. Bay St. and continue west. Turn left on Chippingham Ave. and continue .1mi. Parking lot on left.

Nassau Botanic Gardens (**F**) – *Chippingham Ave., just south of W. Bay St. Open year-round Mon-Fri 8am-4pm, weekends 9am-4pm. Closed major holidays. $1. ⊡ ☎ 242-323-5975.* The wives of British colonial officials established this as a five

Smiling Faces

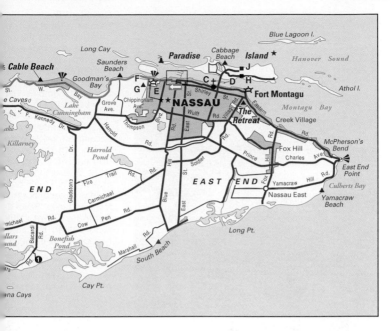

acre coronation garden honoring the crowning of George VI in 1937. Now owned by the government and encompassing 26 acres—12 of them in public gardens— the site features terraced beds, a sunken garden occupying a former rock quarry, and a lovely palm allée. Exotic tropical and subtropical species represent the southern Caribbean, India and Africa.

Continue .2mi south on Chippingham Ave. Turn right at sign for zoo.

Ardastra Gardens and Zoo (G) – *Off Chippingham Ave., just west of Botanic Gardens. Open year-round daily 9am-5pm. Closed Dec 25. $12.* ✕ ⚭ ☏ *242-323-5806.* A 5.5-acre commercial animal park, Ardastra comprises a series of small cages set amid lush vegetation. Fifty-nine animal species are represented, including tropical birds, monkeys and reptiles. A troupe of Marching Caribbean flamingos (the national bird) performs several times daily. The term Ardastra derives from the Latin *per ardua ad astra* ("through endeavor to the stars"), the name given the gardens by Hedley Edwards, a Jamaican horticulturist who began them as a private endeavor in 1937. The Latin phrase also serves as the motto of the Royal Air Force.

Return to W. Bay St., turn left and continue west .5 mi.

Following the curve of the shoreline, you will pass **Saunders Beach,** a narrow but popular roadside beach with views out to Crystal and Long cays. After rounding Brown's Point, the road bends south along **Goodman's Bay,** another roadside beach. A sweeping view here scans the high rises of Cable Beach.

Cable Beach – Sometimes called the Bahamian Riviera, Cable Beach rises in a gleam of towering hotels and casinos that virtually wall off the beach itself. In 1892 a telegraph cable was laid between this point and Jupiter, Florida, providing the first such communication between the Bahamas and the North American mainland and giving the beach its name. Pineapples were cultivated along this stretch of the island until the 1920s, when Americans began building fine vacation homes here. Sir Harry Oakes, a Canadian entrepreneur, began developing Cable Beach as a major resort— complete with casino—in the 1930s. The area remains a mix of tourist facilities along its eastern half and upscale private homes to the north. A lovely stand of casuarina trees overarches portions of the road through the residential section.

Continue west on W. Bay Street.

After crossing the Sandyport Bridge, the road returns to the water's edge. A private pink home hugging a point *(.8mi beyond the bridge)* is recognizable as one of the settings from the James Bond movie *Thunderball.* After .6mi, look to the left for **The Caves,** a limestone labyrinth once used by Lucayan Indians and now home to a colony of bats. Beyond this, the road curves past long, narrow **Orange Hill Beach.** At the intersection of West Bay Street and Blake Road *(.2mi farther on),* notice the *Ficus benjamina* tree in the intersection's grassy triangle. US President John Fitzgerald Kennedy planted the tree in 1962 in commemoration of his meeting on the island with the prime ministers of Canada and Britain.

Continue west 2mi past Blake Rd.

Cable Beach Resort

Gambier Village – This hamlet is one of the oldest settlements on the island. Liberated Africans, freed from Caribbean slave ships by the Royal Navy, established Gambier Village as a farming community shortly after 1807. Recently it has become a tourist destination with the development of Compass Point, a resort identifiable by its small but vividly colored oceanfront cottages. Beyond Compass Point, the road passes the fine houses of **Love Beach** for 3.5mi before reaching the entrance gates to exclusive **Lyford Cay**, a private resort *(not open to the public)* frequented by such stars as Sean Connery, Sidney Poitier and Mick Jagger.

From Lyford Cay continue south 2.5mi. Turn right at turnoff for Pleasant Bay, marked by a sign for Atlantis Submarines.

★**Pleasant Bay** – A lovely crescent beach with easy public access edges the southern half of the small protected bay here, culminating in Clifton Point. The bay's northern half fronts the exclusive homes of Lyford Cay. The dock was used as a set in one of the *Jaws* movies and now serves as a starting point for submarine excursions to the offshore reef.

Return to the main road and continue south 1mi.

Freighters exporting rum from the nearby Bacardi Distillery and importing such commodities as gasoline dock at **Clifton Pier** at the western tip of the island.

> **1 Bacardi Distillery**
> *Map p 329. Southwest side of New Providence on Bacardi Rd. off Carmichael Rd. No public tours available.* A major corporate hub for Bacardi & Co., Ltd., this plant occupies 40 acres and employs 130 people. Five rums, a vodka and a liqueur are produced here; about 95 percent of the total product is shipped to European markets via tankers that tie up at nearby Clifton Pier. A hospitality center located on the grounds offers visitors complimentary drinks and information on the company's history and facilities *(closed weekends; ☒ ☏ 242-362-1412).*

PARADISE ISLAND★

Map p 322
Tourist Information: www.bahamas.com ☏ 242-322-7500

Now a mega-resort complex, the 826-acre island (5.5mi long and .6mi at its widest) on the north side of Nassau Harbour was for centuries known as Hog Island—reportedly so-named by Nicholas Trott after his father's estate in Hog Bay, Bermuda. Sand beaches lining the island's north shore have drawn crowds since the end of the 19C when entrepreneurs operated public "bathing houses" here to serve beachgoers. Two casinos also were constructed during this period. Unlike the present-day Paradise Island casino, these early versions offered dining, dancing, billiards and bowling.

Historical Notes

Early in the 20C, wealthy Americans established a winter colony of vacation homes on the island, and its quiet tenor remained unchanged until 1959, when American grocery-store heir and philanthropist Huntington Hartford bought a large parcel of island from Swedish financier Dr. Axel Wenner-Gren. Determined to develop its resort potential, Hartford successfully petitioned the government to change the name of the island to Paradise in 1962. He went on to open the small, exclusive Ocean Club hotel, a golf course and horse stables, and to complete the quarter-mile-long Versailles Gardens that Wenner-Gren had begun. Though Hartford's endeavors failed financially, they did succeed in establishing the tourist potential of Paradise Island.

In 1967 the current arcing bridge—1,500ft long and 70ft at its pinnacle—was built, connecting the island to Nassau. During the same period the large Paradise Island Resort and Casino opened, as did the Yoga Retreat, a far different type of guest establishment constructed on land bequeathed to Swami Vishnu Devananda. In the following decade, a half-dozen major resort complexes sprang to life, including a Club Med on the western end of the island.

The recent history of Paradise Island, however, has been changeable. Paradise Island Resort and Casino met with financial problems in the early 1990s. Sun International Investments, Ltd., a South Africa-based firm, purchased these properties in 1994 and opened an ambitious $250 million resort and casino called Atlantis, Paradise Island, in December of that year. In addition to Atlantis' 14-acre waterscape, Paradise Island offers a mix of hotels, pristine beaches and remnants of its past.

SIGHTS

A water taxi ($3) runs year-round between the island and Nassau (times vary, depending on demand). The Paradise Island Bridge charges an incoming fee of $2 for rental cars and taxis.

The Cloisters (**H**) – *On Paradise Island Dr., east of Casino Dr. at Cloisters Dr. Open daily year-round.* An unlikely vision of medieval piety, the columned stone Cloisters crown a rise overlooking Nassau Harbour. The structure, once part of a c.14C Augustinian monastery in Montréjeau, France, was disassembled and shipped to Florida in the 1920s by newspaper magnate William Randolph Hearst. Huntington Hartford purchased the still-crated structure from Hearst and had it reassembled on this location in 1962. *Silence*, the marble statue in the Cloisters' center, is the work of American sculptor Dick Reid.

Across Paradise Island Drive from the Cloisters, the seven-tiered gardens of Wenner-Gren's **Versailles** (**J**) lead down to a private swimming pool for guests at the elegant Ocean Club, refurbished in 1994 to reflect its 1960s style.

Paradise Island's north shore is rimmed with stunning white-sand **beaches**. While all beaches on the island are considered public below the low-water mark, access to many is difficult. **Cabbage Beach** *(between the Radisson Grand and Sunrise properties)* offers easy public access.

GRAND BAHAMA ISLAND

Population 40,898 (1990)
Map p 322
Tourist Information: www.grandbahama.bahamas.com ☎ 242-352-6909
or 800-448-3386 (US)

The second-most-visited island in the Bahamas archipelago lies a mere 55mi east of Florida. Measuring 96mi long and 17mi at its widest, Grand Bahama is the fourth-largest island in the chain. Its new towns of Freeport and Lucaya, established in the mid-20C, were specifically developed to attract tourists and commerce.

Historical Notes

Covered in pines for much of its history, Grand Bahama was first home to Lucayan Indians who inhabited the land prior to the Spanish arrival in the Caribbean. After their decimation, the island supported few inhabitants until the 1870s, when sponge fishermen settled here. The West End of the island became a major hub for rumrunners until the repeal of Prohibition in the 1930s, and soon thereafter a blight destroyed Bahamian sponges.

A new boom began in 1944 when the Abaco Lumber Co. relocated here, having exhausted the pine forests on Abaco Island. Four years later, **Wallace Groves**, an American entrepreneur living in the Bahamas, purchased the failing company and made it profitable. In 1955 he entered into the **Hawksbill Agreement** with the Bahamian government, which allowed him to develop a free port on the island, where goods could be imported without heavy duty taxes. Infrastructure for residential and resort areas was eventually laid out around the inland administrative area that was to become Freeport and the oceanside resort area of Lucaya. The island never developed as Groves had hoped. To bolster his failing investment, he opened a casino at the Lucayan Beach Hotel in 1963. Gambling rather than commerce became the lifeblood of the island.

Groves' infrastructure was developed to support half a million people, but only about 46,000 now live on Grand Bahama. The network of roads, intended for residential areas, lead only into the pine barrens. Activity revolves around a handful of resorts, two casinos and the shopping complexes of Freeport and Lucaya. A harbor on the island's southwest edge accommodates a host of cruise and cargo ships.

FREEPORT

Built as the administrative and commercial core of the island, the inland town of Freeport revolves around the business and governmental activities of **Churchill Square** *(intersection of E. Mall Dr. and Pioneers Way)*, the tourist activities at **International Square** *(intersection of W. Sunrise Hwy. and E. Mall Dr.)* and the extensive Bahamas Princess Resort and Casino complex that adjoins it. **Xanadu Beach**, adjacent to the Xanadu Hotel on the south shore of Freeport, offers a lovely stretch of white sand.

Along the island's west end, a string of small towns remains largely the domain of Bahamians, though the hamlet of West End itself, on the far tip of the island, holds a modest marina that attracts boaters and visitors.

Sights

International Bazaar – *Intersection of W. Sunrise Hwy. and E. Mall Dr. Open year-round Mon-Sat 9:30am-5:30pm, Sun hours vary.* This maze of small shops, fronted by a landmark torii (a Japanese ceremonial gate), was designed by American special-effects artist Charles Perrin and completed in 1967. The architecture of the 90-some shops and eateries, as well as their themes and merchandise, reflect the motifs of 25 different countries. Peek behind the scenes at the **Perfume Factory** *(east rear of bazaar)*, where you can tour the facilities and mix your own personal fragrance *(open year-round Mon-Fri 9:30am-5:30pm, Sat noon-4pm; closed major holidays; ☎ 242-352-9391);* or watch jewelers at work at Paris in the Bahamas.

At a local **straw market** occupying a lot behind the bazaar, small stalls of vendors display T-shirts, African-inspired textile items and other souvenirs.

★**Rand Nature Centre** – *E. Settlers Way. Open year-round Mon-Fri 9am-4pm, Sat 9am-1pm. Closed Dec 25-Jan 1. $5.* 🅿 ☎ *242-352-5438. www.bahamasnet.com/ rand.* This 100-acre nature preserve was established in 1969 by Dorothy Rand in memory of her husband, James Henry Rand, an American inventor and founder of the Remington Rand Corp. In the 1960s the Rands moved to the Bahamas, where Mr. Rand established a medical facility and was involved in philanthropic pursuits. Initially operated by Trustees of the Rand Corporation, the Nature Centre was given to the Bahamas National Trust in the early 1990s.

A .4mi trail rambles through the varied native and introduced flora, with a rich display of orchids, pines and palms. At the trail's end a large pond provides habitat for flamingos, herons, egrets and other waterbirds.

Straw Market

LUCAYA AND EAST END

Comprising a small open-air mall of souvenir shops and restaurants overlooking Bell Channel Bay, **Port Lucaya** *(south end of Seahorse Rd.)* reigns as the center of activity here. Headquarters for the **Underwater Explorers Society** (UNEXSO), which runs commercial diving excursions, is located at the west end of the mall. Across Seahorse Road, several large hotels rise along popular **Lucayan Beach.** East of Port Lucaya, **Taino Beach** offers a quieter, less crowded beach experience *(from Port Lucaya, take Midshipman Rd. east to W. Beach Rd.).*

The virtually undeveloped 60mi stretch of island between Lucaya and McLean's Town on the far eastern tip is blessed with spectacular, deserted beaches along its southern edge. Grand Bahama Highway follows the coastline here, cutting through Lucayan National Park and through scrub pine forests that obstruct views of the ocean. The isolation of this area is broken only momentarily by the tiny hamlets of Free Town, High Rock, Pelican Point, Rocky Creek and, finally, McLean's Town.

Sights

★★Garden of the Groves – *On Magellan Dr., northwest of the intersections of E. Sunrise Hwy. and Midshipman Rd. Open year-round daily 9am-4pm. Closed Dec 25. $9.95.* 242-373-5668. www.gardenofthegroves.com. Georgette and Wallace Groves, Freeport's founders, developed this 12-acre botanical preserve in the early 1970s. Situated around a winding man-made lagoon, the site is landscaped with waterfalls, a hibiscus garden, a lush **fern gully**, a hanging garden of exotic potted plants, and walkways edged by crotons, firecracker, crown-of-thorn bushes and towering palms and citrus trees. A small, simple **chapel** overlooking the gardens replicates a Bahamian church that stood in the logging town of Pine Ridge.

★Lucayan National Park – *On Grand Bahama Hwy., 26mi east of Freeport. Open year-round daily 9am-4pm. $3.* 242-352-5438. Watered by Gold Rock Creek and straddling the Grand Bahama Highway, the diverse 42-acre tract is administered by the Bahamas National Trust. On the north side of the road, a park trail *(.3mi)* leads past two limestone caverns. The clear freshwater pool in **Ben's Cavern** supports a recently discovered centipede-like crustacean called *Speleonectes lucayensis*, and its ceiling serves as a summer nursery for migratory bats. In 1986 explorers found the skeletal remains of Lucayan Indians in **Burial Mound Cave**. Both grottoes are part of one of the most extensive underwater cave systems in the world.

On the south side of the park *(across the street from parking lot)*, a half-mile trail loops through a lush mangrove marsh, supporting a variety of birds, bromeliads and orchids, and leads to the oceanfront. Here the island's second-highest coastal dunes—13ft—are dotted by palms, casuarinas, sea grapes and other tropical vegetation. Beyond the dunes lies **Gold Rock Beach**, named for the limestone formation that juts out of the sea offshore and takes on a golden hue at sunset.

The Dolphin Experience – *Departs from Underwater Explorers Society (UNEXSO) dock at Port Lucaya year-round daily 10am, 11:30am, 1pm & 2:30pm. Round-trip 2hrs. Commentary. Reservations required. $45 (swim with dolphins $109).* 242-373-1250 or 888-365-3483. www.dolphinexperience.com. Participants take a 20min boat ride east along the coast to sheltered Sanctuary Bay, home of more than a dozen Atlantic bottlenose dolphins. After an introduction to dolphin behavior, guests are allowed to stand on a submerged platform and touch these docile marine mammals. Participants in the swim program spend about an hour in the water with dolphins *(swimmers must be at least 12 years of age)*.

Sunny Isles Beach, Miami

© Robert Holmes

Practical
Information

Calendar of Events

Listed below is a selection of Florida's most popular annual events; some dates may vary from year to year. For detailed information, contact local tourism offices (numbers listed under individual entries) or **VISIT FLORIDA** (☎ *850-488-5607 or 888-735-2872; www.flausa.com*) .

Date	Event/description	Location

Spring

Date	Event/description	Location
early Mar	**Marlboro Grand Prix** (auto racing)	*Homestead*
early Mar	**Carnaval Miami**	*Miami*
	Sanibel Shell Fair (shell exhibition, crafts)	*Sanibel Island*
	Bike Week	*Daytona Beach*
Mar–Apr	**Springtime Tallahassee** (festivals, parades, crafts)	*Tallahassee*
late Mar–Apr	**Festival of States** (parades, concerts, fireworks, crafts)	*St. Petersburg*
	Winter Equestrian Festival (equestrian competition)	*Tampa*
	Jazz Festival	*Sarasota*
	Bay Area Renaissance Festival	*Largo*
early Apr	**Bausch & Lomb WTA Championships** (tennis)	*Amelia Island*
Apr	**Seven-Mile Bridge Run**	*Marathon*
	Fun 'n Sun Festival (parades, concerts, crafts)	*Clearwater*
	International Kite Festival	*Miami Beach*
Apr–May	**SunFest**	*West Palm Beach*
May	**Florida Folk Festival**	*White Springs*
	Isle of Eight Flags Shrimp Festival	*Fernandina Beach*

Summer

Date	Event/description	Location
early June	**Billy Bowlegs Festival** ("Pirate invasion," treasure hunt)	*Fort Walton Beach*
	Goombay Festival	*Coconut Grove*
June	**Sarasota Music Festival**	*Sarasota*
	Fiesta of Five Flags (ethnic festival, street parades)	*Pensacola*

Giant Frog Windsock, International Kite Festival

	Spanish Night Watch (music and pageantry of colonial times)	St. Augustine
July	Hemingway Days	Key West
late July–early Aug	Florida International Festival (music festival; held every other year)	Daytona Beach
Aug	Shark's Tooth and Seafood Festival	Venice

Fall

Oct	Clearwater Jazz Holiday	Clearwater
mid-Oct	Bicycle Festival	Mount Dora
	National Car Rental Golf Classic	Orlando
late Oct	Guavaween (Latin-style Halloween)	Ybor City
	St. John's Seafood Festival	Madeira Beach
	Fantasy Fest (gay and lesbian festival)	Key West
early Nov	Florida Seafood Festival	Apalachicola
Nov	Jacksonville Jazz Festival	Jacksonville
	Micanopy Fall Festival (antique fair)	Micanopy

Winter

Dec	Winterfest Boat Parade	Fort Lauderdale
late Dec	King Mango Strut	Coconut Grove
	Junkanoo Celebration	Nassau, Bahamas
	Indian Arts Festival, Miccosukee Indian Village	Everglades
Jan 1	FedEx Orange Bowl (college football)	Miami
	Gator Bowl (college football)	Jacksonville
	Outback Bowl (college football)	Tampa
	Florida Citrus Bowl (college football)	Orlando
Jan 6	Festival of Epiphany	Tarpon Springs
mid-Jan	Art Deco Weekend (street festival)	Miami Beach
	Winter Equestrian Festival (equestrian competition)	West Palm Beach
late Jan	Rolex 24 Hours at Daytona (sports car race)	Daytona Beach
Feb	Gasparilla Festival (arts, sporting events, entertainment)	Tampa
mid-Feb	Florida State Fair (livestock, rides, arts and crafts, entertainment)	Tampa
	Miami International Boat Show	Miami
	Daytona 500 (stock car race)	Daytona Beach
late Feb	Medieval Fair, Ringling Museum of Art	Sarasota
	Coconut Grove Arts Festival	Coconut Grove
Feb–Mar	Florida Strawberry Festival	Plant City

Consult individual entries for detailed practical information about the following areas and cities: Bahamas, Everglades, Fort Lauderdale, Jacksonville, the Keys, Key West, Kennedy Space Center, Miami, Orlando, Pensacola, Sanibel and Captiva Islands, Sarasota, St. Augustine, Tallahassee, Tampa and Walt Disney World.

Planning Your Trip

Tourist Information

Tourist Offices – To request the *Florida Vacation Guide* (published annually) or a state map, contact **Visit Florida**, P.O. Box 1100, Tallahassee FL 32302 *(☎ 850-488-5607 or 888-735-2872; www.flausa.com)*. Local tourist offices (telephone numbers listed under each entry) provide information free of charge on accommodations, shopping, entertainment, festivals and recreation. *Florida Travel Saver Guides* provide information about lodging, attractions and shopping, and contain money-saving coupons; they are distributed by official Florida welcome centers and by many businesses and hotels. Other Web addresses that may be useful in planning your trip are:

www.myflorida.com	State of Florida information including state parks
www.flheritage.com	State Division of Historical Resources information includes museum network, preservation news, etc.
www.floridasecrets.com	accommodations, restaurants, fun facts and more
www.see-florida.com	attractions, lodgings, dining and recreation
www.beachdirectory.com	information on accommodations, restaurants and attractions available in five languages

Tips for Special Visitors

Children – *In this guide, sights of particular interest to children are indicated with a* 𝗞𝗶𝗱𝘀 *symbol.* Many sights and attractions offer reduced or free admission for children (usually under 12 years of age), as well as reduced rates for families. When booking accommodations, ask for family rates or discount vacation packages. Restaurants frequently provide a children's menu.

Disabled Travelers – *Wheelchair access to sights described in this guide is indicated in admission information by* ♿. Federal law requires that businesses (including hotels and restaurants) provide access for the disabled, devices for the hearing impaired, and designated parking spaces. Many public buses are equipped with wheelchair lifts; many hotels have rooms designed for visitors with special needs. For further information, contact the **Society for the Advancement of Travel and Hospitality** (SATH), 347 Fifth Ave., Suite 610, New York NY 10016 *(☎ 212-447-7284; www.sath.org)*.

All **national parks** have facilities for the disabled. Free or discounted passes are available from national parks. For details, contact the National Park Service, Office of Public Inquiries, P.O. Box 37127, Room 1013, Washington DC 20013-7127, ☎ 202-208-4747. For **state parks**, check with the **Florida Dept. of Environmental Protection**, Div. of Recreation & Parks, 3900 Commonwealth Blvd., Tallahassee FL 32399-3000 *(☎ 850-488-9872; www.myflorida.com)*.

Passengers who will need assistance with **train** or **bus** travel should give advance notice to Amtrak *(☎ 800-872-7245 or 800-523-6590 (TDD), www.amtrak.com)* or Greyhound *(☎ 800-231-2222 (US only) or 800-345-3109 (TDD); www.greyhound.com)*. Reservations for hand-controlled **rental cars** should be made well in advance with the rental company.

Senior Citizens – Many hotels, attractions and restaurants offer discounts to visitors age 62 or older (proof of age may be required). The **American Association of Retired Persons** (AARP), *(601 E St. N.W., Washington DC 20049 ☎ 202-434-2277; www.aarp.com)*, offers discounts to its members.

When to Go

In the Sunshine State most sights and attractions are open year-round, although peak seasons vary by region. High season in south Florida is during the **winter** (Oct–Apr) when many visitors escape colder climates. Daytime winter temperatures average 70°F/21°C, while in the Everglades and Keys daytime temperatures reach 73°F/23°C. North and central Florida enjoy the traditional four seasons: spring 67°F/19°C; summer 83°F/29°C; fall 69°F/21°C; and winter 55°F/14°C. January is usually the coldest month. Winter, when mosquitoes are tolerable and migratory birds are plentiful, is the best time to view wildlife in parks and reserves. Insect repellent is recommended year round.

Although **summer** months are hot and humid throughout the state, sea breezes moderate temperatures along the coasts. Daytime temperatures average 88°F/31°C and do not vary much between the northern and southern regions. Daily afternoon showers are common between June and September.

The **hurricane season** is generally June to November, with the greatest activity occurring from August to October *(see Nature and Safety)*.

Pleasant water temperatures foster swimming and other water sports year-round. Beaches are most crowded during school holidays, spring breaks and summer vacation periods. Reduced admissions to sights are generally available for senior citizens, students and children under 12.

Casual dress is accepted in most facilities. Better restaurants may request that men wear jackets, but rarely is a tie required. A hat will come in handy while standing in line, especially during the summer heat. A good sunscreen, even on a cloudy day, and sunglasses are recommended.

Average Daily Temperatures

	January	April	July	October
Apalachicola	54°F/12°C	69°F/21°C	82°F/28°C	70°F/21°C
Gainesville	55°F/14°C	70°F/21°C	82°F/28°C	71°F/22°C
Jacksonville	53°F/12°C	69°F/21°C	82°F/28°C	70°F/21°C
Key West	69°F/21°C	78°F/26°C	84°F/29°C	80°F/27°C
Miami	68°F/20°C	76°F/24°C	83°F/29°C	78°F/26°C
Naples	65°F/19°C	73°F/23°C	82°F/28°C	77°F/25°C
Orlando	61°F/16°C	72°F/22°C	83°F/29°C	74°F/23°C
Pensacola	51°F/11°C	68°F/20°C	83°F/29°C	69°F/21°C
Sarasota	60°F/16°C	72°F/22°C	83°F/29°C	75°F/24°C
Tallahassee	51°F/10°C	68°F/20°C	82°F/28°C	68°F/20°C
Tampa	60°F/16°C	68°F/20°C	83°F/29°C	74°F/23°C

International Visitors

Before You Go

In addition to the tourism offices throughout Florida *(see individual entries)*, visitors from outside the US can obtain information in French, German, Japanese, Portuguese and Spanish from the web site of **Visit Florida** www.flausa.com, or from the US embassy or consulate in their country of residence *(partial listing below)*. For a complete list of American consulates and embassies abroad, visit the US State Department Bureau of Consular Affairs listing on the Internet at http://travel.state.gov/links.html.

Country	Address	☎
Belgium	United States Embassy 27, boulevard du Régent 1000 Brussels	02 513 38 30
Canada	American Embassy, Ottawa Consular Section 100 Wellington Street Ottawa, Ontario K1P 5T1	613-238-4470 800-529-4410 (US & Canada)
Germany	Embassy of the United States, Berlin 4-5 Neustaetter Kirchstrasse 10117 Berlin	30 238 5174
Japan	American Embassy 10-5 Akasaka 1-Chome Minato-ku Tokyo 107-8420	0990-5-26160 (call from fax telephone to make visa appointment)
Switzerland	Embassy of the United States, Bern Jubiläumsstrasse 93, 3001 Bern	31 357 7011
United Kingdom	American Embassy, London 24 Grosvenor Square London, W1A 1AE	171 499 9000

Many foreign countries have consular offices in Miami *(for phone numbers, check the yellow pages of the telephone directory under Consulates).*

Entry Requirements – Citizens of countries participating in the Visa Waiver Pilot Program (VWPP) are not required to obtain a visa to enter the US for visits of less than 90 days. For more information, contact the US consulate in your country of residence. Citizens of nonparticipating countries must have a visitor's visa. Upon entry, nonresident foreign visitors must present a **valid passport** and round-trip transportation ticket. Canadian citizens are not required to present a passport or visa, although identification and proof of citizenship may be requested (a passport or Canadian birth certificate and photo identification are usually acceptable). Naturalized Canadian citizens should carry their citizenship papers. Inoculations are generally not required, but check with the US embassy or consulate before departing.

Health Insurance – The US does not have a national health program. Before departing, visitors from abroad should check their health-care insurance to determine if it covers doctors' visits, medication and hospitalization in the US. Prescription drugs should be properly identified and accompanied by a copy of the prescription. Companies offering travel insurance: **Access America** (☎ *800-284-8300; www.access-samerica.com*), **TravelEx** (☎ *800-228-9792; www.travelex.com*), **The Travelers Insured International** (☎ *800-243-3174; www.travelinsured.com*). Physician referrals from a nationwide network are offered by **Housecalls USA** (24hrs/day) (☎ *800-468-3537*).

US Customs – All articles brought into the US must be declared at time of entry. **Exempt** from customs regulations: personal effects; one liter (33.8 fl oz) of alcoholic beverage (providing visitor is at least 21 years old); either 200 cigarettes, 50 cigars or 2 kilograms (4.4 pounds) of smoking tobacco; and gifts (to persons in the US) that do not exceed $100 in value. **Prohibited items** include plant material, firearms and ammunition (if not intended for sporting purposes), and meat and poultry products. For other prohibited items, exemptions and information, contact the **US Customs Service**, 1300 Pennsylvania Ave. N.W., Washington DC 20229 (☎ *202-927-6724; www.customs .gov/travel/travel.htm*). Visitors should also contact the customs service in their country of residence to determine reentry regulations.

General Information

Currency Exchange – *See Money below.*

Driving in the US – Visitors bearing valid driver's licenses issued by their country of residence are not required to obtain an International Driver's License to drive in the US. Drivers must carry vehicle registration and/or rental contract, and proof of automobile insurance at all times. Rental cars in the US are usually equipped with automatic transmission, and rental rates tend to be less expensive than overseas. Gasoline is sold by the gallon (1 gallon=3.8 liters) and is cheaper than in other countries. Most self-service gas stations do not offer car repair, although many sell standard maintenance items. **Road regulations** in the US require that vehicles be driven on the right side of the road. Distances are posted in miles (1 mile=1.6 kilometers).

Electricity – Electrical current in the US is 120 volts AC, 60 Hz. Foreign-made appliances may need voltage transformers and North American flat-blade adapter plugs (available at specialty travel and electronics stores).

Emergencies – In all major US cities dial **911** to telephone the police, ambulance or fire department. Another way to report an emergency is to dial **0** for the operator *(see also Basic Information)*.

Mail – First-class postage rates within the US: letter 34¢ (1oz), postcard 20¢. Overseas: letter 80¢ (1/2oz), postcard 70¢. Letters can be mailed from most hotels as well as from post offices. Stamps and packing material may be purchased at post offices, grocery stores and businesses offering postal and express shipping services located throughout the city *(see the Yellow Pages phone directory under "Mailing Services")*. Most post offices are open Monday–Friday 9am–5pm, some are also open Saturday 9am–noon.

Money – Most banks are members of the network of Automated Teller Machines (ATM), allowing visitors from around the world to withdraw cash using bank cards and major credit cards. ATMs can usually be found in airports, banks, grocery stores and shopping malls. Networks (Cirrus, Honor, Plus) serviced by the ATM are indicated on the machine. To inquire about ATM service, locations and transaction fees, contact your local bank, Cirrus (☎ 800-424-7787) or Plus (☎ *800-843-7587*).

Credit Cards and Traveler's Checks – Rental-car agencies and many hotels require credit cards. Most banks will cash brand-name traveler's checks and process cash advances on major credit cards with proper identification. Traveler's checks are accepted at most stores, restaurants and hotels. **American Express Co. Travel Service** has offices in Jacksonville, Miami and major Florida cities www.americanexpress.com. To report lost or stolen **credit card**, call: American Express (☎ *800-528-4800)*; Diners Club (☎ *800-234-6377)*; Discover Card (☎ *800-347-2683)*; MasterCard (☎ *800-307-7309)* or the issuing bank; Visa (☎ *800-336-8472)*.

Currency Exchange – For a small fee, the main offices of most national banks will exchange foreign currency; contact main or branch offices for information and locations. Some statewide banks (Bank of America, First Union and SunTrust) exchange foreign currency at their local offices. **Thomas Cook Currency Services** operates exchange offices throughout Florida (☎ *800-287-7362; www.thomascook.com)*. Currency exchange offices are located at the international airports in Jacksonville, Miami, Orlando and Tampa.

Taxes and Tips – *See also Basic Information*. Prices displayed or quoted in the US do not generally include **sales tax** (6% in Florida). Sales tax is added at the time of purchase and is not reimbursable as in other countries (it can sometimes be avoided if purchased items are shipped to another country by the seller).

In the US it is customary to give a **tip** (a small gift of money) for services received from waiters/waitresses, porters, hotel maids and taxi drivers.

Telephones/Telegrams – For emergencies (police, fire, ambulance), dial 911. Instructions for using **public telephones** are listed on or near the telephone. Some public telephones accept credit cards, and all will accept long-distance calling cards. For **long-distance calls** in the US and Canada, dial 1 + area code (3 digits) + number (7 digits). To place a **local call**, dial the 7-digit number without 1 or the area code (unless the local calling area includes several area codes). The cost for a local call from a pay phone is generally 35¢ (any combination of nickels, dimes and quarters is accepted). To find a local number (within your area code), check the local telephone directory or dial **411** for information; to find a **long-distance** number, dial 1 + area code + 555-1212 *(there is a charge for both services)*. For operator assistance or information, dial **0** for the local operator or **00** for the long-distance operator.

To place an **international call**, dial 011 + country code + area code + number. A list of country and city codes can be found in the beginning of local phone directories. To place a collect call (person receiving the call pays charges), dial **0** + area code + number and tell the operator you are calling collect. If it is an international call, ask for the overseas operator.

Most telephone numbers in this guide that start with **800** or **888** or **877** are toll-free (no charge) in the US and may not be accessible outside North America. Dial **1** before dialing a toll-free number. The charge for numbers preceded by **900** can range from 50¢ to $15 per minute. Most hotels add a surcharge for local and long-distance calls. You can send a **telegram** or money, or have money telegraphed to you, via the Western Union system (☎ 800-325-6000; www.westernunion.com).

Temperature and Measurement – In the US temperatures are measured in degrees Fahrenheit and measurements are expressed according to the US Customary System of weights and measures.

Equivalents

Degrees Fahrenheit	95°	86°	77°	68°	59°	50°	41°	32°	23°	14°
Degrees Celsius	35°	30°	25°	20°	15°	10°	5°	0°	-5°	-10°

1 inch = 2.54 centimeters	**1 quart** = 0.946 liter
1 foot = 30.48 centimeters	**1 gallon** = 3.785 liters
1 mile = 1.609 kilometers	**1 pound** = 0.454 kilograms

Getting There and Getting Around

Getting to Florida

By Air – Most US airlines offer direct and nonstop flights to Florida. For flight information, contact the airline directly. Nine major international airports—the largest are Miami, Orlando and Tampa International *(see individual entries)*—offer service between Florida and Europe, Central and South America and the Caribbean. Smaller regional airports are usually accessible through commuter carriers.

Airports offer a variety of ground transportation: limousines, shuttle vans, taxis, public transportation and hotel courtesy shuttles. Limousines and shuttles require advance reservations.

By Train – The Amtrak rail network offers a variety of train travel packages that may combine rail, air and bus. Advance reservations are recommended. First-class, coach and sleeping cars are available; on some routes, bi-level Superliner cars with floor-to-ceiling windows permit a panoramic view. Smoking is not permitted on most trains. Information for passengers who require special assistance can be found on p 338. Travelers from Canada should inquire with local travel agents regarding Amtrak/ VIARail connections. The **North America Rail Pass** allows up to 30 days of travel throughout the US and Canada. The **USA RailPass** *(not available to US or Canadian citizens or legal residents)*

Courtesy Orlando/Orange Country CVB

offers unlimited travel within Amtrak-designated regions at discounted rates: 15- and 30-day passes are available.

Daily service is provided on the *Silver Star* (New York-Orlando-Miami), *Silver Palm* (New York-Tampa-Miami) and *Silver Meteor* (New York-Orlando-Miami). The *Sunset Limited* (Orlando-Los Angeles) makes the transcontinental trip three times weekly *(Sun, Tue & Thu; one-way $293/coach)*. A relaxing alternative, the **Auto Train** offers first-class sleeping accommodations, a full-service restaurant, floor-to-ceiling windows in the Sightseer Lounge and a movie presentation—all included in the ticket price *(leaves Lorton, Virginia daily 4pm; arrives Sanford, Florida 9am)*. Only passengers with automobiles are permitted on the train; no cars accepted after 3pm. Check restrictions when making reservations.

Amtrak and United Airlines offer a package allowing passengers to travel one way by plane with three stops along the way. Air-Rail travel is also available from some points in Canada. For information, contact Amtrak Vacations *(☎ 800-321-8684)*.

Amtrak Thruway Bus Connections provide a link to train service. Tickets must be purchased at Amtrak stations, travel agencies or by mail before boarding buses. *(For schedule and route information: ☎ 800-872-7245 (US only), www.amtrak.com.)*

By Bus – Greyhound offers access to most cities in Florida at a leisurely pace. Overall, bus fares are lower than other forms of transportation. The **Discovery Pass** allows unlimited travel for anywhere from 4 to 60 days. Advance reservations are suggested. *(For fares, schedules and routes: ☎ 800-231-2222; www.greyhound.com)*. Most communities have a Greyhound bus station; in small towns the local post office or gas station often doubles as a stop. In the Keys along the Overseas Highway, the bus stops at designated flag stops.

Getting Around in Florida

Distances in Florida are relatively short; it only takes a couple of hours to travel between the east and west coasts (except in the northern part of the state). Even the stretch from the Panhandle to Miami can be driven in one day. Many towns are serviced by Amtrak. In some areas links are maintained with bus connections. Some of the more remote communities, especially along beaches, can only be reached by car. **Florida Department of Transportation** *(☎ 850-414-4100, www.dot.state.fl.us)*.

By Car – Florida has an extensive system of well-maintained major roads, some of which are designated limited-access highways that require a toll *(average toll 6¢/mi)*. Four major interstates traverse Florida: I-10 runs from Jacksonville to Pensacola; I-4 links Daytona Beach and Tampa; I-75 cuts southwest across the state from Georgia; and I-95 travels the length of Florida's east coast, ending at Miami. Located on the interstates, welcome centers greet visitors with samples of free citrus juice and supply answers to your travel questions. Many rest areas have picnic tables; most are open 24 hours and are patrolled by security officers at night. Watch for wildlife on roads in remote areas. Along highways and major urban thoroughfares, many gas stations stay open 24 hours. Most self-service gas stations do not offer car repair although many sell standard maintenance items. For free maps phone the tourist office for your destination *(see individual entries)* or contact **Visit Florida** *(see Planning Your Trip)*.

The **Florida Turnpike** (a toll road) branches off I-75 northwest of Orlando and slants southeastward across the state until it ends below Miami in Florida City *($16.65 for entire distance)*. Toll booths are manned, but for quick travel motorists should carry correct change. Call boxes placed at mile intervals allow travelers to phone for help. For further information ☎ 800-749-7453.

<u>Motoring Safety Tips:</u>

- ■ Do not stop if strangers try to flag your car down.
- ■ If you carry a cellular phone, dial **FHP** (*347) for the Florida Highway Patrol.
- ■ Don't stop if your car is bumped from the rear; instead proceed to the nearest well-lit public area and contact the police.
- ■ Ask the concierge or hotel clerk what parts of the city should be avoided.

Rental Cars – Most large rental companies have offices at major airports and downtown locations. Packages may offer unlimited mileage and discounted prices. If a vehicle is returned at a different location from where it was rented, drop-off charges may be incurred. Reservations are accepted through a toll-free service with a major credit card. Minimum age for rental is 21. A surcharge *($25/day)* for persons up to age 24 is applied to all rentals in Florida. Be sure to check for proper insurance coverage, offered at extra charge. Liability is not automatically included in the terms of the lease. Aside from the national rental agencies listed below, there are local companies that offer reasonable rentals. *See yellow pages of local directories for phone numbers.*

Rental Company	☎ Reservations
Alamo	800-327-9633 www.alamo.com
Avis	800-331-1212 www.avis.com
Budget	800-527-0700 www.budget.com
Dollar	800-800-4000 www.dollar.com
Enterprise	800-325-8007 www.enterprise.com
Hertz	800-654-3131 www.hertz.com
National	800-227-7368 www.nationalcar.com
Thrifty	800-331-4200 www.thrifty.com

(Toll-free numbers may not be accessible outside North America.)

Recreational Vehicle (RV) Rentals – One-way motor-home rentals are offered from several locations in Florida. Some models accommodate up to eight people, and service can include free mileage and airport transfers. Make reservations 2-3 weeks in advance. In the summer months (Jun–Aug) and during holiday seasons, reservations should be made at least 4-6 weeks in advance. Cruise America RV Depot: ☎ 480-464-7300 or 800-327-7778, www.cruiseamerica.com.

Road Regulations and Insurance – The maximum speed limit on interstate highways is 70mph, 60mph on state highways, unless otherwise posted. Speed limits are generally 30mph within city limits and residential areas. Right turns on red are allowed after coming to a complete stop, unless otherwise indicated. Florida law requires that headlights must be turned on when driving in fog and rain. Authorities recommend keeping headlights on at dawn and dusk and when driving through smoke. **Seat belts** must be worn by all front seat occupants. Children under 6 must ride in crash-tested, federally approved child restraint devices (child safety seats are offered by most car-rental agencies; indicate such a need when making reservations). The law requires motorists in both directions to bring their vehicles to a full stop when warning signals on a **school bus** are activated. Parking spaces identified by ♿ are reserved for handicapped persons only. Anyone parking in these spaces without proper identification will be ticketed and/or their vehicle will be towed.

Drivers are required to have personal injury protection and property liability insurance. Carry proof of insurance in the vehicle at all times.

Apart from local authorities, motor clubs (membership required) offer road assistance: **American Automobile Association (AAA)** (☎ *800-222-4357*); **Mobil Auto Club** (☎ *800-621-5581*); **Shell Motorist Club** (☎ *800-852-0555*).

In Case of Accident – If you are involved in an accident resulting in personal injury or property damage, you must notify the local police and remain at the scene until dismissed. If blocking traffic, vehicles should be moved as soon as possible. In the case of property damage to an unattended vehicle, the driver must attempt to locate the owner or leave written notice in a conspicuous place of driver's name, address and car registration number.

Accommodations

Overview

Although Florida's weather permits visiting year-round, rates are lower in **off-season**: South Florida May to October; the Panhandle and northern coastal areas December to February. In some hotels children under 18 stay free when sharing a room with their parents. Some small hotel and many motel rooms include efficiency kitchens. Almost all accommodations are air-conditioned. Typical amenities at hotels and motels include television, smoking/non-smoking rooms, restaurants and swimming pools. The more elegant hotels and resorts may also offer entertainment, gourmet dining, health clubs, private golf courses and tennis clubs. Hotel taxes, which vary according to location, range from 6% to 12.5% and are not included in rates quoted. Contact the local tourist office to request free brochures that give details about accommodations. The Official *Florida Vacation Guide* lists members of the Florida Hotel & Motel Assn. and is available from **Visit Florida** *(see Planning Your Trip)*. State-wide hotel information service: ☏ 888-735-2872, www.flausa .com.

Josephine's Country Inn, Seaside

Gwen Cannon/MICHELIN

Traditional Lodgings

Hotels/Motels – Accommodations range from luxury hotels *($200 and up)* and superior hotels *($125-$200)* to moderate motels *($80-$125)*. Rates vary greatly according to season and location and tend to be higher during holiday and peak seasons. Many hotels and motels offer packages, which can include meals, passes to local attractions, organized trips and theme and weekend specials. Some hotels include breakfast in the room rate. Advance reservations are recommended. Always advise the reservations clerk of late arrival; unless confirmed with a credit card, rooms may not be held after 5pm.

Major hotel and motel chains with locations throughout Florida include:

	☏/www		☏/www
Best Western	800-528-1234 www.bestwestern.com	**ITT Sheraton**	800-325-3535 www.sheraton.com
Clarion, Comfort & Quality Inns	800-228-5150 www.comfortinn.com	**Marriott**	800-228-9290 www.marriott.com
Crowne Plaza	800-227-6963 www.crowneplaza.com	**Omni**	800-843-6664 www.omnihotels.com
Days Inn	800-325-2525 www.daysinn.com	**Radisson**	800-333-3333 www.radisson.com
Hilton	800-445-8667 www.hilton.com	**Ramada**	800-228-2828 www.ramada.com
Holiday Inn	800-465-4329 www.holiday-inn.com	**Ritz-Carlton**	800-241-3333 www.ritzcarlton.com
Howard Johnson	800-446-4656 www.hojo.com	**Westin**	800-848-0016 www.westin.com
Hyatt	800-233-1234 www.hyatt.com		

(toll-free numbers may not be accessible outside of North America)

Bed-and-Breakfasts and Country Inns – Most B&Bs are privately owned and many are located in historic structures in residential sections of a city or in small towns and rural areas. Amenities include complimentary breakfast ranging from continental fare to a gourmet repast; some offer afternoon tea and the use of sitting rooms or garden areas where hosts and guests mingle. Most establishments are small and offer fewer than 10 rooms. Private baths are not always available, and often there is no phone in individual rooms. Smoking indoors may not be allowed. Reservations should be made well in advance, especially during holiday seasons; be sure to ask about minimum stay, cancellation and refund policies. Most establishments accept major credit cards. Rates vary seasonally but range from $70 in low season to $250 in high season for a double room per night. Rates may be higher when amenities such as hot tubs, private entrances and ocean views are offered.

Address	☎/Contact Information
Inn Route	
PO Box 6187,	800-524-1880
Palm Harbor FL 34684	www.florida-inns.com
Superior Small Lodging Assn.	
1809 Silver Valley Ct.	407-880-1707
Apopka FL 32712	

Resorts and Spas – Grand South Florida resorts like The Breakers, The Biltmore or the Boca Raton Resort and Club have been restored and furnished lavishly, offering modern amenities coupled with luxuries of the past. On-site chef-staffed restaurants, indoor and outdoor swimming pools, tennis courts, fitness centers, an 18-hole golf course and perhaps its own marina are often standard features of these large resort hotels. Modern spas offer a variety of programs, from fitness, beauty and wellness, to weight management and stress relief, to relaxation and adventure vacations. Guests are pampered with European mud baths, daily massages, state-of-the-art fitness and exercise programs, cooking classes and nutritional counseling. Spas offer luxurious facilities in beautiful settings that can include championship golf courses and tennis courts. Most offer packages for stays ranging from 2 to 10 nights, which include health and fitness programs and spa treatments. Most spas are informal, but check when making your reservations.

Prices range from $900/week in summer to $4,000/week during the winter season depending on choice of program (price per person, double occupancy). Meals (including special diets), use of facilities, tax, gratuities and airport transfers are usually included. For more information, Spa Finder, Inc., 91 Fifth Ave., New York NY 10003. **Reservation service:** ☎ 800-255-7727, www.spafinder.com.

Other Accommodations

Condominiums – Furnished apartments or houses are more cost-effective than hotels for families with children. Amenities include separate living quarters, fully equipped kitchen with dining area, several bedrooms and bathrooms, and laundry facilities. Most condos provide televisions, basic linens and maid service. Depending on location, properties often include sports and recreational facilities, patios and beach access. Most require a minimum stay of three nights or one week, especially during peak season. When making reservations, ask about cancellation penalties and refund policies. Chambers of commerce and tourist offices have listings of local property management agencies that can assist with the selection. For single-family vacation homes in Naples and the Orlando area, contact **Florida Choice Vacation Home Rentals Inc.** *(☎ 800-847-2731, www.floridachoice.com).*

Hostels – Simple budget accommodations are offered at hostels in such locations as Clearwater Beach, Florida City, Key West, Miami Beach and Kissimmee. Dormitory-style rooms average $14-$17/night for members; non-members pay an additional $3/night. Private rooms are available at additional charge; amenities include swimming pool (Kissimmee), air-conditioning, common living room, laundry facilities, self-service kitchen and dining room. Blankets and pillows are provided; linens can be rented. Reservations are suggested. All hostels accept credit cards. **Hostelling International**, 733 15th St. N.W., Suite 840, Washington DC 20005 *(☎ 202-783-6161; www.hiayh.org; reservations: ☎ 800-909-4776).*

Camping – Campsites are located in national parks, state parks, national forests, along beaches and in private campgrounds. Many camping facilities are located in central Florida near theme park attractions. Most offer full utility hookups, lodges or cabins and recreational facilities. Florida's many rivers and lakes allow boat camping and usually include mooring facilities and marinas. Primitive camping is for the experienced camper only. Because there may be mosquitoes and other creatures present, plan to sleep well-protected in the outdoors. Make sure your tent is waterproof; sudden thunderstorms can soak through quickly. Advance reservations are recommended, especially during holidays and school vacations.

A variety of camping facilities, from full-facility camping to cabins, resort lodges, boat camping and primitive camping, await the outdoor enthusiast in Florida's national and state parks. Some facilities are available on a first-come, first-served basis, while others require advance reservations; permits are required for certain campsites. Reservations for campsites are accepted in advance, cabin rentals up to 11 months in advance.

Rates vary according to season and facilities: cabins *($20–$110/day)*, campsites *($8–$21)*. For reservations *(Mon–Fri8am–5pm)* contact the park directly. For a free brochure listing all state park facilities, contact: **Florida Department of Environmental Protection**, Division of Recreation & Parks, *(☎ 850-488-9872; www.dep.state.fl.us./ parks).*

Campgrounds and Recreational Vehicle (RV) Parks – The Florida Assn. of RV Parks & Campgrounds publishes the annual *Florida Camping Directory*, which lists member sites and gives addresses and details on hookups, laundry facilities, pools, playgrounds, sporting facilities, freeway access and shopping. For a free copy: 1340 Vickers Rd., Tallahassee FL 32303-3041 www.floridacamping.com ☎ 850-562-7151. Parks are family-oriented and open year-round. Most campgrounds offer daily, weekly or monthly occupancy for recreational vehicles. Prices range from $10-$60/night for campsites and average $20-$25/night for RV. Reservations are recommended, especially for longer stays and in popular resort areas, including the Keys. **KOA Kampgrounds** are located all across Florida; some resort properties offer pools, hot tubs, air-conditioned cabins, restaurants, boat ramps, deep-sea fishing and snorkeling. For a directory *($6, includes shipping)*, write to KOA Kampgrounds, PO Box 30558, Billings MT 59114 *(☎ 406-248-7444; www.koa.com).*

Basic Information

General Information

Business Hours – Most businesses operate Monday–Friday 9am–5pm. **Banks:** Monday–Thursday 9am–4:30pm, Friday until 5pm or 6pm; some banks in larger cities may be open Saturday morning. Most retail stores and specialty shops are open Monday–Saturday 10am–6pm (Thursday 9pm). Malls and **shopping centers** are usually open Monday–Saturday 10am–9pm, Sunday noon–6pm. Most **state and federal** government buildings (including city halls) are open Monday–Friday 8:30am–4:30pm. In general, **churches** are open daily, sometimes as early as 7am, until 5pm or 6pm, and later, if evening services; otherwise, inquire at the church office to view the sanctuary, if permitted.

Liquor Laws – The legal minimum age for purchase and consumption of alcoholic beverages is 21; proof of age is normally required. Most restaurants/bars do not serve liquor prior to 1pm on Sunday. Liquor is sold in liquor stores only, while beer and wine is available at grocery stores. Consuming liquor in public places and carrying an open liquor container in a moving vehicle is illegal.

Major Holidays – Most banks and government offices are closed on the following legal holidays *(many retail stores and restaurants remain open on days indicated with*):*

New Year's Day	January 1
Martin Luther King Jr.'s Birthday*	3rd Monday in January
Presidents' Day*	3rd Monday in February
Memorial Day	Last Monday in May
Independence Day	July 4
Labor Day*	1st Monday in September
Columbus Day*	2nd Monday in October
Veterans Day*	November 11
Thanksgiving Day	4th Thursday in November
Christmas Day	December 25

Taxes and Tips – In Florida the sales tax is 6%. Some counties levy an additional local sales tax, and/or a 1%–5% tourist tax. The hotel occupancy tax (6%–12.5%) and tax rate for rental cars vary according to location; additional daily surcharges may be added as well. It is customary in restaurants to tip the server 15%–20% of the bill. At hotels, porters are generally given $1 per suitcase, housekeeping staff $1 per day. Taxi drivers are usually tipped 15% of the fare.

Telephones/Telegrams – A local call from a pay phone generally costs 35¢—or more, depending on the telephone number being called (any combination of nickels, dimes or quarters is accepted). *For more information, see International Visitors.*

Time Zones – Most of Florida is on Eastern Standard Time (EST), 5hrs behind Greenwich Mean Time (GMT). The Panhandle region west of the Apalachicola River adheres to Central Standard Time (CST), 1hr behind EST. Daylight Saving Time (clocks are advanced 1hr) is in effect for most of the US from the first Sunday in April until the last Sunday in October. All the Bahamian islands are on Eastern Standard Time and observe Daylight Saving Time from April through October.

Shopping

General Merchandise – Florida is a shopper's paradise where the sophisticated, practical and curious shopper can indulge. Downtown areas in cities tempt travelers and residents alike with department stores, specialty shops, antique shops and galleries. **Worth Avenue** in Palm Beach attracts well-to-do patrons with its high-fashion boutiques and trendy art galleries. The **Shops at Bal Harbour** and **Streets of Mayfair** in Miami; St. Armands Circle in Sarasota; Galleria at Fort Lauderdale; and Park Avenue in Winter Park are among Florida's popular shopping spots. Beach togs and resort wear can be purchased in every large coastal city in Florida. There's at least one surfer shop (for the latest in surfboards and accessories) in nearly every seaside town, no matter its size.

Shopping venues such as large malls, flea markets and theme-park villages await the adventurous buyer. Bargains galore (reductions up to 75%) can be found in **outlet malls**—Sawgrass Mills (over 200 stores), Fort Lauderdale; Belz Factory Outlet (150 stores), Orlando; and Bay Area Outlet Mall (70 stores), Clearwater—to name just a few. Most stores are reluctant to accept out-of-town checks, however.

Crafts and Souvenirs – Handmade dolls, beaded belts and other **Native American crafts** are sold at the Miccosukee and Seminole reservations in the Everglades. Seashells are offered in countless souvenir shops, especially on Sanibel Island and along the Southwest Coast, where the best seashells can usually be found. The Shell Factory near Fort Myers boasts the largest commercial assortment of shells. Natural sponges from the Gulf of Mexico can be selected at the waterfront in Tarpon Springs. Many of the local bait-and-tackle shops are a good source for sporting and fishing equipment. In historic Ybor City near Tampa, fine hand-rolled cigars make a prized gift for the connoisseur. And don't overlook Downtown Disney Marketplace, which offers merchandise from around the world.

Farm Produce – Agriculture is big business in the Sunshine State and farmers everywhere proffer the fruits of their labor at local markets. Visit these **farmers' markets**, held most Saturday mornings, usually outdoors, in small towns and large city neighborhoods, to shop for produce, fresh fish, and flowers grown in nearby nurseries. Take some of Florida's sunshine with you when you buy oranges, grapefruit and other **citrus fruits**. Many growers have roadside stands and welcome travelers to the orange groves that line many roads. Fruit can be shipped anywhere in the continental US. Inquire about shipping costs; they can run higher than the merchandise.

Antiques – A unique selection of antique shops can be found in north and central Florida. Micanopy features a collection of antique shops clustered along Cholokka Boulevard, as well as Smiley's Antique Mall. The hamlets of Havana and Quincy near Tallahassee are known for their small-town charm and abundance of antiques, art galleries and collectible shops. An assemblage of some 60 shops is located in the Munn Park Historic District in Lakeland, southwest of Orlando. Quaint craft and antique shops line Fifth Avenue and Donnelly Street in Mount Dora, which lies south of Ocala. The Wagon Wheel Flea Market, located in St. Petersburg, claims to be the world's largest **flea market** and is worth a visit. Streets in south Tampa and Ybor City sport antique shops, art galleries and studios. **Vintage clothing** stores, some with a sizable array of apparel, jewelry and accessories, can be found in Sarasota, Ybor City, Micanopy and other Florida towns. **Antique car** buffs will want to visit car shows in Daytona Beach that feature swap meets *(Mar & Nov)* offering vintage car parts and accessories. The Don Garlits' Museums in Ocala has vintage cars for sale.

Gwen Cannon/MICHELIN

Nature and Safety

Protective Measures

Fauna Great and Small – A multitude of creatures such as mosquitoes, chiggers, scorpions, lovebugs, fire ants, sand flies, cockroaches and other wildlife enjoy Florida's subtropical climate as much as most visitors do. When planning outdoor activities, be sure to take necessary precautions. **Mosquitoes** are unavoidable, especially from June to September—the rainy months when humidity is high. In coastal areas mosquitoes are active year-round. Insect repellent, available at supermarkets, pharmacies and most camping stores, is as important as wearing long-sleeved shirts and long pants. When camping, remember that smoke from a campfire is an effective mosquito deterrent. It is unlikely that visitors will encounter **alligators**; they tend to avoid people unless provoked. However, stay clear of a mother guarding her young and do not swim in remote lakes, especially during gator mating season (mid-April). When hiking do not bring your dog; alligators have been known to attack dogs, especially small ones. Florida law prohibits the feeding or molesting of alligators. Forty-four species of **snakes** inhabit the Florida landscape. The poisonous ones *(p 52)* include several species of rattlesnakes and the coral snake. However, like most wildlife, they generally do not pose a threat to people unless provoked. Always wear appropriate footwear and look where you are walking.

Visitor Impact – When visiting a national wildlife refuge, state park or national forest, remember that while the disturbance of a single person may be small, the cumulative impact of a large number of visitors may be disastrous. "Take nothing but pictures; leave nothing but footprints" has been adopted as a slogan and is posted in many parks.

Tips for Visiting Public Lands:

- Enjoy the native vegetation, but please leave it untouched.
- Do not feed animals; they may become ill and die.
- Keep your distance from wildlife.
- Do not walk on sand dunes, but stay on boardwalks.
- Do not litter.
- Remember to pack out everything you pack in.
- Learn to recognize and avoid poisonwood, poison sumac, manchineel *(p 23)*, poison oak and poison ivy; contact may require medical attention.

Weather Watch

Hurricanes – The hurricane season usually lasts from June to November with the greatest activity generally from August to October. Hurricanes begin as tropical depressions and are classified as hurricanes once winds reach 74mph. The National Hurricane Center in Miami, Florida tracks all storms and issues advisories every six hours; stay tuned to radio and television. A hurricane **watch** is announced if hurricane conditions may threaten an area within 36 hours; a hurricane **warning** is issued if sustained winds of at least 74mph are expected within 24 hours.

Hurricane Precautionary Measures:

- Check your car battery and fill up the gas tank.
- Make sure you have a battery-operated radio and extra batteries.
- Collect plenty of fresh water in containers and bathtubs.
- When staying in coastal areas, familiarize yourself with evacuation routes.
- Stay indoors once the hurricane has struck.
- Be aware of storm surges in coastal regions.
- Most importantly, never take a hurricane lightly, and follow instructions issued by local authorities.

Thunderstorms and Lightning – Storms occur almost daily in the summer in Florida (June–Sept) and can pass quickly. Peak lightning season is July to August. Some thunderstorms can be severe, featuring hail and dangerous lightning.

Storm Safety Tips:

- Take cover.
- Stay away from trees, metal objects, doors and windows.
- If riding in a vehicle, remain inside until the storm has passed.
- Avoid being in or near water.
- If in a boat, head for the nearest shore.
- Do not use electrical appliances, especially the telephone.

Seashore Savvy

Beach and Water Safety – In the strong subtropical sun, visitors run the risk of sunburn, even in winter. Reflections from the white sand and water increase the sun's intensity. Use sunglasses to protect your eyes, wear a wide-brimmed hat and drink plenty of liquids. Apply sunscreen even on overcast days, since ultraviolet rays penetrate the cloud cover. Avoid strenuous exercise during midday.

Never swim alone and heed **red warning flags** that indicate dangerous conditions such as riptides, strong underlying currents that pull swimmers seaward. Warning flags are posted every mile along public beaches: blue means calm waters; yellow indicates choppy waters. Most public beaches employ lifeguards seasonally. Take care when swimming at an unguarded beach. Children should be supervised at all times. Scuba diving and snorkeling should never be undertaken alone. Attacks by **sharks**, though rare, have been on the increase along Florida shores recently, particularly off the Northeast Coast. It is strongly advised to be on the alert and to heed instructions from lifeguards.

Stinging creatures such as jellyfish, Portuguese men-of-war and sea urchins inhabit shallow waters. Although most jellyfish stings produce little more than an itchy skin rash, some can cause painful swelling. Treating the affected area with papain-type meat tenderizer will give relief. Stingrays and Portuguese men-of-war can inflict a more serious sting; seek medical treatment immediately. Though rare, **red tides** have occurred off Florida's coast, caused by micro-organisms that release poisons into the water, discoloring it and creating a nauseating odor. The toxins have resulted in the death of thousands of fish and can be irritating to people.

Boating – A good rule of thumb for any water-sports activity is to check with local authorities about conditions before setting out. If you rent a canoe or charter a small yacht, first familiarize yourself with the craft and obtain maps and the latest weather information. When going out on a boat, always advise someone of your itinerary. **Life jackets** should be worn when boating; they must be worn by children under six years of age and are required to be on board for all passengers. Many equipment rental facilities also offer instruction; be sure to choose a reputable outfitter.

© Susan Russell

Sports and Recreation

National, State and Local Facilities

Florida has three national parks, two national seashores, three national forests, two national monuments, two preserves, and more than 100 state parks that preserve and protect the natural and cultural heritage. Recreational activities at most parks include hiking, biking, fishing, swimming, snorkeling, boating, horseback riding and camping (it's best to limit strenuous activities to early morning or late afternoon). Parks are most frequently visited from Memorial Day to Labor Day, although in south Florida they are busiest during the dry season (October–April) when viewing of wildlife and migratory birds is best.

National Parks, Seashores and Monuments – Florida has seven units administered by the National Park Service; entrance fees are charged only at Everglades National Park *($10/vehicle)*, Castillo de San Marcos National Monument *($4/person)* and the

Fort Pickens section of Gulf Islands National Seashore *($6/vehicle)*. Prices are subject to change. All are at least partially accessible to people with disabilities. Camping is permissible *(fees range from $8-$28)* at Everglades, Biscayne and Dry Tortugas national parks and Gulf Islands National Seashore *(for reservations:* ☎ *800-365-2267; www.reservations.nps.gov)*. Most visitor centers offer interpretive exhibits, slide presentations and maps. Picnic areas are provided at parks and seashores. In some cases, visitors can explore the surroundings on self-guided nature trails and participate in ranger-led hikes. Boat rentals may be available. Most park beaches do not have lifeguards. Pets are welcome if kept on a leash, but are not allowed in camping areas or on swimming beaches. For detailed information, contact the individual park or write to National Park Service, 100 Alabama St. S.W., Atlanta GA 30303 *(*☎ *404-562-3123; www.nps.gov)*.

State and Local Parks – Visitors can choose from an ever-expanding state park system, including nature preserves and historic landmarks. **State parks** are generally open year-round daily 8am–dusk. Visitor centers, museums and historic sites may have different opening hours. Entrance fees are usually $3.25-$5/vehicle (up to 8 people), $1/person when entering on foot or by bicycle. Camping fees vary according to season and location (average $8–$19). To request a copy of the guide *Florida State Parks* (free), contact the Department of Environmental Protection, Division of Recreation and Parks *(*☎ *850-488-9872; www.myflorida.com)*; copies are also available at official state welcome centers. **Local parks** are generally open year-round daily 8am–dusk and are free-of-charge.

Specific Activities

For an overview of the many types of recreational activities and facilities available throughout Florida, see the Recreation section in the Introduction at the front of this guide. A comprehensive directory of Florida sports is available online at www. flasports.com.

Biking – Because of the flat terrain, bicycling is popular throughout the state. The cooler months (October–May) are the best cycling "season" since summer temperatures and high humidity can make long rides a challenge. Bicycles are not allowed on highways, limited-access highways, expressways or some bridges. The most pleasant cycling conditions are north of I-4, in central Florida near Gainesville and Ocala, north in the Live Oak area, and on trails and greenways that link local and state parks and national forests. Beach areas from Fernandina Beach to Melbourne and on Captiva and Sanibel Islands offer pleasant riding paths. For more information, contact area tourist offices and local bike rental shops or the **Department of Environmental Protection**, Office of Greenways and Trails in Tallahassee *(*☎ *850-487-4784; www. myflorida .com)*.

Biking Safety Tips:

■ Obey all traffic laws and ride single file.

■ The law requires bicyclists under 16 to wear a helmet.

■ Do not travel at night.

Three bicycle **tours** of varying lengths—from a weekend to a six-day excursion with overnight stops in state parks—have been organized by the Florida Department of Environmental Protection. Other cycling tours: **Outdoor Adventures** *(*☎ *904-393-9030)*; **Brooks Country Cycling Tours** *(*☎ *212-874-5151; www.brookscountrycycling.com)* Other sources for information: **State Bicycle Office**, Florida Department of Transportation in Tallahassee *(*☎ *850-487-1200)* or **Rails-to-Trails**, 2545 Blairstone Pines Dr., Tallahassee FL 32301 *(*☎ *850-942-2379; www.railtrails.org)*.

Fishing – The many rivers, lakes, ponds and wilderness waterways offer experienced and amateur anglers some of the best fishing waters in the US. Enthusiasts do not have to rent expensive boats to enjoy a day of fishing. Many coastal communities have public fishing piers where equipment can be rented from bait-and-tackle shops for a minimal fee. Fish camps along inland waterways offer boat and houseboat rentals and guided fishing trips for the whole family.

Saltwater – Miles of coastline on the Atlantic Ocean and Gulf of Mexico give the saltwater enthusiast the opportunity to catch more than 70 species of fish. For the average fisherman there are opportunities to engage in surf casting and bridge and pier fishing. A variety of boat-charter services can accommodate every level of expertise and budget. Many marinas rent boats ranging from canoes to pontoon boats. Most backcountry channels in the Gulf are unmarked, and it is wise to employ the services of a local guide who can lead you to the best fishing spots. Be sure to choose a licensed outfitter. For additional information on saltwater fishing, visit www.Florida Conservation.org/marine or contact the Florida Fish and Wildlife Conservation Commission, Div. Of Marine Fisheries, 2590 Executive Center Circle East, Suite 204, Tallahassee FL 32301 ☎ 850-488-4676.

Freshwater – There are some 33 species of freshwater fish in Florida that are sought after by practitioners of the sport. For forecasts, fish identification, boat ramp and fishing pier locations, tips and details about licenses www.FloridaFisheries.com. For freshwater **fishing regulations**, limits, seasons and a copy of the *Florida Hunting Handbook* (free), contact Florida Fish and Wildlife Conservation Commission.

Resident and nonresidents must have a **fishing license**; anglers are not required to have both freshwater and saltwater licenses, unless they are taking both freshwater and saltwater species. Licenses can usually be obtained at sporting-goods stores, marinas and some bait-and-tackle shops. To purchase a license: ☎ 888-347-4356 or www.FloridaFisheries.com. To receive a copy of *Florida Fishing & Boating Guidebook* (free), contact the **Florida Sports Foundation** 2964 Wellington Circle North, Tallahassee FL 32308 (☎ 850-488-8347; *www.flasports.com).*

Deep-Sea Fishing – Many species can be found along the Florida Keys year-round offering a great variety of offshore game fishing. Large "party boats" can take up to 20 people. Half-day trips are suitable for beginners, while full-day excursions are designed for the avid angler, allowing the captain to change locations, according to where the fish are biting. Most boats have a fishing license and knowledgeable crew. Prices range from $50–$250/person.

Charter boats specializing in deep-sea sport fishing will appeal to the experienced fisherman who is looking to reel in "thebig one"—sailfish, wahoo, tuna, kingfish and blue or white marlin. Charters are costly but include equipment, bait and fishing licenses. For further information, contact the **Florida Sport Fishing Information Line** ☎ 800-ASK-FISH.

Golf – Ranked one of the nation's top golfing destinations, Florida boasts well over 1,200 golf courses, several designed by such legends as Jack Nicklaus and Arnold Palmer. Florida's balmy climate makes golf accessible year-round. Duffers can practice their driving and putting expertise at numerous public courses or watch professional golfers at one of the numerous tournaments that take place throughout the state. Many hotels and resorts include golf facilities, and some private courses allow nonmembers to play. Numerous courses offer golf clinics and private instruction. Make reservations well ahead of time; teeing off during midday means less-crowded fairways and lower humidity. Greens fees average $75 in winter, $40 in summer. For golf vacation packages that include accommodations at over 250 courses *(starting at $49/person per night, depending on season and location)* statewide, contact World of

Courtesy Biltmore Hotel

Golf Tours (☎ 407-884-8300 or 800-729-1400; www.wogolftours.com). The publication *Play Florida Golf Directory* is available (free) from Florida Sports Foundation *(above).*

Tee Times USA will make reservations (free) for tee times at more than 300 selected golf courses. Discount golf packages are available. Written confirmation and travel directions will be mailed, faxed or e-mailed. To request a brochure or to make reservations, contact Tee Times USA, PO Box 641, Flagler Beach FL 32136 (☎ *800-374-8633; www.teetimesusa.com).*

Hiking – The best time to hike is from late fall to early spring when temperatures are cooler and humidity is lower. When hiking, stay on marked trails; taking shortcuts is dangerous and can cause erosion. Obtain up-to-date weather forecasts; a sudden storm can flood trails in swampy areas. If hiking alone, notify someone of your destination and anticipated return time.

The USDA Forest Service and the Florida Trail Assn. maintain the **Florida National Scenic Trail**, which extends from the Gulf Islands National Seashore in northwestern Florida to the Big Cypress National Preserve in southwestern Florida. All trails are marked; camping is limited. Some segments of the trail may be closed during hunting season. Before setting out, check with the local managing authority or write to: US Forest Service, 325 John Knox Rd., Suite F100, Tallahassee FL 32303 ☎ 850-942-9300 or the Florida Trail Assn., 5415 S.W. 13th St., Gainesville FL 32608 (☎ 352-378-8823 or 800-343-1882; *www.florida-trail.org).*

The Florida Trail Assn. builds and maintains trails, publishes a trail guide and trail maps, provides its members *($25/year)* with a bi-monthly newsletter and offers activities such as day hikes and backpacking and canoeing trips. Hiking and backpacking tips are given in the *Hiking Guide to the Florida Trail*, available from the association. For *A Guide to Your National Scenic Trail*, contact the US Forest Service *(above)*.

Horseback Riding – Many state parks and forests offer miles of unpaved roads and trails for horseback riding. State parks that provide overnight camping for riders and horses are: Florida Caverns, Jonathan Dickinson, Little Manatee River, Lower Wekiva River, Myakka River, O'Leno, Rock Springs Run and Wekiva Springs. Call the park office to inquire about staging areas, camping facilities and trail conditions. Regulations require proof of a recent negative Coggins test for all horses entering park areas. Riders are required to stay on designated trails. The *Florida Horse Trail Directory* is available from the Florida Department of Agriculture, Room 416, Mayo Building, Tallahassee FL 32399-0800 *(☎ 850-488-4132; www.fl-ag.com)*. Contact local chambers of commerce or the Florida Department of Environmental Protection *(above)* for additional information. Horseback riding is allowed on several beaches. Check with local authorities before setting out.

Hunting – Many different types of game await the sports hunter in Florida's forests, grasslands and vast swamps. Rifles and shotguns may be brought into Florida for hunting and sporting purposes (no permit required). Hunting is permitted in Big Cypress National Preserve, wildlife-management areas and most state and national forests. Whether fishing or hunting, sportsmen should be aware that native species of birds are protected by law, as are all endangered and threatened animals. For hunting **regulations**, bag limits, seasons and a copy of the *Florida Hunting Handbook* (free), contact Florida Game and Freshwater Fish Commission, 620 S. Meridian St., Tallahassee FL 32399-1600 *(☎ 850-488-4676)*.

Expeditions and Cruises

Outdoor Adventures – A naturalist-guided expedition that explores the Everglades and the Florida Keys by kayak is a **learning vacation** offered by Sea Kayak Georgia, 1102 Highway 80, Tybee Island GA 31328 *(☎ 912-786-8732 or 888-529-2542; www.seakayakgeorgia.com)*. **Bird-watching** tours in the Keys and Dry Tortugas are led by Victor Emanuel Nature Tours, Austin TX *(☎ 800-328-8368; www.ventbird.com)*. Coastal **kayaking and canoe trips** to the barrier islands and inland waters of North Florida are offered by Outdoor Adventures, Jacksonville FL, *(☎ 904-393-9030; www.outdooradventuresfla.com)*. **Snorkel with manatees** as part of an 8-day excursion offered by Royal Palm Tours, PO Box 60079, Fort Myers FL 33906, *(☎ 941-368-0760 or 800-296-0249; www.discoverfloridatours.com)*.

Cruises – A variety of cruise vacations catering to families and singles are available. Choose from a four-day sail to the Bahamas with ample time to explore the islands; a relaxing cruise to Mexico's Yucatan Peninsula or through the Panama Canal to Los Angeles; or a voyage to some out-of-the-way island that includes educational lectures and on-shore excursions. Most cruise lines offer air/sea packages and discounts for early bookings. Florida has seven ports that offer service year-round. The four largest are the Port of Miami, Port Everglades (Fort Lauderdale), Port Canaveral and Port Tampa. Major cruise lines departing from these ports are Carnival, Cunard, Holland

America, Norwegian, Princess, Royal Caribbean and others. All ports provide parking facilities. For up-to-date information, check with individual cruise lines or contact the National Assn. of Cruise-Oriented Agencies (☎ 305-663-5626; www. nacoa online .com) for a listing of organizations that specialize in cruise vacations.

Fun for Children

Theme parks are the number-one attraction for the young and young-at-heart, offering not only fun and entertainment but also education. Many state parks and nature preserves sponsor activities and programs for children; campsites are often situated so as to allow children to swim, boat, fish or play along sandy beaches. Miniature golf courses for young and old abound in Florida. Local festivals and fairs (see Calendar of Events) can be fun times for youngsters. Many sites offer discounted admission fees to children under 12. When reserving a hotel, check whether it offers organized children's programs that include sports, arts and crafts, beach outings, canoe trips and more. In this guide, sights of particular interest to children are indicated by the 👶 symbol.

Eileen Osteen/MICHELIN

Some Activities for Kids:

👶 Ride a go-kart at Port Orange: **Go-Kart City** (☎ 904-761-2882).

👶 Attend a spring practice (see Spectator Sports) and get your favorite player to sign a baseball for you (have a pen ready).

👶 Tube down five stories or splash around in a wave pool at **Wet'n'Wild** in Orlando (☎ 407-351-1800; www.wetnwild.com) or at **Wild Waters** near Ocala (☎ 352-236-2121; www.silversprings.com).

👶 Wrestle with video or virtual monsters of every kind at **Game Works** in Miami (☎ 305-740-9091).

👶 Learn to scuba dive or ride a surfboard in Cocoa Beach. For scuba lessons and equipment rental, **Ron Jon Surf Shop** (☎ 321-799-8888); for surfing lessons and board rental, **Cocoa Beach Surfing School** (☎ 321-452-0854).

👶 Take a trip to the moon in Space Base, a flight simulator at the **Museum of Discovery and Science** in Fort Lauderdale (☎ 954-467-6637; www.mods.org).

Spectator Sports

For an overview of spectator sports available in Florida, see the Recreation section in the Introduction at the front of this guide. A comprehensive directory of Florida sports is available online at www.flasports.com.

Motor Sports

Daytona International Speedway is home to a number of racing events throughout the year including motorcycle and go-kart racing. Enthusiasts of automobile racing flock here from late January to mid-February when the Rolex 24 at Daytona sports car race and the world-famous **Daytona 500** stock car race take place. Held every spring, Bike Week is a city-wide celebration of motorcycles. Gator-Nationals, the largest drag-racing contest on the Atlantic Seaboard, takes place each March in Gainesville.

Racing and More

Most major metropolitan areas have **greyhound racing** tracks close by. Winter brings the best horses and riders to south Florida. Horse lovers can experience the thrill of **thoroughbred racing** at four tracks in the Greater Miami area and at Tampa Bay Downs. For a listing of pari-mutuel betting establishments, write to the Department of Business and Professional Regulations, 1940 N. Monroe St., Tallahassee FL 32399 (☎ 850-488-3211; www.myflorida.com). Pompano Park hosts **harness racing** from October to June.

West Palm Beach, Boca Raton and Vero Beach present **polo** matches from November to mid-April. **Jai alai** facilities are located in Fort Lauderdale, Fort Pierce, Miami, Ocala and Orlando. For venues check local telephone directories or contact area tourist offices.

Professional Leagues

Team/League Association		City	Location	☎
Miami Dolphins	NFL	Miami	Pro Player Stadium	305-620-2578
Miami Heat	NBA	Miami	American Airlines Arena	786-777-1000
Florida Panthers	NHL	Sunrise	Nat'l Car Rental Center	954-835-7000
Florida Marlins	MLB	Miami	Pro Player Stadium	305-626-7400
Jacksonville Jaguars	NFL	Jacksonville	Alltel Stadium	904-633-2000
Orlando Magic	NBA	Orlando	TD Waterhouse Centre	407-896-2442
Tampa Bay Buccaneers	NFL	Tampa	Raymond James Stadium	813-879-2827
Tampa Bay Lightning	NHL	Tampa	Ice Palace Arena	813-229-2658
Tampa Bay Devil Rays	MLB	St. Petersburg	Tropicana Field	727-825-3120

(for tickets contact the local Ticketmaster office)

Professional Baseball

Spring Training Camps – If it's spring, it must be baseball season, when many of the major-league baseball teams head for training camps in Florida. Warm-up practice starts in late February and "Grapefruit League" exhibition games are played daily through March. Practices are held between 10am–2pm and are free. Tickets for games range from $5–$18. Order tickets early by calling the stadium directly or the local Ticketmaster outlet. For a free schedule, write to Major League Baseball, 350 Park Ave., New York NY 10022. The magazine *Spring Training ($5.99)*, published annually in late January, gives team histories, schedules, ticket details, directions and accommodations. To order, contact Vanguard Publications, PO Box 667, Chapel Hill NC 27514 ☎ 800-473-1656. The *Spring Training Guide* is available (free) from the **Florida Sports Foundation** *(☎ 850-488-8347; www.flasports.com)*.

Team	City	Location	☎/Web
Atlanta Braves	Kissimmee	Disney's Wide World of Sports	407-939-1500 braves.mlb.com
Baltimore Orioles	Fort Lauderdale	Fort Lauderdale Stadium	954-776-1921 orioles.mlb.com
Boston Red Sox	Fort Myers	City of Palms Park	941-334-4700 redsox.mlb.com
Cincinnati Reds	Sarasota	Ed Smith Stadium	941-954-4464 reds.mlb.com

Kids at Baseball Camp

Team	City	Stadium	Contact
Cleveland Indians	Winter Haven	Chain of Lakes Stadium	863-293-3900 indians.mlb.com
Detroit Tigers	Lakeland	Joker Marchant Stadium	863-686-8075 tigers.mlb.com
Florida Marlins	Melbourne	Space Coast Stadium	321-633-9200 marlins.mlb.com
Houston Astros	Kissimmee	Osceola County Stadium	407-933-6500 astros.mlb.com
Kansas City Royals	Davenport	Baseball City Stadium	863-424-2424 royals.mlb.com
Los Angeles Dodgers	Vero Beach	Holman Stadium	561-569-4900 dodgers.mlb.com
Minnesota Twins	Fort Myers	Hammond Stadium	800-33TWINS twins.mlb.com
Montreal Expos	Jupiter	Roger Dean Stadium	561-775-1818 expos.mlb.com
New York Mets	Port St. Lucie	Thomas J. White Stadium	561-871-2115 mets.mlb.com
New York Yankees	Tampa	Legends Field	813-879-2244 yankees.mlb.com
Philadelphia Phillies	Clearwater	Jack Russell Stadium	727-442-8496 phillies.mlb.com
Pittsburgh Pirates	Bradenton	McKechnie Field	941-748-4610 pirates.mlb.com
St. Louis Cardinals	Jupiter	Roger Dean Stadium	561-775-1818 cardinals.mlb.com
Tampa Bay Devil Rays	St. Petersburg	Al Lang Stadium	727-825-3250 devilrays.mlb.com
Texas Rangers	Port Charlotte	Charlotte County Stadium	941-625-9500 rangers.mlb.com
Toronto Blue Jays	Dunedin	Dunedin Stadium at Grant Field	727-733-0429 bluejays.mlb.com

Water Sports

With hundreds of miles of prime coastline bordering the Atlantic and Gulf of Mexico, a multitude of water sports is available year-round to visitors of all ages. Inland lakes, rivers and springs complete the array of opportunities to **swim**, boat or simply enjoy the relaxing sound of rippling water. Although Florida's Atlantic coast is not known for its large waves, **surfing** is popular along Sebastian Inlet south of Melbourne, and around Jacksonville, Flagler Beach and Miami. Surfboards and sailboards can be rented locally. Check water conditions with lifeguards or local authorities before setting out to surf or windsurf.

Selected Beaches *(listed by region)*

	☎	$	🏊	✚	⛺	🎣	⛷	⬛
Panhandle								
Grayton Beach SP	850-231-4210	•	•		•	•		
Henderson Beach SP	850-837-7550	•	•		•	•		
Perdido Key Area Gulf Islands National Seashore	850-934-2600	•	•	•				•
Panama City Beach	850-235-1159		•	•		•	•	
Pensacola Beach	850-932-1500	•	•	•				
Santa Rosa Island	850-934-2600	•		•		•	•	•
St. Andrews SP	850-233-5140	•	•	•		•		
St. George Island SP	850-927-2111	•	•			•		
St. Joseph Peninsula SP	850-227-1327	•	•					•
East Coast	☎	$	🏊	✚	⛺	🎣	⛷	⬛
Amelia Island SP	904-251-2320					•		
Anastasia SP	904-461-2033	•	•			•	•	
Daytona Beach	386-239-6414	•	•	•		•	•	

	$	🏊 swimming	✚ lifeguard	⛺ camping	🎣 fishing	🏄 surfing	🤿 scuba/snorkeling
Flagler Beach	386-517-2086	●	●		●	●	●	●
Fort Pierce Inlet SP	561-468-3985	●	●	●		●	●	●
St. Augustine Beach	904-829-1711	●	●	●	●	●	●	
Sebastian Inlet SP	321-984-4852	●	●	●	●	●	●	●
Vero Beach	561-567-3491		●	●		●	●	●

South Florida and the Keys

	$	🏊	✚	⛺	🎣	🏄	🤿
Bahia Honda SP	305-872-2353	●	●		●	●		●
Bill Baggs Cape Florida SP	305-361-5811	●	●	●	●			
Crandon Park	305-361-5421	●	●	●				
Fort Lauderdale Beach	954-765-4466	●	●	●		●	●	
Haulover Beach	305-947-3525	●	●	●		●		
Hugh Taylor Birch SP	954-564-4521	●	●	●		●		
J. D. MacArthur Beach SP	561-624-6952	●	●			●		●
J. U. Lloyd Beach SP	954-923-2833	●	●	●		●		
John Pennekamp C.R. SP	305-451-1202	●	●		●		●	●
North Shore SP	305-993-2032	●	●				●	●
Miami Beach	305-672-1270		●	●	●		●	

Gulf Coast

	$	🏊	✚	⛺	🎣	🏄	🤿
Coquina Beach	941-729-9177		●			●		
Clearwater Beach	813-461-0011	●	●	●				
Delnor-Wiggins Pass SP	941-597-6196	●	●	●		●		
Gasparilla Island SP	941-964-0375	●	●			●		
Longboat Key	941-383-2466		●			●		
Lovers Key SP	941-463-4588	●	●			●		
St. Petersburg Beach	727-866-2484	●	●			●		
Sanibel Island Beaches	941-472-1080	●	●	●	●			
Venice Beach	941-488-2236		●	●		●		●

Symbols on the above chart indicate: $ admission/parking fee; 🏊 swimming; ✚ lifeguard (seasonally); ⛺ camping; 🎣 fishing; 🏄 surfing; 🤿 scuba/snorkeling.

Pier at Flagler Beach

© Stephen Frink

Canoeing

The Florida Canoe Trail system includes more than 1,000mi of scenic waterways. Canoe trails on rivers and creeks let the outdoor enthusiast paddle along the slow-flowing waters of the Santa Fe River, glide through swampy areas along the upper Suwannee River, or camp on a secluded riverbank. *Florida Recreational Canoe Trails (free from the Office of Greenways and Trails, ☎ 850-487-4784; www.myflorida .com)* lists facilities, camping and local outfitters. You can also contact individual national parks, state parks or preserves for additional information on local canoe trails. Flat-water wilderness canoeing can be experienced along the Wilderness Waterway in the Everglades.

Employ the services of a reputable outfitter to explore Florida's backwaters. Enjoy self-guided family paddle adventures on the Peace River that range from half-day canoe outings to overnight camping trips. For a brochure, contact Canoe Outpost Peace River, 2816 N.W. County Rd. 661, Arcadia FL 34266 *(☎ 863-494-1215 or 800-268-0083; www.canoeoutpost.com)*. Kayak, paddle boats, tubing and canoe excursions can be arranged through Adventures Unlimited, Rte. 6, Box 283 Milton FL 32570 *(☎ 850-623-6197 or 800-239-6864; www.adventuresunlimited.com)*. To request a copy of the canoeing and kayaking directory that lists member outfitters, contact the Office of Greenways and Trails *(above)*. For canoeing in the Ten Thousand Islands area, contact Wilderness Inquiry, 808 14th Ave. S.E., Minneapolis MN 55414, *(☎ 612-676-9400 or 800-728-0719; www.wildernessinquiry.org)* or NACT-Everglades Rentals & Eco Adventures, 107 Camellia St., Everglades City FL 34149 *(☎ 941-695-4666; www.evergladesadventures.com)*.

Canoeing Tips:

■ Law requires that each occupant wear a flotation device.

■ Take an extra paddle.

■ Get a map of canoeing routes and keep abreast of weather conditions.

■ Keep in mind that coastal rivers are affected by tides.

■ Rivers in north Florida run high in spring and summer; in central and south Florida rivers run high in summer and fall.

■ Avoid flooded rivers.

■ Carry drinking water, and always advise someone of your plans.

Scuba Diving and Snorkeling

The most popular areas are the Keys and south Florida, where hundreds of private dive shops offer a variety of diving trips. Most venues rent equipment and organize dive excursions. For a listing of dive shops in the upper Keys, contact the Key Largo Chamber of Commerce *(☎ 305-451-1414 or 800-822-1088; www.floridakeys.org)*. A **Certified Diver's Card** is required in order to scuba dive. Courses to obtain the necessary certification are offered by most diving shops. Choose an instructor who is certified by the Professional Assn. of Dive Instructors (PADI) or the National Assn. of Underwater Instructors (NAUI). *See also Sports and Recreation.*

Snorkelers and scuba divers can enjoy the living coral reef that lies off the Florida Keys. If you feel more at ease staying close to the surface, snorkeling trips are available. Although waters are shallow, you should be a good swimmer. To get close to the reef without the heavy air tank, try **snuba**. Expeditions by Snuba Tours of Key Largo let you explore the reef connected to a 20ft breathing hose that is attached to an air tank secured to a raft on the surface *(1hr lesson; half-day excursion and guided dive; $120/person;* ☎ *305-451-6391; www.snuba.com)*. Make advance reservations for all expeditions.

A few precautions: wear lightweight shoes to protect against sharp rocks; don't wear shiny objects that will attract hungry fish; if you leave the boat, display a red-and-white "diver down" flag, and most importantly **never dive alone**. Seas are usually rougher in winter and can produce poor visibility on the reefs.

Index

N

O

U – V

W

X – Y – Z

Please write to us !
Your input will help us to improve our guides.

Please send this questionnaire to the following address:
Michelin Travel Publications.
Post Office Box 19001, Greenville, SC 29602-9001

---

1. Is this the first time you have purchased THE GREEN GUIDE? ye   n

---

2. Which title did you buy? :

---

3. What influenced your decision to purchase this guide?

	Not important at all	Somewhat important	Important	Very important
Cover				
Clear, attractive layout				
Structure				
Cultural information				
Practical information				
Maps and plans				
Michelin quality				
Loyalty to THE GREEN GUIDE collection				

Your comments :

---

4. How would you rate the following aspects of THE GREEN GUIDE?

	Poor	Average	Good	Excellent
Maps at the beginning of the guide				
Maps and plans throughout the guide				
Description of the sights (style, detail...)				
Depth of cultural information				
Amount of practical information				
Format				

Please comment if you have responded poor or average on any of the above:

5. What do you think about the establishments provided in the guide?

HOTELS :	Not Enough	Sufficient	Too many
All categories			
"Budget"			
"Moderate"			
"Expensive"			
RESTAURANTS :	Not Enough	Sufficient	Too many
All categories			
"Budget"			
"Moderate"			
"Expensive"			

Your comments:

6. On a scale of 1-20, please rate THE GREEN GUIDE (1 being the lowest, 20 being the highest):

How would you suggest we improve these guides?

1. Maps and Plans:

2. Sights:

3. Establishments:

4. Practical Information:

5. Other:

Demographic information: (optional)

	Male	Female	Age

Name:

Address: